THIRD EDITION

The Paralegal Professional

The Essentials

THIRD EDITION

The Paralegal Professional

The Essentials

Thomas F. Goldman, JD

Professor Emeritus
Bucks County Community College

Henry R. Cheeseman, JD, LLM

Clinical Professor of Law
University of Southern California

Prentice Hall
Boston   Columbus   Indianapolis   New York   San Francisco   Upper Saddle River
Amsterdam   Cape Town   Dubai   London   Madrid   Milan   Munich   Paris   Montreal   Toronto
Delhi   Mexico City   Sao Paulo   Sydney   Hong Kong   Seoul   Singapore   Taipei   Tokyo

Editor in Chief: Vernon Anthony
Senior Acquisitions Editor: Gary Bauer
Developmental Editor: Linda Cupp
Editorial Assistant: Megan Heintz
Director of Marketing: David Gesell
Marketing Manager: Thomas Hayward
Thomas Hayward Marketing Assistant: Les Roberts
Senior Managing Editor: JoEllen Gohr
Project Manager: Christina Taylor
Operations Specialist: Deidra Skahill

Senior Art Director: Diane Ernsberger
Cover Designer: Wanda Espana
Cover Art: Frantz Jantzen/U.S. Supreme Court
Full-Service Project Management: Mary Jo Graham and Barb Tucker, S4Carlisle Publishing Services
Composition: S4Carlisle Publishing Services
Printer/Binder: Webcrafters, Inc.
Cover Printer: Coral Graphics
Text Font: Janson Text

Credits: Cover: The Supreme Court of the United States/Franz Jantzen; Page 1: SuperStock, Inc./Ingram Publishing; Page 2: iStockphoto; Page 38: Pearson Education/David Graham; Page 74: Photos.com/Tanya Constantine; Page 126: Shutterstock; Page 175: Getty Images Inc. -Stone Allstock/Bruce Ayres; Page 176: Henry Cheeseman; Page 206: Pearson Education/David Graham; Page 240: Pearson Education/David Graham; Page 284: Photos.com/Image Source; Pages 325, 326: Pearson Education/David Graham; Page 366: Photos.com/Dave and Les Jacobs; Page 410: iStockphoto; Page 445: Getty Images/Yellow Dog Productions/The Image Bank; Pearson Education/David Graham; Page 488: iStockphoto; Page 520: Dreamstime LLC-Royalty Free/Stephen Coburn/Dreamstome.com; Page 554: Getty Images Inc. -PhotoDisc/Triangle Images/Digital Vision; Page 446: CORBIS-NY/Creasource; Page 614: Photos.com/Image Source; Page 656: Photos.com/Steve Allen; Page 708: Fotosearch.Com, LLC/Royalty Free; Page 732: iStockphoto

Library of Congress Cataloging-in-Publication Data
Goldman, Thomas F.
    The paralegal professional: essentials / Thomas F. Goldman, Henry R. Cheeseman. — 3rd ed.
      p. cm.
    Rev. ed. of: The paralegal professional: essentials / Henry R. Cheeseman, Thomas F. Goldman. 2nd. ed. 2008.
    Includes bibliographical references and index.
    ISBN 978-0-13-506401-6
  1. Legal assistants—United States—Handbooks, manuals, etc. I. Cheeseman, Henry R. II. Cheeseman, Henry R. Paralegal professional. III. Title.
    KF320.L4C446 2011
    340.023'73—dc22   2009046202

Pearson Education Ltd.
Pearson Education Singapore Pte. Ltd.
Pearson Education Canada, Ltd.
Pearson Education—Japan

Pearson Education Australia PTY. Limited
Pearson Education North Asia Ltd.
Pearson Educación de Mexico, S.A. de C.V.
Pearson Education Malaysia Pte. Ltd.

10 9 8 7 6 5 4 3 2 1

Prentice Hall
is an imprint of

ISBN 10:   0-13-506401-5
ISBN 13: 978-0-13-506401-6

Dedicated to the memory of my parents,
Morris and Ethel Goldman,
who guided me through life, encouraged me to pursue an education,
and delighted in my becoming a teacher.

—Thomas F. Goldman

In memory of Henry B. and Florence Cheeseman
A grain of sand has been ten thousand mountains.
Who are we to hold it?

—Henry R. Cheeseman

CONTENTS

PART III

PARALEGAL SKILLS 325

CHAPTER 11

Legal Writing and Critical Legal Thinking   410

APPENDIX A

How to Brief a Case

APPENDIX B

National Federation of Paralegal Associations, Inc.

APPENDIX C

Model Standards and Guidelines for Utilization of Legal Assistants— Paralegals

VIDEO CASE STUDY INDEX

Welcome to the third edition of *The Paralegal Professional: The Essentials*. The paralegal profession is a dynamic, evolving, and growing field that requires developing not only concept knowledge, but also professional and analytical skills, and a firm understanding of the ethical values and obligations of the profession to be competitive in an increasingly challenging work environment. Our goal in the third edition is to provide paralegal students and professionals with the foundation on which to grow and excel in this field today and in the future.

In this edition, we have incorporated comments and suggestions from a wide range of adopters of the text, non-users, and our students. Their feedback resulted in several important changes to the Table of Contents and the introduction of several new features that help bring paralegal practice alive and illuminate the roles and tasks paralegals are asked to assume in the legal working environment.

In the third edition we have divided the *Essentials* into three sections that provide a logical grouping of topics. Note that individual chapters on areas of substantive law covered in Part IV of the comprehensive version of this text can be added in a custom publication, as desired.

Part I: The Paralegal Profession focuses on introducing students to the paralegal profession, career opportunities, the paralegal workplace, ethics, regulation, and the use of technology on the job.

Part II: Introduction to Law provides an overview of law and the American legal system and now introduces students to the three areas of procedure: civil, criminal, and administrative procedure in succession. This treatment helps students understand the differences between these three legal arenas early in the course.

Part III: Paralegal Skills focuses on introducing students to interviewing, investigation, traditional and online legal research, and writing and critical thinking in the legal field.

We are particularly excited about the new video case studies that are integrated into the third edition. The third edition includes 34 video scenarios that make it easy to bring the world of the practicing paralegal into the classroom. Videos cover topics such as resume writing and interviewing for a job, working in a small family firm, the courtroom players and their roles, and paralegals performing various procedures and duties. Many of the segments present scenarios dealing with common ethical situations that paralegals will encounter on the job making it easy to integrate ethics education throughout the course.

Our book has been carefully and thoroughly designed to meet the requirements as set forth by the American Bar Association (ABA) and the American Association for Paralegal Education (AAfPE) regarding coverage of paralegal topics, ethical issues, professional skill development, and other educational requirements for an introductory paralegal education course.

Thomas Goldman
Henry Cheeseman

Thomas F. Goldman, JD, is Professor Emeritus of Bucks County Community College, where he was a professor of Law and Management and Director of the Center for Legal Studies and the Paralegal Studies Program. He is currently a member of the Paralegal Studies Advisory Board and mentor at Thomas Edison State College, where he has developed the Advanced Litigation Support and Technology Certificate Program in the School of Professional Studies.

He is an author of textbooks in paralegal studies and technology, including *Technology in the Law Office, Accounting and Taxation for Paralegals, Civil Litigation: Process and Procedures,* and *SmartDraw Tutorial and Guide.*

An accounting and economics graduate of Boston University and of Temple University School of Law, Professor Goldman has an active international law, technology law, and litigation practice. He has worked extensively with paralegals and received the award of the Legal Support Staff Guild. He was elected the Legal Secretaries Association Boss of the Year for his contribution to cooperative education by encouraging the use of paralegals and legal assistants in law offices. He also received the Bucks County Community College Alumni Association Professional Achievement Award. He has been an educational consultant on technology to educational institutions and major corporations and is a frequent speaker and lecturer on educational, legal, and technology issues.

Henry R. Cheeseman is an award-winning author of several business law textbooks published by Prentice Hall, including the definitive, highly regarded *Business Law.* Other textbooks by Professor Cheeseman published by Prentice Hall are *Contemporary Business and Online Commerce Law, The Legal Environment of Business and Online Commerce, Essential of Business and Online Commerce,* and *Introduction to Law.* He has earned six degrees, including a Juris Doctor degree from the UCLA School of Law, an LLM degree from Boston University, and an MBA degree from the University of Chicago. Professor Cheeseman is a Clinical Professor of Law and the Director of Legal Studies at the Marshall School of Business, University of Southern California. Students there voted him the best teacher of the year on many occasions, earning him the "Golden Apple" Teacher Award. He has also served at the Center for Excellence in Teaching at the University. Professor Cheeseman recognizes the importance of the paralegal to the practice of law, and has co-authored this new and exciting edition of *The Paralegal Professional.*

BUILD A SOLID FOUNDATION FOR YOUR PARALEGAL CAREER!

Written by an award-winning team, *The Paralegal Professional: The Essentials*, Third Edition, builds the foundation in substantive and procedural legal knowledge and real-world skills you will need throughout your course of study. The book emphasizes the following:

DEVELOP CRITICAL THINKING AND PROCEDURAL SKILLS!

End-of-chapter material in this edition has been greatly expanded to focus on developing critical thinking and hands-on skills, including the following exercises and assignments:
- Critical thinking and writing case exercises
- Web research exercises
- Ethics analysis and discussion questions
- Collaborative exercises
- Legal analysis and writing cases, cases for briefing
- New portfolio building exercises

LEARN ABOUT TECHNOLOGY APPLICATIONS IN THE LAW OFFICE

To be effective on the job, you will need to become comfortable using computers and common legal office software. Chapter 4, Technology and the Paralegal, introduces you to the types of application programs and their uses commonly found in law offices today.

UNDERSTAND HOW TO HANDLE ETHICAL SITUATIONS IN THE WORKPLACE

The Paralegal Professional: The Essentials, Third Edition, text and package is designed to build a strong foundational understanding of ethical principles for paralegals in the introductory course. Resources include Chapter 2: Ethics and Professional Responsibility, new ethical perspectives boxes integrated throughout the textbook, and 24 ethics-related video segments from the new Paralegal Professional Classroom Video Series Segments.

▶ PARALEGALS AT WORK CHAPTER OPENERS

These opening scenarios offer a hypothetical fact situation that a professional paralegal could encounter on the job. They are designed to stimulate a student's interest in the material to be covered in the chapter.

▶ ETHICAL PERSPECTIVE BOXES

These new boxes present hypothetical fact situations and ethical dilemmas that paralegals might face in their professional careers.

ETHICAL PERSPECTIVE
Paralegal's Duty to Report Sexual Harassment Conduct

Ms. Heath is hired as a paralegal for the law firm of White, Cassel, and Smith, a large law firm. Ms. Heath is assigned as a paralegal professional to assist Mr. White, a partner of the law firm. During the first couple of weeks on the job, on numerous occasions when Ms. Heath was in attorney Mr. White's office on legal and paralegal matters, Mr. White made rude comments such as talking about people having sex, how good he is in bed, making obscene gestures, and touching Ms. Heath on the

▶ NEW! SIDEBAR BOXES

These new boxes provide additional information and commentary on chapter topics.

DIVISION OF MARITAL PROPERTY

Law	Description
Equitable distribution	The marital property is distributed fairly. This does not necessarily mean the equal distribution of the property.

SIDEBAR

▶ NEW! PARALEGALS IN PRACTICE BOXES

For the third edition, we have added profiles of paralegals practicing in a variety of types of practices. Their commentaries provide students with insight into the world of practicing paralegals.

Paralegals *in* Practice
PARALEGAL PROFILE
Annette R. Brown

▶ ADVICE FROM THE FIELD ARTICLES

These articles feature professional advice straight from the experts on interviewing skills, developing your portfolio, professional development, handling clients, and more.

Advice *from the* Field
GETTING CASE ANALYSIS OFF TO A FAST START
by DecisionQuest

From your first conversation with a prospective client, you're learning about the dispute that led the individual or corporation to seek counsel. There are many benefits to taking a systematic approach to analyzing this knowledge. Not least of these is the favorable impression you'll make on those who retain you.

The following article presents a method for organizing and evaluating the facts about any case. And it illustrates how the early results of this dispute analy-

CHRONOLOGY

A chronology of key facts is a critical tool for analyzing any dispute. As you create the chronology, important factual disputes and areas of strength and weakness become obvious.

Begin by listing the fact and the date on which it occurred. As you enter each fact, be sure to make the important details about the fact explicit. For example,

▶ IN THE WORDS OF THE COURT BOXES

Excerpts from key court cases are presented to familiarize students with important legal decisions.

IN THE WORDS OF THE COURT

Alaska Case Law
WHITING V. STATE, A-8755 (ALASKA APP. 10-12-2005)
MANNHEIMER, Judge.

Michael T. Whiting appeals his conviction for felony driving under the influence, . . . the facts . . . : Whiting and his girlfriend and his girlfriend's six-year-old son decided to go fishing in Gastineau Channel. Whiting piloted a skiff into the channel and then turned the motor off. The three occupants of the skiff fished while the skiff drifted in the channel; Whiting sat in the rear of the skiff near the motor. While Whiting was fishing, he was also drinking alcoholic beverages.

▶ PARALEGAL CHECKLISTS

Checklists help students track their personal progress as well as class and job details.

CHECKLIST Website Profile

☐ Address (URL):
☐ Name of organization or site:
☐ Key subject:

THE PARALEGAL PROFESSIONAL VIDEO SERIES ONLINE AND ON DVD

Free to Adopters of Paralegal Professional 3e

The third edition of *The Paralegal Professional: The Essentials* is supported by 34 scenario-based video segments that allow you to bring the world of the practicing paralegal into the classroom. Videos cover topics such as resume writing and interviewing for a job, working in a small family firm, the courtroom players and their roles, and paralegals performing various procedures and duties. All are assignable and can be shown in the classroom from a DVD or viewed online at the Companion Website. For a complete listing of the videos by chapter, consult the Video Case Study Index on page xvii following the Table of Contents.

Getting a Job and Related Video Segments:

These include segments on preparing for a job interview, interviewing advice, and an engaging interview scenario enactment.

Paralegal Practice and Ethics-Related Video Segments:

Many of the segments present situations involving paralegal ethics, such as common UPL, confidentiality, conflict of interest, billing, and zealous representation issues.

PARALEGAL PROFESSIONAL VIDEO CASE STUDIES ON DVD (ISBN:0-13-506610-7)

View the video cases online on the Companion Website: www.pearson highered.com/goldman.

Paralegal Practice Video Segments:

These segments include a combination of interviews with members of the legal team and law office practice scenario-based sections. Topics covered include interviewing and deposition, electronic discovery, legal research, courtroom procedures, courtroom players and etiquette, the independent paralegal, small family practice, and many other topics.

Teaching notes for the videos are in the Instructor's Manual!

INTEGRATE ETHICS INSTRUCTION
INTO THE INTRODUCTORY COURSE!

Many paralegal programs struggle with the question of how to integrate dedicated ethics instruction into a paralegal curriculum already packed with coursework. *The Paralegal Professional: The Essentials*, Third Edition, text and package is designed to build a strong foundational understanding of ethical principles for paralegals in the introductory course. Resources include:

Chapter 2: Ethics, Regulation, and Professional Responsibility

The fundamental ethics issues and principles are presented in chapter 2.

New Ethical Perspectives Boxes Integrated throughout the Textbook

These new boxes present hypothetical fact situations and ethical dilemmas that highlight situations paralegals might face in their professional careers.

ETHICAL PERSPECTIVE
Paralegal Loses $900,000 for Failing to Get a Contract in Writing

Paralegals are sometimes themselves involved in contract disputes. Consider the following case. Barbara Lucinda Sawyer worked as a paralegal for Melbourne Mills, Jr., an attorney at a law firm. Ms. Sawyer proposed that Mr. Mills and the law firm become engaged in class-action lawsuits. Mr. Mills agreed to pay Ms. Sawyer an unspecified bonus when "the ship comes in." After Ms. Sawyer's assistance and persistence, the law firm became involved in class-action litigation—primarily the Fen-Phen class-action litigation. After the law firm received millions of dollars in fees from the Fen-Phen class-action lawsuits, Ms. Sawyer and her husband Steve met with Mills to discuss Ms. Sawyer's bonus. Mr. Mills orally agreed to pay

Paralegal Practice and Ethics-Related Video Segments

Many of the segments present situations involving paralegal ethics, such as common UPL, confidentiality, conflict of interest, billing, and zealous representation issues.

Need More Coverage of Ethics in a Handy Supplemental Guide?

TOP 10 RULES OF ETHICS FOR PARALEGALS, SECOND EDITION
by Deborah Orlik

If more depth in dealing with ethical issues is desired, this handy guide can be packaged with the textbook at low cost.
(ISBN: 0-13-506393-0)

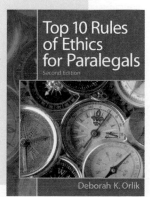

▶ THE PARALEGAL PROFESSIONAL COMPANION WEBSITE:

YOUR 24/7 STUDY AND RESOURCE SITE

At: **www.pearsonhighered.com/goldman**
Use this book-specific Website to prepare for tests, do online research, read full versions of cases discussed in the book, and view the video case studies discussed in your textbook.

* Learning Objectives
* Chapter Summary
* Key Term Flashcards
* Web Exercises
* Video Case Studies Online
* Full Case Versions of Cases in the Book
* Quizzes

▶ TOP 10 RULES OF ETHICS FOR PARALEGALS, SECOND EDITION

by Deborah Orlik

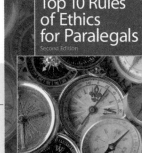

If more depth in dealing with ethical issues is desired, this handy guide can be packaged with the textbook at low cost. (ISBN: 0-13-506393-0)

▶ MOVIE GUIDE FOR LEGAL STUDIES, SECOND EDITION

by Kent Kauffman

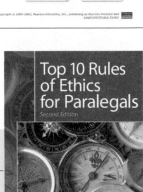

This supplemental movie guide to 33 of the most popular movies that deal with legal issues can be packaged with *The Paralegal Professional: The Essentials*, Third Edition. It includes a synopsis of each movie with notes on key scenes and discussion questions that can be assigned or discussed in class. Teaching notes are included in the Instructor's Manual. (ISBN: 0-13-506375-2)

▶ PEARSON ENGLISH/SPANISH LEGAL DICTIONARY

by Antonio Figueroa, Norma C. Connolly

(2004, 464 pp., Paper) The approximately 1,200 terms presented in this book are up-to-date in their use and interpretation. They are easy to find, use, and correlate in both languages. (ISBN: 0-13-113738-7)

▶ **INSTRUCTOR'S MANUAL WITH TOOLKIT**

FOR NEW INSTRUCTORS

The Instructor's Manual has been dramatically expanded to accommodate the needs of instructors with any level of experience. Whether you are a first-time instructor or an experienced hand, this manual contains a wealth of teaching materials:

- **New Instructor's Toolkit:**
  - Preparing for Class
  - *"First Day of Class"* Notes and PowerPoints

- **Sample Syllabi: 10-, 12-, 15-, 16-Week Courses with Templates on CD**
  - Weekly Assignments
  - Weekly Deadlines
  - Drop-Box Formatted Assignments also on CD

- **Using PowerPoint Quick Guide**

- **Using WebCT and BlackBoard Notes**

- **Transition Notes for Users of Miller 3e and Statsky 6e**

- By Chapter
  - **Chapter Outline**
  - **Teaching Notes**
  - **New! Law in the Movies Teaching Notes**
  - **New! Outcome Assessment Tools**

- **TEST GENERATOR**

  This computerized test generation system gives you maximum flexibility in preparing tests. You can create custom tests and print scrambled versions of a test at one time, as well as build tests randomly by chapter, level of difficulty, or question type. The software also allows online testing and record-keeping and the ability to add problems to the database.

- **POWERPOINT LECTURE PRESENTATION PACKAGE**

  Lecture Presentation screens for each chapter are available online and on the Instructor Resource CD.

- **INSTRUCTOR RESOURCE CENTER**

  The Instructor's Manual, Test Generator, and PPT Package can be downloaded from our Instructor Resource Center. To access supplementary materials online, instructors need to request an instructor access code. Go to www.pearsonhighered.com/irc, where you can register for an instructor access code. Within 48 hours of registering you will receive a confirming e-mail including an instructor access code. Once you have received your code, locate your text in the online catalog and click on the Instructor Resources button on the left side of the catalog product page. Select a supplement and a log-in page will appear. Once you have logged in, you can access instructor material for all Pearson textbooks.

- **THE PARALEGAL PROFESSIONAL VIDEO CASE STUDIES ON DVD**

  All video cases are available for in-class use on DVD free to adopters. Ask your local representative for more information or call 1-800-922-0579 (ISBN: 0-13-506610-7).

COMPLETE ONLINE COURSES: COURSECONNECT!

COURSECONNECT INTRODUCTION TO PARALEGAL STUDIES

ONLINE COURSES

Looking for robust online course content to reinforce and enhance your student learning? We have the solution: CourseConnect! CourseConnect courses contain customizable modules of content mapped to major learning outcomes. Each learning objeive contains interactive tutorials, rich media, discussion questions, MP3 downloadable lectures, assessments, and interactive activities that address different learning styles. CourseConnect courses follow a consistent 21-step instructional design process, yet each course is developed individually by instructional designers and instructors who have taught the course online. Test questions, created by assessment professionals, were developed at all levels of Bloom's Taxonomy. When you buy a CourseConnect course, you purchase a complete package that provides you with detailed documentation you can use for your accreditation reviews. CourseConnect courses can be delivered in any commercial platform such as WebCT, BlackBoard, Angel, or eCollege.

TWO CHOICES IN COURSECONNECT COURSES

Introduction to Paralegal Studies (covers the first 3 parts of the textbook)
Introduction to Paralegal Studies and the Law (covers all 4 parts of the textbook)

For more information regarding which course and platform application is right for your school, please contact your representative or call 800-635-1579.

VERSUSLAW® ONLINE LEGAL RESEARCH ACCESS

Pearson Education has teamed-up with VersusLaw® to provide paralegal and legal studies students with online legal research access. One-semester subscription access code cards (ISBN: 0-13-118514-4) can be packaged with any Pearson Paralegal Studies title. The VersusLaw® subscription allows students to work from the dorm, home, library, or anywhere there is an Internet connection. Receive online access to archives and current opinions from the following courts:

VersusLaw® Ⓥ

- U.S. Supreme Court
- U.S. Circuit Court of Appeals
- Federal District Court
- State Appellate Court
- Tribal Courts
- Foreign Courts

ACKNOWLEDGMENTS

A round of applause to those whose insights contributed to the learning aspects of the book. Special thanks to:

Michael Fitch, for his guidance and encouragement early in the development of the project.

Kathryn Myers, for her generosity and kindness in allowing the use of material on portfolios and for the guidance she unknowingly gave by her example of enthusiasm, dedication, and hard work in support of paralegal education.

Lilian Harris for her constant encouragement and help in developing materials on family law and the needs of tireless paralegal program directors and faculty to teach students the real-world approach.

Richard Opie for sharing his ideas and materials.

Joy Smucker for her encouragement in developing soft skills materials.

Deborah Orlik for help in really understanding the ethics of the paralegal profession.

Bill Mulkeen for his encouragement and insights to the educational needs of students.

Don Swanson, an independent paralegal, for his expertise in the role of the paralegal in e-discovery and total dedication to help paralegal students by volunteering endless hours to help paralegal educators and authors with real-life experiences and paralegal educational needs.

Members of the AAfPE board who have shared ideas and material and offer guidance in developing the materials for this book to meet the needs of the paralegal student and faculty, including Pamela Bailey, Marissa Campbell, Christine Lissitzyn, Bob LeClair, Ed Husted, and Carolyn Smoot.

The inspiring panelists and speakers at the AAfPE annual and regional meetings over the past eleven years, who provided insights, guidance, suggestions, and encouragement.

To the officers and members of the local and national professional associations, including NALA, NFPA, NALS, and ALA, for allowing the use of materials but mostly for their suggestions regarding topics and real-life issues to be covered.

Paralegal Edie Hannah of Tom Goldman's law office, for tireless reviews, detail checking, encouragement and support, countless hours on the phone getting materials, and networking with other professionals to obtain comments and input to make this textbook relevant to working paralegals as well as to students preparing for the profession.

The students in Tom Goldman's classes, for testing the text and online materials in a class setting and graciously providing suggestions and feedback.

Vivi Wang, Tiffany Lee, and Ashley Anderson, Professor Henry Cheeseman's research assistants at the Marshall School of Business at the University of Southern California, for their excellent assistance in conducting legal and paralegal research for this book.

Finally, much gratitude to the reviewers of the second edition, whose thorough comments helped to complete this edition:

Hakim Ben Adjoua, Columbus State Community College
Laura C. Barnard, Lakeland Community College

Karen Betancourt, University of Texas at Brownsville and Texas Southmost College
Carol Brady, Milwaukee Area Tech—Milwaukee
Belinda Clifton, IIA College
Karen Cook, Anne Arundel Community College
Subrina Cooper, University of Southern Mississippi
Jennifer Cote, Madonna University
Brian Craig, Minnesota School of Business—Richfield
Steven A. Dayton, Fullerton College
Robert Donley, Central Pennsylvania College
Jameka Ellison, Florida Metro University—Lakeland
Linda Gassaway, McLennan Community College
Katherine Greenwood, Loyola University
Jennifer Jenkins, South College—Knoxville
Alan Katz, Cape Fear Community College
Elaine Lerner, Kaplan College—Online
Robert McDonald, Franciscan University
Alan Mege, LeHigh Valley College
Hillary Michaud, Stevenson University
Sharla Miller-Fowler, Amarillo College
Anne Murphy Brown, J.D., Ursuline College
Kathryn L. Myers, Saint Mary-of-the-Woods College
Lisa Newman, Brown Mackie College—Atlanta
Deborah Periman, University of Alaska-Anchorage
Beth Pless, Northeast Wisconsin Technical College
Pat Roberson, New Mexico Junior College
Labron Shuman, Delaware County Community College
Kathy Smith, Community College of Philadelphia

REVIEWERS OF THE FIRST EDITION

Mercedes P. Alonso-Knapp, Florida International University
Sue Armstrong, Central Washington University
Linda Cabral Marrero, Mercy College
Chelsea Campbell, Lehman College CUNY
Anderson Castro, Florida International University
Mark A. Ciccarelli, Kent State University, OH
Ernest Davila, San Jacinto College North, Texas
Stephanie Delaney, Highline Community College
Tara L. Duncan, Everest College, Phoenix, AZ
Katharine Greenwood, Loyola University
Louise B. Gussin, University of Maryland University College
Laura J. Hansen-Brown, Kaplan University, Florida
P. Darrel Harrison, Miramar College, San Diego, CA
Linda Hornsby, Florida International University
Dee Janssen Lammers, Pima Community College, Tucson, AZ
Pierre A. Kleff, Jr., The University of Texas at Brownsville
Nance Kriscenski, Manchester Community College
Victoria H. Lopez, Southwestern College, California
Margaret Lovig, Coastline Community College, California
Leslie Miron, Mercy College
R. Eileen Mitchell, University of New Orleans
Kathryn L. Myers, Saint Mary-of-the-Woods, IN
Mary People, Arapahoe Community College, Colorado

Anthony Piazza, Dan N. Myers University
Robin Rossenfeld, Community College of Aurora, Colorado
Wesley K. Sasano, Everest College—Rancho Cucamonga, California
Deborah Vinecour, SUNY Rockland Community College
Alex A. Yarborough, Virginia College at Birmingham

Thomas F. Goldman
Henry R. Cheeseman

THIRD EDITION

The Paralegal Professional

The Essentials

The Paralegal Profession

The paralegal, or legal assistant, profession has seen explosive growth since the late 1960s. In recent years it has evolved into a profession that demands strong professional skills, a firm foundation in ethics, and increasingly higher degrees of knowledge including knowledge of technology applications. Opportunities and career choices for the paralegal have never been better. Possible employers are as diverse as the duties paralegals are asked to perform. Today's paralegals need specialized skills in many areas. Formal programs of study and continuing education programs have developed to help individuals obtain needed skills. As with other professions, ethical rules and regulations have evolved to help paralegals avoid conflicts and possible malpractice. These topics will be discussed in Part I.

The Paralegal Profession

 The great can protect themselves, but the poor and humble require the arm and shield of the law. ”

Andrew Jackson

Paralegals at Work

On the Friday before Thanksgiving, Ariel sits in the bleachers watching her high school alma mater, Lincoln High, take on Newtown. Ariel's brother, Ethan, is a line-backer on the football team and this is his last high school football game.

Ariel graduated from Lincoln in 1995 and went on to get her bachelor's degree with a major in English and a minor in Languages. She spots Mr. Marshall, her high school guid-ance counselor, and goes over to greet him.

As their conversation continues, Ariel asks Mr. Marshall about the career advice he's given to her brother. Ethan is thinking about a legal career but isn't interested in criminal justice or law enforcement. He's not sure about the time and dedication it takes to get through law school. Mr. Marshall gave Ethan information on local paralegal programs.

Ariel has been working as an editorial assistant for a small publisher of medical books. Although she always has plenty of work to do, she's not challenged in her job. She wants to use the language and writing skills she's developed, as well as have more autonomy and control over her work. Ariel asks Mr. Marshall whether a paralegal career makes sense for her.

Consider the issue involved in this scenario as you read the chapter.

INTRODUCTION TO THE PARALEGAL PROFESSION

Prior to the late 1960s, many of the functions of paralegals today were performed by those with titles such as legal secretary, lay assistant, and legal clerk or law clerk (the latter of which usually was reserved for the recent law school graduate who had not yet passed the bar exam). Members of the legal profession and the legal community increasingly see the paralegal as a member of the legal services delivery team. As paralegals' educational level increases, so will the responsibility given to them. In many areas of law, the cost of legal services has increased. The use of paralegals in many cases permits the delivery of quality legal services at a reduced cost to the client.

Opportunities and career choices for the paralegal have never been better. Paralegals are employed in every area of the delivery of legal services. They interview clients, conduct factual investigations, do legal research, prepare legal documents, assist at the counsel table in trials, and even represent clients in some administrative hearings. They are employed in law firms of all sizes, federal, state, and local government, insurance companies, and corporations.

What Is a Paralegal?

Paralegal (legal assistant)
A person qualified by education, training, or work experience who is employed or retained by a lawyer, law office, corporation, governmental agency, or other entity who performs specifically delegated substantive legal work for which a lawyer is responsible; equivalent term is legal assistant.

American Bar Association (ABA) Largest professional legal organization in the United States.

National Federation of Paralegal Associations (NFPA) Professional organization of state and local paralegal associations founded in 1974.

National Association of Legal Assistants (NALA) Professional organization for legal assistants that provides continuing education and professional certification for paralegals, incorporated in 1975.

A great deal of confusion has arisen as to what the professional in this field should be called or what the professionals should call themselves. The most popular terms, **paralegal** and **legal assistant,** have been used in most of the United States. These terms were used interchangeably by the **American Bar Association (ABA),** the **National Federation of Paralegal Associations (NFPA),** and the **National Association of Legal Assistants (NALA).** The confusion stems in part from the shift from the title of "secretary" to "administrative assistant" and, in some offices and educational institutions, "law office assistant."

The exact definition of legal assistant has been the subject of discussions by national organizations including the ABA, NFPA, and NALA, as well as many state legislatures, supreme courts, and bar associations. The trend is toward the use of the term *paralegal* and away from using the term *legal assistant.* Originally called the Standing Committee on Legal Assistants, the American Bar Association changed its name to the Standing Committee on Paralegals, in recognition of this trend.

The American Bar Association's 1997 version of the definition, which also has been adopted by the National Association of Legal Assistants, is:

> A legal assistant or paralegal is a person, qualified by education, training, or work experience who is employed or retained by a lawyer, law office, corporation, governmental agency or other entity and who performs specifically delegated substantive legal work for which a lawyer is responsible.

The National Federation of Paralegal Associations adopted a resolution in 2002 eliminating the term *legal assistant* from its definition of *paralegal* because that term now is being used to refer to positions outside the paralegal definition. Accordingly, NFPA defines a paralegal as follows:

> A paralegal is a person qualified through education, training or work experience to perform substantive legal work that requires knowledge of legal concepts as customarily, but not exclusively performed by a lawyer. This person may be retained or employed by a lawyer, law office, governmental agency or other entity or may be authorized by administrative, statutory or court authority to perform this work.

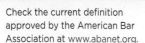

Web Exploration

Check the current definition approved by the American Bar Association at www.abanet.org.

Web Exploration

Review the full NFPA resolution at www.paralegals.org.

What Do Paralegals Do?

The primary function of paralegals is to assist attorneys in preparing for hearings, trials, meetings, and real estate closings. In many cases paralegals do the preparatory work, helping to draft documents, assisting in the preparation of other documents and

Paralegals *in* Practice

PARALEGAL PROFILE
Vicki L. Karayan

During her 12-year paralegal career, Vicki L. Karayan has worked for both law firms and business corporations. She is currently employed in Camarillo, California, at WellPoint, Inc., the nation's second largest company in the health care industry. As an Advanced Certified Paralegal, her present position of Business Change Advisor focuses on compliance reporting and legal research for the company's consumer marketing department.

I became inspired to pursue a paralegal career after going through a difficult, personal legal battle. After graduating with an Associate's degree in Applied Science with a Legal Studies emphasis, I worked in a general practice firm. Later, I worked for a bankruptcy law firm where I eventually became the trainer/staff manager of seven offices. A family move led to a new job in a nationwide bankruptcy firm where I learned to track federal and state regulatory requirements.

In order to work closer to home, I took an Administrative Assistant position in the Medicaid Marketing department for a corporate health care company. What started as an entry level job grew into a whole new position, as I offered better ways to tackle the company's market compliance reporting and legal research, and also helped improve office efficiency and staff training. Three promotions later, I believe I owe much of my career success to actively looking for opportunities to apply knowledge and skills learned from previous jobs and experiences, and from learning how to network with people, building strong working relationships based on ethical practices.

My advice is: try not to limit yourself to traditional paralegal job descriptions. Some of the best opportunities are found by looking "outside the box" and obtaining as many business and technology skills as possible. Finally, find what you love to do, and then network by making new business connections through individuals you already know and others you meet. These contacts can help your work go more smoothly and provide invaluable information in the future.

---

forms, coordinating the activities and functions required in some cases, and in many offices maintaining the financial records of the firm.

People tend to think of paralegals as working in a private law office directly under the supervision of attorneys. Actually, employers of the paralegal are just as diverse as the duties they are asked to perform. Many paralegals are employed by the federal government, as well as state and local governments including regulatory bodies. The paralegal's activities might include analyzing legal material for internal use and collecting and analyzing data, as well as preparing information and explanatory material, for use by the general public.

More and more paralegals are coming to the profession from other professions. For example, they may come from nursing, bringing with them a specialized body of knowledge that they combine with the legal skills they learned in a paralegal program. With this expertise they frequently are hired to analyze case materials for trial attorneys, both plaintiff and defense, and also are employed as case analysts and as claims representatives for health insurance companies. Their knowledge of medicine, combined with their legal knowledge, gives them a unique ability to analyze specialized material.

Other specialties can take the same career path. Those with engineering and other Bachelor of Science degrees bring specialized expertise to the law, such as patent and intellectual property law. A paralegal with a criminal justice or a forensic science background, for example, may well be the ideal paralegal to work with criminal defense attorneys and prosecutors.

Prior to the recognition of a separate paralegal profession, individuals typically had acquired specialized knowledge of a narrow legal field through on-the-job training. Someone working with a lawyer—usually a secretary—learned the daily routine tasks and become knowledgeable about that specific area of law. Many of these individuals became resource sources of information, such as the documentation requirements for real estate settlements, the preparation and filing of estate and trust accountings, and the procedures for preparing and filing cases and appeals. These were the first paralegals. Today, many of the skills and procedures formerly acquired over an

Web Exploration

Review the Model Standards and Guidelines of the National Association of Legal Assistants at http://www.nala.org/stand.htm.

Advice *from the* Field

Kathleen Call is executive director of Robert Half Legal, a leading staffing service specializing in the placement of legal professionals ranging from project attorneys and paralegals to administrators, legal secretaries and other support staff. Robert Half Legal, which works with law firms and corporate legal departments, has offices throughout the United States and Canada.

When you think of which skills will be most important to your career advancement over the next five years, chances are "proficiency with technology" ranks high on your list. Knowledge of key software applications has become a critical success factor in the legal profession. However, to be considered for the best job opportunities in the future, you'll not only need technical competency, but also solid interpersonal skills and problem-solving abilities.

Audio- and video-conferencing, email, corporate Intranets and, of course, the Internet have increased exponentially the amount—and speed—of day-to-day professional communication. The expanded use of technology will make it more important for legal professionals to be able to communicate effectively and articulately.

Another significant development driving the need for strong soft skills is the trend toward a more collaborative workplace. In a team-based office environment, diplomacy, flexibility, persuasiveness and management skills are critical. In a survey we commissioned among executives at the nation's 1,000 largest companies, 79 percent of respondents said self-managed employee work teams will increase productivity for U.S. companies. These productivity gains will only be realized, however, if team members can work together effectively. As a result, firms are placing a premium on excellent interpersonal skills.

WHAT ARE PEOPLE SKILLS?

Since soft skills are intangible and therefore hard to quantify, how do you determine whether you have what it takes to succeed? Our firm has identified a composite of key interpersonal traits represented by the acronym "PEOPLE":

Problem-solving abilities (organization, judgment, logic, creativity, conflict resolution)

Ethics (diplomacy, courtesy, honesty, professionalism)

Open-mindedness (flexibility, open to new business ideas, positive outlook)

Persuasiveness (excellent communication and listening skills)

Leadership (accountability, management and motivational skills)

Educational interests (continuous thirst for knowledge and skills development)

A deficiency in these skills can seriously limit your career prospects, whether you're applying for a new job as a legal assistant or seeking to move upward as an attorney within your current firm. Just as workers who failed to enhance their technical skills were left behind by the digital revolution, those who dismiss the significance of PEOPLE skills can find themselves stagnating in dead-end jobs.

ASSESS YOUR STRENGTHS AND WEAKNESSES

While it's relatively easy to measure the development of your proficiency with technology, it's much more challenging to gauge your progress in enhancing your PEOPLE skills. Again, this is primarily because these qualities are more subjective in nature. Since there are no classes on "flexibility" or "positive outlook" at the typical college or university, how do you acquire and upgrade your interpersonal abilities?

The following steps will help you take an accurate inventory of your strengths and weaknesses:

Honestly evaluate your aptitude in each of the PEOPLE skills. Which seem to come naturally? Is there room for improvement in any area?

Ask trusted friends, family members and coworkers for their opinions. How would they rate your PEOPLE skills?

COMMIT TO LEARNING

It takes time and experience to fully develop interpersonal skills, so don't expect to see improvement overnight. Here are some effective strategies to help you continue your progress:

Develop a list of the characteristics you'd most like to develop in yourself. Then brainstorm specific activities that will boost your abilities in your selected areas. For example, if you'd like to refine your leadership skills, volunteer to work on cases that provide the opportunity to supervise others or manage a project from start to finish.

Observe those who demonstrate strong PEOPLE skills in the areas you'd like to improve. How do they apply their abilities in various situations? How are their responses different than what yours would be?

Select a mentor. The best candidate is someone in the legal field whom you admire. Ask your prospective mentor if he or she would advise you, particularly in those PEOPLE skills that you've determined require enhancement. Since it's difficult to see yourself objectively, a mentor's ongoing support and feedback can be invaluable.

Enhance your listening skills. Concentrate on paying close attention to what others are saying. In general, avoid interrupting but ask for clarification when necessary. To prevent misunderstandings, paraphrase information in your own words when you are given complex instructions.

Become a better writer. Read books on effective writing so that you can develop a more concise style, or consider taking a journalism or business writing course. Proofread everything you write, especially e-mail. Because electronic messages are prepared and sent quickly, they can be inadvertently filled with typographical and grammatical errors. In addition, it's important to employ PEOPLE skills in your writing, explaining yourself diplomatically and courteously.

Refine your verbal communication. Know what you want to say before you speak, and use a tone and style appropriate to the audience. When leaving a voice-mail message, organize your thoughts in advance to avoid being vague or rambling. If you're presenting a report to an attorney or client, rehearse a few times so your delivery will be smooth and your message clear.

Become a volunteer. You can acquire stronger leadership and organizational skills through volunteer work. Whether it's becoming involved in a trade association or helping your favorite charity, the skills you develop can be used on the job in a variety of situations.

Seek growth opportunities outside the workplace. Hobbies and leisure-time activities are an enjoyable way to enrich your PEOPLE skills. By coaching your child's soccer team, for example, you'll develop motivational and managerial skills, and become better at dealing with diverse personalities. If you'd like to enhance your creativity, consider taking an art or music class.

Copyright © Robert Half Legal. Reprinted with permission.

extended time on the job are taught at institutions specializing in the education of paralegals or legal assistants, offering a certificate program, a two-year associate degree program, or a four-year bachelor's degree program.

In 1968 the American Bar Association formed a committee to investigate the use of lay assistants in the legal office. The result was the American Bar Association's forming the Standing Committee on Legal Assistants, later changed to Standing Committee on Paralegals. The ABA gave this committee jurisdiction over training and standards for the education of legal assistants. Within this jurisdiction the Standing Committee on Paralegals monitors trends in the field and recommends to the House of Delegates—the policymaking body of the American Bar Association—training programs that meet its standards for quality education.

Professional Skills

The skills needed by a paralegal are varied and depend, in some cases, on the nature of the legal specialty in which one works. Common to all paralegals are certain professional skills, also known as soft skills, including communication skills, initiative, resourcefulness, problem solving, commitment or "stick-to-itiveness," team working, leadership, and self-motivation, among others.

Everyone has goals in life. You might be an accomplished jogger who longs to win the Boston Marathon, or a skilled writer who has visions of writing the great American novel. Achieving most goals requires some set of skills. If your goal is to be a successful paralegal, you will need certain basic skills. You may possess some of these already, and may need to acquire others. Some of the basic skills you already have are:

- the ability to read English—unless someone is reading this book to you
- the ability to communicate at some level in writing or speaking
- initiative—because you have signed up for this course or have picked up this book to read and learn about the paralegal profession

In addition, you may have skills such as

- facility with computers and the Internet
- the ability to speak a second or third language
- a background in medicine, engineering, business, or other academic or occupational area

Some other skills are less obvious—resourcefulness, commitment or stick-to-itiveness, analytical skills and interpersonal skills including cultural sensitivity—so we will explore them in more depth. We cannot all run a marathon or type 160 words a minute, but we all can acquire most of the basic skills by making an effort to improve ourselves and attain the knowledge base to achieve most, if not all, of our goals.

Many people achieve much more than they, themselves, and others believed they were capable of achieving—by just plain hard work. If you want something bad enough and are willing to work hard enough, you can achieve your personal and professional goals. A good starting point in achieving your goals is to understand your strengths and weaknesses, capitalize on the strengths, and work on improving the weaknesses.

NATIONAL ASSOCIATION OF LEGAL ASSISTANTS MODEL STANDARDS AND GUIDELINES FOR UTILIZATION OF LEGAL ASSISTANTS PARALEGALS

Preamble

Proper utilization of the services of legal assistants contributes to the delivery of cost effective, high-quality legal services. Legal assistants and the legal profession should be assured that measures exist for identifying legal assistants and their role in assisting attorneys in the delivery of legal services. Therefore, the National Association of Legal Assistants, Inc., hereby adopts these Standards and Guidelines as an educational document for the benefit of legal assistants and the legal profession. . . .

III Standards

A legal assistant should meet certain minimum qualifications. The following standards may be used to determine an individual's qualifications as a legal assistant:

(1) Successful completion of the Certified Legal Assistant (CLA)/Certified Paralegal (CP) certifying examination of the National Association of Legal Assistants, Inc.;

(2) Graduation from an ABA approved program of study for legal assistants;

(3) Graduation from a course of study for legal assistants which is institutionally accredited but not ABA approved, and which requires not less than the equivalent of 60 semester hours of classroom study;

(4) Graduation from a course of study for legal assistants, other than those set forth in (2) and (3) above, plus not less than six months of in-house training as a legal assistant;

(5) A baccalaureate degree in any field, plus not less than six months in-house training as a legal assistant;

(6) A minimum of three years of law-related experience under the supervision of an attorney, including at least six months of in-house training as a legal assistant; or

(7) Two years of in-house training as a legal assistant.

For purposes of these Standards, "in-house training as a legal assistant" means attorney education of the employee concerning legal assistant duties and these Guidelines. In addition to review and analysis of assignments, the legal assistant should receive a reasonable amount of instruction directly related to the duties and obligations of the legal assistant.

SOURCE: Copyright 1984, adopted 1984; revised 1991, 1997, 2005. Reprinted with permission of the National Association of Legal Assistants, www.nala.org, 1516 S. Boston, #200, Tulsa, OK 74119.

CHECKLIST Strengths and Weaknesses

- ☐ My strengths:
- ☐ How can I capitalize on my strengths?

- ☐ My weaknesses:
- ☐ How can I overcome my weaknesses?

Resourcefulness

Resourcefulness is the ability to meet and handle a situation and find solutions to problems. It is one of the most valuable skills anyone can have—and one that is not easily taught. A resourceful person in the office is sometimes referred to as the "can-do" person on the team. This is the person who usually finds some creative way to accomplish what everyone else has given up on. Certainly, creativity is involved— solving the problem by thinking outside the box and not limiting the solution to tried-and-true methods.

The skill of organizing includes the ability to

- categorize
- prioritize
- organize
- utilize time efficiently

When everyone else says, "I can't find this witness," the resourceful person tries a new approach and finds the witness. When others use only the standard telephone directories, the resourceful person uses the cross-reference directory. When local telephone directories do not yield results, resourceful people use the national telephone directories on CD and the online Internet telephone directories.

In the legal workplace the person who gets noticed is the one who finds a way to get the job done in time for the hearing, meeting, or arbitration. This is the person who is willing to use unconventional ways to get the job finished, such as when the power goes out or the computer system crashes just before a deadline. Lawyers want resourceful people on their team and reward them to keep them on the team.

Commitment

Commitment means finishing what one starts out to do or complete. From our childhood we remember the story of the tortoise and the hare (rabbit), in which the tortoise wins the race by being "slow and steady." The tortoise wins in part because of commitment— putting everything into the race and not stopping until the job is done. Many people start jobs and don't finish them. Others start what seems to be an insurmountable task and— to their amazement and maybe ours—finish, and finish well. Taking on an assignment in a law office requires commitment. Team members are expected to finish the task, whether it is researching a case, writing a brief, filing a pleading, or organizing a file.

As a professional, you are expected to finish the tasks within the assigned timeframe. There is no excuse for not doing some tasks, such as filing the complaint with the court before the statute of limitations expires, or getting the brief to the court by the court-imposed deadline. Even a simple thing like getting to court on time requires commitment.

Not everyone has the necessary commitment or wants to take on the responsibility of meeting commitments. You have to decide whether you are willing to make the commitment. Others will be depending on you, and if you do not want to commit, admit it to yourself and to the others who are depending on you, and then choose some other activity or profession. Choosing a profession, whether it is the legal profession, the paralegal profession, the medical profession, or the accounting profession, requires a commitment to serve others. As a professional, you are making a commitment to your clients that you will provide the best professional advice, skill, and effort. They depend on this professionalism and the necessary commitment.

Analytical Skills

Analytical skills allow one to follow a step-by-step process to solve a problem. It could be finding a missing witness by looking in telephone books, or determining that the person is part of a group, such as a professional society or an organization that publishes a membership directory. Solving these types of problems requires analytical skills to figure out, for instance, what made a bottle explode, injuring a client. Determining the actual cause requires a step-by-step analysis of the potential reasons and the narrowing down of possible causes.

CREATING AN IMPRESSION

SIDEBAR

Unless you are intentionally trying to create a different impression, try to

- have a positive attitude
- be diplomatic
- be flexible
- establish good rapport with others
- be a team player
- be resourceful
- be adaptable
- be thorough

One of the basic skills that law students and paralegal students are taught is legal analysis, the ability to identify the facts and legal issues and contrast and compare them to the law and to other cases. This is a skill that develops with time. As you learn the elements of crimes, torts, and other areas of law, you will learn the individual parts of each. In contracts law, you will learn what conduct is a valid acceptance of a contract offer, and in tort law, what constitutes reasonable conduct under the circumstances.

Interpersonal Skills

Vital to paralegal success, as well as to success in other endeavors, is the ability to work with people. To categorize people, coworkers, colleagues, and employers might be unfair, but we all do it. We think—and sometimes say—things like, "He's a pleasure to work with" or, "She has clients eating out of her hand." Conversely, we might say things like, "She's the most negative person I know," or "He's only out for himself." These comments reflect the other person's interpersonal skills (or lack thereof), the ability to work with and communicate with others.

How we relate to others can make the job easier or harder. These others include not just coworkers as members of the legal team but also clients, witnesses, and opposing parties. Obviously, everyone in the firm or on the team must have a level of trust and confidence in the others on the team. People who have a good working relationship accomplish more and enjoy doing it. By contrast, conflict and tension make the job harder and can cause people to take shortcuts and avoid contact, which can result in poor performance and potential malpractice.

Not everyone has the personality to deal with every type of situation and every type of personality—for example, dealing with clients. But everyone on the legal team has to develop the skills to work with people and recognize when they may have to have someone else handle certain aspects of a case or client. The skill is in recognizing when and how they can affect relationships and results. Some might call this "sensitivity"—to other people's needs, desires, wants, likes, and dislikes.

Cultural differences are discussed later, but in the American culture, for example, people tend to be sensitive to odors—breath, body, environmental. We do not want to offend. Our use of language is another area of sensitivity. We try to avoid using words that we believe will offend the other person in a specific circumstance, such as telling off-color jokes in a religious setting in front of a person of the cloth.

The starting point in working with attorneys, paralegals, and support staff, clients and opposing counsel, court personnel and others, is to be sensitive to issues such as these. What offends you probably offends others. Being sensitive to how others react to your words, conduct, and actions can provide good clues as to what is acceptable and what is not.

In the past, how we related to others and how others perceived us was measured by direct face-to-face contact, telephone contact, and written communications. Today we have to add to those forms of communication the way we write emails and use electronic communications. These technological advances make our communications more immediate. Too many happy faces and frowning faces, such as:) or :(in an email could be interpreted as overfamiliarity. THE USE OF ALL CAPITAL LETTERS might be interpreted as shouting at the reader. Poor spelling and bad grammar in emails are likely to be seen as less than professional or pure sloppiness or carelessness. In the past, letters were dictated, typed, proofread, and then signed. Today we dash off an email without much thought—and sometimes it reflects just that. How our clients view our capabilities and skill now might be measured by that quick email response.

Communication Skills

Communication means expressing ideas effectively. The practice of law requires good communication, both oral and written. The lawyer and the paralegal who work together must be able to communicate assignments and information with clarity and, frequently, brevity. Over time, communication will improve, as each person comes to understand what the other is really asking or saying.

Communication is made complex by subtleties, nuances, and expressions that may require interpretation or explanation. For example, older attorneys who are used to using traditional methods of research may ask the new paralegal (who has a deep understanding of computer research methods and little traditional book experience) to "check the pocket parts." This means checking for the latest update or change to a statute or case law. Or asking a paralegal to "Shepardize" a case may have no meaning to one who has learned only the West system, in which the method for checking other cases is called KeyCiting, or the Loislaw system, which refers to this as GlobalCiting.

Communication can be a major problem in the fast-paced office when the litigation attorney sends a message from court in the middle of a case to the support paralegal at the office, by a two-way pager, after the other side has brought up an unexpected case in argument to the court. Nowadays, we rarely have the luxury of time to develop a common written and oral language base for communication among the paralegal, clients, opposing attorneys, and court personnel. Letters, pleadings, contracts, and other written documents must be clear and accurate. In many situations, only one document must carefully communicate the idea, request, or demand.

Oral communication also must be clear and precise. The old adage still holds true: First impressions matter. If a first discussion in person or by telephone is filled with slang and poor grammar, the impression may affect the client's or court's view of the firm's professionalism, ability, and legal skills. It can influence the client's decision to stay with the firm or not, the judge's granting the request, or the court clerk's giving you the help you need.

Career Planning

Career planning should include educational planning and a plan for perfecting professional skills. A sound educational plan builds on a sound foundation, at the base of which are general education courses that will assist in any occupational choice and are acceptable in meeting basic core requirements either for an associate's degree or a bachelor's degree. Occupation-related courses such as paralegal specialty courses should be selected with an eye toward transferability and suitability in a higher-level educational pursuit.

This is not to say that all courses must be transferable from school to school or from associate-degree program to bachelor's- or master's-degree program. Something can be learned from every course you take, including the realization that you do not wish to pursue this area of study further. Think of the people you know who have pursued a career only to discover later that they are not interested in this line of work. One of your early educational goals should be to explore areas of your actual or potential interest. Many students even find a career goal after taking one of the dreaded required courses.

Therefore, you should be prepared to explore new areas of specialty and new technology. It is clearer today than ever that successful paralegals have a good foundation in computer skills. Further, you will have to maintain and build upon these skills as ever more sophisticated online service and resources continues.

 Web Exploration

Check the available resources for paralegal students at the different national paralegal organizations:

National Federation of Paralegal Associations
http://www.paralegals.org

National Association of Legal Assistants
http://www.nala.org

Association of Legal Administrators
http://www.alanet.org

International Paralegal Management Association
http://www.paralegal management.org/ipma/

NALS.... the Association for Legal Professionals
http://www.nals.org

CHECKLIST My Career Roadmap

- ☐ Skills I need to acquire:
- ☐ Skills I need to strengthen:
- ☐ Courses I should take:
- ☐ Extracurricular activities for the resume:

- ☐ Interim work experience I should seek:
- ☐ Volunteer activities:
- ☐ Short-term career goals:
- ☐ Long-term career goals:

Paralegal Education in the United States

According to the Department of Labor, occupations requiring a postsecondary vocational award or an academic degree accounted for 25 percent of all jobs in 1998, 29 percent of all jobs in 2000, and will account for 42 percent of total job growth from 2000 to 2010.

The best trained, most skilled individual clearly will be the one to get the job. The challenge in obtaining your first job is to demonstrate that you are the best person for the job. Consider the prospective employer comparing the resumes of a number of paralegal job applicants. One paralegal has a high school diploma and a paralegal certificate. Another applicant has an associate degree or even a bachelor's degree in paralegal studies. Which would you hire?

An estimated 1000 paralegal education programs are available in the United States. These programs are offered in on-site, online, and hybrid format combining online and on-site instruction. Some of these programs have obtained ABA approval of their paralegal education program. Many of the institutions offering these programs are members of the American Association for Paralegal Education (AAfPE), which, as a condition of institutional membership, requires substantial compliance with the ABA guidelines for approval of a paralegal program.

What are the qualifications that permit one to call oneself a paralegal or a legal assistant, and to be billed as a paralegal? The answer is not easy to come by. Just as the practice of law falls to the individual states for regulation, so does regulation of the paralegal profession. Presently regulations lack uniformity, either by statute or by court rules. Without a state law such as the California Statute shown in Exhibit 1.2 on page 23 or a court rule, perhaps the most consistent and universal recognition of minimum qualifications are those established by the educational guidelines of the American Bar Association's Standing Committee on Paralegals and the **American Association for Paralegal Education (AAfPE),** a national association of legal educators. The minimum educational requirements for certification of the educational institutions' program of study have become the de facto standard of the minimum qualifications to call one a paralegal or legal assistant.

The ABA Standing Committee Guidelines require that instruction be at the postsecondary level and contain at least 60 semester hours including general educational and legal specialty courses. Of these 60 hours, at least 18 must be general education courses and at least 18 must be legal specialty courses.

For purposes of the Guidelines, a "legal specialty course" is interpreted in Guideline G-303(c)d as a course (1) in a specific area of law, procedure, or legal process, (2) which has been developed for legal assistants and emphasizes legal assistant skills, forms, documents, procedures, and legal principles and theories, and (3) which is pertinent to the legal assistants' performance of a job.

The American Bar Association and the American Association for Paralegal Education are voluntary programs. As stated by the ABA,

> Seeking approval from the American Bar Association is a voluntary process initiated by the institution offering the program. Therefore, the lack of approval does not necessarily mean a paralegal program is not of good quality and reputable.

The majority of programs may have chosen not to undergo the cost or process for approval by the ABA or for membership in the AAfPE, or offer a majority of courses in online or hybrid format that do not meet the ABA guidelines, which limit the number of such courses that may be offered as part of the program of study.

Types of Educational Programs

The goal of the educational experience is to get a job and be able to perform at a professional level. The demands on paralegals today require them to have higher-level skills and ability than in the past. Whereas basic typing, office, and business communications skills might have been acceptable for a starting position in a law firm

American Association for Paralegal Education (AAfPE) National organization of paralegal educators and institutions offering paralegal education programs.

RELEVANT PARALEGAL SKILLS

Skill Development

- Critical thinking skills
- Organizational skills
- General communication skills
- Interpersonal skills
- Legal research skills
- Legal writing skills
- Computer skills
- Interviewing and investigation skills

Acquisition of Knowledge

- Organization and operation of the legal system
- Organization and operation of law offices
- The paralegal profession and ethical obligations
- Contracts
- Torts
- Business organizations
- Litigation procedures

twenty years ago, these are not the skills demanded for those looking for a paralegal position today.

More and more employers today also are asking for transcripts showing the courses taken and the minimum number of hours of study as spelled out in the ABA guidelines, even for graduates of educational institutions that have not obtained ABA certification of their programs. The reality is that many attorneys do not know the educational requirements to obtain a paralegal degree or certificate. And in many cases they do not know the elements of the ABA, NFPA, or NALA definitions of paralegal or legal assistant.

Paralegal/legal assistant educational programs generally fall into two categories: (a) those offering a certificate, and (b) those offering a degree, either an **associate's degree** or a **bachelor's degree.** These programs of study may be offered by a two-year community college or junior college or a four-year college or university. A number of business and private **(proprietary)** schools also offer paralegal/legal assistant programs of study.

Students' educational and professional backgrounds will determine, in many cases, which of the programs to select. Those with bachelor's and higher academic degrees may need only the legal specialty courses. Those who come from a specialty background, such as nursing or one heavy in science courses, may want to broaden their education by taking courses of a general nature in addition to the legal specialty courses.

Certificate Programs

Most educational institutions with paralegal/legal assistant programs, both public and private, offer a certificate. The **certificate** recognizes completion of a program of study that requires less than is required to receive a degree. Some certificates award college credits; some do not. For students who already possess a baccalaureate degree, obtaining additional college credits probably isn't an issue. For students without an undergraduate degree, programs that do not offer college credit still can be valuable but should be considered carefully. At the very least, the actual time spent in the classroom should be equivalent to the minimums of college credit courses.

Students' concerns should be for what is acceptable in the community in which they intend to work. Those planning to transfer should consider the acceptability of the course for transferring credit to another credit-granting institution. Even if they have no immediate intent to continue in school, they would be wise to plan ahead and not lose the hours and credits they have earned, in the event they later decide to transfer or go on to obtain a degree.

Many professional paralegal organizations are reporting that a bachelor's degree is becoming more necessary to enter the paralegal field and some programs. The U.S. Attorney's Office, for example, is requiring at least a four-year degree to consider individuals for a paralegal position.

Associate's degree A college degree in science (AS) arts (AA), or applied arts (AAS), generally requiring two years of full-time study.

Bachelor's degree A college degree generally requiring four years of full-time study.

Proprietary school Private, as opposed to public, institution, generally for profit, offering training and education.

Certificate A recognition of the completion of a program of study that requires less than that needed for a degree.

Associate Degree Programs

Many community colleges and junior colleges offer an associate degree in science (AS degree) or in arts (AA degree) or applied arts (AAS degree) in paralegal or legal assistant studies. For many students the two-year community college or junior college programs offer a community-based transition into higher education. For others it is a way of getting back into higher education while working at a full-time job or after being in another occupation.

Support services for returning students or students who need additional help are often available. Many of these schools offer English courses for those for whom English is a second language and those returning to school who need a refresher course or help with study skills after years away from school. This also tends to be a cost-effective educational environment for trying different areas of study before finding an area of concentration.

Baccalaureate Programs

Web Exploration

IPMA Position Paper is available at www.paralegalmanagement .org/ipmadocs/education% 20position%20paper.pdf.

Some of the earliest paralegal programs were built on a model in which a bachelor's degree was the prerequisite for entering the paralegal program of study. A number of programs now offer a bachelor's degree in paralegal studies. One national organization—the International Paralegal Management Association (IPMA)—has recommended the bachelor's degree as the minimum qualification to enter the profession. The increase in professional recognition of paralegals has resulted in their gaining more responsibility, as well as a growing demand for the skills required to perform the assigned tasks. As the standing of the paralegal on the legal team rises, so will the demand for those with a broad-based educational background to serve in those positions. Four-year programs of study are attempting to meet that demand by merging traditional four-year study core requirements and legal specialty courses.

Consider the family law attorney or paralegal. In the frequently highly charged emotional environment of custody and divorce, knowledge of family and child psychology is essential. For those in an intellectual-property practice, an understanding of science and engineering is a basic requirement. The four-year timeframe allows more flexibility to explore and build skills and knowledge, as well as to meet the increasing demand for more education for paralegals.

Graduate Programs

A few colleges and universities now offer graduate degrees in legal studies. Others offer advanced degrees in related areas such as legal administration.

Specialty Certificates

Specialty certificates, such as the paralegal certificate or the legal nurse consultant certificate, offer an excellent entry point into a paralegal career. Specialty certificates combined with degrees in other fields of study, such as nursing, journalism, and computer science, are like a capstone program preparing a person for entry into a new career. One of the greatest demands has been for those with a background in nursing combined with a paralegal education. A growing number of colleges are offering a certificate in Legal Nurse Consulting.

Paralegal Advanced Competency Exam (PACE) National Federation of Paralegal Association's certification program that requires the paralegal to have two years of experience and a bachelor's degree and have completed a paralegal course at an accredited school.

Paralegal Certification

The National Federation of Paralegal Associations (NFPA) administers an exam to test the competency level of experienced paralegals known as **Paralegal Advance Competency Exam (PACE),** which requires that:

> . . . the paralegal cannot have been convicted of a felony nor be under suspension, termination, or revocation of a certificate, registration, or license by any entity.

- An associates degree in paralegal studies obtained from an institutionally accredited and/or ABA approved paralegal education program; and six (6) years substantive paralegal experience; OR
- A bachelor's degree in any course of study obtained from an institutionally accredited school and three (3) years of substantive paralegal experience; OR
- A bachelor's degree and completion of a paralegal program with an institutionally accredited school; said paralegal program may be embodied in a bachelor's degree; and two (2) years substantive paralegal experience; OR
- four (4) years substantive paralegal experience on or before December 31, 2000.

Those who successfully pass the exam may use the designation "PACE-Registered Paralegal, or RP." Continued use of the designation requires 12 additional hours of continuing legal or specialty education every 2 years, with at least one hour of legal ethics.

Since 1976, the National Association of Legal Assistants has conferred the **Certified Legal Assistant (CLA)** designation on those who pass its national certification program's two-day comprehensive examination. In 2004, NALA registered the certification mark CP with the U.S. Patent and Trademark Office for those who prefer the term Certified Paralegal. To be eligible to take the exam requires the following.

1. Graduation from a legal assistant program that is:
   - approved by the American Bar Association; or
   - an associate degree program; or
   - a post-baccalaureate certificate program in legal assistant studies; or
   - a bachelor's degree program in legal assistant studies; or
   - a legal assistant program which consists of a minimum of 60 semester hours (900 clock hours or 90 quarter hours) of which at least 15 semester hours (225 clock hours or 22.5 quarter hours) are substantive legal courses.
2. A bachelor's degree in any field plus one year's experience as a legal assistant. Successful completion of at least 15 semester hours (or 22.5 quarter hours or 225 clock hours) of substantive legal assistant courses will be considered equivalent to one year's experience as a legal assistant.
3. A high school diploma or equivalent plus seven (7) year's experience as a legal assistant under the supervision of a member of the Bar, plus evidence of a minimum of twenty (20) hours of continuing legal education credit to have been completed within a two (2) year period prior to the examination date.

To maintain use of the CLA designation, evidence must be submitted of completion of 50 hours of continuing legal assistant education every five years. For those who have achieved the initial designation, NALA also offers specialist credentials for those practicing in a specific area of law, such as bankruptcy, intellectual property, civil litigation, probate, and estate planning. Successful completion of these examinations permits the additional designation CLAS, Certified Legal Assistant–Specialty.

NALS offers members and nonmembers the opportunity to sit for three unique certifications dedicated to the legal services profession—ALS, PLS, and PP. The exams are of varying levels and are developed by professionals in the industry.

1. **ALS**—the basic certification for legal professionals exam—covers:
   Part 1: Written Communications
   Part 2: Office Procedures and Legal Knowledge
   Part 3: Ethics, Human Relations, and Judgment
2. **PLS**—the advanced certification for legal professionals exam—covers:
   Part 1: Written Communications
   Part 2: Office Procedures and Technology
   Part 3: Ethics and Judgment
   Part 4: Legal Knowledge and Skills

Web Exploration

Detailed information on PACE can be obtained at http://www.paralegals.org/displaycommon.cfm?an517.

Certified Legal Assistant (CLA) Designation by National Association of Legal Assistants for those who take and pass NALA certification program two-day comprehensive examination.

Web Exploration

General information about paralegal certification, including requirements, exam subjects, and testing schedule can be found at http://www.nala.org/cert.htm.

ALS (Accredited Legal Secretary) The basic certification for legal professionals from NALS.

PLS (Professional Legal Secretary) The advanced certification for legal professionals from NALS.

PP (Professional Paralegal)
Certification from NALS for those performing paralegal duties.

3. **PP** (Professional Paralegal)—professionals performing paralegal duties. Examination eligibility requires five years' experience performing paralegal/legal assistant duties (a candidate may receive a partial waiver of one year if he or she has a postsecondary degree, other certification, or a paralegal certificate; a candidate with a paralegal degree may receive a two-year partial waiver). The exam covers:

> Part 1: Written Communications
> Part 2: Legal Knowledge and Skills
> Part 3: Ethics and Judgment Skills
> Part 4: Substantive Law

A comparison of the various exams—NALS, NALA, and NFPA—is presented in Exhibit 1.1

Minimum Education

International Paralegal Management Association (IPMA) A North American association for legal assistant managers.

The **International Paralegal Management Association (IPMA)** is an organization for paralegal management professionals. In its position paper on paralegal education it states that "nearly 80% of IPMA member organizations require the bachelor's degree when hiring, and many require specific paralegal education and/or give credit for professional certifications."

Legal assistants have assumed many responsibilities formerly handled by lawyers. Working with complex legal issues requires that a legal assistant possess clear writing, researching, and critical thinking abilities.

National Association of Legal Secretaries (NALS) Since 1999 an association for legal professionals, originally formed in 1949 as an association for legal secretaries.

Making a Personal Assessment and Setting Goals

If you are reading this book, you probably have made at least a tentative career goal to enter the paralegal profession, with the ultimate goal of obtaining a job. It should not be "just a job" but, rather, a job that will give you satisfaction and one that you will get up and go to with anticipation, not dread. The paralegal field offers many and varied specialties. An early goal should be to take courses that will introduce you to the specialty you would enjoy most. Maybe you already are well versed in something that will lead to a specialty, such as nursing, one of the sciences, or law enforcement.

Web Exploration

For the IPMA survey results, go to http://www.paralegalmanagement .org/ipma/detail.asp?linkID =69&heading=Utilization+ Survey+Results.

One of the first steps is to assess your own skills. What are your other educational skills? What are your personality traits? Do you like working under deadlines or working with certain groups of people, such as elderly people or those with disabilities?

As you will find out, the paralegal profession offers opportunities in many areas of legal specialty and in many types of working environments. Understanding your interests, skills, and desired working conditions and job locations will help you select the best educational path toward achieving your professional goals.

Selecting a Specialty

It is never too early to set career goals; although you will find that your final career path will take many bends and turns as you start your first job and learn about the various areas of practice that are available to you. Your ultimate specialty or employer might result from your educational background, such as journalism or medicine, or an area of special interest such as environmental issues, or possibly just a preference to work with certain types of clients such as the elderly or infirm.

And it is never too late to make a career adjustment. Many successful individuals begin a career later in life. Colonel Sanders started Kentucky Fried Chicken late in life. Schools are full of nontraditional students seeking a career change. In the paralegal field we are seeing more and more nurses who, having worked in the medical field for years, are making a career change to the legal field.

Your decision should be based on a self-evaluation of your likes and dislikes, interests, passions, and any physical or geographic limitations. If you hate to fly, you probably will not want a job that requires travel. If you are not comfortable with

Exhibit 1.1 Legal certification comparison chart

Compares the certification exams offered by: NALS . . . the association for legal professionals
National Association for Legal Assistants (NALA), National Federation of Paralegal Associations,
Inc. (NFPA)

	Professional Paralegal (PP)— NALS	PLS . . . the advanced certification for legal professionals (PLS)—NALS	Certified Legal Assistant (CLA)— or Paralegal (CP)—NALA	Paralegal (RP)— Paralegal Advanced Competency Exam (PACE) Registered
Organization Established	1929, incorporated in 1949	1929, incorporated in 1949	1975	1974
Certification Established	2004	1960	1976	1996
Membership	5,000 individual members Regular Member = $135.00 per year (includes state and local dues) International Member = $135.00 per year Retired Member = $45.00 per year National Associate Member = $45.00 per year (educators, judges and attorneys) National Student Member = $19.00 per year (must be a full-time student) Lifetime Member = $750.00 (one time fee) (annual billing for state and local dues)	5,000 individual members	18,000 individual members Active Membership Annual Dues: $125 Associate Membership Annual Dues: $100 Student Membership Annual Dues: $50 Sustaining Membership Annual Dues: $70	11,000 individual members and 50 member associations
Number Certified	402 (eff 03/08)	5,482 (eff 03/08)	over 15,000 (2008)	
Eligibility to Test Education and/or Employment			A paralegal must meet one of the following alternate requirements: 1. Graduation from a paralegal program that is: (a) Approved by the American Bar Association; or (b) An associate degree program; or (c) A post-baccalaureate certificate program in legal assistant studies; or (d) A bachelor's degree program in legal assistant studies; or (e) A legal assistant program which consists of a minimum of 60 semester hours (900 clock hours or 90 quarter hours) of which at least 15 semester hours (225 clock hours or 22.5 quarter hours) are substantive legal courses.	• An associate degree in paralegal studies obtained from an institutionally accredited and/or ABA approved paralegal program; and six (6) years of substantive paralegal experience; or, • A bachelor's degree in any course of study obtained from an institutionally accredited school; and three (3) years of substantive paralegal experience; or, • A bachelor's degree and completion of a paralegal program from an institutionally accredited school,

(continued)

Exhibit 1.1 Legal certification comparison chart *(continued)*

	Professional Paralegal (PP)— NALS	PLS . . . the advanced certification for legal professionals (PLS)—NALS	Certified Legal Assistant (CLA)— or Paralegal (CP)—NALA	Paralegal (RP)— Paralegal Advanced Competency Exam (PACE) Registered
				said paralegal program may be imbedded in a bachelor's degree; and two (2) years of substantive paralegal experience; OR, • Four (4) years substantive paralegal experience on or before December 31, 2000; and, • The paralegal cannot have been convicted of a felony nor be under suspension, termination or revocation of a certificate, registration or license by any entity.
Examination Topics	Part 1—Written Communications: Grammar and word usage, spelling, punctuation, number usage, capitalization, composition, and expression Part 2—Legal Knowledge and Skills: Legal research, citations, legal terminology, the court system and ADR, and the legal skills of interviewing clients and witnesses, planning and conducting investigations, and docketing Part 3—Ethics and Judgment: Ethical situations involving contact with clients, the public, coworkers, and subordinates; other ethical considerations for the legal profession; decisionmaking and analytical ability; and ability to recognize priorities Part 4—All areas of substantive law, including	Part 1—Written Communications: Grammar and word usage, punctuation, number usage, capitalization, spelling, and composition and expression Part 2—Office Procedures and Technology: records management, computer information systems, equipment/ information services, office procedures and practices, office accounting Part 3—Ethics and Judgment: Ethical situations involving contact with clients, the public, coworkers; ethical considerations for legal profession; decisionmaking and analytical ability; ability to recognize priorities	**Communications** • Word usage and vocabulary • Grammar/punctuation • Writing skills • Nonverbal communications • General communications related to interviewing and client communications • General communications related to interoffice office situations This section contains a writing exercise. *The Elements of Style,* Strunk & White, has been adopted by the NALA Certifying Board as the authority for the Communications section. **Ethics** • Ethical responsibilities centering on performance of delegated work including confidentiality, unauthorized practice of law, legal advice, conflict of interest, billing and client communications • Client/public contact including identification as a non-lawyer, advertising and initial client contact • Professional Integrity/ competence including knowledge of legal assistant codes of ethics • Relationships with co-workers and support staff • Attorney codes/discipline	Domain I—Administration of Client Legal Matters: Conflict checks; develop, organize and maintain client files; develop and maintain calendar/tickler systems; develop and maintain databases; coordinate client services. Domain II—Development of Client Legal Matters: Client interviews; analyze information; collaborate with counsel; prepare, file, and serve legal documents and exhibits; prepare clients and witnesses for legal proceedings. Domain III—Factual/Legal Research: Obtain factual and legal information; investigate and compile facts; inspect, evaluate, and analyze evidence; ascertain and analyze legal authority. Domain IV—Factual/Legal Writing: Communicate with client/counsel; draft legal analytical documents. Domain V—Office Administration: Personnel management; acquire technology; coordinate and utilize vendor

Exhibit 1.1 Legal certification comparison chart *(continued)*

Professional Paralegal (PP)— NALS	PLS . . . the advanced certification for legal professionals (PLS)—NALS	Certified Legal Assistant (CLA)— or Paralegal (CP)—NALA	Paralegal (RP)— Paralegal Advanced Competency Exam (PACE) Registered
administrative; business organizations and contracts; civil procedure and litigation; criminal; family; real property; torts; wills, trusts, and estates; admiralty and maritime; antitrust; bankruptcy; environmental; federal civil rights and employment discrimination; immigration; intellectual property; labor; oil and gas; pension and profit sharing; taxation; water; workers' compensation	Part 4—Legal Knowledge and Skills: Legal Knowledge: citations, legal research, and the ability to prepare legal documents based on oral instructions and materials; all areas of substantive law	• Knowledge of the American Bar Association's Rules of Professional Conduct and the NALA Code of Ethics and Professional Responsibility is required by this examination. **Legal Research** • Sources of law including primary authority, secondary authority; understanding how law is recorded • Research skills including citing the law; shepardizing, updating decisions; procedural rules of citations • Analysis of research problem including identification of relevant facts and legal issues *A Uniform System of Citation,* Harvard Law Review Association, has been adopted by the NALA Certifying Board as the authority for the Legal Research section. **Judgment and Analytical Ability** • Comprehension of data—identifying and understanding a problem • Application of knowledge—ability to link facts or legal issues from other cases to the problem at hand, recognizing similarities and differences by analogy • Evaluating and categorizing data • Organizing data and findings in a written document This section contains an essay question which requires analysis of a research request, finding applicable law, and writing a responsive memo. Examinees will be graded on the ability to: • Identify which facts are relevant and state them concisely and accurately; • Identify the threshold or main issue and any secondary issue(s); • Identify the relevant legal authority and apply it to the facts; and • Draw persuasive logical conclusions. **Substantive Law** The substantive law section of the examination is composed of five sub-sections. The first section, Substantive Law-General covers concepts of the American legal system. **All examinees are required to take this section.**	services; create and maintain library and legal resources; develop and maintain billing system.

(continued)

Exhibit 1.1   **Legal certification comparison chart** *(continued)*

Professional Paralegal (PP)— NALS	PLS . . . the advanced certification for legal professionals (PLS)—NALS	Certified Legal Assistant (CLA)— or Paralegal (CP)—NALA	Paralegal (RP)— Paralegal Advanced Competency Exam (PACE) Registered
		Subjects covered within this section include: • Court system including their structure and jurisdiction • Branches of government, agencies, and concepts such as separation of powers • Legal concepts and principles including sources of law, judicial decision making, appellate process • Sources and classifications of law including the constitution, statutes, common law, civil law, statutory law, and equity law The other four sub-sections are selected by the applicants from a list of nine substantive areas of the law. These tests cover general knowledge of the following practice areas: • Administrative Law • Bankruptcy • Business Organizations • Civil Litigation • Contracts • Criminal Law and Procedure • Estate Planning and Probate • Family Law • Real Estate The skills required by these tests involve recall of facts and principles that form the basis of the specialty area. Examinees must also demonstrate an understanding of the structure of the law and procedures to be followed in each specialty area. © 2008, National Association of Legal Assistants 1516 S. Boston, #200, Tulsa, OK 74119 nalanet@nala.org	
Cost $200 (retake $50/section) $250 (retake $60/section) PLS Members Part 4: $150 (retake $50) PLS Nonmember Part 4: $200 (retake $60)		The fee for the CLA/CP examination is $250 for NALA members and $275 for nonmembers	
CLE Required		50 hours (five hours legal ethics)	12 hours continuing legal education including at least one hour in ethics every two (2) years.

Legal Certification Comparison Chart prepared by Kathleen L. McRae, PLS, RP and Lyn M. Hurlbutt, PP, PLS, CLA, RP, CPS. NALS is dedicated to enhancing the competencies and contributions of members in the legal services profession. NALS Resource Center, 314 East Third Street, Suite 210, Tulsa, OK 74120 918.582.5188, 918.582.5907 (fax) © NALS, Inc. Reprinted with permission. All rights reserved.

CHECKLIST Career Planning

☐ My current paralegal job-related skills are:

☐ My special interests are:

☐ My passions are:

☐ My personality traits are:

☐ My geographical work and living desires are:

☐ My willingness to accept responsibility is:

☐ My level of self-motivation is:

strangers, you probably will not want a job as a paralegal investigator for a litigation firm. If you like books and research, you might want to work as the firm's librarian or researcher.

Assessing Your Background

As the law has become more specialized, so has the demand for paralegals with more than just paralegal skills. Law firms specializing in an area such as medical malpractice frequently look for paralegals who also have a medical background such as nursing. Firms with large, complex litigation cases often look for someone with computer database skills who can manage the files. Paralegals with journalism experience and training frequently are sought out for their interviewing and writing skills.

Your personal background can be an asset when added to your paralegal certificate or degree. As you begin your professional training, take stock of your entire educational background, special skills, and talents, as well as personal areas of interest.

Doing a self-assessment early in your studies offers you an opportunity to recognize your strengths and develop them and to acknowledge weaknesses that you need to work on to permit your personal and professional growth.

Assessing Your Skills

You may well have a number of personal skills that will benefit you in the future as a paralegal. You might have great interpersonal skills, communicate well orally and in writing, and be a highly motivated person—all qualities of a good paralegal.

Individuals with language skills are particularly in demand in international law, as well as in working with clients who lack English-language skills. The paralegal who understands a second language and the cultural nuances of the client's background can be invaluable.

Assessing Your Interests

What are your personal interests? Are you an active outdoors person in your free time, for whom working on environmental issues would be of high interest and satisfaction? Do you find yourself drawn to volunteering or working in your free time with shut-ins and elderly people?

Selecting Your Electives

Becoming aware of your interests and background knowledge enables you to select the elective course that can qualify you for work in a specialty field of law. Taking electives is a good way to explore an area in which you think you might be interested, without committing to more than one semester or a few credits of study. Many students find new interests and a potential career direction after taking courses in areas they had not considered previously. For example, you may have been reading in newspapers and magazines, and following on television, stories about the high-technology industries and wondered how your career goal as a paralegal might fit into this growth area.

One of the fastest growing fields is that of intellectual property law. In an age of dot coms, computers, and a growing global marketplace, protection of intellectual property has become a critical concern for individuals and companies alike. Taking a three-credit course in intellectual property may well introduce the paralegal student to a new area of interest in a potential growth area of the paralegal profession. This is also true for other emerging areas in the paralegal profession, such as environmental law and legal nurse consulting.

Regulating the Practice of Law

To protect the public, certain professions, such as law, require state licensure as a method of regulating who can practice. For the lawyer, the rules that must be followed to continue practice are found in the individual states' code or canon of ethics for lawyers, such as the Model Rules of Professional Conduct of the American Bar Association as adopted by many states' highest courts, serious violation of which can result in the loss of the license or right to practice law.

Paralegals, with a few exceptions, have no state license requirement to enter the profession, and no unified code of ethics. State regulations and ethics opinions are neither uniform nor mandatory. At worst, a paralegal runs the risk of a charge of unauthorized practice of law under the state criminal code, which will be discussed in more detail in Chapter 2, and at best the violation of a professional organization's ethics code results in a loss of membership in the organization.

Regulating the Paralegal Profession

Unauthorized Practice of Law (UPL) Giving legal advice, if legal rights may be affected, by anyone not licensed to practice law.

Regulation and licensing of the paralegal profession has been one of the hottest topics in the legal and paralegal communities. Each state, through its respective legislature and court, regulates and licenses the practice of law. The original **Unauthorized Practice of Law (UPL)** issues were simply those of the licensing of attorneys and laws preventing the unauthorized practice of law. With the development of the paralegal profession has come a new set of concerns and controversy surrounding what constitutes the unauthorized practice of law, who should be permitted to render legal services, and under what conditions.

The conflict is between the paralegal profession and the bar organizations, such as the American Bar Association, which does not see the need for the additional time, effort, and cost for certification of paralegals. The ABA position is broadly based on the argument that the public is protected by the attorney's obligation to supervise the paralegal and responsibility to the public.

For the most part, the paralegal profession has sought some level of regulation, certification, or licensure. Somewhere in the middle are increasing numbers of employers of paralegals who want some level of assurance that those they hire who claim to be paralegals are qualified for those positions. As the responsibilities undertaken by paralegals have increased, so have the educational requirements. Within the profession has come a concern that those who hold themselves out as paralegals are truly qualified to perform the work they have undertaken. This is no different from the organized bar monitoring the activities of those holding themselves out as being lawyers.

State Licensing

Some states and others have attempted to set up licensing systems or defining who may use the title paralegal. A case in point is the proposal rejected in 1999 by the New Jersey Supreme Court to license traditional paralegals, which had been developed after five years of study by that court's committee on paralegal education and regulation. If it had been approved, this proposal would have made New Jersey the first state to license traditional paralegals. Another state's approach is that of North Carolina's plan shown below.

- California leads the nation in setting stringent educational requirements that may become a model for other states. In 2000 California amended its Business and Professional Code requiring minimum educational standards for paralegals. See Exhibit 1.2.

Exhibit 1.2   California regulation of paralegals

While other state legislatures and courts wrestle with the minimum standards, California addressed the requirements in a 2000 amendment to the Business and Professional Code that requires a paralegal to possess at least one of the following:

(1) A certificate of completion of a paralegal program approved by the American Bar Association.

(2) A certificate of completion of a paralegal program at an institution that requires a minimum of 24 semester, or equivalent, units in law-related courses, accredited by a national or regional accreditation organization or approved by the Bureau for Private Postsecondary and Vocational Education.

(3) A baccalaureate or advanced degree and minimum of one year of law-related experience under an attorney who is an active member of the State Bar of California.

(4) A high school diploma or general equivalency diploma and a minimum of three years' law-related experience under the supervision of a California attorney, with this training being completed before December 31, 2003.

Other states might look to the California statute in deciding the question of who is qualified by education, training, or work experience.

- After a number of efforts, a Hawaii State Bar Association task force on paralegal certification developed a compromise voluntary certification proposal for consideration by the Hawaii Supreme Court, which recognized the opposition from some segments of the bar.

To some observers it is obvious that the organized bar is fearful in many cases of the incursion of the paralegal profession into the practice of law. For some, the issue is loss of income. Others are concerned for the delivery of quality legal services by all those who hold themselves out as being members of the legal profession.

Florida and Ohio are among the states that have addressed the issue of certification of paralegals.

Florida Registered Paralegal

A Florida Registered Paralegal is a person with education, training, or work experience, who works under the direction and supervision of a member of The Florida Bar and who performs specifically delegated substantive legal work for which a member of The Florida Bar is responsible and who has met the requirements of registration as set forth in Chapter 20 of the Rules Regulating The Florida Bar. A Florida Registered Paralegal is not a member of The Florida Bar and may not give legal advice or practice law. Florida Registered Paralegal and FRP are trademarks of The Florida Bar.

Source: www.floridabar.org

Ohio State Bar Association Certified Paralegal

The Ohio State Bar Association offers a voluntary credentialing program for paralegals. Individuals meeting the OSBA definition of "paralegal," meeting the eligibility requirements and passing a written examination will be designated as an "OSBA Certified Paralegal." This credential, along with a logo provided for the purpose may be used by the paralegal to the extent permitted by the Supreme Court of Ohio's Rules for the Government of the Bar and Rules of Professional Conduct.

OSBA Paralegal Certification provides a valuable credential for paralegals in Ohio through the use of objective standards which measure the training, knowledge, experience and skill of paralegals. It requires a commitment to excellence and will assist lawyers and law firms in identifying the highly qualified paralegal professionals.

Source: http://www.ohiobar.org/pub/?articleid=785

For the paralegal, it is a question of status as well as job opportunities. With the establishment of minimum standards for holding oneself out as a paralegal comes a

Advice *from the* Field

NORTH CAROLINA STATE BAR PARALEGAL CERTIFICATION PROGRAM

I recommend a visit to the North Carolina State Bar's Paralegal website (http://www.nccertifiedparalegal.org), for information on the benefits of paralegal certification. The first page is shown below.

PLAN FOR CERTIFICATION OF PARALEGALS

The State Bar's interest in the paralegal profession promotes proper utilization of paralegals and assures that legal services are professionally and ethically offered to the public. The Plan for Certification of Paralegals approved by the NC State Bar and adopted by the NC Supreme Court in 2004 will assist in the development of paralegal standards, raise the profile of the paralegal profession, and standardize the expectations of the public and other legal professionals.

The State Bar has worked diligently with attorneys and paralegals across our state to establish a voluntary North Carolina certification program with requirements that are properly defined and that will ensure the credential has value. Through education and experience, the North Carolina certification plan will assist lawyers and administrators in distinguishing paralegals that meet or exceed the skills required for certification. As multi-skilled professionals, paralegals have a diverse knowledge base and must practice

effective interpersonal communication skills to maintain collaborative relationships within the legal team. Paralegals, like attorneys, will continue to be held accountable to the highest of ethical and professional standards.

Paralegals certified by the State Bar may use the following designations:

- North Carolina Certified Paralegal
- North Carolina State Bar Certified Paralegal
- Paralegal Certified by the North Carolina State Bar Board of Paralegal Certification
- NCCP

This site has two brochures that may be downloaded,

NC Certified Paralegal—A Primer for Paralegals
NC Certified Paralegal—A Primer for Attorney

Both brochures review the benefits to the public, to the profession, to attorneys and to paralegals. I think that they give a great overall response to "why" become certified. North Carolina began their certification program July 1, 2005, as of February 2006, the Board received 1489 applications and had certified 762. The current applicants are qualifying under the grandfather clause which ends June 30, 2007.

status that members of a profession are entitled to enjoy. For those who have worked hard to develop the necessary paralegal skills by way of education and experience, it eliminates unqualified individuals from taking jobs that should be performed by qualified individuals. The stated goals of the different groups are not that far apart: delivery of quality legal services at affordable prices with a reasonable standard of living for the legal profession and the paralegal profession.

The traditional role of the attorney in advising and representing clients is limited to those who are admitted to practice as lawyers under the applicable state law. Some exemptions do exist that allow nonlawyers to perform certain services under state law, such as document preparation under California law.

Federal Practice

Under federal regulations, nonlawyers may represent parties before the Social Security Administration, the Patent Office, and other agencies. A conflict may arise between the federal law and state law that limit the activity. For example, Florida sought unsuccessfully to enjoin a practitioner authorized to practice before the Patent Office, alleging UPL (*Sperry v. Florida*, 373 U.S. 379 (1963)).

Under federal regulation, a paralegal can, without supervision, represent individuals before the Social Security Administration, including appearing before Administrative Law Judges on behalf of clients. Paralegals may appear as representatives of claimants for disability claims; Medicare parts A, B, and C; and cases of overpayment and underpayment.

As representative of a claimant, the paralegal in practice before the Social Security Administration may obtain information, submit evidence, and make statements and arguments. The difference between the paralegal and the attorney is only in the matter of direct versus indirect payment for services. The Social Security Administration pays the attorney directly, whereas the paralegal must bill the client for services rendered. Within the Social Security Administration, paralegals are employed as decision writers and case technicians.

Opportunities for Paralegals

The U.S. Department of Labor has included the paralegal profession among the fastest growing occupations with employment projected to grow 22 percent between 2006 and 2016, much faster than the average for all occupations. This encompasses additional growth of the occupation as well as the need for individuals to replace existing employees. The Labor Department estimates might be increased further by the de facto requirement found in the court opinions that more paralegals be used to perform services instead of attorneys performing the services.

Web Exploration

Check the latest paralegal statistics in the *Occupational Outlook Handbook* from the Department of Labor, Bureau of Labor Statistics at http://www .bls.gov/oco/home.htm.

Projections data from the National Employment Matrix

Occupational title	SOC Code	Employment, 2006	Projected employment, 2016	Change, 2006–16	
				Number	Percent
Paralegals and legal assistants	23-2011	238,000	291,000	53,000	22

Source: Occupational Outlook Handbook, 2008–09 Edition, U.S. Department of Labor, Bureau of Labor Statistics

Paralegals held about 238,000 jobs in 2006, according to the Bureau of Labor Statistics, U.S. Department of Labor, *Occupational Outlook Handbook*, 2008–09 Edition. In May 2006, full-time wage-and-salary paralegals and legal assistants had median annual earnings, including bonuses, of $43,040. The middle 50 percent earned between $33,920 and $54,690. The top 10 percent earned more than $67,540, and the bottom 10 percent earned less than $27,450. Median annual earnings in the industries employing the largest numbers of paralegals were:

Federal government	$56,080
Management of companies and enterprises	52,220
Local government	42,170
Legal services	41,460
State government	38,020

Source: *Occupational Outlook Handbook*, 2008-09 Edition, U.S. Department of Labor, Bureau of Labor Statistics

In a 1998 survey by the American Bar Association:

- Almost two-thirds of the lawyers who responded, 65.5 percent, employ legal assistants at their firms; 60.2 percent of respondents actively work with paralegals.
- The general responsibilities most often assigned to paralegals are maintaining client files, drafting correspondence, and performing factual research.

- Legal assistants are more likely to be employed by large firms than small firms.
- Lawyers in smaller firms delegate a wider array of responsibilities to legal assistants than do lawyers in bigger firms.
- Lawyers with business/corporate, probate/estate planning, and litigation practices make more extensive use of paralegals than do lawyers in other practice areas.

The ABA survey demonstrates that clients who choose to work with larger firms are much more likely to have a portion of their work completed by paralegals than those who choose a lawyer from a small firm. Almost all (99 percent) of the lawyers practicing in firms with more than 100 lawyers reported that their firms use legal assistants. By contrast, only 34.8 percent of those working at firms of three or fewer lawyers employ paralegals. Of the lawyers who indicated that their firms do not employ paralegals, 56.8 percent reported that the size of their firm would not support legal assistants, and 44.1 percent said that their secretaries assume tasks that otherwise would be assigned to legal assistants.

Compensation for paralegals is as varied as the working environments and regional locations. As with most jobs and professions, salaries tend to be higher in large metropolitan areas and lower in small and rural areas. Large firms tend to pay more, and small firms tend to pay less. At times, these variations in compensation can be justified by the costs of working in certain locations, such as higher taxation and the cost of commuting.

The Future

The future of the paralegal profession may be determined by clients who are unwilling or unable to pay what they see as inflated fees for lawyers. The future also could be dictated by the courts, which, looking at the fairness of charging higher rates for attorneys' tasks that could properly be delegated to a paralegal would result in a lower charge to the client. Two of the future concerns involving paralegals and billings are the following:

1. The cases in which secretarial or clerical tasks are charged to the client as paralegal fees. These tasks are considered overhead (part of the cost of running the office) and should be performed at no additional cost to the client. This is one of the areas in which the definition of paralegal has come into play in the courts. Courts are allowing charges for paralegal fees but not for secretarial fees.
2. The fairness of charging higher rates for attorneys' performing tasks that could properly be delegated to a paralegal, thereby resulting in a lower charge to the client.

For instance, summarizing depositions traditionally has been a task delegated to paralegals. Assume that the paralegal takes two hours to complete the task and the paralegal's time is billed to the client at $75 per hour (don't get excited—that doesn't necessarily have any bearing on what you may be paid); the client would be charged $150. For a lawyer to do the same work, if billed out at $175 per hour, the client would be charged $350. Unless there is good reason for the lawyer to do the work, the decision not to delegate the work to a paralegal seems unfair to the client. A number of court decisions are beginning to draw upon these fundamental questions of the fairness and propriety of attorney billings for their services. As other federal and state courts weigh in on this line of decisions, law firms may have to hire more paralegals.

Getting Started

As you start your legal studies and paralegal career, consider the suggestions and advice in the following *Advice from the Field* by a leading paralegal educator.

Web Exploration

Full article available at the website of NFPA at http://www.paralegals.org/displaycommon.cfm?am=1&subarticlenbr=564.

Web Exploration

The Kathryn Myers' student portfolio article and other information for students can be found on the American Association for Paralegal Education website at www.aafpe.org.

Advice *from the* Field

THE STUDENT PORTFOLIO

Kathryn Myers, Coordinator, Paralegal Studies, Saint Mary-of-the-Woods College, Paralegal Studies Program

A portfolio is a purposeful collection of student work that is accumulated over time. The material reveals the extent of student learning, achievement, and development. The "portfolio system" is intended to specify knowledge and competence in areas considered necessary to successfully work as a paralegal/legal assistant while leaving the selection of means of documentation of competency to the individual student. Documentation of knowledge and skill acquisition can take a variety of forms including, but not limited to,

- letters of support
- diaries
- videotapes and audiotapes of work
- pleadings
- memoranda
- course projects
- registration receipts from continuing education and other conferences attended
- proof of membership in professional organizations
- subscriptions to legal publications

Typically, much of the material can be compiled from projects and activities required within courses.

PROCEDURE

The portfolio shall contain documentation of knowledge and skill acquisition based on the Core Competencies established by the American Association for Paralegal Education. Those core competencies are divided into two areas—skill development and acquisition of knowledge. Within those areas are competencies based on:

SKILL DEVELOPMENT

- critical thinking skills
- organizational skills
- general communication skills
- interpersonal skills
- legal research skills
- legal writing skills
- computer skills
- interviewing and investigation skills

ACQUISITION OF KNOWLEDGE

- organization and operation of the legal system
- organization and operation of law offices
- the paralegal profession and ethical obligations
- contracts
- torts
- business organizations
- litigation procedures

It is understood that the areas may overlap somewhat and that these areas do not cover all competencies associated with the program, student growth, or professional success. However, students who perfect these competencies and who perform from this educational base have a foundation for success.

It is suggested that the student purchase a secure container to collect and organize the material [such as] a hanging file folder or file box. This portfolio may be maintained on computer disk; however, you will not have any graded materials if this is the only method of collection you use.

Students should keep a log of all materials completed. When completing each assignment, [they should] enter the document in the log, with a column to check for inclusion in the campus portfolio and another to check for inclusion in the professional portfolio. Some documents may, of course, overlap in their application.

Students are responsible for the contents of their portfolios. The student should periodically review the contents of the portfolio and add or remove materials based on decisions as to the extent to which the contents adequately represent knowledge and skill acquisition in each of the areas outlined below. This portfolio is not intended to be a compilation of senior level work; rather, it is useful to provide work of varying levels of efficiency to show, among other things, growth and improvement.

CONTENT

To be a successful paralegal/legal assistant, the student must possess a common core of legal knowledge as well as acquire vital critical thinking, organizational, communication, and interpersonal skills. Courses in a student's program should provide the student with

(continued)

the means to develop the competencies, which have been divided into the following sections:

Area 1 Understanding the Profession and Its Ethical Obligations

Area 2 Research

Area 3 Legal Writing

Area 4 Basic Skills

Area 5 Acquisition of Legal Knowledge

Area 6 Professional Commitment Beyond Coursework

Area 7 Evaluation of Professional Growth/ Evaluation of Program

Appendix

GUIDELINES FOR SELECTING ENTRIES

When selecting entries, students should bear in mind that each piece is part of a much larger whole and that, together, the artifacts and rationale make a powerful statement about individual professional development. Asking the following questions may help with decision making.

1. What do I want my portfolio to show about me as a paralegal? What are my attributes as a paralegal?
2. What do I want my portfolio to demonstrate about me as a learner? How and what have I learned?
3. What directions for my future growth and development does my self-evaluation suggest? How can I show them in my portfolio?
4. What points have been made by others about me as a paralegal and learner? How can I show them in my portfolio?
5. What effect does my professionalism have upon my peers? How can I show this in my portfolio?
6. What overall impression do I want my portfolio to give a reviewer about me as a learner and as a paralegal?

When decision-making about what to include becomes a challenge, it may be helpful to look at each artifact and ask yourself, "What would including this item add that has not already been said or shown?" Remember that portfolios create representative records of your professional development; they are not intended to be comprehensive.

VALUES AND ATTITUDES

Values and attitudes determine the choices we make in our lives. They cross the boundaries of subject-matter areas. Thus, in this final section of your portfolio, you are asked to look at your own values and attitudes and then write a one- to three-page paper in which you reflect upon your own values. Identify one or more values that are important to you. Explain how they influence your choices as a person, parent, future paralegal, voter, and/or citizen of the global community. Include specific examples.

The following questions may help you choose a topic for your essay: What does it mean to be honest? fair? tolerant? open to new ideas and experiences? respect evidence? Which is more important—decreasing the production of greenhouse gases or preserving jobs?

The right to choose how many children we want or controlling world population growth? Freedom to produce pornographic art or the right of children to be sheltered from such experiences? Spending more time with your children or getting a second job so you can buy things you want?

There are no easy answers to these questions. Have fun thinking about your own values. Remember to include specific examples from your own life!

TRANSCRIPTS

Include copies of unofficial transcripts from all colleges and universities that you have attended.

Degree evaluation

Graduation evaluation

Awards or recognitions

Include a copy of your degree evaluation, if you received one.

Include a copy of your graduation evaluation.

Include copies of awards or recognitions you have received.

PROFESSIONAL PORTFOLIO

Modify this inclusive portfolio into a professional portfolio. This professional portfolio will be representative, not comprehensive. Each artifact chosen for inclusion should represent at least one significant aspect of you and/or your accomplishments that can be translated into employability. Use these guidelines to prepare your professional portfolio:

1. Prepare your portfolio as a showcase of your best work—your highest achievements. This will involve selecting from artifacts in your portfolio and adding new ones.
2. Do not send your portfolio when you apply for a job. Rather, include in your cover letter a statement concerning your portfolio. For example: "Throughout my paralegal studies program at _____ College, I developed a professional portfolio that clearly and concisely exhibits my attributes as a paralegal. I would be pleased to share this portfolio with you during an interview."
3. If granted an interview, take your portfolio with you. Be prepared to present the highlights. Practice presenting it effectively. In some instances, you might be asked to present it at the beginning of the interview, and in other instances you might

use it as a source of evidence or enhancement of a point you make in the interview. Interviewing practices vary widely from employer to employer. Portfolios are most likely to be reviewed in situations where the employer is familiar with the abilities of a paralegal.

4. If the interviewer(s) is particularly interested and would like to examine your portfolio more closely, offer to leave it if at all possible. You should make explicit arrangements for collecting it and, of course, follow through as planned. It could be that your portfolio will create the impression that tips the scales in your favor.

5. Remember—it is likely that some people in a position to hire are not familiar with professional portfolios as you know them. Take time to concisely explain that developing your portfolio has been a process of reflection and evaluation that has helped you to know yourself as a paralegal and to establish a foundation for career-long professional development. To some extent, presenting

your portfolio will inform the interviewer about both you and the portfolio concept and process.

6. Keep your portfolio up to date. As you continue to gain experience and to grow professionally, alter it to reflect your development. It is not only your first job application that may be enhanced by a well prepared and presented portfolio but developing your portfolio is an excellent foundation for meeting any expectation of continuing legal education.

CONCLUSION

It is my hope and intention that by your creating this portfolio, you have an opportunity to reflect upon your education and to emphasize to yourself and others that you are capable and qualified to perform as a paralegal. It is time to believe in you. Good luck!

Reproduced with permission of Kathryn Myers.

Concept Review *and* Reinforcement

LEGAL TERMINOLOGY

ALS (Accredited Legal Secretary) 15
American Association for Paralegal Education (AAfPE) 12
American Bar Association (ABA) 4
Associate's degree 13
Bachelor's degree 13
Certificate 13
Certified Legal Assistant (CLA) 15

International Paralegal Management Association (IPMA) 16
Legal assistant 4
National Association of Legal Assistants (NALA) 4
National Association of Legal Secretaries (NALS) 16
National Federation of Paralegal Associations (NFPA) 4

Paralegal 4
Paralegal Advanced Competency Exam (PACE) 14
PLS (Professional Legal Secretary) 15
PP (Professional Paralegal) 16
Proprietary school 13
Unauthorized Practice of Law (UPL) 22

SUMMARY OF KEY CONCEPTS

What Is a Paralegal?

Definition	A paralegal, or legal assistant, is "a person qualified by education, training, or work experience who is employed or retained by a lawyer, law office, corporation, governmental agency or other entity who performs specifically delegated substantive legal work for which a lawyer is responsible."

What Do Paralegals Do?

Functions of Paralegals	The primary function of paralegals is to assist attorneys in preparing for hearings, trials, meetings, and closings.

Professional Skills

Definition	Professional skills are also called soft skills. These include communication skills, initiative, resourcefulness, problem solving, commitment, team work, leadership, and self-motivation.
Resourcefulness	The ability to meet and handle a situation and find solutions to problems.
Commitment	The ability to complete what one starts out to do.
Analytical Skills	Analytical skills allow one to follow a step-by-step process to solve a problem.
Interpersonal Skills	The ability to work with people.
Communication Skills	Communication means expressing ideas effectively—both oral and written.

Career Planning

Career Planning	Career planning includes educational planning and a plan for perfecting professional skills.
Paralegal Education in the United States	An estimated 1,000 paralegal education programs are available in the United States. These programs are offered in onsite, online, and hybrid format combining online and on site instruction. Some of these programs have obtained ABA.
Qualifications of a Paralegal	Qualifications were established by the educational guidelines of the American Bar Association's Standing Committee on Paralegals and American Association for Paralegal Education.
Types of Educational Programs	1. Certificate programs 2. Associate degree programs 3. Baccalaureate programs 4. Graduate programs 5. Specialty certificates
Paralegal Certification	PACE (Paralegal Advance Competency Exam) of the National Federation of Paralegal Associations CLA (Certified Legal Assistant) of the National Association of Legal Assistants ALS (the basic certification for legal professionals of NALS) PLS (the advanced certification for legal professionals of NALS) PP (Professional Paralegal certification of NALS)
Making a Personal Assessment and Setting Goals	1. What are your other educational skills? 2. What are your personality traits? 3. Do you like working under deadlines? 4. Do you like working with certain groups of people? 5. What are your personal interests? 6. Recognize your strengths 7. Acknowledge weaknesses
Selecting a Specialty	Your decision should be based on a self-evaluation of your likes and dislikes, interests, passions, and any physical or geographic limitations.
Assessing Your Background	Doing a self-assessment early in your studies offers you an opportunity to recognize your strengths and develop them and to acknowledge weaknesses that you need to address in order to permit your personal and professional growth.

Regulating the Practice of Law

Reasons for Regulating the Practice of Law	The practice of law is regulated by state government and court rule to protect the public from incompetent and unscrupulous practitioners.
Regulating the Paralegal Profession	The traditional role of the attorney in advising and representing clients is limited to those who are admitted to practice as lawyers under the applicable state law. Some exemptions do exist that allow nonlawyers to perform certain services under state law.
State Licensing	Some states have enacted legislation establishing licensure to perform certain paralegal functions to address the issues of the unauthorized practice of law.
Federal Practice	Under federal regulations, nonlawyers may represent parties before the Social Security Administration, the Patent Office, and other agencies.

Opportunities for Paralegals

Compensation Issues for the Paralegal	In 2006, paralegals held about 238,000 jobs in the United States, with median annual earnings of $43,040. The U.S. Department of Labor projects that this profession will continue to be among the fastest growing through the year 2016.

The Future

Career Planning	As courts require the use of paralegals to reduce legal costs, law firms may have to hire more paralegals and delegate work to them in fairness to clients and propriety in billing practice.

WORKING THE WEB

1. Download a copy of the latest edition of the ABA Standing Committee on Paralegals *Update Newsletter* at www.abanet.org/legalservices/paralegals/home.html.
2. What advice does the ABA Standing Committee on Paralegals offer in its publication on *Getting Started As a Pro Bono Legal Assistant?* www.abanet.org/legalservices/paralegals/publications.html
3. The *Occupational Outlook Handbook* is updated regularly. Download a copy of the current version on Paralegals and Legal Assistants and compare the salary ranges with those in this text. Have they changed? www.bls.gov/oco/ocos114.htm
4. One of the significant issues for paralegals over the past years has been whether paralegals are classified as exempt or nonexempt according to the U.S. Department of Labor regulations. Download a copy of the current Overview for Executive, Administrative, Professional, Computer, & Outside Sales Employees, and highlight the information that applies to paralegals. www.dol.gov/esa/regs/compliance/whd/fairpay/main.htm
5. Print out a copy of the Mission Statement or Homepage of each of the major national paralegal associations.
   a. International Paralegal Management Association www.paralegalmanagement.org
   b. NALS . . . the Association for Legal Professionals http://www.nals.org
   c. National Federation of Paralegal Associations www.paralegals.org
   d. National Association of Legal Assistants www.nala.org
   e. Association of Legal Administrators www.alanet.org
6. Compare your skills with the list of knowledge or competencies required of principal legal administrators at http://www.alanet.org/education/knowledgelist.html.

CRITICAL THINKING & WRITING QUESTIONS

1. How does the American Bar Association define the term "paralegal"?
2. What are the minimum qualifications that a paralegal should meet?
3. What is the role of the paralegal in the legal system?
4. Why should those planning to become paralegals or legal assistants get a well-grounded education and develop the necessary skills?
5. How can one satisfy the court that he or she is qualified as a paralegal and not as a legal secretary?
6. What is the advantage to the paralegal in obtaining the PACE or CLA designation?
7. What educational plan makes the most sense for you? Why?
8. How can a paralegal demonstrate the qualifications for employment as a paralegal?
9. Why would an employer, such as the U.S. Attorney's office, require a four-year degree for those seeking a paralegal position?
10. Complete the checklist "Career Planning" and assess your personal skills and professional goals. Based on your answers, how well prepared are you for a career as a paralegal? What skills need development?
11. How does assessing your interests and skills help in choosing a career path?
12. What skills are required to be a paralegal and why are they important?
13. Complete the "Strengths & Weaknesses" checklist in this chapter.
14. Why are good English writing and speaking skills important for the paralegal?
15. Complete the "My Career Roadmap" checklist in this chapter.
16. How can you use the "Strengths & Weaknesses" checklist in preparing your personal career roadmap?
17. What advantages might a person have in entering the paralegal profession later in life?
18. What actions have you observed in other people that demonstrated their resourcefulness? Have others ever told you that you are resourceful?
19. How can you demonstrate the characteristic of commitment?
20. Start to network by setting up a meeting with a working paralegal and preparing a list of questions to ask at that meeting.

Building Paralegal Skills

VIDEO CASE STUDIES

When Friends Ask for Legal Advice

Dante, a paralegal is approached by a friend for legal advice about his apartment lease. His landlord is refusing to allow him to have a dog in his apartment.

After viewing the video case study at www.pearsonhighered.com/goldman answer the following:

1. Would a paralegal working in a real estate office be able to give advice as an incidental activity?
2. Is advising the person that you are a paralegal enough to avoid UPL?
3. What is the law in your state on UPL?

Resume Writing Do's and Don'ts

Two law office human resource directors review some of the resumes they have received and discuss the errors people often make in submitting job applications.

After viewing the video case study at www.pearsonhighered.com/goldman answer the following:

1. Why is a good resume and cover letter so important in getting a paralegal position?
2. What are some of the skills human resource directors look for in new hires?
3. Make a list of skills you need to acquire and courses you should take in pursuing your paralegal studies.

Independent Paralegal

Don Swanson, President of Five Star Legal, an independent paralegal discusses the pros and cons of being an independent paralegal.

After viewing the video case study at www.pearsonhighered.com/goldman answer the following:

1. What are the advantages and disadvantages of working as an independent paralegal?
2. Are there any regulatory issues in your jurisdiction on working as an independent paralegal?

ETHICS ANALYSIS & DISCUSSION QUESTIONS

1. Does your state by statute, regulation, code, ethics rule, or court rule define "Paralegal" or "Legal Assistant"? If it does, what is that definition and where is it so defined? If not, should it formally define the term?
2. Does your state have a statute or court rule on the regulation of the paralegal or legal assistant practice? What are the requirements to practice as a paralegal or legal assistant? Does the law define the practice in some other terminology?
3. Does your state have minimum educational requirements for paralegals? Should there be a set of minimum qualifications?
4. Does having a set of minimum educational requirements eliminate the need for a set of ethical guidelines?

DEVELOPING YOUR COLLABORATION SKILLS

Working on your own or with a group of other students assigned by your instructor, review the scenario at the beginning of the chapter discussing the employment options and educational issues involved.

1. Discuss why or why not Ethan and Ariel should consider a paralegal career. What are the advantages or disadvantages? What strengths or skills do Ethan and Ariel bring to this type of career choice?
2. Working individually or in a group, complete the following:
   a. Summarize, in writing, your career advice to Ethan and/or Ariel.
   b. Share your advice with other students or groups. Does your group have any additional advice or recommendations?
   c. Take on the role of Ethan and/or Ariel. Might they have any other questions for Mr. Marshall about the paralegal profession? Make a list of additional questions. Where might Ethan and Ariel get additional information about the paralegal profession?
3. Select a spokesperson that can summarize and present your recommendations in class.

PARALEGAL PORTFOLIO EXERCISE

Using a three-ring binder with the following tabbed sections listed, start to create a hardcopy portfolio of your work and accomplishments in this course. Please also include any work you are doing in other courses that best represents your growing "skill set." Prepare binder tabs with the following headings listed and insert into your three-ring binder:

A. Understanding the Profession and Its Ethical Obligations
B. Research
C. Legal Writing
D. Basic Skills
E. Acquisition of Legal Knowledge
F. Professional Commitment Beyond Coursework
G. Evaluation of Professional Growth/Evaluation of Program
H. Appendix

LEGAL ANALYSIS & WRITING CASES

Doe v. Condon *532 S.E.2d 879(S.C. 2000)*

The Unauthorized Practice of Law and the Paralegal
A paralegal asked the court if he could conduct unsupervised "wills and trusts" seminars for the public, "emphasizing" living trusts during the course of his presentation and answering estate-planning questions from the audience. He proposed a fee-splitting arrangement with his attorney–employer.

The South Carolina Supreme Court ruled: "The activities of a paralegal do not constitute the practice of law as long as they are limited to work of a preparatory nature, such as legal research, investigation, or the composition of legal documents, which enables licensed attorney–employer to carry a given matter to a conclusion through his own examination, approval, or additional effort.

" . . . The paralegal plays a supporting role to the supervising attorney. Here the roles are reversed. The attorney would support the paralegal. Petitioner would play the lead role, with no meaningful attorney supervision and the attorney's presence and involvement only surfaces on the back end. Meaningful attorney supervision must be present throughout the process. The line between what is and what is not permissible conduct by a non-attorney is sometimes unclear as a potential trap for the unsuspecting client. . . . It is well settled the paralegal may not give legal advice, consult, offer legal explanations, or make legal recommendations."

Questions

1. Why is the practice of law limited to licensed attorneys?
2. What tasks may a paralegal perform?

Sperry v. Florida   373 U.S. 379 (1963)

Petitioner, not a lawyer and not admitted to practice in Florida as a lawyer, was nevertheless authorized to practice before the U.S. Patent Office pursuant to federal statute (35 U.S.C. Sec. 31). The Florida Bar sued to prevent him from representing patent applicants, preparing and prosecuting the patent claims and advising them in the State of Florida.

The Supreme Court, in holding that the Petitioner was permitted to perform tasks incident to prosecuting of patent claims, said, ". . . by virtue of the Supremacy Clause, Florida may not deny to those failing to meet its own qualifications the right to perform the functions within the scope of the federal authority." The Court further stated, ". . . since patent

3. What tasks may a paralegal not perform?
4. Why is the answering of legal questions about the need for a will or a trust the unauthorized practice of law (UPL)?
5. Why is a fee-splitting arrangement between a lawyer and a paralegal prohibited?

Note: If in South Carolina, include the parallel citation: 341 S.C. 22. The Lexis citation for this case is 2000 S.C. LEXIS 125.

practitioners are authorized to practice before the Patent Office, the State maintains control over the practice of law within its borders except to the limited extent for the accomplishment of the federal objective."

Questions

1. Does this decision allow anyone to practice before any federal agency without being licensed?
2. What are the prerequisites for nonlawyers to act on behalf of others before federal agencies?
3. What steps would a paralegal have to take to prosecute patent claims?

WORKING WITH THE LANGUAGE OF THE COURT CASE

Missouri v. Jenkins

491 U.S. 274 (1989)
Supreme Court of the United States

Read the following case excerpts. Information on preparing a briefing is provided in Appendix A: How to Brief a Case. In your brief, prepare a written answer to each of the following questions.

1. What is the difference between "market rates" for paralegals and cost to the attorney for paralegal service?
2. Does billing for paralegal services at market rates unfairly benefit the law firm?
3. According to this court, how is a reasonable attorney's fee calculated?

4. How does the public benefit from allowing paralegals to be billed at market rates?
5. Does this court believe that a reasonable attorney's fee should include paralegal fees?

Brennan, J., delivered the opinion of the Court.

This is the attorney's fee aftermath of major school desegregation litigation in Kansas City, Missouri. We [are hearing this case to decide] should the fee award compensate the work of paralegals and law clerks by applying the market rate for their work?

I

This litigation began in 1977 as a suit by the Kansas City Missouri School District (KCMSD), the school board, and the children of two school board members,

against the State of Missouri and other defendants. The plaintiffs alleged that the State, surrounding school districts, and various federal agencies had caused and perpetuated a system of racial segregation in the schools of the Kansas City metropolitan area. . . . After lengthy proceedings, including a trial that lasted 7½ months during 1983 and 1984, the District Court found the State of Missouri and KCMSD liable. . . . It ordered various intradistrict remedies, to be paid for by the State and KCMSD, including $260 million in capital improvements and a magnet-school plan costing over $200 million.

The plaintiff class has been represented, since 1979, by Kansas City lawyer Arthur Benson and, since 1982, by the NAACP Legal Defense and Educational Fund, Inc. (LDF). Benson and the LDF requested attorney's fees under the Civil Rights Attorney's Fees Awards Act of 1976, 42 U.S.C. § 1988. Benson and his associates had devoted 10,875 attorney hours to the litigation, as well as 8,108 hours of paralegal and law clerk time. For the LDF, the corresponding figures were 10,854 hours for attorneys and 15,517 hours for paralegals and law clerks. Their fee applications deleted from these totals 3,628 attorney hours and 7,046 paralegal hours allocable to unsuccessful claims against the suburban school districts. With additions for postjudgment monitoring and for preparation of the fee application, the District Court awarded Benson a total of approximately $1.7 million and the LDF $2.3 million. . . .

Both Benson and the LDF employed numerous paralegals, law clerks (generally law students working part-time), and recent law graduates in this litigation. The court awarded fees for their work based on Kansas City market rates for those categories. As in the case of the attorneys, it used current rather than historic market rates in order to compensate for the delay in payment. It therefore awarded fees based on hourly rates of $35 for law clerks, $40 for paralegals, and $50 for recent law graduates. [. . .]

III

Missouri's second contention is that the District Court erred in compensating the work of law clerks and paralegals (hereinafter collectively "paralegals") at the market rates for their services, rather than at their cost to the attorney. While Missouri agrees that compensation for the cost of these personnel should be included in the fee award, it suggests that an hourly rate of $15—which it argued below corresponded to their salaries, benefits, and overhead—would be appropriate, rather than the market rates of $35 to $50. According to Missouri, § 1988 does not authorize billing paralegals' hours at market rates, and doing so produces a "windfall" for the attorney.

We begin with the statutory language, which provides simply for "a reasonable attorney's fee as part of the costs." Clearly, a "reasonable attorney's fee" cannot have been meant to compensate only work performed personally by members of the bar. Rather, the term must refer to a reasonable fee for the work product of an attorney.

Thus, the fee must take into account the work not only of attorneys but also of secretaries, messengers, librarians, janitors, and others whose labor contributes to the work product for which an attorney bills her client; and it also must take account of other expenses and profit. The parties have suggested no reason why the work of paralegals should not be similarly compensated, nor can we think of any. We thus take as our starting point the self-evident proposition that the "reasonable attorney's fee" provided for by statute should compensate the work of paralegals, as well as that of attorneys.

The more difficult question is how the work of paralegals is to be valuated in calculating the overall attorney's fee.

The statute specifies a "reasonable" fee for the attorney's work product. In determining how other elements of the attorney's fee are to be calculated, we have consistently looked to the marketplace as our guide to what is "reasonable." In *Blum v. Stenson*, 465 U.S. 886 (1984), for example, we rejected an argument that attorney's fees for nonprofit legal service organizations should be based on cost. We said: "The statute and legislative history establish that 'reasonable fees' under § 1988 are to be calculated according to the prevailing market rates in the relevant community. . . ." A reasonable attorney's fee under § 1988 is one calculated on the basis of rates and practices prevailing in the relevant market, i.e., "in line with those [rates] prevailing in the community for similar services by lawyers of reasonably comparable skill, experience, and reputation," and one that grants the successful civil rights plaintiff a "fully compensatory fee," comparable to what "is traditional with attorneys compensated by a fee-paying client."

If an attorney's fee awarded under § 1988 is to yield the same level of compensation that would be available from the market, the "increasingly widespread custom of separately billing for the services of paralegals and law students who serve as clerks," all else being equal, the hourly fee charged by an attorney whose rates include paralegal work in her hourly fee, or who bills separately for the work of paralegals at cost, will be higher than the hourly fee charged by an attorney competing in the same market who bills separately for the work of paralegals at "market rates." In other words, the prevailing "market rate" for attorney time is not independent of the manner in which paralegal time is accounted for. Thus, if the prevailing practice in a given community were to bill paralegal time separately at market rates, fees awarded the attorney at market rates for attorney time would not be fully compensatory if the court refused to compensate hours billed by paralegals or did so only at "cost." Similarly, the fee awarded would be too high if the court accepted separate billing for paralegal hours in a market where that was not the custom.

(continued)

We reject the argument that compensation for paralegals at rates above "cost" would yield a "windfall" for the prevailing attorney. Neither petitioners nor anyone else, to our knowledge, has ever suggested that the hourly rate applied to the work of an associate attorney in a law firm creates a windfall for the firm's partners or is otherwise improper under § 1988, merely because it exceeds the cost of the attorney's services. If the fees are consistent with market rates and practices, the "windfall" argument has no more force with regard to paralegals than it does for associates. And it would hardly accord with Congress' intent to provide a "fully compensatory fee" if the prevailing plaintiff's attorney in a civil rights lawsuit were not permitted to bill separately for paralegals, while the defense attorney in the same litigation was able to take advantage of the prevailing practice and obtain market rates for such work. Yet that is precisely the result sought in this case by the State of Missouri, which appears to have paid its own outside counsel for the work of paralegals at the hourly rate of $35.

Nothing in § 1988 requires that the work of paralegals invariably be billed separately. If it is the practice in the relevant market not to do so, or to bill the work of paralegals only at cost, that is all that § 1988 requires. Where, however, the prevailing practice is to bill paralegal work at market rates, treating civil rights lawyers' fee requests in the same way is not only permitted by § 1988, but also makes economic sense. By encouraging the use of lower cost paralegals rather than attorneys wherever possible, permitting market-rate billing of paralegal hours "encourages cost-effective delivery of legal services and, by reducing the spiraling cost of civil rights litigation, furthers the policies underlying civil rights statutes."

Such separate billing appears to be the practice in most communities today. In the present case, Missouri concedes that "the local market typically bills separately for paralegal services," and the District Court found that the requested hourly rates of $35 for law clerks, $40 for paralegals, and $50 for recent law graduates were the prevailing rates for such services in the Kansas City area. Under these circumstances, the court's decision to award separate compensation at these rates was fully in accord with § 1988.

IV

The courts correctly granted a fee enhancement to compensate for delay in payment and approved compensation of paralegals and law clerks at market rates. The judgment of the Court of Appeals is therefore Affirmed.

Ethics and Professional Responsibility

LEARNING OBJECTIVES

After studying this chapter, you should be able to:

1. Understand the difference between the attorney's rules of ethics and the paralegal's rules of ethics and the obligations of each profession.
2. Analyze a situation to determine if it involves the unauthorized practice of law.
3. Understand the concept of confidentiality of client communications and the attorney–client privilege.
4. Understand the concept of conflict of interest for the legal profession and methods to protect client confidentiality.
5. Explain the difference between attorney–client privilege and the work-product doctrine.
6. Explain the issues in making inadvertent disclosure of confidential information.

Paralegals at Work

Kelsey and Kathryn became friends when they were studying to be paralegals. Kathryn now works for a large national law firm while Kelsey does freelance paralegal work. They have over the years met frequently for lunch to discuss office issues and client cases. Kelsey asks Kathryn to meet for lunch at a crowded sandwich shop in the office building where she works to discuss a recent office issue. Kathryn can see that something is troubling her friend. After getting a seat at the lunch counter they order lunch and Kelsey begins to confide in Kathryn.

Kelsey regularly does freelance work for two lawyers— one who specializes in intellectual-property issues and one who does mostly personal injury work. Both are working on the same case and both have asked Kelsey to work on the file. One lawyer represents the plaintiff, a close family friend, and the other lawyer represents the defendant. Both lawyers want Kelsey to interview the clients, witnesses, and generally handle the file. Kelsey is wondering if she should be working "both sides of the fence." Kelsey describes to Kathryn the clients and the case in detail while they wait for their lunch to be served.

Kelsey explains that she often does most of the work on the plaintiff lawyer's cases not related to intellectual property, including settling the cases with insurance company adjusters or the lawyers representing the defendants. Kelsey knows the adjuster on this case and he has revealed to her that the insurance company for the defendant wants to settle the case quickly and avoid a trial. Kelsey asks Kathryn for advice.

Consider the issues involved in this scenario as you read the chapter.

INTRODUCTION TO ETHICS AND PROFESSIONAL RESPONSIBILITY

Professions such as law and medicine are regulated for the protection of the public. It may be by licensing or other regulation. Every profession develops a set of guidelines for those in the profession to follow. These may be codes of conduct or **ethical guidelines**, such as the **ABA Model Rules of Professional Conduct** for lawyers. With only a few exceptions, most states have adopted some form of the current or former version of the American Bar Association's Model Rules of Professional Conduct. This provides a high degree of consistency in the ethical guidelines for the legal profession across the country.

Members of national paralegal associations, such as NALA, the National Association of Legal Assistants, and NFPA, the National Federation of Paralegal Associations, have ethics guidelines. These organizations require members to conduct themselves in accordance with these guidelines, observance of which by its members is a condition of continued membership in the organization.

These codes typically set forth the minimum in ethical behavior—the very least each professional should do. In the field of law, these rules are referred to as "the rules of ethics" or "the rules of professional responsibility." Each state controls the right to practice law and, therefore, each state has adopted its own "rules of ethics." The supreme court or legislature of each state has a committee or board that is authorized to enforce state rules of professional responsibility. States typically use a "bar association" to receive and investigate complaints against lawyers.

Regulation of the Practice of Law

Just as the practice of medicine and other professions is regulated, the practice of law is regulated by state government and court rule in an attempt to protect the public from incompetent and unscrupulous practitioners. To protect the public, certain occupations and professions, such as law, require obtaining a license as a method of regulating and monitoring those who offer services to the public. Obtaining a license may be as simple as completing a form and providing proof that the required education and or experience requirements have been satisfied. The profession of law, in most cases, requires taking a qualifying examination after proving that the required educational background has been obtained. This has not always been the case. In the past, admission was possible by satisfying the court that one had studied or, as it was called, "read" the law and had worked under the supervision of a lawyer.

In some states, prior admission for a required period of time allowed admission to the new jurisdiction without taking the examination. Today's rules generally have eliminated these alternative methods of admission to the practice of law. Even seasoned attorneys seeking admission to other states such as California and Florida must retake the examination for that state as a condition for admission.

This examination is generally called the "bar exam." The term "bar" in bar exam has been attributed to the custom of separating the public by a bar from those allowed to pass the bar and approach the judge or court. Most modern courtrooms continue the tradition with a barrier separating the area where spectators sit from where the lawyers, judges, and juries sit. The bar examination tests the applicant's basic legal knowledge and attempts to assure a minimum standard of competency.

Passing the bar exam is the first step in "getting admitted to practice." Admission usually is a ceremonial swearing-in by the court to which the person is "admitted to practice" upon the recommendation of the state or local bar examiners and the introduction and motion for admission by an existing member of the bar of that court.

Admission to practice before one court does not automatically authorize practice before other courts. Each state has its own rules and standards. Generally, admission to the highest court of the state confers admission to all of the other state and municipal and minor judiciary courts of that state. The right to practice before the various federal courts requires separate application and admission to practice. Admission to federal court is generally granted upon motion of an existing member of the court bar upon submission of proof of admission to practice before the highest court of the state of admission and proof of good character.

For the lawyer, the rules that must be followed in the practice of law are found in the individual code of professional responsibility or canons of ethics, such as the Model Rules of Professional Conduct of the American Bar Association, as adopted by the individual state's highest court. The rules of conduct or ethics are enforced by disciplinary committees and their recommendation to the court for sanctions against offending attorneys. Complaints about breaches of ethical behavior normally are referred to a committee for investigation. In some states, minor infractions can subject the lawyer to private reprimand, public reprimand or censure, or in serious cases, temporary or permanent loss of the license to practice law, usually called disbarment.

Breaches of unauthorized practice of law complaint generally are referred to the state attorney or local prosecutor for criminal prosecution as a violation of statute and not a breach of the court rules of ethical behavior. It should be noted that some ethical breaches also may be violations of statute. Attorneys who breach a client's trust by taking the client's fund are guilty of violating an ethical rule and a criminal act of theft.

An appreciation for the system of admission and monitoring of those who seek to practice law can be found in the Preamble to the Illinois Supreme Court Rules of Professional Conduct:

> The practice of law is a public trust. Lawyers are the trustees of the system by which citizens resolve disputes among themselves, punish and deter crime, and determine their relative rights and responsibilities toward each other and their government. Lawyers therefore are responsible for the character, competence and integrity of the persons whom they assist in joining their profession; for assuring access to that system through the availability of competent legal counsel; for maintaining public confidence in the system of justice by acting competently and with loyalty to the best interests of their clients; by working to improve that system to meet the challenges of a rapidly changing society; and by defending the integrity of the judicial system against those who would corrupt, abuse or defraud it.
>
> To achieve these ends, the practice of law is regulated by the following rules. Violation of these rules is grounds for discipline. No set of prohibitions, however, can adequately articulate the positive values or goals sought to be advanced by those prohibitions. This preamble therefore seeks to articulate those values in much the same way as did the former canons set forth in the Illinois Code of Professional Responsibility. Lawyers seeking to conform their conduct to the requirements of these rules should look to the values described in this preamble for guidance in interpreting the difficult issues which may arise under the rules.
>
> The policies which underlie the various rules may, under certain circumstances, be in some tension with each other. Wherever feasible, the rules themselves seek to resolve such conflicts with clear statements of duty. For example, a lawyer must disclose, even in breach of a client confidence, a client's intent to commit a crime involving a serious risk of bodily harm. In other cases, lawyers must carefully weigh conflicting values, and make decisions, at the peril of violating one or more of the following rules. Lawyers are trained to make just such decisions, however, and should not shrink from the task. To reach correct ethical decisions, lawyers must be sensitive to the duties imposed by these rules and, whenever practical, should discuss particularly difficult issues with their peers.

The Paralegal and Licensing

There are, with a few exceptions, no state licensing requirements for one to work as a paralegal—unlike the procedures that lawyers must follow to practice law. Some states, such as California, Maine, and North Carolina, have enacted legislation establishing licensure to perform certain functions frequently performed by paralegals. Generally, these are attempting to regulate the unsupervised performance by freelance or independent paralegals, such as document-completion services.

At best, these laws carve out a small part of the practice of law that can be performed by nonlawyers without risking the performance of acts that constitute the unlawful practice of law. But none allow anyone other than a lawyer properly admitted to practice in the jurisdiction to give legal advice or opinions. Even the selection of the correct form is considered a lawyer's function. (See the California Business Code on the next page.) The client must select the forms.

There is a fine line between lawful activity and unlawful practice of law. Recommending or selecting a form that may impact on a person's legal rights is more likely than not to be treated as practicing law and therefore subject the unlicensed person to a charge of UPL. The dilemma for the paralegal is knowing when giving advice or helping someone fill in blank forms is the **Unauthorized Practice of Law (UPL)**.

Unauthorized Practice of Law (UPL) Giving legal advice, if legal rights may be affected, by anyone not licensed to practice law.

Although each state is free to define the practice of law differently, the statutes have certain elements in common. Typical of the various states' definitions of the Practice of Law is that of *Rule 31, Rules of the Supreme Court of Arizona.*

A. "Practice of law" means providing legal advice or services to or for another by:

(1) preparing any document in any medium intended to affect or secure legal rights for a specific person or entity;

(2) preparing or expressing legal opinions;

(3) representing another in a judicial, quasi-judicial, or administrative proceeding, or other formal dispute resolution process such as arbitration and mediation;

(4) preparing any document through any medium for filing in any court, administrative agency or tribunal for a specific person or entity; or

(5) negotiating legal rights or responsibilities for a specific person or entity . . .

Penalties for the Unauthorized Practice of Law

States such as Pennsylvania have specifically addressed the issue of unauthorized practice of law by paralegals and legal assistants. The Pennsylvania statute on the unauthorized practice of law makes it a misdemeanor for "any person, including, but not limited to, a paralegal or legal assistant who within this Commonwealth, shall practice law . . . " 42 Pa. C.S.A. § 2524.

The Pennsylvania statute seems to address concerns that the general public will misinterpret the title of paralegal or legal assistant as denoting a person admitted to practice law in the commonwealth. An unresolved issue in Pennsylvania, and in other states, is to define what specific conduct the courts will hold to be the practice of law. Because the interpretation will vary from state to state, the paralegal must be aware of the local requirements and limitations that define the unauthorized practice of law within that jurisdiction.

In those states that have enacted legislation regulating paralegal activity some guidance is offered by the defined activity that is permitted. For example, California has included within its Business and Professional Code, licensing of persons as "Unlawful Detainer Assistant" and "Legal Document Assistant" and defining the activity permitted.

Chapter 5.5. Legal Document Assistants and Unlawful Detainer Assistants

Article 1. General Provisions

6400(a) "Unlawful detainer assistant" means any individual who for compensation renders assistance or advice in the prosecution or defense of an unlawful detainer claim or action, including any bankruptcy petition that may affect the unlawful detainer claim or action.

(b) "Unlawful detainer claim" means a proceeding, filing, or action affecting rights or liabilities of any person that arises under Chapter 4 (commencing with Section 1159) of Title 3 of Part 3 of the Code of Civil Procedure and that contemplates an adjudication by a court.

(c) "Legal document assistant" means:

(1) Any person who is not exempted under Section 6401 and who provides, or assists in providing, or offers to provide, or offers to assist in providing, for compensation, any self-help service to a member of the public who is representing himself or herself in a legal matter, or who holds himself or herself out as someone who offers that service or has that authority. This paragraph does not apply to any individual whose assistance consists merely of secretarial or receptionist services.

Avoiding UPL: Holding Oneself Out

With so much uncertainty in what constitutes the unauthorized practice of law the question for every paralegal must be "How Do I Avoid UPL?" Some general guidelines should be followed. A common thread in the law of UPL is the prohibition of holding oneself out as a lawyer when not admitted to practice law. The Florida statute was amended recently to read:

Any person not licensed or otherwise authorized to practice law in this state who practices law in this state or holds himself or herself out to the public as qualified to practice law in this state, or who willfully pretends to be, or willfully takes or uses any name, title, addition, or description implying that he or she is qualified, or recognized by law as qualified, to practice law in this state, commits a felony of the third degree. . . .

Chapter *2004-287*, Senate Bill 1776.

California, in the Business and Professional Code mentioned above, reinforces the concept of not misleading the public into thinking one is a lawyer when he/she provides limited service, by requiring the following statement to prospective clients:

(4) The statement: "I am not an attorney" and, if the person offering legal document assistant or unlawful detainer assistant services is a partnership or a corporation, or uses a fictitious business name, "(name) is not a law firm. I/we cannot represent you in court, advise you about your legal rights or the law, or select legal forms for you."

For the paralegal, the first rule must be to inform the parties with whom they are dealing that they are not lawyers. Paralegals must not hold themselves out as being anything more than a paralegal. Parties with whom the paralegal has contact must know the limited role the person plays as a paralegal on the legal team. Other lawyers, members of the legal team, and courthouse staff are put on notice by being informed of the person's status as paralegal. This may be by oral comment, written statement, such as a letter signed using the title "paralegal," or presentment with a business card clearly showing the title of paralegal.

Advising clients, witnesses, and other members of the general public of the role of the paralegal is not as easy. Those who are not properly educated in the role of the paralegal may believe that a paralegal is someone with advanced training and knowledge who can perform some of the functions normally performed by lawyers, including giving legal advice and opinions. The safest course is to be certain the other party is not misled about the role of the paralegal. Use of the statement from the California Business Code above is a start: "I am not an attorney" . . . "I . . . cannot represent you in court, advise you about your legal rights or the law, or select legal forms for you."

Even this may have its peril when the individual is not aware of the differences in our legal system in the functions of members of the legal team. Some members of the community may come from backgrounds where the distinctions are not clear—for example, those coming from other countries where the legal systems are different and the roles of people in the system are different or where different terms are used for those who perform legal-type functions such as notaries.

For non-native English-speaking people, translation also may play a role in the misunderstanding. To some clients, the paralegal is the "face" or main contact with the law firms. The paralegal may be the first point of contact and the one through whom all documents and information is communicated by the lawyers in the firm.

Paralegals must make it clear that they are paralegals and not lawyers. In a first meeting with anyone—client, witness, opposing counsel, or court personnel—the wisest course of action is to advise them of your position as a paralegal. A short, "I am Miss Attorney's paralegal" may be sufficient to put the other party on notice. Business cards and letterhead, where permitted, should clearly state the title of paralegal. Correspondence always should include the title as part of the signature block.

Never allow the other party to think you are anything other than what you are—a professional who is a paralegal. For those who are not familiar with the role of the paralegal, you may have to clarify what the paralegal can and cannot do in your jurisdiction.

Avoiding UPL: Giving Advice

Every UPL statute or rule prohibits anyone other than a lawyer properly admitted to practice in the state or jurisdiction from preparing or expressing legal opinions. Clearly, then, a paralegal cannot give a legal opinion or give legal advice. It sounds easy, but the reality is that paralegals must be on guard constantly to avoid giving legal advice or rendering a legal opinion. Clients and those seeking "a little free advice" may not want to respect the limitations on the paralegal's role in the legal system.

Certain conduct required or requested by an attorney or client should, at the very least, cause the paralegal to pause. A client who asks you to prepare a power of attorney "without bothering the lawyer," or to "go with me to the support conference" should raise a caution flag in the paralegal's mind. Even in a social setting, you may have to repeat the statement, "I am not an attorney". . . "I/we cannot represent you in court, advise you about your legal rights or the law, or select legal forms for you."

When is giving advice an unauthorized practice of law? If legal rights may be affected, it probably is legal advice. The question of what advice is legal advice is not easy to answer. Consider the seemingly innocent question, "How should I sign my name?" In most circumstances the answer might be: "Just sign it the way you normally write your name." But when a person is signing a document in a representative capacity—for example as the officer of a corporation or on behalf of another person under a power of attorney—telling the client to "just sign your name" might be giving legal advice because the client's legal rights could be affected if he or she does not indicate representative capacity.

Avoiding UPL: Filling Out Forms

Filling out forms for clients also can be a source of trouble. In some jurisdictions, paralegals are permitted to assist clients in preparing certain documents. Other courts, however, view this assistance as rendering legal advice.

> As a general matter, other courts have held that the sale of self-help legal kits or printed legal forms does not constitute the unauthorized practice of law as long as the seller provides the buyer no advice regarding which forms to use or how the forms should be filled out.

Fifteenth Jud. Dis. v. Glasgow, M1996-00020-COA-R3-CV (Tenn.App. 12-10-1999)(FN4)

The Florida court addressed this issue in an unlawful practice of law case, holding the UPL consisted of

> . . . a nonlawyer who has direct contact with individuals in the nature of consultation, explanation, recommendations, advice, and assistance in the provision, selection, and completion of legal forms engages in the unlicensed practice of law; . . . [W]hile a nonlawyer may sell certain legal forms and type up instruments completed by clients, a nonlawyer "must not engage in personal legal assistance in conjunction with her business activities, including the correction of errors and omissions. . . ."

The Florida Bar, petitioner, versus **We The People Forms and Service Center of Sarasota, Inc., et al.**, No. SC02—1675

Avoiding UPL: Representing Clients

Knowing when someone may represent a client before a judicial or quasi-judicial board, such as an administrative agency, is a difficult question to answer. The difficulty is in knowing what the individual courts allow or will permit in individual circumstances. Some jurisdictions and administrative agencies do permit those who are not licensed or admitted to practice to appear in court or before administrative law judges or referees on behalf of clients. Typically, these are law students acting under the guidance and supervision of an attorney under limited circumstances, but they may include paralegals. Depending upon the jurisdiction, nature of the action, and level of the court, the paralegal might be permitted to appear with or on behalf of a client—for example, before a Social Security Administration Administrative Law Judge.

Who may represent clients is not a simple question for lawyers, or for paralegals. Representation of parties traditionally has been the role of lawyers. But even lawyers are not always permitted to represent parties. Appropriate admission to practice in the jurisdiction is typically a requirement. A lawyer admitted to practice in one state may not necessarily represent the same client in another state. Lawyers admitted to practice in one jurisdiction, however, may ask the court of another jurisdiction for permission to appear and try a specific case. This is a courtesy generally granted for a single case, and usually when the trial attorney has retained local counsel who will appear as well to advise on local rules and procedures. But the issue of out-of-state counsel is not without other issues. The complexity of the issue is raised in a portion of a report on the Unauthorized Practice of Law prepared by the Nevada Assistant Bar Counsel.

> The Bar has received complaints of out-of-state counsel participating in the pre-litigation mediation procedures. Writing notification letters, engaging in discovery, and appearing at pre-litigation mediations in a representative capacity is generally the practice of law. In Nevada there is no mechanism to obtain authority from the Supreme Court to appear in pre-litigation cases. Therefore, engaging in legal activities involving Nevada disputes and Nevada parties requires a licensed Nevada attorney. . . .

(Unauthorized Practice of Law, David A. Clark, Assistant Bar Counsel, September 20, 2001)

If the representation of clients is not clear for members of the bar, it certainly is not clear for members of the paralegal profession. Generally, only duly admitted lawyers in the jurisdiction may represent parties. But this rule has been modified to allow law students in some states to represent parties in certain situations, generally under appropriate supervision.

In some states a nonlawyer employee may represent a business in some proceeding before administrative agencies or before the minor judiciary, such as small claims courts. There is no uniformity of rules when nonlawyers may represent parties or before which agencies or courts. Any appearance before a court must be approached carefully. Even the presentation of a request for continuance of a case may be considered by some courts to be the practice of law.

Appearance on behalf of clients before federal and state administrative agencies is no less lacking in uniformity than appearances before courts. But it frequently is easier to determine the ability to appear as a paralegal representing a client. Some federal agencies specifically permit nonlawyers to appear. Most notable is the Social Security Administration, which allows representation by nonlawyers with few differences from representation by lawyers. The U.S. Patent Office also specifically permits nonlawyer practice. Some states, by specific legislation or administrative rule, also permit representation by nonlawyers.

Avoiding UPL: Guidelines

The National Association of Legal Assistants, Inc. Model Standards and Guidelines for the Utilization of Legal Assistants provides guidelines on conduct that may prevent UPL.

Guideline 1

Legal Assistants Should:

1. Disclose their status as legal assistants at the outset of any professional relationship with a client, other attorneys, a court or administrative agency or personnel thereof, or members of the general public.

Guideline 2

Legal Assistants Should Not:

1. Establish attorney–client relationships; set legal fees; give legal opinions or advice; or represent a client before a court, unless authorized to do so by said court; nor
2. Engage in, encourage, or contribute to any act that could constitute the unauthorized practice of law.

Guideline 3

Legal Assistants May Perform Services for an Attorney in the Representation of a Client, Provided:

1. The services performed by the legal assistant do not require the exercise of independent professional legal judgment;
2. The attorney maintains a direct relationship with the client and maintains control of all client matters;
3. The attorney supervises the legal assistant;
4. The attorney remains professionally responsible for all work on behalf of the client, including any actions taken or not taken by the legal assistant in connection therewith; and
5. The services performed supplement, merge with, and become the attorney's work product.

Ethical Obligations

Ethical behavior is expected and required of every member of the legal team, attorney, paralegal, litigation support, information technologist, and outside consultant. What is sometimes not clear in the minds of nonlawyer members of the legal team is what ethical obligations they have and how the ethics rules are to be followed and enforced.

Duty to Supervise

The attorney is ultimately responsible for the ethic conduct of everyone on the legal team. The supervising attorney is the one in charge of a case and those working on the case.

The duty of supervision is required of partners and lawyers with managerial authority in the firm to ensure other lawyers' conduct conforms to the ethical code. Rule 5.1. Direct supervising attorneys with authority over nonlawyers have an ethical obligation to ensure those persons' conduct is compatible with the obligations of the lawyer. Rule 5.3(b). What happens in the handling and processing of a case by the legal team is ultimately the responsibility of the supervising attorney. Any ethical breaches or lapses are ultimately the responsibility of the attorney under the ethical guidelines and under common law principles of agency law. (The principal is responsible for the acts of the agent when the agent is acting within the scope of their employment.) The attorney is the one to whom the client looks for professional advice and the outcome of the case. The attorney will suffer any sanctions that result from a failure to follow and enforce the ethical rules by members of the legal team. As noted in the *opinion of the magistrate judge in the Qualcomm v. Broadcom* case:

> . . . Producing 1.2 million pages of marginally relevant documents while hiding 46,000 critically important ones does not constitute good faith and does not satisfy either the client's or attorney's discovery obligations. Similarly, agreeing to produce certain categories of documents and then not producing all of the documents that fit within such a category is unacceptable. Qualcomm's conduct warrants sanctions.

C. Sanctions

> The Court's review of Qualcomm's declarations, the attorneys' declarations, and Judge Brewster's orders leads this Court to the inevitable conclusion that Qualcomm intentionally withheld tens of thousands of decisive documents from its opponent in an effort to win this case and gain a strategic business advantage over Broadcom.
>
> Qualcomm could not have achieved this goal without some type of assistance or deliberate ignorance from its retained attorneys. Accordingly, the Court concludes it must sanction both Qualcomm and some of its retained attorneys . . ,

QUALCOMM INCORPORATED, v. BROADCOM CORPORATION, and RELATED COUNTER-CLAIMS. Case No. 05cv1958-B (BLM)

Ethical obligations of lawyers are enforced by the court in the jurisdiction where the attorney is practicing or where the case is being tried. The supervising attorney of every legal team must follow the ethics rules and ensure the members of the legal team follow the same rules as the supervising attorney. The obligation to ensure ethical conduct is that of the **supervising attorney** under the ethical obligation to supervise all who work on the case for the attorney, under Rules 5.1 and 5.3.

These rules are as much a part of the administration of justice as the rules of civil or criminal procedure and the rules of evidence. The bigger issue is who has the responsibility to instruct the nonlawyer members of the legal or trial team and who is responsible for ensuring their compliance. While it is ultimately the responsibility of the lawyer to supervise the nonlawyers support staff, such as secretaries, investigators, litigation support staff, and technical consultants, in many cases this obligation falls to the paralegal or litigation manager on the legal team. Each person working for or supervised by the attorney is in fact the **agent** of the attorney. Under fundamentals of agency law, the agent and the **principal**—the attorney—have a **fiduciary relationship** to each other. The agent must obey the reasonable instructions of the principal and the principal is presumed to know everything the agent learns in the ordinary course of working for the attorney on the case. The attorney is ultimately responsible for the ethical conduct of the agent.

Supervising attorney The member of the legal team to whom all others on the team report and who has the ultimate responsibility for the actions of the legal team.

Agent A party who acts on behalf of another.

Principal A party who employs another person to act on his or her behalf.

Fiduciary relationship A relationship under which one party has a duty to act for the interest and benefit of another while acting within the scope of the relationship.

By definition, the paralegal works under the supervision of an attorney. As such, the paralegal is the agent of the attorney and therefore owes a duty to the supervising attorney similar to that of the traditional agent–servant relationship found in agency law—that of a fiduciary obligation. Among the fiduciary obligations of an agent are the duty to exercise reasonable care, skill, and diligence.

The agent also owes a duty of loyalty to the principal. This includes the obligation to act for the employer's benefit rather than for his or her own benefit or the benefit of another whose interest may be adverse to that of the employer.

Ethical Guidelines and Rules

Lawyers generally need to follow only one set of ethics guidelines. Although it may be a set enacted by the state legislature, it usually is one adopted by the supreme court of the state in which they practice.

The most widely adopted is the Model Rules of Professional Conduct, prepared by the American Bar Association and originally released in 1983. The prior release, the Model Code of Professional Conduct (Model Code), is still in use in some jurisdictions. Procedurally, each state reviews the Model Rules or Model Code and adopts the entire recommended set of Model Rules or the Model Code, or portions as it thinks appropriate for its jurisdiction.

Unlike the ABA for lawyers, no single source of ethical rules is set out for the legal assistant. Absent a single unified body of ethical rules, legal assistants must follow state statutes and conduct themselves in conformity with the rules of professional conduct applicable to attorneys and with the ethics opinions of their professional associations. The two major legal assistant organizations providing an ethical code for their members are the National Federation of Paralegal Associations (NFPA) and the National Association of Legal Assistants (NALA).

Although legal assistants are not governed directly by the American Bar Association ethical rules, there is an intertwined relationship between the lawyer, the client, and the paralegal. What the paralegal does or does not do can have a real impact on the lawyer's duty and obligation to the client. Under the Model Rules, the lawyer ultimately is responsible for the actions of the legal assistant.

Model Guidelines for the Utilization of Legal Assistant Services A set of guidelines by ABA policymaking body, the House of Delegates, intended to govern conduct of lawyers when utilizing paralegals or legal assistants.

ABA Model Guidelines for the Utilization of Paralegal Services

In 1991, the American Bar Association's policymaking body, the House of Delegates, initially adopted a set of guidelines intended to govern the conduct of lawyers when utilizing paralegals or legal assistants. These guidelines were updated in 2002 to reflect the legal and policy developments that had taken place since 1991.

Attorneys are bound by the ethical code adopted by the state in which they practice. The ethical guidelines for the paralegal are a combination of the ethical rules imposed on the supervising attorney and the paralegal professional association rules imposed on paralegals. As a general rule, whatever the ethical rules forbid the attorney from doing, they also forbid the paralegal from doing. Paralegals, therefore, can look to their state's adopted set of rules, or code, of professional responsibility for guidance in deciding what is appropriate or inappropriate from an ethical perspective.

By extension of the rule of agency, the paralegal, as a subagent of the supervising attorney, becomes an agent of the client. The attorney is an agent of the client, and the paralegal is a subagent. As an agent of the client, the same duties that are owed to the law firm as the employer are also owed to the client.

One of the questions that arise in firms engaged in corporate practice and in securities practice is whether the paralegal can purchase stock (securities) in a client corporation. Some firms have written policies prohibiting members of the firm, including

Paralegals *in* Practice

PARALEGAL PROFILE
Vicki Voisin

Vicki Voisin, an Advanced Certified Paralegal, is nationally recognized as an author and speaker on ethical issues related to the paralegal profession. She is the creator and presenter of EthicsBasics, a program designed to raise awareness of ethical concerns by legal professionals and corporate employees. She also publishes an e-magazine titled Strategies for Paralegals Seeking Excellence (www .paralegalmentor.com). Vicki is a past president of the National Association of Legal Assistants (NALA), and presently serves on NALA's Advanced Certification Board. She has over 20 years of paralegal experience and is currently employed by Running, Wise & Ford in Charlevoix, Michigan.

The most important paralegal skills needed in the law office where I work are a familiarity with court rules and ethical issues, the ability to communicate clearly with clients, excellent organizational skills, and an attentiveness to detail and accuracy.

I also believe that technology plays an important role in the legal profession. Although technology allows attorneys and paralegals to work faster, it does not necessarily guarantee that all of the work results are accurate. Paralegals should be aware of the potential ethical hazards that technology can introduce, especially in the areas of confidentiality and conflicts of interest. For example, unless done properly, redaction (editing) on electronically filed documents can be uncovered, resulting in the disclosure of confidential and/or privileged information to third parties.

All paralegals should be aware of their ethical obligations and those of an attorney. My advice is to familiarize yourself with the American Bar Association's *Model Rules of Professional Conduct*, as well as its *Guidelines for the Utilization of Paralegal Services*. Then, become acquainted with the related *Model Rules and Guidelines* for your particular state, if available. Also, join professional associations to keep abreast of trends, and attend continuing education programs as often as possible.

paralegals, from purchasing the securities (stock) of client corporations. At the forefront is the propriety of using the information leading to the purchase or the transaction in client securities. Among the issues is whether the purchase was made based upon material inside information, information not generally available to the public, the knowledge of which would cause a person to buy or sell a corporate security. Use of material inside information of publicly traded stocks is generally a violation of federal securities laws prohibiting insider transactions.

For the attorney, guidance is available from Model Rule 1.7 and the comments to the Model Rule and under the previous Model Code DR 5–101A, which provides that an attorney must refuse employment when personal interests, including financial interests, might sway professional judgment. To the extent that this rule applies to the attorney, good judgment would dictate that it applies to the paralegal as well.

Uniformity of Paralegal Ethics

The paralegal profession has no unified code of ethics. State regulations and ethics opinions are not uniform. National organizations such as the National Association of Legal Assistants and the National Federation of Paralegal Associations each provide a uniform code of ethical conduct for members.

Ethics Codes of Paralegal Associations

The two leading national paralegal membership organizations are the National Federation of Paralegal Associations and the National Association of Legal Assistants. Each of these groups has formulated a set of ethical guidelines for its respective membership, as well as for others looking for ethical guidance in regulating the paralegal profession.

 Web Exploration

The National Associations Ethics Codes and ethical guidelines can be reviewed at:

National Federation of Paralegal Associations
www.paralegals.org/display
common.cfm?an=1&subarti
clenbr=330

National Association of Legal Assistants
www.nala.org/

NALS. . . . the Association for Legal Professionals
http://www.nals.org

Association of Legal Administrators
www.alanet.org

National Federation of Paralegal Associations

The National Federation of Paralegal Associations, Inc. is a professional organization composed of paralegal associations and individual paralegals throughout the United States and Canada. Members of NFPA have varying backgrounds, experiences, education, and job responsibilities that reflect the diversity of the paralegal profession. NFPA promotes the growth, development, and recognition of the paralegal profession as an integral partner in the delivery of legal services.

In April 1997, NFPA adopted the Model Disciplinary Rules (Model Rules) to make possible the enforcement of the Canons and Ethical Considerations contained in the NFPA Model Code. At present, unlike a violation by an attorney of the state-adopted rules that can result in loss of the right to practice (disbarment), no such sanction exists for the paralegal breach of association rules except loss of membership.

National Association of Legal Assistants

The National Association of Legal Assistants, formed in 1975, is a leading professional association for legal assistants. NALA provides continuing professional education, development, and certification. It may best be known in the profession for its Certified Legal Assistant (CLA) examination. The ABA Standing Committee on Paralegals has recognized the CLA designation as a designation marking a high level of professional achievement.

A proper coverage of the ethical rules and guidelines is the subject for a course by itself. This overview highlights some key ethical issues that the paralegal must be aware of as a member of a legal team. As a part of the legal team, the paralegal is required to follow the same rules as the supervising attorney. In a majority of jurisdictions these ethical rules are based on the ABA Model Rules of Professional Conduct. Among the ethical obligations of the attorney, and the legal team acting as agent of the attorney, which will be discussed below, are those of:

- Competency, Model Rules of Professional Conduct Rule 1.1,
- Confidentiality, Model Rules of Professional Conduct Rule 1.6(A),
- Conflicts Of Interest, Model Rules of Professional Conduct Rule 1.7,
- Candor, Model Rules of Professional Conduct Rule 3.3,
- Fairness To Opposing Party And Counsel, Model Rules of Professional Conduct Rule 3.4, and
- Duty to Supervise, Model Rules of Professional Conduct Rules 5.1 and 5.3.

Related to the ethical obligation of confidentiality are the related rules of evidence that limit the obligation of the members of the legal team from having to testify under the attorney–client privilege and protect the work product of the legal team prepared for trial from disclosure (Federal Rules of Evidence 501). Paralegals and other nonlawyers also must be concerned with the ethical issues as discussed in the Advice from the Field by Betty Wells.

Competence

Competence/competent The minimum level of knowledge and skill required of a professional.

Rules of court A court's rules for the processing and presentation of cases.

ABA Model Rule of Professional Conduct 1.1 requires that lawyers provide competent representation to a client. **Competent** representation requires the legal knowledge, skill, thoroughness, and preparation reasonably necessary for the representation. Few ethics opinions have been written on the subject of competent representation required under Rule 1.1 as it relates to nonspecific legal issues of workload and legal knowledge. However, the minimum standards clearly require an understanding of the **rules of court**. These rules continue to grow in number and complexity including the adoption of rules regarding electronic discovery. New rules require a new level of knowledge to competently represent clients. Further, lawyers

Advice *from the* **Field**

ETHICS THROUGH THE EYES OF A NON-LAWYER
Betty Wells, PP, PLS, TSC

Betty Wells, PP, PLS, TSC, is currently employed in the Austin, Texas, office of Cox Smith Matthews Incorporated, a San Antonio law firm. She joined NALS in 1994, is a NALS Life Member, and is serving as webmaster for her local chapter, Corresponding Secretary for her state association, Chair of the NALS Foundation, as well as a non-voting Board Member of NALS. She received the Member of the Year in 1997–98 and 2001–02 from her local chapter, the Legal Professional of the Year award in 1997–98 from her state association and the NALS Award of Excellence in 2003. In 2004–05 she received the Mentor of the Year award from her local chapter.

This article was originally published in the Winter 2002–3 issue of *@Law*, the NALS magazine for legal professionals. It is printed with the permission of *@Law* and NALS, the association for legal professionals. © NALS, Inc. Reprinted with permission. All rights reserved.

The American Bar Association and NALS . . . *the association for legal professionals* uses this definition for a legal assistant or paralegal: "A legal assistant or paralegal is a person, qualified by education, training or work experience who is employed or retained by a lawyer, law office, corporation, governmental agency or other entity and who performs specifically delegated substantive legal work for which a lawyer is responsible."

In simple language, a legal assistant is a non-lawyer who provides substantive legal services and is supervised by a lawyer. Legal services performed by non-lawyers differ from firm to firm but may include anything from answering the phone to complex research. Just as the description of legal tasks the non-lawyer may be asked to perform varies from firm to firm, so do non-lawyer classifications. In one firm, a legal secretary may simply answer the attorney's phone and revise documents, while in another firm a legal secretary may prepare complex wills and research case law. You may be "classed" as a legal secretary in your firm while you are actually asked to perform "legal assistant or paralegal" work while working under the supervision of an attorney.

Non-lawyers should be aware of how their conduct could affect not only themselves, but also the lawyer and firm for whom they work. Although legal assistants or paralegals are not directly subject to any rules of professional conduct promulgated by courts, legislatures, or government agencies, those non-lawyer personnel could loose [sic] their job for not following the rules of ethical conduct. In addition, the supervising lawyer could be reprimanded, suspended, or even disbarred, depending on the severity of the unethical conduct of the non-lawyer. Legal assistants or paralegals who are members of national and/or local paralegal associations are required to follow the ethical codes of those associations.

Possibly the biggest ethical situation a non-lawyer faces is the unauthorized practice of law ("UPL"). If you are "tenured," you may find you know more about a particular area of the law than some newly "sworn" lawyers. Because of your knowledge, you may get dangerously close to crossing or may have already crossed the UPL line. Tasks a non-lawyer may perform are limited by statutory or court authority, and the lawyer's determination of the non-lawyer's competency. As the legal profession has evolved so has the role of non-lawyers. Today a non-lawyer is well-educated and well-trained with a variety of backgrounds and experience. The practice of law includes accepting cases, setting fees, giving legal advice, preparing or signing legal documents, and appearing before a court or other judicial body in a representative capacity. The unauthorized practice of law occurs when a non-lawyer engages in activities which affect the legal rights and obligations of clients. The biggest risk for a non-lawyer is giving legal advice instead of general legal information especially when the request comes from a family member or friend. Family members are typically the hardest to convince that you cannot give them legal advice, and they can be relentless in their pursuit of advice. Be aware: Your willingness to dispense legal advice to the family member or friend could potentially result in your unemployment.

How can the non-lawyer avoid UPL? The best way is to always identify oneself as a legal secretary, legal assistant or paralegal who has posed the specific question to a supervising lawyer and as one who is relaying information gleaned from that lawyer. Make certain all legal documents and correspondence that could be considered legal opinion are reviewed, approved and signed by your supervising lawyer or another lawyer in the firm that is familiar with the matter. If you do not know what the UPL provisions are in your state, call your state bar and ask them for the guidelines non-lawyers must follow. Find out today before you are forced to explain what you have done, not only to your employer but to the bar association in your state.

Confidentiality is another area non-lawyers are faced with each and every day. It is important to a lawyer's practice that his clients are able to speak freely with the lawyer's support personnel and for the clients to know the information they are relaying through you will be held in the strictest of confidence. Did the firm where you are employed ask you to sign a confidentiality statement when you were hired? If they did, did they explain to you what client confidentiality meant? If they didn't, ask them for the form and ask them to explain client confidences.

If the firm doesn't have a confidentiality form for non-lawyers, ask them to create one—their malpractice insurance carrier will love you for it. In simple

(continued)

terms, protecting a client's confidence means you do not talk about clients or cases in your firm with anyone, anywhere, especially in public places—the ethics rules require the lawyer to exercise reasonable care to prevent his employees or associates from violating the obligation regarding client confidences or secrets. In other words, the non-lawyer must follow the same rules as the lawyer when it comes to protecting client confidentiality.

Have you ever interviewed for a position at a law firm only to find yourself conflicted out of employment? More and more often, law firms are asking support personnel to provide a list of clients they have worked with. On occasion a non-lawyer has not been hired due to a conflict of interest that cannot be resolved. Have you been hired by a firm, or found yourself doing temp work in a firm and realized you have knowledge from your past job that could change the outcome of the matter on which you are working? Did you immediately go to the supervising lawyer or HR department and tell them of the possibility of a conflict? You should never make the decision that the information you have is inconsequential or take it for granted simply because you are "just a temp." Remember, it is important for you to inform your employer of the potential conflict to avoid potential problems as the matter progresses, not only for you but for the lawyer and their firm as well.

What about receiving legal fees? Can you "troll" for clients and be compensated when your firm is hired? Remember, you are not allowed to set fees, you must not practice law or give the appearance of practicing law, so therefore, you must not accept fees. The reasoning behind this is to protect the lawyer's professional independence of judgment. The obligations of the lawyer to the client do not change simply because you "brought" the client to the firm.

Your unethical behavior may cause you to loose [sic] your job *and* it may cost your employer his or her career. Stay current with ethical requirements in your profession by attending continuing legal education seminars offered by local and state bar associations, as well as through your local, state, and national association. You and your employer will be glad you did.

must be able to communicate with clients in the language of technology about methods of creation and sources of electronic documents and the methods for retrieving them and processing them for submission to opposing counsel and the court. Consider the need to use "interpreters of the language of technology" as similar to the use of language interpreters as explained in the Formal Opinion of the Association of the Bar of the City of New York in the following Ethical Perspective and the notes to the Wisconsin rules on competence when the lawyer is not knowledgeable about a particular issue.

Conflict of Interest

Conflict of interest The representation of one client being directly adverse to the interest of another client.

A **conflict of interest** exists if the representation of one client will be adverse to the interest of another client. Conflict of interest may best be explained by the adage that no one can serve two masters. If the master is entitled to complete loyalty, any conflict in loyalties presents a conflict of interest in which neither master can be certain of the loyalty of his or her servant. It's easy to see the conflict that would arise in a lawyer's going to court representing both the plaintiff and the defendant.

Less obvious are situations in which the attorney represents two parties with a common interest, such as a husband and wife purchasing a new home. In most cases, the interests would be the same and no conflict would exist. When these clients are seeking counseling for marital problems, however, the conflict becomes more obvious as one of them seeks a greater share of the common property or other rights and the lawyer is called upon to give legal advice as to the right to the parties. Finally, lawyers clearly cannot represent both husband and wife in court in the marital dissolution trial.

The American Bar Association Model Rules of Professional Conduct provide a guideline in Rule 1.7, Conflict of Interest: General Rule, which provides in part that a lawyer shall not represent a client if the representation of that client will be directly adverse to another client, unless the lawyer reasonably believes the representation will not adversely affect the relationship with the other client; and each client consents after

Web Exploration

The complete version of the Formal Opinion at: http://www.nycbar.org/Ethics/eth1995-12.htm.

ETHICAL PERSPECTIVE

*The Association of the Bar of the City of New York
Formal Opinion 1995-12
Committee on Professional and Judicial Ethics
July 6, 1995
Action: Formal Opinion*

. . . DR 6-101(A)(2) mandates that "[a] lawyer shall not . . . [h]andle a legal matter without preparation adequate in the circumstances." Adequate preparation requires, not only that a lawyer conduct necessary legal research, but also that he or she gather information material to the claims or defenses of the client. See *Mason v. Balcom*, 531 F.2d 717, 724 (5th Cir. 1976). The lawyer's inability, because of a language barrier, to understand fully what the client is telling him or her may unnecessarily impede the lawyer's ability to gather the information from the client needed to familiarize the lawyer with the circumstances of the case. This makes communication via the interpreter vital since it may be the only practical way that a free-flowing dialogue can be maintained with the client, and the only means by which the lawyer can actually and substantially assist the client.

The duty to represent a client competently, embodied in DR 6-101(A)(1), requires a lawyer confronted with a legal matter calling for legal skills or knowledge outside the lawyer's experience or ability, to associate with lawyers with skills or knowledge necessary to handle the legal matter. When a lawyer is confronted with a legal matter requiring nonlegal skills or knowledge outside the lawyer's experience or ability and these skills or knowledge are necessary for the proper preparation of the legal matter, DR 6-101(A)(2) appears to require that the lawyer associate with professionals in other disciplines who possess the requisite skills or knowledge needed by the lawyer to prepare the legal matter. The interpreter appears to be the type of professional envisioned by EC 6-3's observation that "[p]roper preparation and representation may require the association by the lawyer of professionals in other disciplines." When the need for an interpreter is apparent or it is reasonable to conclude that an interpreter is required for effective communication, failure to take steps with the client to secure an interpreter may be a breach of the duty to represent the client competently.

The Association of the Bar of the City of New York, 42 W. 44th, New York, NY. 10036, (212) 382–6600

consultation. The essence of the rule is that of loyalty to the client. The 1981 version of the American Bar Association Model Code of Professional Responsibility provides in Canon 5:

A lawyer should exercise independent professional judgment on behalf of a client.

The ethical considerations comment to Canon 5 states:

EC–1 The professional judgment of a lawyer should be exercised, within the bounds of the law, solely for the benefit of his client and free of compromising influences and loyalties. Neither his personal interests, the interests of other clients, nor the desires of third persons should be permitted to dilute his loyalty to his client.

Clearly, a lawyer should not accept the employment if the lawyer's personal interests or desires will, or if there is a reasonable probability that they will, adversely affect the advice to be given or services to be rendered to the prospective client. The

WISCONSIN RULES OF PROFESSIONAL CONDUCT FOR ATTORNEYS

SIDEBAR

SCR 20:1.1 Competence
A lawyer shall provide competent representation to a client. Competent representation requires the legal knowledge, skill, thoroughness and preparation reasonably necessary for the representation. Contrast and compare the **Wisconsin Rules of Professional Conduct for Attorneys** at http://www.legis .state.wi.us/rsb/scr/5200 .pdf2006, with the American Bar Association Model Rules of Professional Responsibility at http://www.abanet.org/cpr/ mrpc/mrpc_toc.html, and the ethical rules in your jurisdiction.

Ethical wall An environment in which an attorney or a paralegal is isolated from a particular case or client to avoid a conflict of interest or to protect a client's confidences and secrets.

information that may be considered to create a conflict of interest is not limited solely to that of the attorney representing a client. It also includes the information held by another member of the legal team, including the legal assistant.

The National Federation of Paralegal Associations Model Code of Ethics provides in Canon 8:

> A paralegal shall avoid conflicts of interest and shall disclose any possible conflict to the employer or client, as well as to their prospective employers or clients.

The ultimate obligation to determine the conflict of interest of the paralegal or legal assistant rests with the supervising attorney. Standard procedure in law firms is to check for conflicts of interest within the law firm before accepting a new client or undertaking a new matter for an existing client. Just as other attorneys are asked to review lists of new clients and new matters, so must paralegals check to be certain they do not have a conflict of interest.

Conflicts of interest may arise for paralegals when they change from one employer to another. If the previous employer represented a client or handled certain matters for a client during the period in which the paralegal was employed, a conflict of interest may exist. A more difficult concern for the paralegal is the conflict of interest that can arise from a law firm's representation of family members and personal friends. Paralegals frequently refer family and friends to the attorney or the law firm where they work. The mere relationship or friendship itself might not create conflict, but in some cases could give rise to a claim of undue influence wherein the paralegal may stand to benefit from the action of the law firm. Examples are the drafting of wills and trusts in which the paralegal may be named as a beneficiary or instances in which the paralegal may be named as the executor of the estate or as a trustee receiving compensation.

Ethical Wall

Law firms use the term **"ethical wall"**—also called a Chinese wall (after the Great Wall of China)—to describe an environment in which an attorney or a paralegal is isolated from a particular case or client to avoid a conflict of interest or to protect a client's confidences and secrets. By creating this boundary or wall, any potential communications, whether written or oral, are prevented between members of the legal team handling a particular matter or client and the person with whom there may be a conflict of interest.

In an age of consolidation of law firms in many areas, the number of individual employers has diminished while the number of clients has increased. As a result, professionals today may find themselves in firms that were on the opposite side of cases in the past. Creating an ethical wall permits the professional to accept employment with the other firm. It also permits greater mobility by professionals, as they can go to a new firm in which there may have been a conflict.

Freelance or Independent Paralegal

Freelance or independent paralegals who work for more than one firm or attorney face the potential problem of conflict of interest. Special caution has to be taken to avoid accepting employment in cases where conflicts may exist. Freelance and independent paralegals are keenly aware of this and generally take precautions to prevent conflicts. The law firms and attorneys for whom they work usually are aware of the potential and also take special precautions to isolate potential conflict situations. Full-time paralegals who seek outside income should pay special attention to potential conflicts that may arise.

Not all of these conflicts are obvious. Consider the case of a paralegal working for a plaintiff's negligence firm handling cases against a major retail store. That

HISTORY: SUP. CT. ORDER NO. 04–07, 2007 WI 4, 293 WIS. 2D XV. ABA COMMENT: LEGAL KNOWLEDGE AND SKILL

1. In determining whether a lawyer employs the requisite knowledge and skill in a particular matter, relevant factors include the relative complexity and specialized nature of the matter, the lawyer's general experience, the lawyer's training and experience in the field in question, the preparation and study the lawyer is able to give the matter and whether it is feasible to refer the matter to, or associate or consult with, a lawyer of established competence in the field in question. In many instances, the required proficiency is that of a general practitioner. Expertise in a particular field of law may be required in some circumstances.

2. A lawyer need not necessarily have special training or prior experience to handle legal problems of a type with which the lawyer is unfamiliar. A newly admitted lawyer can be as competent as a practitioner with long experience. Some important legal skills, such as the analysis of precedent, the evaluation of evidence and legal drafting, are required in all legal problems. Perhaps the most fundamental legal skill consists of determining what kind of legal problems a situation may involve, a skill that necessarily transcends any particular specialized knowledge. A lawyer can provide adequate representation in a wholly novel field through necessary study. Competent representation can also be provided through the association of a lawyer of established competence in the field in question.

3. In an emergency a lawyer may give advice or assistance in a matter in which the lawyer does not have the skill ordinarily required where referral to or consultation or association with another lawyer would be impractical. Even in an emergency, however, assistance should be limited to that reasonably necessary in the circumstances, for ill-considered action under emergency conditions can jeopardize the client's interest.

4. A lawyer may accept representation where the requisite level of competence can be achieved by reasonable preparation. This applies as well to a lawyer who is appointed as counsel for an unrepresented person. See also Rule 6.2.

Thoroughness and Preparation

5. Competent handling of a particular matter includes inquiry into and analysis of the factual and legal elements of the problem, and use of methods and procedures meeting the standards of competent practitioners. It also includes adequate preparation. The required attention and preparation are determined in part by what is at stake; major litigation and complex transactions ordinarily require more extensive treatment than matters of lesser complexity and consequence. An agreement between the lawyer and the client regarding the scope of the representation may limit the matters for which the lawyer is responsible. See Rule 1.2(c).

Maintaining Competence

6. To maintain the requisite knowledge and skill, a lawyer should keep abreast of changes in the law and its practice, engage in continuing study and education and comply with all continuing legal education requirements to which the lawyer is subject.

SOURCE: http://www.legis.state.wi.us/rsb/scr/5200.pdf2006

paralegal's acceptance of employment at the retail store the firm is suing presents a conflict of interest. Knowledge of the strategy of the case would be of interest to the retail store employer. But divulging the information would breach the confidence of the law firm and the confidence of the law firm's client. Failing to disclose information to the retail store that directly affects its business breaches the duty of loyalty to that employer.

The Duty of Confidentiality, Attorney–Client Privilege, and Work–Product Doctrine

The three concepts—duty of confidentiality, attorney–client privilege, and work–product doctrine—have something in common: they are all connected to the legal profession's obligation to protect the secrets of the client so that the client can provide all the information necessary for the legal team to conduct an effective representation of the client.

ETHICAL PERSPECTIVE

Wyoming Rules of Professional Conduct for Attorneys at Law

RULE 1.6 CONFIDENTIALITY OF INFORMATION

(a) A lawyer shall not reveal confidential information relating to the representation of a client unless the client makes an informed decision, the disclosure is impliedly authorized in order to carry out the representation or the disclosure is permitted by paragraph (b).

(b) A lawyer may reveal such information to the extent the lawyer reasonably believes necessary:

(1) to prevent the client from committing a criminal act;

(2) to secure legal advice about the lawyer's compliance with these Rules;

(3) to establish a claim or defense on behalf of the lawyer in a controversy between the lawyer and the client, to establish a defense to a criminal charge or civil claim against the lawyer based upon conduct in which the client was involved, or to respond to allegations in any proceeding concerning the lawyer's representation of the client;

(4) to comply with other law or a court order; or

(5) to protect the best interests of an individual when the lawyer has been appointed to act as a guardian ad litem or as an attorney for the best interests of that individual.

Attorney–client privilege
A rule that says a client can tell his or her lawyer anything about the case without fear that the attorney will be called as a witness against the client.

Web Exploration

Review the most current version of Rule 1.6 on Confidentiality in your jurisdiction with the American Bar Association Model Rules of Professional Conduct at the American Bar Association website at www.abanet.org/cpr/mrcp/rule1.6.html.

Attorney–client privilege is founded on the belief that clients should be able to tell their attorneys everything about their case so the attorney can give proper legal advice to the client. For the attorney, the ABA Model Rules provide in Rule 1.6, Confidentiality of Information, that a lawyer shall not reveal information relating to representation of a client unless the client consents after consultation, except for disclosures that are impliedly authorized. What is confidential information is also defined in the ABA model rules: "all information, regardless of the source, gained in the representation of the client." Even information that may be published in the newspaper is confidential for the lawyer and paralegal working for the client and may not be discussed with others. The article may or may not be accurate and any discussion with others could result in discussion of items not in the newspaper story, therefore the lawyer or paralegal cannot confirm or deny anything.

As stated by the federal court in the case of Claus Von Bulow, the attorney–client privilege extends to those working on the case for the attorney representing the client.

> The law is clear in this circuit the person claiming the attorney–client privilege has the burden of establishing all the essential elements thereof. The question is a simple one: Was Reynolds [a friend of Claus Von Bulow claiming that information given to her by the defendant was privileged] an agent of an attorney and has she presented sufficient evidence of this relationship? In other words, were communications made to her, in confidence, in her capacity as an agent of an attorney for the purpose of obtaining legal advice from that attorney? We think not.
>
> The attorney–client privilege is founded on the assumption that encouraging clients to make the fullest disclosure to their attorneys enables the latter to act more effectively. We have recognized that an attorney's effectiveness depends upon his ability to rely on the assistance of various aides, be they secretaries, file clerks, telephone operators, messengers, clerks not yet admitted to the bar, and aides of other sorts. The privilege must include all the persons who act as the attorney's agents. *Von Bulow v. Von Bulow*, 811 F. 2d 136 (2d Cir. 1987)

In every case there are two sides, each represented by an attorney. The attorney for each party to a case has a competing interest, either to obtain information or to protect information from the other. Attorneys want to protect the information received from their clients, or developed in the process of preparing for litigation. The conflict over protecting or releasing information has intensified in recent years as private counsel and government counsel challenge the attorney's obligation to maintain in confidence information obtained directly and through use of agents such as paralegal, and public relations consultants in criminal and civil matters before commencement of litigation. Increased regulatory obligations have created additional obligations on businesses to conduct internal investigations, which has resulted in a new area of federal and state privilege—"the audit privilege."

Increased use of electronic communications tools, such as email and text messaging, has created the era of the instant message, and with it the instant inadvertent disclosure of potentially privileged material with the press of a key. Lawyers and paralegals must know what action the courts will require of the attorney or paralegal to preserve confidential and privileged information that is inadvertently disclosed and, when possible, prevent a loss of the confidentiality privilege that could result in a potential loss of the case and a possible malpractice claim against the law firm. Email has become a universal form of communication, not only for personal communication but also for business and between attorneys and client. Consider the frequent situation where an email is sent to the wrong party by accident. It may be necessary to avoid using electronic communications in jurisdictions that take a hard line that all disclosure, inadvertent or intentional, is a breach of confidentiality or privilege.

Confidentiality

The duty of **confidentiality** is just that for the legal team, a duty. It is a duty imposed on the attorney and each member of the legal team working under the supervision of the attorney to enable clients to obtain legal advice by allowing the client to freely and openly give the members of the legal team all the relevant facts without fear of disclosure of these facts except in limited situations, such as to prevent commission of a crime or to defend against a client's suit.

Attorneys, and the members of the legal team, have a duty to treat client information obtained in the course of representation of a client in confidence under ABA Rule 1.6.[i] Members of the legal team cannot tell anyone the client's information. The duty does not end when the case ends but continues forever and precludes discussing the information with friends, spouses, strangers, or anyone else who might inquire about the case.

The duty of confidentiality also extends to paralegals under ethical guidelines of the major national paralegal organizations such as NALA.[ii] Although these ethical rules are not mandatory on the paralegal, in most states the paralegal's position as an agent creates an obligation to the attorney and to the client.

In the modern practice of law, the attorney must rely on others, such as paralegals, legal secretaries, investigators, law clerks, and the like, to assist in vigorous representation of the client. These "agents" also must be covered by the attorney–client privilege. To do otherwise would require the attorney to guard every document,

Confidentiality A duty imposed on the attorney to enable clients to obtain legal advice by allowing the client to freely and openly give the attorney all the relevant facts.

---

[i] American Bar Association Model Rules of Professional Conduct Rule 1.6, Confidentiality of Information (a) A lawyer shall not reveal information relating to the representation of a client unless the client gives informed consent, the disclosure is impliedly authorized in order to carry out the representation or the disclosure is permitted by paragraph (b).

[ii] NALA Code of Ethics and Professional Responsibility *Canon* 7. A legal assistant must protect the confidences of a client and must not violate any rule or statute now in effect or hereafter enacted controlling the doctrine of privileged communications between a client and an attorney.

NALA Code of Ethics and Professional Responsibility Canon 7

A legal assistant must protect the confidences of a client and must not violate any rule or statute now in effect or hereafter enacted controlling the doctrine of privileged communications between a client and an attorney.

exhibit, and pretrial memorandum from the eyes of everyone on the legal team and perform every task personally from interviews of clients and witnesses, to the typing of reports and memorandum of law, to the conduct of fact and legal research to the preparation of trial exhibits and documents. This is clearly not desirable or cost effective for the client or the administration of justice.

Attorney–Client Privilege

The attorney–client privilege differs from the duty of confidentiality because it applies only to information obtained from the client—for example, the client's confession of commission of the crime. This privilege is found in the state or federal evidence code. It is a rule of evidence that applies in cases where the Rules of Evidence apply: a court of law, a deposition, or other places where a witness is under oath, such as interrogatories, responses to requests for documents, or grand jury hearings. The attorney–client privilege is a part of both state and federal law. The law of each jurisdiction must be consulted to determine the extent of the privilege. In the federal courts the rule determining which privilege rules are followed is governed under the Federal Rules of Evidence Rule 501.

> Except as otherwise required by the Constitution of the United States or provided by Act of Congress or in rules prescribed by the Supreme Court pursuant to statutory authority, the privilege of a witness, person, government, State, or political subdivision thereof shall be governed by the principles of the common law as they may be interpreted by the courts of the United States in the light of reason and experience. However, in civil actions and proceedings, with respect to an element of a claim or defense as to which State law supplies the rule of decision, the privilege of a witness, person, government, State, or political subdivision thereof shall be determined in accordance with State law. (Jan. 2, 1975, P.L. 93–595, § 1, 88 Stat. 1933)[iii]

For example, Pennsylvania is typical of many states in treating the privilege as part of the state common law tradition that has been incorporated in state law (*Commonwealth v. Noll*, 662 A.2d 1123, 1126 (Pa.Super. 1995), appeal denied, 543 Pa. 726, 673 A.2d 333 (1996)).

The "privilege" belongs to the client, not to the attorney. The client may waive the privilege and allow the attorney or paralegal to reveal the information; however, the

---

[iii] Rule 501 General Rule Except as otherwise required by the Constitution of the United States or provided by Act of Congress or in rules prescribed by the Supreme Court pursuant to statutory authority, the privilege of a witness, person, government, State, or political subdivision thereof shall be governed by the principles of the common law as they may be interpreted by the courts of the United States in the light of reason and experience. However, in civil actions and proceedings, with respect to an element of a claim or defense as to which State law supplies the rule of decision, the privilege of a witness, person, government, State, or political subdivision thereof shall be determined in accordance with State law. (Jan. 2, 1975, P.L. 93–595, §1, 88 Stat. 1933).

attorneys or paralegals may not of themselves waive the privilege when asked what the client has told them. In a court proceeding, an appropriate answer to the question of what the client said would be: "I declined to answer because of the attorney–client privilege." If the client had revealed or released the same information to someone else, the privilege is lost. Thus, the client must really keep the information secret for the privilege to apply.

The concept of privilege also extends to persons while acting within certain roles as discussed by the U.S. Supreme Court:

> The privileges between priest and penitent, attorney and client, and physician and patient limit protection to private communication. These privileges are rooted in the imperative need for confidence and trust. The priest-penitent privilege recognizes the human need to disclose to a spiritual counselor, in total and absolute confidence, what are believed to be flawed acts or thoughts and to receive priestly consolation and guidance in return. The lawyer-client privilege rests on the need for the advocate and counselor to know all that relates to the client's reasons for seeking representation if the professional mission is to be carried out. Similarly, the physician must know all that a patient can articulate in order to identify and to treat disease; barriers to full disclosure would impair diagnosis and treatment.

Trammell v. United States, 445 U.S. 40 (1980)

Additional relationships include:

1. Spouse[iv]
2. Psychotherapist–patient. *Jaffe v. Redmond*, 518 US 1[v]
3. Participants in settlement negotiations. *Federal Rules of Evidence* 408[vi]

Claim of Privilege

Privilege is not automatically invoked. The person claiming the privilege—usually the client—has the burden to establish the existence of the privilege.

Privilege A special legal right.

> To sustain a claim of privilege, the party invoking it must demonstrate that the information at issue was a communication between client and counsel or his employee, that it was intended to be and was in fact kept confidential, and that it was made in order to assist in obtaining or providing legal advice or services to the client[vii]

Extension of Attorney–Client Privilege to Others

It is now accepted that the efficient administration of justice requires lawyers to engage others, such as legal assistants, accountants, and other experts. This would not be possible if the privilege did not extend to these agents of the attorney including, most recently, public relations firms.

The U.S. District Court for the Southern District of New York summarized the law, stating:

> . . . the privilege in appropriate circumstances extends to otherwise privileged communications that involve persons assisting the lawyer in the rendition of legal services. This principle has been applied universally to cover office personnel, such as secretaries and law clerks, who assist lawyers in performing their tasks. But it has been

[iv] *Trammell v. U.S.* 445 U.S. 40 (1980).
[v] *Jaffe v. Redmond*, 518 US 1 (1996).
[vi] Rule 480 FRE: . . . evidence of conduct or statements made in compromise negotiation is . . . not admissible. Also see *The Goodyear Tire and Rubber Company v Chiles Power Supply, Inc, et al*, 2003 Fed App 0197P (6th Cir).
[vii] *SR International Bus. Ins. Co v. World Trade Center* Prop No 01 Civ 9291 (S.D.N.Y. 2002), quoting *Browne of New York City, Inc v. Ambase Corp.*

applied more broadly as well. For example, In *United States v Kovel*, the Second Circuit held that a client's communication with an accountant employed by his attorney were privileged where made for the purpose of enabling the attorney to understand the client situation in order to provide legal advice.

(IN RE Grand Jury Subpoenas dated March 24, 2003 directed to (A) Grand Jury Witness Firm and (B) Grand Jury Witness, M11-188 (USDC, S.D.N.Y.) (June 2, 2003)).

Common Interest Privilege

Common interest privilege To permit a client to share confidential information with the attorney for another who shares a common legal interest.

Another variation of privilege is the **common interest privilege**. "The purpose of the common interest privilege is to permit a client to share confidential information with the attorney for another who shares a common legal interest, such as the attorney for a co-defendant who has separate counsel.

> The key consideration is that the nature of the interest be identical, *not similar* [emphasis added], and be legal, not solely commercial.[viii-ix]

Work–Product Doctrine

Work–product doctrine A qualified immunity from discovery for "work product of the lawyer" except on a substantial showing of "necessity or justification" of certain written statements and memoranda prepared by counsel in representation of a client, generally in preparation for trial.

The **work–product doctrine** is different from both the attorney–client privilege and the duty of confidentiality. The attorney–client privilege and the duty of confidentiality relate to the information provided by the clients regardless of whether they involve potential litigation. The U.S. Supreme Court recognized the work–product doctrine and its importance saying:

> Proper preparation of a client's case demands that he assemble information, sift what he considers to be the relevant from the irrelevant facts, prepare his legal theories and plan his strategy without undue and needless interference. That is the historical and the necessary way in which lawyers act within the framework of our system of jurisprudence to promote justice and to protect their clients' interests.
>
> This work is reflected, of course, in interviews, statements, memoranda, correspondence, briefs, mental impressions, personal beliefs, and countless other tangible and intangible ways—aptly though roughly termed by the Circuit Court of Appeals in this case as the "work product of the lawyer." Were such materials open to opposing counsel on mere demand, much of what is now put down in writing would remain unwritten.
>
> An attorney's thoughts, heretofore inviolate, would not be his own. Inefficiency, unfairness and sharp practices would inevitably develop in the giving of legal advice and in the preparation of cases for trial. The effect on the legal profession would be demoralizing. And the interests of the clients and the cause of justice would be poorly served.
>
> . . . where relevant and non-privileged facts remain hidden in an attorney's file and where production of those facts is essential to the preparation of one's case, discovery may be properly had.
>
> *Hickman v. Tayler,* 329 U.S. 495 (1947) at page 511

The work–product doctrine provides a limited protection for material prepared by the attorney or those working for the attorney in anticipation of litigation or for trial, such as research on theories of law or defenses that may be raised in the trial or trial strategy for the order of presentations or methods of impeaching the credibility of witnesses for the other side.

[viii] *International Bus. Ins. Co. v. World Trade Center Prop* No 01 Civ 9291 (S.D.N.Y. 2002), quoting North River Insurance Co. v. Columbia Casualty Company No. 9 Civ 2518, 1995 WL 5792.

[ix] Also see the interesting article on the issue of providing privileged information to insurers. Guarding privileged documents poses challenge to "utmost good faith" doctrine, *National Underwriter; Eranger, April 28, 2003; Sally Agel; Felton Newell.*

The work–product doctrine is narrower than the attorney–client privilege in that it protects only materials prepared "in anticipation of litigation," Fed. R. Civ. P. 26(b)(3), whereas the attorney–client privilege protects confidential legal communications between an attorney and client regardless of whether they involve possible litigation.[x]

The work–product doctrine is codified in the Federal Rules of Civil Procedure Rule 26 (B) (3),[xi] and in Rule 16 (B) (2) of the Federal Rules of Criminal Procedure.[xii]

FRCP 26 (b) Discovery Scope and Limits

Unless otherwise limited by order of the court in accordance with these rules, the scope of discovery is as follows:

(1) In General. Parties may obtain discovery regarding any matter, not privileged, that is relevant to the claim or defense of any party, including the existence, description, nature, custody, condition, and location of any books, documents, or other tangible things and the identity and location of persons having knowledge of any discoverable matter. For good cause, the court may order discovery of any matter relevant to the subject matter involved in the action. Relevant information need not be admissible at the trial if the discovery appears reasonably calculated to lead to the discovery of admissible evidence. All discovery is subject to the limitations imposed by Rule 26(b)(2)(i),(ii), and (iii).

Exceptions and Limitations to the Work–Product Doctrine

The work–product doctrine has some exceptions. It does not cover documents prepared in the normal operation of the client's business, such as sales reports, data analysis, or summaries of business operations.

The work–product doctrine does not extend to documents in an attorney's possession that were prepared by a third-party in the ordinary course of business and that would have been created in essentially similar form irrespective of any litigation anticipated by counsel.[xiii]

In other words, the client cannot obtain protection for internal business documents by giving them to the attorney and thereby protect them from discovery by the other side because they are in the possession of the attorney.

Exception to the Third-Party Document Exception

The courts have made an exception to the exception in which a lawyer is trying to find out the other party's strategy by asking about documents already in his/her possession that would not be protected under the third-party exception. To protect the lawyer's trial strategy, the court may impose a privilege where it would not otherwise exist. We, too, have observed that

Where a request is made for documents already in the possession of requesting party, with precise goal of warning what the opposing attorney's thinking or strategy may be, even **third-party documents** may be protected. Id[xiv]

Third-party documents
Documents prepared by a third party in the ordinary course of business that would have been prepared in similar form if there was no litigation.

---

[x] *Electronic Data Systems Corporation v. Steingraber Case* 4:02 CV 225 USDC, E.D. Texas (2003).
[xi] FRCP 26 (b) Discovery Scope and Limits. Unless otherwise limited by order of the court in accordance with these rules, the scope of discovery is as follows:
(1) In General. Parties may obtain discovery regarding any matter, not privileged, that is relevant to the claim or defense of any party, including the existence, description, nature, custody, condition, and location of any books, documents, or other tangible things and the identity and location of persons having knowledge of any discoverable matter. For good cause, the court may order discovery of any matter relevant to the subject matter involved in the action. Relevant information need not be admissible at the trial if the discovery appears reasonably calculated to lead to the discovery of admissible evidence. All discovery is subject to the limitations imposed by Rule 26(b)(2)(i),(ii), and (iii).
[xii] Fed. R. Crim. P. 16.
[xiii] In Re Grand Jury Subpoenas, 318 F. 3d 379 (2nd Cir 2002) at page 385.
[xiv] Id page 385.

Governmental Attorney Exception

The attorney–client privilege does not extend to government attorneys. Individuals and corporations are both subject to criminal liability for their transgressions. Individuals will not talk and corporations will have no incentive to conduct or cooperate in internal investigations if they know that any information disclosed may be turned over to the authorities. . . . A state agency, however, cannot be held criminally liable. . . . A government attorney should have no privilege to shield relevant information from the public citizens to whom she owes ultimate allegiance, as represented by the grand jury.[xv]

Inadvertent Disclosure of Confidential Information

Inadvertent disclosure of confidential or privileged information does happen. It may be the slip of the finger in sending an email, an accidental pushing of the wrong number on the speed dial of a fax machine or the sending of a misaddressed envelope.

The admissibility of the inadvertently disclosed documents may hinge on the steps the firm takes before and after the disclosure. Having a proper screening policy in place and monitoring this policy may prevent a claim of negligence.[xvi]

The treatment will depend on the individual jurisdiction. The courts follow no single policy.

Judicial Views

There are three judicial views on handling the inadvertent disclosure under the attorney–client privilege: (1) Automatic waiver; (2) no waiver; (3) and balancing test.[xvii]

Automatic Waiver
These cases hold that once the confidentiality is breached, the privilege is therefore waived.

No Waiver
There can only be a waiver when a client makes a knowing voluntary waiver of the privilege. Therefore, the attorney's inadvertent disclosure does not constitute a waiver.

Balancing Test
The courts using the balancing test looked to the nature of the methods taken to protect the information, efforts made to correct the error, the extent of the disclosure and fairness. Remedies under this test range from unlimited use of the disclosed materials, to court-ordered return of documents, to disqualification of attorneys who have reviewed inadvertently disclosed privileged documents.

ABA Ethics Opinion

The American Bar Association has issued a formal opinion modifying the long-standing opinion 92-368, which advocated for confidentiality of privileged materials to protect the client, and imposing a burden upon receiving attorneys not to review privileged material and return it following instructions given to them by the disclosing attorney, issuing a clarifying formal opinion 05-437, which states:

A lawyer who receives a document from opposing parties or their lawyers and knows or reasonably should know that the document was inadvertently sent should promptly notify the sender in order to permit the sender to take protective measures. To the extent that Formal Opinion 92-368 opined otherwise, it is hereby withdrawn.

[xv] *In Re a Witness*, 288 F.3d 289 (7th Cir.2002) at pages 293–294.
[xvi] *VLT Inc. Lucent Technologies*, no 00–11049-PBS (D. Mass. 01/21/03).
[xvii] Inadvertent Disclosure: Approaches and Remedies, *The Practical Lawyer*, Philadelphia, April 2001, by Kevin M. McCarthy.

Internal Investigations and Evidentiary Privileges

Businesses, and particularly corporations with publicly traded stocks, are under state and federal requirement to take a proactive approach to determine wrongdoing and identify violations of statutes and regulations. These investigations and "audits" create a body of documents all, some, or none of which may be subject to evidentiary privilege.

Candor and Fairness in Litigation

Litigation is the practice of advocacy, advocating a legal position to the court or trying to persuade a **trier of facts** to accept the facts as presented. It is the duty of the advocate to avoid any conduct that undermines the integrity of the process. The duty to the client to persuasively present the case is a qualified duty, qualified by the ethical obligation (**candor**) to not mislead the court or opposing counsel with false statements of law or of facts which the lawyer knows to be false. Without mutual respect, honesty, and fairness the system cannot function properly. It may be a simple ethical duty to competently research and present the current case and statutory law, even when the most current version is not favorable to the position taken. In the technology age, this duty requires making a complete search for ALL the law, statutory enactments and case law, and not just the part that is favorable to the client's position. In an age of vast numbers of electronic cases, it is easy to lose a few or not run the search as professionally as possible. Not making the proper inquiry of the client's staff to find all of the law may lead to sanctions and potentially worse, disbarment.

Trier of facts The trier of facts decides what facts are to be accepted and used in making the decision. It is usually a jury, but may be a judge who hears a case without a jury and decides the facts and applies the law.

Candor A duty of honesty to the court.

Fairness to Opposing Party and Counsel

Fairness in the practice of law has been an issue probably as long as there has been an adversarial justice system. A number of states have established professionalism commissions and committees. Attorneys are advocates for their clients and occasionally forget that the purpose of the legal system is justice for all. The ethical rule of fairness to opposing counsel and parties is an attempt to set the guidelines to ensure justice is done even if one's client loses the case. Each side is expected to use its best skills and knowledge and present fairly their position in the form of evidence for the trier of fact to determine where the truth lies. Destroying, falsifying, or tampering with evidence destroys the fabric of the system. If people lose confidence in the system because of these unfair tactics society loses confidence in the system and it breaks down. Just consider the criminal cases where the prosecutor does not turn over, as required, **exculpatory evidence** that might show the defendant innocent.

The obligation of the supervising attorney to the court and to the other side may extend not only to the legal term but also in insuring that the client and the client's staff fully comply with the rules of court. Sanctions for failure to properly supervise can come from two sources: the court hearing the underlying action (as in the *Qualcomm*

Exculpatory evidence Evidence which tends to prove the innocence of the accused or prove the facts of the defendant's case.

ETHICAL PERSPECTIVE
One Last Word About Integrity

Model Rule 8.1 states that legal professionals should be persons of integrity. The more integrity each of us brings to the profession, the better the legal system will be. Regardless of a person's expertise or extraordinary gift for the law, the person still will be held to high standards of moral ethical conduct, as has been the case historically. (See also EC8-7)

Ethics: Ten Top Rules for Paralegals, by Deborah K. Orlik. © 2006, Pearson Education, Upper Saddle River, N.J. Reproduced by permission.

Web Exploration

A list of commissions and committees may be seen at www.ABANET.org/cpr/professionals/profcommissions.htm.

case above) and the attorney disciplinary agency. The court typically punishes this sort of misbehavior with monetary sanctions, the purpose of which is to recompense the other side for the time and effort they have expended or will expend because of the discovery abuse. The attorney disciplinary agency's punishment can include, in extreme cases, disbarment or suspension from practice before the court for a period of time, or in less extreme cases public or private censure. In addition, under some circumstances "unfair" litigation tactics may result in a suit for malpractice by the client against the attorney and the law firm.

Concept Review *and* Reinforcement

LEGAL TERMINOLOGY

ABA Model Rules of Professional Conduct   40
Agent   48
Attorney–client privilege   56
Candor   63
Common interest privilege   60
Competence/competent   52
Confidentiality   57
Conflict of interest   52

Ethical guidelines   40
Ethical wall   54
Exculpatory evidence   63
Fiduciary relationship   48
Model Guidelines for the Utilization of Legal Assistant Services   49
Principal   48
Privilege   59

Rules of court   52
Supervising attorney   48
Third-party documents   61
Trier of facts   63
Unauthorized Practice of Law (UPL)   43
Work–product doctrine   60

SUMMARY OF KEY CONCEPTS

Regulation of the Practice of Law

Purpose of Regulation	The practice of law is regulated by state government and court rule in an attempt to protect the public from incompetent and unscrupulous practitioners.
The Paralegal and Licensing	There are, with a few exceptions, no state licensing requirements for one to work as a paralegal—unlike the procedures that lawyers must follow to practice law.
Penalties for the Unauthorized Practice of Law	States such as Pennsylvania have specifically addressed the issue of unauthorized practice of law by paralegals and legal assistants. The Pennsylvania statute on the unauthorized practice of law makes it a misdemeanor for "any person, including, but not limited to, a paralegal or legal assistant who within this Commonwealth, shall practice law."

Avoiding UPL: Holding Oneself Out

Avoiding UPL: Holding Oneself Out	Parties with whom the paralegal has contact must know the limited role the paralegal plays on the legal team.
Avoiding UPL: Giving Advice	A paralegal cannot give a legal opinion or give legal advice. If legal rights may be affected, it is probably legal advice.
Avoiding UPL: Filling Out Forms	UPL may consist of a nonlawyer who explains, recommends, advises, and assists in the selection, completion, and corrections of errors and omissions of legal forms.

Avoiding UPL: Representing Clients	1. Some jurisdictions and administrative agencies do permit those who are not licensed or admitted to practice to appear in court or before administrative law judges or referees on behalf of clients. 2. No uniformity of rules exists outlining when nonlawyers may represent parties or the specific agencies or courts before which nonlawyers can appear. Any appearance before a court must be approved carefully. 3. The presentation of a request for continuance of a case may be considered by some courts to be the practice of law. 4. Some federal agencies specifically permit nonlawyers to appear. Most notable are the Social Security Administration and the U.S. Patent Office.
Avoiding UPL: Guidelines	**Guideline 1** Legal assistants should: 1. disclose their status as legal assistants at the outset of any professional relationship with a client, other attorneys, a court or administrative agency or personnel thereof, or members of the general public. **Guideline 2** Legal assistants should not: 1. establish attorney–client relationships; set legal fees, give legal opinions or advice, or represent a client before a court, unless authorized to do so by said court; nor 2. engage in, encourage, or contribute to any act that could constitute the unauthorized practice of law. **Guideline 3** Legal assistants may perform services for an attorney in the representation of a client, provided that 1. the services performed by the legal assistant do not require the exercise of independent professional legal judgment; 2. the attorney maintains a direct relationship with the client and maintains control of all client matters; 3. the attorney supervises the legal assistant; 4. the attorney remains professionally responsible for all work on behalf of the client, including any actions taken or not taken by the legal assistant in connection therewith.

Ethical Obligations

Expected Behavior	Ethical behavior is expected and required of every member of the legal team, attorney, paralegal, litigation support, information technologist, and outside consultant.
Duty to Supervise	The obligation to ensure ethical conduct is that of the supervising attorney under the ethical obligation to supervise all who work on the case for the attorney. Ethical behavior is expected and required of every member of the legal team, attorney, paralegal, litigation support, information technologist, and outside consultant. Ethical obligations of lawyers are enforced by the court in the jurisdiction where the attorney is practicing or where the case is being tried.

Ethical Guidelines and Rules

Every profession develops a set of guidelines for those in the profession to follow. These may be codes of conduct or ethical guidelines. These codes typically set forth the minimum in ethical behavior—the very least each professional should do.

ABA Model Guidelines for the Utilization of Paralegal Services	A set of guidelines intended to govern the conduct of lawyers when utilizing paralegals or legal assistants.
Uniformity of Paralegal Ethics	No single source of ethical rules is set out for the paralegal. At present, unlike a violation by an attorney of the state-adopted rules that can result in loss of the right to practice (disbarment), no such sanction exists for the paralegal breach of association rules except loss of membership.
Ethics Codes of Paralegal Associations	1. National Federation of Paralegal Associations, Inc. 2. National Association of Legal Assistants
Competence	Competent representation requires the legal knowledge, skill, thoroughness, and preparation reasonably necessary for the representation.
Conflict of Interest	1. A conflict of interest exists if the representation of one client will be adverse to the interest of another client. 2. Conflicts of interest may arise for paralegals when they change from one employer to another if the previous employer represented a client or handled certain matters for a client during the period in which the paralegal was employed.
Ethical Wall	This is an environment in which an attorney or a paralegal is isolated from a particular case or client to avoid a conflict of interest or to protect a client's confidences and secrets.
Freelance or Independent Paralegal	Freelance or independent paralegals who work for more than one firm or attorney face the potential problem of conflict of interest.

The Duty of Confidentiality, Attorney–Client Privilege, and the Work–Product Doctrine

Attorney–Client Privilege	1. This privilege is found in the state or federal evidence code and is a rule of evidence that applies in cases where the Rules of Evidence apply: a court of law, a deposition, or other places where a witness is under oath: such as interrogatories, responses to requests for documents or grand jury hearings. 2. The "privilege" belongs to the client not to the attorney. 3. The person claiming the privilege, usually the client, has the burden to establish the existence of the privilege.
Confidentiality	This is a duty imposed on the attorney and each member of the legal team working under the supervision of the attorney to enable clients to obtain legal advice by allowing the client to freely and openly give the members of the legal team all the relevant facts without fear of disclosure of these facts except in limited situations, such as to prevent commission of a crime or to defend against a client's suit.
Claim of Privilege	The person claiming the privilege, usually the client, has the burden to establish the existence of the privilege.
Extension of Attorney–Client Privilege to Others	The efficient administration of justice requires the privilege to extend to agents of the attorney.
Work–Product Doctrine	1. The work–product doctrine provides a limited protection for material prepared by the attorney or those working for the attorney in anticipation of litigation or for trial. 2. The work–product doctrine is different from both the attorney–client privilege and the duty of confidentiality. The attorney–client privilege and the duty of confidentiality relate to the information provided by the clients regardless of whether they involve potential litigation.

Exceptions and Limitations to the Work–Product Doctrine	Does not cover documents prepared in the normal operation of the client's business, such as sales reports, data analyses, or summaries of business operations.
Exception to the Third-Party Document Exception	Courts have made an exception when a lawyer is trying to find out the other party's strategy by asking about documents already in his/her possession.
Governmental Attorney Exception	Government attorneys should have no privilege to shield relevant information from the public citizens to whom they owe ultimate allegiance, as represented by the grand jury.
Inadvertent Disclosure of Confidential Information	The treatment will depend on the individual jurisdiction. The courts follow no single policy.
Judicial Views	The three judicial views on handling the inadvertent disclosure under the attorney–client privilege are 1. automatic waiver 2. no waiver 3. balancing test
Internal Investigations and Evidentiary Privilege	Internal investigations and audits mandated by state and federal regulation create a body of documents, some or none of which may be subject to evidentiary privilege.

Candor and Fairness in Litigation

	It is the duty of the advocate to avoid any conduct that undermines the integrity of the process. The duty to the client to persuasively present the case is a qualified duty, qualified by the ethical obligation (candor) to not mislead the court or opposing counsel with false statements of law or of facts which the lawyer knows to be false.
Fairness to Opposing Party and Counsel	The ethical rule of fairness to opposing counsel and parties is an attempt to set the guidelines to ensure justice is done even if one's client loses the case.

WORKING THE WEB

1. Download the latest ethics opinions and guidelines from the NALA website at www.NALA.org.
2. Download any ethics updates from the NFPA website at www.paralegal.org.
3. Download a personal reference copy of the Model Rules of Professional Conduct from the ABA Center for Professional Responsibility at www.abanet.org.
4. Use a web browser or search engine to find the URL (web address) for your state or local bar association website that provides guidance or opinions on legal ethics. Three popular search engines are www.google.com, www.yahoo.com, or www.ask.com and www.bing.com.
5. Use the NFPA website to find the names of agencies that allow nonlawyer practice. www.paralegals.org/Development/Roles/allow.html

CRITICAL THINKING & WRITING QUESTIONS

1. What is the general theory for regulating the practice of law? How is this applied?
2. Why is "just giving advice" potentially the unauthorized practice of law?
3. How would regulation of the paralegal profession assure the public of quality legal services?
4. When may nonlawyers represent clients?
5. How can the paralegal avoid UPL?
6. How do unauthorized-practice-of-law statutes protect the public?
7. Why should the paralegal be familiar with the ABA Model Rules of Professional Conduct?

8. How do the ABA Model Guidelines for the Utilization of Legal Assistant Services define the role of the paralegal in the law office?
9. Does a paralegal's violation of the ethics rules of the national paralegal associations have the same impact as violating the ethical rules of attorneys on the right to practice?
10. Would a paralegal dating a client have a conflict of interest caused by compromising influences and loyalties?
11. What is the reason for creating privileged communications?
12. Under what circumstances might a paralegal have a conflict of interest in taking a new job in a law firm?
13. How does an ethical wall protect the client?
14. What is a "Chinese wall"?
15. What are the potential dangers in paralegal's moonlighting?
16. What is a conflict of interest under the Model Rules of Professional Conduct?
17. Does a client have an attorney–client privilege regarding information given to a paralegal during the preparation of a case?
18. What duty does a paralegal owe to the supervising attorney?
19. How is a paralegal an agent of the client?
20. In possible conflict of interest, with whom does the ultimate decision rest?
21. Under what circumstance must a lawyer or a paralegal refuse employment?
22. What is required to invoke the attorney–client privilege?
23. What is covered under the work–product doctrine?
24. Should a paralegal be considered an "other representative" under the Federal Rules of Civil Procedure, Rule 26? Why or why not?
25. What is the duty of the trier of fact?
26. What is exculpatory evidence?

Building Paralegal Skills

VIDEO CASE STUDIES

Disclosure of Status

 A client is meeting with his new attorney and the attorney's paralegal. He expresses some concerns about confidentiality of information given to the paralegal.

After viewing the video case study at www.pearsonhighered.com/goldman answer the following:

1. Does the paralegal have a duty to reveal their status as a paralegal? Does the supervising attorney have the duty?
2. Is the paralegal bound by the same rules of confidentiality as the lawyer?
3. Is the paralegal covered under the attorney client privilege?

Confidentiality Issue: Family Exception?

 Paralegal Judy meets with her mother in a public coffee shop and tells her mother details of the case she is working on that has her stressed out.

After viewing the video case study at www.pearsonhighered.com/goldman answer the following:

1. Does being stressed out change the rules of confidentiality?
2. Is there a privilege that permits discussing the facts of a case with a family member?
3. Can the facts be discussed if names are left out?

Confidentiality Issue: Public Information

 A law firm has a case that has received coverage in the local newspaper. Two of the paralegals from the same law firm are having coffee in a public coffee shop. One of the paralegals who is not assigned to the case reads an article about the client and asks her friend who is working on the case about the accuracy of the article.

After viewing the video case study at www.pearson highered.com/goldman answer the following:

1. How does public disclosure of information about a client or a case change the paralegals responsibility to maintain confidentiality?
2. Are there any ethical issues in discussing cases in a public area?
3. Is the paralegal who was not working on the case under any duty of confidentiality?

ETHICS ANALYSIS & DISCUSSION QUESTIONS

1. Are paralegals held to the same standard as attorneys when there is no supervising attorney?
2. What is the paralegal's duty to the client when the paralegal's employer breaches its duty to the client?
3. Who is responsible for the quality of the legal work performed for a client—the attorney or the paralegal?
4. Assume you have graduated from a paralegal program at a local college. While you are looking for a job where your talents can be properly utilized, a friend asks you to help him fill out a set of bankruptcy forms using a computer program he purchased at the local office supply mega warehouse. The program is designed to pick out the exemptions after the requested information is plugged in. [*In Re Kaitangian*, Calif. 218 BR 102 (1998).] Is this the unauthorized practice of law?

Paralegal Ethics in Practice

5. Assume you are offered the opportunity to work with a local law firm providing living trust services to the public. Your responsibility would be to make a presentation to community groups and in other public meetings on the advantages of living trusts. After the general session, any interested person would meet with you and you would fill out the forms, collect the fee, and send the completed form and half the fee collected to the law firm for review and transmittal to the client. You would retain half the amount collected as your fee. [*Cincinnati Bar Assn. v. Kathman*, 92 Ohio St.3d 92 (2001).] What ethical issues are involved? Explain.

DEVELOPING YOUR COLLABORATION SKILLS

Working on your own or with a group of other students assigned by your instructor, review the scenario at the beginning of the chapter.

1. In a group or individually, identify all the potential ethical issues involved in this scenario.
2. Imagine that a local lawyer who knows both Kathryn and Kelsey was sitting next to them and overheard their conversation. The lawyer sends a letter to the local Ethics Board. Let one group represent the Ethics Board, one group represent Kathryn's employer, and another Kelsey's employers.
   a. How should the Ethics Board respond?
   b. How should the lawyers Kelsey works for respond?
3. Write or discuss a summary of the advice the group would give to Kathryn and Kelsey, and the law firms that employ them.

PARALEGAL PORTFOLIO EXERCISE

Prepare a memorandum of law for submission to a potential employer, outlining the existing regulations in your state for paralegals, and the application of any unauthorized practice of law statutes. Include complete citations to any cases, statutes or regulations, and the Internet address of any state or local ethics sites for lawyers and/or paralegals.

LEGAL ANALYSIS & WRITING CASES

In Re Estate of Devine   263 Ill. App.3d 799 (1994)

A paralegal working in a small office became friendly with a client of the attorney and assisted the client in personal matters outside of the office, including helping him to shop and handle personal finances. In that role, the paralegal was given power to sign checks for the client. After the client died, the paralegal withdrew $165,958 from the joint account with the deceased client. Is a lawyer responsible for the actions of a paralegal?

The court held both the paralegal and the attorney liable for breach of fiduciary duty, holding that if the attorney, who performed work including writing a will leaving a bequest to the attorney and the paralegal, was a fiduciary, so then was the paralegal as a matter of law. Further, the court noted that the law in a number of states holds the attorney liable for a paralegal's acts including the responsibility for unethical conduct by nonlawyer employees of the lawyer. The Illinois court quoted New York and New Jersey cases holding the employing attorney in violation of the Code of Professional Conduct for failing to properly supervise employed paralegals.

Questions

1. Does this case effectively extend the lawyer's ethical rules to the conduct of paralegals?
2. May a paralegal maintain a personal relationship with a client of the firm?
3. Should a paralegal be as familiar as the supervising (employing) attorney with the ABA Model Rules of Professional Conduct?

In the Matter of JOHN A. ARETAKIS, an Attorney, Respondent.   791 N.Y.S.2d 687
COMMITTEE ON PROFESSIONAL STANDARDS, Petitioner.

An attorney made certain statements public from a complaint filed against him with the state committee on disciplinary standards in violation of the rules on confidentiality of proceeding on complaints against attorneys.

The court stated . . . "The Court of Appeals has observed that Judiciary Law § 90 and its counterparts reflect a policy of keeping disciplinary proceedings involving licensed professionals confidential until they are finally determined. The policy serves the purpose of safeguarding information that a potential complainant may regard as private or confidential and thereby removes a possible disincentive to the filing of complaints of professional misconduct. The State's policy also evinces a sensitivity to the possibility of irreparable harm to a professional's reputation resulting from unfounded accusations—a possibility which is enhanced by the more relaxed nature of the [proceedings] . . . Indeed, . . . Professional reputation 'once lost, is not easily restored.'"

Questions

1. Can the reputation of a professional be tarnished by disclosure of unsubstantiated claims of ethical breaches?
2. Once tarnished can a professional reestablish his or her professional integrity?
3. Is the greater good to allow all complaints to be made public?

WORKING WITH THE LANGUAGE OF THE COURT CASE

Tegman v. Accident and Medical Investigations

30 P.3d 8 (Wash. Ct. App. 2001)
Court of Appeals of Washington, Division One

Read the following case excerpted from the Court of Appeals opinion. Review and brief the case. In your brief, answer the following questions.

1. How does this court define "the practice of law"?
2. What is the standard or duty of care that this court imposes on a paralegal who does not have a supervising attorney?
3. What action does this court suggest that a paralegal take when it becomes clear that there is no supervising attorney?
4. Why should a paralegal contact the supervising attorney immediately upon being given a case to handle?
5. Based on this case, should a paralegal advise the client that he or she is a paralegal? If so, when? Why?

Becker, Mary K., A.C.J.

Between 1989 and 1991, plaintiffs Maria Tegman, Linda Leszynski, and Daina Calixto were each injured in separate and unrelated automobile accidents. After their accidents, each plaintiff retained G. Richard McClellan and Accident & Medical Investigations, Inc.

(AMI) for legal counsel and assistance in handling their personal injury claims. . . . Each plaintiff signed a contingency fee agreement with AMI, believing that McClellan was an attorney and AMI a law firm. McClellan has never been an attorney in any jurisdiction. McClellan and AMI employed Camille Jescavage, . . . [a] licensed attorney. . . .

Jescavage . . . learned that McClellan entered into contingency fee agreements with AMI's clients and that McClellan was not an attorney. [Attorneys for AMI] settled a number of cases for AMI, and learned that McClellan processed settlements of AMI cases through his own bank account. . . .

In July 1991, McClellan hired Deloris Mullen as a paralegal. Mullen considered Jescavage to be her supervising attorney, though Jescavage provided little supervision. Jescavage resigned from AMI in the first week of September 1991. McClellan told Mullen that her new supervising attorney would be James Bailey. Mullen did not immediately contact Bailey to confirm that he was her supervising attorney. [He] later told Mullen he was not.

While at AMI, Mullen worked on approximately 50–60 cases, including those of [the] plaintiffs. . . . Mullen was aware of some of McClellan's questionable practices and knew that there were substantial improprieties involved with his operation. Mullen stopped working at AMI on December 6, 1991, when the situation became personally intolerable to her and she obtained direct knowledge that she was without a supervising attorney.

When she left, she did not advise any of the plaintiffs about the problems at AMI. After Mullen left, McClellan settled each plaintiff's case for various amounts without their knowledge or consent, and deposited the funds in his general account by forging their names on the settlement checks.

The "practice of law" clearly does not just mean appearing in court. In a larger sense, it includes "legal advice and counsel, and the preparation of legal instruments and contracts by which legal rights are secured." Mullen contends that her status as a paralegal precludes a finding that she was engaged in the practice of law. She argues that a paralegal is, by definition, someone who works under the supervision of an attorney, and that it is necessarily the attorney, not the paralegal, who is practicing law and owes a duty to the clients. Her argument assumes that she had a supervising attorney.

The trial court's determination that Mullen was negligent was dependent on the court's finding that Mullen knew, or should have known, that she did not have a supervising attorney over a period of several months while she was at AMI. . . . The label "paralegal" is not in itself a shield from liability. A factual evaluation is necessary to distinguish a paralegal who is working under an attorney's supervision from one who is actually practicing law. A finding that a paralegal is practicing law will not be supported merely by evidence of infrequent contact with the supervising attorney.

As long as the paralegal does in fact have a supervising attorney who is responsible for the case, any de-

ficiency in the quality of the supervision or in the quality of the paralegal's work goes to the attorney's negligence, not the paralegal's.

In this case, Mullen testified that she believed James Bailey was her supervising attorney after Jescavage left. The court found Mullen was not justified in that belief. . . . Mullen testified that she had started to distrust McClellan before he informed her that Bailey would be her supervising attorney. Mullen also testified that she did not contact Bailey to confirm that he was supervising her. Bailey testified at a deposition that he did not share Mullen's clients and she did not consult him regarding any of her ongoing cases. He also said that one of the only conversations he remembers having with Mullen with respect to AMI is one where he told her that he was not her supervising attorney after she raised the issue with him. This testimony amply supports the trial court's finding that Mullen was unjustified in her belief that Bailey was her supervising attorney.

[Mullen] continued to send out demand and representation letters after Jescavage left AMI. Letters written by Mullen before Jescavage's departure identify Mullen as a paralegal after her signature, whereas letters she wrote after Jescavage's departure lacked such identification. Even after Mullen discovered, in late November 1991, that Bailey was not her supervising attorney, she wrote letters identifying "this office" as representing the plaintiffs, neglecting to mention that she was a paralegal and that no attorney was responsible for the case. This evidence substantially supports the finding that Mullen engaged in the practice of law.

Accordingly, we conclude the trial court did not err in following Bowers and holding Mullen to the duty of an attorney. The duty of care owed by an attorney is that degree of care, skill, diligence, and knowledge commonly possessed and exercised by a reasonable, careful, and prudent lawyer in the practice of law in Washington. . . .

The court found that the standard of care owed by an attorney, and therefore also by Mullen, required her to notify the plaintiffs of: (1) the serious problems concerning the accessibility of their files to persons who had no right to see them, (2) the fact that client settlements were not processed through an attorney's trust account but, rather, McClellan's own account, (3) the fact that McClellan and AMI, as nonlawyers, had no right to enter into contingent fee agreements with clients and receive contingent fees, (4) the fact that McClellan was, in fact, engaged in the unlawful practice of law, and that, generally, (5) the clients of McClellan and AMI were at substantial risk of financial harm as a result of their association with AMI. Mullen breached her duty to her clients in all of these particulars.

(continued)

We conclude the finding is supported by substantial evidence. Accordingly, the trial court did not err in concluding that Mullen was negligent. . . .

Although Mullen was a paralegal, she is held to an attorney's standard of care because she worked on the plaintiffs' cases during a period of several months when she had no supervising attorney. The fact that she did not render legal advice directly does not excuse her; in fact, her failure to advise the plaintiffs of the improper arrangements at AMI is the very omission that breached her duty. Under these circumstances it is not unjust to hold her accountable as a legal cause of the plaintiffs' injuries. As all the elements of negligence have been established, we affirm the judgment against Mullen.

Affirmed.

WE CONCUR: AGID, J., COLEMAN, J.

This case also was scheduled to be published in the Washington Appellate Reports, and if cited in the courts of Washington, would require that citation as well. This case has a Lexis number of 2001 Wash. App. LEXIS 1890.

Rubin v. Enns

23 S.W.3d 382 Tex. App.-Amarillo (7th Dist. 2000)

1. Does the court's "rebuttable presumption" test work? Would any other test work better?
2. Using the court's "rebuttable presumption" test, would there be some temptation on the part of the second law firm to obtain confidential information that the paralegal learned at the first law firm?
3. Do the ethics standards of the American Bar Association and paralegal associations adequately address ethical conflicts that paralegals face? Discuss.

FACTS

Inda Crawford was employed as a legal assistant by the law firm of Hicks, Thomas & Lilienstern (HTL) for a number of years prior to May 1999. During her employment with the HTL law firm, HTL represented Michael Rubin and other real estate agents in a lawsuit against Westgate Petroleum and other defendants. Crawford worked on this case as a legal assistant for HTL and billed 170 hours of work on the case.

In May 1999, Crawford left her employment at HTL and went to work for the law firm Templeton, Smithee, Hayes, Fields, Young & Heinrich (Templeton). Templeton represented Westgate Petroleum and the other defendants in the previously mentioned lawsuit. Rubin and the other real estate agents in this case filed a writ of mandamus with trial court judge the Honorable Ron Enns to have the Templeton firm disqualified as counsel for Westgate et al. because Crawford had now switched firms.

Rubin argued that because Crawford had previously worked on the case for the HTL firm, the opposing counsel she now worked for should be disqualified from representing the opposing side in the lawsuit. The trial court judge denied the petitioners' writ of mandamus. The petitioners appealed.

ISSUE

Should the writ of mandamus be approved disqualifying a law firm that represents one side of a lawsuit because a legal assistant who worked for the law firm that represented the other side of the lawsuit has now switched firms and works for the law firm sought to be disqualified?

Boyd, Chief Justice

In *Phoenix Founders, Inc. v. Marshall*, 887 S.W.2d 831, 835 (Tex. 1994), the court had occasion to discuss at some length circumstances such as the one before us in which a paralegal has changed employment from a law firm on one side of a case to a law firm on the other side of the case. In doing so, it recognized the countervailing interests involved and noted with approval the ABA suggestion that any restrictions on the nonlawyer's employment should be held to the minimum standard necessary to protect confidentiality of client information. In the course of its discussion, the court held that a paralegal or legal assistant who changes employment and who has worked on a case is subject to a conclusive presumption that confidences and secrets were imparted. While the presumption that a legal assistant obtained confidential information is not rebuttable, the presumption that the information was shared with a new employer is rebuttable.

Such distinction was created to ensure that a nonlawyer's mobility would not be unduly restricted.

However, the court emphasized that the only way the rebuttable presumption could be overcome would be (1) to instruct the legal assistant not to work on any matter on which the paralegal worked during the prior employment, or regarding which the paralegal had information relating to the former employer's representation; and (2) "to take other reasonable steps to ensure that the paralegal does not work in connection with the matters on which the paralegal worked during the prior employment, absent client consent."

The trial court also had before it copies of a May 17, 1999, memo from Joe Hayes, managing partner of the Templeton firm, addressed to all the lawyers and staff of the Templeton firm. In the memo, Hayes designated two cases (one of which underlies this proceeding) as those about which Crawford might possess confidential information. In the memo, the recipients were instructed that Texas Disciplinary Rules 1.05(b)(1) and 5.03(a) prohibited them, as Crawford's supervising employers, "from revealing any confidential information she might have regarding the cases." The memo also advised that to satisfy the requirements of the Disciplinary Rules, as well as those set forth by the supreme court in the *In Re American Home Products Corporation* case, the firm was implementing the following six policies and procedures, effective immediately:

1. Inda shall not perform any work or take any action in connection with the *Westgate* case or the *Seger* case [the second, unrelated, case].
2. Inda shall not discuss the *Westgate* case or the *Seger* case, or disclose any information she has concerning these cases, with anyone.
3. No lawyer or staff member shall discuss the *Westgate* case or the *Seger* case with Inda, or in her presence.
4. All computer information relating to the *Westgate* case and the *Seger* case shall be removed from the firm's computer system. No future information concerning either the *Westgate* case or the *Seger* case shall be stored in any electronic medium but, rather, kept solely in hard copy form with the files in the respective case.
5. The files in the *Westgate* case and the *Seger* case shall be kept in locked files under my supervision. No one shall have access to those files other than me, and those to whom I have given specific authority to access these files. Inda shall not have access to these files or the area where the files are to be maintained. At the close of each business day, all documents relating to these cases shall be placed in their respective files, which shall be returned to their storage places, which shall then be locked.
6. Inda shall not be given access to any of the files pertaining to the *Westgate* case or the *Seger* case, or their contents. None of the documents pertaining to either of these cases shall be disclosed to Inda, discussed with her, or discussed in her presence.

Our review of the record before the trial court convinces us that we cannot say he abused his discretion in arriving at his decision to deny the motion to disqualify the Templeton law firm. Accordingly, relators' petition seeking mandamus relief must be, and is, denied.

DECISION AND REMEDY

The court of appeals affirmed the trial court's denial of the writ of mandamus, thus permitting Crawford to work for the second law firm, which had imposed sufficient safeguards to assure that confidential information obtained at the first law firm was not disclosed to the second law firm.

The court also may find that the lower court has made an error that can be corrected, by sending the case back to the lower court, and **remand** the case to the lower court, to take additional action or conduct further proceedings. For example, the lower court may be directed to hold further proceedings in which a jury hears testimony related to the issue of damages and makes an award of monetary damages.

An appellate court will reverse a lower court decision if it finds an *error of* law the record. An error of law occurs if the jury was improperly instructed by the trial court judge, prejudicial evidence was admitted at trial when it should have been excluded, prejudicial evidence was obtained through an unconstitutional search and seizure, and the like. An appellate court will not reverse a finding of fact unless such finding is unsupported by the evidence or is contradicted by the evidence.

The Paralegal Workplace

DIGITAL RESOURCES

Chapter 3 Digital Resources at *www.pearsonhighered.com/goldman*

- Video Case Studies:
  - Preparing for a Job Interview: Resume Advice
  - Preparing for a Job Interview: Interviewing Advice
  - Interviewing: The Good, the Bad, and the Ugly
- Chapter Summary • Web Links • Court Opinions • Glossary • Comprehension Quizzes
- Technology Resources

> " A lawyer's time and advice are his stock in trade. "
>
> *Abraham Lincoln*

After studying this chapter, you should be able to:

1. Describe the different types of practice arrangements of lawyers and law firms.
2. Explain the organizational structure of law offices.
3. Describe the administrative procedures found in most law offices.
4. Understand the purpose and the importance of conflict checking in the law office.
5. Explain why knowledge of accounting is important in a law practice.
6. Describe the emerging fields in paralegal specialty practice.
7. Be able to prepare a traditional resume and an electronic resume.
8. Create an effective cover letter submitting your resume for employment.
9. Understand the planning needed for a successful job interview.

Paralegals at Work

Law Offices
Goldenberg, Craigie, and Luria

INTEROFFICE MEMO

TO: Natasha Weiser
FROM: Cary Moritz, Office Manager
SUBJECT: Mentoring for New Hires

All of us at Goldenberg, Craigie, and Luria welcome you to our firm. We know you had other job opportunities but believe you will be professionally satisfied and challenged by working here.

The paralegal profession has changed dramatically since I first started in this field, and the one thing we can count on is more change. Please know that you can call on me at any time for advice and guidance. No question is too big or too small.

After all these years I have seen a number of major changes in the profession. When I started out, we were hired based on our keyboarding skills and basically operated as secretaries. Today, more and more lawyers treat us as a part of the legal team and demand as much, if not more, of us than they do new law graduates.

In your new job as a paralegal for Goldenberg, Craigie, and Luria, you frequently will represent our firm as the client's first point of contact and be responsible for conducting initial interviews with clients. As you prepare your interview strategies, please use me as a sounding board. It is important to build rapport so clients will feel comfortable sharing sensitive and personal information with someone who is, at first, a complete stranger. As time goes on, clients often become most comfortable with the paralegal assigned to their case.

As a paralegal, you will be expected to follow a case and do much of the administrative work, such as keeping track of the time and costs associated with each case. Bookkeeping and accounting skills can be a real plus! When I first started, I did only litigation work. When the lawyers in my firm found out that I had been a bookkeeper and had taken accounting classes, I was asked not only to work in the estates area but also was given responsibility for some of the in-office accounting. This is something to think about

75

as you look to develop your professional skill set. Getting a Bachelor's degree eventually led to my job as Office Manager. Additional education is always a plus!

Please know that you can count on me to help you succeed in the present and also to plan and prepare for future endeavors here at Goldenberg, Craigie, and Luria.

Consider the issues involved in this scenario as you read the chapter.

INTRODUCTION FOR THE PARALEGAL

As the paralegal profession has evolved, so, too, have the duties and roles of the paralegal within the legal system and elsewhere. The earliest legal assistant was probably a legal secretary who developed specialized skills while working for an attorney in one of the legal specialties. As the need for specialized skills became more obvious, legal assistant programs and paralegal programs were created to teach the requisite skills.

In the classic sense, a paralegal performs those tasks and activities that assist the supervising attorney in representing clients. In the broader view, the paralegal performs many of the same functions that attorneys perform, under the supervision of an attorney but limited by laws and regulations on the unauthorized practice of law (UPL). The paralegal's actual tasks and functions vary according to the type of practice, size of the firm or organization, and skill of the individual paralegal.

Arrangements and Organization of Law Offices and Firms

The classic image of the law firm was of the practitioner working alone in a small office in a small town. The more modern view portrayed in movies and on TV is that of a large national or global law firm. In between are small partnerships and other environments—corporations, insurance companies, government agencies, and consulting firms composed of accountants, lawyers, and management consultants. Exhibit 3.1 shows organization charts for four typical types of arrangements in which the paralegal may find work.

Solo Practice

Solo practice One lawyer practicing alone without the assistance of other attorneys.

Solo practice refers to one lawyer practicing alone without the assistance of other attorneys. The solo practitioner still exists, not only in small towns but in large metropolitan areas as well. The solo practitioner may well be the employer who most depends on the skills of the paralegal in running the office, working with clients, and assisting at trial. A solo practice offers perhaps the greatest challenge for the paralegal who wishes to be involved in every aspect of a law practice. Tasks that otherwise might be assigned to an associate will fall to the paralegal to perform.

In a litigation practice or a practice in which the attorney is frequently out of the office attending meetings, the paralegal becomes the main point of contact and coordination between clients and the supervising attorney. Jobs that might be done in larger firms by an accounting staff, such as preparation of payroll and maintenance of client escrow accounts, frequently are done by the paralegal in solo practices. Many solo practitioners consider their paralegal to be a key resource in the practice of law.

Small Offices

Small offices Small-office arrangements range from individual practitioners sharing space to partnerships.

Small-office arrangements range from individual practitioners sharing space to partnerships. For the small practitioner, the cost of maintaining an adequate law library,

Exhibit 3.1 Typical organization charts for various-sized firms

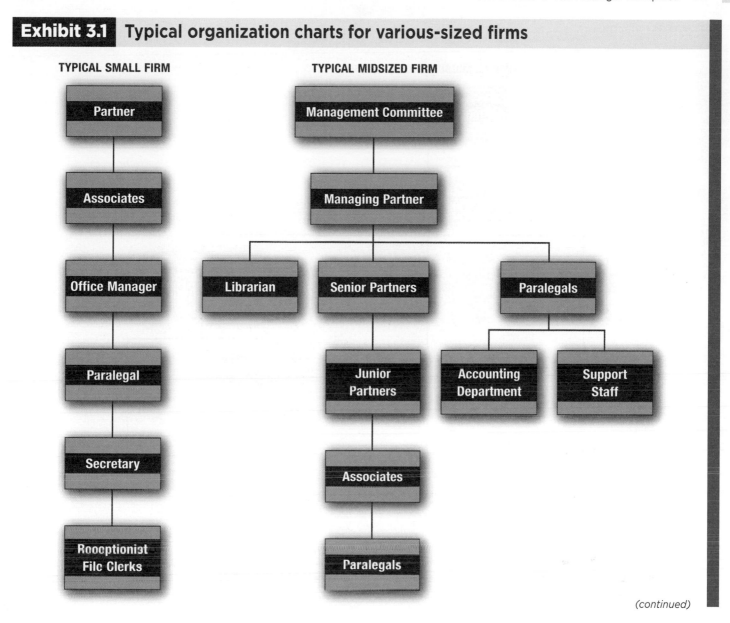

TYPICAL SMALL FIRM

- Partner
- Associates
- Office Manager
- Paralegal
- Secretary
- Receptionist File Clerks

TYPICAL MIDSIZED FIRM

- Management Committee
- Managing Partner
  - Librarian
  - Senior Partners
    - Junior Partners
      - Associates
        - Paralegals
  - Paralegals
    - Accounting Department
    - Support Staff

(continued)

conference room, office space, and office support services such as photocopy and fax machines is daunting. Therefore, practices frequently share these common services while separating client practices. The lawyers might have a similar type of practice, such as criminal law or family law, or dissimilar practices, such as family law and insurance defense work. Depending upon the arrangement, the practitioners might refer clients back and forth. The responsibility for the client and the client relationship is a personal one for the attorney.

Depending upon the arrangement, personnel, such as the receptionist, secretary, or paralegal, might be shared. In these situations the paralegal must be certain which of the attorneys is the supervising attorney with regard to each client. The paralegal who is working for more than one attorney in a sharing arrangement might be privy to confidential information that may not be shared with the other attorneys in the office unless they are working on the same case. In some respects this can be thought of as an "ethical wall" environment. At the very least, the paralegal and the attorneys must clearly understand the ethical issues involved.

Exhibit 3.1 Typical organization charts for various-sized firms *(continued)*

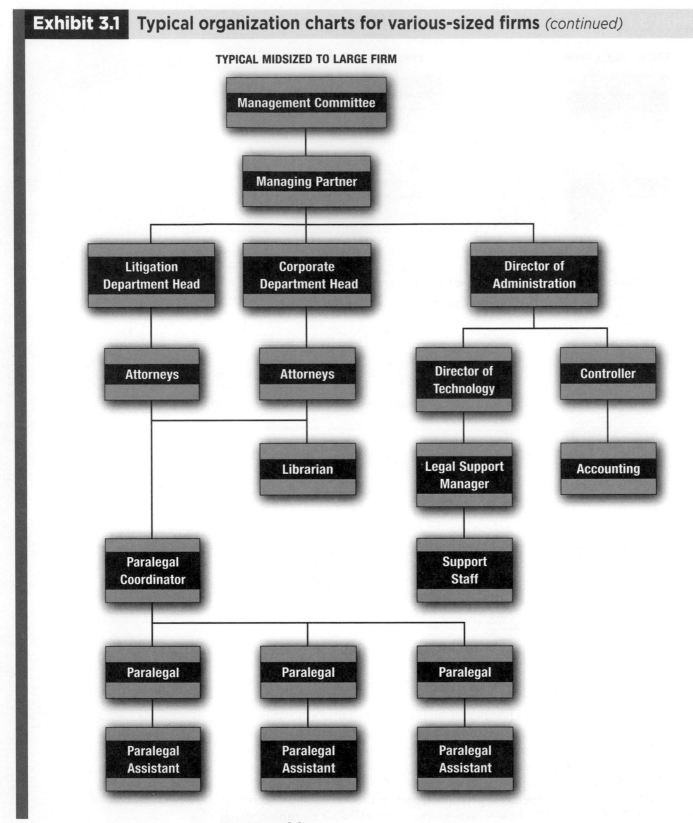

Partnerships

Partnership Two or more natural (human) or artificial (corporation) persons who have joined together to share ownership and profit or loss.

In a **partnership** arrangement, two or more natural (human) or artificial (corporation) persons have joined together to share ownership and profit or loss. Partnerships in small-office arrangements may take the form of true partnerships, sharing all aspects of the practice, or may be partnerships in name only. In the latter case, the same ethical issues that the paralegal faces in the pure office-sharing arrangement must be considered.

Exhibit 3.1 Typical organization charts for various-sized firms *(continued)*

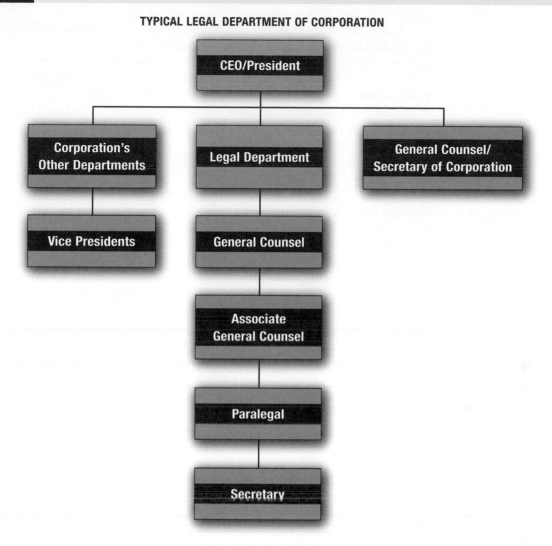

TYPICAL LEGAL DEPARTMENT OF CORPORATION

Source: Wagner, Andrea, How to Land Your First Paralegal Job: Insiders, 3rd, © 2001. Electronically reproduced by permission of Pearson Education, Inc., Upper Saddle River, New Jersey.

If all of the attorneys are partners with complete responsibility for each other and the practice, paralegals may find themselves working for more than one of the partners. In effect, the partners share the paralegal's services. This can give rise to certain issues for the paralegal when more than one of the partners demand something at the same time with the same sense of urgency. The fact that each of the partners will consider himself or herself to be "boss" can create a delicate situation for the paralegal.

A common solution in many offices is for one of the partners to be the primary supervising attorney for the paralegal, through whom the other partner (or partners) funnels work and requests. From an ethical point of view this solves the problem of who the supervising attorney is for the clients and files on which the paralegal is working and at the same time clarifies the lawyers' responsibilities under the lawyers' Rules of Professional Conduct.

Large Offices

Historically, what are now viewed as **large law offices** are an outgrowth of traditional law offices that have expanded over the years, adding partners and associates along the way. Initially, the larger law firms were regional, confined to major cities such as

Large law offices Large law offices are an outgrowth of traditional law offices that have expanded over the years, adding partners and associates along the way.

New York, Chicago, Philadelphia, and Los Angeles. With the growth of government at the national level, many firms found themselves establishing offices in the nation's capital to service clients appearing before federal agencies.

Continued growth of the national economy and business and corporate clients around the country resulted in many firms establishing offices in other large cities, giving them a presence on each of the coasts as well as central locations such as Chicago, with offices in Washington, D.C., and elsewhere. Growth of the global economy has taken us one step farther, with law firms establishing offices in foreign countries. As a result, the large law firm has taken on the characteristics of many corporations, with firms merging to bring specialty areas of law within one firm while expanding the global availability of legal services.

For the paralegal the large office can be an exciting and dynamic area of practice. Paralegals may be called upon to travel with other members of the legal team or on their own as part of the practice. Even when no travel is required, the paralegal might be called upon to work with clients who have diverse backgrounds, both domestically and internationally. One of the values of the large law firm for clients is the availability of a number of legal specialties within one legal services provider. For the paralegal this offers the opportunity to work in different areas of legal specialty.

Working in a large law firm also has some disadvantages. The larger the firm, the greater is the potential for fewer personal relationships and contacts with clients and other members of the legal team. In some firms, just as in any large organization, "playing politics" becomes very real. A paralegal's status, as well as some of the perks and benefits of the job, may depend on the status of the individual's supervising attorney. At the same time, the opportunities for advancement in a large firm might outweigh the disadvantages.

Large Firms

Unlike the small office, in which the paralegal also might be the bookkeeper, office manager, receptionist, and second chair in litigation, a department within a large firm typically hires support staff for each of these functions. The first contact for a paralegal with a large firm may be with the human resources department as part of the job-application process. Bookkeeping or accounting departments usually handle payroll, check requests, and other financial issues. In the larger firms, even the function of making copies takes place in a duplicating department, and the firm might have a mailroom for handling incoming and outgoing mail.

The large law firm has specialized components. In some ways this is similar to the structure of the English legal system, in which the solicitor deals directly with clients and the barrister litigates the cases. United States law firms frequently have litigation specialists who spend their time in the actual litigation of cases while other attorneys within the same firm rarely, if ever, go to court. The role of the latter is to work with clients and, when the need arises, prepare the materials for the litigation department.

Just as the law has become more complex, lawyers also have come to specialize in narrow areas of practice such as environmental law, intellectual-property law, health-care law, insurance law, tort law, and family law. This means that paralegals in large law firms also become specialists within their supervising attorney's primary field of law. Large-practice firms encourage clients to use the firm for all of their legal needs, so a lawyer within the firm frequently refers clients to other specialists in the firm while maintaining primary contact with the clients. Some firms have lawyers whose expertise is in getting new clients. These lawyers, often former politicians and government officials, frequently are referred to as the "rainmakers." They use their contacts to obtain clients and then refer the clients to the specialists within the firm.

Compensation for attorneys within large firms is generally based on how much new business the attorney has brought in, as well as how many billable hours the supervising attorneys have been able to bill for themselves and their paralegals. In this kind of environment, the paralegal who is able to maintain relationships with clients is an invaluable asset to the firm.

ETHICAL PERSPECTIVE
Lawyers Who Share Offices

It is "impermissible for unaffiliated attorneys to have unrestricted access to each other's electronic files (including email and word-processing documents) and other client records. If separate computer systems are not utilized, each attorney's confidential client information should be protected in a way that guards against unauthorized access and preserves client confidences and secrets."

Source: District of Columbia Ethics Opinion 303.

General Practice

A **general law practice** is one that handles all types of cases. This is what people usually think of as the small-town lawyer, the generalist to whom everyone in town comes for advice. The reality is that the same generalists practice in cities as well as small towns throughout the country. Their practices are as diverse as the law itself, handling everything from adoptions to zoning appeals. As general practitioners, they serve the same function in law as the general family practice doctor does in medicine.

Lawyers in this type of practice often work in several areas of law within the same day—attending a hearing in small-claims court in the morning, preparing a will before lunch, having a luncheon meeting with an opposing attorney to discuss settlement of an accident case, then helping someone who is forming a corporation, and finally appearing at a municipal government meeting in the evening to seek a zoning approval. For many, the general practice is the most exciting type of practice, with a continually changing clientele offering all sorts of legal challenges. The paralegal in this environment has the opportunity to work with different types of clients on different types of legal matters on a constant basis. The challenge in this type of practice is to stay current in each of the areas of law of the practice.

General law practice A general law practice is one that handles all types of cases.

Specialty Practice

A **specialty practice** is involved in one area of law. Lawyers with specialty backgrounds, such as engineering, might choose to work in patent law or intellectual-property law. Those coming into the legal profession with accounting backgrounds might specialize in tax matters. Others have special interests and passions such as working with senior

Specialty practice A specialty practice is involved in practice in one area of law.

Paralegals *in* Practice

PARALEGAL PROFILE
Ann W. Price

Ann W. Price, RP, has been a paralegal for over 25 years, working in different sized law firms in diverse practice areas. Ann is currently employed as a Litigation Paralegal Specialist in the U.S. Department of Justice's Environment and Natural Resources Division in Washington, D.C. She is a PACE™ Registered Paralegal which means she has passed the Paralegal Advanced Competency Exam, a certification test developed by the National Federation of Paralegal Associations (NFPA).

In my first few paralegal positions, I was either the only paralegal in the office, or one of two paralegals supporting several attorneys. Because these were small law firms, I was given a large degree of responsibility right from the start. I routinely prepared client correspondence, assisted with discovery (gathering and managing evidence), interviewed clients, and attended trials.

Next, I worked in larger law firms, specializing in food and drug law and environmental law. As a food and drug law paralegal, I researched congressional reports, the Federal Register, and other news and legal databases to summarize findings that might be of interest to the firm's clients. As an environ-

mental law paralegal, I worked on all phases of discovery, trial preparation, and arbitration proceedings in Superfund cases that mostly involved municipal landfill clean-ups.

My next two jobs were both related to paralegal management for large law firms with hundreds of attorneys. In one of these positions, I was an active paralegal in addition to my management duties. Eventually, I became a paralegal manager where my duties were entirely managerial. I currently work for the U.S. Department of Justice's Environment and Natural Resources Division where I provide litigation support to approximately 60 attorneys.

There are pros and cons in every type of legal work setting. Paralegals in large law firms are usually paid a larger salary, but the work they perform is often far less substantive than the work performed by paralegals in smaller firms. Large firms often give the most substantive work to the associate attorneys, particularly those right out of law school. In smaller firms, every person is expected to be able to meet any need the case requires. Also, in larger firms, there is often pressure to meet a specified number of client billable hours; many smaller law firms do not even set a minimum.

In my various jobs, the basic skills used and the work performed did not change significantly from practice area to practice area. However, the terminology and legal resources varied considerably. Continuing legal education opportunities are more prevalent in larger law firms than smaller ones. In smaller firms, education is generally limited to on-the-job training. Most law firms in the metro D.C. area, particularly the large ones, require a four-year degree, and many want a paralegal certificate as well. Individuals with two-year degrees are more likely to find employment at smaller firms, at least for their first paralegal job.

citizens in an elder law practice, or protecting the interests of children as child advocates, or practicing criminal law.

With the increasing complexity of the law, legal specialists frequently are receiving referrals from attorneys in other specialties or in general practice. The paralegal working for a specialist often acquires such a high level of knowledge in a specific area of law that it rivals that of many general practitioners. One of the dangers for the paralegal with this extent of specialty knowledge is that other attorneys could ask the paralegal questions to which the answers border on, or actually result in, the unauthorized practice of law.

Because the paralegal in a specialty law practice is dependent—as are the supervising attorney and the practice—on referrals from other attorneys, the natural tendency is to accommodate referral attorneys by trying to answer questions of a legal nature. To avoid a potential claim of UPL, the paralegal must diplomatically avoid giving legal advice even to an attorney from another firm.

Maintaining relationships with other law firms and their paralegals and secretaries becomes a primary job function for the paralegal in a specialty practice. The paralegal commonly obtains referrals for the supervising attorney and the firm as a result of relationships developed in professional associations with other paralegals who recommend their friend who works for a lawyer specializing in the area sought.

In many areas of specialty, the paralegal has become a vital team member. Paralegals with specialty skills in specific substantive areas perform services that allow the attorney to concentrate on other substantive issues of law. In addition, the paralegal handles office management tasks and functions. These encompass intraoffice support including coordination between members of the professional team and the client.

Legal Nurse Consultants and Nurse Paralegals

Nurse paralegals or legal nurse consultants Nurses who have gained medical work experience and combine it with paralegal skills.

Nurse paralegals or **legal nurse consultants** are nurses who have gained medical work experience and combine it with paralegal skills. Becoming a legal nurse consultant or a nurse paralegal is an ideal career opportunity for nurses with clinical nursing experience who want to work in the legal environment. Entry to most education programs requires a current license as a Registered Nurse and a minimum of 2,000 to 6,000 hours of clinical nursing experience, usually one to three years. Some programs are open to those with an associate degree in nursing, but usually a bachelor's degree in nursing is requested or desired.

Nurse paralegals draw upon their knowledge of medical terminology, medical procedures, and nursing practice to decipher medical records for the legal community. The most obvious advantage is their ability to analyze medical records from both medical and legal standpoints. Their experience also enables them to conduct more effective interviews with clients, fact witnesses, and expert witnesses in cases of medical malpractice and cases involving injury and damage investigation. Graduates of these programs often work as independent nurse consultants for law firms and insurance companies. Others find positions with insurance companies and law firms specializing in medical malpractice and personal injury.

Although the ABA considers the nurse paralegal and legal nurse consultant to be part of the paralegal profession, the American Association of Legal Nurse Consultants (AALNC) views this role as a subspecialty of nursing. In March 1998, the then named Standing Committee on Legal Assistants of the American Bar Association, now named the Standing Committee on Paralegals, decided that "legal nurses and legal nurse consultants fall squarely within the ABA definition of 'paralegal/legal assistant.'" By contrast, AALNC has defined the legal nurse consultant as a specialty practitioner of nursing whose education should be developed and presented as specialty nursing curricula by nurse educators in partnership with legal educators. The ethical code and regulations that must be followed may depend on which profession they are associated with.

Web Exploration

Further information on Legal Nurse Consulting can be obtained at www.Aalnc.org.

Real Estate

Paralegals with real estate experience in sales or from title insurance agencies can perform many of the tasks associated with a real estate practice, such as communicating between buyers and sellers, coordinating the documentation for settlement, and preparing documents for recording purposes. In most jurisdictions, becoming a licensed salesperson or a real estate broker requires completion of a course of study that provides a foundation in the practices and procedures of real estate practice and equips the paralegal with a terminology base that facilitates effective communication with the supervising attorney.

Complex Litigation

Complex litigation takes many forms, from class-action lawsuits to complex product-liability cases. Paralegals working in complex litigation typically oversee the requests for document production and maintain indexes, usually on computer databases, of the paperwork generated from litigation. In large cases the paralegal might supervise a staff of other paralegals or law students in summarizing discovery documents. At trial, these paralegals frequently coordinate the production of exhibits.

Complex litigation Cases involving many parties as in a class action or multiple or complex legal issues.

Environmental Law

Environmental law covers everything from toxic waste dumps to protection of wildlife and the environment. A challenge for the environmental paralegal is in locating and obtaining public records and other documents necessary to establish the areas of concern and claims, some of which predate computer records, such as toxic waste dumps created during World War II and the early 1950s.

Environmental law An area of the law dealing with the protection of the environment.

Intellectual Property

In a survey by The Affiliates, a company providing temporary and full-time legal personnel, 48 percent of the surveyed attorneys indicated **intellectual property** as the fastest growing field in law. The intellectual-property paralegal is concerned with the formalities of protecting intellectual-property interests including patent rights, trade secrets, and copyrights and trademarks. The two main areas are (a) prosecution, which involves establishing the priority of the claims that will result in granting of the patent or copyright, and (b) litigation, which protects those rights against claims by others, such as in patent-infringement cases.

Intellectual property Protection of intellectual-property interests like patents, trademarks, and copyrights.

Elder Law

With the aging of the population has come an increased need to protect the rights of the elderly and obtain all the benefits to which they are entitled. This includes simple tasks such as helping individuals to apply for Social Security, Medicare, or Medicaid benefits. It also entails working with the elderly to create estate plan documents, powers of attorney, and health-care directives. More and more, the paralegal or legal assistant is becoming an advocate for the elderly, in many cases working in a pro bono capacity or through social service agencies. **Elder law** has come to include the additional issues of helping the elderly work through the maze of health care and government benefits.

Elder law Advocacy for the elderly.

Paralegal Managers

As paralegal staffs have grown, even at some of the smaller firms, the position of **paralegal manager** has emerged. With higher turnover rates and increased specialization comes the associated need for someone to hire, supervise, train, and evaluate paralegals. In many firms this person is the interface between the paralegal and the attorneys.

Paralegal manager Someone who hires, supervises, trains, and evaluates paralegals.

As paralegals gain specialized knowledge in specific fields, they find themselves working for different attorneys in specialties, such as intellectual property, real estate, or securities law that require paralegals with specific expertise. Attorneys, for the most part, do not have the time to handle the nonlegal aspects of managers, such as acting as leader, mentor, employee advocate, supervisor, trainer, evaluator, problem solver, and resource manager.

The largest firms appoint a managing partner to handle the management tasks and human resources issues. In many smaller firms, these duties fall to the individual with the title of paralegal manager. This new specialty is well recognized and supported by its own organization, the International Paralegal Management Association.

Web Exploration

Check the latest IPMA News at the IPMA website www.ipma.org.

Pro bono Working without compensation on behalf of individuals and organizations that otherwise could not afford legal assistance.

Government employment Working for federal, state, and local government agencies and authorities.

Pro Bono Paralegals

Pro bono means working without compensation on behalf of individuals and organizations that otherwise could not afford legal assistance. Increasingly, the legal profession has taken on the role of working without compensation in legal aid offices and community legal service programs. As members of professional associations, paralegals participate in pro bono activities at varying levels and time commitments. For example, the Massachusetts Paralegal Association supports a number of pro bono projects. In one of these, the Family Law Project, paralegals partner with attorneys to help handle domestic violence cases without compensation. Pro bono work is seen as part of an ethical obligation of the legal profession.

Government Employment

Federal, state, and local governments are large employers of paralegals, and paralegals are expected to be utilized even further in **government employment** at every level in the future. Many of the federally employed paralegals are found in administrative agencies. A good example is the work of paralegals in the Social Security Administration as decision writers, case schedulers, and case specialists. Just as the private law firm has discovered the value of the paralegal on the legal team, so have government law offices such as the U.S. Attorney's Office and the Office of the Solicitor General. These offices are involved with both criminal prosecutions and civil litigation where the government is a party. Many other agencies that conduct administrative hearings utilize paralegals at all levels.

Legal Departments of Corporations

Many people think of a corporate legal department as a laid-back, conservative environment with little activity other than drafting minutes of meetings and filing corporate records with federal and state governments. The reality today is that, in the global economy, more and more corporations with in-house staffs are engaged in international trade. A whole body of law relates to compliance for imports and exports.

For example, the transfer and sale of certain high-tech equipment and technology must have prior government approval. Sales involving shipments to other countries require letters of credit and currency conversion. International trade creates a host of unique issues related to the laws of the countries with which the domestic corporation may be doing business.

The paralegal is in the middle of these transactions, juggling the requirements from both the legal perspective and the sales/marketing perspective. Paralegals with foreign language skills find themselves in even greater demand in handling communication issues. Those with cultural ties to, or background in, the countries with which the corporation is doing business will find their knowledge frequently tapped to avoid cultural mistakes resulting from miscommunication.

DuPont is one of the largest corporations in the United States. In an effort to reduce costs, DuPont changed the way it uses legal assistants—elevating the work, positions, and numbers of legal assistants. Legal assistants have been given more responsibility in handling documents, technology, and investigations. In doing so, DuPont reportedly reduced by almost 90 percent the number of outside law firms and services it formerly used.

As of 2000, the DuPont legal department had 51 paralegals working with 140 lawyers. In the DuPont model, the legal department acts as counsel to the other DuPont-owned companies and deals with them as clients much in the way that the outside law firms did in the past.[1]

Self-Employment

The paralegal has some opportunities to be self-employed, although state regulation may limit the opportunities or restrict paralegal **self-employment.** Where authorized by federal law, the paralegal may actively represent clients without the supervision of an attorney, such as before the U.S. Patent Office or Social Security Administration. Many paralegals work as freelancers for different attorneys, usually on a case-by-case basis. In addition to the normal ethical obligations regarding confidentiality and conflict of interest, the freelance paralegal must observe the ethical guidelines on advertising in the local jurisdiction and avoid creating the appearance of being available to render legal advice except where authorized.

Self-employment Working independently either as a freelance paralegal for different lawyers or, when authorized by state or federal law, performing services for the public.

Networking

Regardless of the size or type of working environment, **networking** is important for the individual. It establishes contact with others with whom questions and information are shared. Many paralegals develop a referral list of other paralegals they can call to get a quick answer in their own jurisdiction and in others. Most paralegals facing a deadline are not too proud to call their contacts—whether they are across the street, across the state, or across the country—to meet a deadline or get the necessary form. During interviews, hiring attorneys have been known to ask about the paralegal's networking activity.

For the paralegal, networking may also be the key to obtaining a job. As you've heard no doubt, it is not what you know but whom you know. Knowing the right person or a person who can refer you to the right person is a valuable asset.

Networking The establishment of contact with others with whom questions and information are shared.

Paralegal Tasks and Functions

The actual tasks and functions the paralegal performs vary according to the type of practice, size of the firm or organization, and skill of the individual paralegal. Some of the more generic tasks include

- conducting interviews
- maintaining written and verbal contacts with clients and counsel
- setting up, organizing, and maintaining client files
- preparing pleadings and documents
- reviewing, analyzing, summarizing, and indexing documents and transcripts
- assisting in preparing witnesses and clients for trial
- maintaining calendar and tickler systems
- conducting research, both factual and legal
- performing office administrative functions including maintaining time and billing records

Client Interviews

Many paralegals act as the first line of contact with clients. Although paralegals may not ethically or legally give legal advice or set legal fees, they frequently conduct the initial interview with the client. This might involve taking the initial client information

---

[1]"The DuPont Experience," from *Paralegals Are Part of DuPont's Legal Team*, by D. L. Hawley. As seen in the March 2000 issue of *Legal Assistant Today.* Copyright 2000 James Publishing, Inc. Reprinted courtesy of *Legal Assistant Today* magazine. For subscription information call (800) 394-2626, or visit www.legalassistanttoday.com.

and preparing the client data sheet (see Exhibit 3.2) or conducting a more in-depth interview to determine the facts of the matter for the attorney's review. Frequently, the paralegal continues to function as the contact point with the client and the supervising attorney or the law firm. Paralegals frequently establish rapport with clients and earn their confidence.

The paralegal always must be keenly aware of the ethical limitations in dealing with clients. This is especially true when the client develops a high level of confidence in dealing with the paralegal. Clients come to the attorney for advice. When they have confidence in a paralegal, they might tend to ask the paralegal for advice and recommendations instead of "bothering" the attorney. Providing such advice or recommendations may be in violation of UPL restrictions.

Exhibit 3.2	**Client data sheet**

CLIENT DATA SHEET

ACTION TAKEN/REQUIRED

1. Client Name:

2. Client/Matter Number:

3. Client Address:

4. Phone: Work:

   Home:

   Fax:

5. Email address:

6. Social Security No.:

7. Date of Birth:

8. Marital Status:

9. Client Contact:

10. Matter:

(a) Adverse Party:

(b) Date of Incident:

(c) Statute of Limitations Period:

(d) Statute of Limitations Date:

11. Opposing Counsel:

12. Opposing Counsel Address:

13. Opposing Counsel Phone:

For example, to the client, the question, "Should I make my son my power of attorney?" seems simple. But the answer is not so simple and involves many legal consequences, so it must be referred to the supervising attorney. Another UPL might be to help the client complete blank legal forms, such as bankruptcy forms or will forms purchased at a retail store.

Investigations

The paralegal may be asked to act as the direct representative of the supervising attorney in conducting an investigation into a pending case. A paralegal trained in the specific area of law understands the factual needs of a case and the sources of information available. A paralegal who has had the opportunity to observe or work with an attorney and has watched the presentation of evidence in a trial obtains a good sense of what will make good demonstrative evidence, such as models and photographs.

In the case of photos, an understanding of the kind of questions that might be asked in direct examination and cross-examination about the photographs offered as evidence enables the paralegal to be certain that the photographs are taken from the correct angles with the correct landmarks or measurements included. Interviews conducted by the paralegal in preparation for trial could qualify as privileged for the attorney–client privilege just as they do when conducted by attorneys. The paralegal must be aware of how interview material may be used and potentially obtained by opposing parties and act to protect clients' privileged communication with the paralegal as a representative of the supervising attorney.

Legal Writing

Paralegals frequently are called upon to maintain the written communications with clients, opposing attorneys, and the court. These may be in the form of correspondence, memos of law, or briefs for the court. Many paralegals become extremely adept at drafting complaints and supporting memoranda of law and briefs. Although the content is the ultimate responsibility of the supervising attorney, the paralegal with good writing skills is an invaluable asset. Well-written and well-reasoned documentation is easy to review for signature and transmittal and is a major time-saver for the attorney.

Legal Research

In the modern law office, legal research is conducted with hardcopy books and also with electronic media, including extensive use of the Internet. The ability to conduct research into case law, statutory enactments, and regulatory rules and procedures gives the paralegal a major advantage in getting the job in the first place and advancing in most firms. Legal research today requires the ability to use online legal services such as Lexis, Westlaw, VersusLaw, and Loislaw, as well as the ability to find information on government websites and private websites.

What Paralegals in Legal Specialties Do

In addition to the various generic tasks that most paralegals or legal assistants perform, paralegals working in specialty areas find themselves performing additional and more specialized tasks that frequently require special knowledge, education, or skill beyond the basic skills and knowledge required of all paralegals. Following are some of the tasks that paralegals in specialty practice perform.

General business practice:

- Draft lease agreements
- Draft partnership agreements
- Draft noncompetition agreements
- Prepare agreements of sale and attend real estate settlements

- Draft contracts for business arrangements and new ventures
- Draft employee agreements

Debtor rights and creditor remedies:

- Draft correspondence complying with state and federal regulations concerning debt collection
- Prepare documentation to support garnishment proceedings
- Arrange for execution and support judgments, including publication of notice of sales and levies on personal property
- Transfer judgments to other jurisdictions
- Prepare, file, and terminate Uniform Commercial Code financing statements
- Assist clients in filing bankruptcy petitions, including the preparation of schedules and proofs of claim
- Prepare Chapter 11 debtor's financial statements
- Attend Chapter 13 confirmation hearings

Corporate practice:

- Determine availability and reserve fictitious or corporate name
- Prepare and file fictitious name registrations
- Prepare articles of incorporation, minutes, and bylaws for corporation
- Prepare, issue, and transfer stock certificates
- Prepare shareholder agreements
- Prepare applications and file for employer identification numbers and tax registration numbers
- Prepare and file annual reports
- Prepare and file articles of dissolution
- Prepare and file securities registrations and required filings with state regulatory agencies and with the United States Securities & Exchange Commission

Environmental law:

- Track information with regard to Superfund sites
- Determine applicability of brown fields to client property
- Research history of properties to determine environmental activity
- Obtain the appropriate information about sites from state and federal environmental agencies
- Obtain documentation and assist in the preparation of environmental audits
- Organize and index documentation

Family law:

- Collect information from clients with regard to marital status and prior marital status
- Interview client and collect information with regard to child support (see Exhibit 3.3)
- Draft prenuptial agreements
- Draft divorce complaints and responsive pleadings
- Prepare motions for support
- Prepare motions for custody and visitation
- Prepare property settlement agreements
- Prepare protection-from-abuse petitions
- Prepare petitions for termination of parental rights
- Prepare adoption petitions

| Exhibit 3.3 | Child support data form |

_____ v. _____ No. _____

THIS FORM MUST BE FILLED OUT

(If you are self-employed or if you are salaried by a business of which you are owner in whole or in part, you must also fill out the Supplemental Income Statement which appears on the last page of this Income and Expense Statement.)

INCOME AND EXPENSE STATEMENT OF
_____

I verify that the statements made in this Income and Expense Statement are true and correct. I understand that false statements herein are made subject to the penalties of 18 Pa.C.S. §4904 relating to unsworn falsification to authorities.

Date: _____ Plaintiff or Defendant: _____

INCOME

Employer: _____

Address: _____

Type of Work: _____

Payroll Number: _____

Pay Period (weekly, biweekly, etc.): _____

Gross Pay per Pay Period: $ _____

Itemized Payroll Deductions:	Federal Withholding	$ _____
	Social Security	_____
	Local Wage Tax	_____
	State Income Tax	_____
	Retirement	_____
	Savings Bonds	_____
	Credit Union	_____
	Life Insurance	_____
	Health Insurance	_____
	Other (specify)	_____
	_____	
	Net Pay per Pay Period	$ _____

OTHER INCOME: (Fill in Appropriate Column)

	Weekly	Monthly	Yearly
Interest	$ _____	$ _____	$ _____
Dividends	_____	_____	_____
Pension	_____	_____	_____
Annuity	_____	_____	_____
Social Security	_____	_____	_____
Rents	_____	_____	_____
Royalties	_____	_____	_____
Expense Account	_____	_____	_____
Gifts	_____	_____	_____
Unemployment Comp.	_____	_____	_____
Workmen's Comp.	_____	_____	_____
_____	_____	_____	_____
Total	_____	_____	_____
TOTAL INCOME			$ _____

Immigration law:

- Prepare applications and petitions for filing with the Immigration and Naturalization Service (INS) (see Exhibit 3.4 for a sample)
- Coordinate translation of foreign documents
- Prepare immigration and nonimmigration visa applications
- Coordinate activities with clients in foreign jurisdictions seeking visa and entry into the United States

Exhibit 3.4 **Sample immigration and naturalization service form**

U.S. Department of Justice
Immigration and Naturalization Service

Notice of Entry of Appearance as Attorney or Representative

Appearances - An appearance shall be filed on this form by the attorney or representative appearing in each case. Thereafter, substitution may be permitted upon the written withdrawal of the attorney or representative of record or upon notification of the new attorney or representative. When an appearance is made by a person acting in a representative capacity, his personal appearance or signature shall constitute a representation that under the provisions of this chapter he is authorized and qualified to represent. Further proof of authority to act in a representative capacity may be required. **Availability of Records** - During the time a case is pending, and except as otherwise provided in 8 CFR 103.2(b), a party to a proceeding or his attorney or representative shall be permitted to examine the record of proceeding in a Service office. He may, in conformity with 8 CFR 103.10, obtain copies of Service records or information therefrom and copies of documents or transcripts of evidence furnished by him. Upon request, he/she may, in addition, be loaned a copy of the testimony and exhibits contained in the record of proceeding upon giving his/her receipt for such copies and pledging that it will be surrendered upon final disposition of the case or upon demand. If extra copies of exhibits do not exist, they shall not be furnished free on loan; however, they shall be made available for copying or purchase of copies as provided in 8 CFR 103.10.

In re:
    Lim Chi

Date: 09-15-2002
File No. A1357

I hereby enter my appearance as attorney for (or representative of), and at the request of the following named person(s):

Name: Lim chi
☑ Petitioner ☐ Applicant
☐ Beneficiary

Address: (Apt. No.)   (Number & Street)   (City)   (State)   (Zip Code)
275 Swamp Road   Newtown   Pa 18940

Name:
☐ Petitioner ☐ Applicant
☐ Beneficiary

Address: (Apt. No.)   (Number & Street)   (City)   (State)   (Zip Code)

Check Applicable Item(s) below:

☑ 1. I am an attorney and a member in good standing of the bar of the Supreme Court of the United States or of the highest court of the following State, territory, insular possession, or District of Columbia
Pennsylvania   Supreme Court   and am not under a court or administrative agency
Name of Court
order suspending, enjoining, restraining, disbarring, or otherwise restricting me in practicing law.

☐ 2. I am an accredited representative of the following named religious, charitable, social service, or similar organization established in the United States and which is so recognized by the Board:

☐ 3. I am associated with
the attorney of record previously filed a notice of appearance in this case and my appearance is at his request. (*If you check this item, also check item 1 or 2 whichever is appropriate.*)

☐ 4. Others (Explain Fully.)

SIGNATURE

COMPLETE ADDRESS
138 North State Street
Newtown, pa 18940

NAME (Type or Print)
Thomas F. Goldman

TELEPHONE NUMBER
215 555 4321

PURSUANT TO THE PRIVACY ACT OF 1974, I HEREBY CONSENT TO THE DISCLOSURE TO THE FOLLOWING NAMED ATTORNEY OR REPRESENTATIVE OF ANY RECORD PERTAINING TO ME WHICH APPEARS IN ANY IMMIGRATION AND NATURALIZATION SERVICE SYSTEM OF RECORDS:
Thomas F. Goldman
(Name of Attorney or Representative)
THE ABOVE CONSENT TO DISCLOSURE IS IN CONNECTION WITH THE FOLLOWING MATTER:

Name of Person Consenting   Signature of Person Consenting   Date

(NOTE: Execution of this box is required under the Privacy Act of 1974 where the person being represented is a citizen of the United States or an alien lawfully admitted for permanent residence.)

This form may not be used to request records under the Freedom of Information Act or the Privacy Act. The manner of requesting such records is contained in 8CFR 103.10 and 103.20 Et.SEQ.   Form G-28 (09/26/00)Y

- Assist clients in obtaining work visa to work in foreign countries
- Assist clients in the preparation of documentation to prove claim of marital status for submission to INS

Intellectual property:

- Prepare patent search
- Prepare trademark search
- Prepare applications for patent, trademark, or copyright (Exhibit 3.5 is a sample)
- Assist in preparation of documentation in opposition, interference, infringement, and similar proceedings
- Coordinate activities and filings with foreign patent, trademark, and copyright attorneys and agents
- Work with engineers in preparation of applications and defense of patents and trade secrets
- Draft licensing agreements for intellectual property items

Exhibit 3.5   Copyright form

FEE CHANGES
Fees are effective through June 30, 2002. After that date, check the Copyright Office Website at www.loc.gov/copyright or call (202) 707-3000 for current fee information.

FORM TX
For a Nondramatic Literary Work
UNITED STATES COPYRIGHT OFFICE

REGISTRATION NUMBER

TX   TXU
EFFECTIVE DATE OF REGISTRATION

Month   Day   Year

DO NOT WRITE ABOVE THIS LINE. IF YOU NEED MORE SPACE, USE A SEPARATE CONTINUATION SHEET.

1 TITLE OF THIS WORK ▼

PREVIOUS OR ALTERNATIVE TITLES ▼

PUBLICATION AS A CONTRIBUTION If this work was published as a contribution to a periodical, serial, or collection, give information about the collective work in which the contribution appeared.   Title of Collective Work ▼

If published in a periodical or serial give: Volume ▼   Number ▼   Issue Date ▼   On Pages ▼

2 a NAME OF AUTHOR ▼   DATES OF BIRTH AND DEATH
                                                Year Born ▼   Year Died ▼

Was this contribution to the work a "work made for hire"? ☐ Yes ☐ No   AUTHOR'S NATIONALITY OR DOMICILE Name of Country OR { Citizen of ▶ USA / Domiciled in▶   WAS THIS AUTHOR'S CONTRIBUTION TO THE WORK Anonymous? ☐ Yes ☐ No Pseudonymous? ☐ Yes ☐ No   If the answer to either of these questions is "Yes," see detailed instructions.

NOTE NATURE OF AUTHORSHIP Briefly describe nature of material created by this author in which copyright is claimed. ▼
Sole Author

Under the law, the "author" of a "work made for hire" is generally the employer, not the employee (see instructions). For any part of this work that was "made for hire" check "Yes" in the space provided, give the employer (or other person for whom the work was prepared) as "Author" of that part, and leave the space for dates of birth and death blank.

b NAME OF AUTHOR ▼   DATES OF BIRTH AND DEATH
                                                Year Born ▼   Year Died ▼

Was this contribution to the work a "work made for hire"? ☐ Yes ☐ No   AUTHOR'S NATIONALITY OR DOMICILE Name of Country OR { Citizen of ▶ / Domiciled in▶   WAS THIS AUTHOR'S CONTRIBUTION TO THE WORK Anonymous? ☐ Yes ☐ No Pseudonymous? ☐ Yes ☐ No   If the answer to either of these questions is "Yes," see detailed instructions.

NATURE OF AUTHORSHIP Briefly describe nature of material created by this author in which copyright is claimed. ▼

c NAME OF AUTHOR ▼   DATES OF BIRTH AND DEATH
                                                Year Born ▼   Year Died ▼

Was this contribution to the work a "work made for hire"? ☐ Yes ☐ No   AUTHOR'S NATIONALITY OR DOMICILE Name of Country OR { Citizen of ▶ / Domiciled in▶   WAS THIS AUTHOR'S CONTRIBUTION TO THE WORK Anonymous? ☐ Yes ☐ No Pseudonymous? ☐ Yes ☐ No   If the answer to either of these questions is "Yes," see detailed instructions.

NATURE OF AUTHORSHIP Briefly describe nature of material created by this author in which copyright is claimed. ▼

3 a YEAR IN WHICH CREATION OF THIS WORK WAS COMPLETED This information must be given ◀ Year in all cases.   **b** DATE AND NATION OF FIRST PUBLICATION OF THIS PARTICULAR WORK Complete this information ONLY if this work has been published. Month ▶   Day ▶   Year ▶ USA   ◀ Nation

4 COPYRIGHT CLAIMANT(S) Name and address must be given even if the claimant is the same as the author given in space 2. ▼

See instructions before completing this space.

TRANSFER If the claimant(s) named here in space 4 is (are) different from the author(s) named in space 2, give a brief statement of how the claimant(s) obtained ownership of the copyright. ▼
By written agreement.

APPLICATION RECEIVED

ONE DEPOSIT RECEIVED

TWO DEPOSITS RECEIVED

FUNDS RECEIVED

DO NOT WRITE HERE OFFICE USE ONLY

MORE ON BACK ▶ • Complete all applicable spaces (numbers 5-9) on the reverse side of this page.   • See detailed instructions.   • Sign the form at line 8.   DO NOT WRITE HERE Page 1 of _____ pages

(continued)

Exhibit 3.5 Copyright form *(continued)*

Human resources law:

- Draft plan documents for tax-sheltered employee benefit plans
- Draft deferred compensation plans
- Prepare and file for Internal Revenue Service determination letters of plans
- Prepare and file annual reports including 5500 series Internal Revenue Service forms
- Calculate employer and employee contribution levels and limitations
- Draft, review, and distribute summary plan descriptions

Litigation:

- Investigate factual allegations of case
- Help to locate witnesses and physical evidence
- Draft summons, complaint, answers, and other defenses and responsive pleadings

Exhibit 3.6 Subpoena

Commonwealth of Pennsylvania
County of Philadelphia

In the matter of:

Henry Thomas
(Plaintiff)   _(Demandante)_

vs.

Thomas Cheese
(Defendant)   _(Demandado)_

COURT OF COMMON PLEAS

October _____ Term, Yr. 2007

No. 68-96874

Subpoena

To: Elizabeth Rhodes
     (Name of Witness)   _(Nombre del Testigo)_

1. YOU ARE ORDERED BY THE COURT TO COME TO _(El tribunal le ordena que venga a)_
Court room 654 _____, AT PHILADELPHIA, PENNSYLVANIA ON _(en Filadelfia,
Pennsylvania el)_ November 4, 2007 _____, AT _(a las)_ 10 O'CLOCK A .M., TO
TESTIFY ON BEHALF OF _(para atestiguar a favor de)_ Henry Thomas _____ IN THE ABOVE
CASE, AND TO REMAIN UNTIL EXCUSED _(en el caso arriba mencionado y permanecer hasta que le autoricen irse)._

2. AND BRING WITH YOU THE FOLLOWING _(Y traer con usted lo siguiente)_:

_____
_____
_____

NOTICE	AVISO
If you fail to attend or to produce the documents or things required by this subpoena, you may be subject to the sanctions authorized by Rule 234.5 of the Pennsylvania Rules of Civil Procedure, including but not limited to costs, attorney fees and imprisonment.	Si usted falla en comparecer o producir los documentos o cosas requeridas por esta cita, usted estara sujeto a las sanciones autorizadas por la regla 234.5 de las reglas de procedimiento civil de Pensilvania, incluyendo pero no limitado a los costos, remuneracion de abogados y encarcelamiento.

INQUIRIES CONCERNING THIS SUBPOENA SHOULD BE ADDRESSED TO _(Las preguntas que tenga acerca de esta Citacion deben ser dirigidas a)_:
ISSUED BY:

Edith Hannah
     (Attorney)   _(Abogado/Abogada)_

ADDRESS _(Direccion)_ 8 North Broad Street, Philadelphia, PA

TELEPHONE NO. _(No. de Telefono)_ 215 555 9999

ATTORNEY _(Abogado ID #)_ A5B6

BY THE COURT _(Por El Tribunal)_
JOSEPH H. EVERS
PROTHONOTARY _(Protonotario)_

PRO _____
     (Clerk)   _(Escribano)_

10-200 (Rev. 7/99)   Completed Subpoena must be signed and sealed by the Prothonotary (Room 266 City Hall) before service.

- Organize and maintain litigation files
- Assist in the preparation of trial notebooks
- Gather, review, summarize, and index documents for use at trial
- Locate and arrange for interviews with expert witnesses
- Prepare written interrogatories

- Assist in preparing and conducting oral depositions, including videotape depositions
- Prepare or obtain subpoenas (see sample in Exhibit 3.6) and arrange for service upon witnesses
- Coordinate, assist, and arrange for trial exhibits
- Obtain jury-pool information, and assist in the selection of appropriate jury members
- Attend trial and assist in the handling of witnesses, exhibits, and evidence
- Prepare contemporaneous summaries of witness statements during trial

Administrative Procedures in Law Offices and Firms

Certain administrative procedures, such as conflict checking and time keeping, are common to most, if not all, law offices. Depending on the size of the law firm and the nature of the practice, a paralegal also may be called upon to perform what might be thought to be accounting or financial activities, such as preparing invoices, maintaining client escrow accounts, maintaining trust accounts, preparing payroll records, preparing court required accounting, and completing real estate settlement forms.

Conflict Checking

Conflict checking Verifying that the attorneys in the firm do not have a personal conflict and have not previously represented and are not currently representing any party with an adverse interest or conflict with the potential client.

Conflict checking is necessary to verify that current and prior representations of parties and matters handled will not present a conflict of interest for the firm in accepting a new client or legal matter. Checking for conflicts of interest is an essential function designed to avoid the ethical violations of representing competing interests. Many offices use computer database software for conflict checking. Names of clients, opposing parties, counsel, and law firms can be quickly searched electronically. Some firms still rely on a manual check of paper lists and file-card indexes containing the names of clients, opposing parties, and opposing attorneys in cases. To determine conflicts where there has been only indirect representation is difficult.

Attorneys and paralegals who change firms may have to do a preliminary conflict check before they accept or start employment. The conflict comes when the former firm and the new firm are, or were, on opposite sides of a case. It may be a conflict for someone who has had access to information about a case to switch to the firm representing the opposing party. Confidential disclosure for the limited purpose of checking for a conflict before starting employment could prevent a serious or perceived ethical breach in the form of a breach of confidentiality or conflict of interest. In some cases, the conflict of interest may result from a financial interest such as stock ownership or investments. Making full disclosure of these potential conflict situations to the supervising attorney or to the appropriate conflict checker with the firm is important.

In many cases, the conflict can be resolved by isolating the individual from information about the case—sometimes called building an ethical wall. An ethical wall, also known as a Chinese wall, is an attempt to shield a paralegal or lawyer from access to information about a case when there is the possibility of a conflict of interest. Most courts permit the establishment of an ethical wall to protect the parties from the conflict of interest or breach of confidentiality. As commented by a Connecticut trial court in an unpublished opinion:

> . . . The court does not subscribe to the argument that, as a matter of law, screening would be ineffective when a nonlawyer switches employment to 'the other side.' The ABA opinions indicate that a law firm can set up appropriate screening and administrative procedures to prevent nonlawyers from working on the other side of those common cases and disclosing confidential information. . . .
>
> *Source:* Devine v. Beinfield, *1997 Ct. Sup. 7674, 1997 Conn Super Lexis 1966, No. CV93 0121721 S (Jul. 1, 1997).*

The Nevada Supreme Court specifically addresses the issue of paralegals in the *Leibowitz* case.

IN THE WORDS OF THE COURT

LEIBOWITZ V. DIST. CT., 119 NEV. ADV. OP. NO. 57, 39683 (2003) 78 P.3D 515

The Nevada Supreme Court in overturning a 1994 ethics opinion [*Ciaffone v. District Court*, 113 Nev. 1165 (1997), 945 P.2d 950] that prohibited paralegals from working for a firm that represents any client that had an adversarial relationship to any client of the former employer law firm, summarized the rationale for the ethical wall and provided an instructive guide . . .

. . . As pointed out by the amici's brief, the majority of professional legal ethics commentators, ethics tribunals, and courts have concluded that nonlawyer screening is a permissible method to protect confidences held by nonlawyer employees who change employment. Nevada is in a minority of jurisdictions that do not allow screening for nonlawyers moving from private firm to private firm.

Imputed disqualification is considered a harsh remedy that "should be invoked if, and only if, the [c]ourt is satisfied that real harm is likely to result from failing to invoke it."

This stringent standard is based on a client's right to counsel of the client's choosing and the likelihood of prejudice and economic harm to the client when severance of the attorney–client relationship is ordered. It is for this reason that the ABA opined in 1988 that screening is permitted for nonlawyer employees, while conversely concluding, through the Model Rules of Professional Conduct, that screening is not permitted for lawyers. The ABA explained that "additional considerations" exist justifying application of screening to nonlawyer employees (*i.e.,* mobility in employment opportunities which function to serve both legal clients and the legal profession) versus the Model Rule's proscription against screening where lawyers move from private firm to private firm. In essence, a lawyer may always practice his or her profession regardless of an affiliation to a law firm. Paralegals, legal secretaries, and other employees of attorneys do not have that option.

We are persuaded that *Ciaffone* misapprehended the state of the law regarding nonlawyer imputed disqualification. We therefore overrule *Ciaffone* to the extent it prohibits screening of nonlawyer employees.

When a law firm hires a nonlawyer employee, the firm has an affirmative duty to determine whether the employee previously had access to adversarial client files. If the hiring law firm determines that the employee had such access, the hiring law firm has an absolute duty to screen the nonlawyer employee from the adversarial cases irrespective of the nonlawyer employee's actual knowledge of privileged or confidential information.

Although we decline to mandate an exhaustive list of screening requirements, the following provides an instructive minimum:

(1) *"The newly hired nonlawyer [employee] must be cautioned not to disclose any information relating to the representation of a client of the former employer."*
(2) *"The nonlawyer [employee] must be instructed not to work on any matter on which [he or] she worked during the prior employment, or regarding which [he or] she has information relating to the former employer's representation."*
(3) *"The new firm should take . . . reasonable steps to ensure that the nonlawyer [employee] does not work in connection with matters on which [he or] she worked during the prior employment, absent client consent [i.e., unconditional waiver] after consultation."*

In addition, the hiring law firm must inform the adversarial party, or their counsel, regarding the hiring of the nonlawyer employee and the screening mechanisms utilized. The adversarial party may then: (1) make a conditional waiver (*i.e.,* agree to the screening mechanisms); (2) make an unconditional waiver (eliminate the screening mechanisms); or (3) file a motion to disqualify counsel.

(continued)

IN THE WORDS OF THE COURT *(continued)*

However, even if the new employer uses a screening process, disqualification will always be required—absent unconditional waiver by the affected client—under the following circumstances:

(1) *"[W]hen information relating to the representation of an adverse client has in fact been disclosed [to the new employer]"; or, in the absence of disclosure to the new employer,*

(2) *"[W]hen screening would be ineffective or the nonlawyer [employee] necessarily would be required to work on the other side of a matter that is the same as or substantially related to a matter on which the nonlawyer [employee] has previously worked."*

Once a district court determines that a nonlawyer employee acquired confidential information about a former client, the district court should grant a motion for disqualification unless the district court determines that the screening is sufficient to safeguard the former client from disclosure of the confidential information. The district court is faced with the delicate task of balancing competing interests, including: (1) "the individual right to be represented by counsel of one's choice," (2) "each party's right to be free from the risk of even inadvertent disclosure of confidential information," (3) "the public's interest in the scrupulous administration of justice," and (4) "the prejudices that will inure to the parties as a result of the [district court's] decision."

Time Keeping and Billing

Keeping track of billable time is a critical function to ensure that the law firm will be compensated properly for its advice and efforts on behalf of clients. Tracking time extends beyond just the efforts of attorneys to paralegals and, in some cases, secretaries and clerks.

Billing is the most important function in a law firm. Without billings there is no revenue to pay expenses and salaries. As important as it is, in many offices billing is not treated with enough importance. Time records are the basis for most law firm billings. Without accurate time records, billings cannot be made.

The propriety of fees is addressed in Rule 1.5 of the Model Rules of Professional Conduct.

The Utah Rules of Professional Conduct provide:

Rule 1.5. Fees.

(a) A lawyer shall not make an agreement for, charge or collect an unreasonable fee or an unreasonable amount for expenses. The factors to be considered in determining the reasonableness of a fee include the following:

(a)(1) the time and labor required, the novelty and difficulty of the questions involved and the skill requisite to perform the legal service properly;

(a)(2) the likelihood, if apparent to the client, that the acceptance of the particular employment will preclude other employment by the lawyer;

(a)(3) the fee customarily charged in the locality for similar legal services;

(a)(4) the amount involved and the results obtained;

(a)(5) the time limitations imposed by the client or by the circumstances;

(a)(6) the nature and length of the professional relationship with the client;

(a)(7) the experience, reputation and ability of the lawyer or lawyers performing the services; and

(a)(8) whether the fee is fixed or contingent.

(b) The scope of the representation and the basis or rate of the fee and expenses for which the client will be responsible shall be communicated to the client, preferably in writing, before or within a reasonable time after commencing the representation, except when the lawyer will charge a regularly represented client on the same basis or rate. Any changes in the basis or rate of the fee or expenses shall also be communicated to the client.

(c) A fee may be contingent on the outcome of the matter for which the service is rendered, except in a matter in which a contingent fee is prohibited by paragraph (d) or other law. A contingent fee agreement shall be in a writing signed by the client and shall state the method by which the fee is to be determined, including the percentage or percentages that shall accrue to the lawyer in the event of settlement, trial or appeal; litigation and other expenses to be deducted from the recovery; and whether such expenses are to be deducted before or after the contingent fee is calculated. The agreement must clearly notify the client of any expenses for which the client will be liable whether or not the client is the prevailing party. Upon conclusion of a contingent fee matter, the lawyer shall provide the client with a written statement stating the outcome of the matter and, if there is a recovery, showing the remittance to the client and the method of its determination.

(d) A lawyer shall not enter into an arrangement for, charge or collect:

    (d)(1) any fee in a domestic relations matter, the payment or amount of which is contingent upon the securing of a divorce or upon the amount of alimony or support, or property settlement in lieu thereof; or

    (d)(2) a contingent fee for representing a defendant in a criminal case.

(e) A division of a fee between lawyers who are not in the same firm may be made only if:

    (e)(1) the division is in proportion to the services performed by each lawyer or each lawyer assumes joint responsibility for the representation;

    (e)(2) the client agrees to the arrangement, including the share each lawyer will receive, and the agreement is confirmed in writing; and

    (e)(3) the total fee is reasonable.

Web Exploration

View the comments to the Utah rules at http://www.utcourts.gov/resources/rules/ucja/ch13/1_5.htm.

The billing of clients is not limited to the time of lawyers but may include that of paralegals as the 11th Circuit Court of Appeals has stated:

> We have held that paralegal time is recoverable as part of a prevailing party's award for attorney's fees and expenses, [but] only to the extent that the paralegal performs work traditionally done by an attorney." Quoting from *Allen v. United States Steel Corp.*, 665 F.2d 689, 697 (5th Cir. 1982): "To hold otherwise would be counterproductive because excluding reimbursement for such work might encourage attorneys to handle entire cases themselves, thereby achieving the same results at a higher overall cost.

> *Jean v. Nelson*, 863 F. 2d 759 (11th Cir. 1988).

Client expense records, by contrast, are usually well maintained because a check is usually written, which provides a documented record for billing purposes. But the time record must come from the recording of time spent by the attorney, paralegal, or legal team member. This information frequently is maintained manually on pieces of paper called time slips or time records. Client bills are prepared manually from these records.

More frequently, the client billing is prepared using a computer time and billing program, such as the popular AbacusLaw program. Most of these programs allow for random entry of the individual time record information and then automatically sort by client and project or case. These programs also allow for the entry and inclusion in the final billing report or printout of the costs expended in the current period and the costs and fees received from previous billing periods and the application of retainers.

Accounting in the Law Office

In the law office working environment, your ability to understand basic financial issues makes you a more valuable member of the law office team. A law firm is a business that, as Abraham Lincoln said, deals in time and advice, unlike retail, wholesale, or manufacturing businesses that trade in goods or commodities.

A major function of the legal support staff is to keep track of the time the lawyers and support staff spend on a case and then bill the client for the time expended. Financial account records must be kept accurately both for internal office activities and for matters related to specific clients. Expenses may be associated with specific clients or part of the overall cost of running the office. If accurate records are not kept for the law office operation, it may fail or close.

When the funds involved belong to clients, errors can result in malpractice claims for improperly prepared documentation and the filing of inaccurate court documents and tax returns. At worst, errors may result in a loss or misappropriation of client funds, which can lead to sanctions, including disbarment or even criminal prosecution.

In addition to understanding the internal operations accounting needs of a law firm is the need to understand the accounting and financial affairs of clients. Understanding accounting and financial reports and documents is essential in many areas of law today.

Family Law

Every domestic relations case has concerns related to property settlement, support, and alimony. In today's marital climate, there is an increasing demand for full financial disclosure in prenuptial agreements. A basic understanding of the nature and the sources of the family financial information will enable you to prepare the necessary documents. As an example, Exhibit 3.7 shows selected pages from the New Jersey Family Part Case Information.

Commercial Litigation

Commercial litigation typically involves actions resulting from claims of breach of contract or interpretations of provisions of a contract stating the obligations of the parties. It has become more complex—in no small matter because of the financial implications of contract breaches and remedies. The tasks of finding, analyzing, and presenting financial matters increasingly fall on litigation paralegals.

Litigation

Even in the simplest of litigation matters, a measure of damages has to be computed. Calculations of wages lost, projection of future losses, and the current or present value may have to be computed or reviewed for accuracy.

Maintaining Law Firm Financial Information

Law firms, like any other business, have numerous forms of financial obligations. Utility bills and employees have to be paid on a regular basis. Accurate records have to be maintained to determine which costs are chargeable to individual clients. Office operations frequently involve record keeping for client funds in the form of escrow accounts.

Records of the various receipts and disbursements are used to prepare the firm's tax returns, including quarterly and annual employee withholding and employer tax returns, income tax returns, and informational tax returns, such as reports for nonemployee compensation and independent contractors such as freelance paralegals, or reporters and investigators.

Regular use of a systematic system simplifies the completion of financial reports. By using a standard system of accounting, lawyers, bookkeepers, paralegals, and secretarial personnel can easily communicate, contributing information of charges and revenues that are usable for all concerned including the outside accountants and auditors.

Reconstructing the financial information is a common task in many law offices. In many cases, clients deliver piles of financial documents and expect the law office personnel to sort, classify, and organize seemingly unrelated pieces of paper into tax returns, estate tax returns, and documents with which settlements and major decisions will be made. Knowing how to attack the piles of paper can save time, stress, and frustration.

Safekeeping of client property and segregation of client funds from those of the law firm is an ethical obligation imposed under Rule 1.15 of the Model Rules of Professional Conduct of which that of South Dakota provides in part:

Rule 1.15. Safekeeping Property.

(a) A lawyer shall hold property of clients or third persons that is in a lawyer's possession in connection with a representation separate from the lawyer's own property.

Exhibit 3.7 New Jersey family case information

PART D - MONTHLY EXPENSES (computed at 4.3 wks/mo.)

Joint Marital Life Style should reflect standard of living established during marriage. Current expenses should reflect the current life style. Do not repeat those income deductions listed in Part C–3.

	Joint Marital Life Style Family, including _____ children	Current Life Style Yours and _____ children
SCHEDULE A: SHELTER		
If Tenant:		
Rent	$_____	$_____
Heat (if not furnished)	$_____	$_____
Electric & Gas (if not furnished)	$_____	$_____
Renter's Insurance	$_____	$_____
Parking (at Apartment)	$_____	$_____
Other Charges (Itemize)	$_____	$_____
If Homeowner:		
Mortgage	$_____	$_____
Real Estate Taxes (if not included w/mortgage payment)	$_____	$_____
Homeowners Ins. (if not included w/mortgage payment)	$_____	$_____
Other Mortgages or Home Equity Loans	$_____	$_____
Heat (unless Electric or Gas)	$_____	$_____
Electric & Gas	$_____	$_____
Water & Sewer	$_____	$_____
Garbage Removal	$_____	$_____
Snow Removal	$_____	$_____
Lawn Care	$_____	$_____
Maintenance	$_____	$_____
Repairs	$_____	$_____
Other Charges (Itemize)	$_____	$_____
Tenant or Homeowner:		
Telephone	$_____	$_____
Mobile/Cellular Telephone	$_____	$_____
Service Contracts on Equipment	$_____	$_____
Cable TV	$_____	$_____
Plumber/Electrician	$_____	$_____
Equipment & Furnishings	$_____	$_____
Internet Charges	$_____	$_____
Other (Itemize)	$_____	$_____
TOTAL	$_____	$_____
SCHEDULE B: TRANSPORTATION		
Auto Payment	$_____	$_____
Auto Insurance (number of vehicles)	$_____	$_____
Registration, License	$_____	$_____
Maintenance	$_____	$_____
Fuel and Oil	$_____	$_____
Commuting Expenses	$_____	$_____
Other Charges (Itemize)	$_____	$_____
TOTAL	$_____	$_____

(continued)

Exhibit 3.7 **New Jersey family case information** *(continued)*

PART E - BALANCE SHEET OF ALL FAMILY ASSETS AND LIABILITIES STATEMENT OF ASSETS

Description	Title to Property (H, W, J)	Date of purchase/acquisition. If claim that asset is exempt, state reason and value of what is claimed to be exempt	Value $ Put * after exempt	Date of Evaluation Mo./Day/Yr.
1. Real Property				
2. Bank Accounts, CDs				
3. Vehicles				
4. Tangible Personal Property				
5. Stocks and Bonds				
6. Pension, Profit Sharing, Retirement Plan(s) 401(k)s, etc. [list each employer]				
7. IRAs				
8. Businesses, Partnerships, Professional Practices				
9. Life Insurance (cash surrender value)				
10. Loans Receivable				
11. Other (specify)				

TOTAL GROSS ASSETS: $_____

TOTAL SUBJECT TO EQUITABLE DISTRIBUTION: $_____

TOTAL NOT SUBJECT TO EQUITABLE DISTRIBUTION: $_____

Funds shall be kept in a separate account maintained in the state where the lawyer's office is situated, or elsewhere with the consent of the client or third person. Other property shall be identified as such and appropriately safeguarded. Complete records of such account funds and other property shall be kept by the lawyer and shall be preserved for a period of five years after termination of the representation. A lawyer may deposit the lawyer's own funds in a client trust account for the sole purpose of paying bank service charges on that account, but only in an amount necessary for that purpose. A lawyer shall deposit into a client trust account legal fees and expenses that have been paid in advance, to be withdrawn by the lawyer only as fees are earned or expenses incurred.

(b) Upon receiving funds or other property in which a client or third person has an interest, a lawyer shall promptly notify the client or third person. Except as stated in this Rule or otherwise permitted by law or by agreement with the client, a lawyer shall promptly deliver to the client or third person any funds or other property that the client or third person is entitled to receive and, upon request by the client or third person, shall promptly render a full accounting regarding such property.

(c) When in the course of representation a lawyer is in possession of property in which two or more persons (one of whom may be the lawyer) claim interests, the property shall be kept separate by the lawyer until the dispute is resolved. The lawyer shall promptly distribute all portions of the property as to which the interests are not in dispute.

(d) Preserving Identity of Funds and Property of Client.

(1) All funds of clients paid to a lawyer or law firm, including advances for costs and expenses, shall be deposited in one or more identifiable bank accounts maintained in the state in which the law office is situated and no funds belonging to the lawyer or law firm shall be deposited therein except as follows:

(i) Funds reasonably sufficient to pay bank charges may be deposited therein.

(ii) Funds belonging in part to a client and in part presently or potentially to the lawyer or law firm must be deposited therein, but the portion belonging to the lawyer or law firm may be withdrawn when due unless the right of the lawyer or law firm to receive it is disputed by the client, in which event the disputed portion shall not be withdrawn until the dispute is finally resolved.

(2) A lawyer shall:

(i) Promptly notify a client of the receipt of his funds, securities, or other properties.

(ii) Identify and label securities and properties of a client promptly upon receipt and place them in a safe deposit box or other place of safekeeping as soon as practicable.

(iii) Maintain complete records of all funds, securities, and other properties of a client coming into the possession of the lawyer and render appropriate accountings to his client regarding them.

(iv) Promptly pay or deliver to the client as requested by a client the funds, securities, or other properties in the possession of the lawyer which the client is entitled to receive. . . .

Web Exploration

The complete rule may be viewed at http://www.sdbar.org/Rules/Rules/PC_Rules.htm.

Accounting for Client Retainers and Costs

Law firms frequently request a **retainer**—a payment at the beginning of handling a new matter for a client. This amount may be used to offset the fees for services rendered or costs advanced on behalf of the client. Unless there is some other arrangement, agreed upon in conformity with applicable court rules and ABA guidelines, these funds belong to the law firm only when they have been earned by rendering of the service or actual cost expenditure. Unused amounts may have to be returned to the client and those expended accounted for to the client.

Increasingly, under the rules of professional conduct, many states also require a written fee agreement in contingent-fee cases, whereas in other types of cases, it is preferred but not required.

A new approach to providing legal services is sometimes called "unbundled" legal services or discrete task representation. The term refers to a broad range of discrete tasks that an attorney might undertake, such as advice, negotiation, document review, document preparation, and limited representation. A sample retainer agreement under Maine Bar Rule 3.4(I) is shown in Exhibit 3.8.

Retainer A payment at the beginning of the handling of a new matter for a client. This amount may be used to offset the fees for services rendered or costs advanced on behalf of the client.

Exhibit 3.8 Limited representation agreement

Date:_____, 20_____
1. The client, _____, retains the attorney, _____, to perform limited legal services in the following matter: _____ v. _____.

2. The client seeks the following services from the attorney (indicate by writing "yes" or "no"):

a. _____ Legal advice: office visits, telephone calls, fax, mail, e-mail;
b. _____ Advice about availability of alternative means to resolving the dispute, including mediation and arbitration;
c. _____ Evaluation of client self-diagnosis of the case and advising client about legal rights and responsibilities;
d. _____ Guidance and procedural information for filing or serving documents;
e. _____ Review pleadings and other documents prepared by client;
f. _____ Suggest documents to be prepared;
g. _____ Draft pleadings, motions, and other documents;
h. _____ Factual investigation: contacting witnesses, public record searches, in-depth interview of client;
i. _____ Assistance with computer support programs;
j. _____ Legal research and analysis;
k. _____ Evaluate settlement options;
l. _____ Discovery: interrogatories, depositions, requests for document production;
m. _____ Planning for negotiations;
n. _____ Planning for court appearances;
o. _____ Standby telephone assistance during negotiations or settlement conferences;
p. _____ Referring client to expert witnesses, special masters, or other counsel;
q. _____ Counseling client about an appeal;
r. _____ Procedural assistance with an appeal and assisting with substantive legal argument in an appeal;
s. _____ Provide preventive planning and/or schedule legal checkups:
t. _____ Other:

_____
_____

3. The client shall pay the attorney for those limited services as follows:
a. Hourly Fee:

The current hourly fee charged by the attorney or the attorney's law firm for services under this agreement are as follows:
 i. Attorney: $_____
 ii. Associate: $_____
 iii. Paralegal: $_____
 iv. Law Clerk: $_____

Unless a different fee arrangement is established in clause b. of this paragraph, the hourly fee shall be payable at the time of the service. Time will be charged in increments of one-tenth of an hour, rounded off for each particular activity to the nearest one-tenth of an hour.

b. Payment from Deposit:

For a continuing consulting role, client will pay to attorney a deposit of $_____, to be received by attorney on or before _____, and to be applied against attorney fees and costs incurred by client. This amount will be deposited by attorney in attorney trust account. Client authorizes attorney to withdraw funds from the trust account to pay attorney fees and costs as they are incurred by client. The deposit is refundable. If, at the termination of services under this agreement, the total amount incurred by client for attorney fees and costs is less than the amount of the deposit, the difference will be refunded to client. Any balance due shall be paid within thirty days of the termination of services.

Exhibit 3.8   **Limited representation agreement** *(continued)*

c. Costs:

Client shall pay attorney out-of-pocket costs incurred in connection with this agreement, including long distance telephone and fax costs, photocopy expense and postage. All costs payable to third parties in connection with client case, including filing fees, investigation fees, deposition fees, and the like shall be paid directly by client. Attorney shall not advance costs to third parties on client behalf.

4. The client understands that the attorney will exercise his or her best judgment while performing the limited legal services set out above, but also recognizes:

a. the attorney is not promising any particular outcome,
b. the attorney has not made any independent investigation of the facts and is relying entirely on the client limited disclosure of the facts given the duration of the limited services provided, and
c. the attorney has no further obligation to the client after completing the above described limited legal services unless and until both attorney and client enter into another written representation agreement.

5. If any dispute between client and attorney arises under this agreement concerning the payment of fees, the client and attorney shall submit the dispute for fee arbitration in accordance with Rule 9(e)-(k) of the Maine Bar Rules. This arbitration shall be binding upon both parties to this agreement.

WE HAVE EACH READ THE ABOVE AGREEMENT BEFORE SIGNING IT.
Signature of client _____
Signature of attorney _____

A lawyer may request a nonrefundable retainer. This is a common practice when the client does not want the law firm to be able to represent the opposing party in a pending legal action. This is seen most commonly in family law or divorce actions. Legal ethics prohibit taking on a client where there is a conflict of interest. In cases of nonrefundable retainers, a statement of application of the funds may or should be made as a matter of the financial accounting practice.

Costs Advanced

Law firms typically pay directly to the court any fees for filing documents for the client. In some cases, the cost of stenographers, expert witnesses, and duplication of records, travel, phone, and copying also will be advanced. The firm must keep proper accounting for these items to be able to bill a client properly or charge the amounts expended against prepaid costs or retainers. Good practice is to include in the initial client fee letter the nature and amount of costs that will be charged for these various items.

Civil Practice: Fee and Cost Billing

In a civil litigation practice, fees may be calculated on an hourly rate, a contingent fee, or a combination of the two. The time records for each member of the firm must be obtained, either from the hard copies of time records or the computer printout of hours spent working on the case. The actual time may be reported to the client chronologically, with all activity by each person who worked on the file integrated with all the others, but may be listed separately by the individual.

The difficulty is in calculating the correct amount for each person at his/her respected hourly rate. It is not unusual to have a senior partner bill at one rate, a junior partner at another rate, and a paralegal at a third rate. It is good practice to calculate the total for each billable person separately, and then collectively. The totals of the individuals, of course, must equal the grand total. Therefore, the comparison acts as a check on mathematical accuracy.

Client bills can be prepared manually from paper copies of time records or other office records. More frequently, the client billing is prepared using a computer program. Most of these programs allow input of the individual time record in a random order that can be sorted automatically by client and project. In addition to the time billing, these programs allow for entry and inclusion in the final billing of costs expended in the current billing period and costs and payments received from previous billing periods and retainers.

Timely Disbursements

As part of the settlement of a case for a client, the opposing side may pay the amount of the cash settlement to the lawyer. These funds must be disbursed to the client and until disbursed, retained in a separate escrow account and not commingled with the lawyer's own funds. Records of the receipt and disbursement of these funds must be maintained properly to avoid charges of misuse of client funds.

A lawyer is not required to make disbursements until the draft or check has cleared. A check or draft is deemed cleared when the funds are available for disbursement. But, lawyers cannot retain the amount for an unreasonable time. The client is entitled to earn the potential interest on the amount to be dispersed. The lawyer is not entitled to keep the amount and earn interest for his/her own account.

Trust Accounts

Trust account The funds of the client.

A **trust account** or fiduciary account contains the client's funds and should never be commingled with those of the firm or the individual attorney. A clear record of all trust transactions must be maintained. In many cases, such as trusts, estates, or cases involving children, detailed reports must be filed with the court following the court-imposed rules as shown in Exhibit 3.9 for the Probate Courts of the State of New Hampshire. When a checking account has been established, the check register is a primary source for creating any required or desired reports. With some larger accounts, checking accounts may not have been set up. Many trust and estate accounts are invested in money market funds, stocks, bonds, and mutual funds.

Keeping a clear record is made more difficult by the potential for periodic increases and decreases in value that are not actually realized—referred to as paper gains and losses. They exist on paper but have not been realized by the actual sale or transfer of the asset. For the attorney, the client or state law must authorize any investments of assets held in trust. Separate records should be maintained showing the activity in each of the trust accounts, including all deposits, interest earned, and disbursements, including bank charges.

Exhibit 3.9	**Selected provisions of the rules of practice and procedure in the probate courts of the state of New Hampshire**

RULE 108. FIDUCIARY ACCOUNTING STANDARDS

The following standards shall be applicable to all interim and final accountings of Administrators, trustees, guardians and conservators, required or permitted to be filed with the Court.

A. Accounts shall be stated in a manner that is understandable by Persons who are not familiar with practices and terminology peculiar to the administration of estates, trusts, guardianships and conservatorships. . . .

B. A Fiduciary account shall begin with a concise summary of its purpose and content. The account shall begin with a brief statement identifying the Fiduciary, the subject matter, the relationship of Parties interested in the account to the account, and, if applicable, appropriate notice of any limitations on or requirements for action by Parties interested in the account. . . .

C. A Fiduciary account shall contain sufficient information to put parties interested in the account on notice as to all significant transactions affecting administration during the accounting period. . . .

IOLTA Accounts

Many states, by court rule, impose an obligation to deposit client funds, when the amount is too small to earn interest, into a special interest-bearing account, the **IOLTA account** (Interest on Lawyers Trust Accounts). Interest generated from these small accounts is paid to the court-designated agency, usually the local legal aid agency, to fund their activities. Because the cost of setting up individual small accounts is greater than the interest earned, or the amount deposited is so small that no interest would accrue to the client, everyone wins by having these funds generate some income for the public good. Reconciliation of this account is simpler because no accounting for the interest to the client has to be made.

IOLTA account Where the amount is too small to earn interest, court rules require the funds be deposited into a special interest-bearing account, and the interest generally paid to support legal aid projects (Interest on Lawyers Trust Accounts).

Interest-Bearing Escrow Accounts

Lawyers frequently are asked to act as escrow agents or to retain client funds for future disbursements. In some cases the amounts may be significant. Prudent handling of the client's monies dictates that the fiduciary treat them in the same manner as would any prudent investor. If the amount is sufficient to earn interest, the amount earned belongs to the client, not to the attorney, and must be accounted for, to the client.

If earning interest, it is good practice and expected to open up separate accounts for each client. In opening these accounts, the client's Social Security number or other employer identification number should be used. If the law firm maintains the account under its tax identification number, it will have to report interest annually to the client and to the federal and state government.

A significant body of law has emerged to avoid money-laundering. In a law firm this may require reporting when significant amounts of cash are received. The problem is balancing the money-laundering rules and the attorney–client privilege. When amounts in excess of $10,000 are received in cash from a client, current legislation and regulation must be consulted.

To open an account with a financial institution requires a federal identification number. This identification number may be that of the client, the trust, the estate, or other legal entity having a current identification number. In some cases the financial institution may require copies of any documentation that created the client entity, such as the trust documents, death certificate, or decedent's will. The concern of the financial institution is to properly comply with existing regulations on federal withholding and money-laundering or large-deposit reporting obligations. A state requirement is to complete the federal form W-9.

Court Accounting

In addition to the preparation of filing federal and state estate tax returns, the fiduciary often has to file an accounting with the local court that administers or supervises trust and estate matters. These **court accounting** reports are designed to show that the fiduciary has administered the estate or trust properly.

Court accounting An accounting with the local court that administers or supervises trust and estate matters. These reports are designed to show that the fiduciary has properly administered the estate or trust.

Reports to the court also are required in many jurisdictions in civil cases involving minors. Approval of tort actions involving a minor may be negotiated between the lawyers for the insurance company or defendant and the minor's parent or guardian, subject to the approval of the court. This usually requires submitting a brief accounting of the expenses, including counsel fees, and the proposed disbursements to compensate for out-of-pocket expenses and proposed investments of the proceeds until the minor reaches a set age or by other order of court.

All of the parties are considered as acting as fiduciaries in the best interest of the minor. Local practice and court rules will furthermore dictate the form and methods of fiduciary accounting. The uniform system of accounts has been accepted by some jurisdictions without formal court rule and others by inclusion in the local court rules.

The basic objective of the uniform system of accounts is to present the financial information in a consistent manner that is understandable to the court and all the interested parties. The parties are entitled to full disclosure, clarity, and, when appropriate, supplemental information. Exhibit 3.10 is a sample of a model executor's account template using the uniform system of accounts.

Exhibit 3.10	Model executor's account template sample—Pennsylvania Orphan's Court

ORPHANS' COURT RULES

MODEL EXECUTOR'S ACCOUNT

First and Final Account

FIRST AND FINAL ACCOUNT OF

William C. Doe, Executor

For

ESTATE OF John Doe, Deceased

Date of Death: November 14, 1978
Date of Executor's Appointment: November 24, 1978
Accounting for the Period: November 24, 1978 to November 30, 1979

Purpose of Account: William C. Doe, Executor, offers this account to acquaint interested parties with the transactions that have occurred during his administration.

The account also indicates the proposed distribution of the estate.[1]
It is important that the account be carefully examined. Requests for additional information or questions or objections can be discussed with:

[Name of Executor, Counsel or other appropriate person]
[address and telephone number]

[*Note:* See discussion under Fiduciary Accounting Principle II with respect to presentation of collateral material needed by beneficiaries.]

Note

In Pennsylvania the date of first advertisement of the grant of letters should be shown after the date of the personal representative's appointment.

[1] Optional—for use if applicable.

SUMMARY OF ACCOUNT

	Page	Current Value	Fiduciary Acquisition Value
Proposed Distribution to Beneficiaries[1]	645	$102,974.56	$ 90,813.96
Principal			
Receipts	636		$160,488.76
			2,662.00
Net Gain (or Loss) on Sales or Other Disposition	638		$163,150.76
Less Disbursements:			
Debts of Decedent	639	$ 485.82	
Funeral Expenses	639	1,375.00	
Administration Expenses	639	194.25	
Federal and State Taxes	639	5,962.09	
Fees and Commissions	639	11,689.64	19,706.80
Balance before Distributions			$143,443.96

Exhibit 3.10 **Model executor's account template sample—Pennsylvania Orphan's Court** (continued)

FIDUCIARY ACCOUNTING STANDARDS

Distributions to Beneficiaries	641	52,630.00
Principal Balance on Hand	641	$ 90,813.96
For Information:		
Investments Made	642	
Changes in Investment Holdings	642	
Income		
Receipts	643	$ 2,513.40
Less Disbursements	643	178.67
Balance Before Distributions		$ 2,334.73
Distributions to Beneficiaries	644	2,334.73
Income Balance on Hand		-0-
Combined Balance on Hand		$ 90,813.96

[1]Optional—for use if applicable.

RECEIPTS OF PRINCIPAL

Assets Listed in Inventory (Valued as of Date of Death)		Fiduciary Acquisition Value
Cash:		
First National Bank—checking account	$ 516.93	
Prudent Saving Fund Society—savings account	2,518.16	
Cash in possession of decedent	42.54	$ 3,077.63
Tangible Personal Property:		
Jewelry—		
1 pearl necklace		515.00
Furniture—		
1 antique highboy	$ 2,000.00	
1 antique side table	60.00	
1 antique chair	55.00	2,115.00
Stocks:		
200 shs. Home Telephone & Telegraph Co., common	$ 25,000.00	
50 shs. Best Oil Co., common	5,000.00	
1,000 shs. Central Trust Co., capital	50,850.00	
151 shs. Electric Data Corp., common	1,887.50	
50 shs. Fabulous Mutual Fund	1,833.33	
200 shs. XYZ Corporation, common	6,000.00	90,570.83
Realty:		
Residence— 86 Norwood Road West Hartford, CT		$ 50,000.00
Total Inventory		$146,278.46

Receipts Subsequent to Inventory (Valued When Received)

2/22/79	Proceeds of Sale—Best Oil Co., rights to subscribe received 2/15/79	$ 50.00[1]	
3/12/79	Fabulous Mutual Fund, capital gains dividend received in cash	32.50	
5/11/79	Refund of overpayment of 1978 U.S. individual income tax	127.80	
9/25/79	From Richard Roe, Ancillary Administrator, net proceeds on sale of oil and gas leases in Jefferson Parish, Louisiana	10,000.00	$ 10,210.30

[1]Proceeds of sale of rights may be treated as an additional receipt, as illustrated here, or may be applied in reduction of carrying value as illustrated on page 646 of the Model Trustee's Account. Either method, consistently applied, is acceptable.

Preparing Your Resume

Getting a job requires presenting your credentials including education and experience; a well-prepared resume is usually the first impression you will make on a prospective employer.

A **resume** is a short description of a person's education, a summary of work experience, and other related and supporting information that potential employers use in evaluating a person's qualifications for a position in a firm or an organization. Exhibits 3.11 and 3.12 provide examples. You should prepare a resume as you see yourself today. Look at your resume from the perspective of a future employer. What areas do you need to strengthen to demonstrate your ability to perform the type of job you would like to have?

You should look at your resume as being a continuing work in progress. Constantly update your resume to include any new job responsibilities, part-time employment skills and qualifications, and special achievements. Add meaningful items to your resume in the form of courses, skills, and outside interests that will land you that first paralegal job after you complete your training.

After you have gathered all of the necessary information, put it into a proper resume form, then review it. Does the resume reflect the information you want to communicate to a prospective employer? Try to look at it with an open, objective mind.

Resume A short description of a person's education, a summary of work experience, and other related and supporting information that potential employers use in evaluating a person's qualifications for a position in a firm or an organization.

Exhibit 3.11 Sample functional resume

SARA MARKS

2222 Market Way
Brooklyn, NY 11223
(212) 555-8634 (Home)
(212) 555-9234 (Office)

EDUCATION
Reading College, Brooklyn, NY, 2008
    Associate of Science degree, GPA 4.0
        Paralegal Major—ABA-approved program
    Dean's List, Vice President of the Honor Society

EMPLOYMENT HISTORY
Paralegal field work, Brooklyn, NY, 2006 to 2008
    Advisor, Small Claims Court and the Brooklyn Department of
Consumer Affairs
- Assisted claimants with small claim forms
- Counseled individuals on consumer affairs issues

Registration and admissions clerk, Brooklyn, NY, 2004 to 2006
    Reading College
- Registered incoming and returning students
- In charge of organizing the filing system, creating more efficiency in the office

Cosmetologist and Barber, Brooklyn, NY, 2000 to 2004
- Self-employed
- Handled all phases of business, including purchasing, bookkeeping, and payroll

SPECIAL SKILLS
- WordPerfect, Microsoft Office Suite
- Excellent ability to communicate with general public

PROFESSIONAL AFFILIATIONS
Manhattan Paralegal Association

Excellent references available upon request

Exhibit 3.12 Sample chronological resume

MICHAEL C. SMITH

2345 Oregon Street, #A
Portland, OR 98765
(363) 282-7890

EDUCATION
Paralegal Certificate, General Litigation, 2008
University of Portland (ABA approved)
Curriculum included:

Family Law	Paralegal Practices and Procedures
Criminal Law	Legal Research and Writing
Civil Litigation	Estates, Trusts, and Wills

Bachelor of Science Degree,
 Transportation and Distribution Management
 Golden Gate University, San Francisco, CA

EXPERIENCE
Paralegal Practice
- Drafted memos to clients
- Prepared notice of summons
- Conducted research for misdemeanor appeal cases
- Prepared points and authorities for motions
- Observed bankruptcy and family law court proceedings
- Completed necessary documents for probate
- Wrote legal memorandum

Administration and Management
- Participated in new division startup
- Dispatched and routed for the transportation of 80 to 120 special education students daily
- Supervised between 20 and 25 drivers
- Designed and implemented daily operation logs
- Liaison between drivers and school officials or parents
- Evaluated various conditions when assigning routes and equipment

EMPLOYMENT HISTORY

Susan Hildebrand, Attorney, Portland, OR Paralegal Intern	2008
Laidlaw Transit, Inc., San Francisco, CA Dispatch Manager	2002 to 2008
Hayward Unified School District Teaching Assistant	2001 to 2002
San Mateo Union High School District Office Clerk	2000 to 2001

Employers are looking for individuals who demonstrate a good work ethic, willingness to accept responsibility and take direction, and the skills necessary for the job for which they are applying.

Set your roadmap for the job you wish to obtain. What additional educational skills are required? This will determine your future course of study. Work–study programs in your field and cooperative education are good ways of demonstrating on-the-job training. Depending upon your goals, resources, and timeframe, a specialized certificate such as a paralegal certificate, an associate's degree in paralegal studies, or a bachelor's degree in paralegal studies will certainly demonstrate your level of interest and ability to achieve the minimum level of education for the job.

Resume Formats

Many formats may be used in preparing a resume: functional, chronological, reverse chronological, combination, technical, and electronic.

The **chronological resume format** presents education and job history in a time sequence with the most recent experience listed first. An alternative format is the reverse chronological resume format, with the latest job listed last. The **functional resume format** usually gives a summary of the individual's qualifications and current experience and education without emphasizing dates of employment. The combination resume format combines the chronological and functional resume formats.

There are no hard and fast rules for choosing a proper resume format, except perhaps to put your name and contact information at the top. Some suggest that the chronological resume is the form used most commonly in the legal field. Always remember that the main purpose of the resume is to get a job interview and, you hope, employment.

If responding to an ad in the paper, tailor your resume to the job description or to the job listing of the individual employer. You may have to develop resumes in more than one format if the employment opportunities presented require different skill sets. For example, the resume sent to an employer looking for someone with specific computer skills should show that functional skill first. A job description looking for depth of experience probably should use the chronological approach.

Common elements of most resumes include:

- Heading, with your name and contact information
- Career objective, concise and to the point, geared to the job description of the position you seek
- Education, generally at the beginning of the resume if you are a recent graduate, including specific academic honors and awards if applicable to the job
- Experience, including paid and unpaid activities showing the employer the skills you have to offer
- Activities, a brief listing unless directly related to the job description, including professional organizations and educational and volunteer activities

Cover Letters

Always include a **cover letter** with your resume. This applies to email applications, too. The cover letter creates the first impression. Brief though it is, it represents a sample of your writing skills and ability to communicate in writing. Take the time to be sure it properly reflects who you are and your skills. The cover letter should be brief, as your qualifications will be covered in the accompanying resume.

The cover letter should describe the job you are seeking, summarize your qualifications, request an interview, and express a desire for the job. If possible, address the cover letter directly to the person who is responsible for the hiring decision. Be sure to spell the person's name correctly and include the correct job title.

Just as you may need different resumes for different jobs, you should personalize each letter for each job application.

References

References may be requested in responses to advertisements or you may wish to add them to your resume. Select your references carefully, they are frequently called or contacted for comment as part of the hiring process. Those you select must be contacted before you use their names and their permission secured. Faculty members and former employers are frequently asked to be used as references. In some schools and workplaces, there is a policy that limits the information that may be given out about dates or work or attendance. An employer following up on one of these references may take a negative inference from the limited information given. Keep in touch with those who do agree to give a reference and who will say good things about you to a potential

---

Chronological resume format Presents education and job history in chronological order with the most recent experience listed first.

Functional resume format Lists a summary of the individual's qualifications with current experience and education without any emphasis on dates of employment.

Cover letter A brief letter sent with a document identifying the intended recipient and the purpose of the attachment.

employer. Keep them informed on your latest work and other extracurricular activities like charity or pro bono work so they may speak knowledgeably about you if contacted.

Creating an Electronic Resume

A growing number of employers are using computers to search the Internet for job applicants and to sort electronically through the resumes they receive. Human resources managers search through resumes received online or through Internet sites by entering a few words or phrases that describe the required skills and qualifications for the position they are trying to fill. Only the resumes in the computer system that match these electronic sorting terms and phrases are considered for the job offered. To have your resume considered, you will need an electronic resume in addition to the traditional printed resume.

Computer programs that are used to search resumes generally look for certain descriptive words in the resume, these are called key words, like the key words used to conduct legal or actual research. For example, to highlight your initiative use words like initiated, started, created, introduced; for leadership skills, use words like directed, guided, organized; to attract interest to problem-solving skills, uses words like evaluated, reorganized, simplified, solved, eliminated. Be sure to use these types of key words in your electronic resume where appropriate to make your accomplishments stand out from the other resumes. A starting point is to gather all the information as shown in the Resume Checklist.

Converting a Traditional Resume into an Electronic Resume

If you plan to send your resume as an attachment to an email, the only way you can be sure the person you are sending it to can read it is if you send it as an ASCII file or in a universally usable format such as Rich text file RTF. If you already have created a resume using a word-processing program, open the file containing your resume and save it as a plain ASCII text file or RTF file. You will want to change the name of the new text file to distinguish it from the file name used for the traditional printed version.

Text-only files cannot accommodate type formatting and special characters, so be sure that your electronic resume appears in one simple font and one font size. You also

CHECKLIST Resume

PERSONAL INFORMATION
- ☐ Name
- ☐ Address

EDUCATION
- ☐ High school
  - ☐ Year of graduation
- ☐ College
  - ☐ Year of graduation
  - ☐ Degree
  - ☐ Grade point average or class rank

WORK EXPERIENCE
- ☐ Current or last employer
  - ☐ Position(s) held

- ☐ Prior employer
  - ☐ Position held and dates

SPECIFIC SKILLS
- ☐ Office skills
- ☐ Computer skills
- ☐ Language skills
- ☐ Other job-related skills

OTHER
- ☐ Organizational memberships
- ☐ Licenses/certifications

must remove line justification, tables, rules (lines), and columns. Align all text at the left to avoid indentation problems. Exhibit 3.13 is an example of an electronic resume.

The first line of your resume should contain only your full name. Type your street address, phone and fax numbers, and email address on separate lines below your name.

Because many human resource managers search by key words, you'll want to include a key word section near the top of your resume. List nouns that describe your job-related skills and abilities. If you have work experience with specific job titles such as "paralegal," list these key words as well. Also include language proficiency or other specialty qualifications such as "nurse–paralegal" or "fluent in Spanish."

Exhibit 3.13   Sample electronic resume

JANE DOE
1234 N. Maple Street
Anytown, USA 90000
Home: (213) 555-1111 * Work: (213) 555-3333
Jane.doe@att.net

LITIGATION PARALEGAL

Education
University of Paralegal Studies, Fremont, CA
Paralegal Specialist Certificate, 2002, Honors graduate
Approved by ABA
Course of study: Legal Research and Writing, Contracts, Torts, Ethics, Litigation Specialization

University of California at Berkeley
Bachelor of Arts Degree in History, 2001
Graduated Cum Laude

Skills and Abilities
• Ability to analyze documents, digest depositions, draft discovery, and prepare cases for trial
• Knowledge of torts and contract law, legal research techniques, and basic civil procedure
• Fluent in French, both written and spoken
• Proficient in Word for Windows, WordPerfect 6.0, and Excel

Legal Internship
Jones, Smith, Smythe and Smooth, Los Angeles, 2001–2002
• Digested depositions for complex litigation case
• Organized multiple documents using several software programs

Work Experience
Los Angeles Unified School District, 1998–1999
Secondary School Teacher
• Arranged classroom materials
• Supervised student teachers
• Chaired English Department
• Created curricula for advanced students

Professional Associations
Los Angeles Paralegal Association
University of Paralegal Studies Alumni Association

References and writing samples available upon request.

Source: Wagner, Andrea, How to Land Your First Paralegal Job: Insiders, 3rd, © 2001. Electronically reproduced by permission of Pearson Education, Inc., Upper Saddle River, New Jersey.

After you have created your resume, save it again as an ASCII plain text file. Email the resume to yourself or to a friend to see how it looks when sent over the Internet.

Think of getting a job as a process that starts with the resume and continues through the interview and the follow-up to the interview as shown in the Checklist for Interview Strategies.

CHECKLIST Interview Strategies

GETTING READY

☐ Write resume.

☐ Make contacts.

☐ Network.

☐ Make appointments from mass mailings, telephone solicitations, and network contacts.

BEFORE THE INTERVIEW

☐ Know your resume.

☐ Be familiar with a typical application form.

☐ Know something about the company or firm. Check the Martindale-Hubbell or Standard and Poor's directories.

☐ Have a list of good questions to ask the interviewer, and know when to ask them.

☐ Rehearse your answers to possible interview questions, then rehearse again.

☐ Plan a "thumbnail" sketch of yourself.

☐ Know the location of the interview site and where to park, or become familiar with the public transportation schedule.

☐ Be at least 10 minutes early.

☐ Go alone.

☐ Bring copies of your resume, list of references, and writing samples in a briefcase or portfolio.

☐ Check local salary ranges for the position.

☐ Be prepared to answer questions regarding your salary expectations.

☐ Try to anticipate problem areas, such as inexperience or gaps in your work history.

☐ Be prepared to handle difficult questions, and know how to overcome objections.

THE INTRODUCTION

☐ Dress the part.

☐ Do not smoke, eat, chew gum, or drink coffee prior to or during the interview.

☐ Maintain good eye contact and good posture.

☐ Shake hands firmly.

☐ Establish rapport and be cordial without being overly familiar.

☐ Be positive—convert negatives to positives.

☐ Keep in mind that the first impressions are lasting impressions.

THE INTERVIEW

☐ Provide all important information about yourself.

☐ Sell yourself—no one else will.

☐ Use correct grammar.

☐ Do not be afraid to say, "I don't know."

☐ Ask questions of the interviewer.

☐ Do not answer questions about age, religion, marital status, or children unless you wish to. Try to address the perceived concern.

☐ Find out about the next interview or contact.

☐ Find out when a decision will be made.

☐ Shake hands at the end of the interview.

AFTER THE INTERVIEW

☐ Immediately document the interview in your placement file.

☐ Send personalized thank-you letters to each person who interviewed you.

☐ Call to follow up.

Source: Andrea Wagner, *How to Land Your First Paralegal Job* (Upper Saddle River, NJ: Prentice Hall, 2001), pp. 163–164.

Advice *from the* Field

THE PARALEGAL'S PORTFOLIO

Kathryn Myers, Coordinator, Paralegal Studies, Saint Mary-of-the-Woods College, Paralegal Studies Program

INTERVIEW

Q: How did the practice of assembling a portfolio come about?

A: This portfolio is actually based on the old concept of the "artist's portfolio." Anyone who is involved in a "hands-on" profession has utilized this concept for years.

Q: Instead of pictures, what do you mean when you speak of a portfolio for paralegal students?

A: A portfolio for paralegal students consists of two parts. One part is for my use in the program. The students have growth papers for each class, plus a series of other papers. I look at the collection of work to determine whether the paralegal program is doing what it says it will and whether it needs to be changed. I have modified a number of classes based on the material in this portfolio.

The other part is a professional portfolio. The students pull material from the above portfolio and create their own professional portfolio to take on interviews. This contains a copy or copies of their resume, transcripts, selected writing samples, projects, or any other document they believe would be useful at the interview. Employers have been very impressed with this presentation.

Q: Do potential employers ever balk at seeing something that bulky? If so, how would you suggest handling it?

A: This has not been a problem for my students. As indicated earlier, we "create" two portfolios—one program-related and the other for professional purposes. I think this eliminates any problems at the interview.

Q: What is the most important thing about a portfolio?

A: The most important thing in the professional portfolio appears to be that the employer has another tool to assess the quality of the potential employee. Grades do not mean that much anymore. An "A" at [our college] may well come from a more demanding curriculum than an "A" at another institution. There is no basis for comparison unless the employer knows the grading scales/demands of the different programs. However, having a portfolio of material allows the employer to see what an interviewee can do.

Q: With that in mind, what should a paralegal student keep in mind when putting together the portfolio?

A: How a student puts a portfolio together says a lot about the student. I encourage students to incorporate both good and "not so good" work. That shows the employer that the interviewee can learn and can improve. Students collect material as they go through the program rather than waiting until the end.

Students should highlight their growth, their abilities, and their determination. They need to provide documentation that can show abilities that counter any poor grades that might appear on the transcript. This shows potential employers that test-taking is not necessarily the be-all, end-all to grades.

Most of all, the students need to let themselves shine through within the portfolio materials. Each student is unique and each has different talents to highlight. That is the value of the portfolio.

Kathryn Myers is Coordinator, Paralegal Studies, Saint Mary-of-the-Woods College, Paralegal Studies Program. Used by permission.

Interviewing for a Job

Most students today work at part-time or full-time jobs while pursuing their education. These might be summer jobs, holiday fill-in positions, or full-time jobs. The interview for a part-time, summer, or holiday position, or the interview for a new full-time position provides an opportunity to perfect your interviewing skills. Interviewing for a job can be highly stressful but careful preparation can reduce the stress and help you put your best foot forward so you can get that dream job you want.

After the interview, you should review what happened and the results of the interview as a way of learning how to improve your interviewing skills. Even if you obtain the job, you'll want to learn what you did correctly that helped you to get the job, as well as what you could have done better, to prepare for future interviews.

The Interview

An interview for a job need not be intimidating. With a little preparation and research you can appear confident and make a good impression. The starting point is careful reading of the job description and the employer's requested qualifications. Be sure that you can answer questions related to these qualifications, such as your experience in the particular area of law or special training in the use of specialty legal software. Research the firm by finding articles about the firm or lawyers online and by looking at its website. Prepare a list of questions that you want to ask that shows your interest in the firm and the particular job as shown in the Checklist of Interview Questions. After you leave the interview analyze how you did in the interview by reviewing the Checklist below. Then, prepare and send the thank-you note to the person with whom you interviewed to make a positive, lasting impression.

CHECKLIST Questions to Ask at the Interview

☐ How does the firm evaluate paralegals?

☐ What is the growth potential for a paralegal in the firm?

☐ Why did the prior paralegal leave?

☐ How is work assigned?

☐ What support services are available to paralegals?

☐ What consideration is given for membership in paralegal associations?

☐ Does the firm provide any assistance for continuing education for paralegals?

CHECKLIST Analyzing How I Handled the Interview

☐ I arrived early for the interview.

☐ I greeted the interviewer warmly, with a smile and a firm handshake.

☐ I maintained good posture.

☐ I did not smoke or chew gum during the interview.

☐ I spoke clearly, using good grammar.

☐ I demonstrated enthusiasm and interest.

☐ I was able to answer questions asked of me.

☐ I sent a thank-you note within 24 hours after the interview.

Concept Review *and* Reinforcement

LEGAL TERMINOLOGY

Chronological resume format   110

Complex litigation   83

Conflict checking   94

Court accounting   105

Cover letter   110

Elder law   83

Environmental law   83

Functional resume format   110

General law practice   81

Government employment   84

Intellectual property   83

IOLTA account   105

Large law offices   79

Networking   85

Nurse paralegals or legal nurse consultants   82

Paralegal manager   83

Partnership   78

Pro bono   84

Resume   108

Retainer   101

Self-employment   85

Small offices   76

Solo practice   76

Specialty practice   81

Trust account   104

SUMMARY OF KEY CONCEPTS

Arrangements and Organization of Law Offices and Firms

Solo Practice	One lawyer practicing alone without the assistance of other attorneys.
Small Offices	Range from individual practitioners sharing space to partnerships.
Partnerships	Two or more natural (human) or artificial (corporation) persons who have joined together to share ownership and profit or loss.
Large Offices	An outgrowth of traditional law offices that have expanded over the years, adding partners and associates along the way.
General Practice	Handles all types of cases.

Specialty Practice

Legal Nurse Consultants and Nurse Paralegals	Nurses who have gained medical work experience and combine it with paralegal skills.
Real Estate	Paralegals with real estate experience in sales or from title insurance agencies.
Complex Litigation	Requires document production and maintaining indexes, usually on computer databases, of the paperwork generated from litigation.
Environmental Law	Covers everything from toxic waste dumps to protection of wildlife and the environment.
Intellectual Property	Concerned with the formalities of protecting intellectual-property interests including patent rights, trade secrets, and copyrights and trademarks.
Elder Law	Protecting the rights of the elderly and obtaining all the benefits to which they are entitled.
Paralegal Managers	Hire, supervise, train, and evaluate paralegals.
Pro Bono Paralegals	Work without compensation on behalf of individuals and organizations that otherwise could not afford legal assistance.
Government Employment	Paralegals are found in administrative agencies and federal offices involved with both criminal prosecutions and civil litigation.
Legal Departments of Corporations	Paralegals handle documents, technology, and investigations juggling legal, sales, and marketing perspectives.
Self-Employment	State regulation may limit the opportunities or restrict paralegal self-employment. Where authorized by federal law, the paralegal may actively represent clients without the supervision of an attorney.
Networking	Establishing contact with others to exchange questions and information.

Paralegal Tasks and Functions

1. Conducting interviews
2. Maintaining written and verbal contacts with clients and counsel
3. Setting up, organizing, and maintaining client files
4. Preparing pleadings and documents
5. Reviewing, analyzing, summarizing, and indexing documents and transcripts
6. Assisting in preparing witnesses and clients for trial
7. Maintaining calendar and tickler systems
8. Conducting research, both factual and legal
9. Performing office administrative functions including maintaining time and billing records

Administrative Procedures in Law Offices and Firms

Conflict Checking	To verify that current and prior representations of parties and matters handled will not present a conflict of interest for the firm in accepting a new client or legal matter.
Time Keeping and Billing	Keeping track of billable time.

Accounting in the Law Office

Maintaining Law Firm Financial Information	A paralegal needs to understand the internal accounting needs of the firm and to understand and prepare client financial information.
Accounting for Client Retainers and Costs Advanced	A payment at the beginning of the handling of a new matter for a client. This amount may be used to offset the fees for services rendered or costs advanced on behalf of the client.
Civil Practice: Fee and Cost Billing	May be calculated on an hourly rate, a contingent fee, or a combination of the two.
Timely Disbursements	Lawyers cannot retain settlement funds for an unreasonable time.
Trust Accounts	The client's funds.
IOLTA Accounts	Where the amount is too small to earn interest, court rules require that the funds be deposited into a special interest-bearing account, and the interest generally paid to support legal aid projects (Interest on Lawyers Trust Accounts).
Interest-Bearing Escrow Accounts	If the amount held for a client is sufficient to earn substantial interest it should be deposited in an interest-bearing account for the benefit of the client.
Court Accounting	An accounting with the local court that administers or supervises trust and estate matters; these reports are designed to show that the fiduciary has properly administered the estate or trust.

Preparing Your Resume

Resume Formats	Brief description of a person's education, a summary of work experience, and other related and supporting information that potential employers use in evaluating a person's qualifications for a position in a firm or an organization.
	Chronological Resume Format
	1. Presents education and job history in chronological order with the most recent experience listed first.
	Functional Resume Format
	2. Gives a summary of the individual's qualifications with current experience and education without emphasizing dates of employment.
Cover Letters	The cover letter creates the first impression, and is a sample of your writing skills and ability to communicate in writing.
Creating an Electronic Resume	A growing number of employers use computers to search the Internet for job applicants, sorting resumes electronically.
Converting a Traditional Resume into an Electronic Resume	Traditional word-processing documents may not be readable in electronic form and need to be converted to a readable format.

Interviewing for a Job

The Interview	Careful interview preparation can help to eliminate some of the stress and help you put your best foot forward.

WORKING THE WEB

1. Download the Tips for Networking Success from the NALS website at http://www.nals.org/students/reading/networkingsuccess.html.
2. Review some of the job opportunities posted on the American Alliance of Paralegals. What are the common qualifications? http://aapipara.org/Jobbank.htm
3. Check and download from the websites of the various paralegal professional associations information on paralegal occupational opportunities:
   a. National Association of Legal Assistants at www.nala.org
   b. National Federation of Paralegal Associations at www.paralegals.org
   c. Legal Assistant Management Association at www.lamanet.org
   d. American Association of Legal Nurse Consultants at www.aalnc.org
   e. The American Association of Nurse Attorneys at www.taana.org
   f. American Corporate Legal Assistants Association at www.aclaa.org
4. What paralegal opportunities are posted at www.monster.com?
5. What online resources are available to help in creating resumes?
   a. Purdue University at www.owl.English.purdue.edu
   b. College of William and Mary at www.wm.edu/csrv/career/stualum/resmdir
6. What online career sources are available at:
   a. Career Resource Library at www.labor.state.ny.us
   b. America's Job Bank at www.ajb.dni.us/index.html
   c. Wall Street Journal at www.careers.wsj.com
   d. CareerWEB at www.employmentguide.com
7. What law firms in your area have a website that offers employment opportunities? Use the Martindale-Hubbell Legal Directory to find the law firms.

CRITICAL THINKING & WRITING QUESTIONS

1. What are the different forms of practice arrangements that lawyers use?
2. What are the advantages and disadvantages of working for a lawyer in solo practice?
3. What are the advantages and disadvantages of working in a small multi-lawyer office or partnership?
4. What are the advantages and disadvantages of working in large law offices or firms?
5. Would working in a specialty practice be less stressful than working in a general practice?
6. What are the advantages and disadvantages of working in a corporate legal department?
7. Why would a law firm want to hire nurse paralegals?
8. What additional costs might a paralegal incur in working in a large-city practice in contrast to a small-town office?
9. Why would a paralegal who specializes in one legal field be at greater risk for unauthorized practice of law?
10. Other than revealing potential employment opportunities, what advantages does networking have for a paralegal?
11. Are interviews conducted by paralegals privileged?
12. Why is doing a conflict check important?
13. Is it necessary to do a conflict check before starting employment at a new law firm? Why?
14. When is an ethical wall required?
15. What steps should be taken to ensure that a proper ethical screen is in place?
16. Why is accurate time keeping important to the paralegal and the law firm?
17. What is a retainer?
18. What is an IOLTA account, and what is the reason behind maintaining IOLTA?
19. What is the purpose of filing a court accounting?
20. What is the objective of the Uniform System of Accounts?
21. Prepare the resume you would like to have five years from now. How would this resume help you in selecting courses, extracurricular activities, and interim employment?
22. Prepare your current resume in print form. What format did you use? Why?
23. Convert a print resume to an electronic resume. Email a copy to your instructor if requested.
24. How does assessing your interests and skills help in preparing your personal resume?

Building Paralegal Skills

Preparing for a Job Interview: Resume Advice

Paralegal student Reed meets with a college counselor for advice about preparing his resume and obtains some suggestions for enhancing his resume and preparing a cover letter.

After viewing the video case study at www.pearsonhighered.com/goldman answer the following:

1. Prepare an outline of your resume with the appropriate sections, and save it as a template for future use.
2. Complete the resume using the template by adding your current qualifications and experience.
3. Prepare and print out a copy of the resume using the paper you would use for submitting a resume to a potential employer.
4. Prepare the resume for electronic submission with an email. Prepare and send the email to yourself as if you were the potential employer.

Preparing for a Job Interview: Interviewing Advice

Paralegal student Reed meets with his college counselor to obtain advice about interviewing for a job. His counselor helps him with some of the questions he may be asked that trouble him.

After viewing the video case study at www.pearsonhighered.com/goldman answer the following:

1. Pair up with another student and role-play with one of you acting as the human resource director and the other the applicant.
2. Make a list of questions you would ask as the interviewer.
3. Make a list of questions you would ask as the applicant.
4. Conduct the interview in front of the class or another person who can offer comments and critiques of the interview.
5. Prepare a follow-up note to the interviewer.
6. What are questions that cannot be asked? If they are asked how will you answer them.

Interviewing: The Good, The Bad, and the Ugly

Three paralegals are applying for a job at a prestigious law firm. Each presents themselves in a different manner and with a distinctive style.

After viewing the video case study at www.pearsonhighered.com/goldman answer the following:

1. Make a list of suggestions for each of the three applicants on what they should have done or can do in their next interview to make the most positive impression.
2. What interviewing rules did each applicant make?
3. How important is the way you dress for an interview, why?

1. In changing jobs from one firm to another, how does the paralegal avoid a conflict of interest?
2. What ethical and UPL problems do freelance paralegals face that those working in a single firm do not?
3. What ethical issues might arise in determining the paralegal's supervising attorney when the paralegal is working in a small firm of three attorneys?
4. Say you are working as a paralegal in a small law office, shared by three attorneys, each of whom is a solo practitioner. To save money, they share a law library and a fax machine, and they use a common computer network with separate workstations but with a common file server to save files because it has an automatic backup system. You work for each of the lawyers as the need arises, answering phones and generally performing paralegal services. [District of Columbia Ethics Opinion 303.] What issues of confidentiality should be considered? As the office paralegal, do you have any conflict of interest problems?

Paralegal Ethics in Practice

5. You hold a bachelor's degree in paralegal studies from a prestigious college. You want to work as an independent paralegal. May you advertise in the local newspaper and put a sign on the door of your office that uses the term "paralegal," according to your state law?

DEVELOPING YOUR COLLABORATION SKILLS

Working on your own or with a group of other students assigned by your instructor, review the scenario at the beginning of the chapter discussing the changes and the opportunities in the paralegal profession.

1. Dividing the class into groups of three, one person will play the role of Cary Moritz and another the role of Natasha Weiser; the third person will act as recorder and presenter.
2. Role-play Natasha's first day on the job. She receives the memo from Cary and goes to her office to offer her thanks.

a. What additional questions could Natasha ask Cary?
b. What additional advice could Cary offer?
3. The recorder keeps detailed notes of the conversation.
4. Once the role-play is completed, the group summarizes the expectations that Natasha and Cary would have of the other in their working relationship.
5. Now it is Natasha's turn to prepare a memo thanking Cary and summarizing their conversation.

PARALEGAL PORTFOLIO EXERCISE

Develop your resume, using the functional format to prepare the resume you would like to have when you finish your education as a paralegal. List the skills you expect to develop or learn before you apply for your desired paralegal position.

LEGAL ANALYSIS & WRITING CASES

Jean v. Nelson   863 F.2d 759 (11th Cir. 1988)

Reimbursement for Paralegal Time under Federal Statute

The district court awarded, and the 11th Circuit Court of Appeals upheld, reimbursement for time spent by paralegals and law clerks where the work normally was done by an attorney. The hourly rate awarded was $40, the rate at which the law firm whose paralegals and clerks were involved bills its clients.

The government challenges the rate awarded, and contends that paralegal time is compensational only at the actual cost to the plaintiff's counsel. In the context of a Title VII case, [the court] held that paralegal time is recoverable as "part of a prevailing party's award for attorney's fees and expenses, [but]

only to the extent that the paralegal performs work traditionally done by an attorney. To hold otherwise would be counterproductive because excluding reimbursement for such work might encourage attorneys to handle entire cases themselves, thereby achieving the same results at a higher overall cost."

Questions
1. Does this rationale encourage lawyers to use paralegals?
2. Does this decision facilitate the availability of lower-cost quality legal services?
3. Should an attorney be allowed to charge more than out-of-pocket costs for paralegal services?

In Re Busy Beaver Bldg. Centers, Inc.   19 F.3d 833 (3rd Cir. 1994)

Paralegal Fees Based on Skill Level
In deciding the propriety of awarding paralegal fees in bankruptcy cases, the court held:

As is true with recently graduated attorneys, entry-level paralegals perform the more mundane tasks in the paralegal work spectrum, some of which may resemble those tasks generally deemed "clerical" in nature. Yet, even with these

tasks, paralegals may have to bring their training or experience to bear, thereby relieving attorneys of the burden of extensive supervision and ensuring the proper completion of tasks involving the exercise, or potential exercise, of some paraprofessional judgment. Of course, the appropriate rate the attorney will command for paralegal services will ordinarily parallel the paralegal's credentials and the degree of experience, knowledge, and skill the task at hand calls for. . . . [P]urely clerical or secretarial tasks should not be billed at a paralegal rate, regardless of who performs them.

The short of it is that the market-driven approach of the [bankruptcy act] § 330 permits compensation for relatively low-level paralegal services if and only if analogous non-bankruptcy clients agree to pay for the same, and then only at that rate. [T]hose services not requiring the exercise of professional legal judgment . . . must be included in "overhead."

We cannot agree that in all cases the general ability of a legal secretary to perform some particular task determines whether a paralegal or a legal secretary is the appropriate, most efficient, employee to perform it at any given instant.

At times temporal constraints may foreclose the delegation option. At other times a paralegal—or, for that matter, an attorney—can more productively complete a clerical task, such as photocopying documents, than can a legal secretary.

Questions

1. How can the attorney prove the skill level of paralegals when seeking compensation for paralegal services?
2. Will this kind of reasoning by the court force attorneys to hire more skilled paralegals?
3. Would the existence of a certificate or degree in paralegal studies be useful in proving that the person who worked on a case was a paralegal?

WORKING WITH THE LANGUAGE OF THE COURT CASE

Phoenix Founders Inc. v. Marshall

887 S.W.2d 831 (Tex. 1994)
Supreme Court of Texas

Read the following case, excerpted from the state supreme court's opinion. Review and brief the case. In your brief, answer the following questions.

1. What is the danger in hiring a paralegal who has worked at a competing law firm when handling a case on appeal?
2. What is the supervising attorney's responsibility in hiring a paralegal who has worked at another law firm?
3. What steps must be taken when hiring a paralegal who worked at another law firm that represents an opposing party?

4. What instructions should the paralegal who worked at another firm be given when hired?
5. Under what general circumstances will a law firm be disqualified after hiring a paralegal?

Spector, Justice, delivered the opinion of the Court, in which Hillips, Chief Justice, and Gonzalez, Hightower, Hecht, Doggett, Cornyn, and Gammage, Justices join.

In this original proceeding, we consider whether a law firm must be disqualified from ongoing litigation because it rehired a legal assistant who had worked for opposing counsel for three weeks. We hold that disqualification is not required if the rehiring firm is able to establish that it has effectively screened the paralegal from any contact with the underlying suit. Because this standard had not been adopted in Texas prior to the trial court's disqualification order, we deny mandamus relief without prejudice to allow the trial court to reconsider its ruling in light of today's opinion.

The present dispute arises from a suit brought by Phoenix Founders, Inc. and others ("Phoenix") to collect a federal-court judgment against Ronald and Jane Beneke and others. The law firm of Thompson & Knight represented Phoenix in the original federal-court suit, which began in 1990 and ended in 1991, and has also represented them in the collection suit since its commencement in 1992. The Benekes have been represented in the latter suit by the firm of David & Goodman.

In July of 1993, Denise Hargrove, a legal assistant at Thompson & Knight, left her position at that firm to begin working for David & Goodman as a paralegal. While at David & Goodman, Hargrove billed six-tenths of an hour on the collection suit for locating a pleading. She also discussed the case generally with

(continued)

Mark Goodman, the Benekes' lead counsel. After three weeks at David & Goodman, Hargrove returned to Thompson & Knight to resume work as a paralegal. At the time of the rehiring, Thompson & Knight made no effort to question Hargrove in regard to potential conflicts of interest resulting from her employment at David & Goodman.

Three weeks after Hargrove had returned, counsel for the Benekes wrote to Thompson & Knight asserting that its renewed employment of Hargrove created a conflict of interest. The letter demanded that the firm withdraw from its representation of Phoenix. Hargrove resigned from Thompson & Knight the next week, after having been given the option of either resigning with severance pay or being terminated. The firm itself, however, refused to withdraw from the case. The Benekes then filed a motion to disqualify.

This Court has not previously addressed the standards governing a disqualification motion based on the hiring of a nonlawyer employee. With respect to lawyers, however, this Court has adopted a standard requiring disqualification whenever counsel undertakes representation of an interest that is adverse to that of a former client, as long as the matters embraced in the pending suit are "substantially related" to the factual matters involved in the previous suit. This strict rule is based on a conclusive presumption that confidences and secrets were imparted to the attorney during the prior representation [Coker, 765 S.W.2d at 400].

We agree that a paralegal who has actually worked on a case must be subject to the presumption set out in Coker; that is, a conclusive presumption that confidences and secrets were imparted during the course of the paralegal's work on the case. We disagree, however, with the argument that paralegals should be conclusively presumed to share confidential information with members of their firms. The Disciplinary Rules require a lawyer having direct supervisory authority over a nonlawyer to make reasonable efforts to ensure that the nonlawyer's conduct is compatible with the professional obligations of the lawyer.

The Texas Committee on Professional Ethics has considered the application of these rules in the context of a "right hand" legal secretary or legal assistant leaving one small firm and joining another that represents an adverse party. The Committee concluded that the Rules do not require disqualification of the new law firm, provided that the supervising lawyer at that firm complies with the Rules so as to ensure that the nonlawyer's conduct is compatible with the professional obligations of a lawyer. This view is consistent with the weight of authority in other jurisdictions.

The American Bar Association's Committee on Professional Ethics, after surveying case law and ethics opinions from a number of jurisdictions, concluded that the new firm need not be disqualified, as long as the firm and the paralegal strictly adhere to the screening process set forth in the opinion, and as long as the paralegal does not reveal any information relating to the former employer's clients to any person in the employing firm. A number of courts have since relied on the ABA's opinion to allow continued representation under similar conditions.

Underlying these decisions is a concern regarding the mobility of paralegals and other nonlawyers. A potential employer might well be reluctant to hire a particular nonlawyer if doing so would automatically disqualify the entire firm from ongoing litigation. This problem would be especially acute in the context of massive firms and extensive, complex litigation. Recognizing this danger, the ABA concluded "any restrictions on the nonlawyer's employment should be held to the minimum necessary to protect confidentiality of client information" [ABA Op. 1526].

We share the concerns expressed by the ABA, and agree that client confidences may be adequately safeguarded if a firm hiring a paralegal from another firm takes appropriate steps in compliance with the Disciplinary Rules. Specifically, the newly hired paralegal should be cautioned not to disclose any information relating to the representation of a client of the former employer. The paralegal should also be instructed not to work on any matter on which the paralegal worked during the prior employment, or regarding which the paralegal has information relating to the former employer's representation. Additionally, the firm should take other reasonable steps to ensure that the paralegal does not work in connection with matters on which the paralegal worked during the prior employment, absent client consent after consultation. Each of these precautions would tend to reduce the danger that the paralegal might share confidential information with members of the new firm. Thus, while a court must ordinarily presume that some sharing will take place, the challenged firm may rebut this presumption by showing that sufficient precautions have been taken to guard against any disclosure of confidences.

Absent consent of the former employer's client, disqualification will always be required under some circumstances, such as (1) when information relating to the representation of an adverse client has in fact been disclosed, or (2) when screening would be ineffective or the nonlawyer necessarily would be required to work on the other side of a matter that is the same as or substantially related to a matter on which the nonlawyer has previously worked. Ordinarily, however, disqualification is not required as long as "the practical effect of formal screening has been achieved."

In reconsidering the disqualification motion, the trial court should examine the circumstances of Hargrove's employment at Thompson & Knight to determine whether the practical effect of formal screening has been achieved. The factors bearing on such a determination will generally include the substantiality of the relationship between the former and current matters; the time elapsing between the matters; the size of the firm; the number of individuals presumed to have confidential information; the nature of their involvement in the former matter; and the timing and features of any measures taken to reduce the danger of disclosure. The fact that the present case involves representation of adverse parties in the same proceeding, rather than two separate proceedings, increases the danger that some improper disclosure may have occurred. Evidence regarding the other factors, however, may tend to rebut the presumption of shared confidences.

The ultimate question in weighing these factors is whether Thompson & Knight has taken measures sufficient to reduce the potential for misuse of confidences to an acceptable level. Because we have modified the controlling legal standard, the writ of mandamus is denied without prejudice to allow the trial court to reconsider the disqualification motion in light of today's opinion. The stay order previously issued by this Court remains in effect only so long as necessary to allow the trial court to act.

Ramirez v. Plough, Inc.

12 Cal. Rptr. 2d 423 (Cal. Ct. App. 1992)*
Court of Appeal of California

Read, and if assigned, brief this case. Prepare a written answer to each of the following questions. Note the words of the California Supreme Court on appeal.

1. How does this case illustrate clients' cultural differences?
2. Are the views and conduct of the parent in this case the same as you have and would have taken?
3. What ethical obligation does the paralegal have to be sure the client who does not speak the same language understands the advice given? Does it matter if it is medical directions, as in this case, or legal advice?
4. Does a law firm have a higher duty to a non-English-speaking client than a drug company, such as the defendant in this case, does in selling a product?
5. Does the law firm have a duty to explain cultural differences in the American legal system and its procedures to non-English-speaking, non-native born clients?

Thaxter, Judge

Jorge Ramirez, a minor, by his guardian ad litem Rosa Rivera, appeals from a summary judgment in favor of Plough, Inc. Appellant sued Plough alleging negligence, product liability, and fraud. The action sought damages for injuries sustained in March of 1986 when Jorge, who was then four months old, contracted Reye's Syndrome after ingesting St. Joseph Aspirin for Children (SJAC). Plough marketed and distributed SJAC.

Reye's Syndrome is a serious disease of unknown cause characterized by severe vomiting, lethargy, or irritability, which may progress to delirium or coma.

In December 1985, the Food and Drug Administration (FDA) requested that aspirin manufacturers voluntarily place a label on aspirin products warning consumers of the possible association between aspirin and Reye's Syndrome. Plough voluntarily complied and began including a warning and insert in SJAC packaging. On June 5, 1986, the Reye's Syndrome warning became mandatory.

In March 1986, SJAC labeling bore the following warning: "Warning: Reye's Syndrome is a rare but serious disease which can follow flu or chicken pox in children and teenagers. While the cause of Reye's Syndrome is unknown, some reports claim aspirin may increase the risk of developing this disease. Consult a doctor before use in children or teenagers with flu or chicken pox." In addition, the SJAC package insert included the following statement: "The symptoms of Reye's Syndrome can include persistent vomiting,

*If citing in a California court, add "15 Cal. App. 4th 1110" after the case name and before the citation from the California Reporter, set off by commas. Ramirez v. Plough, Inc., 15 Cal. App. 4th 1110, 12 Cal. Rptr. 2d 423 (1992)

(continued)

sleepiness and lethargy, violent headaches, unusual behavior, including disorientation, combativeness, and delirium. If any of these symptoms occur, especially following chicken pox or flu, call your doctor immediately, even if your child has not taken any medication. Reye's Syndrome is serious, so early detection and treatment are vital."

Rosa Rivera purchased SJAC on March 12, 1986, and administered it to appellant, who was suffering from what appeared to be a cold or upper respiratory infection. She gave appellant the aspirin without reading the directions or warnings appearing on the SJAC packaging. The packaging was in English and Ms. Rivera can speak and understand only Spanish. She did not seek to have the directions or warnings translated from English to Spanish, even though members of her household spoke English.

The trial court granted Plough's motion for summary judgment on the grounds that "there is no duty to warn in a foreign language and there is no causal relationship between plaintiff's injury and defendant's activities."

It is undisputed that SJAC was marketed and intended for the treatment of minor aches and pains associated with colds, flu, and minor viral illnesses. The SJAC box promised "fast, effective relief of fever and minor aches and pains of colds." . . . In March 1986, federal regulations requiring a Reye's Syndrome warning had been promulgated and were final, although not yet effective. . . . The scientific community had already confirmed and documented the relationship between Reye's Syndrome and the use of aspirin after a viral illness. There is no doubt Plough had a duty to warn of the Reye's Syndrome risk.

The question thus is whether the warning given only in English was adequate under the circumstances. Respondent argues that, as a matter of law, it has no duty to place foreign-language warnings on products manufactured to be sold in the United States and that holding manufacturers liable for failing to do so would violate public policy.

While the constitutional, statutory, regulatory, and judicial authorities relied on by respondent may reflect a public policy recognizing the status of English as an official language, nothing compels the conclusion that a manufacturer of a dangerous or defective product is immunized from liability when an English-only warning does not adequately inform non-English literate persons likely to use the product.

Plough's evidence showed that over 148 foreign languages are spoken in the United States and over 23 million Americans speak a language other than English in their homes. That evidence plainly does not prove that Plough used reasonable care in giving an English-only warning. Plough, then, resorts to arguing that the burden on manufacturers and society of requiring additional warnings is so "staggering" that the courts should preclude liability as a matter of law. We are not persuaded.

Certainly the burden and costs of giving foreign-language warnings is one factor for consideration in determining whether a manufacturer acted reasonably in using only English. The importance of that factor may vary from case to case depending upon other circumstances, such as the nature of the product, marketing efforts directed to segments of the population unlikely to be English-literate, and the actual and relative size of the consumer market which could reasonably be expected to speak or read only a certain foreign language. Plough presented no evidence from which we can gauge the extent of the burden under the facts of this case.

Ramirez submitted evidence that Plough knew Hispanics were an important part of the market for SJAC and that Hispanics often maintain their first language rather than learn English. SJAC was advertised in the Spanish media, both radio and television. That evidence raises material questions of fact concerning the foreseeability of purchase by a Hispanic not literate in English and the reasonableness of not giving a Spanish-language warning. If Plough has evidence conclusively showing that it would have been unreasonable to give its label warning in Spanish because of the burden, it did not present that evidence below.

. . . [I]f we accepted Plough's arguments in this case, in effect we would be holding that failure to warn in a foreign language is not negligence, regardless of the circumstances. Such a sweeping grant of immunity should come from the legislative branch of government, not the judicial. In deciding that Plough did not establish its right to judgment as a matter of law, we do not hold that manufacturers are required to warn in languages other than English simply because it may be foreseeable that non-English-literate persons are likely to use their products. Our decision merely recognizes that under some circumstances the standard of due care may require such warning.

Because the evidence shows triable issues of material fact and because Plough did not establish its immunity from liability as a matter of law, its motion for summary judgment should have been denied.

California Supreme Court on Appeal—Ramirez v. Plough, Inc.

6 Cal.4th 539 (1993), 863 P.2d 167, 25, Cal.Rptr.2d 97

Opinion

Kennard, J.

IV

. . . We recognize that if a Spanish language warning had accompanied defendant's product, and if plaintiff's mother had read and heeded the warning, the tragic blighting of a young and innocent life that occurred in this case might not have occurred. Yet, as one court has aptly commented, "The extent to which special consideration should be given to persons who have difficulty with the English language is a matter of public policy for consideration by the appropriate legislative bodies and not by the Courts." (*Carmona* v. *Sheffield* (N.D.Cal. 1971) 325 F. Supp. 1341, 1342, affd. *per curiam* (9th Cir. 1973) 475 F.2d 738.) **(4b)** We hold only that, given the inherent limitations of the judicial process, manufacturers of nonprescription drugs have no presently existing legal duty, within the tort law system, to include foreign-language warnings with their packaging materials. . . .

Mosk, J.

I concur. I write separately to emphasize the majority's caveat that "We do not . . . foreclose the possibility of tort liability premised upon the *content* of foreign-language advertising. For example, we do not decide whether a manufacturer would be liable to a consumer who detrimentally relied upon foreign-language advertising that was materially misleading as to product risks and who was unable to read English language package warnings that accurately described the risks. No such issue is presented here. . . ."

. . . Evidence of the content, timing, duration, and scope of distribution of foreign-language advertising bears substantially on the question whether a non-English-literate consumer has been materially misled about product risks, and a trial court must consider that evidence if properly presented.

The majority do not define "materially misleading as to product risks," leaving that issue for another day—a day likely to arrive soon, given the high probability that foreign-language media will continue to expand in California.

Technology and the Paralegal

DIGITAL RESOURCES

Chapter 4 Digital Resources at *www.pearsonhighered.com/goldman*

- Video Case Studies:
  - Attorney Meet and Confer
  - Remote Videoconference Taking Witness Video Deposition
  - Privilege Issue: Misdirected E-mail
- Chapter Summary • Web Links • Court Opinions • Glossary • Comprehension Quizzes
- Technology Resources

Laws too gentle are seldom obeyed; too severe, seldom executed. *"*

Benjamin Franklin,
Poor Richard's Almanack (1756)

LEARNING OBJECTIVES

After studying this chapter, you should be able to:

1. Explain why computer skills are essential in the law office and court system.
2. Explain the importance of understanding the language of technology.
3. Explain the functions of the components of a computer system in the law office.
4. Describe the types of software and the functions they perform in a law office.
5. Describe the kinds of specialty applications software used in the law office.
6. Describe the features of the electronic courtroom and the paperless office.
7. Describe how a computer network and the Internet are used in the practice of law and the importance of maintaining security.

Paralegals at Work

Edith Hannah and Alice Hart, Attorneys at Law, have decided to combine their practices to create the Hannah Hart Law Office. Miss Hannah has had a thriving practice for 35 years, and Miss Hart has been in practice for only 5 years. Both attorneys rely heavily on their paralegal staff to run their businesses. Elma Quinn has worked for Miss Hannah for 25 years, and Cary Moritz has been with Miss Hart for only 3 years. The Hannah law firm was located across the street from the county courthouse and the Hart office a block from the federal courthouse and government complex in a neighboring city 20 miles away.

When Elma first visited the Hart office, she was surprised to see how small the Hart library was compared to Miss Hannah's library. She also noticed that the Hart office had many fewer filing cabinets and boxes and no large ledger books.

Elma sat down next to Cary's workstation and asked: "Where do you store all of your files? We have at least a dozen heavy fireproof file cabinets and a rented warehouse room full of boxes of closed files. I've heard of the paperless office, but you must have records somewhere and how do you do legal research without a decent law library?" Cary explained how they were able to access almost everything needed to research cases online and use the Internet and online research subscriptions to find all of the latest cases, statutes, and regulations. And, that all the client files and records were also kept on the computer system.

Elma expressed her real concern to Cary: "I come from the old school, we use paper files and ledger books. How much will I have to learn if they decide to use your computer system? It takes an hour to get between the offices; I don't want to have to be the one to travel between the offices to exchange documents.

The attorneys spend most of their time in court; I just don't see how they will be able to find the time to work together."

When they combine their offices, do you think they will have any problems combining files, clients, and office procedures? Consider the issues involved in this scenario as you read this chapter.

INTRODUCTION FOR THE PARALEGAL

The increased use of technology and computers in the law office, the court system, and the courtroom has changed the way many traditional procedures are performed. The computer and the Internet are increasingly used, not just for traditional document preparation, but also for maintaining client databases, keeping office and client accounting records, engaging in electronic communications, research and filing documents with the court, and trial presentation as shown in Exhibit 4.1.

Computer technology is used in the following ways in the law office:

Word processing—Prepare documents

Electronic spreadsheets—Perform financial calculations and financial presentations

Time and billing programs—Record accurate client time and billing

Accounting programs—Manage firm financial records, payroll, and client escrow accounts

Calendaring—Track deadlines, appointments, and hearing dates

Graphic presentation software—Prepare persuasive presentations

Trial presentation software—Organize trial presentations

Internet search engines—Search for accurate and current legal information and factual information to support a case

Databases—Maintain records and documents

Document scanning—Convert documents to electronic format

Document search features—Locate relevant material in documents and exhibits

Email and document delivery—Communicate electronically

Web Exploration

Compare the results of the latest survey information with the data listed to the right. The full survey may be viewed at the International Paralegal Management Association website at http://www.paralegalmanagement.org/ipma/.

Exhibit 4.1 IPMA survey results

Technology Most Often Used by Paralegals

In a survey by the International Paralegal Management Association (IPMA), the most frequently used programs as reported by respondents were:

General

Microsoft Word	99%
Document management programs	83%
General Internet research	74%
Spreadsheets	57%
Databases	57%
Billing applications	53%

Litigation

Litigation support	75%
Electronic court filing	42%
Online docket programs	33%
Trial preparation	25%

Source: 2005 Utilization Survey IPMA.

Paralegals *in* Practice

PARALEGAL PROFILE
Vanessa A. Lozzi

Vanessa A. Lozzi specializes in litigation, or law suit proceedings, in the areas of securities, class actions, appellate law, and labor and employment law. Her current position is Litigation Technology Specialist for Butzel Long, a law firm in Detroit, Michigan with about 250 attorneys.

As the Litigation Technology Specialist for my firm, I am responsible for understanding, supporting, and training firm employees to use litigation software; assisting with technology aspects of trials and arbitration; project management for document intensive cases; and staying up-to-date on the best and most cost-effective technology products and tools available.

Technology is a significant part of paralegal work. In litigation, probably 75% of the job involves some sort of technology. For example, at my firm:

- All time and billing is done electronically through a software application.
- The paralegals and secretaries work together to complete e-filings, the electronic filing of court documents.
- Paralegals are involved with electronic discovery, or e-discovery. This is the process of collecting, reviewing, managing, producing, and exchanging electronic data as evidence in a legal case.
- Paralegals are often asked to conduct legal research and locate other information. Since books are hardly used, they often use LexisNexis® and Westlaw®, online legal and factual research tools. Both offer a host of databases.
- Case-related information is managed electronically in many ways, including an internal electronic filing system for the firm's records; electronic calendars; and software used to manage document productions, transcripts, and trial presentations.

In the future, I believe that paralegals will be expected more and more to be technology experts. Since many paralegal educational programs have difficulty keeping up with technology's rapid changes, you can help educate yourself by participating in your local or state bar associations, subscribing to technology newsletters and magazines, and participating in Webinars (online seminars) and software demonstrations.

Online collaboration—Use the Internet to work collaboratively

Online electronic document repositories—Use for remote storage and access to documents

Need for Computer Skills

Computers are being used with greater frequency to share information in **digital format** between remote offices, courthouses, government agencies, and clients. Computer files are shared today more and more by the use of the Internet as well as in the form of CDs, DVDs, and as **attachments** to emails. In the past, paper had to be physically copied and sent, frequently by costly messenger service or express mail service. Today large files can be quickly, almost instantaneously, exchanged electronically, anywhere in the world, without any paper **(hardcopy).** Whereas formerly the physical safety of the delivery of paper documents was a concern, today the security and confidentiality of documents sent in electronic format are increasing concerns.

The legal team is increasingly using the Web and the Internet for more than just pure legal research. Access to most government information is obtained online through Internet websites. Finding businesses and individuals through private service providers, such as the yellow pages and white pages, is now handled most efficiently through Web search engines such as Google and Yahoo!. Though legal firms are increasingly developing and using websites for their own businesses as shown in Exhibit 4.2, only the best of these sites are created in a way that effectively helps to retain clients and attract new clients.

The implementation of new federal court rules on electronic discovery, the use of electronically stored documents in litigation, and emerging electronic discovery case law is creating increased demand for skills and knowledge in the use of technology in civil litigation. Increasingly the legal team must be able to interface with technology professionals in maximizing the efficiency of internal computer usage, and in obtaining and handling client and trial data electronically. Everyone on the legal team must now

Digital format A computerized format utilizing a series of 0's and 1's.

Attachment A popular method of transmitting text files and graphic images by attaching the file to an email.

Hardcopy Paper copies of documents.

Exhibit 4.2 A typical law firm website, the new yellow pages

Source: Reprinted with permission from Mellon, Webster, & Shelly Law Offices.

---

have a working familiarity with computers and the types of computer programs used in the law office. Not too many years ago, the average law office had a typewriter, an adding machine, and a duplicating machine of some type. Paper was king, with every document typed, edited, retyped—and frequently retyped again. In each instance, a paper copy was produced and delivered to the supervising attorney for review and additional changes. It then was returned for retyping and eventually sent to the client, to the opposing counsel, or filed with the court. File cabinets abounded in the law office, and the storage of paper files created back rooms, warehouses, and other storage locations filled with box after box of paper. The trend is toward eliminating paper in the law office through the use of computer technology and software.

Members of the legal team frequently find themselves working from locations outside the traditional office. In some cases, the legal team members are located in different offices of the firm or are from different firms located in different parts of the country or world. Each member of the team may need access to the case data or electronic files. One solution is to have all of the files stored electronically in an **electronic repository** on a secure, protected file server to which everyone authorized has access over the Internet.

Members of the team may use the Internet to work collaboratively using **online collaboration** software that allows each person to see the documents and, in some cases, each other, and make on-screen notes and comments. A number of companies provide services and software for converting case documents to electronic format and storing of the documents on a secure server. Collaboration software is provided for the individual members of the legal or litigation team. Exhibit 4.3 shows a typical, secure remote litigation network.

Electronic repository An off-site computer used to store records that may be accessed over secure Internet connections.

Online collaboration Using the internet to conduct meetings and share documents.

| **Exhibit 4.3** | **Secure remote access for the legal profession** |

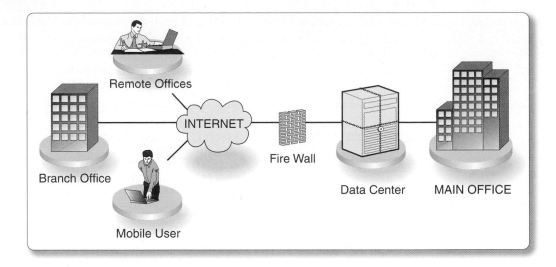

Technology Usage in the Law

The role of technology in the law has evolved in a very few years from a minor function, such as the stand-alone word processor, to a ubiquitous element in the management of law offices of all sizes. Computers are now being used for everything from word processing to computerized timekeeping, payroll productions, and tax return preparation. In some offices computerized telephone systems even use a computerized attendant to answer the phone without human intervention. The use of technology in litigation was once limited to large law firms working on large cases for wealthy clients who could pay the cost of the technology. Today even the smallest law firm and litigator must use technology. Some courts are demanding computerized filing. Records previously available in paper form, such as medical records in litigation cases, are now provided electronically. The result is that offices of all sizes need to have computer or technology support, in some cases with dedicated technologists or support of the computerized infrastructure and others dedicated to providing litigation support.

Outsourcing

Outsourcing has become a buzzword for shipping work out of the office or overseas to save money. Some of the services that can be performed in-house may, in fact, be better outsourced. For years, many law firms have outsourced the payroll function instead of preparing payroll checks and tax returns in-house. The confidentiality of information about salaries may dictate that an outside firm handle the payroll process so that only a few people in the office have access to the critical payroll information. In a similar vein, the accounting functions may be outsourced to an outside bookkeeping or accounting firm. Using an outside computer consultant to help with support for the hardware and software of the office is a form of outsourcing and may involve a help desk located in a foreign location to answer questions.

Outsourcing Use of persons or services outside of the immediate office staff.

How Much Do I Really Need To Know

No one can be an expert in everything. What is important is to know enough to know what you do not know and be able to find someone who does. The need is to understand the basic concepts and be able to communicate with those who are the experts. Having a basic understanding of the different programs used in the legal environment is a starting point. Know the functions of the programs used in daily support of the legal team, such as word processing, spreadsheet, database, and the like. Understand the differences in the software and computer tools used by the litigation specialist from those used by the in-house legal support team. Most important is the ability to communicate with the legal side and the technology side of a firm. Learn the language of the other, what some refer to as "geek talk." Keep current by reading the professional journals and legal papers for new tools and services being offered to make the job of legal and litigation teams more efficient. Attend the local, regional, and national technology shows for the legal industry to see the products and services and ask questions to learn enough to make the suggestions for updating and changing the tools of your profession.

Understanding the Language of Technology

An understanding of the terminology of technology is a prerequisite to understanding the technology found in the law office, the courthouse, and the clients' business. Law has developed its own lexicon of terms that enables those in the legal community to communicate effectively and with precision. The technology world also has developed its own lexicon. The legal team and the technology support team must learn one another's language to communicate their needs and solutions. Each group thinks it is communicating, but the same word sometimes has different meanings. For example, the word *protocol*. To the legal team, *protocol* is defined as "A summary of a document or treaty; or, a treaty amending another treaty, or the rules of diplomatic etiquette" (*Black's Law Dictionary*—West Group). To the technology specialist, *protocol* is defined as "A set of formal rules describing how to transmit data, especially across a network. Low level protocols define the electrical and physical standards to be observed, bit- and byte-ordering and the transmission and error detection and correction of the bit stream. High level protocols deal with the data formatting, including the syntax of messages, the terminal to computer dialogue, character sets, sequencing of messages etc." (Free On-Line Dictionary of Computing [http://foldoc.org/]).

Another example is the word *cell*. To the criminal lawyer, a cell is a place where clients are held in jail. To the computer support staff, it is a space on a spreadsheet where a piece of data is displayed. Lawyers, paralegals, and other members of the legal team, and the members of the technology support team must learn one another's language in order to effectively meet the needs of clients and work together productively.

Computer Hardware

Computer hardware is the term used to describe the tangible or physical parts of a computer system; a **computer system** includes at least one input device, a computer processor, and at least one output device. A system may be as small and portable as a digital watch or as large as a **mainframe** computer requiring a large room to house it.

Older models of computers, many of which are still found in many law offices, are large, ugly metal boxes connected to large, bulky, and heavy desktop monitors, sometimes taking up half of a desktop. Newer models are smaller and less obtrusive. In some offices the computer system consists of a portable laptop computer, weighing as little as three to four pounds, the size of a large book, used at the user's desk with a docking station to connect it to a flat-screen monitor, external keyboard and mouse, Internet connection, and network.

With the reduction in size have come increased speed and functionality. On older models, opening more than one document uses most of the computer system resources, slowing them down or even "freezing" or stopping the processing of data. The newer models typically run well while allowing the display of multiple documents from multiple applications all running at the same time—Word files, Excel spreadsheets, calendaring programs, and timekeeping applications. Exhibit 4.4 shows a monitor display of four programs running at the same time.

Computer hardware Hardware is the term that encompasses all of the tangible or physical items including computers, monitors, printers, fax machines, duplicators, and similar items that usually have either an electrical connection or use batteries as a power source.

Computer system A combination of an input device, a processor, and an output device.

Mainframe A large computer system used primarily for bulk processing of data and financial information.

Exhibit 4.4 — 4-page display in Microsoft Office suite

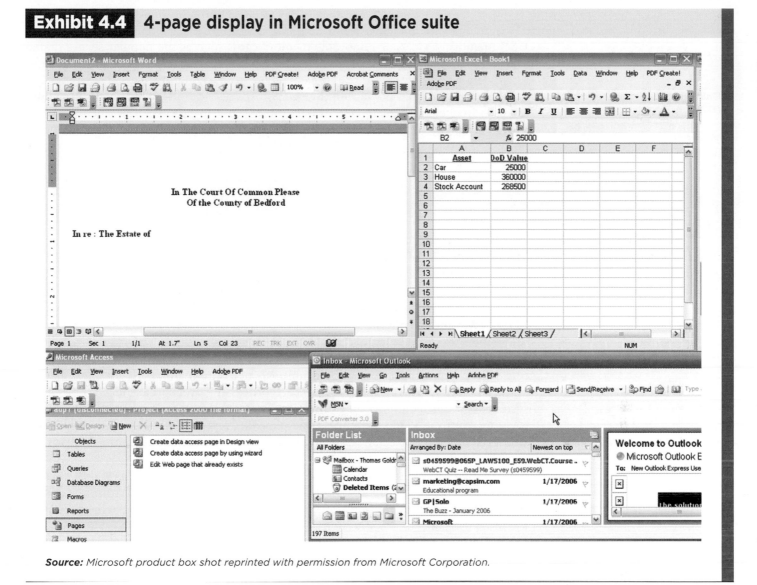

Source: Microsoft product box shot reprinted with permission from Microsoft Corporation.

The ability to perform multiple functions simultaneously is in part the result of the increase in processing speed permitted by newer **central processing units (CPUs)**, also called processors, and the availability of inexpensive dynamic or volatile computer memory, **random access memory (RAM)**. A CPU is the computer "chip" that interprets computer instructions and processes data, and RAM is the temporary computer memory that stores work in progress.

Hardware of all sizes requires software instructions to run and perform desired functions. **Operating system** software provides the basic instructions for starting up the computer and processing the basic input and output activity. The processing of data requires additional applications software such as that used for word processing and financial data processing.

All computer components must have a power source (electrical outlet or battery) to operate, including the basic CPU, the dynamic memory modules used for temporary storage of data (RAM), and output devices like the computer monitor and printer. Just as an automobile depends on fuel to continue to operate, so is the computer dependent on a power source to operate. Computers cannot remember data or information that appears on the computer screen (work in process) after the power is turned off—unless it has been saved to a permanent memory device. The transfer of the information in the

Central processing unit (CPU) The computer chip and memory module that perform the basic computer functions.

Random access memory (RAM) Temporary computer memory that stores work in processs.

Operating system The operating system is a basic set of instructions to the computer on how to handle basic functions—how to process input from "input devices" such as the keyboard and mouse, the order in which to process information, and what to show on the computer monitor.

form of electrical signals also requires power to write the information on devices such as magnetic tape, floppy disks, or hard disk drives, or to portable memory devices like USB memory devices, or removable memory cards such as the popular secure digital (SD) cards, CDs, or DVDs. These permanent memory devices do not require power to retain data—only to write or read the data to or from a computer.

Uninterruptible power supply (UPS) A battery system that can supply power to a computer or computer peripheral for a short period of time.

Uninterruptible power supply (UPS) battery backup systems for the computer are used frequently to guard against loss of the "work-in-process" files when there is a short-term power loss or long-term outage. A UPS is a battery system that can supply power to a computer or computer peripheral for a short period of time. The length of time the computer will continue to work after loss of its permanent power supply depends on the size of the battery in the UPS, and may be as short as a few minutes or as long as an hour or more. The UPS is designed to allow time to save the current work-in-process files and shut down the computer normally in the event of a major power outage.

Operating Systems

The two most popular computer systems are the PC, or personal computer, and the Apple. The original designs of these two systems were built around different central processor system chips manufactured by different companies—Intel in the case of the PC, and Motorola in the case of Apple. Each computer system requires its own unique operating system.

Software Refers to programs containing sets of instructions that tell the computer and the other computer-based electronic devices what to do and how to do it.

Although both computer systems have advocates, the PC has a dominant position in the legal and business communities where the main use is text and mathematical computations in the form of word processing and spreadsheets. The Apple system achieved the dominant position in the graphic and artistic communities, and to some extent among computer game players. New models of both systems have **software** that permits the other computer system software to run on the competitive machine.

In 2006, Apple started to utilize the same CPU manufacturer as the PC manufacturers use, allowing the new Apple computers to use software for both systems on its computers without any additional software to interpret the software instruction of the other system.

Microsoft Windows™ is the most commonly used computer operating system for the personal computer. A number of different versions of the Windows operating system are found in the workplace with the latest versions, such as Windows XP, Vista, and Windows 7, designed to take advantage of increased computer operating speeds and to better display screen graphics. The original PC operating systems did not provide for the **graphic user interface (GUI)**, which everyone has now come to expect. Exhibit 4.5 shows a command line interface and a graphic user interface.

Graphic user interface (GUI) A set of screen presentations and metaphors that utilize graphic elements such as icons in an attempt to make an operating system easier to operate.

Among the newer computer systems gaining followers is the Linux opperative system. It is offered as an alternative to Microsoft operating systems and provided without a license or royalty fee with the agreement that any improvements will be made available without a fee to anyone using the system.

Applications Software

Applications software Applications programs are software that perform generic tasks such as word processing.

Applications software programs are those that perform specific tasks, such as prepare documents, sort information, perform computations, and create and present graphic displays. These are the software programs used in the management of the law office and the management of client cases.

Word Processing

Written communication and document preparation are at the heart of every law office. It may be preparation of letters to clients, other counsel or the court, or contracts and agreements, or pleadings. To achieve written clarity and accuracy frequently

Exhibit 4.5 A Windows screen showing the command line within a GUI interface

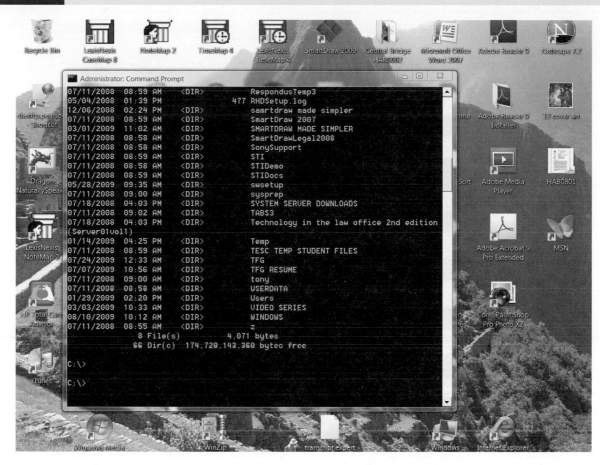

Source: *Microsoft product box shot reprinted with permission from Microsoft Corporation.*

means writing, rewriting, and correcting the same document, sometimes multiple times and by a number of different members of the legal team. The ability to easily make even minor changes in language has a direct impact on the willingness of those reviewing the document to suggest changes and make them in the final document. Computerized word processing makes this possible. Word processing files are sent electronically to the appropriate members of the legal team for review. Changes or revisions are frequently made to the electronic file copy by the reviewer. Where multiple parties may be working on a document, changes made to the original document by each person on the legal team may be monitored by using built-in features such as MS Word's **"Track Changes"** tool. This feature shows the original text, the deleted text, and the new text by a series of lines that show as a strike through the deleted text and by margin notes on the document. When the final document is completed it may be sent by email, fax (frequently directly from the computer without any intermediate paper), and in some jurisdictions filed electronically with the court. Exhibit 4.6 shows the original word file, the changes inserted and old text with a strike through it, and the final version with the changes still showing in the margin of the document.

Today the most commonly used software program in the law office is the word processor. Although many different word processing programs are available, the legal community most commonly uses either WordPerfect™ or Microsoft Word™. In addition to the usual typing functions, these programs have built-in software tools that check spelling and grammar and allow customized formatting using a variety of

Track Changes Track Changes, as found in MS Word, shows the original text, the deleted text, and the new text as well as a strike through for deleted text, underlining or highlighting of new text, as well as margin notes on the document.

Exhibit 4.6 Microsoft Word track changes

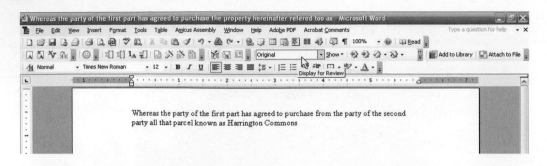

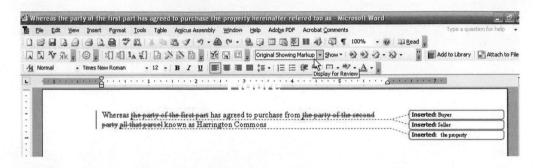

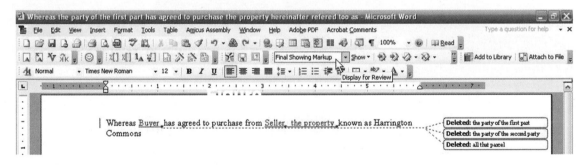

Source: Microsoft product box shot reprinted with permission from Microsoft Corporation.

ETHICAL PERSPECTIVE

Document Comparison Software

When using Track Changes or similar comparison programs, be sure to remove the history of the changes and other information from the document before sending it to the opposing counsel, the client, or the court. The history of changes and other document information is called *metadata*.

The history of the changes may offer the reader insight into the strategy of the case—for example, showing the final price the client is willing to pay, which appeared in the original draft and not the first offer that appeared in the final version sent to the opposing party. Word Help offers instructions on how to remove this information. WordPerfect X4 allows documents to be saved without the metadata, using a file save option—**Save without Metadata**—making it easy to quickly remove private or sensitive data that can be hidden in, but easily extracted from, office productivity documents.

type sizes and font styles in the same document—functions that have not been possible with a typewriter. Some offices even use different programs, each with its own file format.

Most word processing programs allow the opening and saving of files in the file formats of other word processing programs. When a file is saved, a **file extension** (a period followed by characters) is added to the end of the filename that identifies the program or format in which the file has been saved.

For example:

the file name NAME	the extension EXT
Microsoft Word 2003	filename.doc
Microsoft Word 2007	filename.docx
WordPerfect	filename.wpd
Microsoft Works	filename.wps
Web documents	filename.htm
Generic (rich text file) word processing format	filename.rtf
Generic (text file) word processing format	filename.txt

The newer versions of WordPerfect even permit simulation of the Microsoft Word workspace. Word processor files are saved with the document properties such as type font and type size, and document formatting details. The saved files also include instructions to the computer on how to display the document, security features, and hidden information such as the "Track Changes information."

Spreadsheet Programs

Many areas of legal practice involve the calculation and presentation of financial information. For example, in family law practice, the preparation of family and personal balance sheets and income and expense reports are routinely prepared for support and equitable distribution hearings; estate lawyers must submit an "accounting" to the court for approval, showing details of how the fiduciary handled the financial affairs of the estate or trust; and litigation firms must prepare documentation showing the receipts and disbursements of cases, sometime for court approval.

As shown in Exhibit 4.7, in an estate, the calculation involved may be as simple as multiplying the number of shares owned by a decedent by the value on the date of death (D of D), then calculating the profit or loss when the stock was sold. Without a computerized spreadsheet, all of the calculations would have to be done manually,

File extension When a file is saved, a file extension (a period followed by three characters) is added to the end of the filename to identify the program or format in which the file has been saved.

Spreadsheet programs Programs that permit the calculation and presentation of financial information in a grid format of rows and columns.

Exhibit 4.7   **Excel spreadsheet**

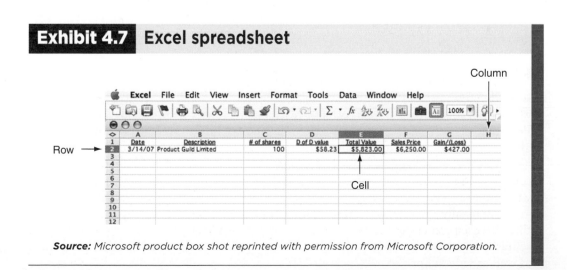

Source: *Microsoft product box shot reprinted with permission from Microsoft Corporation.*

using a multicolumn form known as a spreadsheet or accountant's working papers. The information then has to be typed in a report format for submission to the court, the beneficiaries, or the taxing authorities.

Using a computerized spreadsheet such as Microsoft Excel or Corel Quattro Pro, the numbers are entered in cells, as identified in Exhibit 4.7, and a formula assigned to the cell in which the result is to be displayed, such as "multiply column c by column d," and the result displayed in column e. The computerized spreadsheet, when laid out in the format acceptable to the court, can be printed without reentering the data, or copied into word documents using a simple "Cut and Paste" operation.

The use of computer spreadsheets reduces the errors associated with manual mathematical calculations and errors in retyping the information. Caution must be taken to make sure that the formula is accurate and performs the desired calculation. Even expert spreadsheet users use a set of sample numbers to test the formulas, knowing what the result should be, based on prior use or calculations.

Many offices save spreadsheet templates in the same way that sample forms are saved in word processing. For example, a real estate settlement spreadsheet with formulas and headings may be saved without numbers. Because the formulas do not change and the form has proven accurate, it may be used as a template for other clients' real estate settlements.

Database Programs

Database program A database program is an electronic repository of information of all types that can be sorted and presented in a meaningful manner.

A **database program** is a repository of information of all types that can be sorted and presented in a desired meaningful manner. Some offices use a manual card system to keep track of the names of clients and opposing parties, these cards are searched to determine possible conflicts of interest in representing new clients. For the small office this system works. But for the larger office with multiple attorneys and possibly multiple offices, timely entry and searching of large amounts of information is not realistic. Computerized database software, such as Microsoft Access and Corel DB, will facilitate timely, accurate access to information by every authorized member of the legal team. For example, information may be stored on the law firm's server in an information database that includes the names, addresses, contact information, personal data such as birthdates of every client, every opposing party, every fact witness and expert witness, and every opposing counsel with whom any member of the firm has ever had contact in litigation, contract negotiations, or counseling session, or met in any business or legal setting. With a few keystrokes, a list can be prepared for manually checking for conflicts of interest, or a computer search can be performed with a printout of any matter or litigation where a name appears.

In addition to the obvious use in avoiding accepting a client with a potential conflict of interest, the information frequently is used in maintaining client relations. Many firms use the information to send birthday and anniversary greetings and updates on specific changes in the law for which the client has consulted the firm previously.

Presentation Graphics Programs

It has been said that a picture is worth a thousand words. Presentation graphics software programs, such as WordPerfect Presentation X4 (see Exhibit 4.8) and Microsoft PowerPoint, are being used to create high-quality slide shows and drawings. These graphic presentations can include text, data charts, and graphic objects.

One of the advantages of these programs is their flexibility. They can be used to prepare and present the graphic presentation electronically, using a computer, with or without a projector, and to print out paper copies for distribution. Presentation programs typically provide stock templates of graphics, artwork, and layout as a sample that the user can easily modify. More advanced users can add sound clips to the presentation, include still photos, and incorporate custom graphics from other programs, as well as video clips.

| **Exhibit 4.8** | **WordPerfect presentation X4** |

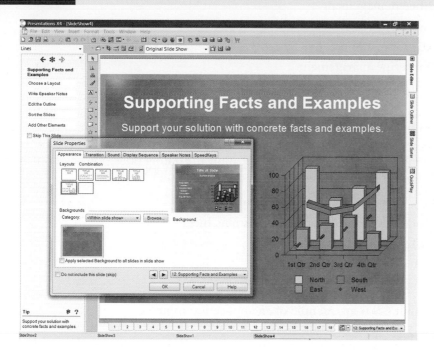

Source: WordPerfect screen shot reprinted with permission of Corel. All rights reserved.

Office Software Suites

Office software suites are sets of commonly used office software programs that manage data and database programs; manipulate financial or numeric information, spreadsheet programs; or display images and presentation graphics programs. Some of the tools in the two most common program suites, Microsoft Office and Corel WordPerfect, are:

	Microsoft Office	**Corel WordPerfect Office X4**
Word processor	Word	WordPerfect
Spreadsheet	Excel	Quattro Pro X4
Database	Access	Paradox
Presentation graphics	PowerPoint	Presentation X4
Graphics	Visio	Presentation Graphics X4

The software suites usually are delivered on one CD, enabling all the programs to be loaded at one time, which simplifies and saves installation time. With common features and appearance, it is easier to switch between programs and copy information between the programs, like copying part of a spreadsheet into a word processing document.

Specialty Application Programs

Every year, computers become more powerful, operating faster with more operating and storage memory. Software programs are getting more powerful and capable of performing more complex functions on more data. Whereas older models of computers can perform only basic word processing and data management, newer, more powerful computers can perform complex functions seamlessly, thereby permitting management of law office functions and management of cases and litigation.

Specialty application programs combine many of the basic functions found in software suites, word processing, database management, spreadsheets, and graphic presentations to perform law office case and litigation management. They simplify the operation with the use of customized input screens and preset report generators.

Office software suites This software consists of commonly used office software programs that manage data and database programs; manipulate financial or numeric information, spreadsheet programs; or display images and presentation graphics programs.

Specialty applicaton programs Specialty programs combine many of the basic functions found in software suites, word processing, database management, spreadsheets, and graphic presentations to perform law office, case, and litigation management.

Web Exploration

For a self-running video demo of Tabs 3, go to http://www.tabs3.com/products/video.html.

Web Exploration

Information on the features of Abacuslaw may be found at http://www.abacuslaw.com.

Web Exploration

Details and additional sample screen graphics about PCLaw are available at http://www.pclaw.com/.

Case and litigation management software Case and litigation management programs are used to manage documents and the facts and issues of cases.

Legal specialty software programs fall generally into the following categories:

Office management

Case management

Litigation support

Transcript management

Trial presentation

Of the office management specialty application programs, the most basic are the time and billing programs. These provide a standard input screen to record the time spent on a client's case, store the information and, with a request for an invoice for a given client, automatically sort the data, apply the billing rates, and print out an invoice.

Among the popular programs in this group are:

Tabs 3 from Software Technology, Inc.

Abacuslaw from Abacus Data Systems Inc.

ProLaw from Thomson Elite

PCLaw from LexisNexis

Timeslips from Sage

Exhibit 4.9 is an example of an application input screen.

Early versions of time reporting software are limited to timekeeping. With faster computers and greater memory capacity, most of these programs have other features integrated into them, such as accounting functions to track costs and expenses, and practice management functions such as calendar and contact management.

Exhibit 4.10 shows the multiple functions integrated in Abacuslaw Accounting.

Case and Litigation Management Software

Paper has long been the bane of the litigation attorney. Even simple cases can involve hundreds of pages of documents. Complex litigation may involve millions of documents and hundreds of witnesses and, in the case of class-action litigation, potentially millions of clients. Keeping track of all of the documentation and parties is an overwhelming task even with a large staff of assistants and endless rows of organized file cabinets and file boxes.

Before the availability of fast computers with inexpensive memory-running case and litigation management software, most case management work was done manually, usually by a team of paralegals and junior associate attorneys. In two of the most notable cases—the IBM antitrust suit and the Ford Pinto negligence suit—teams of law students were hired, some for multiyear positions, to read through and identify the documents, manually index them, and look for a document that would make the case, sometimes referred to as the "smoking gun" document. In the Ford Pinto case, in a serendipitous discovery just such a smoking gun document was found, which detailed the engineering cost savings and the inherent risk by eliminating a specific part that led to the fire that engulfed the Pinto when it was struck by another car from the rear.

The use of computers for email and document storage by business and government has caused a massive increase in the number of potential documents that may have to be reviewed, tracked, and made available to opposing counsel in a case. Managing cases and litigation with the massive amount of data has become increasingly difficult. As the number of documents has increased and cases have become more complex, the number of members of the legal team working on a given case also has increased. These factors have led to greater use of the computer to manage the case files and the litigation process.

In pre-computer days, attorneys frequently concentrated on one case, personally working on all of the documentation, pleadings, and discovery, and learning every detail of the case in anticipation of trying the case with little backup support except in the largest cases in the larger firms. The legal-team approach to case management and

Exhibit 4.9   Tabs3 time and billing screens

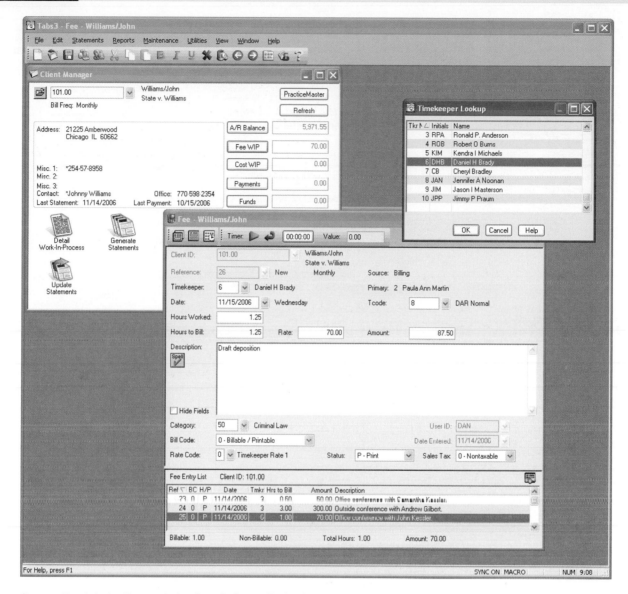

Source: *Reprinted with permission from Software Technology, Inc.*

litigation has allowed, in some ways, for specialization within the legal team. Some members of the litigation team may specialize in discovery of documents. Others may be concerned with locating, interviewing, and preparing witnesses. Still others concentrate on investigative matters and legal research.

Effective case management, therefore, requires some central repository of the information gathered by each of the team members, as well as the ability of each to access the case information input by others. Computer systems today even permit members of the legal team to access the same information from remote locations across town, across the country, and sometimes around the world.

A typical case file contains documentation of the:

Interview of the client

Interviews of fact and expert witnesses

Investigation reports

Expert reports

Exhibit 4.10 Abacus Accounting input screens

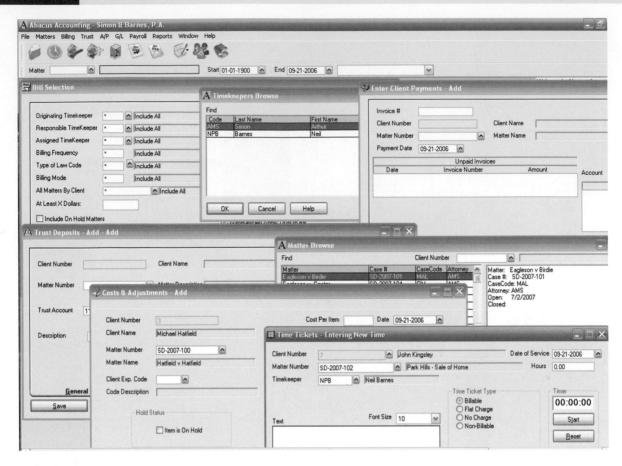

Source: *Reprinted with permission from Abacus Data Systems.*

Research memoranda

Pleadings

Trial preparation material

The trial team frequently has to quickly find a document or information on a specific issue from among potentially thousands of pages of documents. With a computer and the proper specialty software program, this is possible. Some of the litigation and case management specialty software programs found in the law office are discussed below.

CaseMap

CaseMap™ from LexisNexis® CaseSoft is a case management and analysis software tool that acts as a central repository for critical case knowledge. As facts are gathered, parties identified, and documents and research assembled, they may be entered into the program, allowing for easy organization and exploration of the facts, the cast of characters, and the issues by any member of the legal team.

Typical of integrated software applications, CaseMap allows seamless transfer of data to other programs such as TimeMap™, a timeline graphic program, and word processor programs. It also allows for creating specialty reports and documents including trial notebook information. Exhibit 4.11 shows the flow of information in a typical case, using CaseMap as a case management tool.

Web Exploration

Demonstration versions of CaseSoft products and Webinar tutorials on their use can be found at http://www.casesoft.com/student.asp.

Exhibit 4.11 Managing case information using CaseMap case management and analysis software

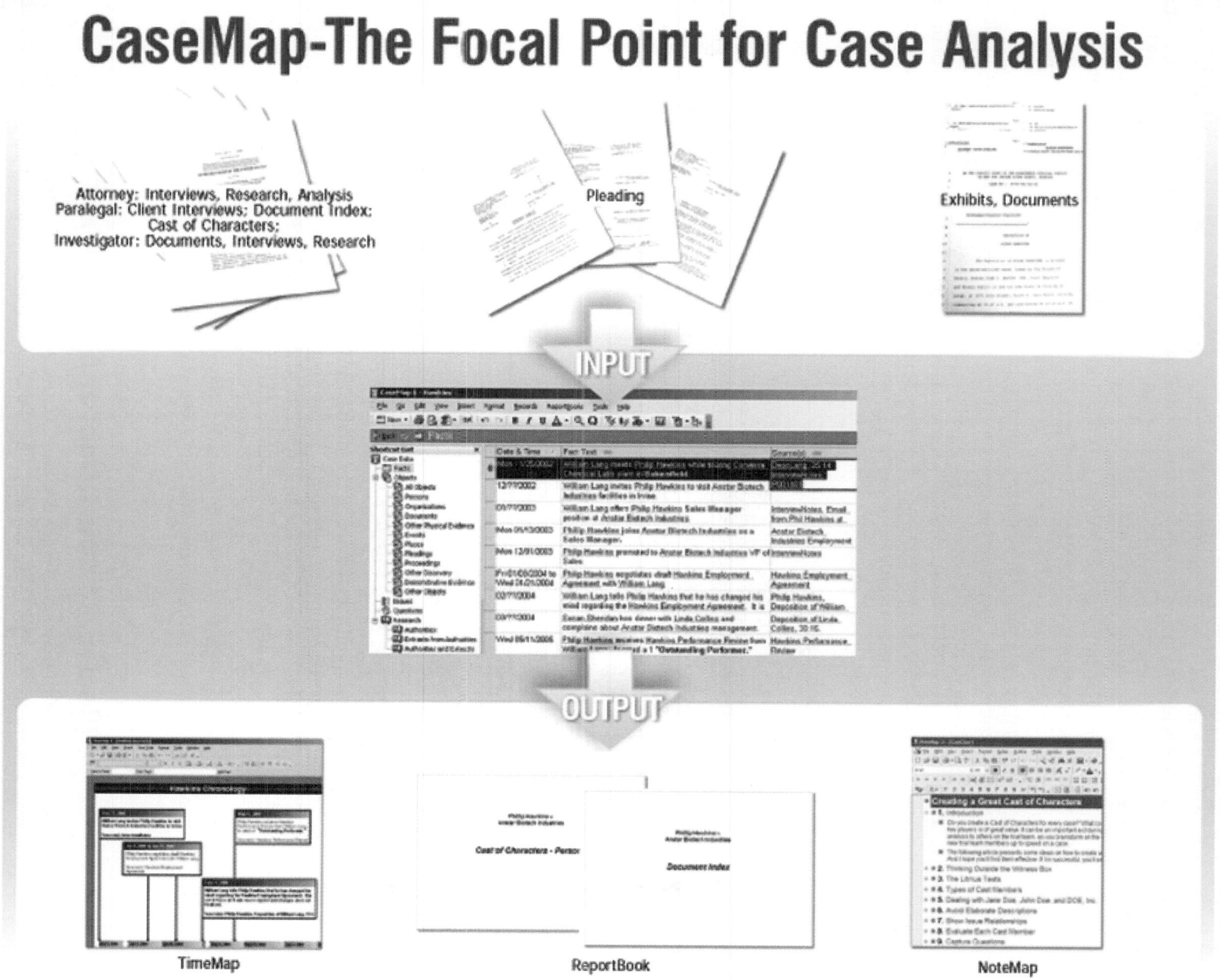
CaseMap-The Focal Point for Case Analysis
Attorney: Interviews, Research, Analysis
Paralegal: Client Interviews; Document Index; Cast of Characters;
Investigator: Documents, Interviews, Research
Pleading
Exhibits, Documents
INPUT
OUTPUT
TimeMap
ReportBook
NoteMap

Source: Reprinted with permission of LexisNexus. All rights reserved.

Summation

The Summation family of products, from CT Summation, Inc. (a Wolters Kluwer business) and similar software applications programs are classified as litigation support systems. As the number of documents increases in a case, the ability to locate relevant documents in a timely fashion becomes more and more critical. Managing the documents is critical to successful litigation outcomes. In cases involving potentially millions of documents, it is essential to be able to find the relevant information quickly, sometimes in the middle of the direct or cross-examination of a witness.

Summation-type programs allow for easy search and retrieval of all of the evidence, whether documents, testimony, photographs, or electronic files, with a single command. Documents associated with a case are stored on the computer in electronic folders. These folders may be set up to include transcripts, pleadings, text files (from OCR or otherwise), casts of characters, and core databases. Some versions of these programs are designed to work on stand-alone systems such as a laptop carried into court. Others permit concurrent use by many users over a network, and some permit remote access over the Internet.

Concordance

LexisNexis Concordance is a litigation support system program that provides document management. Early versions of Concordance were limited to storing and handling 4 gigabytes of data, or approximately 280,000 documents. The newer version allows the management of 128 times that amount, or more than 35 million documents. Like other document support tools, Concordance has a powerful search engine that allows searches by word, phrase, date, email address, or document type, as well as Boolean, using the fuzzy and wildcard searches.

A Boolean search uses connectors between words such as AND, OR, or NOT to narrow the search. A fuzzy or fuzzy string search is the name for a search that looks for strings or letters or characters that approximately match some given pattern. A wildcard search allows the use of a "wild" character such as the symbol * to replace a letter in the search word that allows you to search for plurals or variations of words using a wildcard character. It also is a good way to search if you do not know the spelling of a word. For example: Book* finds Booking and Books.

Sanction II by Verdict Systems and TrialDirector by inData

These multifaceted trial presentation programs offer a comprehensive approach to presenting all types of exhibits in the courtroom, including documents, photographs, graphic images, video presentations, and recorded depositions.

Unlike PowerPoint, which requires the creation of individual slides, these programs allow existing documents and files to be presented without any more effort than copying them into the program data file and making a selection for presentation. Trial presentation programs, like Sanction, are databases of the documents in either a case file or on a computer.

Electronic Courtroom and Paperless Office

Computer technology is changing the way that law offices and court systems perform traditional functions. The ease of creating documents, including traditional letters and contracts and electronic communications in the form of emails, has resulted in a document explosion. At the same time, cases are coming to trial faster because of the demand for "quicker justice," which allows less time to prepare and present a case in court. The result has been growth in the use of electronic documentation and computerized case management and the use of computers in litigation.

Web Exploration

View an online demo of Summation®LG at http://info.summation.com/demo/modules.htm.

Web Exploration

Learn more about Concordance at http://www.dataflight.com.

Web Exploration

An interactive demo of TrialDirector showing how trial presentation software can be used in litigation at http://www.indatacorp.com/flash/tdstutorial.swf.

The Electronic Courtroom

Increasingly, judges are embracing the use of electronics and computer-based systems in the courts. The initial reluctance to allow the "newfangled" technology is giving way to acceptance of tools that enhance the speedy administration of justice. One of the earliest uses of technology in the courtroom was the playing of videotaped depositions of expert witnesses on TV monitors in court.

To get experts to testify is difficult when the schedule for their testimony is uncertain because of uncertain trial schedules. Many experts, such as noted surgeons and medical forensics experts, have active lucrative practices and demand compensation that can range in the thousands of dollars per hour for time lost waiting to testify. The average litigant can rarely afford this litigation cost. A videotape, or electronic recording, of a deposition can be used in trial as a cost-effective method of presenting expert witnesses or for witnesses who for reasons of health or distance, could not otherwise be available to testify personally at a trial.

As judicial budgets allow, courtrooms are being outfitted with computers and audiovisual presentation systems. Exhibit 4.12 shows the U.S. Tax Court's electronic courtroom in Virginia. Computerized courtrooms can be seen frequently on Court TV televised trials, in which computer terminals are present at each lawyer's table, the judge's bench, for each of the court support personnel, and monitors for the jury.

Litigation support software is used in trial to display documentary evidence, graphic presentations, and simulations of accident cases. Relevant portions of documents can be displayed for everyone to see at the same time without passing paper copies to everyone, as the witness testifies and identifies the document. Lawyers can rapidly search depositions and documents, sometimes in the tens of thousands of pages, on their laptop computer to find pertinent material for examination or cross-examination of the witness.

The electronic courtroom also is used in many jurisdictions in criminal cases for preliminary matters in which the judge is located at a central location, and the defendants at various lock-up facilities with video cameras and monitors recording and displaying the parties to each other.

Exhibit 4.12 **U.S. Tax Court's electronic courtroom**

The Paperless Office

To some people, the ideal office is one that has no paper documents, or hardcopy, as they are sometimes referred to. The office where documents are created and stored electronically is sometimes referred to as the **"paperless office,"** or "electronic office." Difficult as it may seem for some who have grown up in the paper world, the paperless office is rapidly approaching reality. In the traditional office, documents are created electronically with word processing software, or received by fax or email and then printed. In the paperless office, documents are created using computer-based word processor programs such as Microsoft Word or Corel WordPerfect. These electronic files then are sent electronically to the attorney for review.

The reviewer frequently makes changes or revisions to the electronic file copy and when multiple parties are working on a document; changes made to the original document by each person on the legal team may be monitored by using built-in features such as Track Changes in MS Word. This feature shows the original text, the deleted text, and the new text by a strike through the deleted text, underlining of new text, and by margin notes on the document. When the final document is completed, it may be sent by email, fax (frequently directly from the computer without any intermediate paper) and, in some jurisdictions, filed electronically with the court.

Electronic portability requires inexpensive portable computer memory, a computer to store and transport the documents, and small, lightweight computers to display them. Conversion of existing paper documents requires the availability of scanners and software that converts the documents to an acceptable format that cannot be easily changed.

The paperless law office indeed is becoming the norm with the advent of modern scanning technology, secured methods for transmission of documents, accepted protocols for use of electronic replacements for paper documents, and rules of court permitting electronic submission of documents.

Portable Document Format (PDF)

The ability to save documents in a format that cannot be easily changed through use of the computer is one of the basic requirements of a system that allows for electronic documentation. Anyone who has received a word processing document file knows that they may change it, save it, and present it as an original. Now, documents may be saved in a graphic image format or portable document format (PDF), developed by Adobe Systems. The recipient cannot easily or readily change these graphic images.

Although creating documents in PDF format requires specialty software such as Adobe Acrobat, everyone can download a free Adobe Reader to view these documents. With the acceptance of this format has come a willingness to scan and store documents electronically in this format, eliminating or returning to the client the original paper copies. Companies such as Adobe Systems frequently provide free, limited versions of their programs, downloadable from their website, that allow the opening and reading of files created using their proprietary software formats, such as Adobe's PDF file format.

Many websites that provide programs using these proprietary formats, such as the Internal Revenue Service forms website, contain links to these programs. They are limited in that they allow the user to open and read the files but do not allow changes or the creation of new document files, which requires the full version of the program.

Scanning

Scanning and storing of paper documents has become easier with the development of software such as PaperPort by Nuance. This software provides easy-to-use, high-speed scanning and document capture. As a document management software application, it allows for organizing, finding, and sharing paper and digital documents, which permits the elimination of paper documents.

The original scanning hardware was costly and frequently unreliable. Modern scanners provide double-sided (front and back) scanning of documents with a high degree of accuracy at a relatively low cost. Scanning today has become a common feature in office printers and copy machines. Double-sided scanning is found today in multi-function devices featuring printing, scanning, copying, and faxing, at prices under $100. These devices, when coupled with application software such as PaperPort, allow virtually anyone to create electronic documents.

OCR

Obviously, at times, documents have to be converted from a graphic image to a format that allows for editing or other use in an office suite of applications. These software applications have come to be referred to as OCR, or optical character recognition. Products such as OmniPage, by Nuance, provide document-conversion solutions by permitting any scanned page, PDF file, or other image or document file to be converted quickly and accurately into one of a number of different editable formats including Microsoft Word or Corel WordPerfect.

Networks

The first computers in law offices, as we said, generally consisted of a computer, a monitor, and a printer. In the contemporary law office this is called a **workstation**. A **computer network** is a group of workstations connected together. This may be as little as two workstations, or in large law firms, hundreds of workstations and other peripheral devices such as shared printers and fax machines all connected through a network file server. Exhibit 4.13 is a typical computer network system in a law office.

A **network file server** is generally a separate computer that acts as the traffic cop of the system, controlling the flow of information between workstations and the file server and other peripheral devices and requests to use the resources of the system or access data stored on the system.

Like the computer that requires an operating system to run, the server requires network operating software that tells it how to communicate with the connected workstations and peripheral devices. These computers and devices are referred to as "connections."

Workstation A computer connected to a network that is used for access consisting of a monitor, input device, and computer.

Computer network A set of workstations connected together.

Network file server A separate computer in a network that acts as the traffic cop of the system controlling the flow of data.

Exhibit 4.13	Typical network system

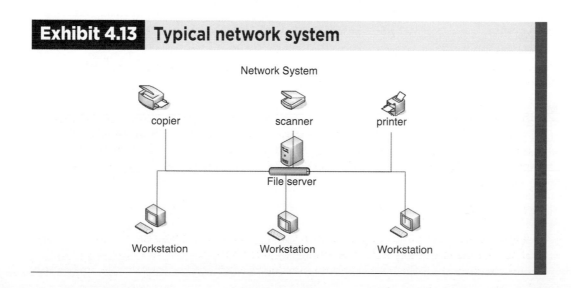

Network Rights and Privileges

Network software programs have security protocols that limit access to the file server, peripherals such as printers, or other workstations. These rights to access the server and the other devices are sometimes called "**network rights and privileges.**" The rights or privileges determine who has access to the server, the data stored on the server, and the flow of information between connections.

Network Administrator

Generally the person with the highest level access is called the **network administrator.** Law offices that use network servers generally use these servers as the central repository for all electronic files. Although an individual workstation can store documents or data on the workstation, it is usually stored centrally. This offers a level of protection by limiting access to those who have the proper authorization, most often requiring a password for access. It also makes backing up data easier.

The ability to limit access to files on a file server is one method to ensure confidentiality in a large office. File access can be limited by password-protecting files and granting password access only to those with a need to access and work on those specific files. Because each file or set of files, called folders, can be password-protected separately, ethical walls can be established by restricting access to just those on the legal team who are working on a case.

Advice *from the* Field

TECHNOLOGY IS A TOOL, NOT A CASE STRATEGY IN THE COURTROOM
Michael E. Cobo

The latest legal technology products such as animations and courtroom presentation systems can be very alluring to lawyers. After learning about these products, you may be anxious to use them. But you should keep in mind that technology products are only tools to implement a solution and are not solutions in themselves. The key issue is: What is your case strategy and what do you need to present?

An expensive, ill-planned use of technology may result in losses at trial. These losses, or even an uncomfortable implementation of a technology product, may ultimately cause some to feel the experiment was unsuccessful and abandon future use of courtroom technology.

On the other hand, such potentially devastating results can be avoided by carefully planning a case strategy with the same care as you would plan a general trial strategy. The pitfalls will be avoided and you will present a more effective case to the trier of fact.

The trial team must remember that it is the message, not the medium, that wins at trial. Take this opportunity to vary the presentation media and develop some exhibit boards or utilize an overhead. Certain exhibits are displayed best as foamcore boards. Timelines or chronologies generally lend themselves to a board, as do other exhibits that need to be larger and hold more visual or textual information. Strategically, some exhibits need to be used in conjunction with others or need to be in the view of the jury more often than not.

ASSESS YOURSELF

Before you spend a dime to develop the visual strategy, create a presentation or invest in any technology, make a critical self-assessment. Will you be comfortable with the strategy and the technological tools that will be developed for the trial? The most effective visual communication strategy will never be effective if it is never implemented or is delivered without conviction because you are not comfortable using the tools.

The effective use of technology involves (1) creating an inventory of the visual requirements, (2) selecting the proper technologies, medium and tools, and (3) being prepared to properly use the products to implement your case strategy.

Backing Up Data

With everything on one file server, the **backup of data** can be automated to make copies of everyone's files and not just the files on workstations of those who remember to back up their computer. Backing up data regularly is an essential function to prevent loss of critical files and office data in the event of a disaster such as a flood, fire, earthquake, or tornado.

   Good backup policy is to back up the file server daily and store the duplicate copy in a safe location away from the server location, such as a fireproof safe or a bank safe deposit box. Imagine trying to reconstruct files, court-filed documents, and other essential information after a devastating hurricane and resultant flood that destroys a law firm's and courthouse paper records, as occurred in New Orleans in 2005 as a result of Hurricane Katrina!

Backup of data Making a copy of critical files and programs in case of a loss of the original computer files.

Wide Area and Wireless Networks

Time can be saved by electronically sharing information instead of by personal delivery or by having a courier deliver paper copies of documents, whether on a different floor, building, or city. Many firms—some as small as two people—maintain multiple office sites, such as a center-city and a suburban office location, or a main office and a satellite office across from the courthouse. Each of these offices may have a separate computer network.

   With high-speed communications lines, these separate networks may be connected to form a "network of networks." Access to a workstation on one of the networks allows access to the other networks in the system and the peripherals attached to the network, including network printers. This allows a person in one office to print documents on a printer in another office. Files may be shared among all the members of the legal team regardless of the office in which they are physically located.

Wide area network A wide area network is a network of networks. Each network is treated as if it were a connection on the network.

Wireless network A wireless network uses wireless technology instead of wires for connecting to the network.

The Internet

In its most basic form, the **Internet** or the World Wide Web may be thought of as nothing more than a group of computers linked together with the added ability to search all the connections for information. If you work in an office in which all of the computers are networked together, you have a small version of the Internet. Each person's computer is connected to other people's computers, generally with a main computer on which resides the frequently shared data files and the software (network operating system) that controls the connections and how the requests from each computer are handled and directed. This main control computer usually is referred to as the file server (see Exhibit 4.14).

Internet The Internet or the World Wide Web is a group of computers linked together with the added ability to search all the connections for information.

Exhibit 4.14   Network system

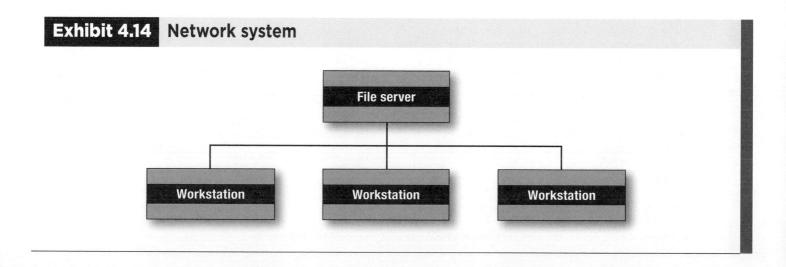

Local area network (LAN)
A network of computers at one location.

Internet service provider (ISP) The company providing the connection between the user and the Internet.

Modem A device to translate electrical signals to allow computers to communicate with each other.

The **local area, or office, network (LAN)** search tool is usually a program such as Microsoft Windows Explorer—not to be confused with the Internet browser Internet Explorer—which permits files to be found on the local computer or the other computers with shared access, by location or other characteristics. Exhibit 4.15 shows the Explorer screen, and Exhibit 4.16 shows search companion. **Internet service providers (ISPs)** provide local or toll-free access numbers that most people use to connect to their service. Larger offices and companies may have a direct connection (hardwired, or by dedicated telephone line) that eliminates the need to dial up the ISP. A device called a **modem** is used to translate the electrical signals for transmission over these connections so the computers can "talk" to each other. The modem converts (modulates) the information from the keyboard and computer into a form that can be transferred electronically over telephone lines, cable connections, and radio waves.

At the receiving end of the signal is another modem that reconverts (demodulates) the signal into a form usable by the computer. Depending on the modem and the ISP service, speeds of transmission vary widely. The slower the connection provided by the modem and the service, the longer it takes to transmit and receive information. As with most services, the higher the speed, the higher is the cost. It is easy to see that a multipage document will take longer to transmit or receive than a single-page document. The reasonableness of the cost of a high-speed connection depends upon the volume of pages regularly sent or received.

Perhaps less obvious is the size of the files and those that are in graphic format. Most government forms are available in a graphic form rather than a text form. A single one-page form in graphic format may be the equivalent of a 10-page text document. Again depending upon the frequency of downloads of forms, it might be advisable to upgrade to a high-speed line.

Online Computer Resources

The number of online or Internet resources increases daily. Finding the desired information is easy when you know the specific source and piece of information. In these cases, you can enter the computer address of the specific page or document and obtain

Exhibit 4.15 Explorer screen

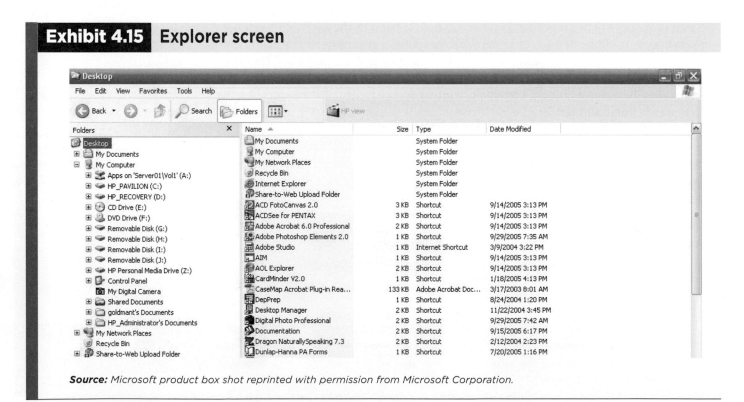

Source: *Microsoft product box shot reprinted with permission from Microsoft Corporation.*

Exhibit 4.16 Search companion

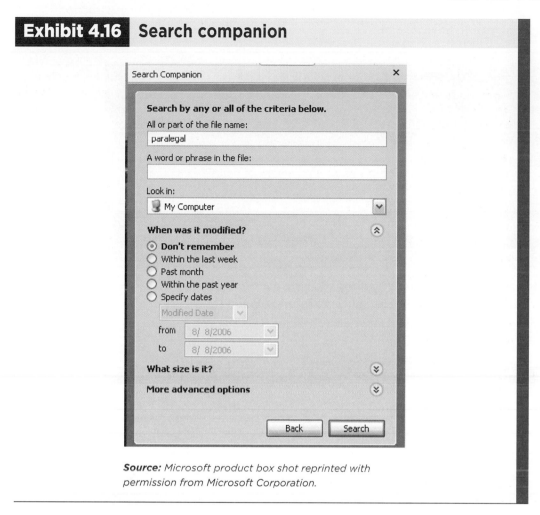

Source: *Microsoft product box shot reprinted with permission from Microsoft Corporation.*

your result almost instantly. More frequently, you will have to locate information about a specific item without knowing where to find it.

Internet Browsers

The solution is found in **Internet (Web) browsers** such as AOL and Internet Explorer. These browsers provide a search feature, usually referred to as a search engine, that allows a search of available Web resources. These searches require only inputting into the search engine a word or phrase to obtain a listing of potentially relevant information. Also useful are specialized search engines such as Google and Yahoo!, which use highly developed algorithms to search for relevant information and return a listing in order of relevancy with amazing accuracy.

An Internet or Web browser is a software program that allows a person to use a computer to access the Internet. Unless you have a direct connection to a computer database, you will be working with a software program known as a Web browser. The two most popular Web browsers are Microsoft Internet Explorer and AOL, both of which provide content. These browsers typically are used with Internet service providers that do not themselves provide any content but, rather, act as an intermediary between the user and the World Wide Web. Some services, such as America OnLine (AOL) and MSN, provide content, such as news and weather and specialty sections for sharing information, along with providing the traditional Internet connections and email.

All of the browsers basically provide two main screens—one to display email (see Exhibit 4.17) and to display content and Internet search results (see Exhibit 4.18.)

Internet (Web) browsers An Internet or Web browser is a software program that allows a person to use a computer to access the Internet. The two most popular Web browsers are Microsoft Internet Explorer and AOL.

 **Web Exploration**

Obtain a copy of the current AOL browser at www.daol.aol.com/software.

Exhibit 4.17 Email display

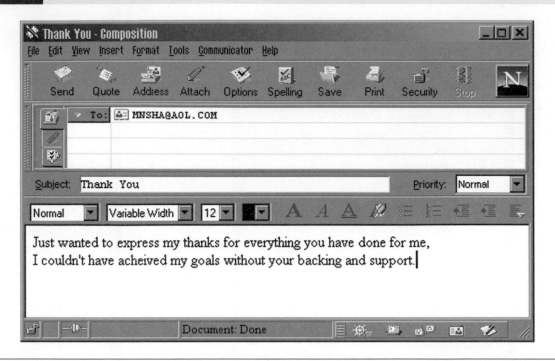

Exhibit 4.18 AOL Internet browser

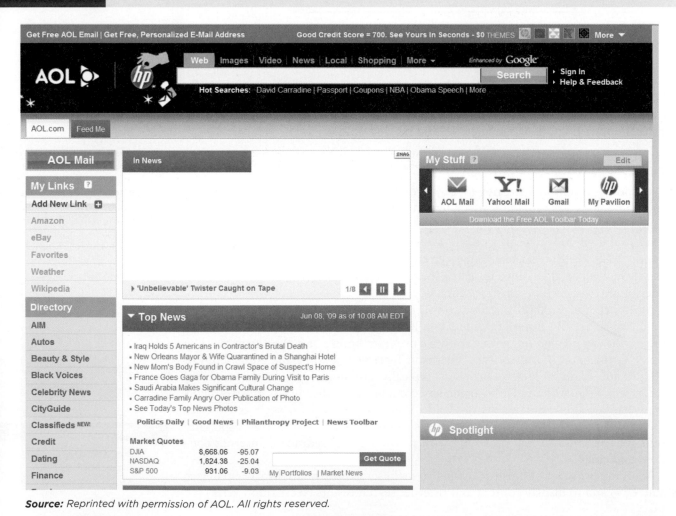

Search Engines

An **Internet search engine** is a program designed to take a word or set of words and search websites on the Internet. Of the available Internet search engines, each searches in a different fashion. The same search request may generate totally different results on different search engines. The number of search engines is expanding constantly. Some search engines are more suitable than others for legal searches. Many search engines are designed for use by children and families, so they may not return the results needed in the professional areas.

It is useful to create a search query and run the query through a number of different search engines, then compare the results. For example, you may wish to search the topic "regulation of paralegals." Each of the search engines shown below may be accessed by entering its **URL (uniform resource locator)** in your Web browser:

AltaVista	www.altavista.com
Ask.com	www.ask.com
Dogpile	www.dogpile.com
Excite	www.excite.com
Google	www.google.com
MetaCrawler	www.metacrawler.com
Yahoo!	www.yahoo.com

Some of the information is shown on the screen and will not require any more searching. The data—such as a phone number, address, or other limited information—will appear and may be copied manually or printed out to capture the displayed page. Other information may be in the form of large text or graphic files. These may be many pages long or involve use of graphic display programs such as the popular Adobe. Typical of the graphic images are the tax forms available from the Internal Revenue Service.

A word of caution: Addresses of websites tend to change frequently. It is a good idea to keep a list of frequently used websites handy and update it regularly.

Addresses and Locations

Obviously, finding something requires knowing where it resides. We find people by looking for their home or business address or by their telephone number. The modern equivalent of a telephone number is the **computer address and location**. Web pages also have addresses, known as uniform resource locators, or URLs.

The URL is made up of three parts:

Protocol://Computer/Path

The **protocol** is usually http (hypertext transfer protocol). The computer is the Internet computer name, such as **www.bucks.edu.** And the path is the directory or subdirectory on the computer where the information can be found.

The URL may be thought of as a file cabinet, in which the protocol is the name of the file cabinet, the computer is the drawer in the file cabinet, and the path is the file folder in the drawer. Not all URLs have a path as part of the address.

Part of the naming protocol is a domain nomenclature, with extensions such as the "edu" in www.bucks.edu. Common extensions are:

.org	organizations
.edu	educational institutions
.com	commercial operations
.gov	government agencies
.bus	business
.mil	military

In addition, there are extensions such as

.jp	Japan
.fr	France
.uk	United Kingdom

Internet search engine An Internet search engine is a program designed to take a word or set of words and locate websites on the Internet.

Uniform resource locator (URL) The address of a site on the Internet.

Web Exploration

Internal Revenue Service: Obtain copies of tax forms at www.irs.gov.

Computer address and location The modern equivalent of a person's telephone number is the email address. Pages on the Internet also have addresses known as the Uniform Resource Locator (URL), made up of three parts: protocol, computer, and path.

Protocol In a URL the required format of the Web address.

These designations refer to the country where the computer is located.

Many people save information on websites for future use, which may be in hard-copy, on cards, or in a database. The Website Profile Checklist below provides suggested headings.

CHECKLIST Website Profile

☐ Address (URL):

☐ Name of organization or site:

☐ Key subject:

☐ Secondary subject:

☐ Cost:

☐ Comments:

In determining the authenticity of information found on the Internet, knowing if the computer is a commercial site (.com or .bus) or a government site (.gov) is sometimes useful. Some websites may appear to be official government websites or may appear to contain official information but actually are private sites.

For example, the official URL for the Internal Revenue Service is **www.irs.gov.** This is not to be confused with the unofficial private website www.irs.com. To obtain the official Internal Revenue Service forms and information, you must use the official site, **www.irs.gov.**

Potentially, one of the biggest time-savers for the paralegal is the ready availability of information, forms, and files on the Internet or World Wide Web. Public information that would have required a trip to the courthouse or other government office is instantly available without leaving the office. This information may come from public or private sources. Government information typically is available without cost or at minimum cost. Private information may be free to all, or at a cost per use, per page, or per time period (such as a month).

Legal Research

Web Exploration

Check the free resources of the Cornell Law School website at http://www.law.cornell.edu/.

A major use of the Internet in the law office is to perform research, both factual and legal. Using powerful search engines such as Google, Yahoo!, and Ask can help the paralegal locate almost any information that is available on the Internet. More and more legal research is being conducted on the Internet as law offices reduce the size of paper-based law libraries in favor of online resources. A number of companies provide access to case law, statutory material, and other secondary legal sources for a fee. Among the most widely used of these are Westlaw, LexisNexis, Loislaw, and Versus-Law. Although some websites offer information without charge, most do not have the depth of available resources that the for-fee sites offer. The Cornell University Law school site is among the most popular of the no-fee sites.

Formats of Available Information

Most of the items that are displayed can be printed to a printer attached to a computer. At the top of most Web browsers is a printer icon or a Print command in the FILE icon at the top of the page. Clicking on the icon or word PRINT in the FILE pull-down menu will initiate the print process. Patience may be necessary, as the computer may have to take some time to access the original source of the information. Clicking several times will not speed up the process and actually may result in several copies of the same information being printed.

File Attachments

A popular method for transmitting text files and graphic images is by **attachment** of the file to an email. This is much easier than it sounds. Today, almost everyone has an email address, whether at home or at work, or both. To send or receive emails requires the use of an Internet service provider and a browser such as Internet Explorer, Netscape, or one of the other specialty email programs. In the traditional email, text is entered on the keyboard and transmitted to the email account of a recipient, who reads it online. Virtually any file can be attached (linked) and sent with an email. The receiver needs only to click the mouse on the attachment, which may appear as an icon. In most cases, the file will open using the same program from which it was created, such as Microsoft Word, Corel WordPerfect, or Adobe Acrobat. Occasionally a file may be transmitted in a format that the receiver does not have the software to open. This is particularly true with regard to graphic images, pictures, and drawings.

File attachment The attachment is a popular method for transmitting text files, and occasionally graphic images, by attaching the file to an email.

Receiving and Downloading Files and Attachments

The method for downloading files and attachments is the same. Users first should determine the directory (folder) into which they will be downloading these files. In Windows this usually is a folder called My Download Files or My Files. If there is no existing folder, Windows Explorer can be used to create a file with a name such as Download. Windows Explorer is a program in the Start directory under Programs. (This is not the same as Windows Internet Explorer, which is an Internet browser.)

CHECKLIST To Retrieve and Download a Form

- ☐ Select a file format.
- ☐ Select the file(s) you wish to receive. To select multiple items, hold the Control button down while selecting.
- ☐ Click the Review Selected Files button. A Results page will be displayed with links to the file(s) you requested.
- ☐ Select the file title to retrieve.

Most of the files attached as part of email will be document files created and saved as either Microsoft Word documents or WordPerfect documents. The user may want to save these files directly into the Word or WordPerfect directory. Saving them in the computer download is one option, as is opening the file on the screen immediately instead of saving it for later use. Alternative file formats may be offered, such as MS Word or WordPerfect or PDF, so be sure you have the appropriate program on your computer that can open and view the file.

Normally, text files and graphic images are static files; that is, by themselves they do not perform any function but are merely data-usable within another program such as a word processor or graphic image viewer. It has become common, however, to send, as attachments, files that have within them miniprograms such as macros that perform functions when activated, such as those used to calculate sums in spreadsheets. Others are self-contained software programs such as screensavers containing animation and animated cartoons.

Some program files have an extension of either ".exe" or ".com." Files with these extensions may run automatically after downloading. Therefore, greater caution must be taken in downloading any file, particularly files with these or other unknown file extensions, which may contain macros (mini files), such as Excel files, which may contain formulas that run automatically and may contain computer viruses, as discussed below. Remember that it is not enough to rely on the sender being a reliable source, as even the most reliable source can have a security breach that allows a virus to be attached to a file, or the source may be forwarding files from other, less reliable sources without checking the files before sending them to you.

ETHICAL PERSPECTIVE

Arizona Law Firm Domain Names Opinion No. 2001-05 (March 2001) Summary.

A law firm domain name does not have to be identical to the firm's actual name, but it must comply with the Rules of Professional Conduct, including refraining from being false or misleading. And it may not imply any special competence or unique affiliation unless this is factually true. A for-profit law firm domain name should not use the domain suffix ".org" nor should it use a domain name that implies that the law firm is affiliated with a given nonprofit organization or governmental entity. [ERs 7.1, 7.4, 7.5]

Sending Files

Some Internet Service Providers (ISPs) limit the amount of information that may be sent at one time, depending on the speed of the connection and how busy the system is at different times of the day. This may limit the number of pages that may be sent at one time. With increased transmission speed, also referred to as bandwidth, comes the ability to transmit much larger files and more pages in the same time.

Increasingly, large-size graphics files and images such as photographs are sent or attached to emails. The larger files being transmitted require more bandwidth (the pipeline) to avoid slowing down the system. Bandwidth may be thought of as the amount of data that can be sent in a given timeframe. For example:

Telephone dial-up service	24–56 kilobits (amount of data) per second (kps)
Digital Subscriber Line (DSL)	up to 750 kps
Fiber Optic Service (FIOS)	up to 15 megabits

As with any pipeline, only a limited amount of product can be transmitted at any one time. To more equitably share the limited pipeline resource, ISPs and network operators permanently—or temporarily during peak usage times—limit the number of files or the size of files that one user may transmit. In some offices, the same limitations may be imposed to overcome the size limitation; files may be transmitted in a compressed format, frequently referred to as zip files. Large files are run through a program that compresses them before being sent. The recipient of the compressed file then must uncompress the file before being able to read it.

A number of programs are available to compress and decompress files. Some of these require several steps, and other programs perform the task automatically. For occasional use, the manual method is acceptable, but with the increasing number of compressed files, it may be more time-efficient to purchase one of the automatic programs. Limited time-trial versions of some of these decompression programs may be downloaded without charge over the Internet from software companies who are encouraging users to buy the full version after the trial period expires.

ETHICAL PERSPECTIVE

Ohio Rule on Commercial Law-Related Websites

Ohio lawyers may not participate in a commercial law-related website that provides them with clients if the arrangement entails prohibited payment for referrals or if the business is engaged in the unauthorized practice of law. (Ohio Supreme Court Board of Commissioners on Grievances and Discipline opinion 2001–2)

Electronic Filing

A number of courts have established procedures for the electronic filing of pleadings. Each court is free to set up its own rules and procedures and must be consulted before attempting to use this service. The Internal Revenue Service and some states have combined in a joint effort to allow electronic filing of both the federal and state individual income tax returns in one step. The local or state tax authority retrieves the information from the Internal Revenue Service. A feature of this service, known as IRS e-file, is the return receipt when the federal and state governments receive the form.

Types of Image Formats

With increasing frequency, the Internet is being used to obtain needed forms. These may be government agency forms, tax forms, or court forms. Even the best-equipped office will require one form or another that is not in the office supply room for completing a case. This may be an unusual federal tax form or a form from your state or another state.

The most popular format for the federal government forms is PDF form, and many state agencies also use the PDF format for document delivery. Other options may be presented for selection.

Computer and Network Security

Security has become a critical issue as law offices, courts, and clients become more dependent upon the use of the computer and the Internet. With only a single computer, the security concern is limited to introducing a program that does not work properly. With computer networks, the potential is introduced to adversely impact every workstation on the network and the network file server itself. On a network, any workstation is a potential input source of problems in the form of software programs that could corrupt the system or the files stored on the system. Though not common, there are instances of employees introducing annoying or potentially harmful programs as a method of getting even with an employer. Part of the solution to these kinds of issues is to limit access to the network, including limiting the ability to access the file server from workstations and limiting the ability or right to make changes to operating systems and limit other activity to saving of documents.

Use of the Internet from workstations has introduced the security concern about unauthorized parties gaining access to the computer network—referred to informally as "**hacking**." In some instances, the unauthorized party wants to gain access to information in files stored on the network. In other cases, it is to undermine the integrity of the system by causing files and programs to be modified or to introduce computer viruses that can cause minor inconvenience or even destroy entire systems by deleting files, programs, and operating systems.

Hacking Unauthorized access to a computer or computer network.

Firewalls

A **firewall** is a program designed to limit access to a computer or to a computer network system. Depending upon the complexity of the program, it may restrict total access without proper validation in the form of passwords, or limit all access to the system for certain kinds of programs or sources not deemed to be acceptable to the network or system administrator. For example, many parents use a form of a firewall designed to limit children's access to certain kinds of programs and certain sites on the Internet that are deemed to be unacceptable.

Firewalls Programs designed to limit access to authorized users and applications.

A firewall can be a two-edged sword for the paralegal: It prevents unauthorized access to the network, and it may prevent the paralegal working at an offsite location such as a courthouse, client's office, or opposing counsel's offices from accessing files on the firm's computer or other Internet connection. It is important to check a connection to be sure it will allow data to be accessed from a remote location and sent as planned before it is needed for trial, depositions, or presentation. With enough time, any issue may be resolved with the local system administrator.

Encryption Technology

Encryption Encryption is technology that allows computer users to put a "lock" around information to prevent discovery by others.

Encryption technology permits a computer user to basically put a lock around its computer information to protect it from being discovered by others. Encryption technology is like a lock on a house. Without the lock in place, unwanted persons can easily enter the house and steal its contents; with the lock in place, it is more difficult to enter and take the house's contents. Encryption software serves a similar function in that it lets computer users scramble information so only those who have the encryption code can enter the database and discover the information.

Encryption

Confidential or privileged information sent over the Internet is frequently encrypted by the sender and unencrypted by the receiver because of the concerns that it will be intercepted when transmitted over the Internet. Encryption programs use algorithms (mathematical formulas) to scramble documents. Without the proper password or encryption key, unauthorized persons are not able to read the files and determine their content.

To understand the levels of protection offered by the different encryption programs, think of the protection offered by a combination lock. The least security is provided by a two-number combination lock frequently found with inexpensive luggage. As the numbers required for opening the lock increase to two, three, four or more numbers, the security also increases. It is not hard to see how the two-digit combination lock can be quickly opened while the four-digit lock requires more time and effort. For an amateur computer hacker with a simple encryption-breaking program, a basic encryption program might be thought to be the equivalent of a two- or three-number combination lock. The higher-level program with tougher algorithms designed to thwart a professional code-breaker would require the four or more number combinations. As computers become faster, more sophisticated methods will be required.

ETHICAL PERSPECTIVE
Interception of Electronic Communications

Interception or monitoring of email communications for purposes other than assuring quality of service or maintenance is illegal under the Electronic Communications Privacy Act of 1986, as amended in 1994. [18 U.S.C. B2511(2)(a)(i)]

Computer Viruses

Computer viruses Viruses are programs that attack and destroy computer programs, internal computer operating systems, and occasionally the hard disk drives of computers.

Unfortunately, some computer-knowledgeable people take sadistic pleasure in developing and disseminating programs that attack and destroy computer programs, internal computer-operating systems, and occasionally even the hard disk drives of computers. These programs are known as **computer viruses**. Viruses range from those that create minor inconvenience to those that can destroy data and cause computer shutdowns.

Some simple precautions can prevent disaster. A virus-protection program, such as those sold by Norton, McAfee, and others, is as important to have on your computer as the computer operating system itself. This should be the first program loaded on a new computer.

Anti-virus programs scan the computer to identify the presence of viruses, and the better programs eliminate the virus. Every disk should be scanned with a virus program before being used. Files that are downloaded from other computers or over the Internet also should be checked. As good as these programs are, they quickly go out of date as new viruses are created and unleashed. Therefore, these virus checking programs should be updated regularly.

Future Trends in Law Office Technology

The pressure is on law offices to be more productive. The increased cost of operating law offices is a major factor in law office managers looking for new ways to use technology to increase productivity. Clients and the courts are not willing to approve fees and costs where more cost-effective methods are available. The demand for speedy justice in the courts has resulted in less time to prepare and present cases, requiring the legal team to use technology to become faster and more productive with less time in which to do it. Advances in computer technology are providing solutions to the productivity and cost issues.

Looking ahead to what's on the technological horizon is imperative to the smooth and profitable functioning of the law office. Anticipating change and incorporating it requires IT knowledge and savvy, whether it comes in the form of in-house staff or external technology consultants. Corporate law firms might have a chief information officer or chief technology officer whose role includes anticipating change and planning for it in concrete as well as visionary ways. Those responsible for IT at smaller firms, as well, have the responsibility to be well-informed of technology trends in order to assess when a new tool should be added to their technology repertoire—and when it should be avoided.

The legal team is an increasingly mobile workforce. Working out of the office is a fact of life for trial attorneys and their support staff. The litigation team may spend much of their time in courthouses and outside the office taking depositions as close as across the street or across the country and around the globe. Increasingly, the support staff is also located or working outside the traditional law office.

In some cases it is because of outsourcing of activity to other firms or companies in remote locations, such as the legal support firms in India. It is also lawyers, paralegals, and litigation support members of the legal team who, for various reasons, work from home. With advances in technology it is possible to connect with the traditional office and access all the needed files and electronic resources on a computer at home; these workers are sometimes referred to as **teleworkers**. The following sections describe emerging technology that is available now and in use at some law firms and technology that is available but not fully deployed. The list is not exhaustive but rather illuminative of what businesses might expect in the near and distant future. How soon is a matter of conjecture, but we know from recent technology trends that it will be sooner than we could have expected even a few years ago.

Teleworker People who work from remote locations, typically home.

As Raymond Kurzweil writes in his essay, "The Law of Accelerating Returns" (2001), "An analysis of the history of technology shows that technological change is exponential, contrary to the common-sense "intuitive linear" view. So we won't experience 100 years of progress in the 21st century—it will be more like 20,000 years of progress (at today's rate). The "returns," such as chip speed and cost-effectiveness, also increase exponentially. There's even exponential growth in the rate of exponential growth."

Videoconferencing

Videoconferencing is the use generally of the Internet, or in some cases telephone lines or special satellite systems, to transmit and receive video and audio signals in real time to allow parties to see and hear each other. It is defined in the Wisconsin court rules (subchapter III of Wis. Stat. chapter 885) as; *Videoconferencing*, as defined in section 885.52(3) of the new rule, means an interactive technology that sends video, voice, and data signals over a transmission circuit so that two or more individuals or groups

Videoconferencing Conferencing from multiple locations using high speed Internet connections to transmit sound and images.

can communicate with each other simultaneously using video monitors. It is a live, real-time, interactive form of communication and does not include the presentation of prerecorded video testimony pursuant to subchapter II of Wis. Stat. chapter 885. The definition is intended to encompass emerging technologies such as Web-based solutions, as they appear, so long as the functional requirements of the definition are met.

The Wisconsin Supreme Court adopted a rule effective July 1, 2008, entitled "Use of Videoconferencing in the Circuit Courts," one of the most advanced rules on the use of this technology in the country. Videoconferencing has been used in many courts for criminal proceedings at various stages of the process, usually at the beginning of the process. The Wisconsin rule advances the use to all aspects of criminal and civil litigation.

Many law firms and their clients use videoconferencing on a regular basis as a method of "face-to-face" communication when parties are at remote sites. With Wisconsin leading the way it can be expected to be an important new tool in the litigation practice.

VoIP

VoIP Voice over internet protocol is a computer internet replacement for traditional telephone connections.

Voice over Internet Protocol **(VoIP)** is a protocol for using the Internet as a method of communication instead of traditional telephone company services. A computer with a microphone and headset or speaker is used to complete a call to another computer or telephone over the Internet. It may be a voice connection or voice and image.

Software is installed on the computer that facilitates the desired activity. An example of a popular service for VoIP is Yahoo Messenger, which has provisions for traditional telephone calling and short message service to cell phone and other portable devices. The initial limitation of VoIP was the inability to call a traditional phone or receive a call. Services like Yahoo Messenger provide options that permit calling traditional phones at a very nominal rate, sometimes as low as one cent per minute.

The relative ease of use of these services and the low cost make conferencing, including videoconferencing, a reality. The days of going to a special location and paying substantial fees to conduct a videoconference are gone. Anyone with an Internet connection, a laptop with built-in microphone and speakers, and an inexpensive video camera can set up a videoconference from almost anywhere there is an Internet connection.

Voice Recognition

Voice recognition Computer programs for converting speech into text or commands without the use of other in/out devices such as keyboards.

Voice recognition software has been around for a number of years. Many will remember trying out an earlier version of a speech recognition program as a possible alternative to typing. More computer technology has brought this software to the point of accuracy approaching, and in some cases exceeding, the accuracy of typing.

Speech-enabled devices include cell phones, personal digital assistants (PDAs), and other handheld devices. It is now possible with programs like Dragon Naturally Speaking Legal Version to dictate working drafts of legal documents directly into almost any program, including word processors, spreadsheets, and databases, without touching a computer keyboard, and send the document to another member of the legal team electronically over a network or by email, as shown in Exhibit 4.19. So advanced have the systems become, portable dictation devices can be used out of the office and then connected to the office computer, on which the speech recognition program has been installed, and the documents transcribed without the intervention of a typist. At up to 160 words a minute for speech input, for the average typist on the legal team the savings are significant. The underlying technology that enables voice technology to perform is now being used in automated response systems, like automatic call attendants that replace operators and receptionists in some firms. It is also a technology that permits those with physical disabilities that prevent using a keyboard, such as carpal tunnel syndrome, to remain or become productive in a world of word processors.

Miniaturization and Portability

The trend in computers and related computer devices has been toward miniaturization and portability. Smaller devices are becoming more powerful than some of the older

Exhibit 4.19   **Dictation using theBoom noise reduction microphone with Dragon NaturallySpeaking legal software**

theBoom is a registered trademark of UmeVoice Inc. Dragon NaturallySpeaking is a registered trademark of Nuance Communications.

desktop systems and laptops. Even the telephone has been reduced to a pocket-sized wireless communication device that is also capable of taking and displaying photo images, video, documents, and emails and accessing the Internet—many functions that formerly were reserved to large hardwired computer devices.

The Apple iPhone is an example of a device that can perform many functions formerly requiring a computer. Laptops have been reduced in size, with some weighing less than three pounds. They include all of the features previously mentioned together with built-in Web camera for videoconferencing and have built-in and removable memory greater than many file servers in some small offices.

Wireless Technology

Hardware in many offices today includes the wireless telephone and the laptop computer with built-in wireless Internet capability. The worldwide availability of inexpensive high-speed Internet connections has expanded the availability and use of new technologies. These tools allow constant communication and enable work to be performed virtually anywhere—home, courthouse, airport lounge, or coffee shop. The connection to the office may be by wireless network using the cell phone, or by a wireless connection with built-in wireless network hardware on the computer, or using an adapter card plugged into the computer that uses a wireless Internet connection.

Unlike a few years ago, wires are not necessary to access networks or to set up network connections. Today they may be set up using wireless technology in a wireless network. Just as the cell phone has enabled communications without wires, so has wireless technology allowed networks to be set up where workstations, servers, and peripherals connect over a wireless connection. Remote access is also possible by the use of wireless Internet connection using laptops and other personal computing devices including cell phones with built-in Web or Internet access.

Remote Access

Remote access allows members of the legal team working on cases out of the office to connect with the office file server to retrieve documents, work on them, and send them to other members of the team anywhere in the world. If hardcopy is needed, documents may be printed on any printer accessible over the Internet, including printers in remote office locations, public access points in airports, clients' offices, and courthouses.

Remote Collaboration

Remote collaboration Working on a common document utilizing remote access by two or more parties.

Remote collaboration means that members of the team can work collaboratively from multiple locations as if in the same physical location. This is possible through software conferencing programs that allow the sharing of files while communicating and seeing each other on the same screen using small desktop cameras or cameras built into laptop computers. The same remote access technology allows for the taking of witness statements from remote locations while the parties can see each other or view exhibits on the computer screen.

With higher-speed Internet connections the reality of true real-time videoconferencing has become a reality. Formerly, limited-speed connections restricted how much information could be transmitted. In the simplest form, slower speed increased the time to send a document. If not fast enough it prevented full-motion, full-screen video. With the introduction of fiber optic and cable Internet services in offices and in homes, videoconferencing from multiple locations, which requires a high-speed Internet connection to simultaneously transmit both the sound and the images, is now available on-site at many offices.

Wireless Computer Networks

Wireless computer networks A wireless network uses wireless technology in place of wires for connecting to the network.

Wireless computer networks are like cell phone networks in that both use radio waves to transmit signals to a receiver. Cell phone systems use cell towers located at strategic points all over the world to receive the signals from the cell phone subscriber's cellular device. The wireless network uses wireless access points, which are essentially receivers of radio signals that convert them so they can be transmitted over a connecting wire to a computer or other connection to the Internet.

Unlike cell phone towers, these access points are more limited. With the exception of a few cities that have access points over a large portion of the city these access points are local, often with a range limited to a few hundred feet. Many of these access points are provided in coffee shops, airport lounges, hotels, libraries, and bookstores without charge or at a nominal fee to encourage customers to use the facility instead of a competitor's.

Hot spot A wireless access point, generally in a public area.

With the growth of wireless **"hot spot"** locations, the wire connection has been cut. Lawyers and their paralegals may be connected anywhere in the world and send documents electronically back and forth with the same ease as sending them within the same building. With the growth of Internet connections to portable devices over cell phone connections, computers with built-in devices or with the use of plug-in devices can access the Internet over wide areas not previously possible.

Wireless Laptop Connections

Laptops may be used wirelessly to connect to the Internet without the limitation of use of a "hot spot" by using plug-in devices such as the AT&T Laptop Connect Card, Sierra Wireless Air Card, and a subscription to the service provided by most major providers like AT&T, Verizon, and Sprint. These services essentially provide service virtually anywhere there is a cellular connection. The popularity of these wireless services has resulted in many newer-generation laptops having the feature built in, eliminating the need for the external cards.

Thin Client

Thin client A computer system where programs and files are maintained on a centralized server.

A trend called **"thin client"** or cloud computing is emerging where programs and files are maintained on a centralized server and each user has access through a dumb terminal (one without programs or data). The thin client model offers some additional level of control and prevents loss of information through the loss of a computer. This general concept also includes Software as a Service (SaaS) and Web 2.0. It can be expected that the increased usage of the smaller, lighter computers, commonly called netbooks, designed for accessing the Internet will increase the demand for software and data repositories to minimize the need to support software and large data devices on these very portable computers.

ETHICAL PERSPECTIVE

Unauthorized Eavesdropping

With the increased freedom of communication comes an increased risk of eavesdropping by unauthorized parties accessing the wireless signals. Security measures, such as encryption and access restricted by password, are essential to prevent ethical breaches in confidentiality. Use of public access points, such as the coffee shop with wireless access, the airport lounge, or other public location, invites the curious to eavesdrop and look over the shoulder at the screen of the laptop user. With the growing availability of Internet access on airplanes, the eyes of the adjoining seatmate may be those of a member of the opposing team traveling to the same destination on the same case.

Concept Review *and* Reinforcement

LEGAL TERMINOLOGY

Applications software 134
Attachment 129
Backup of data 149
Case and litigation management software 140
Central processing unit (CPU) 133
Computer addresses and locations 153
Computer hardware 132
Computer network 147
Computer system 132
Computer viruses 158
Database program 138
Digital format 129
Electronic repository 130
Encryption 158
File attachment 155
File extension 137
Firewalls 157
Graphic user interface (GUI) 134

Hacking 157
Hardcopy 129
Hot spot 162
Internet 149
Internet (Web) browsers 151
Internet search engine 153
Internet service provider (ISP) 150
Local area network (LAN) 150
Mainframe 132
Modem 150
Network administrator 148
Network file server 147
Network rights and privileges 148
Office software suites 139
Online collaboration 130
Operating system 133
Outsourcing 131
Paperless office 146
Protocol 153
Random access memory (RAM) 133

Remote collaboration 162
Software 134
Specialty application programs 139
Spreadsheet programs 137
Teleworker 159
Thin client 162
Track Changes 135
Uniform resource locator (URL) 153
Uninterruptible power supply (UPS) 134
Videoconferencing 159
Voice recognition 160
VoIP 160
Wide area network 149
Wireless computer networks 162
Wireless network 149
Workstation 147

SUMMARY OF KEY CONCEPTS

Need for Computer Skills

The Need	Computers are being used with greater frequency to share information in digital format between remote offices, courthouses, government agencies, and clients.
Technology Usage in the Law	Computers are now being used for everything from word processing to computerized timekeeping, payroll productions, and tax return preparation. Today even the smallest law firm and litigator must use technology. Some courts are demanding computerized filing.
Outsourcing	Outsourcing has become a buzzword for shipping work out of the office or overseas to save money. Using an outside computer consultant to help with support for the hardware and software of the office is a form of outsourcing and may involve a help desk located in a foreign location to answer questions.
How Much Do I Really Need to Know	No one can be an expert in everything. What is important is to know enough to know what you do not know and be able to find someone who does.

Understanding the Language of Technology

Why	An understanding of the terminology of technology is a prerequisite to understanding the technology found in the law office, the courthouse, and the clients' business.

Computer Hardware

Computer Hardware	Hardware is the term that encompasses all of the tangible or physical items including computers, monitors, printers, fax machines, duplicators, and similar items that usually have either an electrical connection or use batteries as a power source.

Operating Systems

	The operating system is a basic set of instructions to the computer on how to handle basic functions—how to process input from "input devices" such as the keyboard and mouse, the order in which to process information, and what to show on the computer monitor.

Applications Software

Applications Software Programs	Applications programs are software that perform generic tasks such as word processing.
Word Processing Programs	Programs for creating written documents in electronic format.
Track Changes	Track Changes, as found in MS word, shows the original text, the deleted text, and the new text as well as a strike through for deleted text, underlining or highlighting of new text, as well as margin notes on the document.
File Extensions	When a file is saved, a file extension (a period followed by three characters) is added to the end of the filename to identify the program or format in which the file has been saved.
Spreadsheet Programs	Programs that permit the calculation and presentation of financial information in a grid format of rows and columns.
Database Programs	A database program is an electronic repository of information of all types that can be sorted and presented in a meaningful manner.

Presentation Graphic Programs

Software programs used to create high quality slide shows and drawings.

Specialty Application Programs

Specialty applications programs combine many of the basic functions found in software suites, word processing, database management, spreadsheets, and graphic presentations to perform law office, case, and litigation management.

Case and Litigation Management Software	Case and litigation management programs are used to manage documents and the facts and issues of cases.

The Electronic Courtroom and Paperless Office

Electronic Courtroom	The use of electronics and computer-based systems are used in the electronic courtroom.
Paperless Office	The paperless office is one in which documents are created and stored electronically.

Networks

Workstation	A workstation generally consists of a computer, a monitor, and a printer.
Computer Network	A network is a set of workstations connected together.
Network Server	The network file server generally is a separate computer that acts as the traffic cop of the system controlling the flow of information; it requests to use the resources of the system or data, between the connected workstations and other peripherals that are part of the network. These servers usually are the central repository for all electronic files.
Network Rights and Privileges	Rights or privileges determine who has access to the server, the data stored on the server, and the flow of information between connections.
Network Administrator	The network administrator usually is the person with the highest-level access to the network file server.
Backup of Data	Backing up data—making copies of files—regularly is an essential function to prevent loss of critical files and office data in the event of a disaster.
Wide Area Network	A wide area network is a network of networks. Each network is treated as if it were a connection on the network.
Wireless Network	A wireless network uses wireless technology instead of wires for connecting to the network.

The Internet

What Is It?	The Internet or the World Wide Web is a group of computers linked together with the added ability to search all the connections for information.

Online Computer Resources

Internet Browsers	An Internet or Web browser is a software program that allows a person to use a computer to access the Internet. The two most popular Web browsers are Microsoft Internet Explorer and AOL.
Search Engines	An Internet search engine is a program designed to take a word or set of words and locate websites on the Internet.

Addresses and Locations	The modern equivalent of a person's telephone number is the email address. Pages on the Internet also have addresses known as the Uniform Resource Locator (URL), made up of three parts: protocol, computer, and path.

Formats of Available Information

File Attachments	The attachment is a popular method for transmitting text files, and occasionally graphic images, by attaching the file to an email.
Receiving and Downloading Files and Attachments	The method for downloading files and attachments is the same. They are downloaded into a directory (a folder), which in Windows usually is called My Download Files or My Files. If there is no existing folder, Windows Explorer can be used to create a file with a name, such as Download.

Electronic Filing

Courts	Many courts have established procedures for the electronic filing of pleadings. Each court is free to set up its own rules and procedures and must be consulted before attempting to use this service.
IRS	The Internal Revenue Service and some states have combined in a joint effort to allow the filing of both the federal and state individual income tax returns.
Types of Image Formats	The most popular format for computerized forms is PDF.

Computer and Network Security

Security	Security is a critical issue in law offices and for the court as they become more and more dependant on computers and the Internet.
Firewalls	A firewall is a software program designed to limit access to a computer network system.
Encryption	Encryption is technology that allows computer users to put a "lock" around information to prevent discovery by others.
Computer Viruses	Viruses are programs that attack and destroy computer programs, internal computer operating systems, and occasionally the hard disk drives of computers.
Precautions	Virus-protection programs such as Norton or McAfee should be updated regularly.

Future Trends in Law Office Technology

	Looking ahead to what's on the technological horizon is imperative to the smooth and profitable functioning of the law office. Anticipating change and incorporating it requires IT knowledge and savvy, whether it comes in the form of in-house staff or external technology consultants.
Videoconferencing	Use, generally, of the Internet, or in some cases telephone lines or special satellite systems, to transmit and receive video and audio signals in real time to allow parties to see and hear each other.
VoIP	Voice over Internet Protocol (VoIP) is a protocol for using the Internet as a method of communication instead of traditional telephone company services. A computer with a microphone and headset or speaker is used to complete a call to another computer or telephone over the Internet. It may be a voice connection or voice and image.
Voice Recognition	More computer technology has brought this software to the point of accuracy, approaching, and in some cases exceeding, the accuracy of typing.

Miniaturization and Portability	Smaller devices are becoming more powerful than some of the older desktop systems and laptops. Even the telephone has been reduced to a pocket-sized wireless communication device.
Wireless Technology	Hardware in many offices today includes the wireless telephone and the laptop computer with built-in wireless Internet capability. The worldwide availability of inexpensive high-speed Internet connections has expanded the availability and use of new technologies.
Remote Access	Remote access allows members of the legal team working on cases while out of the office to connect with the office file server to retrieve documents, work on them, and send them to other members of the team anywhere in the world.
Remote Collaboration	Remote collaboration means that members of the team can work collaboratively from multiple locations as if in the same physical location. This is possible through software conferencing programs that allow the sharing of files while communicating and seeing each other on the same screen.
Wireless Computer Networks	Like cell phone networks that use radio waves to transmit signals to a receiver.
Wireless Laptop Connections	Laptops may be used wirelessly by using plug-in devices to connect to the Internet without the limitation or use of a "hot spot."
Thin Client	A trend called "thin client" or cloud computing is emerging where programs and files are maintained on a centralized server and each user has access through a dumb terminal (one without programs or data).

WORKING THE WEB

1. Download the latest 1040 tax form and instructions from the Internal Revenue Service website at www.irs.gov.
2. Use one of the search engines listed below to find information on your school or local government:
   a. AltaVista: http://www.altavista.com
   b. Ask.com: http://www.ask.com
   c. Dogpile: http://www.dogpile.com
   d. Excite: http://www.excite.com
   e. Google: http://www.google.com
   f. MetaCrawler: http://www.metacrawler.com
   g. Netscape: http://www.netscape.com
   h. Yahoo!: www.yahoo.com
3. Use the Google search engine to find information on how firewalls work, and print out the first page of the results. Using one of the results, print out a copy of the information that is most responsive to the search, and write a short summary describing what a firewall does. http://www.google.com
4. Use a search engine of your choice to run a search for legal research resources. Print a copy of the first 10 results.

Mark each result you think will be useful in the future as a paralegal and state why.
5. Prepare a step-by-step list of how to find the Code of Federal Regulations on the Government Printing Office website. http://www.access.gpo.gov
6. Prepare a list of the legislative information available from the Library of Congress online. http://www.LOC.gov
7. Use any search engine or browser search tool to find the document "How Our Laws Are Made," as revised and updated by Charles W. Johnson-Parliamentarian, on a federal government website. Hint: use quotation marks around the names. Print out the specific query you used and the URL of the source where the document was found.
8. Print out a copy of the results of the search for "firewall" using Yahoo!, and compare the results to the result from Google. How many of the first 20 listings are the same?

CRITICAL THINKING & WRITING QUESTIONS

1. How can the computer and the Internet increase a paralegal's productivity?
2. What is meant by the term "computer hardware"?
3. What is the danger in using the word processing feature "Track Changes"?
4. What are applications software programs? Give an example.
5. What are the advantages of using office suite programs?
6. How can database programs be used to avoid ethical issues?
7. How can legal office management programs help prevent malpractice?
8. What is meant by the "paperless office"? What changes in law office administration have encouraged this?
9. What is the function of a network server?
10. Why is making a backup essential in a law office?
11. What is the advantage to the legal team in having a wide area network or wireless network?
12. How has the availability of the high-speed Internet impacted the use of the Internet in the law office?
13. What is an Internet browser? How is this different from Windows Explorer?
14. How reliable are forms and documents obtained over the Internet?
15. What advantages does knowing how to use the Internet provide the paralegal in the law office?
16. What are the limitations of using a website to attract new clients to your state?
17. Do cross-jurisdictional boundary websites present any problems for the law firm using the Internet? If so, why?
18. What are some of the ways in which using an Internet browser can assist the paralegal working on a file or a case? How are URLs used in conducting Internet searches?
19. What copyright issues must a paralegal consider in using the Internet to prepare written documents and reports?
20. How can authenticity of information obtained on the Internet be validated? Explain the issues in downloading information.
21. What is the purpose of a firewall? What are the implications to the law office of not having a firewall?
22. What is a computer virus, and what should a paralegal do to protect the firm against computer viruses?
23. Should encryption software be used regularly in transmitting files electronically? Why?
24. Why would the legal team want to use encryption when transmitting a document?
25. What is a wireless access point? How could this be used in a law firm?
26. What ethical issues arise in the use of "hot spots" or public access points?

Building Paralegal Skills

VIDEO CASE STUDIES

Attorney Meet and Confer

Opposing counsel are meeting as required under the Federal Rules of Civil Procedure to discuss discovery issues in the case. Defense counsel has recently taken over the file and is not familiar with its contents and asks for additional time to complete discovery.

After viewing the video case study at www.pearsonhighered .com/goldman answer the following:

1. What is the purpose of the meet and confer under the Federal Rules of Civil Procedure.
2. If the lawyers are not familiar with some of the electronic discovery issues, do they have an ethical obligation to have someone there who is more knowledgeable?
3. How important is it for the lawyers and paralegals to be aware of the issues in the electronic discovery?

Remote Videoconference Taking Witness Video Deposition

The parent of an accident victim is not available locally for deposition. To save time and costs his deposition is being taken by videoconferencing.

After viewing the video case study at www.pearsonhighered.com/goldman answer the following:

1. What arrangements must be made to take a deposition using video conferencing?
2. What are the advantages and disadvantages of using video conferencing for taking depositions of fact witnesses?
3. What is the role of the court reporter in a video conference deposition?

Privilege Issue: Misdirected E-mail

The paralegal working on a confidential memo for a client has accidentally sent it to opposing counsel. The supervising attorney, visibly upset, gives instructions on how to handle the situation.

After viewing the video case study at www.pearsonhighered .com/goldman answer the following:

1. What is the potential of fact of the e-mail and confidential information to the opposing party?
2. What steps should be taken in your jurisdiction when e-mail is inadvertently sent to the wrong party?
3. Who is ultimately responsible and what are the penalties for inadvertent disclosure of confidential information by e-mail?

ETHICS ANALYSIS & DISCUSSION QUESTIONS

1. What are the ethical issues related to a law firm website that is available around the world when the firm is licensed to practice only in one jurisdiction?
2. Explain the ethical implication of the following: "In today's society, with the advent of the information superhighway, federal and state legislation and regulations, as well as information regarding industry trends, are easily accessed."
3. What are the ethical issues of erroneously sending or receiving by email or fax a confidential trial strategy memorandum?
4. What ethical issues arise for the law firm when it does not maintain an off-premises copy of files and client records? Does a major catastrophe, such as the flooding caused by Hurricane Katrina in New Orleans in 2005, excuse not having backup files and records?
5. What role do security protocols have in ethical compliance?
6. What ethical issues are involved in combining law practices as discussed in the opening scenario? What specific steps should be taken? Explain how these steps will prevent ethical breaches.

7. You are working in a sophisticated law firm that has the latest computers and software. You have not been trained in the use of the firm's computer encryption software for transmitting email and other electronic documents to clients and other offices of the firm. You live a few blocks from the office and consent to stay late on Friday night before a major holiday weekend when everyone has left early to avoid the rush hour traffic.

   A client calls and asks for a copy of the trial strategy memorandum for a major case to take with him for review over the weekend. He advises that he is getting ready to get on a plane but has a computer with him that has reverse encryption software the firm gave him and tells you he wants to read the memo while he is on the plane for the next 14 hours on his way to Tokyo. He hangs up and you do not have his cell phone number. You send the email without using the encryption software. [*U.S. v. Thomas*, 74 F.3d. 701 (1996), ABA Ethics Opinion, Utah Ethics Opinion 00-01.] Have you breached any rules on client confidentiality by sending unencrypted email containing confidential client information?

DEVELOPING YOUR COLLABORATION SKILLS

Working on your own or with a group of other students assigned by your instructor, review the scenario at the beginning of the chapter that deals with combining a paper-based office and an electronic office.

1. Divide into two teams, one team playing the role of the junior paralegal and the other the senior paralegal. Put yourself in that person's place, and make a list of the benefits of the type of office system (electronic or paper) that they are accustomed to working in.
2. Share your list with the other team. As a group, decide what systems/practices you think will be most efficient

and effective to use in the combined office to perform the following activities:

- Manage conflicts of interest
- Perform legal research
- Manage cases
- Handle client files
- Communicate with clients
- Manage financial accounts

3. As a group, identify areas of ethical concern in a merger, and discuss how best to handle these issues.

PARALEGAL PORTFOLIO EXERCISE

Prepare a memo for a potential law office manager, outlining the advantages and disadvantages of the paperless office. What security and confidentiality issues must be considered?

What potential solutions or office procedures should be put in place? Reference and cite any applicable ethical rules or opinions from your local or state court or bar association.

LEGAL ANALYSIS & WRITING CASES

Issue: Are Images Displayed on the Internet as a Result of a Search Protected by Copyright?

Defendant operates a "visual search engine" on the Internet that allows a user to obtain a list of related Web content in response to a search query entered by the user. Unlike other Internet search engines, defendant's search engine, the "Ditto" crawler, retrieves images instead of descriptive text. It produces a list of reduced, "thumbnail" pictures related to the user's query. By clicking on the desired thumbnail, a user could view the "image attributes" window displaying the full-size version of the image, a description of its dimensions, and an address for the website where it originated. By clicking on the address, the user could link to the originating website for the image. The search engine works by maintaining an indexed database of approximately two million thumbnail images obtained through a "crawler"—a computer program that travels the Web in search of images to be converted into thumbnails and added to the index.

Plaintiff Kelly is a photographer specializing in photographs of California Gold Rush country and photographs related to the works of Laura Ingalls Wilder. He does not sell the photographs independently, but his photographs have appeared in several books. Plaintiff also maintains two websites, one of which (www.goldrush1849.com) provides a "virtual tour" of California's Gold Rush country and promotes plaintiff's book on the subject. The other (www.showmethegold.com) markets corporate retreats in California's Gold Rush country.

Thirty-five of plaintiff's images were indexed by the Ditto crawler and put in defendant's image database. As a result, these images were made available in thumbnail form to users of defendant's visual search engine. After being notified of plaintiff's objections, Ditto removed the images from its database.

Plaintiff filed a copyright-infringement action. One of the questions of first impression is whether the display of copyrighted images by a "visual search engine" on the Internet constitutes fair use under the Copyright Act. The court found that defendant never held out plaintiff's work as its own, or even engaged in conduct specifically directed at plaintiff's work. Plaintiff's images were swept up along with two million others available on the Internet, as part of defendant's efforts to provide its users with a better way to find images on the Internet. Defendant's purposes were and are inherently transformative, even if its realization of those purposes was at times imperfect. Where, as here, a new use and new technology are evolving, the broad transformative purpose of the use weighs more heavily than the inevitable flaws in its early stages of development.

Questions

1. As the use of the Internet matures, will courts view use of information from the Web differently?
2. What are the implications in taking material off the Internet and including it in reports, memos, and briefs?
3. Would the decision have been different if the items were copyrighted legal forms also located by a "crawler" and displayed as a visual image such as a PDF file?

WORKING WITH THE LANGUAGE OF THE COURT CASE

CoStar Group Inc. v. LoopNet, Inc.

164 F. Supp. 2d 688 (D.C. Md. 2001)
United States District Court, Maryland

Read, and if assigned, brief this case. In your brief, include answers to the following questions.

1. What is a "contributory infringer" under the Digital Millennium Copyright Act?
2. Who is an online service provider as defined by the Digital Millennium Copyright Act (DMCA)?

3. When does a service provider lose its immunity under the DMCA?
4. What is a "safe harbor" under the DMCA?
5. What conduct takes a service provider out of the safe harbor?

Deborah K. Chasanow

I. BACKGROUND

Plaintiffs CoStar Group, Inc. and CoStar Realty Information, Inc. (collectively CoStar) filed suit against LoopNet, Inc. (LoopNet) alleging copyright infringement. CoStar is a national provider of commercial real estate information services . . . which includes photographs. . . .

LoopNet is an Internet-based company offering a service through which a user . . . may post a listing of commercial real estate available for lease. . . . To include a photograph, . . . it is uploaded into a separate "folder," . . . where it is reviewed by a LoopNet employee to determine that it is . . . a photograph of commercial property and that there is no obvious . . . violation of LoopNet's terms and conditions. If the photograph meets LoopNet's criteria . . . it is automatically posted. . . . CoStar claims that over 300 of its copyrighted photographs have appeared on LoopNet's site (the number has increased over time). . . .

Application of copyright law in cyberspace is elusive and perplexing. The World Wide Web has progressed far faster than the law and, as a result, courts are struggling to catch up. Legislatures and courts endeavor in this growing area to maintain the free flow of information over the Internet while still protecting intellectual property rights. . . .

Contributory Copyright Infringement

1. OVERVIEW

It is, today, a given that: one who, with knowledge of the infringing activity, induces, causes, or materially contributes to the infringing conduct of another, may be held liable as a "contributory" infringer. . . . Put differently, liability exists if the defendant engages in "personal conduct that encourages or assists the infringement." . . .

CoStar does not claim that LoopNet had knowledge of its users' infringements prior to its giving notice. . . . Given the nature of the infringements in this

case, it was impossible for LoopNet to have knowledge of the alleged infringement before receiving notice from CoStar. CoStar does not attach a copyright notice to its photos and even CoStar's own expert could not identify a CoStar photo simply by reviewing it. . . . Thus, LoopNet cannot be charged with . . . knowledge before receiving claims of infringement from CoStar. . . . CoStar does not claim that LoopNet had knowledge of infringement prior to receiving notice from CoStar. [T]here remain . . . disputes about [its] knowledge . . . after receiving the claims of infringement. CoStar alleges that once it gave LoopNet notice that its photographs were being infringed, LoopNet can be charged with knowledge of continuing infringements. . . .

The DMCA was enacted both to preserve copyright enforcement in the Internet and to provide immunity to service providers from copyright infringement liability for "passive," "automatic" actions in which a service provider's system engages through a technological process initiated by another without the knowledge of the service provider. . . . The DMCA's protection of an innocent service provider disappears at the moment the service provider loses its innocence, i.e., at the moment it becomes aware that a third party is using its system to infringe. At that point, the Act shifts responsibility to the service provider to disable the infringing matter, "preserving the strong incentives for service providers and copyright owners to cooperate to detect and deal with copyright infringements that take place in the digital networked environment."

The DMCA seeks to strike a balance by shielding online service providers from liability in damages as long as they remove or prevent access to infringing material. . . . The initial inquiry is whether LoopNet can be considered a service provider for the purposes of the DMCA.

a. Service Provider

In order to qualify for the safe harbor in the DMCA, LoopNet must meet the definition of "online service provider." Under § 512 (k)(1)(A), a service provider is "an entity offering the transmission, routing, or providing of connections for digital online communications, between

(continued)

or among points specified by a user, of material of the user's choosing, without modification to the content of the material as sent or received." 17 U.S.C. § 512(k)(1)(A)(1998). . . . For the other safe harbor provisions, including (c), which is at issue here, the definition is broader: "a provider of online services or network access, or the operator of facilities therefore.". . .

"Online services" is surely broad enough to encompass the type of service provided by LoopNet that is at issue here. The term is, of course, only a threshold to the protections of the Act. Even if LoopNet qualifies as a service provider, it must meet the other criteria.

b. Stored at the Instance of the User

A service provider is only protected from liability by the DMCA, "for infringement of copyright by reason of its storage at the direction of user of material." 17 U.S.C. § 512(c)(1) . . . [The photographs at issue] are uploaded at the volition of the user and are subject . . . to a mere screening to assess whether they are commercial property and to catch any obvious infringements. . . . Although humans are involved rather than mere technology, they serve only as a gateway and are not involved in a selection process . . . Therefore, this threshold requirement is met and LoopNet is not disqualified from the safe harbor on these grounds.

c. Knowledge

The safe harbor protects service providers from liability unless they have knowledge of copyright infringement. There are three types of knowledge of infringement that can take a service provider out of the safe harbor: (1) the service provider can have actual knowledge of infringement; (2) it can be aware of facts which raise a "red flag" that its users are infringing; or (3) the copyright owner can notify the service provider in a manner "substantially" conforming with § 512 (c)(3) that its works are being infringed. . . . The service provider does not automatically lose its liability shield upon receiving notice, but "the Act shifts responsibility to the service provider to disable the infringing matter. . . ."

. . . LoopNet received notification of claimed infringement . . . so the adequacy of LoopNet's removal policy must be assessed to determine whether LoopNet is protected by the safe harbor.

d. Adequacy of Termination and "Take Down" Policy

Once a service provider has received notification of a claimed infringement as described in [the Act] . . . the service provider can remain in the safe harbor if it "responds expeditiously to remove, or disable access to, the material that is claimed to be infringing or to be the subject of infringing activity." 17 U.S.C. § 512 (c)(1)(C) (1998). . . .

There are several material factual disputes remaining as to whether the removal of allegedly infringing photographs was satisfactorily expeditious and whether LoopNet's termination policy was reasonable and effective. CoStar's infringement claims are based on the posting of specific photographs. Additionally, LoopNet's knowledge of the alleged infringements and its "take down" and termination policies have changed over time in fairly significant ways. In order to resolve this issue, the factfinder will have to focus on each photo and the policy in effect prior to the posting of each photo. Hence, neither party is entitled to summary judgment on this issue. . . .

3. LIABILITY FOR CONTRIBUTORY INFRINGEMENT

With regard to the photographs that were infringed before the safe harbor applied . . . and in case LoopNet's termination policy and take down of infringing photographs is found to be inadequate so as to remove it from the safe harbor, the analysis shifts from the DMCA back to contributory infringement. The determination of contributory infringement liability turns on a different issue of knowledge than the standard used to determine LoopNet's eligibility for the safe harbor. Here, the question is whether CoStar's notice of claimed infringement was sufficient to satisfy the knowledge prong of the test for contributory infringement either by providing actual knowledge, a "red flag" that infringement was occurring, or constructive knowledge.

. . . [T]he fact finder must determine along a continuum the adequacy of the policy in place prior to the posting of each specific photograph. Therefore, neither party is entitled to summary judgment on this issue.

e. Preemption of Non-Copyright Claims

. . . The Copyright Act preempts state law that is "equivalent to any of the exclusive rights within the general scope of copyright as specified by section 106." 17 U.S.C. § 301(a) (1996) . . . "To determine whether a state claim is preempted by the Act, courts must make a two-part inquiry: (1) the work must be within the scope of the subject matter of copyright, and (2) the state law rights must be equivalent to any exclusive rights within the scope of federal copyright." *Fischer v. Viacom Intern Corp.*, 115 F. Supp. 2d 535. 540 (D.Md. 2000). . . . The critical question, then, is whether CoStar's unfair competition claim contains an additional element or whether it is based solely on the alleged copying.

. . . Essentially, CoStar's claim is that LoopNet is exhibiting as its own photographs on its website that CoStar has an exclusive right to exhibit or license for exhibition. This type of reverse passing off is, in effect, a "disguised copyright infringement claim.". . . Therefore, this claim does not satisfy the "extra-element" test and so is equivalent to CoStar's claim under the Copyright Act. Accordingly, it is preempted. . . .

V. CONCLUSION

For the foregoing reasons; by separate order, both motions concerning the safe harbor defense of the DMCA will be denied, . . . both motions concerning contributory infringement will be denied, . . . summary judgment will be granted in favor of LoopNet on the . . . preemption of the state law claims.

II

Introduction to Law

The aspiring paralegal professional must become familiar with American legal heritage, including how the law developed in this country over the centuries. This includes learning the historical and current sources of law of federal and state law. In addition, a professional paralegal should have knowledge of the Constitution of the United States of America and how it created the federal government, delegating powers to the federal government, reserving powers to the states, and protecting us from unwelcomed government intrusion into our lives. A paralegal professional must have knowledge of the American court system and the process of judicial and non-judicial dispute resolution. A working knowledge of the civil litigation process, criminal litigation and procedure, and administrative law is a necessary part of a paralegal professional's education. Part II "Introduction to Law" provides the paralegal professional student with this knowledge.

Chapter 5
American Legal Heritage and Constitutional Law

Chapter 6
The Court System and Alternative Dispute Resolution

Chapter 7
Civil Litigation

Chapter 8
Criminal Procedure and Administrative Law

American Legal Heritage and Constitutional Law

DIGITAL RESOURCES

Chapter 5 Digital Resources at *www.pearsonhighered.com/goldman*

- Video Case Studies:
  - Difference Between a Criminal and a Civil Trial
  - A School Principal Reacts: Student Rights versus School's Duty
  - Confidentiality Issue: Attorney–Client Privilege
- Chapter Summary • Web Links • Court Opinions • Glossary • Comprehension Quizzes
- Technology Resources

" We the People of the United States, in Order to form a more perfect Union, establish Justice, insure domestic Tranquility, provide for the common defense, promote the general Welfare, and secure the Blessings of Liberty to ourselves and our Posterity, do ordain and establish this Constitution for the United States of America."

Preamble to the Constitution of the United States of America

After studying this chapter, you should be able to:

1. Recognize the professional opportunities for paralegals in the constitutional law area.
2. Define *law* and describe the functions of law.
3. Describe the fairness and flexibility of the law.
4. List and describe the sources of law in the United States.
5. Describe and apply important clauses of the U.S. Constitution.
6. Describe and apply the protections of the Bill of Rights and other amendments to the U.S. Constitution.
7. Explain a paralegal's duty to avoid conflicts of interest.

Paralegals at Work

As a paralegal, you are working for a large law firm that specializes in handling constitutional law issues for clients. You work for Vivian Kang, a senior partner of the law firm. One day Ms. Kang calls you into her office and tells you that a new client, Mr. Hayward Storm, has retained the law firm. Ms. Kang asks you to sit in with her during an interview with Mr. Storm. Mr. Storm arrives on the day of the interview, and Ms. Kang, Mr. Storm, and you go into the conference room.

Mr. Storm tells the following story: For more than twenty years he has been on radio and television, primarily as a disc jockey and talk show host. Mr. Storm most recently hosted television shows where he did outlandish things such as using vulgar language, having guests appear on the show nude, telling disgusting jokes, and doing other things that offend many people. Mr. Storm also hosted a radio show in which he used profanity and offensive language. The Federal Communications Commission (FCC), a federal government agency, is responsible for regulating radio and television. Mr. Storm tells you that the FCC has fined him and his employer for his engaging in such conduct over the television and radio airwaves.

In addition, Mr. Storm explains that he will be leaving regular radio and television, which is regulated by the FCC, and has been hired to be a disc jockey for satellite radio broadcasts. He is making this change because satellite radio currently is not regulated by the FCC. Mr. Storm plans to continue his usual offensive programming on satellite radio and says he will expand his extreme language and conduct because satellite radio is not regulated by the FCC but is concerned that Congress will enact a federal statute granting the FCC power to regulate satellite radio.

Consider the issues involved in this scenario as you read the chapter.

INTRODUCTION FOR THE PARALEGAL

A paralegal must have a foundation in the basic sources of the law of the United States. Our society makes and enforces laws that govern the conduct of the individuals, businesses, and other organizations that function within it. In the words of Judge Learned Hand, "Without law we cannot live; only with it can we insure the future which by right is ours. The best of men's hopes are enmeshed in its success" (*The Spirit of Liberty*, 1960).

Although U.S. law is based primarily on English common law, other legal systems, such as Spanish and French civil law, also influenced it. The sources of law in this country are the U.S. Constitution, state constitutions, federal and state statutes, ordinances, administrative agency rules and regulations, executive orders, and judicial decisions by federal and state courts.

Paralegals should be renaissance men and women, who have an understanding of this country's founding, its constitutional protections, and the current debates concerning the application of the constitutional language in these modern times. This chapter covers the nature and definition of law, the history and sources of law, and the U.S. Constitution.

The following section discusses the career opportunities for paralegal professionals in the constitutional law area.

Web Exploration

Go to www.nps.gov/archive/stli/prod02.htm to read a history of the Statute of Liberty. Visit the World Heritage website describing the Statute of Liberty at www.unesco.org/en/list/307.

CAREER OPPORTUNITIES FOR PARALEGALS IN CONSTITUTIONAL LAW

Some members of the paralegal profession will work on cases that involve constitutional law issues. The Constitution of the United States of America is one of the most important documents ever drafted. The U.S. Constitution created a new country, one that was not ruled by kings, queens, monarchs, or dictators. The country was created as the world's first democracy—a crucial change in the history of the world.

The Constitution has been continually implemented since its ratification more than two centuries ago. The Constitution is considered a "living document" that has been interpreted by the United States Supreme Court and other courts to apply to an ever-changing society.

Paralegals who work in the constitutional law field will be called upon to conduct legal research relating to provisions and amendments to the U.S. Constitution, find relevant cases that interpret constitutional language, and assist lawyers who present cases to the courts regarding constitutional law issues. This is an exciting field of law to participate in as a paralegal professional. Some members of the paralegal profession will be fortunate to work on cases that will be heard and decided by the U.S. Supreme Court.

Several of the major provisions and protections of the U.S. Constitution and its amendments that paralegals should know, and which are covered in this chapter, are:

- Supremacy Clause
- Commerce Clause
- Freedom of speech
- Freedom of religion
- Due Process Clause
- Equal Protection Clause

The U.S. Constitution has many other important provisions as well. Paralegals should be fully informed citizens, and because of their position, understand how the Constitution created the federal government, built in checks and balances, granted powers to the federal government, and established protections for us against unconstitutional intrusions into our lives by the government. The Constitution of the United States of America is set forth in its entirety in Appendix F to this book.

What Is Law?

The first question a paralegal studying American legal heritage must answer is "What is law?" The law consists of rules that regulate the conduct of individuals, businesses, and other organizations within society. Laws are intended to protect persons and their property from unwanted interference from others and forbid persons from engaging in certain undesirable activities.

The concept of **law** is broad. Although it is difficult to state a precise definition, *Black's Law Dictionary*, 5th edition, gives one that is sufficient for this text:

> Law, in its generic sense, is a body of rules of action or conduct prescribed by controlling authority, and having binding legal force. That which must be obeyed and followed by citizens subject to sanctions or legal consequences is a law.

Law That which must be obeyed and followed by citizens subject to sanctions or legal consequences; a body of rules of action or conduct prescribed by controlling authority, and having binding legal force.

Fairness of the Law

On the whole, the American legal system is one of the most comprehensive, fair, and democratic systems of law ever developed and enforced. Nevertheless, some misuses and oversights of our legal system—including abuses of discretion and mistakes by judges and juries, unequal applications of the law, and procedural mishaps—allow some guilty parties to go unpunished.

In *Standefer v. United States* [447 U.S.10, 100 S.Ct.1999 (1980)] the Supreme Court *affirmed* (let stand) the criminal conviction of a Gulf Oil Corporation executive for aiding and abetting the bribery of an Internal Revenue Service agent. The agent had been acquitted in a separate trial. In writing the opinion of the Court, Chief Justice Warren Burger stated, "This case does no more than manifest the simple, if discomforting, reality that different juries may reach different results under any criminal statute. That is one of the consequences we accept under our jury system."

Flexibility of the Law

An important fact for a paralegal professional to learn is that American law is flexible. The law is generally responsive to cultural, technological, economic, and social changes.

Example Laws which are no longer viable—such as those that restricted the property rights of women—are often repealed.

Laws cannot be written in advance to anticipate every dispute that could arise in the future. Therefore, *general principles* are developed to be applied by courts and juries to individual disputes. This flexibility in the law leads to some uncertainty in predicting

---

FUNCTIONS OF THE LAW

The law is often described by the functions it serves within a society. The primary functions served by U.S. law are:

1. Keeping the peace (e.g., making certain activities crimes).
2. Shaping moral standards (e.g., enacting laws that discourage drug and alcohol abuse).
3. Promoting social justice (e.g., enacting statutes that prohibit discrimination in employment).
4. Maintaining the status quo (e.g., passing laws that prevent the forceful overthrow of government).
5. Facilitating orderly change (e.g., passing statutes only after considerable study, debate, and public input).
6. Facilitating planning (e.g., designing commercial laws to allow businesses to plan their activities, allocate their productive resources, and assess the risks they take).
7. Providing a basis for compromise (approximately 90 percent of all lawsuits are settled prior to trial).
8. Maximizing individual freedom (e.g., the rights of freedom of speech, religion, and association granted by the First Amendment to the U.S. Constitution).

results of lawsuits. The following quote by Judge Jerome Frank addresses the value of the adaptability of law (*Law and the Modern Mind*, 1930):

> The law always has been, is now, and will ever continue to be, largely vague and variable. And how could this be otherwise? The law deals with human relations in their most complicated aspects. The whole confused, shifting helter-skelter of life parades before it—more confused than ever, in our kaleidoscopic age.
>
> Men have never been able to construct a comprehensive, eternalized set of rules anticipating all possible legal disputes and formulating in advance the rules which would apply to them. Situations are bound to occur which were never contemplated when the original rules were made. How much less is such a frozen legal system possible in modern times?
>
> The constant development of unprecedented problems requires a legal system capable of fluidity and pliancy. Our society would be straightjacketed were not the courts, with the able assistance of the lawyers, constantly overhauling the law and adapting it to the realities of ever-changing social, industrial, and political conditions; although changes cannot be made lightly, yet rules of law must be more or less impermanent, experimental and therefore not nicely calculable.
>
> Much of the uncertainty of law is not an unfortunate accident; it is of immense social value.

Sometimes it takes years before the law reflects the norms of society. Other times, society is led by the law.

Schools of Jurisprudential Thought

The philosophy or science of the law is referred to as **jurisprudence**. Several different philosophies have been advanced about how the law developed, ranging from the classical natural theory to modern theories of law and economics and critical legal studies. Legal philosophers can be grouped into the following major categories.

- The **natural law school of jurisprudence** postulates that the law is based on what is "correct." Natural law philosophers emphasize a *moral theory of law*—that is, law should be based on morality and ethics. People "discover" natural law through reasoning and choosing between good and evil. Documents such as the U.S. Constitution, the Magna Carta, and the United Nations Charter reflect this theory.
- The **historical school of jurisprudence** believes that the law is an aggregate of social traditions and customs that have developed over the centuries. Changes in the norms of society will be reflected gradually in the law. The law is an evolutionary process. Thus, historical legal scholars look to past legal decisions (precedent) to solve contemporary problems.
- The **analytical school of jurisprudence** maintains that the law is shaped by logic. Analytical philosophers believe that results are reached by applying principles of logic to the specific facts of the case. The emphasis is on the logic of the result rather than how the result is reached.
- The **sociological school of jurisprudence** asserts that the law is a means of achieving and advancing certain sociological goals. Followers of this philosophy, known as *realists*, believe that the purpose of law is to shape social behavior. Sociological philosophers are unlikely to adhere to past law as precedent.
- The philosophers of the **command school of jurisprudence** believe that the law is a set of rules developed, communicated, and enforced by the ruling party rather than reflecting the society's morality, history, logic, or sociology. This school maintains that the law changes when the ruling class changes.
- The **critical legal studies school of jurisprudence** proposes that legal rules are unnecessary and are used as an obstacle by the powerful to

maintain the status quo. Critical legal theorists (the "*Crits*") argue that legal disputes should be solved by applying arbitrary rules based on broad notions of what is "fair" in each circumstance. Under this theory, subjective decision making by judges would be permitted.

- The **law and economics school** proposes that promoting market and economic efficiency should be the central goal of legal decision making. This school is called the "Chicago School" of jurisprudence because it had its roots at the University of Chicago. This school proposes, for example, that free-market principles, cost–benefit analysis, and supply-and-demand theories should be used to determine the passage of legislation and the outcome of lawsuits.

Web Exploration

Read the opinion of Chief Justice Warren of the U.S. Supreme Court in *Brown v. Board of Education* at http://www .nationalcenter.org/brown.html.

History of American Law

Paralegals need to know the history of the law in the United States and how the law developed to be what it is today. Every person in the United States, and paralegals in particular, should have knowledge of this country's legal history.

When the American colonies were first settled, the English system of common law was generally adopted as the system of jurisprudence. English common law became the source of much of the law of the American colonies and eventually of the United States of America. This was the foundation from which American judges developed a common law in the United States.

English Common Law

English **common law** was law developed by judges who issued their opinions when deciding a case. The principles announced in these cases became precedent for later judges deciding similar cases. The English common law can be divided into cases decided by the following courts:

- **Law courts**. After 1066, William the Conqueror and his successors to the throne of England replaced various local laws with one uniform system of law. The king or queen appointed loyal followers as judges in all local areas. These judges were charged with administering the law in a uniform manner in what were called **law courts**. Law at this time tended to emphasize form (legal procedure) over the substance (merit) of the case. The only relief available in law courts was a monetary award for damages.

- **Chancery (equity) courts**. Because of the sometimes unfair results and the limited remedy available in the law courts, a second set of courts— the **Court of Chancery** (or **equity court**)—was established, under the authority of the Lord Chancellor. Those who believed that the decision of the law court was unfair or that the law court could not grant an appropriate remedy could seek relief in the Court of Chancery. The Chancery Court inquired into the merits of the case rather than emphasize legal procedure. The Chancellor's remedies were called *equitable remedies* because they were shaped to fit each situation. Equitable orders and remedies of the Court of Chancery took precedence over the legal decisions and remedies of the law courts.

- **Merchant courts**. As trade developed in the Middle Ages, the merchants who traveled around England and Europe developed certain rules to solve their commercial disputes. These rules, known as the "law of merchants" or the *law merchant*, were based upon common trade practices and usage. Eventually, a separate set of courts, called the **merchant court,** was established to administer these rules. In the early 1900s, the merchant court was absorbed into the regular law court system of England.

Common law Developed by judges who issue their opinions when deciding cases. The principles announced in these cases became precedent for later judges deciding similar cases.

Adoption of the English Common Law in America

All the states of the United States of America (except Louisiana) base their legal systems primarily on the English *common law*. In the United States, the law, equity, and merchant courts have been merged. Thus, most U.S. courts permit the aggrieved party to seek both law and equitable orders and remedies.

The importance of common law to the American legal system is described in the following excerpt from Justice William Douglas's opinion in the 1841 case of *Penny v. Little* [4 Ill. 301, 1841 Ill. Lexis 98 (Ill. 1841)]:

> The common law is a beautiful system, containing the wisdom and experiences of ages. Like the people it ruled and protected, it was simple and crude in its infancy, and became enlarged, improved, and polished as the nation advanced in civilization, virtue, and intelligence. Adapting itself to the conditions and circumstances of the people and relying upon them for its administration, it necessarily improved as the condition of the people was elevated. The inhabitants of this country always claimed the common law as their birthright, and at an early period established it as the basis of their jurisprudence.

Civil Law System

In addition to the Anglo-American common law system, one of the other major legal systems that has developed in the world is the Romano-Germanic **civil law system**. This legal system, commonly called the *civil law*, dates to 450 B.C., when Rome adopted a code of laws applicable to the Romans. A compilation of Roman law, called the *Corpus Juris Civilis* (the Body of Civil Law), was completed in A.D. 534. Later, two national codes—the French Civil Code of 1804 (the Napoleonic Code) and the German Civil Code of 1896—became models for countries that adopted civil codes.

In contrast to the Anglo-American common law, in which laws are created by the judicial system as well as by congressional legislation, the Civil Code and parliamentary statutes that expand and interpret it are the sole sources of the law in most civil law countries. Thus, the adjudication of a case is simply the application of the Code or the statutes to a specific set of facts. In some civil law countries, court decisions do not have the force of law.

Some states in America, particularly states that have a French or Spanish heritage, such as Louisiana and states of the southwestern United States, have incorporated civil law into their legal systems.

U.S. Congress, Washington, DC. The U.S. Congress, which is a bicameral system made up of the U.S. Senate and the U.S. House of Representatives, creates federal law by enacting statutes. Each state has two senators and is allocated a certain number of representatives, based on population.

Sources of Law in the United States

In more than 230 years since the founding of this country and adoption of the English common law, U.S. lawmakers have developed a substantial body of law. The laws of the United States are extremely complex.

Paralegals must have knowledge of the source of the laws that govern their work assignments. Paralegals often are called upon to conduct legal research to find relevant laws and judicial decisions that affect the cases or projects to which they are assigned. This chapter provides a detailed discussion of the sources of law in this country.

The sources of modern law in the United States are discussed in the following sections.

Constitutions

The **Constitution of the United States of America** is the *supreme law of the land*. This means that any law—federal, state, or local—that conflicts with the U.S. Constitution is unconstitutional and, therefore, unenforceable.

The principles enumerated in the Constitution are extremely broad, because the founding fathers intended them to be applied to evolving social, technological, and economic conditions. The U.S. Constitution often is referred to as a "living document" because it is so adaptable.

States also have their own constitutions, often patterned after the U.S. Constitution, though many are more detailed. Provisions of state constitutions are valid unless they conflict with the U.S. Constitution or any valid federal law.

> **Constitution of the United States of America** The supreme law of the United States. The Constitution of the United States of America establishes the structure of the federal government, delegates powers to the federal government, and guarantees certain fundamental rights.

Treaties

The U.S. Constitution provides that the President, with the advice and consent of the U.S. Senate, may enter into **treaties** with foreign governments. Treaties become part of the supreme law of the land. With increasing international economic relations among nations, treaties will become an even more important source of law affecting business in the future.

> **Treaty** A compact made between two or more nations.

Codified Law

Statutes are written laws that establish certain courses of conduct to which the covered parties must adhere. The U.S. Congress is empowered by the Commerce Clause and other provisions of the U.S. Constitution to enact **federal statutes** to regulate foreign and interstate commerce.

> **Statute** Written law enacted by the legislative branch of the federal and state governments that establishes certain courses of conduct that the covered parties must adhere to.

Examples   Federal antitrust laws, securities laws, bankruptcy laws, labor laws, equal employment opportunity laws, environmental protection laws, consumer protection laws, and such.

State legislatures also enact **state statutes**.

Examples   State corporation laws, partnership laws, workers' compensation laws, and the Uniform Commercial Code.

The statutes enacted by the legislative branches of the federal and state governments are organized by topic into code books, often called **codified law**. Paralegals are often called upon to conduct research to find appropriate codified law for cases that they are assigned to.

State legislatures often delegate lawmaking authority to local government bodies, including cities and municipalities, counties, school districts, water districts, and so on. These governmental units are empowered to adopt **ordinances**.

Examples   Traffic laws, local building codes, and zoning laws. Ordinances are also codified.

Administrative Agencies

The legislative and executive branches of federal and state governments are empowered to establish **administrative agencies** to enforce and interpret statutes enacted by Congress and state legislatures. Many of these agencies regulate business.

> **Example** Congress has created the Securities and Exchange Commission (SEC) and the Federal Trade Commission (FTC), among others.

The U.S. Congress or the state legislatures usually empower these agencies to adopt administrative rules and regulations to interpret the statutes that the agency is authorized to enforce. These rules and regulations have the force of law. Administrative agencies usually have the power to hear and decide disputes. Their decisions are called *orders*. Because of their power, administrative agencies often are informally called the "fourth branch" of government.

Executive Orders

The executive branch of government, which consists of the President of the United States and state governors, is empowered to issue executive orders.

This power is derived from express delegation from the legislative branch and is implied from the U.S. Constitution and state constitutions.

> **Example** On October 8, 2001, President George W. Bush by Executive Order established within the Executive Office of the President an Office of Homeland Security to be headed by the Assistant to the President for Homeland Security.

Judicial Decisions

Judicial decision A ruling about an individual lawsuit issued by federal and state courts.

When deciding individual lawsuits, federal and state courts issue **judicial decisions**. In these written opinions, the judge or justice usually explains the legal reasoning used to decide the case. These opinions often include interpretations of statutes, ordinances, administrative regulations, and the announcement of legal principles used to decide the case. Many court decisions are printed (reported) in books available in law libraries.

ETHICAL PERSPECTIVE

Paralegal's Duty to Perform an Assignment

Mr. Harrington, a paralegal, works for attorney Ms. Zhou. Ms. Zhou represents a client who has been charged with insider trading in violation of federal securities laws. Ms. Zhou assigns Mr. Harrington the responsibility of conducting research and finding any relevant court decisions that would apply to the case and any administrative agency rules of the Securities and Exchange Commission (SEC) that might apply to the case as well. Mr. Harrington is to prepare a memorandum summarizing his findings for Ms. Zhou.

Mr. Harrington conducts computer research using Lexis and finds the U.S. Supreme Court and U.S. Court of Appeals decisions that are relevant to the case. But because researching of administrative agency rules is more difficult to conduct, Mr. Harrington fails to check these sources. Mr. Harrington reports his findings of relevant case law to Ms. Zhou, but reports that he has found no relevant SEC administrative rules relevant to the case.

Here, Mr. Harrington has been derelict in his duties in not performing the task he has been given. He has also engaged in deceit by reporting to Ms. Zhou, his supervising attorney, that he has found no relevant SEC agency rules when in fact he has not conducted such research at all. And finally, Mr. Harrington may cause damage to the client who may suffer a loss in court because the supervising attorney Ms. Zhou does not have all of the relevant information to properly prepare her defense for her client.

Priority of Law in the United States

Again, the U.S. Constitution and treaties take precedence over all other laws. Federal statutes take precedence over federal regulations, and valid federal law takes precedence over any conflicting state or local law. State constitutions rank as the highest state law, and state statutes take precedence over state regulations. Valid state law takes precedence over local laws.

The following feature discusses a paralegal's ethical duty to perform lawful duties that are assigned to him or her.

The Doctrine of *Stare Decisis*

Based on the common law tradition, past court decisions become precedent for deciding future cases. Lower courts must follow the precedent established by higher courts. That is why all federal and state courts in the United States must follow the precedents established by U.S. Supreme Court decisions.

The courts of one jurisdiction are not bound by the precedent established by the courts of another jurisdiction, although they may look to each other for guidance. Thus, state courts of one state are not required to follow the legal precedent established by the courts of another state.

Adherence to precedent is called *stare decisis* ("to stand by the decision"). The doctrine of *stare decisis* promotes uniformity of law within a jurisdiction, makes the court system more efficient, and makes the law more predictable for individuals and businesses. A court may change or reverse its legal reasoning later if a new case is presented to it and change is warranted.

> *Stare decisis* Latin: "to stand by the decision." Adherence to precedent.

The doctrine of *stare decisis* is discussed in the following excerpt from Justice Musmanno's decision in *Flagiello v. Pennsylvania* [208 A.2d 193, 1965 Pa. Lexis 442 (Pa.1965)].

> Without *stare decisis*, there would be no stability in our system of jurisprudence. Stare decisis channels the law. It erects lighthouses and flies the signals of safety. The ships of jurisprudence must follow that well-defined channel which, over the years, has been proved to be secure and worthy.

Constitution of the United States of America

Prior to the American Revolution, each of the thirteen original colonies operated as a separate sovereignty under the rule of England. In September 1774, representatives of the colonies met as a Continental Congress. In 1776, the colonies declared their independence from England, and the American Revolution ensued.

The Constitutional Convention was convened in Philadelphia in May 1787, with the primary purpose of strengthening the federal government. After substantial debate, the delegates agreed to a new U.S. Constitution, reported to Congress in September 1787. State ratification of the Constitution was completed in 1788. Since that time, many amendments, including the Bill of Rights, have been added to the Constitution.

The U.S. Constitution serves several major functions:

1. It creates the three branches of the federal government (executive, legislative, and judicial) and allocates powers to these branches.
2. It grants the federal government certain authority to enact laws and enforce those laws.
3. It protects individual rights by limiting the government's ability to restrict those rights.

The Constitution itself provides that it may be amended to address social and economic changes. The first page of the Constitution of the United States of America is provided in Exhibit 5.1.

Exhibit 5.1 The Constitution of the United States

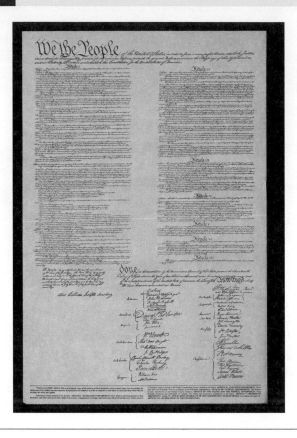

Federalism and Delegated Powers

The U.S. form of government is referred to as **federalism,** which means that the federal government and the 50 state governments share powers. When the states ratified the Constitution, they *delegated* certain powers to the federal government. These **delegated powers,** also called **enumerated powers,** authorize the federal government to deal with national and international affairs. State governments have powers that are not specifically delegated to the federal government by the Constitution and are empowered to deal with local affairs.

Doctrine of Separation of Powers

The first three Articles of the Constitution divide the federal government into three branches:

1. **Article I** of the Constitution establishes the **legislative branch** of government, which is bicameral—consisting of the Senate and the House of Representatives—collectively referred to as *Congress.* Each state is allocated two senators. The number of representatives to the House of Representatives is determined by the population of each state. The current number of representatives is determined from the 2000 census.
2. **Article II** of the Constitution establishes the **executive branch** of government by providing for the election of the President and Vice President. The President is not elected by popular vote but, instead, by the *electoral college*, whose representatives are appointed by state delegations.
3. **Article III** establishes the **judicial branch** of the government in the Supreme Court and provides for the creation of other federal courts by Congress.

Web Exploration

Read the article, "The Power of the Courts—*Marbury v. Madison*, 1803." At the top of the page shown, click on the sixth icon from the left, at http://archives .gov/national-archives-experience/ charters/charters.htm. What was the decision in this case?

Web Exploration

Read the section "How It Works" and answer the following question: "If no candidate for President receives an absolute electoral majority, how is the President of the United States elected?" at http://en.wikipedia.org/wiki/u.s. _electoral_college.

Checks and Balances

Certain **checks and balances** are built into the Constitution to ensure that no one branch of the federal government becomes too powerful. Some of the checks and balances in our system of government are as follows:

1. The judicial branch has authority to examine the acts of the other two branches of government and determine whether these acts are constitutional.
2. The executive branch can enter into treaties with foreign governments only with the advice and consent of the Senate.
3. The legislative branch is authorized to create federal courts and determine their jurisdiction and to enact statutes that change judicially made law.
4. The President has veto power over bills passed by Congress. The bill goes back to Congress, where a vote of two-thirds of each the Senate and the House of Representatives is required to override the President's veto.
5. The President nominates persons to be U.S. Supreme Court justices, and many other federal judges, but the U.S. Senate must confirm the candidate before he or she becomes a judge.
6. The House of Representatives has the power to impeach the President for certain activities, such as treason, bribery, and other crimes. The Senate has the power to try the impeachment case, which requires a two-thirds vote of the Senate to impeach the President.

Supremacy Clause

The **Supremacy Clause** establishes that the federal Constitution, treaties, federal laws, and federal regulations are the supreme law of the land [Article VI, Section 2]. State and local laws that conflict with valid federal law are unconstitutional. The concept of federal law taking precedence over state or local law is called the **preemption doctrine**.

> **Supremacy Clause** A clause of the U.S. Constitution that establishes that the federal Constitution, treaties, federal laws, and federal regulations are the supreme law of the land.

Congress may expressly provide that a specific federal statute *exclusively* regulates a specific area or activity. No state or local law regulating the area or activity is valid if there is such a statute. More often, though, federal statutes do not expressly provide for exclusive jurisdiction. In these instances, state and local governments have *concurrent jurisdiction* to regulate the area or activity. But any state or local law that "directly and substantially" conflicts with valid federal law is preempted under the Supremacy Clause.

> **Example** The United States government entered into treaties with other countries that established the size and length of oil tanker ships. Thus, oil tankers can transport oil between different countries using the same oil tankers. The state of Washington enacted a law that only permitted smaller oil tankers to enter its Puget Sound watercourse, which flows from waters of the Pacific Ocean. Oil tanker companies sued the state of Washington, arguing that the state law was unconstitutional. The U.S. Supreme Court held that the state law conflicted with federal law and was therefore preempted by the Supremacy Clause.

Commerce Clause

The **Commerce Clause** of the U.S. Constitution grants Congress the power "to regulate commerce with foreign nations, and among the several states, and with Indian tribes" [Article I, Section 8, Clause 3]. Because this clause authorizes the federal government to regulate commerce, it has a greater impact on business than any other provision in the Constitution. Among other things, this clause is intended to foster the development of a national market and free trade among the states.

> **Commerce Clause** A clause of the U.S. Constitution that grants Congress the power "to regulate commerce with foreign nations, and among the several states, and with Indian tribes."

The U.S. Constitution grants the federal government the power to regulate three types of commerce. These are:

1. Commerce with Indian tribes
2. Commerce with foreign nations
3. Interstate commerce

Native Americans

Web Exploration

Visit the website of the National Museum of the American Indian at www.nmai.si.edu. Go to http://www.youtube.com/watch?v=Gve7avdld78&feature=related and view the video about the "Trail of Tears." When did this occur?

Before Europeans arrived in the "New World," the land had been occupied for thousands of years by who we now refer to as Native Americans. When the United States was first founded over two centuries ago, it consisted of the original thirteen colonies, all located in the east, primarily on the Atlantic Ocean. At that time, these colonies (states), in the U.S. Constitution, delegated to the federal government the authority to regulate commerce with the Indian tribes. This included the original thirteen states as well as the territory that was to eventually become the United States of America.

> **Example**   The federal government enacted the Indian Gaming Regulatory Act[1] wherein the federal government authorized Native American tribes to operate gaming facilities. This act sets the terms of casino gambling and other gaming activities on tribal land. Today, casinos operated by Native Americans can be found in many states. Profits from the casinos have become an important source of income for members of certain tribes.

Foreign Commerce

The Commerce Clause gives the federal government the exclusive power to regulate commerce with foreign nations. Direct or indirect regulation of foreign commerce by state or local governments violates the Commerce Clause and is therefore unconstitutional.

> **Example**   Suppose the state of Michigan imposes a 20 percent sales tax on foreign automobiles sold in Michigan but only 6 percent tax on domestic automobiles sold in Michigan. This state act violates the Commerce Clause because Michigan has regulated foreign commerce differently than state commerce. If Michigan placed a 20 percent sales tax on all automobiles sold in Michigan, this would not violate the Commerce Clause. Under its Foreign Commerce Clause power, the federal government could enact a federal law that places a 20 percent tax on foreign automobiles sold in the United States.

Interstate Commerce

The Commerce Clause gives the federal government the authority to regulate **interstate commerce**. Originally, the courts interpreted this clause to mean that the federal government could regulate only commerce that moved *in* interstate commerce. The modern rule, however, allows the federal government to regulate activities that *affect* interstate commerce.

Web Exploration

Go to www.uscis.gov/portal/site/uscis. Find information on this website that shows how to become a citizen of the United States of America.

Under the *effects on interstate commerce test*, the regulated activity does not itself have to be in interstate commerce. Thus, any **intrastate** (local) **commerce** that has an effect on interstate commerce is subject to federal regulation. Theoretically, this test subjects a substantial amount of business activity in the United States to federal regulation.

> **Example**   In the famous case of *Wickard, Secretary of Agriculture v. Filburn* [317 U.S. 111, 63 S.Ct. 82, 87 L.Ed. 122, 1942 U.S. Lexis 1046 (U.S.)] a federal statute limited the amount of wheat a farmer could plant and harvest for home consumption. Filburn, a farmer, violated the law. The U.S. Supreme Court

[1] 25 U.S.C. Sections 2701–2721.

upheld the statute on the grounds that it prevented nationwide surpluses and shortages of wheat. The Court reasoned that wheat grown for home consumption would affect the supply of wheat available in interstate commerce.

State Police Power

The states did not delegate all power to regulate business to the federal government. They retained the power to regulate intrastate and much interstate business activity that occurs within their borders. This is commonly referred to as states' **police power**.

Police power permits states (and, by delegation, local governments) to enact laws to protect or promote the *public health*, *safety*, *morals*, *and general welfare*. This includes the authority to enact laws that regulate the conduct of business.

Examples State environmental laws, corporation and partnership laws, property laws, and local zoning ordinances and building codes are enacted under this power.

Bill of Rights and Other Amendments

In 1791, the states approved the 10 amendments commonly referred to as the **Bill of Rights,** and they became part of the U.S. Constitution (see Exhibit 5.2). The Bill of Rights guarantees certain fundamental rights to natural persons and protects these rights from intrusive government action. Most of these rights, or "freedoms," also have been found applicable to so-called artificial persons (i.e., corporations).

The First Amendment to the Constitution guarantees the rights of free speech, assembly, and religion. In addition to the Bill of Rights, seventeen amendments have been added to the Constitution. Two important clauses from these amendments are the Due Process Clause and the Equal Protection Clause. Because these amendments are continually litigated and are frequent subjects of U.S. Supreme Court opinions, they are singled out for discussion in the following paragraphs.

Bill of Rights The first 10 amendments to the Constitution. They were added to the U.S. Constitution in 1791.

Web Exploration

Go to http://www.youtube.com/watch?v=ENiBuwkScEA to listen to a reading of the Bill of Rights.

Exhibit 5.2 Bill of Rights

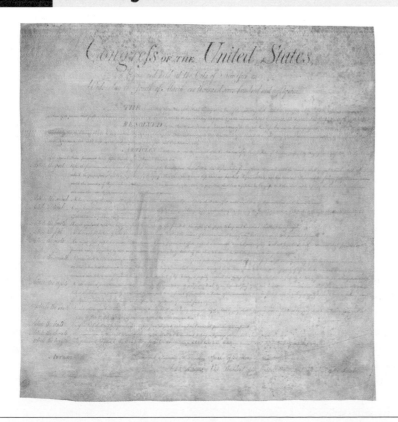

Freedom of Speech

One of the most honored freedoms guaranteed by the Bill of Rights is the **freedom of speech** of the First Amendment. Many other constitutional freedoms would be meaningless without it. The First Amendment's Freedom of Speech Clause protects speech only, not conduct. The U.S. Supreme Court places speech into three categories: (1) fully protected, (2) limited protected, and (3) unprotected speech.

Fully Protected Speech

Fully protected speech is speech that the government cannot prohibit or regulate. Political speech is an example of such speech.

> **Example**   The government could not enact a law that forbids citizens from criticizing the current President.

> The First Amendment protects oral, written, and symbolic speech.

> **Example**   If a person burns the American flag in protest of a current government policy, this is symbolic speech that is protected by the First Amendment.

Limited Protected Speech

The Supreme Court has held that certain types of speech are only **limited protected speech** under the First Amendment. Although the government cannot forbid this type of speech, it can subject this speech to restrictions of time, place, and manner. The following types of speech are accorded limited protection:

- **Offensive speech** is speech that offends many members of society. (It is not the same as obscene speech, however.) The Supreme Court has held that offensive speech may be restricted by the government under time, place, and manner restrictions.

  > **Example**   The Federal Communications Commission (FCC) can regulate the use of offensive language on television by limiting such language to times when children would be unlikely to be watching (e.g., late at night).

- **Commercial speech** is speech such as advertising and business solicitation. The Supreme Court has held that commercial speech is subject to proper time, place, and manner restrictions.

  > **Example**   A city could prohibit billboards along its highways for safety and aesthetic reasons as long as other forms of advertising (e.g., print media) are available to the commercial advertiser.

Unprotected Speech

There are certain types of speech that the U.S. Supreme Court has held has no protection under the Freedom of Speech Clause. These types of speech may be entirely prohibited by the government. The Supreme Court has held that the following types of speech are **unprotected speech** under the First Amendment and may be totally forbidden by the government:

- Dangerous speech (including such things as yelling "fire" in a crowded theater when there is no fire)
- Fighting words that are likely to provoke a hostile or violent response from an average person
- Speech that incites the violent or revolutionary overthrowing of the government; the mere abstract teaching of the morality and consequences of such action is protected
- Defamatory language
- Child pornography
- Obscene speech

Definition of Obscene Speech

The definition of **obscene speech** is quite subjective. One Supreme Court justice stated, "I know it when I see it" [Justice Stewart in *Facobellis v. Ohio*, 378 U.S. 184, 84 S.Ct. 1676 12 L.Ed.2d 793, 1964 U.S. Lexis 822 (U.S.)]. In *Miller v. California*, the Supreme Court determined that speech is obscene under the following circumstances.

1. The average person, applying contemporary community standards, would find that the work, taken as a whole, appeals to the prurient interest.
2. The work depicts or describes, in a patently offensive way, sexual conduct specifically defined by the applicable state law.
3. The work, taken as a whole, lacks serious literary, artistic, political, or scientific value. [413 U.S. 15, 93 S.Ct. 2607, 37 L.Ed.2d 419, 1973 U.S. Lexis 149 (U.S.)]

States are free to define what constitutes obscene speech. Movie theaters, magazine publishers, Web operators, and so on are often subject to challenges that the materials they display or sell are obscene and, therefore, not protected by the First Amendment.

Free Speech in Cyberspace

Paralegals are at the forefront of witnessing development and application of traditional laws to the digital age. This is nowhere more relevant than the application of constitutional provisions—drafted centuries ago—to the modern age. Once or twice a century a new medium seems to come along that presents new problems in applying freedom-of-speech rights. This time it is the Internet. The following is a U.S. Supreme Court case that addressed free speech in cyberspace.

The U.S. Congress enacted the *Computer Decency Act* to regulate the Internet. This statute made it a felony to knowingly make "indecent" or "patently offensive" materials available on computer systems, including the Internet, to persons under 18 years of age. The Act provided for fines, prison terms, and loss of licenses for anyone convicted of violating its terms.

Immediately, cyberspace providers and users filed lawsuits challenging these provisions of the Act as violating their free speech rights granted under the First Amendment to the Constitution. Proponents of the Act countered that these provisions were necessary to protect children from indecent materials.

The U.S. Supreme Court decided to hear this issue. The Supreme Court came down on the plaintiff's side, overturning the challenged provisions of the Computer Decency Act. The Court found that the terms "indecent" and "patently offensive" were too vague to define and criminally enforce. The Supreme Court reasoned that limiting the content on the Internet to what is suitable for a child resulted in unconstitutional limiting of adult speech. The Court stated that parents can regulate their children's access to the Internet and can install blocking and filtering software programs to protect their children from seeing adult materials.

The Supreme Court declared emphatically that the Internet must be given the highest possible level of First Amendment free-speech protection. The Supreme Court stated,

> As the most participatory form of mass speech yet developed, the Internet deserves the highest protection from government intrusion.

The Court also reasoned that because the Internet is a global medium, there would be no way to prevent indecent material from flowing over the Internet from abroad.[2]

---

[2]*Reno v. American Civil Liberties Union*, 521 U.S. 844, 117 S.Ct. 2329, 138 L.Ed.2d 874, **Web** 1997 U.S. Lexis 4037 (Supreme Court of the United States).

Protest, Los Angeles, California. The Freedom of Speech Clause of the First Amendment to the U.S. Constitution protects the right to engage in political speech. Freedom of speech is one of Americans' most highly prized rights.

Freedom of Religion

The U.S. Constitution requires federal, state, and local governments to be neutral toward religion. The First Amendment actually contains two separate religion clauses:

Establishment Clause A clause to the First Amendment that prohibits the government from either establishing a state religion or promoting one religion over another.

1. The **Establishment Clause** prohibits the government from either establishing a state religion or promoting one religion over another. Thus, it guarantees that there will be no state-sponsored religion.

   Example The U.S. Supreme Court ruled that an Alabama statute that authorized a one-minute period of silence in school for "meditation or voluntary prayer" was invalid.[3] The Court held that the statute endorsed religion.

   Example The U.S. Supreme Court held that copies of the Ten Commandments that were prominently displayed in large, gold-frames, and hung alone in the McCreary County courthouse and the Pulaski County courthouse in Kentucky, so that visitors could see them, violated the Establishment Clause.[4]

Free Exercise Clause A clause to the First Amendment that prohibits the government from interfering with the free exercise of religion in the United States.

2. The **Free Exercise Clause** prohibits the government from interfering with the free exercise of religion in the United States. Generally, this clause prevents the government from enacting laws that either prohibit or inhibit individuals from participating in or practicing their chosen religion.

   Example The federal, state, or local governments could not enact a law that prohibited all religions or that prohibited churches, synagogues, mosques, or temples. The government could not prohibit religious practitioners from celebrating their major holidays and high holy days. Of course, this right to be free from government intervention in the practice of religion is not absolute.

   Example Human sacrifices are unlawful and are not protected by the First Amendment.

---

[3]*Wallace v. Jaffree*, 472 U.S. 38, 105 S.Ct. 2479, 86 L.Ed.2d 29, **Web** 1985 U.S. Lexis 91 (Supreme Court of the United States).
[4]*McCreary County, Kentucky v. American Civil Liberties Union*, 545 U.S. 844, 125 S.Ct. 2722, 162 L.Ed.2d 729, **Web** 2005 U.S. Lexis 5211 (Supreme Court of the United States).

Paralegals *in* Practice

Charlotte A. Sheraden-Baker started her legal career as a legal secretary after graduating from high school. After taking time out to raise a family, she resumed work as a legal secretary while attending night school to obtain her paralegal degree. In 2000, she graduated as Paralegal of the Year with an Associate of Applied Science degree, the oldest person in her class. After convincing her firm they needed another paralegal, Charlotte was promoted and continued evening classes to obtain her Bachelor of Arts degree. She currently works for the law firm of Warner, Smith & Harris in Fort Smith, Arkansas, where she has been employed for the last 14 years.

I work for a general practice that has 13 partners and three associates. I recently assisted in a constitutional law case that was appealed to the Arkansas Supreme Court over a First Amendment issue. Our client was a party to a lawsuit between two groups of a local temple. Both thought they were entitled to make governing rules for the temple, and maintain its original assets and location. Since the matter could not be resolved between the opposing parties, the state court judge was asked to do so, and determined that an election should be held, whereby the temple members would decide.

In the process, my firm's attorneys contended that the judge overstepped his duties by overriding the already-established governing documents of the temple and assigning a different definition as to who was a member of the congregation and entitled to vote. It was argued that the judge had prohibited the free exercise of religion, as guaranteed by the First Amendment of both the federal and state constitutions. Our case was lost on appeal because it was determined the judge did not intrude into anyone's religious rights. Nonetheless, the case was a great learning experience in my legal career.

At the state court level, some of my pretrial duties included preparing, gathering, and duplicating exhibits; copying and keeping up-to-date on important documents; making lists of witnesses and exhibits; and more. At trial, my primary job was to ensure that the judge, court clerk, and court reporter had all the necessary documents; monitor exhibits offered, admitted, or rejected; organize witnesses and keep track of their appearances and testimony; and take notes of testimony to help with the attorney's upcoming examinations.

My duties at the state Supreme Court level were slightly different. For any case that is appealed, each party gets to prepare a brief, and respond to the other party's brief within a short time. Then, the case is set for oral argument before the state Supreme Court. Preparation of appellate briefs is complicated and precise, as the Supreme Courts require specific style, format, and contents. I was asked to monitor filing deadlines, obtain the local trial transcripts and submit them to the Supreme Court, prepare an extensive summary of the pertinent trial testimony for the appeal brief, and verify or "Shepardize" all cases cited in the brief itself.

Due Process Clause

The **Due Process Clause** provides that no person shall be deprived of "life, liberty, or property" without due process of the law. It is contained in both the Fifth and the Fourteenth Amendments. The Due Process Clause of the Fifth Amendment applies to federal government action; that of the Fourteenth Amendment applies to state and local government action. The government is not prohibited from taking a person's life, liberty, or property, but the government must follow due process to do so. There are two categories of due process: *substantive* and *procedural*.

Due Process Clause A clause that provides that no person shall be deprived of "life, liberty, or property" without due process of the law.

Substantive Due Process

Substantive due process requires that government statutes, ordinances, regulations, or other laws be clear on their face and not overly broad in scope. The test of whether substantive due process is met is whether a "reasonable person" could understand the law to be able to comply with it. Laws that do not meet this test are declared *void for vagueness*.

> **Example**   A city ordinance that makes it illegal for persons to wear "clothes of the opposite sex" would be held unconstitutional as void for vagueness because a reasonable person could not clearly determine whether his or her conduct violates the law.

Procedural Due Process

Web Exploration

How does Louisiana law differ from the other 49 states? Go to: http://www.la-legal.com/history_louisiana_law.htm.

Procedural due process requires that the government give a person proper *notice* and *hearing* of the legal action before that person is deprived of his or her life, liberty, or property. The government action must be fair.

> **Example**   If the federal government or a state government brings a criminal lawsuit against a defendant for the alleged commission of a crime, the government must notify the person of its intent (by charging the defendant with a crime) and provide the defendant with a proper hearing (a trial).

> **Example**   If the government wants to take a person's home by eminent domain to build a highway, the government must (1) give the homeowner sufficient notice of its intention, and (2) provide a hearing. Under the **Just Compensation Clause** of the Fifth Amendment, the government must pay the owner just compensation for taking the property.

Equal Protection Clause

Equal Protection Clause

A clause that provides that state, local, and federal governments cannot deny to any person the "equal protection of the laws."

The **Equal Protection Clause** of the Fourteenth Amendment to the Constitution, as interpreted by the U.S. Supreme Court, provides that state, local, and federal governments cannot deny to any person the "equal protection of the laws." The clause prohibits governments from enacting laws that classify and treat similarly situated persons differently. The clause is designed to prohibit invidious government discrimination. Natural persons and businesses are protected.

The Equal Protection Clause has not been interpreted literally by the U.S. Supreme Court. The Supreme Court has held that some government laws that treat people or businesses differently are constitutional. The Supreme Court has adopted three different standards for determining whether a government action that treats some persons or businesses differently than others is lawful:

1. *Strict scrutiny test.* Any government activity or regulation that classifies persons based on a *suspect class* (i.e., race) is reviewed for lawfulness using a strict scrutiny test. Under this standard, most government classifications of persons based on race are found to be unconstitutional.

   > **Example**   A government rule that permitted persons of one race, but not of another race, to receive government benefits such as Medicaid, would violate this test. But affirmative action programs that give racial minorities a "plus factor" when considered for public university admission is lawful, as long as it does not constitute a quota system.

2. *Intermediate scrutiny test.* The lawfulness of government classifications based on *protected classes* other than race (such as sex or age) is examined using an intermediate scrutiny test. Under this standard, the courts determine whether the government classification is "reasonably related" to a legitimate government purpose.

   > **Example**   A rule prohibiting persons over a certain age from military combat would be lawful, but a rule prohibiting persons over a certain age from acting as government engineers would not be. With regard to a person's gender, the U.S. Supreme Court has held that the federal government can require males, but not females, to register with the military for a possible draft.

3. ***Rational basis test***. The lawfulness of all government classifications that do not involve suspect or protected classes is examined using a rational basis test. Under this test, the courts will uphold government regulation as long as there is a justifiable reason for the law. This standard permits much of the government regulation of business.

Example   Providing government subsidies to farmers but not to those in other occupations is permissible.

The ethical duty and social responsibility of a paralegal professional to avoid conflicts of interest is discussed in the following feature.

ETHICAL PERSPECTIVE
Paralegal's Duty to Avoid Conflicts of Interest

Ms. Jennifer Adams is hired as a paralegal at a law firm with expertise in real estate development law. She recently left a paralegal position at another law firm to take the new paralegal position with the current law firm.

At the new firm, Ms. Adams is assigned to work as the paralegal for Mr. Humberto Cruz, a senior partner of the law firm. Mr. Cruz is an expert in complex real estate transactions representing clients in the purchase, development, and leasing of large shopping malls. One client whom Mr. Cruz represents is Modern Properties L.P., a limited partnership that constructs and operates retail shopping malls across the country.

One day Mr. Cruz asks Ms. Adams to attend a meeting with himself and the president of Modern Properties L.P. At the meeting, the president of Modern Properties L.P. discloses a dispute that the partnership has with a tenant, Third National Bank, concerning the lease of a building by Third National Bank at a mall constructed and operated by Modern Properties L.P. The president explains that Third National Bank has filed a lawsuit against Modern Properties L.P. concerning this dispute. The president further explains that the partnership wants Mr. Cruz to represent the partnership in this lawsuit.

Ms. Adams realizes that her prior law firm represented Third National Bank in many lawsuits, and that she had worked as the paralegal on several of the cases involving Third National Bank. During the course of this work, she became privy to confidential information about Third National Bank, including its financial condition, operations, and legal strategy.

Does Ms. Adams have a conflict of interest? If so, what should she do?

Model and state paralegal Code of Ethics and Professional Responsibility provide that a paralegal is under a duty to avoid conflicts of interest. Thus, a paralegal cannot conduct work on any matter where there would be a conflict of interest with a present or past employer or with a client.

PARALEGAL'S ETHICAL DECISION

Thus, Ms. Adams must immediately disclose the fact that she previously worked on cases involving Third National Bank at the prior law firm where she was employed, and that because of that employment she possesses confidential information about Third National Bank. Because of this conflict of interest, Ms. Adams must excuse herself from working on the *Third National Bank v. Modern Properties L.P.* case.

Concept Review *and* Reinforcement

LEGAL TERMINOLOGY

Administrative agencies   184

Analytical school
   of jurisprudence   180

Bill of Rights   189

Court of Chancery
   (or equity court)   181

Checks and balances   187

Civil law system   182

Codified law   183

Command school of
   jurisprudence   180

Commerce Clause   187

Commercial speech   190

Common law   181

Constitution of the United States
   of America   183

Critical legal studies school
   of jurisprudence   180

Delegated powers   186

Due Process Clause   193

Enumerated powers   186

Equal Protection Clause   194

Establishment Clause   192

Executive branch   186

Federal statutes   183

Federalism   186

Free Exercise Clause   192

Freedom of speech   190

Fully protected speech   190

Historical school
   of jurisprudence   180

Intermediate scrutiny test   194

Interstate commerce   188

Intrastate commerce   188

Judicial branch   186

Judicial decision   184

Jurisprudence   180

Just Compensation Clause   194

Law   179

Law and economics school   181

Law courts   181

Legislative branch   186

Limited protected speech   190

Merchant court   181

Natural law school of
   jurisprudence   180

Obscene speech   191

Offensive speech   190

Ordinances   183

Police power   189

Preemption doctrine   187

Procedural due process   194

Rational basis test   195

Separation of powers   186

Sociological school of
   jurisprudence   180

Stare decisis   185

State statutes   183

Statutes   183

Strict scrutiny test   194

Substantive due process   193

Supremacy Clause   187

Treaty   183

Unprotected speech   190

SUMMARY OF KEY CONCEPTS

What Is Law?

Definition	Law consists of a body of rules of action or conduct prescribed by controlling authority and having binding legal force.
Functions of Law	1. Keep the peace 2. Shape moral standards 3. Promote social justice 4. Maintain the status quo 5. Facilitate orderly change 6. Facilitate planning 7. Provide a basis for compromise 8. Maximize individual freedom
Fairness	Although the American legal system is one of the fairest and most democratic systems of law, abuses and mistakes in the application of the law still occur.
Flexibility	The law must be flexible to meet social, technological, and economic changes.

Schools of Jurisprudential Thought

Natural Law	Postulates that law is based on what is "correct"; it emphasizes a moral theory of law— that is, law should be based on morality and ethics.
Historical	Believes that law is an aggregate of social traditions and customs.
Analytical	Maintains that law is shaped by logic.
Sociological	Asserts that the law is a means of achieving and advancing certain sociological goals.
Command	Believes that the law is a set of rules developed, communicated, and enforced by the ruling party.
Critical Legal Studies	Maintains that legal rules are unnecessary and that legal disputes should be solved by applying arbitrary rules based on fairness.
Law and Economics	Believes that promoting market efficiency should be the central concern of legal decision making.

History of American Law

English Common Law	English common law (judge-made law) forms the basis of the legal systems of most states in this country. Louisiana bases its law on the French civil code.

Sources of Law in the United States

Constitutions	The U.S. Constitution establishes the federal government and enumerates its powers. Powers not given to the federal government are reserved to the states. State constitutions establish state governments and enumerate their powers.
Treaties	The President, with the advice and consent of the Senate, may enter into treaties with foreign countries.
Codified Law	1. *Statutes* are enacted by Congress and state legislatures. 2. *Ordinances* and statutes are passed by municipalities and local government bodies to establish courses of conduct that must be followed by covered parties.
Administrative Agencies	Administrative agencies are created by the legislative and executive branches of government; they may adopt rules and regulations that govern the conduct of covered parties.
Executive Orders	Executive orders, issued by the President and governors of states, regulate the conduct of covered parties.
Judicial Decisions	Courts decide controversies by issuing decisions that state the holding of each case and the rationale the court used to reach that decision.

Doctrine of Stare Decisis

Definition	*Stare decisis* means "to stand by the decision." This doctrine provides for adherence to precedent.

Constitution of the United States of America

Scope	The Constitution consists of seven articles and 27 amendments. It establishes the three branches of the federal government, enumerates their powers, and provides important guarantees of individual freedom. The Constitution was ratified by the states in 1788.

Basic Constitutional Concepts

1. *Federalism:* The Constitution created the federal government, which shares power with the state governments.
2. *Delegated powers:* When the states ratified the Constitution, they delegated certain powers, called *enumerated powers*, to the federal government.
3. *Reserved powers:* Those powers not granted to the federal government by the Constitution are reserved to the states.
4. *Separation of powers:* Each branch of the federal government has separate powers.
    a. Legislative branch—power to make the law
    b. Executive branch—power to enforce the law
    c. Judicial branch—power to interpret the law
5. *Checks and balances:* Certain checks and balances are built into the Constitution to ensure that no one branch of the federal government becomes too powerful.

Supremacy Clause

The Supremacy Clause stipulates that the U.S. Constitution, treaties, and federal law (statutes and regulations) are the *supreme law of the land*. State or local laws that conflict with valid federal law are unconstitutional. This is called the *preemption doctrine*.

Commerce Clause

1. *Commerce Clause:* Authorizes the federal government to regulate commerce with foreign nations, among the states, and with Indian tribes.
2. *Interstate commerce:* Under the broad *effects test*, the federal government may regulate any activity (even intrastate commerce) that *affects* interstate commerce.
3. *Police Powers:* Power reserved to the states to regulate commerce.

Bill of Rights and Other Amendments

1. *Bill of Rights:* The Bill of Rights consists of the first 10 amendments to the Constitution. They establish basic individual rights. The Bill of Rights was ratified in 1791.
2. *Other amendments:* In addition to the 10 amendments of the Bill of Rights, there are seventeen other amendments to the U.S. Constitution.

Freedom of Speech

Freedom of Speech Clause of the First Amendment guarantees that the government shall not infringe on a person's right to speak. Protects oral, written, and symbolic speech. This right is not absolute—that is, some speech is not protected and other speech is granted only limited protection. The U.S. Supreme Court has placed speech in the following three categories:

1. *Fully protected speech:* Speech that cannot be prohibited or regulated by the government
2. *Limited protected speech:* Types of speech that are granted only limited protection under the Freedom of Speech Clause—that is, they are subject to governmental *time, place, and manner restrictions*:
    a. Offensive speech
    b. Commercial speech
3. *Unprotected speech:* Speech that is not protected by the Freedom of Speech Clause:
    a. Dangerous speech
    b. Fighting words
    c. Speech that advocates the violent overthrow of the government
    d. Defamatory language
    e. Child pornography
    f. Obscene speech

Freedom of Religion

There are two religion clauses in the First Amendment. They are:
1. *Establishment Clause.* Prohibits the government from establishing a state religion or promoting religion
2. *Free Exercise Clause.* Prohibits the government from interfering with the free exercise of religion. This right is not absolute: for example, human sacrifices are forbidden.

Due Process Clause

Due Process Clause provides that no person shall be deprived of "life, liberty, or property" without due process. There are two categories of due process:
1. *Substantive due process:* Requires that laws be clear on their face and not overly broad in scope. Laws that do not meet this test are *void for vagueness.*
2. *Procedural due process:* Requires that the government give a person proper *notice* and *hearing* before that person is deprived of his or her life, liberty, or property. An owner must be paid *just compensation* if the government takes his or her property.

Equal Protection Clause

Equal Protection Clause prohibits the government from enacting laws that classify and treat "similarly situated" persons differently. This standard is not absolute and the government can treat persons differently in certain situations. The U.S. Supreme Court has applied the following tests to determine if the Equal Protection Clause has been violated:
1. *Strict scrutiny test.* Applies to *suspect classes* (e.g., race, national origin)
2. *Intermediate scrutiny test.* Applies to other *protected classes* (e.g., sex, age)
3. *Rational basis test.* Applies to government classifications that do not involve a suspect or protected class

WORKING THE WEB

1. Go to the website http://www.usconstitution.net/const.html. Scroll down to "Amendment 7." When was this amendment ratified? What does this amendment provide? Explain.
2. Visit the website http://www.archives.gov/exhibits/charters/charters.html. A page entitled "The Charters of Freedom—A New World is at Hand" will appear on your computer screen. Do the following exercises:
   a. On the page shown, click on the third icon from the left. Read the article entitled, "The Spirit of the Revolution—The Declaration of Independence." What did the Declaration of Independence do? Explain.
   b. On the page shown, click on the sixth icon from the left. Read the article "The Constitutional Convention—Creation of the Constitution." How many states were required to ratify the Constitution for it to be enacted?
   c. At the top of the page shown, click on the second-to-the-last icon from the right. Read the article "Expansion of Rights and Liberties—The Right of Suffrage." What amendment to the U.S. Constitution gave women the right to vote? What year was this amendment ratified?
3. Visit the website http://www.senate.gov/. Click on the word "Senators." Who are the two senators who represent your state in the U.S. Senate? Go to each senator's website and email the senator, expressing your view on a legal issue in which you are interested.
4. Visit the website http://www.house.gov/. Who is the person who represents your home district? Go to that representative's website and read about his or her position on a current legal issue. What is the issue, and what is your representative's view on it?
5. Go to http://google.com. Choose a country in which you are interested and search for a treaty of this country (e.g., "China treaty"). Briefly describe this treaty.

CRITICAL THINKING & WRITING QUESTIONS

1. Define the "law." Is this an easy concept to define? Why?
2. What functions does the law serve? Which of these functions do you think is the most important?
3. Is the law always fair? Give an example of where you think the law was applied unfairly.
4. Should the language of the U.S. Constitution be applied in its original meaning, or should it be applied in a more expansive sense? Explain.
5. What is the power of the legislative branch of government? What is a statute?
6. Do you think that the U.S. Supreme Court makes law when it interprets the U.S. Constitution? Explain.
7. What is the doctrine of *stare decisis*? Why is this doctrine important?
8. What does the doctrine of federalism provide?
9. What does the doctrine of separation of powers provide? Can you give any examples where the separation of the powers of the three branches of government is blurred?
10. What does the doctrine of checks and balances provide? Can you give any examples where one branch of the government checks the power of another branch of the government?
11. What does the Supremacy Clause provide? What would be the consequences if the Supremacy Clause did not exist? Explain.
12. What does the Commerce Clause of the U.S. Constitution do? Explain.
13. The First Amendment to the U.S. Constitution contains the Freedom of Speech Clause. Explain the difference between fully protected speech, partially protected speech, and unprotected speech.
14. The U.S. Constitution guarantees freedom of religion. Explain the difference between the Establishment Clause and the Free Exercise Clause. Can you give an example of a legitimate government restriction of a possible religious practice?
15. What is the difference between substantive due process and procedural due process? Explain.
16. What does the Equal Protection Clause provide? Explain the differences between the (a) strict scrutiny test, (b) intermediate scrutiny test, and (c) rational basis test.

Building Paralegal Skills

VIDEO CASE STUDIES

Difference Between a Criminal and a Civil Trial

An interview with Judge Kenney, a trial court judge, who discusses the difference between a civil and a criminal trial.

After viewing the video case study at www.pearsonhighered.com/goldman answer the following:

1. What are the differences in the burden of proof between a criminal and civil matter?
2. What protections does the U.S. Constitution afford those accused of criminal acts?

A School Principal Reacts: Student Rights Versus School's Duty

As the result of an altercation in a school bus, and a claim that the student involved had a contraband knife on his person, the principal has ordered that he be searched for the knife.

After viewing the video case study at www.pearsonhighered .com/goldman answer the following:

1. Does a student have a constitutional right of privacy?
2. Does the school have a right to search a student?
3. Is the school district and those working for it immune from suit for the actions taken?

Confidentiality Issue: Attorney–Client Privilege

Paralegal Alicia Jackson meets with a client to review answers to documents that must be sent to opposing counsel. While reviewing the answers he tells her about a potentially fraudulent claim.

After viewing the video case study at www.pearsonhighered .com/goldman answer the following:

1. Does the attorney–client privilege apply to information given to a paralegal?
2. To whom does the privilege belong?
3. How is the attorney–client privilege different from the duty of confidentiality?

ETHICS ANALYSIS & DISCUSSION QUESTIONS

1. Are there any ethical issues in allowing one's personal feelings to be expressed in working on a case? What if you have strong feelings against the client's position?
2. Does the American system of law depend on the legal team to put aside its personal beliefs and work diligently on unpopular cases or issues? How does this ensure equal justice and allow for change in the system?
3. You are working in a law firm for an attorney who has had a series of strokes that have caused a permanent reading disability and memory impairment. Do you have any ethical obligation to the attorney's clients? Do you have any ethical obligation to the firm and to the attorney? [Philadelphia Ethics Opinion 2002-12 (2000); also, see Texas Ethics Opinion 522 (1997)].

DEVELOPING YOUR COLLABORATION SKILLS

With a group of other students, selected by you or as assigned by your instructor, review the facts of the following case. As a group, discuss the following questions.

1. What does the federal Driver's Privacy Protection Act mandate?
2. Was the federal Driver's Privacy Protection Act (DPPA) properly enacted by the U.S. Congress pursuant to the Commerce Clause power granted to the federal government by the U.S. Constitution?
3. Did the sale of drivers' personal information by the states violate a driver's right to privacy?

Reno, Attorney General of the United States v. Condon, Attorney General of South Carolina

State Departments of Motor Vehicles (DMVs) register automobiles and issue driver's licenses. State DMVs require automobile owners and drivers to provide personal information, which includes a person's name, address, telephone number, vehicle description, Social Security number, medical information, and a photograph, as a condition for registering an automobile or obtaining a driver's license.

Many states' DMVs sold this personal information to individuals, advertisers, and businesses which then used this information to solicit business from the registered automobile owners and drivers. Sales of automobile owners' and drivers' personal information generated significant revenues for the states.

After receiving thousands of complaints from individuals whose personal information had been sold, the Congress of the United States enacted the **Driver's Privacy Protection Act of 1994 (DPPA)**. This federal statute prohibits a state from selling the personal information of a person unless the state obtains that person's affirmative consent to do so. South Carolina sued the United States, alleging that the federal government did not have power under the Commerce Clause of the U.S. Constitution to adopt the federal DPPA that prohibits the state from selling personal information of its registered automobile owners and drivers.

Source: *Reno, Attorney General of the United States v. Condon, Attorney General of South Carolina*, 528 U.S. 141, 120 S.Ct. 666, 145 L.Ed.2d 587, **Web** 2000 U.S. Lexis 503 (Supreme Court of the United States, 2000)

PARALEGAL PORTFOLIO EXERCISE

Research and find an article that discusses a Federal Communications Commission (FCC) clash with a radio, cable, or television station regarding the subject matter that it may broadcast. Write a memorandum, no longer than two pages, that discusses this dispute and the outcome of the case.

Youngstown Co. v. Sawyer, Secretary of Commerce

343 U.S. 579, 72 S.Ct. 863, 96 L.Ed.2d 1153, Web 1952 U.S. Lexis 2625

Supreme Court of the United States

In 1951, a dispute arose between steel companies and their employees about the terms and conditions that should be included in a new labor contract. At the time, the United States was engaged in a military conflict in Korea that required substantial steel resources from which to make weapons and other military goods.

On April 4, 1952, the steelworkers' union gave notice of a nationwide strike called to begin at 12:01 A.M. on April 9. The indispensability of steel as a component in weapons and other war materials led President Dwight D. Eisenhower to

believe that the proposed strike would jeopardize the national defense and that governmental seizure of the steel mills was necessary to ensure the continued availability of steel. Therefore, a few hours before the strike was to begin, the President issued Executive Order 10340, which directed the Secretary of Commerce to take possession of most of the steel mills and keep them running. The steel companies obeyed the order under protest, and brought proceedings against the President.

Question

1. Was the seizure of the steel mills constitutional?

Bonito Boats, Inc. v. Thunder Craft Boats, Inc.

489 U.S. 141, 109 S.Ct. 971, 103 L.Ed.2d 118, Web 1989 U.S. Lexis 629

Supreme Court of the United States

Article 1, Section 8, Clause 8 of the U.S. Constitution grants Congress the power to enact laws to give inventors the exclusive right to their discoveries. Pursuant to this power, Congress enacted federal patent laws that establish the requirements to obtain a patent. Once a patent is granted, the patent holder has exclusive rights to use the patent.

Bonito Boats, Inc. developed a hull design for a fiberglass recreational boat that it marketed under the trade name Bonito Boats Model 5VBR. The manufacturing process involved creating a hardwood model that was sprayed with fiberglass to create a mold. The mold then served to produce the finished fiberglass boats for sale. Bonito did not file a

patent application to protect the utilitarian or design aspects of the hull or the manufacturing process.

After the Bonito 5VBR was on the market for six years, the Florida legislature enacted a statute prohibiting the use of a direct molding process to duplicate unpatented boat hulls and forbade the knowing sale of hulls so duplicated. The protection afforded under the state statute was broader than that provided for under the federal patent statute.

Subsequently, Thunder Craft Boats, Inc. produced and sold boats made by the direct molding process. Bonito sued Thunder Craft under Florida law.

Question

1. Is the Florida statute valid?

Rostker, Director of the Selective Service v. Goldberg

453 U.S. 57, 101 S.Ct. 2646, 69 L.Ed.2d 478, 69 L.Ed.2d 478, Web 1981 U.S. Lexis 126

Supreme Court of the United States

In 1975, after the war in Vietnam, the U.S. government discontinued draft registration for men in this country. In 1980, after the Soviet Union invaded Afghanistan, President Jimmy Carter asked Congress for funds to reactivate draft registration. President Carter suggested that males and females alike be required to register. Congress allocated funds only for the registration of males. Several men who were subject to draft registration brought a lawsuit that challenged the law as being unconstitutional in violation of the Equal Protection Clause of the U.S. Constitution. The U.S. Supreme Court upheld the constitutionality of the draft registration law, reasoning as follows:

The question of registering women for the draft not only received considerable national attention and was the subject of wide-ranging public debate, but also was extensively considered by Congress in hearings, floor debate, and in committee. The foregoing clearly establishes that the decision to exempt women from registration was not the "accidental by-producer of a traditional way of thinking about women."

This is not a case of Congress arbitrarily choosing to burden one of two similarly situated groups, such as would be the case with an all-black or all-white, or an all-Catholic or all-Lutheran, or an all-Republican or all-Democratic registration. Men and women are simply not similarly situated for purposes of a draft or registration for a draft.

Justice Marshall dissented, stating that "The Court today places its imprimatur on one of the most potent remaining public expressions of 'ancient canards about the proper role of women.' It upholds a statute that requires males but not females to register for the draft, and which thereby categorically excludes women from a fundamental civic obligation. I dissent."

Question

1. Was the decision fair? Was the law a "progressive science" in this case? Was it ethical for males, but not females, to have to register for the draft?

Van Orden v. Perry, Governor of Texas — 125 S.Ct. 2854 162 L.Ed.2d 607, Web 2005 U.S. Lexis 5215

Supreme Court of the United States

The 22 acres surrounding the Texas State Capital contains seventeen monuments and twenty-one historical markers. The monuments and markers commemorate the people and historical events of Texas. Some of the monuments are: Heroes of the Alamo, confederate Soldiers, a Texas Cowboy, Texas Pioneer Women, Disabled Veterans, and Texas Police Officers. One monument is a 6-feet high and 3-feet wide monument on which is carved an eagle grasping an American flag, an eye inside a pyramid, Stars of David, Greek letters, and the Ten Commandments. This monument has been on the grounds for more than 40 years.

Thomas Van Orden, a native Texan and resident of Austin, Texas, where the Texas State Capitol is located,

sued to have the Ten Commandments' monument removed, alleging that the monument violated the Establishment Clause of the U.S. Constitution. The U.S. District Court held that the monument did not violate the Establishment Clause, finding that the monument had a secular purpose. The U.S. Court of Appeals affirmed. Van Orden appealed to the U.S. Supreme Court.

Question

1. Does the monument containing the Ten Commandments, which is located with other monuments on the grounds of the Texas State Capitol, violate the Establishment Clause?

Grutter v. Bollinger, Dean of the University of Michigan Law School — 539 U.S. 306, 123 S.Ct. 2325, 156 L.Ed.2d 304, Web 2003 U.S. Lexis 4800

Supreme Court of the United States

Barbara Grutter, a Caucasian resident of the state of Michigan, applied to the Law School of the University of Michigan, a state government–supported institution. She had a 3.8 undergraduate grade point average and a 161 LSAT score. The Law School rejected her application. The Law School received 3,500 applications for a class of 350 students. The Law School used race as one of the factors in considering applicants for admission to law school. The race of minority applicants, defined as Blacks, Hispanics, and Native Americans, was considered as a "plus factor" in considering their applications to law school. Caucasians and Asians were not given such a plus factor. The Law School stated that it used race as a plus factor to obtain a critical mass of underrepresented minority students, to create diversity at the school.

Grutter brought a class action lawsuit against the Law School of the University of Michigan, alleging that its use of a minority's race as a plus factor in admissions violated the Equal Protection Clause of the Fourteenth Amendment to the U.S. Constitution. The District Court held that the Law School's use of race as a factor in admissions violated the Equal Protection Clause. The Court of Appeals reversed. The U.S. Supreme Court granted certiorari to hear the appeal.

Question

1. Does the University of Michigan Law School's use of race as a plus factor in accepting minority applicants for admission to the Law School violate the Equal Protection Clause of the Fourteenth Amendment to the U.S. Constitution?

WORKING WITH THE LANGUAGE OF THE COURT CASE

Lee v. Weisman

505 U.S. 577, 112 S.Ct. 2649 120 L.Ed.2d. 467, Web 1992 U.S. Lexis 4364
Supreme Court of the United States

Read the following case, excerpted from the U.S. Supreme Court's opinion. Review and brief the case. In your brief, answer the following questions.

1. Who are the plaintiff and defendant?
2. What does the Establishment Clause provide?
3. What test did the court use to determine if the practice violates the Establishment Clause?
4. Was the fact that the prayer was nonsectarian important to the Supreme Court's decision?
5. Is nonsectarian prayer permitted under the Establishment Clause?
6. How close was the vote by the justices in this case?

(continued)

Kennedy, Justice (joined by Blackmun, Stevens, O'Connor, and Souter)

Deborah Weisman graduated from Nathan Bishop Middle School, a public school in Providence, Rhode Island, at a formal ceremony in June 1989. She was about 14 years old. For many years it has been the policy of the Providence school committee and the Superintendent of Schools to permit principals to invite members of the clergy to give invocations and benedictions at middle school and high school graduations. Many, but not all, of the principals elected to include prayers as part of the graduation ceremonies. Acting for himself and his daughter, Deborah's father, Daniel Weisman, objected to any prayers at Deborah's middle school graduation, but to no avail. The school principal, petitioner Robert E. Lee, invited a rabbi to deliver prayers at the graduation exercises for Deborah's class. Rabbi Leslie Gutterman, of the Temple Beth El in Providence, accepted.

It also has been the custom of Providence school officials to provide invited clergy with a pamphlet entitled "Guidelines for Civic Occasions," prepared by the National Conference of Christians and Jews. The Guidelines recommended that public prayers at nonsectarian civic ceremonies be composed with "inclusiveness and sensitivity," though they acknowledge that "prayer of any kind may be inappropriate on some civic occasions." The principal gave Rabbi Gutterman the pamphlet before the graduation and advised him that the invocation and benediction should be nonsectarian.

Deborah's graduation was held on the premises of Nathan Bishop Middle School on June 29, 1989. Four days before the ceremony, Daniel Weisman, in his individual capacity as a Providence taxpayer and as next friend of Deborah, sought a temporary restraining order in the United States District Court for the District of Rhode Island to prohibit school officials from including an invocation or a benediction in the graduation ceremony. The court denied the motion for lack of adequate time to consider it. Deborah and her family attended the graduation, where the prayers were recited.

In July 1989, Daniel Weisman filed an amended complaint seeking a permanent injunction barring petitioners, various officials of the Providence public schools, from inviting the clergy to deliver invocations and benedictions at future graduations.

The case was submitted on stipulated facts. The District Court held that petitioners' practice of including invocations and benedictions in public school graduations violated the Establishment Clause of the First Amendment, and it enjoined petitioners from continuing the practice. The court applied the three-part Establishment Clause test. Under that test, to satisfy the Establishment Clause a governmental practice must (1) reflect a clearly secular purpose, (2) have a primary effect that neither advances nor inhibits religion, and (3) avoid excessive government entanglement with religion. On appeal, the United States Court of Appeals for the First Circuit affirmed.

These dominant facts mark and control the confines of our decision: State officials direct the performance of a formal religious exercise at promotional and graduation ceremonies for secondary schools. Even for those students who object to the religious exercise, their attendance and participation in the state-sponsored religious activity are in a fair and real sense obligatory, though the school district does not require attendance as a condition for receipt of the diploma.

The controlling precedents as they relate to prayer and religious exercise in primary and secondary public schools compel the holding here that the policy of the city of Providence is an unconstitutional one. It is beyond dispute that, at a minimum, the Constitution guarantees that government may not coerce anyone to support or participate in religion or its exercise, or otherwise act in a way which "establishes a state religion or religious faith, or tends to do so."

We are asked to recognize the existence of a practice of nonsectarian prayer within the embrace of what is known as the Judeo-Christian tradition, prayer which is more acceptable than one which, for example, makes explicit references to the God of Israel, or to Jesus Christ, or to a patron saint. If common ground can be defined which permits once conflicting faiths to express the shared conviction that there is an ethic and a morality which transcend human invention, the sense of community and purpose sought by all decent societies might be advanced. But though the First Amendment does not allow the government to stifle prayers which aspire to these ends, neither does it permit the government to undertake that task for itself.

The sole question presented is whether a religious exercise may be conducted at a graduation ceremony in circumstances where, as we have found, young graduates who object are induced to conform. No holding by this Court suggests that a school can persuade or compel a student to participate in a religious exercise. That is being done here, and it is forbidden by the Establishment Clause of the First Amendment.

For the reasons we have stated, the judgment of the Court of Appeals is affirmed.

The Court System and Alternative Dispute Resolution

> " I was never ruined but twice; once when I lost a lawsuit, and once when I won one. "
>
> *Voltaire*

Paralegals at Work

You have applied for a position as a paralegal at a law firm that specializes in litigation. Most of the law firm's practice is in the area of tort litigation, particularly representing plaintiffs in negligence cases. The firm has scheduled an interview with you. On the day you arrive for the interview, you are called into the office of Ms. Harriet Green, a senior partner in the firm. Ms. Green wants to determine your knowledge of judicial and nonjudicial dispute resolution. Ms. Green informs you that she will tell you the facts of a case and will ask you several questions about the case.

Ms. Green explains that Ms. Heather Andersen has retained the law firm as the plaintiff to represent her in an accident case. Ms. Green explains that Ms. Andersen was driving her automobile on the main road of your city when Mr. Joseph Burton, driving another automobile, ran a red street light and hit Ms. Andersen's vehicle, causing her severe physical injuries, as well as pain and suffering. The law firm plans to file a lawsuit for the tort of negligence on behalf of Ms. Andersen, the plaintiff, against Mr. Burton, the defendant. Ms. Andersen is a resident of your state. Mr. Burton is a resident of another state who was visiting your state when the accident occurred.

Ms. Green asks you the following questions: "What is a complaint?" "In what court or courts can our law firm file the complaint on behalf of Ms. Andersen?" "If we lose the case at trial, to what court can our law firm, on behalf of Ms. Andersen, appeal the trial court's decision?" "After the case is filed in the court, is there any way of resolving the case in favor of Ms. Andersen before the case goes to trial?"

Consider the issues involved in this scenario as you read the chapter.

INTRODUCTION FOR THE PARALEGAL

A paralegal often assists attorneys who represent clients in the courts of this country. The court systems and the procedure to bring and defend a lawsuit are complicated, and a paralegal should be knowledgeable of court systems and how a lawsuit proceeds to trial and is decided in court.

Also, some parties to a dispute will choose to settle a case, or have the case reviewed or determined by a private party rather than by the courts. Thus, a paralegal should be knowledgeable of the manner and procedures for having disputes resolved outside of the court system.

The two major court systems in the United States are: (1) the federal court system, and (2) the court systems of the 50 states and the District of Columbia. Each of these systems has jurisdiction to hear different types of lawsuits. The process of bringing, maintaining, and defending a lawsuit is called **litigation**. Litigation is a difficult, time-consuming, and costly process that must comply with complex procedural rules. Although it is not required, most parties employ a lawyer to represent them when they are involved in a lawsuit.

Several forms of *nonjudicial* dispute resolution have developed in response to the expense and difficulty of bringing a lawsuit. These methods, collectively called alternative dispute resolution (ADR), are being used more and more often to resolve commercial disputes.

Paralegals are especially valuable in providing support to lawyers who are engaged in litigation and alternative dispute resolution. Paralegals interview clients, prepare documents submitted to courts, conduct legal research, and assist lawyers during trial and alternative dispute resolution.

This chapter focuses on the various court systems, the jurisdiction of courts to hear and decide cases, the litigation process, and alternative dispute resolution.

The following feature discusses the career opportunities for paralegal professionals in courts and litigation.

State Court Systems

Paralegal professionals should be familiar with the **state court system** in which he or she could be involved in assisting attorneys who practice before one of these state

CAREER OPPORTUNITIES FOR PARALEGALS IN COURTS AND LITIGATION

Paralegals are an extremely fortunate group of individuals because many of them get to work in a special environment—the court system. Paralegals are often hired by state and federal courts to assist judges in the preparation of trial. Paralegals often assist a judge or justice by conducting research, briefing arguments, preparing documents, and such.

In addition to working for the courts directly, many more paralegals are employed by attorneys who represent clients who are involved in litigation in the courts. These paralegals may work for plaintiffs' attorneys and defendants' attorneys in civil litigation lawsuits such as breach of contract, negligence and product liability, business litigation, and other civil lawsuits. These civil lawsuits may be either in state courts or federal courts.

Paralegals are also hired to work for prosecuting attorneys and defense attorneys in the criminal law area. Paralegals assist prosecuting and defense attorneys to prepare for trial and assist the attorney during trial. Criminal law cases are brought both in state and federal courts, depending on the jurisdiction of the court.

A paralegal who works for the courts or litigation attorneys must have a detailed knowledge of the court systems that serve the relevant jurisdiction that he or she works in. Paralegals who work in positions that are not directly involved in supporting lawsuits in court should still have knowledge of the court systems in this country and the jurisdiction of such court systems.

Courthouse, St. Louis, Missouri. State courts hear and decide the majority of cases in the United States.

courts. Each state and the District of Columbia have separate court systems. Most state court systems include:

- Limited-jurisdiction trial courts
- General-jurisdiction trial courts
- Intermediate appellate courts
- Supreme court (or highest state court)

Limited-Jurisdiction Trial Court

State **limited-jurisdiction trial courts**, which sometimes are referred to as *inferior trial courts*, hear matters of a specialized or limited nature.

Examples Traffic courts, juvenile courts, justice-of-the-peace courts, probate courts, family law courts, and courts that hear misdemeanor criminal law cases and civil cases involving lawsuits of less than a certain dollar amount. Because these courts are trial courts, evidence can be introduced and testimony given. Most limited-jurisdiction courts keep a record of their proceedings. Their decisions usually can be appealed to a general-jurisdiction court or an appellate court.

Many states also have created **small-claims courts** to hear civil cases involving small dollar amounts (e.g., $5,000 or less). Generally, the parties must appear individually and cannot have a lawyer represent them. The decisions of small-claims courts are often appealable to general-jurisdiction trial courts or appellate courts.

General-Jurisdiction Trial Court

Every state has a **general-jurisdiction trial court**. These courts often are called **courts of record** because the testimony and evidence at trial are recorded and stored for future reference. These courts hear cases that are not within the jurisdiction of

Web Exploration

Use www.google.com and find out if your state has a small-claims court. If so, what is the dollar limit for cases to qualify to be heard by the small-claims court?

General-jurisdiction trial court (courts of record) A court that hears cases of a general nature that are not within the jurisdiction of limited-jurisdiction trial courts.

limited-jurisdiction trial courts, such as felonies, civil cases above a certain dollar amount, and so on. Some states divide their general-jurisdiction courts into two divisions, one for criminal cases and another for civil cases.

General-jurisdiction trial courts hear evidence and testimony. The decisions these courts hand down are appealable to an intermediate appellate court or the state supreme court, depending on the circumstances.

Intermediate Appellate Court

Intermediate appellate court An intermediate court that hears appeals from trial courts.

In many states, **intermediate appellate courts** (also called *appellate courts* or *courts of appeal*) hear appeals from trial courts. These courts review the trial court record to determine any errors at trial that would require reversal or modification of the trial court's decision. Thus, the appellate court reviews either pertinent parts or the entire trial court record from the lower court. No new evidence or testimony is permitted. The parties usually file legal briefs with the appellate court, stating the law and facts that support their positions. Appellate courts usually grant a short oral hearing to the parties.

Appellate court decisions are appealable to the state's highest court. In less populated states that do not have an intermediate appellate court, trial court decisions can be appealed directly to the state's highest court.

Highest State Court

Highest state court The top court in a state court system; it hears appeals from intermediate state courts and certain trial courts.

Each state has a **highest state court** in its court system. Most states call this highest court *supreme court*. The function of a state supreme court is to hear appeals from intermediate state courts and certain trial courts. The highest court hears no new evidence or testimony. The parties usually submit pertinent parts of or the entire lower court record for review. The parties also submit legal briefs to the court and typically are granted a brief oral hearing. Decisions of state supreme courts are final, unless a question of law is involved that is appealable to the U.S. Supreme Court.

Exhibit 6.1 portrays a typical state court system. Exhibit 6.2 lists the websites for the court systems of 50 states and jurisdictions associated with the United States.

Web Exploration

Go to Exhibit 6.2. Find the website for your state or district or territory and go to this website. What is the name of the highest court? In what city is the highest court located?

Federal Court System

Paralegal professionals are sometimes involved in assisting attorneys who practice before one of the many federal courts. Article III of the U.S. Constitution provides that the federal government's judicial power is vested in one "supreme court." This court is the U.S. Supreme Court. The Constitution also authorizes Congress to establish "inferior" federal courts in the **federal court system**. Pursuant to this power, Congress has established special federal courts, the U.S. district courts, and the U.S. courts of appeal. Federal judges are appointed for life by the President with the advice and consent of the Senate (except bankruptcy court judges, who are appointed for 14-year terms, and U.S. Magistrate Judges, who are appointed for an 8-year term).

Special Federal Courts

Web Exploration

Go to http://www.uscourts.gov/courtlinks/. Choose and click on "Bankruptcy Court." Place the cursor on your state and click. What is the location of the Bankruptcy Court closest to you?

The **special federal courts** established by Congress have limited jurisdiction. They include:

- **U.S. Tax Court**: Hears cases involving federal tax laws
- **U.S. Court of Federal Claims**: Hears cases brought against the United States
- **U.S. Court of International Trade**: Hears cases involving tariffs and international commercial disputes
- **U.S. Bankruptcy Court**: Hears cases involving federal bankruptcy laws

Exhibit 6.1 | Typical state court system

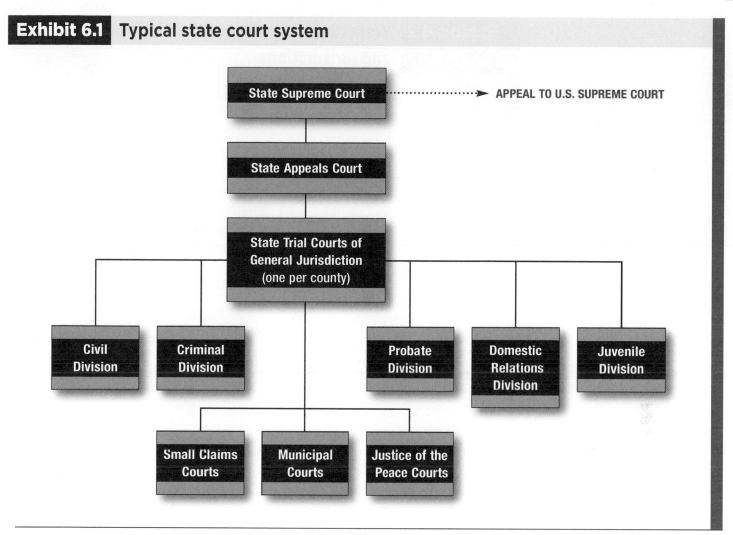

U.S. District Courts

The **U.S. District Courts** are the federal court system's trial courts of general juris-diction. The District of Columbia and each state have at least one federal district court; the more populated states have more than one. The geographical area that each court serves is referred to as a *district*. At present there are 94 federal district courts. The fed-eral district courts are empowered to impanel juries, receive evidence, hear testimony, and decide cases. Most federal cases originate in federal district courts.

U.S. Courts of Appeals

The **U.S. Courts of Appeals** are the federal court system's intermediate appellate courts. The federal court system has 13 circuits. **Circuit** refers to the geographical area served by a court. Eleven are designated by a number, such as the "First Circuit," "Second Circuit," and so on. The Twelfth Circuit court is located in Washington, D.C., and is called the District of Columbia Circuit.

As appellate courts, these circuit courts hear appeals from the district courts located in their circuit, as well as from certain special courts and federal administrative agencies. The courts review the record of the lower court or administrative agency proceedings to determine if any error would warrant reversal or modification of the lower court decision. No new evidence or testimony is heard. The parties file legal briefs with the court and are given a short oral hearing. Appeals usually are heard by a three-judge panel. After the panel renders a decision, a petitioner can request a review *en banc* by the full court.

U.S. District Courts The federal court system's trial courts of general jurisdiction.

Web Exploration

Go to http://www.uscourts.gov/courtlinks/. Choose and click on "District Court." Place the cursor on your state and click. What is the location of the U.S. District Court closest to you?

U.S. Courts of Appeals The federal court system's intermediate appellate courts.

Web Exploration

Visit the website of the U.S. Court for the Federal Circuit at www.fedcir.gov/.

Exhibit 6.2 Websites for state court systems and jurisdictions

State	Website
Alabama	www.judicial.state.al.us
Alaska	www.state.ak.us/courts
Arizona	www.supreme.state.az.us
Arkansas	www.courts.state.ar.us
California	www.courtinfo.ca.gov/courts
Colorado	www.courts.state.co.us
Connecticut	www.jud.state.ct.us
Delaware	www.courts.state.de.us
District of Columbia	www.dccourts.gov
Florida	www.flcourts.org
Georgia	georgiacourts.org
Guam	www.guamsupremecourt.com
Hawaii	www.courts.state.hi.us
Idaho	www.isc.idaho.gov
Illinois	www.state.il.us/court
Indiana	www.in.gov/judiciary
Iowa	www.judicial.state.ia.us
Kansas	www.kscourts.org
Kentucky	www.courts.ky.gov
Louisiana	www.lasc.org
Maine	www.courts.state.me.us
Maryland	www.courts.state.md.us
Massachusetts	www.mass.gov/courts
Michigan	www.courts.michigan.gov
Minnesota	www.courts.state.mn.us
Mississippi	www.mssc.state.ms.us
Missouri	www.courts.mo.gov
Montana	www.montanacourts.org
Nebraska	court.nol.org
Nevada	www.nvsupremecourt.us
New Hampshire	www.courts.state.nh.us
New Jersey	www.judiciary.state.nj.us
New Mexico	www.nmcourts.com
New York	www.courts.state.ny.us
North Carolina	www.nccourts.org
North Dakota	www.ndcourts.com
Ohio	www.sconet.state.oh.us
Oklahoma	www.oscn.net/oscn/schome
Oregon	www.ojd.state.or.us
Pennsylvania	www.courts.state.pa.us

Exhibit 6.2   Websites for state court systems and jurisdictions (continued)

State	Website
Puerto Rico	www.tribunalpr.org
Rhode Island	www.courts.state.ri.us
South Carolina	www.judicial.state.sc.us
South Dakota	www.sdjudicial.com
Tennessee	www.tsc.state.tn.us
Texas	www.courts.state.tx.us
Utah	www.utcourts.gov
Vermont	www.vermontjudiciary.org
Virginia	www.courts.state.va.us
Virgin Islands	www.visuperiorcourt.org
Washington	www.courts.wa.gov
West Virginia	www.wv.gov
Wisconsin	www.wicourts.gov
Wyoming	www.courts.state.wy.us

Exhibit 6.3   Map of the federal circuit courts

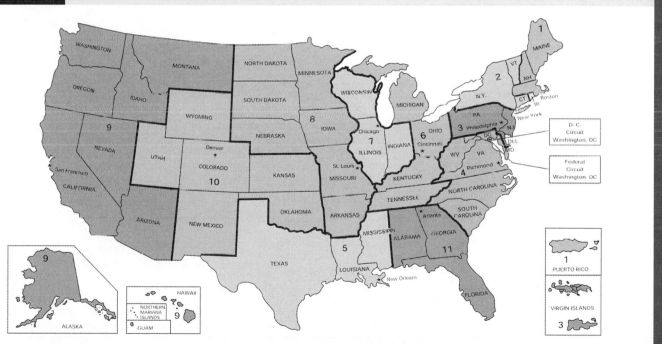

The Thirteenth Circuit court of appeals was created by Congress in 1982. Called the **Court of Appeals for the Federal Circuit** and located in Washington, D.C., this court has special appellate jurisdiction to review the decisions of the Court of Federal Claims, the Patent and Trademark Office, and the Court of International Trade. This court of appeals was created to provide uniformity in the application of federal law in certain areas, particularly patent law.

The map in Exhibit 6.3 shows the 13 federal circuit courts of appeals. Exhibit 6.4 lists the websites of the 13 U.S. courts of appeals.

 Web Exploration

Go to http://www.uscourts.gov/ courtlinks/. Choose and click on "Court of Appeals." Place the cursor on your state and click. What is the location of the U.S. Court of Appeals closest to you?

Exhibit 6.4   Websites for federal courts of appeals

United States Court of Appeals	Main Office	Website
First Circuit	Boston, Massachusetts	www.ca1.uscourts.gov
Second Circuit	New York, New York	www.ca2.uscourts.gov
Third Circuit	Philadelphia, Pennsylvania	www.ca3.uscourts.gov
Fourth Circuit	Richmond, Virginia	www.ca4.uscourts.gov
Fifth Circuit	Houston, Texas	www.ca5.uscourts.gov
Sixth Circuit	Cincinnati, Ohio	www.ca6.uscourts.gov
Seventh Circuit	Chicago, Illinois	www.ca7.uscourts.gov
Eighth Circuit	St. Paul, Minnesota	www.ca8.uscourts.gov
Ninth Circuit	San Francisco, California	www.ca9.uscourts.gov
Tenth Circuit	Denver, Colorado	www.ca10.uscourts.gov
Eleventh Circuit	Atlanta, Georgia	www.ca11.uscourts.gov
District of Columbia	Washington, DC	www.dcd.uscourts.gov
Court of Appeals for the Federal Circuit	Washington, DC	www.cafc.uscourts.gov

Supreme Court of the United States, Washington, DC. The highest court in the land is the Supreme Court of the United States, located in Washington, DC. The U.S. Supreme Court decides the most important constitutional law cases and other important issues it deems ripe for review and decision. The Supreme Court's unanimous and majority decisions are precedent for all the other courts in the country.

Supreme Court of the United States

Paralegals should be familiar with Supreme Court of the United States, its jurisdiction, the types of cases it hears, how cases are determined to be heard by the Supreme Court, and the voting of the Supreme Court justices. The highest court in the land is the **Supreme Court of the United States** located in Washington, D.C. This court is composed of nine justices who are nominated by the President and confirmed by the

Exhibit 6.5 Federal court system

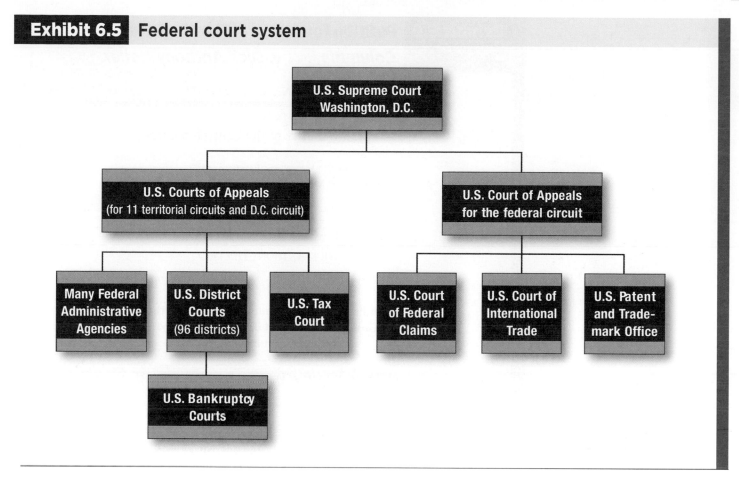

Senate. The President appoints one justice as **chief justice**, responsible for the administration of the Supreme Court. The other eight justices are **associate justices**.

The **U.S. Supreme Court**, which is an appellate court, hears appeals from federal circuit courts of appeals and, under certain circumstances, from federal district courts, special federal courts, and the highest state courts. The Supreme Court hears no evidence or testimony. As with other appellate courts, the lower court record is reviewed to determine whether an error has been committed that warrants a reversal or modification of the decision. Legal briefs are filed, and the parties are granted a brief oral hearing. The Supreme Court's decision is final.

Exhibit 6.5 illustrates the federal court system.

U.S. Supreme Court The Supreme Court was created by Article III of the U.S. Constitution. The Supreme Court is the highest court in the land. It is located in Washington, DC.

Petition for *Certiorari*

A petitioner must file a **petition for** *certiorari* asking the Supreme Court to hear the case. If the Court decides to review a case, it will issue a *writ of certiorari.* Because the Court issues only about 100 opinions each year, *writs* usually are granted only in cases involving constitutional and other important issues.

The justices meet once a week to discuss what cases merit review. The votes of four justices are necessary to grant an appeal and schedule an oral argument before the Court ("rule of four"). Written opinions by the justices usually are issued many months later.

The U.S. Constitution gives Congress the authority to establish rules for the appellate review of cases by the Supreme Court, except in the rare case where mandatory review is required. Congress has given the Supreme Court discretion to decide what cases it will hear.

Exhibit 6.6 shows a petition for certiorari to the U.S. Supreme Court.

Petition for *certiorari* A petition asking the Supreme Court to hear one's case.

Writ of certiorari An official notice that the Supreme Court will review one's case.

Exhibit 6.6   Petition for certiorari for the case *District of Columbia, . . . v. Dick Anthony Heller*

No. 07-

IN THE

Supreme Court of the United States

DISTRICT OF COLUMBIA AND
ADRIAN M. FENTY, MAYOR OF THE DISTRICT OF COLUMBIA,

Petitioners,

v.

DICK ANTHONY HELLER,

Respondent.

**On Petition for a Writ of Certiorari to the
United States Court of Appeals for the
District of Columbia Circuit**

PETITION FOR A WRIT OF CERTIORARI

THOMAS C. GOLDSTEIN	LINDA SINGER
CHRISTOPHER M. EGLESON	*Attorney General*
Akin Gump Strauss Hauer	ALAN B. MORRISON
& Feld LLP	*Special Counsel to the*
1333 New Hampshire	*Attorney General*
Avenue, NW	TODD S. KIM
Washington, DC 20036	*Solicitor General*
	Counsel of Record
WALTER DELLINGER	EDWARD E. SCHWAB
MATTHEW M. SHORS	*Deputy Solicitor General*
MARK S. DAVIES	DONNA M. MURASKY
GEOFFREY M. WYATT	LUTZ ALEXANDER PRAGER
O'Melveny & Myers LLP	Office of the Attorney General
1625 Eye Street, NW	for the District of Columbia
Washington, DC 20006	441 Fourth Street, NW
	Washington, DC 20001
	(202) 724-6609

Attorneys for Petitioners

QUESTION PRESENTED

Whether the Second Amendment forbids the District of Columbia from banning private possession of handguns while allowing possession of rifles and shotguns.

ii

PARTIES TO THE PROCEEDING

Petitioners District of Columbia and Mayor Adrian M. Fenty were defendants-appellees below. Mayor Fenty was substituted automatically for the previous Mayor, Anthony A. Williams, under Federal Rule of Appellate Procedure 43(b)(2).

Exhibit 6.6 **Petition for certiorari for the case _District of Columbia, . . . v. Dick Anthony Heller_** (continued)

Respondent Dick Anthony Heller was the only plaintiff-appellant below held by the court of appeals to have standing. The other plaintiffs-appellants were Shelly Parker, Tom G. Palmer, Gillian St. Lawrence, Tracey Ambeau, and George Lyon.

iii

TABLE OF CONTENTS

Page(s)

Vote of the U.S. Supreme Court

Each justice of the Supreme Court, including the chief justice, has an equal vote. The Supreme Court can issue the following types of decisions:

- **Unanimous decision**. If all of the justices voting agree as to the outcome and reasoning used to decide the case, it is a unanimous opinion. Unanimous decisions are precedent for later cases.

  Example   Suppose all nine justices hear a case, and all nine agree to the outcome (the petitioner wins) and the reason why (the Equal Protection Clause of the U.S. Constitution had been violated); this is a unanimous decision.

- **Majority decision**. If a majority of the justices agree to the outcome and reasoning used to decide the case, it is a majority opinion. Majority decisions are precedent for later cases.

  Example   If all nine justices hear a case, and five of them agree as to the outcome (the petitioner wins) and all of these five justices agree to the same reason why (the Equal Protection Clause of the U.S. Constitution has been violated), it is a majority opinion.

- **Plurality decision**. If a majority of the justices agree to the outcome of the case, but not to the reasoning for reaching the outcome, it is a plurality opinion. A plurality decision settles the case but is not precedent for later cases.

  Example   If all nine justices hear a case, and five of them agree as to the outcome (the petitioner wins), but not all of these five agree to the reason why (suppose that three base their vote on a violation of the Equal Protection Clause and two base their vote on a violation of the Freedom of Speech Clause of the U.S. Constitution), this is a plurality decision. Five justices have agreed to the same outcome, but those five have not agreed for the same reason. The petitioner wins his or her case, but the decision is not precedent for later cases.

- **Tie decision**. Sometimes the Supreme Court sits without all nine justices present because of illness or conflict of interest, or because a justice has not been confirmed to fill a vacant seat on the court. In the case of a tie vote, the lower court decision is affirmed. These votes are not precedent for later cases.

  Example   A petitioner won her case at the court of appeals. At the U.S. Supreme Court, only eight justices hear the case. Four justices vote for the petitioner, and four justices vote for the respondent. This is a tie vote. The petitioner remains the winner because she won at the court of appeals. The decision of the Supreme Court sets no precedent for later cases.

A justice who agrees with the outcome of a case but not the reason proffered by other justices can issue a **concurring opinion**, setting forth his or her reasons for deciding the case. A justice who does not agree with a decision can file a **dissenting opinion** that sets forth the reasons for his or her dissent.

Jurisdiction of Federal and State Courts

Subject-matter jurisdiction
Jurisdiction over the subject matter of a lawsuit.

A federal or state court must have **subject-matter jurisdiction** to hear a case. Article III, Section 2, of the U.S. Constitution sets forth the jurisdiction of federal courts. Federal courts have *limited jurisdiction* to hear cases involving federal questions and cases involving diversity of citizenship. State courts have jurisdiction to hear certain types of cases. Jurisdiction of federal and state courts to hear cases is discussed in the following paragraphs.

Web Exploration

Go to the website of the U.S. Supreme Court at www .supremecourtus.gov. Who are the nine justices of the U.S. Supreme Court? Who is the Chief Justice? What President appointed each justice and what political party (e.g., Democrat, Republican) did that President belong to?

Subject-Matter Jurisdiction of Federal Courts

Federal courts have jurisdiction to hear cases based on the subject matter of the case. The federal courts have jurisdiction to hear cases involving "federal questions." **Federal question** cases are cases arising under the U.S. Constitution, treaties, and federal statutes and regulations. There is no dollar-amount limit on federal question cases that can be brought in federal court.

> **Example** A lawsuit involving federal securities law concerns a federal question (a federal statute) and will be heard by a U.S. district court.

Federal question A case arising under the U.S. Constitution, treaties, or federal statutes and regulations.

Subject-Matter Jurisdiction of State Courts

State courts have jurisdiction to hear cases involving subject matters that federal courts do not have jurisdiction to hear. These usually involve state laws.

> **Examples** Real estate law, corporation law, partnership law, limited liability company law, contract law, sales and lease contracts, and negotiable instruments are state law subject matters.

Diversity of Citizenship

A case involving a state court subject matter may be brought in federal court if there is **diversity of citizenship**. Diversity of citizenship occurs if the lawsuit involves (a) citizens of different states, (b) a citizen of a state and a citizen or subject of a foreign country, and (c) a citizen of a state and a foreign country is the plaintiff. A corporation is considered to be a citizen of the state in which it is incorporated and in which it has its principal place of business. The reason for providing diversity of citizenship jurisdiction was to prevent state court bias against nonresidents. The federal court must apply the appropriate state's law in deciding the case. The dollar amount of the controversy must exceed $75,000 to be brought in federal court. If this requirement is not met, the action must be brought in the appropriate state court.

Diversity of citizenship A case between (1) citizens of different states, (2) a citizen of a state and a citizen or subject of a foreign country, and (3) a citizen of a state and a foreign country where a foreign country is the plaintiff.

> **Example** Henry, a resident of the state of Idaho, is driving his automobile in the state of Idaho when he negligently hits Mary, a pedestrian. Mary is a resident of the state of New York. There is no federal question involved in this case; it is an automobile accident that involves state negligence law. However, there is diversity of citizenship in this case: Henry is from the state of Idaho, while Mary is from another state, the state of New York. Usually the case must be brought in the state in which the automobile accident occurred because this is where most of the witnesses and evidence will be from. In this case, Mary, the plaintiff, may bring her lawsuit in federal court in Idaho, and if she does so the case will remain in federal court. If Mary brings the case in Idaho state court it will remain in Idaho state court if Henry agrees; however, Henry can move the case to federal court.

Exclusive and Concurrent Jurisdiction

Federal courts have **exclusive jurisdiction** to hear cases involving federal crimes, antitrust, bankruptcy, patent and copyright cases, suits against the United States, and most admiralty cases. State courts cannot hear these cases.

State and federal courts have **concurrent jurisdiction** to hear cases involving diversity of citizenship and federal questions over which federal courts do not have exclusive jurisdiction (e.g., cases involving federal securities laws). If a plaintiff brings a case involving concurrent jurisdiction in state court, the defendant can remove the case to federal court. If a case does not qualify to be brought in federal court, it must be brought in the appropriate state court.

The following feature discusses a paralegal's duty to investigate in what court a particular action should be brought.

ETHICAL PERSPECTIVE

Duty of a Paralegal to Investigate What Court in Which to Bring a Lawsuit

Mya is driving her automobile in St. Ignace, Michigan, when her car is rear-ended by another automobile driven by Pierre. Mya is injured in the accident. The accident was caused by Pierre's negligence in driving above the speed limit and not paying attention to the road. Mya comes to attorney Paula Johnson's office to consult about suing Pierre to recover monetary damages for her physical injuries and also to recover damages for the pain and suffering.

You work as the paralegal for Attorney Johnson. Attorney Johnson asks you to investigate the facts and determine in what court the case could be brought. You correctly determine that the subject matter of the case—negligence in causing an automobile accident—belongs in state court. And because the accident occurred in Michigan you automatically assume that the case should be brought in Michigan state court. However, you fail to determine what states the plaintiff and defendant are residents of.

You report to Attorney Johnson that the case should be brought in Michigan state court. Here, you have failed to conduct the proper investigation necessary to determine the proper court for the case to be brought in. You have failed to find out what states the parties are residents of, or if one of the parties is a resident of a foreign country. If the parties are from different states, or one of the parties is from a foreign country, the case qualifies to be brought in federal court because of diversity of citizenship. By failing to conduct a proper investigation you have been negligent and have breached your ethical duty as a paralegal that you owe to your supervising attorney. By failing to discover whether the case involves diversity of citizenship, the case may end up being brought in Michigan state court when in fact the case qualifies to be brought in federal court as well. Without this information, Attorney Johnson is lacking sufficient information to decide the benefits of bringing the case in either state or federal court.

Personal Jurisdiction and Other Issues

Not every court has the authority to hear all types of cases. First, to bring a lawsuit in a court, the plaintiff must have *standing to sue*. In addition, the court must have *jurisdiction* to hear the case, and the case must be brought in the proper *venue*. These topics are discussed in the following paragraphs.

Standing to Sue

To bring a lawsuit, a plaintiff must have **standing to sue**. This means the plaintiff must have some stake in the outcome of the lawsuit.

> **Example**   Linda's friend Jon is injured in an accident caused by Emily. Jon refuses to sue. Linda cannot sue Emily on Jon's behalf because she does not have an interest in the result of the case.

In Personam Jurisdiction

In personam (personal) jurisdiction Jurisdiction over the parties to a lawsuit.

Jurisdiction over a person is called *in personam* **jurisdiction**, or **personal jurisdiction**. A *plaintiff*, by filing a lawsuit with a court, gives the court *in personam* jurisdiction over himself or herself. The court must also have *in personam* jurisdiction over the *defendant*, which is usually obtained by having a summons served to that person within the territorial boundaries of the state (i.e., **service of process**). Service of process is usually accomplished by personal service of the summons and complaint on the defendant.

If personal service is not possible, alternative forms of notice, such as mailing of the summons or publication of a notice in a newspaper, may be permitted. A corporation is subject to personal jurisdiction in the state in which it is incorporated, has its principal office, and is doing business.

A party who disputes the jurisdiction of a court can make a *special appearance* in that court to argue against imposition of jurisdiction. Service of process is not permitted during such an appearance.

In Rem Jurisdiction

A court may have jurisdiction to hear and decide a case because it has jurisdiction over the property of the lawsuit: This is called *in rem* **jurisdiction** ("jurisdiction over the thing").

> **Example** A state court would have jurisdiction to hear a dispute over the ownership of a piece of real estate located within the state. This is so even if one or more of the disputing parties lives in another state or states.

In rem jurisdiction Jurisdiction to hear a case because of jurisdiction over the property of the lawsuit.

Quasi in Rem Jurisdiction

Sometimes a plaintiff who obtains a judgment against a defendant in one state will try to collect the judgment by attaching property of the defendant that is located in another state. This is permitted under *quasi in rem* **jurisdiction**, or **attachment jurisdiction**.

> **Example** If a plaintiff wins a monetary judgment against a defendant in a Florida state court, but the defendant's only property to satisfy the judgment is located in Idaho, the Idaho state court has *quasi in rem* jurisdiction to order the attachment of the defendant's property in Idaho to satisfy the Florida court judgment.

Quasi in rem (attachment) jurisdiction Jurisdiction allowed a plaintiff who obtains a judgment in one state to try to collect the judgment by attaching property of the defendant located in another state.

Long-Arm Statutes

In most states, a state court can obtain jurisdiction over persons and businesses located in another state or country through the state's **long-arm statute**. These statutes extend a state's jurisdiction to nonresidents who were not served a summons within the state. The nonresident must have had some *minimum contact* with the state [*International Shoe Co. v. Washington*, 326 U.S. 310, 66 S.Ct. 154, 90 L.Ed. 95, 1945 U.S. Lexis 1447 (1945)]. In addition, maintenance of the suit must uphold the traditional notions of fair play and substantial justice.

Long-arm statute A statute that extends a state's jurisdiction to nonresidents who were not served a summons within the state.

The exercise of long-arm jurisdiction is generally permitted over nonresidents who have (1) committed torts within the state (e.g., caused an automobile accident in the state), (2) entered into a contract either in the state or that affects the state (and allegedly breached the contract), or (3) transacted other business in the state that allegedly caused injury to another person.

Venue

Venue requires lawsuits to be heard by the court with jurisdiction nearest the location in which the incident occurred or where the parties reside.

Venue A concept that requires lawsuits to be heard by the court with jurisdiction that is nearest the location in which the incident occurred or where the parties reside.

> **Example** Harry, a Georgia resident, commits a felony crime in Los Angeles County, California. The California Superior Court, located in Los Angeles, is the proper venue because the crime was committed in Los Angeles County and the witnesses are probably from the area, and so on.

Occasionally, pretrial publicity may prejudice jurors located in the proper venue. In these cases, a **change of venue** may be requested so a more impartial jury can be found. The courts generally frown upon *forum shopping* (i.e., looking for a favorable court without a valid reason).

Forum-Selection and Choice-of-Law Clauses

Parties sometimes agree in their contract as to what state's courts, federal courts, or country's court will have jurisdiction to hear a legal dispute should one arise. Such clauses in contracts are called **forum-selection clauses**.

In addition to agreeing to a forum, the parties also often agree in contracts as to what state's law or country's law will apply in resolving a dispute. These clauses are called **choice-of-law clauses**.

Alternative Dispute Resolution (ADR)

Alternative dispute resolution (ADR) Methods of resolving disputes other than litigation.

The use of the court system to resolve business and other disputes can take years and cost thousands, if not millions, of dollars in legal fees and expenses. In commercial litigation, the normal business operations of the parties are often disrupted. To avoid or lessen these problems, businesses are increasingly turning to methods of **alternative dispute resolution (ADR)** and other aids to resolving disputes. The most common form of ADR is *arbitration*. Other forms of ADR are *negotiation, mediation, conciliation, minitrial, fact-finding,* and using a *judicial referee*.

The following feature discusses the career opportunities for paralegal professionals in alternative dispute resolution.

Negotiation

Negotiation A procedure in which the parties to a dispute engage in negotiations to try to reach a voluntary settlement of their dispute.

The simplest form of alternative dispute resolution is engaging in negotiation between the parties to try to settle a dispute. **Negotiation** is a procedure whereby the parties to a dispute engage in discussions to try to reach a voluntary settlement of their dispute. Negotiation may take place either before a lawsuit is filed, after a lawsuit is filed, or before other forms of alternative dispute resolution are engaged in.

In a negotiation, the parties, who often are represented by attorneys, negotiate with each other to try to reach an agreeable solution to their dispute. During

CAREER OPPORTUNITIES FOR PARALEGALS IN ALTERNATIVE DISPUTE RESOLUTION

The growth in using alternative dispute resolution to solve disputes has been phenomenal. Alternative dispute resolution is just that—an alternative to using the litigation process and court systems to resolve disputes.

The major form of alternative dispute resolution is arbitration. The United States Supreme Court has upheld the use of arbitration in many types of disputes. Arbitration is used particularly in contract disputes, because many contracts contain arbitration clauses—that is, the parties to the contract have agreed in their contract not to use the court systems to solve their disputes. Instead, they have expressly agreed that an arbitrator, and not a jury, will resolve their dispute.

Most major companies have placed arbitration agreements in their contracts.

Examples Arbitration clauses appear in contracts to purchase goods, to lease automobiles, to employ services, and in other types of contracts. Also, arbitration clauses are included by employers in many employment contracts. Thus, if an employee has a dispute with his or her employer, the dispute goes to arbitration for resolution because the employee has given up his or her right to use the court system by agreeing to the arbitration clause.

Mediation also has become an indispensable method of helping to solve disputes. In mediation, the mediator does not act as a decision-maker but, instead, acts as a facilitator to try to help the disputing parties reach a settlement of their dispute. Mediation often is used in family law matters, particularly in helping reach a settlement in divorce cases.

Paralegals who work for lawyers in business law-related matters, contract disputes, and family law matters should have a thorough understanding of alternative dispute resolution. Paralegals often are called upon to help attorneys prepare for arbitration, mediation, and other forms of alternative dispute resolution. This chapter addresses the major forms of alternative dispute resolution.

negotiation proceedings, the parties usually make offers and counteroffers to one another. The parties or their attorneys also may provide information to the other side that would assist the other side in reaching an amicable settlement.

Many courts require that the parties to a lawsuit engage in settlement discussions prior to trial to try to negotiate a settlement of the case. The judge must be assured that a settlement of the case is not possible before he or she permits the case to go to trial. Judges often convince the parties to engage in further negotiations if the judge determines that the parties are not too far apart in the negotiations of a settlement.

If a settlement of the dispute is reached through negotiation, a settlement agreement is drafted that contains the terms of the agreement. A **settlement agreement** is an agreement that is voluntarily entered into by the parties to a dispute that settles the dispute. Each side must sign the settlement agreement for it to be effective. The settlement agreement usually is submitted to the court, and the case will be dismissed based on execution of the settlement agreement.

Settlement agreement An agreement voluntarily entered into by the parties to a dispute that settles the dispute.

Arbitration

Paralegals working in many areas of the law—litigation, contract law, business law, and such—will encounter arbitration clauses in some of the cases that they are working on. In **arbitration**, the parties choose an impartial third party to hear and decide the dispute. This neutral party is called the **arbitrator**. Arbitrators usually are selected from members of the American Arbitration Association (AAA) or another arbitration association.

Arbitration A form of ADR in which the parties choose an impartial third party to hear and decide the dispute.

Labor union agreements, franchise agreements, leases, and other commercial contracts often contain **arbitration clauses** that require disputes arising out of the contract to be submitted to arbitration. If there is no arbitration clause, the parties can enter into a **submission agreement**, whereby they agree to submit a dispute to arbitration after the dispute arises.

The benefits of arbitration are that it is less expensive than litigation, is completed faster than a lawsuit, and is decided by a person who is knowledgeable in the area of law that is in dispute. Some consumers and employees who are subject to arbitration agreements argue that arbitration unfairly favors businesses and employers over them.

In the past, some courts were reluctant to permit arbitration of a dispute or found that arbitration agreements were illegal. However, in a series of cases the U.S. Supreme Court upheld the validity of many types of arbitration clauses or agreements.

Exhibit 6.7 is the form for a Demand for Arbitration.

Federal Arbitration Act

The **Federal Arbitration Act (FAA)** was originally enacted by Congress in 1925 to reverse the longstanding judicial hostility to arbitration agreements that had existed as English common law and had been adopted by American courts [9 U.S.C. Sections 1 et. seq.]. The Act provides that arbitration agreements involving commerce are valid, irrevocable, and enforceable contracts, unless some grounds exist at law or equity (e.g., fraud, duress) to revoke them. The FAA permits one party to obtain a court order to compel arbitration if the other party has failed, neglected, or refused to comply with an arbitration agreement.

About half of the states have adopted the **Uniform Arbitration Act**, which promotes the arbitration of disputes at the state level. Many federal and state courts have instituted programs to refer legal disputes to arbitration or another form of alternative dispute resolution.

ADR Providers

ADR services usually are provided by private organizations or individuals who qualify to hear and decide certain disputes. For example, the **American Arbitration Association (AAA)** is the largest private provider of ADR services. The AAA employs persons

Exhibit 6.7 Demand for arbitration

American Arbitration Association
Dispute Resolution Services Worldwide

_____ **ARBITRATION RULES**
(ENTER THE NAME OF THE APPLICABLE RULES)
Demand for Arbitration

MEDIATION: *If you would like the AAA to contact the other parties and attempt to arrange mediation, please check this box.* ☐
There is no additional administrative fee for this service.

Name of Respondent			Name of Representative (if known)		
Address:			Name of Firm (if applicable):		
			Representative's Address		
City	State	Zip Code	City	State	Zip Code
Phone No.		Fax No.	Phone No.		Fax No.
Email Address:			Email Address:		

The named claimant, a party to an arbitration agreement dated _____, which provides for arbitration under the
_____Arbitration Rules of the American Arbitration Association, hereby demands arbitration.

THE NATURE OF THE DISPUTE

Dollar Amount of Claim $	Other Relief Sought: ☐ Attorneys Fees ☐ Interest
	☐ Arbitration Costs ☐ Punitive/ Exemplary ☐ Other _____

AMOUNT OF FILING FEE ENCLOSED WITH THIS DEMAND (please refer to the fee schedule in the rules for the appropriate fee) $

PLEASE DESCRIBE APPROPRIATE QUALIFICATIONS FOR ARBITRATOR(S) TO BE APPOINTED TO HEAR THIS DISPUTE:

Hearing locale_____   (check one) ☐ Requested by Claimant   ☐ Locale provision included in the contract

Estimated time needed for hearings overall: _____hours or _____days	Type of Business: Claimant _____ Respondent_____

Is this a dispute between a business and a consumer?   ☐Yes ☐ No
Does this dispute arise out of an employment relationship?   ☐Yes ☐ No

If this dispute arises out of an employment relationship, what was/is the employee's annual wage range? Note: This question is required by California law. ☐Less than $100,000 ☐ $100,000 - $250,000 ☐ Over $250,000

You are hereby notified that copies of our arbitration agreement and this demand are being filed with the American Arbitration Association's Case Management Center, located in (check one) ☐ Atlanta, GA ☐ Dallas, TX   ☐ East Providence, RI ☐ Fresno, CA ☐ International Centre, NY, with a request that it commence administration of the arbitration. Under the rules, you may file an answering statement within the timeframe specified in the rules, after notice from the AAA.

Signature (may be signed by a representative) Date:			Name of Representative		
Name of Claimant			Name of Firm (if applicable)		
Address (to be used in connection with this case):			Representative's Address:		
City	State	Zip Code	City	State	Zip Code
Phone No.		Fax No.	Phone No.		Fax No.
Email Address:			Email Address:		

To begin proceedings, please send two copies of this Demand and the Arbitration Agreement, along with the filing fee as provided for in the Rules, to the AAA. Send the original Demand to the Respondent.

Please visit our website at www.adr.org if you would like to file this case online. AAA Customer Service can be reached at 800-778-7879

Source: Reprinted with permission of American Arbitration Association

---

Web Exploration

Go to the website of the American Arbitration Association (AAA) at http://www.adr.org/sp.asp?id= 28749 and read the article entitled "Arbitration and Mediation."

who are qualified in special areas of the law to provide mediation and arbitration services in those areas. These persons are called **neutrals**.

For example, if parties have a contract dispute involving an employment contract, a construction contract, an Internet contract, or other commercial contract or business dispute, the AAA has a special group of neutrals that can hear and decide these cases. Other mediation and arbitration associations are located throughout the United States and internationally.

ADR Procedure

An arbitration agreement often describes the specific procedures that must be followed for a case to proceed to and through arbitration. If one party seeks to enforce an arbitration clause, that party must give notice to the other party. The parties then select an arbitration association or arbitrator as provided in the agreement. The parties usually agree on the date, time, and place of the arbitration. This can be at the arbitrator's offices, at a law office, or at any other agreed-upon location.

At the arbitration, the parties can call witnesses to give testimony, and introduce evidence to support their case and refute the other side's case. Rules similar to those followed by federal courts usually are adhered to at the arbitration. Often, each party pays a filing fee and other fees for the arbitration. Sometimes the agreement provides that one party will pay all of the costs of the arbitration. Arbitrators are paid by the hour or day, or other agreed-upon method of compensation.

Decision and Award

After the hearing is complete, the arbitrator reaches a decision and issues an **award**. The parties often agree in advance to be bound by an arbitrator's decision and remedy. This is called **binding arbitration**. In this situation, the decision and award of the arbitrator cannot be appealed to the courts. If the arbitration is not binding, the decision and award of the arbitrator can be appealed to the courts. This is called **non-binding arbitration**. Courts usually give great deference to an arbitrator's decision and award.

If a decision and award has been rendered by an arbitrator but a party refuses to abide by the arbitrator's decision, the other party may file an action in court to have the arbitrator's decision enforced.

> **Example** Assume that there has been a contract dispute between NorthWest Corporation and SouthEast Corporation that goes to binding arbitration. The arbitrator issues a decision that awards SouthEast Corporation $5 million against NorthWest Corporation. If NorthWest Corporation fails to pay the award, SouthEast Corporation can file an action in court to have the award enforced by the court.

Other Forms of ADR

As mentioned, in addition to arbitration and negotiation, the other forms of ADR are *mediation, conciliation, minitrial, fact-finding*, and using a *judicial referee*. These forms of ADR are discussed in the following paragraphs.

Mediation

Mediation is a form of negotiation in which a neutral third party assists the disputing parties in reaching a settlement of their dispute. The neutral third party is called a **mediator**. The mediator usually is a person who is an expert in the area of the dispute, or a lawyer or retired judge. The mediator is selected by the parties as provided in their agreement, or as otherwise selected by the parties. Unlike an arbitrator, however, a mediator does not make a decision or an award.

A mediator's role is to assist the parties in reaching a settlement. The mediator usually acts as an intermediary between the parties. In many cases the mediator will meet with the two parties at an agreed-upon location, often the mediator's office or one of the offices of the parties. The mediator then will meet with both parties, usually separately, to discuss their side of the case.

After discussing the facts of the case with both sides, the mediator will encourage settlement of the dispute and will transmit settlement offers from one side to the other. In doing so, the mediator points out the strengths and weaknesses of each party's case and gives his or her opinion to each side why they should decrease or increase their settlement offers. The mediator's job is to facilitate settlement of the case.

Mediation A form of negotiation in which a neutral third party assists the disputing parties in reaching a settlement of their dispute.

Mediator A neutral third party who assists the disputing parties in reaching a settlement of their dispute. The mediator cannot make a decision or an award.

Paralegals *in* Practice

PARALEGAL PROFILE
Kathleen A. Stradley

Kathleen A. Stradley is a Certified Arbitrator and Certified Mediator with 26 years of paralegal experience. She also is an Advanced Certified Paralegal and Civil Litigation Specialist. Since 1998, Kathleen has worked as an independent contractor of litigation support and consulting services in North Dakota and Minnesota. She assists trial attorneys and corporations with case management and trial preparation. She also serves as a private arbitrator and mediator in legal disputes.

Becoming involved in alternative dispute resolution (ADR) has been an interesting process. Before starting my own business, I worked for several law firms and a corporation in Ohio and North Dakota. During that time, I was aware that ADR could save a lot of time and money. However, I did not know much about putting ADR into practice. So, I enrolled in an intense course that allowed me to obtain my mediator certification after 40 hours of training.

A short time later, I trained for a new binding arbitration program for the North Dakota Workers' Compensation Bureau. This program provided employees and employers with the option of binding arbitration rather than a formal administrative hearing or judicial solution. Instead, a hearing was held in front of three arbitrators, one from each of three societal areas: labor, industry, and the public. For about a year, I served as a public sector arbitrator and chairperson for the panel. After the panel was reduced to one person, I continued to serve as an arbitrator for Workers' Compensation hearings.

Later, I served as an arbitrator and mediator through the American Arbitration Association (AAA) for family, commercial, personal injury, employment/workplace, and construction industry claims. In 1997, after a terrible flood destroyed my hometown of Grand Forks, North Dakota, I mediated in many disaster-related commercial and construction disputes, as well as family law cases. In more recent years, I spoke with a number of disaster victims who experienced an ADR process. Most of them agreed that ADR was a valuable course of action that helped them rebuild their homes and lives.

Due to mandatory arbitration provisions in most contracts, and the trend of court ordered dispute resolution proceedings, I think there will be fewer trials in the future. Instead, I believe more and more lawsuits will be resolved with alternative methods. Cases using ADR proceedings typically involve fewer documents. However, these documents need to be prepared much earlier, and in greater detail than cases that are tried in court with a jury. In mediation, each party submits their statement of the case and its value to the mediator in advance of the mediation. In arbitration, the evidence is submitted to the arbitrator in advance of the arbitration. ADR proceedings usually occur after discovery is completed and well in advance of the scheduled trial.

Source: Stradley, Kathleen A., "ADR: Changing Ground." *Facts & Findings, the Journal for Legal Assistants* XXXI.4 (January 2005): 16–17. Career Chronicle Edition 2004, NALA.

The mediator gives his or her opinion to the parties as to what he or she believes to be a reasonable settlement of the case, and usually proposes settlement of the dispute. The parties are free to accept or reject such proposal. If the parties agree to a settlement, a settlement agreement is drafted that expresses their agreement. Execution of the settlement agreement ends the dispute. The parties, of course, must perform their duties under the settlement agreement.

Example Parties to a divorce action often use mediation to try to help resolve the issues involved in the divorce, including property settlement, payment of alimony and child support, custody of children, visitation rights, and other issues.

Exhibit 6.8 is the form for a Request for Mediation.

Conciliation A form of dispute resolution in which a conciliator transmits offers and counteroffers between the disputing parties in helping to reach a settlement of their dispute.

Conciliator A third party in a conciliation proceeding who assists the disputing parties in reaching a settlement of their dispute. The conciliator cannot make a decision or an award.

Conciliation

Conciliation is another form of alternative dispute resolution. In conciliation, a party named a **conciliator** helps the parties to try to reach a resolution of their dispute. Conciliation often is used when the parties refuse to face each other in an adversarial setting. The conciliator schedules meetings and appointments during which information can be transferred between the parties. A conciliator usually carries offers and counteroffers for a settlement back and forth between the disputing parties. A conciliator cannot make a decision or an award.

Although the role of a conciliator is not to propose a settlement of the case, many often do. In many cases, conciliators are neutral third parties, although in some

Exhibit 6.8 Request for mediation

American Arbitration Association
Dispute Resolution Services Worldwide

REQUEST FOR MEDIATION

Name of Responding Party	Name of Representative (if known)
Address:	Name of Firm (if applicable)
	Representative's Address:

City	State	Zip Code	City	State	Zip Code
Phone No.		Fax No.	Phone No.		Fax No.
Email Address:			Email Address:		

The undersigned party to an agreement contained in a written contract dated _____, providing for mediation under the _____ Mediation Procedures of the American Arbitration Association, hereby requests mediation

THE NATURE OF THE DISPUTE

CLAIM OR RELIEF SOUGHT (amount, if any):

AMOUNT OF FILING FEE ENCLOSED WITH THIS REQUEST: $

Mediation locale_____ (check one) ☐ Requested by Filing Party ☐ Locale provision included in the contract

Type of Business: Filing Party _____ Responding Party_____

You are hereby notified that copies of our mediation agreement and this request are being filed with the American Arbitration Association's Case Management Center, located in (check one) ☐ Atlanta, GA ☐ Dallas, TX ☐ East Providence, RI ☐ Fresno, CA ☐ International Centre, NY, with a request that it commence administration of this mediation.

Signature (may be signed by a representative) Date:	Name of Representative
Name of Filling Party	Name of Firm (if applicable)
Address (to be used in connection with this case):	Representative's Address:

City	State	Zip Code	City	State	Zip Code
Phone No.		Fax No.	Phone No.		Fax No.
Email Address:			Email Address:		

To begin proceedings, please send two copies of this Request and the Mediation Agreement, along with the filing fee as provided for in the Rules, to the AAA. Send the original Request to the responding party.

Please visit our website at www.adr.org if you would like to file this case online. AAA Customer Service can be reached at 800-778-7879

Source: Reprinted with permission of American Arbitration Association.

circumstances the parties may select an interested third party to act as the conciliator. If the parties reach a settlement of their dispute through the use of conciliation, a settlement agreement is drafted and executed by the parties.

Minitrial

A **minitrial** is a voluntary private proceeding in which the lawyers for each side present a shortened version of their case to the representatives of the other side. The representatives of each side who attend the minitrial have the authority to settle the

Minitrial A voluntary private proceeding in which the lawyers for each side present a shortened version of their case to representatives of the other side, and usually to a neutral third party, in an attempt to reach a settlement of the dispute.

dispute. In many cases, the parties also hire a neutral third party, often someone who is an expert in the field concerning the disputed matter or a legal expert, who presides over the minitrial. After hearing the case, the neutral third party often is called upon to render an opinion as to how the court would most likely decide the case.

During a minitrial, the parties get to see the strengths and weaknesses of their own position and that of the opposing side. Once the strengths and weaknesses of both sides are exposed, the parties to a minitrial often settle the case. The parties also often settle a minitrial based on the opinion rendered by the neutral third party. If the parties settle their dispute after a minitrial, they will enter into a settlement agreement setting forth their agreement.

Minitrials serve a useful purpose in that they act as a substitute for the real trial, but they are much briefer and not as complex and expensive to prepare for. By exposing the strengths and weaknesses of both sides' cases, the parties usually are more realistic regarding their own position and the merits of settling the case prior to an expensive, and often more risky, trial.

Fact-Finding

In some situations, called fact-finding, the parties to a dispute will employ a neutral third party to act as a fact-finder to investigate the dispute. The fact-finder is authorized to investigate the dispute, gather evidence, prepare demonstrative evidence, and prepare reports of his or her findings.

A fact-finder is not authorized to make a decision or award. In some cases, a fact-finder will recommend settlement of the case. The fact-finder presents the evidence and findings to the parties, who then may use such information in negotiating a settlement if they wish.

Judicial Referee

If the parties agree, the court may appoint a **judicial referee** to conduct a private trial and render a judgment. Referees, who often are retired judges, have most of the powers of a trial judge, and their decisions stand as a judgment of the court. The parties usually reserve their right to appeal.

Online ADR

Web Exploration

Go to the website of the American Arbitration Association (AAA) at http://www.adr.com. Does the AAA provide online dispute resolution?

Several services now offer **online arbitration**. Most of these services allow a party to a dispute to register the dispute with the service and then notify the other party by email of the registration of the dispute. Most online arbitration requires the registering party to submit an amount that the party is willing to accept or pay to the other party in the online arbitration. The other party is afforded the opportunity to accept the offer. If that party accepts the offer, a settlement has been reached. The other party, however, may return a **counteroffer**. The process continues until a settlement is reached or one or both of the parties remove themselves from the online ADR process.

Also, several websites offer **online mediation** services. In an online mediation, the parties sit before their computers and sign onto the site. Two chat rooms are assigned to each party. One chat room is used for private conversations with the online mediator, and the other chat room is for conversations with both parties and the mediator.

Online arbitration and mediation services charge fees for their services. The fees are reasonable. In an online arbitration or mediation, a settlement can be reached rather quickly without paying lawyers' fees and court costs. The parties also are acting through a more objective online process than meeting face-to-face or negotiating over the telephone, either of which could conclude with verbal arguments.

The ethical duty and social responsibility of a paralegal professional to provide *pro bono* services to the public is discussed in the following feature.

ETHICAL PERSPECTIVE

A Paralegal's Duty to Provide Pro Bono *Services to the Public*

Mr. Alvarez is a paralegal in a law firm and works directly with Ms. Dawson, a partner in the law firm. In addition to her law practice with the law firm, Ms. Dawson volunteers to work one evening per week at a domestic abuse center that serves women and children.

At the center, Ms. Dawson interviews domestic abuse victims and pursues whatever legal actions that can be taken to assist the victims and their families. This often includes doing the legal work for obtaining restraining orders, government assistance, and spousal and child support. All of Ms. Dawson's services at the domestic abuse center are provided *pro bono*, that is, for free.

One day Ms. Dawson asks her paralegal, Mr. Alvarez, if he would be interested in volunteering to help her one night each month at the domestic abuse shelter. Ms. Dawson explains that she could use Mr. Alvarez's assistance as a paralegal to help conduct interviews, prepare documents, and obtain government and other assistance for the domestic abuse victims and their families. Mr. Alvarez would be under the supervision of Ms. Dawson while working at the center.

Does a paralegal owe an ethical duty to provide *pro bono* services to the public?

Model and state paralegal Code of Ethics and Professional Responsibility provide that a paralegal has an ethical duty to provide *pro bono* services. Thus, a paralegal should strive to provide *pro bono* services under the authority of an attorney or as authorized by a court. It is best if these services are provided to assist the poor, persons with limited education, charitable programs, or protect civil rights.

PARALEGAL'S ETHICAL DECISION

Because a paralegal owes an ethical duty to provide *pro bono* services to the public, Mr. Alvarez should agree to assist Ms. Dawson at the domestic abuse shelter one evening each month in order to fulfill his duty to the public. This would be an excellent way for Mr. Alvarez to satisfy his ethical duty as a paralegal professional.

Concept Review *and* Reinforcement

LEGAL TERMINOLOGY

SUMMARY OF KEY CONCEPTS

State Court Systems

Limited-Jurisdiction Trial Court	This state court hears matters of a specialized or limited nature (e.g., misdemeanor criminal matters, traffic tickets, civil matters under a certain dollar amount). Many states have created small-claims courts that hear small-dollar-amount civil cases (e.g., under $5,000) in which parties cannot be represented by lawyers.
General-Jurisdiction Trial Court	This is a state court that hears cases of a general nature that are not within the jurisdiction of limited-jurisdiction trial courts.
Intermediate Appellate Court	This state court hears appeals from state trial courts. The appellate court reviews the trial court record in making its decision; no new evidence is introduced at this level.
Highest State Court	Each state has a highest court in its court system. This court hears appeals from appellate courts and, where appropriate, trial courts. This court reviews the record in making its decision; no new evidence is introduced at this level. Most states call this court the *supreme court.*

Federal Court System

Special Federal Courts	Federal courts that have specialized or limited jurisdiction. They include: 1. *U.S. Tax Court:* hears cases involving federal tax laws 2. *U.S. Court of Federal Claims:* hears cases brought against the United States 3. *U.S. Court of International Trade:* hears cases involving tariffs and international commercial disputes 4. *U.S. Bankruptcy Court:* hear cases involving federal bankruptcy law
U.S. District Courts	Federal trial courts of general jurisdiction that hear cases that are not within the jurisdiction of specialized courts. Each state has at least one U.S. district court; more populated states have several district courts. The area served by one of these courts is called a *district.*

U.S. Courts of Appeals	Intermediate federal appellate courts that hear appeals from district courts located in their circuit, and in certain instances from special federal courts and federal administrative agencies. There are 12 geographical *circuits* in the United States. Eleven serve areas composed of several states, and another is located in Washington, DC. A thirteenth circuit court—the *Court of Appeals for the Federal Circuit*—is located in Washington, DC, and reviews patent, trademark, and international trade cases.

Supreme Court of the United States

U.S. Supreme Court	Highest court of the federal court system; hears appeals from the circuit courts and, in some instances, from special courts and U.S. district courts. The Court, located in Washington, DC, comprises nine justices, one of whom is named Chief Justice.
Decisions by U.S. Supreme Court	*Petition of certiorari and writ of certiorari:* To have a case heard by the U.S. Supreme Court, a petitioner must file a *petition for certiorari* with the Court. If the Court decides to hear the case, it will issue a *writ of certiorari*.
Voting by the U.S. Supreme Court	1. *Unanimous decision:* All of the justices agree as to the outcome and reasoning used to decide the case; the decision becomes precedent. 2. *Majority decision:* A majority of justices agrees as to the outcome and reasoning used to decide the case; the decision becomes precedent. 3. *Plurality decision:* A majority of the justices agrees to the outcome but not to the reasoning; the decision is not precedent. 4. *Tie decision:* If there is a tie vote, the lower court's decision stands; the decision is not precedent. 5. *Concurring opinion:* A justice who agrees as to the outcome of the case but not the reasoning used by other justices may write a concurring opinion setting forth his or her reasoning. 6. *Dissenting opinion:* A justice who disagrees with the outcome of a case may write a dissenting opinion setting forth his or her reasoning.

Jurisdiction of Federal and State Courts

Subject-Matter Jurisdiction	The court must have jurisdiction over the subject matter of the lawsuit; each court has limited jurisdiction to hear only certain types of cases.
Limited Jurisdiction of Federal Courts	Federal courts have jurisdiction to hear the following types of cases: 1. *Federal question:* cases arising under the U.S. Constitution, treaties, and federal statutes and regulations; no dollar-amount limit. 2. *Diversity of citizenship:* cases between (a) citizens of different states, (b) a citizen of a state and a citizen or subject of a foreign country; and (c) a citizen of a state and a foreign country where the foreign country is the plaintiff. The controversy must exceed $75,000 for the federal court to hear the case.
Jurisdiction of State Courts	State courts have jurisdiction to hear cases that federal courts do not have jurisdiction to hear.
Exclusive Jurisdiction	Federal courts have exclusive jurisdiction to hear cases involving federal crimes, antitrust, and bankruptcy; patent and copyright cases; suits against the United States; and most admiralty cases. State courts may not hear these matters.
Concurrent Jurisdiction	State courts hear some cases that may be heard by federal courts. State courts have concurrent jurisdiction to hear cases involving diversity of citizenship cases and federal question cases over which the federal courts do not have exclusive jurisdiction. The defendant may have the case removed to federal court.

Personal Jurisdiction and Other Issues

Standing to Sue	To bring a lawsuit, the plaintiff must have some stake in the outcome of the lawsuit.
In Personam Jurisdiction (or Personal Jurisdiction)	The court must have jurisdiction over the parties to a lawsuit. The plaintiff submits to the jurisdiction of the court by filing the lawsuit there. Personal jurisdiction is obtained over the defendant by serving that person *service of process*.
In Rem Jurisdiction	A court may have jurisdiction to hear and decide a case because it has jurisdiction over the property at issue in the lawsuit (e.g., real property located in the state).
Quasi In Rem Jurisdiction (or Attachment Jurisdiction)	A plaintiff who obtains a judgment against a defendant in one state may utilize the court system of another state to attach property of the defendant's located in the second state.
Long-Arm Statutes	These statutes permit a state to obtain personal jurisdiction over an out-of-state defendant as long as the defendant had the requisite minimum contact with the state. The out-of-state defendant may be served process outside the state in which the lawsuit has been brought.
Venue	A case must be heard by the court that has jurisdiction nearest to where the incident at issue occurred or where the parties reside. A *change of venue* will be granted if prejudice would occur because of pretrial publicity or another reason.
Forum-Selection Clause	This clause in a contract designates the court that will hear any dispute that arises out of the contract.
Choice-of-Law Clause	This clause in a contract designates what state's law or country's law will apply in resolving a dispute.

Alternative Dispute Resolution (ADR)

ADR	ADR consists of *nonjudicial* means of solving legal disputes. ADR usually saves time and money required by litigation.

Negotiation

Negotiation	A procedure whereby the parties to a dispute engage in discussions to try to reach a voluntary settlement of their dispute.

Arbitration

Arbitration	Arbitration is a form of ADR where an impartial third party, called the arbitrator, hears and decides the dispute. The arbitrator makes an award. The award is appealable to a court if the parties have not given up this right. Arbitration is designated by the parties pursuant to: 1. *Arbitration clause:* Agreement contained in a contract stipulating that any dispute arising out of the contract will be arbitrated. 2. *Submission agreement:* Agreement to submit a dispute to arbitration after the dispute arises.
Federal Arbitration Act (FAA)	Federal statute that provides that arbitration agreements involving commerce are valid, irrevocable, and enforceable contracts, unless some grounds exist at law or equity (e.g., fraud, duress) to revoke them.

Other Forms of ADR

Mediation	In mediation, a neutral third party, called a *mediator*, assists the parties in trying to reach a settlement of their dispute. The mediator does not make an award.
Conciliation	In conciliation, an interested third party, called a *conciliator*, assists the parties in trying to reach a settlement of their dispute. The conciliator does not make an award.
Minitrial	A minitrial is in a short session, the lawyers for each side present their case to representatives of each party who has the authority to settle the dispute.

| Fact-Finding | In fact-finding, the parties hire a neutral third person, called a *fact-finder*, to investigate the dispute and report his or her findings to the adversaries. |
| Judicial Referee | With the consent of the parties, the court can appoint a judicial referee (usually a retired judge or lawyer) to conduct a private trial and render a judgment. The judgment stands as the judgment of the court and may be appealed to the appropriate appellate court. |

Online ADR

| Online ADR | A form of alternative dispute resolution where the parties use an online provider of ADR services. This could be online arbitration, online mediation, and other forms of online ADR. |

WORKING THE WEB

1. Visit the website http://www.clickNsettle.com. What services are offered by this website? What are the costs of using this site's services?
2. Visit the website http://www.internetneutral.com. What services are offered by this site? What are the costs of these services?
3. Visit the website http://www.abanet.org/published/preview/briefs/home.html. Select one of the case names. Find the "Petitioner's Brief" for the selected case and either print out or write down the "Question Presented" for that case.
4. Visit the website http://www.law.cornell.edu/supct/index.html. Find the most recent decision of the U.S. Supreme Court. Read the case heading and the summary of the case. Who are the parties? What issue was presented to the Supreme Court? What was the decision of the Supreme Court?
5. Go to the website http://www.adr.org.overview. Read "A Brief Overview of the American Arbitration Association." Define a "neutral."
6. Find the homepage for the courts in your state. What are the names of the courts in your state? Draw a diagram of the courts of your state. Include limited-jurisdiction courts, general-jurisdiction trial courts, appellate courts, and the highest state court.

CRITICAL THINKING & WRITING QUESTIONS

1. Describe the difference between state limited-jurisdiction courts and general-jurisdiction courts.
2. What are the functions of the state intermediate courts and the highest state courts? Explain.
3. List the special federal courts, and describe the types of cases that each of these courts can hear.
4. What is the function of U.S. District Courts? How many are there?
5. What is the function of U.S. Courts of Appeals? How many U.S. Courts of Appeals are there? How does the Court of Appeals for the Federal Circuit differ from the other U.S. Courts of Appeals?
6. What is the function of the U.S. Supreme Court? How many justices does the Supreme Court have? How does the Chief Justice differ from Associate Justices?
7. Explain the difference between the following types of decisions by the U.S. Supreme Court: (1) unanimous decision, (2) majority decision, (3) plurality decision, and (4) tie decision. Which types of decision or decisions establish precedent? What are concurring opinions and dissenting opinions?
8. Explain the difference between a federal court's jurisdiction to hear a case based on (1) federal question jurisdiction and (2) diversity of citizenship jurisdiction.
9. Explain the difference between subject-matter jurisdiction and *in personam* jurisdiction. Explain the difference between *in rem* jurisdiction and *quasi in rem* jurisdiction.
10. What is a long-arm statute? What is the purpose of a long-arm statute?
11. What is venue? When can a change of venue be granted?
12. What is the difference between judicial dispute resolution and nonjudicial alternative dispute resolution? Why would one be preferred over the other, and who would have a preference?
13. Define arbitration. Describe how the process of arbitration works. What is an award?
14. Describe the difference between mediation and conciliation. How do these differ from arbitration?
15. Describe minitrial and fact-finding.

Building Paralegal Skills

VIDEO CASE STUDIES

Meet the Courthouse Team

An interview with Judge Kenney, a trial judge, who introduces members of the courthouse and the roles they serve as members of the courtroom team.

After viewing the video case study at www.pearsonhighered.com/goldman answer the following:

1. What type of relationship should the paralegal develop with the courthouse team?
2. In addition to the courtroom team, what other members of the courthouse should the paralegal know about?

Jury Selection: Potential Juror Challenged for Cause

Trial counsel for a case, which is going to be tried before a jury, are interviewing the individual potential jurors to select an appropriate jury member.

After viewing the video case study at www.pearsonhighered.com/goldman answer the following:

1. What is the role of the jury in the justice system?
2. Why are the attorneys allowed to request that certain individuals not be allowed to serve on a jury?
3. Is everyone guaranteed a right to a jury trial and the American system of justice?

Settlement Conference with Judge

Opposing counsel are meeting with Judge Lee prior to the start of the trial. The trial judge is presenting the strengths and weaknesses of each side in an attempt to get the parties to settle the case.

After viewing the video case study at www.pearsonhighered.com/goldman answer the following:

1. How is a settlement conference with a judge before trial like an alternative method of dispute resolution?
2. Is the judge in the settlement conference being unfair to one side or the other?
3. Why is the judge trying to settle the case before trial?

ETHICS ANALYSIS & DISCUSSION QUESTIONS

1. May a paralegal represent a client in court?
2. Are a paralegal's time records or calendar subject to the attorney–client privilege?
3. You have been appointed as a trustee of a client's children's educational trust. You need to petition the court for a release of the funds for noneducational purposes—paying the taxes on the trust income. [*Ziegler v. Harrison Nickel*, 64 Cal. App. 4th 545; 1998 Lexis 500.] May you appear alone as the trustee and represent the trust in the court proceedings? Would a nonlawyer, nonparalegal be permitted to appear?

DEVELOPING YOUR COLLABORATION SKILLS

With a group of other students, selected by you or as assigned by your instructor, review the facts of the following case. As a group, discuss the following questions.

1. What is a forum-selection clause?
2. Is putting a forum-selection clause (or choice-of-law clause) in a contract good practice?
3. If there had not been a forum-selection clause in the contract, would the state of Washington have jurisdiction over Carnival Cruise Lines to make it answer the Shute's lawsuit in Washington?

Carnival Cruise Lines, Inc. v. Shute

Mr. and Mrs. Shute, residents of the State of Washington, purchased passage for a seven-day cruise on the *Tropicale*, a cruise ship operated by Carnival Cruise Lines. Inc. (Carnival). They paid the fare to the travel agent, who forwarded the payment to Carnival's headquarters in Miami, Florida. Carnival prepared the tickets and sent them to the Shutes. Each ticket consisted of five pages, including contract terms. The ticket contained a forum-selection clause that designated the State of Florida as the forum for any lawsuits arising under or in connection with the ticket and cruise. The Shutes boarded the *Tropicale* in Los Angeles, which set sail for Puerto Vallarta, Mexico. While the ship was on its return voyage and in international waters off the coast of Mexico, Mrs. Shute was injured when she slipped on a deck mat during a guided tour of the ship's galley. Upon return to the State of Washington, she filed a negligence lawsuit against Carnival in U.S. district court in Washington, seeking damages. Carnival defended, arguing that the lawsuit could only be brought in a court located in the State of Florida pursuant to the forum-selection clause contained in its ticket.

The U.S. Supreme Court held that the forum-selection clause contained in Carnival Cruise Lines' ticket was enforceable against Mrs. Shute. The Supreme Court stated that including a reasonable forum clause in a form contract is permissible for several reasons. First, a cruise line has a special interest in limiting the number of jurisdictions in which it potentially could be subject to a lawsuit. Because a cruise ship typically carries passengers from many locales, it is likely that a mishap on a cruise could subject the cruise line to litigation in several different jurisdictions. Secondly, a clause establishing the forum for dispute resolution dispells any confusion as to where lawsuits arising from the contract must be brought and defended, sparing litigants the time and expense of pretrial motions to determine the correct forum, and conserving judicial resources needed to decide such issues. Finally, passengers who purchase tickets containing a forum-selection clause benefit in reduced fares reflecting the savings that the cruise line enjoys by limiting the forum in which it may be sued.

The Supreme Court held that the forum-selection clause in Carnival Cruise Lines' ticket was fair and reasonable, and therefore enforceable against Mrs. Shute. If Mrs. Shute wished to sue Carnival Cruise Lines, she must do so in a court in the State of Florida, not in a court in the State of Washington.

Source: *Carnival Cruise Lines, Inc. v. Shute*, 499 U.S. 585, 111 S.Ct. 1522, 113 L.Ed.2d 622, **Web** 1991 U.S. Lexis 2221 (Supreme Court of the United States)

PARALEGAL PORTFOLIO EXERCISE

Based on the facts of the case described in the Opening Scenario, prepare and complete the following documents as well as you can from the facts of the scenario.

1. A complaint to file the case on behalf of the plaintiff against the defendant in the appropriate trial court of your state.
2. The defendant's answer to the complaint.

LEGAL ANALYSIS & WRITING CASES

Ashcroft, Attorney General v. The Free Speech Coalition
535 U.S. 234, 122 S.Ct. 1389, 152 L.Ed.2d 403, Web 2002 U.S. Lexis 2789

Supreme Court of the United States

Congress enacted the Child Pornography Prevention Act (CPPA). Section 2256(8)(B) of the act prohibits "any visual depiction, including any photograph, film, video, picture, or computer-generated image or picture" that "is, or appears to be, of a minor engaging in sexually explicit conduct." This section includes computer-generated images known as "virtual child pornography." A first-time offender may be imprisoned for 15 years; repeat offenders face prison sentences up to 30 years. The Free Speech Coalition, a trade association for the adult-entertainment industry, sued the United States, alleging that Section 2256(8)(B) violated their constitutional free speech rights. The District Court granted summary judgment to the United States government, but the court of appeals reversed. The U.S. Supreme Court granted certiorari.

Question

1. Does Section 2256(8)(B), which criminalizes virtual child pornography, violate the Freedom of Speech Clause of the First Amendment to the U.S. Constitution?

Carnival Cruise Lines, Inc. v. Shute
499 U.S. 585, 111 S.Ct. 1522, 113 L.Ed.2d 622, Web 1991 U.S. Lexis 2221

Supreme Court of the United States

Mr. and Mrs. Shute, residents of the state of Washington, purchased passage for a seven-day cruise on the *Tropicale*, a cruise ship operated by the Carnival Cruise Lines, Inc. (Carnival). They paid the fare to the travel agent, who forwarded the payment to Carnival's headquarters in Miami, Florida. Carnival prepared the tickets and sent them to the Shutes. Each ticket consisted of five pages, including contract terms. The ticket contained a forum-selection clause that designated the state of Florida as the forum for any lawsuits arising under or in connection with the ticket and cruise.

The Shutes boarded the *Tropicale* in Los Angeles, which set sail for Puerto Vallarta, Mexico. While the ship was on its return voyage and in international waters off the Mexican coast, Mrs. Shute was injured when she slipped on a deck mat during a guided tour of the ship's galley. Upon return to Washington, she filed a negligence lawsuit against Carnival in U.S. district court in Washington, seeking damages. Carnival filed a motion for summary judgment contending that the suit could be brought only in a court located in the state of Florida. The District Court granted Carnival's motion. The court of appeals reversed, holding that Mrs. Shute could sue Carnival in Washington. Carnival appealed to the U.S. Supreme Court.

Question

1. Is the forum-selection clause in Carnival Cruise Lines' ticket enforceable?

Allison v. ITE Imperial Corporation
729 F.Supp. 45, Web 1990 U.S. Dist. Lexis 607

United States District Court for the Southern District of Mississippi

James Clayton Allison, a resident of Mississippi, was employed by the Tru-Amp Corporation as a circuit breaker tester. As part of his employment, Allison was sent to inspect, clean, and test a switch gear located at the South Central Bell Telephone Facility in Brentwood, Tennessee. One day he attempted to remove a circuit breaker manufactured by ITE Corporation (ITE) from a bank of breakers when a portion of the breaker fell off. The broken piece fell behind a switching bank and, according to Allison, caused an electrical fire and explosion. Allison was severely burned in the accident. Allison brought suit against ITE in Mississippi state court, claiming damages.

Question

1. Can this suit be removed to federal court?

AMF Inc. v. Brunswick Corporation
621 F.Supp. 456, Web 1985 U.S. Dist. Lexis 14205

United States District Court for the Eastern District of New York

AMF Incorporated and Brunswick Corporation both manufacture electric and automatic bowling center equipment. The two companies became involved in a dispute over whether Brunswick had advertised certain automatic scoring devices in a false and deceptive manner. The two parties settled the dispute by signing an agreement that any future problems between them involving advertising claims would be submitted to the National Advertising Council for arbitration. Two years later Brunswick advertised a new product, Armor Plate 3000, a synthetic laminated material used to make bowling lanes. Armor Plate 3000 competed with wooden lanes produced by AMF. Brunswick's advertisements claimed that bowling centers could save up to $500 per lane per year in maintenance and repair costs if they would switch to Armor Plate 3000 from wooden lanes. AMF disputed this claim and requested arbitration.

Question

1. Is the arbitration agreement enforceable?

Calder v. Jones
465 U.S. 783, 104 S.Ct. 1482, 79 L.Ed.2d 804, Web 1984 U.S. Lexis 41

Supreme Court of the United States

The National Enquirer, Inc., a Florida corporation, has its principal place of business in Florida. It publishes the *National Enquirer*, a national weekly newspaper with a circulation of more than 5 million copies. About 600,000 copies, almost twice the level of the next highest state, are sold in California. The *Enquirer* published an article about Shirley Jones, an entertainer. Jones, a California resident, filed a lawsuit in California state court against the *Enquirer* and its president, a resident of Florida. The suit sought damages for alleged defamation, invasion of privacy, and intentional infliction of emotional distress.

Question

1. Are the defendants subject to suit in California?

Burnham v. Superior Court of California
495 U.S. 604, 110 S.Ct. 2105, 109 LEd.2d 631, Web 1990 U.S. Lexis 2700

Supreme Court of the United States

Dennis and Francis Burnham were married and lived in New Jersey, where their two children were born. Ten years later the Burnhams decided to separate. Mrs. Burnham, who intended to move to California, was to have custody of the children. Mr. Burnham agreed to file for divorce on grounds of "irreconcilable differences." Mr. Burnham threatened to file for divorce in New Jersey on grounds of "desertion." After unsuccessfully demanding that Mr. Burnham adhere to the prior agreement, Mrs. Burnham brought suit for divorce in California state court. One month later Mr. Burnham visited California on a business trip. He then visited his children in the San Francisco Bay area, where his wife resided. He took the older child to San Francisco for the weekend. Upon returning the child to Mrs. Burnham's home, he was served with a California court summons and a copy of Mrs. Burnham's divorce petition. He then returned to New Jersey. Mr. Burnham made a special appearance in the California court and moved to quash the service of process.

Question

1. Did Mr. Burnham act ethically in trying to quash the service of process? Did Mrs. Burnham act ethically in having Mr. Burnham served on his visit to California? Is the service of process good?

WORKING WITH THE LANGUAGE OF THE COURT CASE

Adler v. Duval County School Board

112 F.3d 1475, Web 1997 U.S. App. Lexis 10000
United States Court of Appeals for the Eleventh Circuit

Read the following case, excerpted from the court of appeals opinion. Review and brief the case. In your brief, answer the following questions.

1. What is the doctrine of mootness?
2. What was the action the plaintiffs complained of?
3. When would the plaintiffs have had to file and have their case heard for the court to rule on their claim?
4. How would bringing the cases as a class action have allowed the court to hear the case under the Case or Controversy requirement?
5. How does this case differ from the case of *Lee v. Weisman* in Chapter 5?

Tjoflat, Circuit Judge

Appellants are four former high school students in the Duval County, Florida, school system who brought this action under 42 U.S.C. § 1983 (1994), alleging that a Duval County school policy permitting student-initiated prayer at high school graduation ceremonies (the "policy") violated their rights under the First and Fourteenth Amendments.

On June 7, 1993, three of the appellants graduated from Mandarin, one of the schools in the Duval County system. A fourth appellant graduated in June 1994. Because all four appellants have graduated, we find that to the extent they seek declaratory and injunctive relief, their case is moot. The only justiciable controversy in this case is the appellants' claim for money damages. We affirm the District Court's grant of summary judgment for the appellees on this claim, but we do so without reviewing the merits of the District Court's constitutional analysis. We begin by noting that appellants' claims for declaratory and injunctive relief are moot. All appellants have graduated, and none is threatened with harm from possible prayers in future Duval County graduation ceremonies. . . .

Article III of the Constitution limits the jurisdiction of the federal courts to the consideration of certain "Cases" and "Controversies.". . . The doctrine of mootness is derived from this limitation because an action that is moot cannot be characterized as an active case or controversy. "[A] case is moot when the issues presented are no longer 'live' or the parties lack a legally cognizable interest in the outcome." Any decision on the merits of a moot case would be an impermissible advisory opinion.

To apply the doctrine of mootness to this case, we must distinguish the appellants' claims for equitable relief from their claim for money damages. . . .

(continued)

Equitable relief is a prospective remedy, intended to prevent future injuries. In contrast, a claim for money damages looks back in time and is intended to redress a past injury. The plaintiff requests money damages to redress injuries caused by the defendant's past conduct and seeks equitable relief to prevent the defendant's future conduct from causing future injury. When the threat of future harm dissipates, the plaintiff's claims for equitable relief become moot because the plaintiff no longer needs protection from future injury. This is precisely what happened in this case.

Appellants argue that, despite their graduation from high school, their claims for declaratory and injunctive relief are not moot because the original injury is "capable of repetition, yet evading review." This exception to the mootness doctrine is narrow. In the absence of a class action, the "capable of repetition, yet evading review" doctrine is limited to the situation where two elements combine: (1) the challenged action [is] in its duration too short to be fully litigated prior to its cessation or expiration, and (2) there is a reasonable expectation that the same complaining party will be subjected to the same action again. This case does not satisfy the second element. Because the complaining students have graduated from high school, there is no reasonable expectation that they will be subjected to the same injury again.

Having disposed of the appellants' claims for equitable relief, we are left with their claim for money damages, which we now address. Because the appellants' claim for money damages does not depend on any threat of future harm, this claim remains a live controversy. We accordingly turn our focus to the basis for the appellants' claim for damages. The complaint alleges that a "senior class chaplain" delivered a prayer at the June 7, 1993, Mandarin graduation ceremony at which appellants Adler, Jaffa, and Zion graduated. The only past injury for which the appellants could seek redress is being subjected to this prayer at their graduation ceremony. To prove that the appellees caused this injury, the appellants alleged in their complaint that the prayer was "a direct consequence" of the school's policy. In their answer, the appellees admitted that a student said the prayer, but denied that the prayer was a consequence of the policy.

The only issue the appellants raise on appeal is whether the District Court erred in holding the policy constitutional. While the constitutionality of the policy may have been central to the now moot issue of whether equitable relief is warranted to prevent the policy from being implemented at future graduations, it does not dispose of the issue of whether the appellants should be awarded money damages for being subjected to the prayer at their graduation. In other words, any claim for damages does not depend on the constitutionality of the policy in the abstract or as applied in other Duval County schools.

Even if the policy is unconstitutional, the defendants might not be liable if, for example, they did not implement the policy at the ceremony in question or if the prayer would have been delivered without the policy. On the other hand, if the District Court was correct in finding the policy constitutional, defendant Epting, Mandarin's principal, might nonetheless be liable if he implemented the policy in an unconstitutional manner.

The constitutionality of the policy, therefore, has little independent relevance to the appellants' damages claim. Whether they are entitled to damages depends entirely on the circumstances under which the prayer was delivered at their graduation ceremony. In order to prevail, the appellants must have some theory connecting the individual defendants to the prayer. For these reasons, even if we were to find fault with the district court's constitutional analysis of the policy, this conclusion by itself would not answer the question of whether the court erred in granting the appellees summary judgment on the damages claim. The appellants offer no other grounds in their briefs for finding trial court error.

After considering the appellants' briefs and oral argument, we are convinced that they either fail to understand the basis for their damages claim or do not seriously seek damages. They have offered us no connection between the prayer and their damages claim; their briefs offer no indication as to any of the circumstances surrounding the Mandarin graduation prayer. They failed to argue that the prayer was a "direct consequence" of the policy, or any other theory connecting the defendants' actions to the Mandarin prayer. Their briefs do not even include the allegation made in their complaint that a prayer was delivered at Mandarin.

For all these reasons, we hold that they have waived their damages claim on appeal. We therefore affirm the District Court's order to the extent it denied the appellants' motion for summary judgment and granted the appellees' motions for summary judgment on the appellants' damages claim. For the foregoing reasons, we vacate the district court's order granting the appellees summary judgment on the appellants' claims for declaratory and injunctive relief and remand the case with instructions that the District Court dismiss those claims. We affirm the District Court's denial of the appellants' motion for summary judgment and its grant of summary judgment for the appellees on the appellants' damages claim. It is so ordered.

UPDATE TO CASE

After a rehearing en banc the court, upon a majority vote of the judges of the court, issued a subsequent opinion on June 3, 1999, and on March 15, 2000, on further proceeding the Court ruled that the policy on prayer did not violate the Establishment Clause. On June 19, 2000, the Supreme Court rendered a decision in *Santa Fe Independent School District v. Doe*, 530 U.S. 290, which invalidated a Texas school board's policy permitting students to vote on a prayer subject to officials' approval at home football games. The Duval Court proceeded to rehear the case based on the *Santa Fe* decision and ruled again in favor of the Duval School Board because the prayer there was not subject to official approval or input [*Adler v. Duval County School Board*, 250 F.3d 1330, 2001 U.S. App. Lexis 8880 (United States Court of Appeals for the Eleventh Circuit)].

Civil Litigation

DIGITAL RESOURCES

Chapter 7 Digital Resources at *www.pearsonhighered.com/goldman*

- Video Case Studies:
  - Videotaped Deposition: Deposing an Expert Witness for Use at Trial
  - Trial: Direct and Cross-examination of a Witness
  - Preparing for Trial: Preparing a Fact Witness
- Chapter Summary • Web Links • Court Opinions • Glossary • Comprehension Quizzes
- Technology Resources

> Discourage litigation. Persuade your neighbors to compromise whenever you can. Point out to them how the nominal winner is often a real loser—in fees, and expenses, and waste of time. As a peacemaker, the lawyer has a superior opportunity of being a good man. There will still be business enough.

> *Abraham Lincoln,*
> *Notes on the Practice of Law (1850)*

LEARNING OBJECTIVES

After studying this chapter, you should be able to:

1. Complete a set of basic documents used in civil litigation.
2. Describe the discover process and its purposes.
3. Explain the purposes of pretrial motions.
4. Explain what happens in a settlement conference.
5. Describe the steps in a trial.
6. Explain how verdicts and judgments are rendered at trial.
7. Describe how a case is appealed and what decisions can be rendered by an appellate court.

Paralegals at Work

Rowan, a middle school student, and his sister Isis, a high school student, were passengers on the last school bus of the day on their way home after Rowan's basketball practice and his sister's choir practice. The bus had made its regular stops and was on a public highway when it was struck by a large commercial truck. Rowan's injuries were severe enough to prevent him from playing basketball for the rest of the season on his school team and local club team that was in the championship. Isis had been practicing and eagerly looking forward to traveling with the school choir on an invitational European tour.

Their parents have retained your law firm, on a contingent fee basis, to pursue a claim for their children's injuries and their out-of-pocket expenses. A review of the medical bills shows expenses in excess of $75,000 for each child. Because of the nature of the accident it was investigated by the National Transportation Safety Board, which issued a report indicating the probable cause of the accident was the failure of the brakes on the truck. The truck driver in his initial police statement indicated that he had had no problems with the vehicle before the accident and that he relied upon the mechanics in the maintenance facility to maintain the vehicle, and especially the brakes. The trucking company has denied any liability. No initial reports or documentation were provided by the trucking company to the police because all of the truck and maintenance records were kept in electronic format at the company's corporate headquarters in another state. The first decision is deciding in which court to commence suit.

Consider the issues involved in this scenario as you read the chapter.

INTRODUCTION FOR THE PARALEGAL

Litigation The process of bringing, maintaining, and defending a lawsuit.

Paralegals often work for lawyers who specialize in civil litigation, seeking monetary damages or other remedies, or in the prosecution or defense of criminal cases. The bringing, maintaining, and defense of a lawsuit comprise the litigation process, or **litigation**.

Civil litigation is an area in which a paralegal's talents can shine. The paralegal's analytical ability, expertise in legal research, ability to draft pleadings and documents, and other skills are truly put to the test. Paralegals who choose to work in the litigation field must have excellent knowledge of the various facets of the litigation process, the rules of evidence, and court procedure.

A paralegal's first introduction to a new lawsuit will be when a client employs the law firm for whom the paralegal works to represent the client in a civil lawsuit. The client may be either the plaintiff or the defendant. Many times the paralegal's first work assignment is to sit in on conferences between the attorney and the client, and to take notes of pending issues.

Then the paralegal usually is notified to "start a file" for the lawsuit. This means obtaining available evidence, documents, and other items relevant to the case. Each attorney has his or her own system for preparing a case for trial (or settlement), and the paralegal has his or her own way of preparing the file as well.

The paralegal often is assigned to help draft the pleadings for the case. In addition, the paralegal may interview the client, contact the client for information, draft documents to obtain production of documents and other evidence, and assist in the preparation of depositions to be taken or attended by his or her supervising attorney.

At this stage, the paralegal is involved in the case as much as his or her supervising attorney. Because of their knowledge of a case, paralegals can be indispensable in the proper preparation for lawyer–client meetings, discovery, depositions, and settlement conferences.

If the case is to go to trial, the paralegal usually is called upon to help conduct the legal research that will be placed in the brief of the case to be submitted to the court. The paralegal's responsibility is to help organize the case for trial, and to use all available technology to prepare the case for trial. At trial, the paralegal becomes indispensable in assisting the attorney to present his or her case on behalf of the client.

Civil Litigation

Civil litigation involves legal action to resolve disputes between parties, as contrasted with criminal litigation, which is brought by the government against a party accused of violating the law. The parties to civil litigation may be individuals, businesses, or in some cases, government agencies. Although the fundamental process is the same, the court and the procedure may vary.

Many lawyers specialize in civil litigation, in which a plaintiff sues a defendant to recover money damages or other remedy for the alleged harm the defendant causes the plaintiff. This may be an automobile accident case, a suit alleging a breach of a contract, a claim of patent infringement, or any of a myriad of other civil wrongs.

In a civil case, either party can appeal the trial court's decision once a final judgment is entered. In a criminal case, only the defendant can appeal. The appeal is made to the appropriate appellate court. This chapter discusses civil litigation and the appellate process; the criminal process is covered in Chapter 8.

Pleadings

Pleadings The paperwork that is filed with the court to initiate and respond to a lawsuit.

The paperwork that is filed with the court to initiate and respond to a lawsuit is referred to as the **pleadings**. The major pleadings are the complaint, or petition in some states, the answer, the cross-complaint, and the reply.

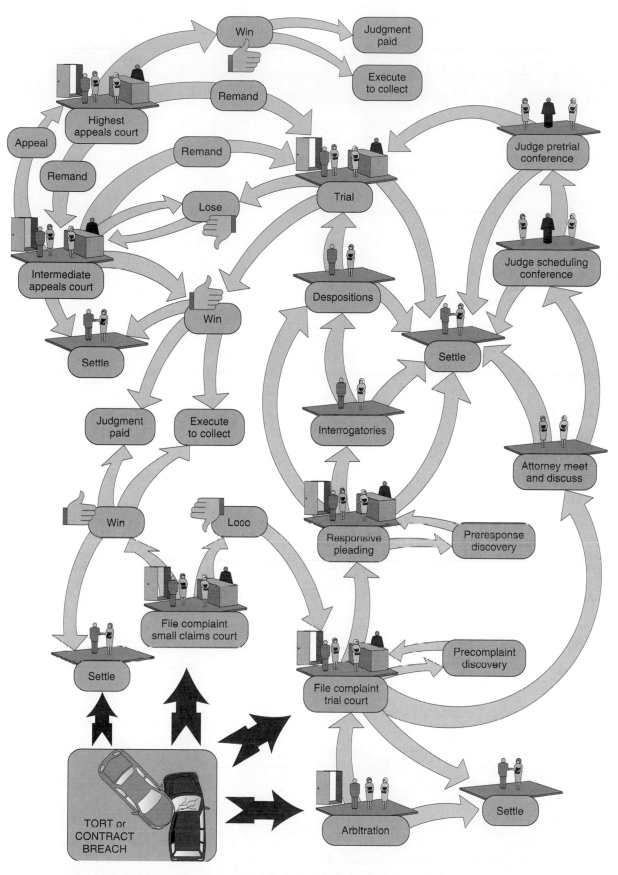

Advice *from the* Field

From your first conversation with a prospective client, you're learning about the dispute that led the individual or corporation to seek counsel. There are many benefits to taking a systematic approach to analyzing this knowledge. Not least of these is the favorable impression you'll make on those who retain you.

The following article presents a method for organizing and evaluating the facts about any case. And it illustrates how the early results of this dispute analysis process can be used to great effect in an initial case analysis session with your client.

When you take this approach to case analysis, you'll gain a thorough understanding of the dispute and clarify your thinking about it. And, as you sort out what you do know about the case, you'll find it easy to identify what you don't know and need to find out.

The process focuses on creating four analysis reports: a Cast of Characters, a Chronology, an Issue List, and a Question List. These reports provide a framework for organizing and evaluating critical case knowledge. If multiple people are involved in the analysis process, the reports provide a way to divide responsibility and share results. Moreover, once you standardize the analysis work product, it's easy to compare the findings in one matter to the analysis results from other similar disputes.

You should create your case analysis reports using database software, not a word-processor. Database software makes the knowledge you're organizing far easier to explore and evaluate. For example, using database software, it's easy to filter your Chronology so it displays only facts that have been evaluated as being particularly troublesome.

CAST OF CHARACTERS

Create a Cast of Characters that lists the individuals and organizations you know are involved in the dispute. This report should also catalog key documents and other important pieces of physical evidence. Capture each player's name and a description of the role the person, organization, or document plays in the case.

Also include a column in which you can indicate your evaluation of cast members. Even if you don't evaluate every player, it's essential to note the people and documents that are particularly worrisome, as well as the basis for your concerns. If you follow my recommendation that you build your dispute analysis reports using database software, you will find it easy to filter the entire cast list down to the problem players you've identified.

CHRONOLOGY

A chronology of key facts is a critical tool for analyzing any dispute. As you create the chronology, important factual disputes and areas of strength and weakness become obvious.

Begin by listing the fact and the date on which it occurred. As you enter each fact, be sure to make the important details about the fact explicit. For example, rather than simply stating "Gayle phoned David," write "Gayle phoned David, and asked him to shred the Fritz Memo." Remember that your chronology should be a memory replacement, not a memory jogger.

Since you're analyzing the case within weeks of being retained, there will be many facts for which you have only partial date information. For example, you may know that Gayle called David about the Fritz Memo sometime in June of 1993, but be unsure as to the day within June. When you run into this problem, a simple solution is to substitute a question mark for the portion of the date that's undetermined, e.g., 6/?/99.

In addition to capturing the fact and the date, be sure to list a source or sources for each fact. Now, in the early days of a case, it's likely that the sources of many of the facts you are entering in your chronology are not of a type that will pass muster come trial. However, by capturing a source such as "David Smith Interview Notes," you know to whom or what you will need to turn to develop a court-acceptable source.

The mission in early dispute analysis is to take a broad look at the potential evidence. Therefore, your chronology should be more than a list of undisputed facts. Be sure to include disputed facts and even prospective facts (i.e., facts that you suspect may turn up as the case proceeds toward trial). You'll want to distinguish the facts that are undisputed from those that are disputed or merely prospective. Include in your chronology a column that you use for this purpose.

Finally, include a column that you use to separate the critical facts from others of lesser importance. A simple solution is to have a column titled "Key" that you set up as a checkbox (checked means the fact is key, unchecked means its not). If you're using database software, filtering the chronology down to the key items should take you about 2 seconds.

ISSUE LIST

Build a list of case issues including both legal claims and critical factual disputes. If the case has yet to be filed, list the claims and counter-claims or cross-claims you anticipate. Rather than listing just the top-level issues, consider breaking each claim down to its component parts. For example, rather than listing Fraud, list Fraud: Intent, Fraud: Reliance, and so on as separate dimensions.

In addition to listing a name for each issue, create a more detailed description of it. The description might include a brief summary of each party's position on the issue and, if it's a legal issue, the potential language of the judge's instruction.

As your case proceeds to trial, your Issue List will increase in importance. You'll use the Issue List to return to the Cast of Characters and Chronology and establish relationships between each fact, each witness, each document, and the issue or issues to which it relates. Once you've made these links, it will be easy to focus on the evidence that's being developed regarding each issue and to make decisions about case strategy based on this analysis.

QUESTION LIST

When you start case analysis early, your knowledge of the dispute is sure to be incomplete. But as you map out what is known about the case, what is unknown and must be determined becomes clear.

Each time you come up with a question about the case that you can't readily answer, get it into your Question List. You'll want your report to include a column for the question and another column where you can capture notes regarding the answer. Also include a column for evaluating the criticality of each question. Use a simple A (extremely critical), B, C, and D scale to make your assessment. Other columns to consider for your Question List are "Assigned To" and "Due Date."

The analysis reports you've begun are "living" ones. As you head toward trial, keep working on your Cast of Characters, your Chronology, your Issue List, and your Question List. These analysis reports will do far more than help you think about your case. They'll serve a myriad of concrete purposes. They'll help you keep your client up-to-date, plan for discovery, prepare to take and defend depositions, create motions for summary judgment, and make your case at settlement conferences and at trial.

Copyright DecisionQuest 1994, 2006. Michael E. Cobo is a founding member of DecisionQuest, the nation's leading trial consulting firm. The principals of DecisionQuest have retained on over 12,500 high-stakes, high-risk litigation cases spanning a wide range of industries. Discover more at www.decisionquest.com.

Complaint

The party who is suing—the **plaintiff**—must file a **complaint**, also called a plaintiff's original petition or summons in some jurisdictions, with the proper court. The content and form of the complaint will vary depending on local courts' procedural rules. Many courts follow the federal practice of "notice pleading." Other state courts follow the traditional form requiring detailed allegations of the basis for the action.

A complaint must name the parties to the lawsuit, allege the ultimate facts and law violated, and state the remedy desired and the "prayer for relief" to be awarded by the court. The complaint can be as long as necessary, depending on the case's complexity. Exhibit 7.1 is a sample state trial court complaint filed in Pennsylvania. Exhibit 7.2 is a federal complaint. Exhibit 7.3 is a bilingual notice to plead a complaint.

In some jurisdictions, after a complaint has been filed with the court, the court issues a **summons**, a court order directing the **defendant** to appear in court and answer the complaint. A fundamental requirement is that notice be given to the defendant. A sheriff, another government official, or a private process server may serve the complaint and, where required, the summons on the defendant. In some cases, the defendant may be served by other means, such as by publication when the defendant cannot otherwise be found to be served personally.

Plaintiff The party who files the complaint.

Complaint The document the plaintiff files with the court and serves on the defendant to initiate a lawsuit.

 Web Exploration

Go to www.eff.org/IP/digitalradio/XM_complaint.pdf to view a copy of a complaint filed in U.S. district court.

Summons A court order directing the defendant to appear in court and answer the complaint.

Defendant The party who files the answer.

Fact and Notice Pleading

In the federal courts and in some state courts, the complaint need only provide a general allegation of the wrongful conduct alleged, this is called **notice pleading**. The sample complaint in Exhibit 7.2 is an example of a notice pleading in federal court. In other states, the plaintiff must plead specific facts alleged to have been committed that constitute the wrong complained of, this is known as **fact pleading**. The sample state complaint in Exhibit 7.1 is an example of a fact pleading.

Court rules require an attorney to sign the documents filed unless a person is filing on his or her own behalf, called a *pro se* filing. In federal court, Rule 11 governs the attorney's obligations and the potential penalties, as discussed in the following case.

IN THE WORDS OF THE COURT

Notice Pleading

CONLEY V. GIBSON, 355 U.S. 41, 47-48 (1957) 78 S.CT. 99

. . . The respondents also argue that the complaint failed to set forth specific facts to support its general allegations of discrimination and that its dismissal is therefore proper. The decisive answer to this is that the Federal Rules of Civil Procedure do not require a claimant to set out in detail the facts upon which he bases his claim. To the contrary, all the Rules require is "a short and plain statement of the claim" that will give the defendant fair notice of what the plaintiff's claim is and the grounds upon which it rests. The illustrative forms appended to the Rules plainly demonstrate this. Such simplified "notice pleading" is made possible by the liberal opportunity for discovery and the other pretrial procedures established by the Rules to disclose more precisely the basis of both claim and defense and to define more narrowly the disputed facts and issues. Following the simple guide of Rule 8(f) that "all pleadings shall be so construed as to do substantial justice," we have no doubt that petitioners' complaint adequately set forth a claim and gave the respondents fair notice of its basis. The Federal Rules reject the approach that pleading is a game of skill in which one misstep by counsel may be decisive to the outcome and accept the principle that the purpose of pleading is to facilitate a proper decision on the merits. Cf. *Maty v. Grasselli Chemical Co., 303 U.S. 197* . . .

IN THE WORDS OF THE COURT

Federal Rule 11

LEAHY V. EDMONDS SCHOOL DISTRICT (W.D.WASH. 3-2-2009)

. . . C. Rule 11 Sanctions

Defendants also argue that Plaintiff's counsel should personally be liable for attorney's fees under Rule 11. Rule 11 generally provides guidelines for attorneys to follow when submitting a pleading to the court. The rule "imposes a duty on attorneys to certify that they have conducted a reasonable inquiry and have determined that any papers filed with the court are well grounded in fact, legally tenable, and not interposed for any improper purpose." *Cooter & Gell v. Hartmarx Corp.*, 496 U.S. 384, 393 (1990). "The central purpose of Rule 11 is to deter baseless filing in district court[.]" *Id.* (internal quotations omitted). Additionally, "[s]anctions must be imposed on the signer of a paper if the paper is 'frivolous.'" *In re Keegan Mgmt. Co., 78 F.3d 431, 434* (9th Cir. 1996). Although the word "frivolous" does not appear in the text of the rule, it is well-established that it denotes "a filing that is *both* baseless *and* made without a reasonable and competent inquiry." *Id.* (citation omitted) (emphasis in original). The Ninth Circuit has explained that "there are basically three types of submitted papers which warrant sanctions: factually frivolous (not 'well grounded in fact'); legally frivolous (not 'warranted by existing law or a good faith argument for the extension, modification, or reversal of existing law'); and papers 'interposed for an improper purpose.'" *Business Guides, Inc. v. Chromatic Commc'ns Enterprises, Inc., 892 F.2d 802, 808* (9th Cir. 1989) (quoting FRCP *11*). . . .

Exhibit 7.1 Sample state

IN THE COURT OF COMMON PLEAS OF BUCKS COUNTY, PA.
CIVIL ACTION-LAW

COUNTY LINE FENCE CO., INC.   :   NO.
2051 W. County Line Road
Warrington, PA 18976   :

    V.   ATTORNEY I.D. #12204

WAYNE YARNELL   :
5707 Dunbar Court
Bensalem, PA 19020   :

<u>COMPLAINT</u>

1. Plaintiff is County Line Fence Company, Inc., a Pennsylvania corporation duly authorized to do business in Pennsylvania, with a place of business at 2051 W. County Line Road, Warrington, Bucks County, Pennsylvania.

2. Defendant, WAYNE YARNELL, is an adult individual residing at 5707 Dunbar Court, Bensalem, Pennsylvania.

3. On or about April 30, 2002, Defendant entered into a contract with the Plaintiff for a 140 ft. Bufftech fence to be installed on Defendant's property at 5707 Dunbar Court, Bensalem, PA 19020. (See Exhibit "A")

4. Plaintiff properly and adequately installed the fencing per the contract.

5. Defendant agreed to pay a total of $5,300.00 for the fence.

6. Demand was made upon the Defendant by Plaintiff for payment of the amount due for fencing and installation.

7. In spite of the demand for payment, Defendant has failed and refused, and continues to fail and refuse to pay Plaintiff the balance due.

WHEREFORE, Plaintiff demands judgment in the amount of $5,300.00, together with attorneys fees, costs of suit and any additional amounts as the court deems proper.
THOMAS F. GOLDMAN & ASSOCIATES

Thomas F. Goldman

Thomas F. Goldman, Esquire
Attorney for Plaintiff

Exhibit 7.2 **Complaint filed in federal court**

UNITED STATES DISTRICT COURT
FOR THE DISTRICT OF COLUMBIA

UNITED STATES OF AMERICA) Plaintiff,) v.) ENHANCED SERVICES BILLING, INC.) BILLING CONCEPTS, INC.,) Delaware Corporations,) both with their principal place of business at) 7411 John Smith Drive, Suite 200) San Antonio, Texas 78229,) NEW CENTURY EQUITY HOLDINGS CORP.) A Delaware Corporation,) 10101 Reunion Place, Suite 450) San Antonio, Texas 78216) Defendants.)	CASE NUMBER 1:01CV01660 JUDGE: Ricardo M. Urbina DECK TYPE: General Civil DATE STAMP: 08/01/2002 Civ. No. COMPLAINT FOR CIVIL PENALTIES, PERMANENT INJUNCTION, CONSUMER REDRESS AND OTHER EQUITABLE RELIEF

Plaintiff, the United States of America, acting upon notification and authorization to the Attorney General by the Federal Trade Commission ("FTC" or "Commission"), for its complaint alleges that:

1. Plaintiff brings this action under Sections 5(a)(1), 5(m)(1)(A), 9, 13(b), 16(a) and 19 of the Federal Trade Commission Act, 15 U.S.C. §§45(a)(1),

Exhibit 7.2 **Complaint filed in federal court** *(continued)*

45(m)(1)(A), 49, 53(b), 56(a) and 57b, and the Telephone Disclosure and Dispute Resolution Act of 1992 ("TDDRA"), 15 U.S.C. §§ 5701 *et. seq.*, to obtain injunctive relief and consumer redress for violations of Section 5(a)(1) of the Federal Trade Commission Act, 15 U.S.C. § 45(a)(1), and to obtain monetary civil penalties, consumer redress and injunctive and other relief for Defendants' violations of the Commission's Trade Regulation Rule Pursuant to the Telephone Disclosure and Dispute Resolution Act of 1992 ("900-Number Rule"), 16 C.F.R. Part 308.

JURISDICTION AND VENUE

2. This court has jurisdiction over this matter under 28 U.S.C. §§ 1331, 1337(a), 1345 and 1355 and under 15 U.S.C. §§ 45(m)(1)(A), 49, 53(b), 56(a), 57b, 5721 and 5723. This action arises under 15 U.S.C. § 45(a)(1).

3. Venue in the District of Columbia is proper under 15 U.S.C. § 53(b) and 28 U.S.C. §§ 1391(b) and (c) and 1395(a).

DEFENDANTS

4. Defendant Enhanced Services Billing, Inc. is a Delaware corporation with its principal place of business at 7411 John Smith Drive, Suite 200, San Antonio, Texas 78229. Enhanced Services Billing, Inc. provides or provided billing and collection services for vendors who market Internet Web sites, psychic memberships, voice mail and hospital telephone and television rental, and other enhanced services. Enhanced Services Billing, Inc. was incorporated on March 17, 1994. Enhanced Services Billing, Inc. transacts or has transacted business in this district.

5. Defendant Billing Concepts, Inc. is a Delaware corporation with its principal place of business at 7411 John Smith Drive, Suite 200, San Antonio, Texas 78229. Billing Concepts, Inc. provides or provided billing and collection services for vendors who market . . .

Exhibit 7.3 **Bilingual notice to plead a complaint**

IN THE COURT OF COMMON PLEAS
OF PHILADELPHIA COUNTY, PENNSYLVANIA
CIVIL ACTION LAW

KATHRYN KELSEY   : NO.

vs.   : ATTORNEY I.D. NO.

KATHRYN CARROLL   : COMPLAINT IN EQUITY

COMPLAINT – CIVIL ACTION

NOTICE

You have been sued in court. If you wish to defend against the claims set forth in the following pages, you must take action within twenty (20) days after this complaint and notice are served, by entering a written appearance personally or by attorney and filing in writing with the court your defenses or objections to the claims set forth against you. You are warned that if you fail to do so the case may proceed without you and a judgment may be entered against you by the court without further notice for any money claimed in the complaint or for any other claims or relief requested by the plaintiff. You may lose money or property or other rights important to you.

You should take this paper to your lawyer at once. If you do not have a lawyer or cannot afford one, go to or telephone the office set forth below to find out where you can get legal help.

Philadelphia Bar Association
Lawyer Referral and
Information Service
One Reading Center
Philadelphia, Pennsylvania 19107
215-238-1701

AVISO

Le han demandado a usted en la corte. Si usted quiere defenderse de estas demandas expuestas en las paginas siguientes, usted tiene veinte (20) dias de plazo al partir de la fecha de la demanda y la notificacion. Hace falta asentar una compancia escrita o en persona o con un abogado y entregar a la corte en forma escrita sus defensas o sus objeciones a las demandas en contra de su persona. Sea avisado que si usted no se defiende, la corta tomara medidas y puede continuar la demanda en contra suya sin previo aviso o notificacion. Ademas, la corte puede decidir a favor del demandante y requiere que usted cumpla con todas las provisiones de esta demanda. Usted puede perer dinero o sus propiedades u oetros derechos importantes para usted.

Lieva esta demanda a un abogado immediatamente. Si no tiene abogado o si no tiene el dinero suficiente de pagartal servicio, vaya en persona o llame por telefono a la oficina cuya direccion se encuentra escrita abajo para averiguar donde se puede conseguir asistencia legal.

Asociacion de Licenciados de Filadelfia
Servicio de Referencia e
Informacion Legal
One Reading Center
Filadelfia, Pennsylvania 19107
215-238-1701

Pleading Deadlines

After filing the complaint and having the summons issued, the plaintiff must serve the defendant, in federal court within 120 days, state courts vary but typically 30 to 60 days after the initial filing. Failure to serve the complaint within the time limit can result in the complaint being dismissed. Alternatively, the plaintiff may file a motion seeking the court's permission to reinstate the complaint and reissue the summons. The time for the defendant to file a responsive pleading begins to run when the complaint is served, not on the last day the complaint could have been served. If served with the traditional means—in federal cases by U.S. Marshall, or in state courts by the sheriff, private process server, or other authorized person—the defendant has a time limit within which to respond to the complaint, for example in federal court it is 20 days or if served by notice and waiver, 60 days. Failure to respond in a timely fashion permits the plaintiff to obtain a default judgment against the defendant. Default is not an automatic procedure but a right the plaintiff may enforce. Calculating for the due date is important for the plaintiff as well as the defendant. The defendant also must know the rule and properly calculate the due date to avoid a **default judgment** for nonaction. All pleadings after the initial complaint and answer have a response time. This includes the plaintiff's response to counterclaims or affirmative defenses asserted by the defendant and the response to any motion.

Default judgment Judgment obtained by the plaintiff against the defendant where the defendant has failed to respond in a timely fashion to the complaint.

Responsive Pleadings

Upon receipt of the complaint, petition, or summons, the defendant, the responding party, and counsel have some critical decisions to make. In many instances, defendants know that a lawsuit may be filed against them. Being served with a complaint may not be a surprise, but the quickly approaching deadlines can be intimidating for the legal defense team, if it is not promptly advised by the client. If served personally, the defendant has a limited time in which to file a responsive pleading, in federal court, if the defendant was personally served it is 20 days, which is probably insufficient time to thoroughly investigate and respond. Just as plaintiffs frequently wait until the last date before the statute of limitations is filed, defendants frequently wait to meet with an attorney until the date the response is due to be filed in court. The first step may be to request an **extension of time to respond** from opposing counsel. If that request is granted, the team, if in federal court and some state courts, must prepare and file a stipulation with the court, if refused, a motion to extend the time asks the court to grant an extension of time to respond.

Answer

The defendant is required to respond to the allegations contained in the plaintiff's complaint. This is done by preparing, filing, and serving an **answer** to the complaint. Like a complaint, an answer is made up of the same sections, whether in federal or state court: caption, numbered paragraphs, prayer for relief, and alternative defenses.

When responding to the averments of the complaint, there are two basic choices:

1. **Admitted**—the facts of the averment in the complaint are true, or
2. **Denied**—the facts of the averment in the complaint are not true.

In some jurisdictions, simply denying averments of the complaint is not sufficient. In those jurisdictions, the word "Denied" with nothing more is a **general denial** and the averment of the complaint is treated as if it were "Admitted." In those jurisdictions where the reason for the denial is crucial to any defense, the reasons for the denial must be listed and include:

1. Denied as the facts are not as stated and set forth specifically the alternate facts.
2. Denied as after reasonable investigation the defendant lacks adequate knowledge to determine whether the information is true.
3. Denied as the averment represents a conclusion of law to which no response is required.

RECOGNIZING A FRIVOLOUS LAWSUIT

Although paralegals are not lawyers, they should still have some concept of whether a lawsuit has merit or not. Consider the following case. The Chungs are Korean residents who came to the United States. The Chungs opened a dry cleaning store and eventually owned three dry cleaning stores in the Washington, D.C. (D.C.) area. Roy L. Pearson was a District of Columbia administrative judge who was a customer at one of the Chungs' dry cleaning stores. Pearson walked to the Chungs' store because he did not have a car.

The Chungs had signs in the window of their store that stated "Satisfaction Guaranteed" and "Same Day Service." Pearson claimed that the Chungs lost a pair of his pants. He sued the Chungs $67 million in damages alleging that they violated the D.C. consumer protection act. Pearson later reduced his demand to $54 million. Pearson demanded $3 million for violation of the "Satisfaction Guaranteed" sign, $2 million for mental suffering and inconvenience, $500,000 in legal fees for representing himself, $6 million for ten years of rental car fees to drive to another cleaners, and $51 million to help similarly dissatisfied D.C. customers. Pearson stated that he had no choice but to take on "the awesome responsibility" for suing the Chungs on behalf of every D.C. resident. A website was set up to accept donations for the Chungs' legal fees of $83,000, which was eventually paid by donations.

Do you think plaintiff Pearson had a legitimate legal case, or was this a frivolous lawsuit?

In some instances, particularly when there are multiple defendants to whom the complaint is directed, there may be paragraphs to the complaint that do not require an answer. In that event, the appropriate response would be:

No answer is required as the averments are addressed to another defendant.

Cross-Complaint and Reply

A defendant who believes that he or she has been injured by the plaintiff can file a **cross-complaint**, or counter petition as it is called in some jurisdictions, against the plaintiff in addition to an answer. In the cross-complaint, the defendant (now the **cross-complainant**) sues the plaintiff (now the **cross-defendant**) for damages or some other remedy. The original plaintiff must file a **reply**, or answer to the cross-complaint. Exhibit 7.4 is a sample state answer. The reply—which can include affirmative defenses—must be filed with the court and served on the original defendant.

Exhibit 7.5 illustrates the pleadings process.

Intervention and Consolidation

If other persons have an interest in a lawsuit, they may step in and become parties to the lawsuit—called an **intervention**. For instance, a bank that has made a secured loan on a piece of real estate can intervene in a lawsuit between parties who are litigating ownership of the property.

If several plaintiffs have filed separate lawsuits stemming from the same fact situation against the same defendant, the court can initiate a **consolidation** of the cases into one case if it would not cause undue prejudice to the parties. Suppose, for example, that a commercial airplane crashes, killing and injuring many people. The court could consolidate all of the lawsuits against the defendant airplane company.

Statute of Limitations

Some crimes, such as murder, have no limitation on the time in which a defendant can be charged. In civil actions, however, the plaintiff must bring suit within a certain period of time after the action that gives rise to the complaint or lose the right to use the courts to enforce the civil right and remedy. This period is called the **statute of limitations**.

If a lawsuit is not filed in keeping with the statute of limitations, the plaintiff loses his or her right to sue. A statute of limitations usually begins to "run" at the time the plaintiff first has the right to sue the defendant (e.g., when the accident happens, or when the breach of contract occurs). Depending on state law, it also may begin to run when the plaintiff knows or should have known of the defendant's wrongful action that gives rise to a cause of action. In the case of minors, the statute may not begin to run—regardless of the time of discovery of the accrual of the cause of action—until the minor reaches the age of majority.

Federal and state governments have established statutes of limitations for each type of lawsuit. Most are from one to four years, depending on the type of lawsuit. A one-year statute of limitations is common for some ordinary negligence actions. For example, if on July 1, 2010, Otis negligently causes an automobile accident in which Cha-Yen is injured, Cha-Yen has until July 1, 2012, to bring a negligence lawsuit against Otis. If she waits longer than that, she loses her right to sue him.

Procedural time limits in the rules of court are similar to the statute of limitations for filing a cause of action. Each court may establish the times within which actions must be taken, such as the number of days within which a plaintiff must serve the complaint and/or summons on the defendant, or the time limit for the defendant to file a responsive pleading, such as an answer. Software, such as AbacusLaw, use rules-based calendaring programs to calculate these deadlines. Deadlines on Demand™ is an internet based program that calculates the various time deadlines based on the different state and federal rules as shown in the sample for a school-bus accident case in Exhibit 7.6.

Exhibit 7.4 Sample state answer

DATZ and GOLDBERG

BY: MARC C. BENDO, ESQUIRE

IDENTIFICATION NO. 80075   ATTORNEY FOR DEFENDANT

1311 SPRUCE STREET

PHILADELPHIA, PENNSYLVANIA 19107

(215) 545-7960

COUNTY LINE FENCE CO., INC. 2051 W. County Line Road Warrington, PA 18976 vs. WAYNE YARNALL 5707 Dunbar Court Bensalem, PA 19020	*COURT OF COMMON PLEAS* BUCKS COUNTY DIVISION *TERM* NO. 99004879-23-1

<u>ANSWER OF DEFENDANT, WAYNE YARNALL, TO PLAINTIFF'S CIVIL ACTION WITH NEW MATTER</u>

1. Denied. Plaintiff is without knowledge or information sufficient to form a belief as to the truth or falsity of this averment. Accordingly, same is denied with strict proof demanded at time of Trial.

2. Admitted. By way of further answer, however, Plaintiff's Civil Action has misspelled Defendant's proper name, which is Wayne Yarnall.

3. Denied. These allegations constitute conclusions of law to which no response is required pursuant to the applicable Pennsylvania Rules of Civil Procedure . . .

Exhibit 7.5 Pleadings process

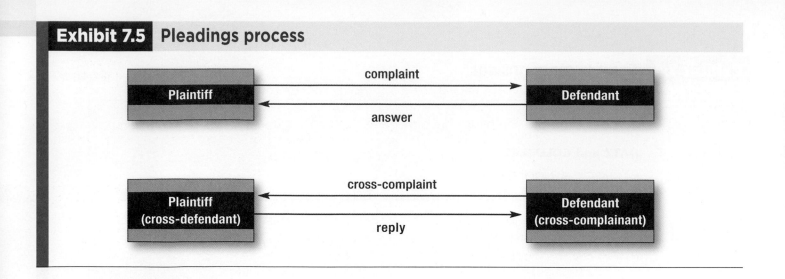

	complaint →	
Plaintiff		Defendant
	← answer	

	← cross-complaint	
Plaintiff (cross-defendant)		Defendant (cross-complainant)
	reply →	

Exhibit 7.6 Sample time deadlines using Deadlines On Demand™

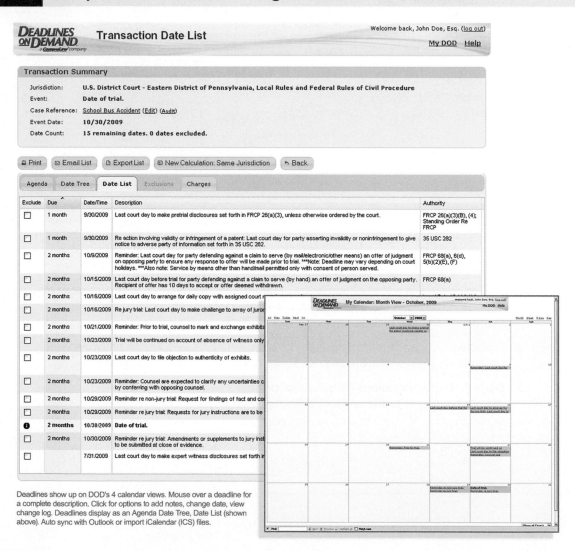

DEADLINES ON DEMAND — Transaction Date List

Welcome back, John Doe, Esq. (log out)

My DOD   Help

Transaction Summary

Jurisdiction: U.S. District Court - Eastern District of Pennsylvania, Local Rules and Federal Rules of Civil Procedure

Event: Date of trial.

Case Reference: School Bus Accident (Edit) (Audit)

Event Date: 10/30/2009

Date Count: 15 remaining dates. 0 dates excluded.

Print | Email List | Export List | New Calculation: Same Jurisdiction | Back

Agenda | Date Tree | **Date List** | Exclusions | Charges

Exclude	Due	Date/Time	Description	Authority
☐	1 month	9/30/2009	Last court day to make pretrial disclosures set forth in FRCP 26(a)(3), unless otherwise ordered by the court.	FRCP 26(a)(3)(B), (4); Standing Order Re FRCP
☐	1 month	9/30/2009	Re action involving validity or infringement of a patent: Last court day for party asserting invalidity or noninfringement to give notice to adverse party of information set forth in 35 USC 282.	35 USC 282
☐	2 months	10/9/2009	Reminder: Last court day for party defending against a claim to serve (by mail/electronic/other means) an offer of judgment on opposing party to ensure any response to offer will be made prior to trial. ***Note: Deadline may vary depending on court holidays. ***Also note: Service by means other than hand/mail permitted only with consent of person served.	FRCP 68(a), 6(d), 5(b)(2)(E), (F)
☐	2 months	10/15/2009	Last court day before trial for party defending against a claim to serve (by hand) an offer of judgment on the opposing party. Recipient of offer has 10 days to accept or offer deemed withdrawn.	FRCP 68(a)
☐	2 months	10/16/2009	Last court day to arrange for daily copy with assigned court r...	
☐	2 months	10/16/2009	Re jury trial: Last court day to make challenge to array of juror...	
☐	2 months	10/21/2009	Reminder: Prior to trial, counsel to mark and exchange exhibits...	
☐	2 months	10/23/2009	Trial will be continued on account of absence of witness only ...	
☐	2 months	10/23/2009	Last court day to file objection to authenticity of exhibits.	
☐	2 months	10/23/2009	Reminder: Counsel are expected to clarify any uncertainties c... by conferring with opposing counsel.	
☐	2 months	10/29/2009	Reminder re non-jury trial: Request for findings of fact and co...	
☐	2 months	10/29/2009	Reminder re jury trial: Requests for jury instructions are to be ...	
❶	2 months	10/30/2009	Date of trial.	
☐	2 months	10/30/2009	Reminder re jury trial: Amendments or supplements to jury inst... to be submitted at close of evidence.	
☐		7/31/2009	Last court day to make expert witness disclosures set forth i...	

Deadlines show up on DOD's 4 calendar views. Mouse over a deadline for a complete description. Click for options to add notes, change date, view change log. Deadlines display as an Agenda Date Tree, Date List (shown above). Auto sync with Outlook or import iCalendar (ICS) files.

E-Filings in Court

When litigation ensues, the clients, lawyers, and judges involved in the case usually are buried in paper—pleadings, interrogatories, documents, motions to the court, briefs, and memoranda; the list goes on and on. By the time a case is over, reams of paper are stored in dozens, if not hundreds, of boxes. Further, court appearances, no matter how small the matter, must be made in person. For example, lawyers often wait hours for a 10-minute scheduling or other conference with the judge. Additional time is required to drive to and from court, which in an urban area may amount to hours.

Paralegals are at the forefront of e-litigation where many of the documents filed in court are done electronically. The technology currently is available for implementing electronic filing—**e-filing**—of pleadings, briefs, and other documents related to a lawsuit. E-filing would include using CD-ROMs for briefs, scanning evidence and documents into a computer for storage and retrieval, and emailing correspondence and documents to the court and the opposing counsel. Scheduling and other conferences with the judge or opposing counsel could be held via telephone conferences and email.

Some courts have instituted e-filing already. For example, in the Manhattan bankruptcy court, e-filing is now mandatory. Other courts around the world are doing the same. Companies such as Microsoft and LexisNexis have developed systems to manage e-filings of court documents. Some forward-thinking judges and lawyers envision a day when the paperwork and hassle are reduced or eliminated in a "virtual courthouse."

Discovery

Discovery is a step in the litigation process where the plaintiff and the defendant share information relevant to their dispute. The discovery process can be a time-consuming and sometimes frustrating phase in litigation. Successful discovery requires familiarity with the rules of court that apply to discovery and an organized approach. Increasingly important are the rules relating to discovery of electronic files that may be the source of information needed in the litigation process. The methods used to locate, preserve, and produce these cyber documents require a new set of skills for the legal team and the paralegal. Paralegals on the litigation team are often charged with coordinating discovery requests and responses from clients and opposing parties and working with information technology experts.

Discovery serves a number of purposes: understanding and evaluating the client's case, focusing the legal team on the strengths and weaknesses of its case; understanding and evaluating the strengths and weaknesses of the opponent's case; preserving testimony; potentially facilitating settlement; and learning information that may be used to impeach a witness, such as showing inconsistencies in testimony.

Case Evaluation

By answering each other's questions, the parties share information about the facts, documents, and statements of fact and expert witnesses related to the legal dispute. By openly sharing information that may be used at trial, each side is forced to evaluate its case and the opponent's case and determine the ability to meet its burdens of proof. With each side fully aware of the potential evidence that can be presented, including potential damages, the legal team can, based on prior experience or reported similar cases, put a potential value on a trial outcome. In many cases the decision to try a case or settle a case is a business decision.

Is the cost of a trial outweighed by the potential recovery? With two well-prepared legal teams, the evaluation is surprisingly close and settlement is more likely than not.

Preparing for Trial

Properly completed discovery eliminates the potential for surprises in evidence presented at trial. In fact, many of the "surprises" one sees on television trial dramas are not possible under rules that are designed to prevent the introduction of surprise witnesses and evidence.

Cross-complaint Filed by the defendant against the plaintiff to seek damages or some other remedy.

Reply Filed by the original plaintiff to answer the defendant's cross-complaint.

 Web Exploration

Locate the U.S. District Court that serves the county or parish in which you live. Go to that court's website and find and review the "Court Forms" for that court. http://uscourts.gov/.

Statute of limitations A law that establishes the period during which a plaintiff must bring a lawsuit against a defendant.

 Web Exploration

Go to http://www.statutes-of-limitations.com/state/Alabama. On the right-hand side of the page there is a list of states. Click on your state to find out what the statute of limitations is for filing a negligence action in your state.

E-filing The electronic filing of pleadings, briefs, and other documents related to a lawsuit with the court.

 Web Exploration

Visit www.abanet.org/tech/ltrc/research/efiling/ for a discussion of e-filings and the use of electronic documents in federal courts.

Discovery A legal process during which both parties engage in various activities to elicit facts of the case from the other party and witnesses prior to trial.

Advice *from the* Field

COULD THIS BE THE FIRST DAY OF EMPLOYMENT FOR A RECENT PARALEGAL PROGRAM GRADUATE?

Maria was up before the alarm went off, ready to begin her new job and her new career. The newest paralegal at one of California's most prestigious law firms was ready to go to work. She still was amazed at how easily she had completed the interviews and had proceeded through the hiring process of the past few weeks. To be hired by such a prominent law firm was beyond her wildest dreams. She knew that her good grades, her excellent work samples and her technology skills would help her look for a position but never thought she would be so successful so quickly. The knowledge and sophisticated skill set she had acquired in her paralegal studies had paid immediate dividends.

Clutching a small portfolio embossed with her paralegal school's logo, she took the elevator to the thirty-fifth floor, got off and went through the big glass doors. Maria's legal degree and her newly acquired Certificate in Legal Information Management were about to be tested.

She knew that this potent combination of legal content and legal information management had been her key to success yet she was still very apprehensive about this new venture. Little did Maria know, but her new employers were as apprehensive as she was on her first day at the office. They had created the title of Paralegal Information Manager and that sign on the door was the first thing that caught Maria's eyes as she was showed her new office.

Maria remembered the interview a few weeks ago when she was led through a large conference room full of file boxes that she thought contained the information on the major cases she would be working on at the firm. She had asked, "Is that the Magnate case materials?" And the answer was "No, they will be accessed through the computer workstation in your new office." She remembered the senior partner telling her that the judge in the Magnate case had ordered the case to be handled electronically as much as possible. All of the documents had either been imaged or produced in native file format and a basic index of all documents had been created. The firm had chosen to optically character recognize the imaged documents for full text search capability. The trial exhibit list had to be filed electronically and the pre-trial order directed that the attorneys use all the technology available in the electronic courtroom to locate and display every document for the judge and jury.

Here she was, the Paralegal Information Manager, the gatekeeper of the management and the flow of information, the one who was primarily responsible for getting the information processed and presented. She felt overwhelmed but was ready to begin. Maria sat down and turned on the computer. She had taken the first step.

Can this happen to a paralegal school graduate? Will this happen in the near future? How can paralegal students be prepared best? What are the implications for paralegals? And what paralegal school courses and programs should the paralegal take to be prepared?

This scenario is already occurring in small ways throughout the country. Paralegals must start thinking about the training and skills necessary to work on the electronic civil litigation team emerging in the present, for many the future is here now. The process of electronic discovery; the gathering and acquisition of electronic records; the filing and preparation of this discovery; and the presentation of it in electronic courtrooms is already upon us. Demand for advanced litigation skills including an understanding of the role of electronic databases and the management of electronic documents is becoming commonplace. Paralegals must understand the technology and the ethical considerations and implications of these technological advances.

Source: © Student Counseling Service, Texas A&M University. Reprinted with permission.

Preserving Oral Testimony

Discovery is also a method for preserving oral testimony. There are times when witnesses may not be available to attend trial to testify. Examples include witnesses who are gravely ill and not expected to live until trial, those who are elderly or incapacitated and physically unable to come to the courthouse, and those who are outside the geographical jurisdiction of the court. Under limited circumstances, the deposition testimony of these unavailable witnesses may be presented at trial. The deposition of witnesses is given the same treatment as if the witness was in court testifying in person.

IN THE WORDS OF THE COURT

United States District Court, S.D. New York

**SECURITIES AND EXCHANGE COMMISSION, PLAINTIFF,
V. COLLINS & AIKMAN CORP., ET AL., DEFENDANTS
NO. 07 CIV. 2419(SAS). JAN. 13, 2009**

II. The Discovery Disputes

This opinion addresses four distinct but related discovery disputes. Stockman served a document request pursuant to Rule 34, asking the SEC to "produce for inspection and copying the documents and things identified" in fifty-four separate categories.[FN4] In response, the SEC produced 1.7 million documents (10.6 million pages) maintained in thirty-six separate Concordance databases-many of which use different metadata protocols.[FN5] Stockman raises the following objections. *First,* the SEC failed to identify documents responsive to requests for documents supporting particular factual allegations in the Complaint, preferring instead to "dump" 1.7 million potentially responsive documents on Stockman and then suggesting that he is capable of searching them to locate those that are relevant. *Second,* the SEC failed to perform a reasonable search for documents relating to accounting principles governing supplier rebates-both in general and with respect to the automobile industry. Instead, the SEC unilaterally limited its search to three of its divisions-and only if those divisions possessed "centralized compilations of non-privileged documents dealing specifically with rebates or accounting for rebates in the automobile industry."[FN6] *Third,* the SEC improperly asserted the deliberative process privilege with regard to certain documents. *Fourth,* the SEC failed to search its own e-mails, attachments thereto, and other records created and maintained solely in an electronic format that related to either "(i) the investigation and litigation of this matter or (ii) the handling of several large cases unrelated to C & A and the Commission's regulatory role in matters relating to rebates and rebate accounting."[FN7] The objections were raised in a series of letters rather than by formal motion.[FN8]

1. Attorney Work Product Protection Applied to Selection and Compilation

The Second Circuit has recognized that the selection and compilation of documents may fall within the protection accorded to attorney work product, despite the general availability of documents from both parties and non-parties during discovery.[FN18] However, it has labeled this protection a "narrow exception"[FN19] aimed at preventing requests with "the precise goal of learning what the opposing attorney's thinking or strategy may be."[FN20] Moreover, equity favors rejection of work product protection to a compilation of documents that are otherwise unavailable or "beyond reasonable access."[FN21] The Circuit has suggested that a court may permit *ex parte* communication of the strategy the withholding party wishes to conceal and *in camera* review of documents, so that the court may make an educated assessment whether production of the compilation will reveal a party's litigation strategy.[FN22]

C. Discussion

1. Work Product Protection

It is first necessary to determine the level of protection afforded to the *selection* of documents by an attorney to support factual allegations in a complaint. Such documents are not "core" work product. Core work product constitutes legal documents drafted by an attorney-her mental impressions, conclusions, opinions, and legal theories. This highest level of protection applies to a compilation only if it is organized by legal theory or strategy. The SEC's theory-that every document or word reviewed by an attorney is "core" attorney work product-leaves nothing to surround the core.[FN35] The first step in responding to any document request is an attorney's assessment of relevance with regard to potentially responsive documents. It would make no sense to then claim that an attorney's determination of relevance shields the selection of responsive documents from production.

(continued)

With few exceptions, *Rule 26(f)* requires the parties to hold a conference and prepare a discovery plan. The Rule specifically requires that the discovery plan state the parties' views and proposals with respect to "the subject on which discovery may be needed . . . and whether discovery should be conducted in phases or be limited to or focused on particular issues"[FN66] and "any issues about disclosure or discovery of electronically stored information. . . ."[FN67] Had this been accomplished, the Court might not now be required to intervene in this particular dispute. I also draw the parties' attention to the recently issued Sedona Conference Cooperation Proclamation, which urges parties to work in a cooperative rather than an adversarial manner to resolve discovery issues in order to stem the "rising monetary costs" of discovery disputes.[FN68] The Proclamation notes that courts see the discovery rules "as a mandate for counsel to act cooperatively."[FN69] Accordingly, counsel are directly to meet and confer forthwith and develop a workable search protocol that would reveal *at least some* of the information defendant seeks. If the parties cannot craft an agreement, the Court will consider the appointment of a Special Master to assist in this effort. . . . The logic of *Rule 34* supports this limitation. When records do not result from "routine and repetitive" activity, there is no incentive to organize them in a predictable system. The purpose of the Rule is to facilitate production of records in a useful manner and to minimize discovery costs; thus it is reasonable to require litigants who do not create and/or maintain records in a "routine and repetitive" manner to organize the records in a usable[FN55] fashion prior to producing them.

. . . By rough analogy to *Rule 803(6)*, the option of producing documents "as they are kept in the usual course of business" under *Rule 34* requires the producing party to meet either of two tests. *First,* this option is available to commercial enterprises or entities that function in the manner of commercial enterprises. *Second,* this option may also apply to records resulting from "regularly conducted activity."[FN53] Where a producing party's activities are not "routine and repetitive" such as to require a well-organized record-keeping system-in other words when the records do not result from an "ordinary course of business"-the party must produce documents according to the sole remaining option under *Rule 34*: "organize[d] and label[ed] . . . to correspond to the categories in the request."[FN54]

B. Applicable Law

"A district court has wide latitude to determine the scope of discovery."[FN62] The general scope of discovery in civil litigation is defined by *Rule 26(b)(1)*.

> **FN62. In re Agent Orange Product Liab. Litig., 517 F.3d 76, 103 (2d Cir.2008).**

Parties may obtain discovery regarding any nonprivileged matter that is relevant to any party's claim or defense.. . . For good cause, the court may order discovery of any matter relevant to the subject matter involved in the action. Relevant information need not be admissible at the trial if the discovery appears reasonably calculated to lead to the discovery of admissible evidence.

. . . A court must limit the "frequency or extent of discovery" if one of three conditions in *Rule 26(b)(2)(C)* is present. The third limits production when "the burden or expense of the proposed discovery outweighs its likely benefit, considering the needs of the case, the amount in controversy, the parties' resources, the importance of the issues at stake in the action, and the importance of the discovery in resolving the issues."[FN63] The burden or expense may be defined in terms of time, expense, or even the "adverse consequences of the disclosure of sensitive, albeit unprivileged material."[FN64] . . .

VII. Conclusion

When a government agency initiates litigation, it must be prepared to follow the same discovery rules that govern private parties (albeit with the benefit of additional privileges such as deliberative process and state secrets). For the reasons set forth above, the SEC is ordered to produce or identify documents organized in response to Stockman's requests; to negotiate an appropriate search protocol to locate documents responsive to requests described above in Part IV; to submit materials allegedly covered by the deliberative process privilege to the Court for *in camera* review, together with a supporting memorandum within twenty days of the date of this Order;

and to negotiate an appropriately limited search protocol with respect to agency e-mail. While the SEC has raised legitimate concerns about the burdens imposed by particular requests, it cannot unilaterally determine that those burdens outweigh defendants' need for discovery. At the very least, the SEC must engage in a good faith effort to negotiate with its adversaries and craft a search protocol designed to retrieve responsive information without incurring an unduly burdensome expense disproportionate to the size and needs of the case. The parties are therefore directed to engage in a cooperative effort to resolve the scope and design of a search with respect to the rebate issues and a search of e-mail created and maintained by the SEC. A conference is scheduled for February 13, at 5:00 pm, by which date the parties should have completed the meet and confer process in the hope of establishing an acceptable discovery program. If the parties remain at an impasse, the Court will be prepared to resolve further disputes and will consider the appointment of a Special Master to supervise the remaining discovery in this case.

SO ORDERED.

Federal Rules of Civil Procedure—Rule 26(a) Disclosure Requirements

Rule 26(a) makes mandatory the disclosure of certain information that for years was available only after a formal written discovery request was issued. For many cases, no action was taken on a file until one side moved the case forward with a formal discovery request. Under current rules, everything the legal team intends to rely upon to prove its claims must be disclosed early in the litigation. Insufficient time to investigate the claim is not a valid excuse for failure to comply. The benefits of mandatory disclosure are twofold: 1. It provides for the early evaluation and settlement of claims; and 2. it reduces the amount, nature, and time necessary to conduct formal discovery. From a practical standpoint, the plaintiff's legal team must be prepared for disclosure at or shortly after filing the complaint. While the new rules contemplate a specific time frame for disclosure, they do permit the attorneys to agree to some other time frame for the disclosure. Although the attorneys may agree to extend that time, the judge at the scheduling conference may encourage them to conclude the disclosure at a faster pace. The investigation that might have occurred under prior rules must now be completed before filing suit. For the defense team, the time to investigate and comply is very short. There is no time for procrastination in investigating and establishing the grounds to defend the claims.

Information Subject to Mandatory Disclosure

Almost anything relied upon in developing the claim, regardless of whether it is admissible at trial, must be disclosed. This disclosure includes the identity of witnesses, copies of documents, a computation of damages, and a copy of any insurance policy that may be used to satisfy a judgment obtained in the litigation.

In the past, information used to compute damages represented the plaintiff attorney's thought process and was typically not released as part of discovery under the work–product privilege. Under the current rule, the attorney's value on the case is made known within months of the complaint being filed.

From the defense standpoint, the disclosure of insurance coverage, which is not admissible at trial, is a significant change from traditional discovery. A key element in settling most cases is the existence of and limitations on insurance coverage. With both the plaintiff's calculation of damages and the defendant's ability to pay based upon disclosure of insurance coverage known within months of filing the lawsuit, the chances for fruitful settlement discussions are enhanced.

Experts and Witnesses

Expert witnesses expected to be called at trial must also be identified, accompanied by a copy of the expert's qualifications as an expert including a list of publications for which the witness has written from the preceding 10 years, a statement of compensation, and a list of other cases in which the expert has testified. The most critical element to be shared is the written report of the expert's opinion. The report represents what the expert is expected to say at trial. The written report must include the opinion of the expert, the basis of that opinion including the information relied upon, and any assumptions made. The disclosure of the expert and his or her report must be made at least 90 days prior to trial. Some courts require the disclosure of the expert at the time of the initial disclosure or within 30 days of receipt of the expert's report. Many lawsuits become a battle of the experts. The early disclosure of the expert and his or her opinion often leads to early resolution of the case.

Depositions

Deposition Oral testimony given by a party or witness prior to trial. The testimony is given under oath and is transcribed.

A **deposition** is the oral testimony given, under oath, by a party or witness prior to trial. The person giving the deposition is called the **deponent**. The *parties* to the lawsuit must give their depositions, if the other party calls them to do so. The deposition of a **witness** can be given voluntarily or pursuant to a **subpoena** (court order). The deponent can be required to bring documents to the deposition.

Depositions are used to preserve evidence (e.g., if the deponent is deceased, ill, or otherwise not available at trial) and to impeach testimony given by witnesses at trial. Most depositions are taken at the office of one of the attorneys. The deponent is placed under oath and then asked oral questions by the attorneys for one or both parties to the lawsuit. The questions and answers are recorded in written form by a court reporter. Depositions also can be videotaped. The deponent is given an opportunity to correct his or her answers prior to signing the deposition, depending on local practice or rules.

Interrogatories

Interrogatories Written questions submitted by one party to another party. The questions must be answered in writing within a stipulated time.

Interrogatories are written questions submitted by one party to a lawsuit to another party. The questions can be highly detailed, as illustrated by the sample interrogatory in Exhibit 7.7. In addition, in some jurisdictions certain documents have to be attached to the answers. A party is required to answer the interrogatories in writing within a specified time period (e.g., 60 to 90 days). An attorney usually helps with preparation of the answers. The answers are signed under oath.

Production of Documents

Production of documents Request by one party to another party to produce all documents relevant to the case prior to the trial.

Often, particularly in complex business cases, a substantial portion of the lawsuit is based on information contained in documents (e.g., memoranda, correspondence, company records). One party to a lawsuit may request that the other party produce all documents that are relevant to the case prior to trial. This is called **production of documents**. If the documents sought are too voluminous to be moved or are in permanent storage, or if moving the documents would disrupt the ongoing business of the party who is to produce them, the requesting party may be required to examine the documents at the other party's premises. Exhibit 7.8 is an example of a request for production of documents.

Physical and Mental Examination

Physical and mental examinations (in some jurisdictions called an **Independent Medical Examination** or **IME**) of the parties to the lawsuit are permitted where the physical or mental condition of one of the parties is an element of the cause of action. In a personal injury action, the physical injuries suffered and the damages that result from those injuries are elements of the cause of action for negligence. Thus, the defense

Exhibit 7.7 Sample interrogatory

THOMAS F. GOLDMAN & ASSOCIATES
138 N. State Street
Newtown, PA 18940
(123) 555-1234

KATHRYN KELSEY	: COURT OF COMMON PLEAS
	: PHILADELPHIA COUNTY
	:
vs.	: APRIL TERM, 2011
	:
KATHRYN CARROLL	: NO. 1234

INTERROGATORIES ADDRESSED TO KATHRYN KELSEY

You are to answer the following interrogatories under oath or verification pursuant to the Pa. R.C.P. 4005 and 4006 within thirty days from the service hereof. The answering party is under a duty to supplement responses to any questions with information discovered after these answers were given.

Also, a party or expert witness must amend prior responses if he/she obtains information upon the basis of which:

(a) he/she knows the response was incorrect when made; or

(b) he/she knows that the response, though correct when made, is no longer true.

The words "your vehicle" as used in the following interrogatories are defined as the motor vehicle you were operating at the time of the accident.

When a Standard Interrogatory uses the word: "identify", the party served with the Interrogatory must identify all documents, things and persons known to that party or to that party's attorney, and the address of all persons identified MUST be set forth.

Where a Standard Interrogatory is marked with an asterisk (*), a Request for Production may accompany the Interrogatory.

**STANDARD INTERROGATORIES PURSUANT TO
PHILADELPHIA RULE OF CIVIL PROCEDURE *4005**

INJURIES AND DISEASES ALLEGED

1. State in detail the injuries or diseases that you allege that you suffered as a result of the accident referred to in the Complaint.

MEDICAL TREATMENT & REPORTS*

2. If you received medical treatment or examinations (including x-rays) because of injuries or diseases you suffered as a result of the accident, identify:

(a) Each hospital at which you were treated or examined;

(b) The dates on which each such treatment or examination at a hospital was rendered and the charges by the hospital for each;

(c) Each doctor or practitioner by whom you were treated or examined;

(d) The dates on which each such treatment or examination by a doctor or practitioner was rendered and the charges for each;

(e) All reports regarding any medical treatment or examinations, setting forth the author and date of such reports.

* This document can be viewed in its entirety on the companion website.

Exhibit 7.8 **Sample request for production of documents**

THOMAS F. GOLDMAN & ASSOCIATES
138 N. State Street
Newtown, PA 18940
(123) 555-1234

KATHRYN KELSEY	:	COURT OF COMMON PLEAS
	:	PHILADELPHIA COUNTY
vs.	:	APRIL TERM, 2011
KATHRYN CARROLL	:	NO. 1259

REQUEST TO PRODUCE UNDER PA R.C.P. 4033 and 4009
<u>DIRECTED TO PLAINTIFFS</u>

Within thirty (30) days of service, please produce for inspection and copying at the office of THOMAS F. GOLDMAN & ASSOCIATES, 138 North State Street, Newtown, Pennsylvania 18940, the following:

1. All photographs and/or diagrams of the area involved in this accident or occurrence, the locale or surrounding area of the site of this accident or occurrence, or any other matter or things involved in this accident or occurrence.

2. All property damage estimates rendered for any object belonging to the Plaintiffs which was involved in this accident or occurrence.

3. All property damage estimates rendered for any object belonging to the Defendant which was involved in this accident or occurrence.

4. All statements concerning this action or its subject matter previously made by any party or witness. The statements referred to here are defined by Pa. R.C.P. 4003.4.

5. All transcriptions and summaries of all interviews conducted by anyone acting on behalf of the Plaintiff or Plaintiff's insurance carrier of any potential witness and/or person(s) who has any knowledge of the accident or its surrounding circumstances.

6. All inter-office memorandum between representative of Plaintiffs' insurance carrier or memorandum to Plaintiffs' insurance carrier's file concerning the manner in which the accident occurred.

7. All inter-office memorandum between representative of Plaintiffs' insurance carrier or memorandum to Plaintiffs' insurance carrier's file concerning the injuries sustained by the Plaintiffs.

8. A copy of any written accident report concerning this accident or occurrence signed by or prepared by Plaintiff for Plaintiffs' insurance carrier or Plaintiff's employers.

9. A copy of the face sheet of any policy of insurance providing coverage to Plaintiffs for the claim being asserted by Plaintiff in this action.

10. All bills, reports, and records from any and all physicians, hospitals, or other health care providers concerning the injuries sustained by the Defendants from this accident or occurrence.

11. All photographs and/or motion pictures of any and all surveillance of Defendant performed by anyone acting on behalf of Plaintiff, Plaintiffs' insurer and/or Plaintiffs' attorney.

12. All photographs taken of Plaintiffs' motor vehicle which depict any damage to said vehicle which was sustained as a result of this accident.

13. All photographs taken of defendant's motor vehicle which depict any damage to said vehicle which was sustained as a result of this accident.

14. Any and all reports, writings, memorandum, Xeroxed cards and/or other writings, lists or compilations of the Defendant and others with similar names as indexed by the Metropolitan Index Bureau, Central Index Bureau or other Index Bureau in possession of the Plaintiffs or the Plaintiffs' insurance carrier.

team may obtain a physical examination of the plaintiff from a doctor of its choosing. In a guardianship proceeding, the plaintiff seeks to be appointed guardian over someone who lacks mental capacity to handle financial and other matters. The cause of action is dependent on the mental state of the individual. Therefore, a mental examination would be appropriate.

Requests for Admission

Requests for admission are written requests issued by one party to the lawsuit to the other asking that certain facts or legal issues be admitted as true. Properly used, requests for admission can narrow the focus of trial and streamline the testimony. Some facts are generally not in controversy, such as names, addresses, and other personal information.

Locations of accidents, time of day, and related facts may also be admitted without calling witnesses. Who was speeding, not observant, or otherwise negligent are facts rarely admitted because they represent an admission of liability. However, if liability is admitted the only issue left is damages. Where the damages are minimal, parties may admit to the facts of liability to avoid the time and cost of trial to obtain a finding of fact of something obvious.

The remaining issue of how much monetary value is assigned to the wrong may be agreed upon between the parties or determined by the trier of fact in very short order at little time or expense.

Example: If the defendant admits as true his liability for the automobile accident, then that issue is no longer in dispute. No evidence as to the cause of the accident will be required at trial. The trial will be limited to determining damages only, making a more focused and streamlined case.

E-Discovery

The use of email, electronic retention of records, establishment of websites, selling goods and services online, and other digital technologies has exploded in conducting business. This technology is used extensively in conducting personal affairs as well. Therefore, in many lawsuits, much of the evidence is in digital form. The winning or losing of lawsuits may lie in the ability of a party to conduct **electronic discovery**, or **e-discovery**.

e-discovery The discovery of emails, electronically stored data, e-contracts, and other electronically stored records.

Modern discovery practices permit the electronic discovery of evidence. Most federal and state courts have adopted rules that permit the e-discovery of emails, electronically stored data, e-contracts, and other electronic records. E-discovery is fast becoming a burgeoning part of the preparation of a case for trial or settlement.

The lawyer and the paralegal must have a sound understanding of permissible e-discovery. Courts have resoundingly permitted the discovery of emails and electronic databases where relevant to a court case. A party seeking e-discovery must prepare the proper requests for such discovery as required by court rules.

In addition to discovery of email and electronic information, courts permit the use of electronic interrogatories to be proffered to the other side, as well as the electronic response to such e-interrogatories. Some courts also permit the taking of depositions electronically. This requires that the questions by the lawyers and answers of the deponent be communicated electronically by email.

Federal and state courts have established rules of evidence that require the parties to a lawsuit not to destroy or delete documents or other evidence that is relevant to the pending lawsuit. This prohibition is particularly important when the documents and evidence are digital. The destruction or deletion of e-evidence may subject the violating party to civil and criminal penalties.

In the case where digital evidence has been destroyed or deleted from electronic files, it may be possible to reconstruct the evidence. The use of computer experts will be necessary to find the missing evidence and digitally reconstruct it.

Paralegals *in* Practice

Emily A. Ewald is a graduate of Xavier University with a Bachelor of Science degree. She also has a Paralegal Certificate from Davenport University. Emily currently works in the area of civil/commercial and appellate litigation at the large law firm of Dickinson Wright in Grand Rapids, Michigan.

Although I have been a paralegal for six years, the first three were spent focused on one enormous case. During that period, I reviewed, organized, and managed over 450,000 documents, 1,650 deposition exhibits, a 98-page trial exhibit list, deposition designations from over 70 depositions, and other numerous assignments to assist attorneys preparing for discovery and trial. In this case, our client, the defendant, was being sued for $74 million. However, three weeks before the scheduled trial date, the case was settled for a much lower amount.

My current work duties include drafting interrogatories, interrogatory responses, motions and briefs, witness lists, juror questionnaires, and verdict forms. I also help prepare for and attend depositions, hearings, mediations, arbitrations, and trials. Additionally, I go to client meetings, expert witness meetings, and deposition preparation sessions.

More and more legal documents are being digitally produced and exchanged. For instance, we are required by all federal courts to file everything electronically through an online program called PACER (Public Access to Court Electronic Records). For e-discovery purposes, we use Summation®, a software program used to summarize case documents and search them for specific data. TrialDirector® software is used to load case exhibits, videos, and other documents onto a laptop computer, which can later be projected onto a courtroom screen for judge and jurors to see.

My main advice to new paralegals is to be flexible. You should expect to be asked to go back and forth between different case assignments, at a moment's notice. You are also likely to get some assignments in which you have little or no interest. However, always do them to the best of your ability because you will gain from the experience.

E-discovery will continue to increase as an important feature in many lawsuits. The recovery of emails, mining of electronic databases, and reconstructing thought-to-be destroyed electronic evidence will play an ever more important part of discovery in current and future lawsuits. E-discovery is clearly an important part of the digital law office and the virtual courtroom.

Pretrial Motions

Pretrial motion A motion a party can make to try to dispose of all or part of a lawsuit prior to trial.

Paralegals employed in the civil litigation field are often called upon to prepare **pretrial motions** to try to dispose of all or part of a lawsuit prior to trial. The three major pretrial motions are the motion to dismiss, the motion for judgment on the pleadings, and the motion for summary judgment.

Motion to Dismiss

Motion to dismiss A motion that alleges that the plaintiff's complaint fails to state a claim for which relief can be granted. Also called a *demurrer*.

A defendant can file a **motion to dismiss** the plaintiff's complaint for failure to state a claim for which relief can be granted. A motion to dismiss is sometimes called a *demurrer*. A motion to dismiss a case alleges that even if the facts as presented in the plaintiff's complaint are true, there is no reason to continue the lawsuit. For example, a motion to dismiss would be granted if the plaintiff alleges that the defendant was negligent but the facts as alleged do not support a claim of negligence.

A motion to dismiss can be filed with the court prior to the defendant's having filed an answer in the case. If the motion to dismiss is denied, the defendant is given further time to answer. If the court grants the motion to dismiss, the defendant does not have to file an answer. The plaintiff usually is given time to file an amended complaint. If the plaintiff fails to file an amended complaint, judgment will be entered against the plaintiff. If the plaintiff files an amended complaint, the defendant must answer the complaint or file a new motion to dismiss.

Motion for Judgment on the Pleadings

Once the pleadings are complete, either party can make a **motion for judgment on the pleadings**. This motion alleges that if all of the facts presented in the pleadings are true, the party making the motion would win the lawsuit when the proper law is applied to these facts. In deciding this motion, the judge cannot consider any facts outside the pleadings.

Motion for Summary Judgment

The trier of the fact (i.e., the jury, or, if no jury, the judge) determines *factual issues*. A **motion for summary judgment** asserts that there are no factual disputes to be decided by the jury and that the judge should apply the relevant law to the undisputed facts to decide the case. Motions for summary judgment, which can be made by either party, are supported by evidence outside the pleadings. Affidavits from the parties and witnesses, documents (e.g., a written contract between the parties), depositions, and such are common forms of evidence.

If, after examining the evidence, the court finds no factual dispute, it can decide the issue or issues raised in the summary judgment motion. This may dispense with the entire case or with part of the case. If the judge finds that a factual dispute exists, the motion will be denied and the case will go to trial.

Settlement Conference

Federal court rules and most state court rules permit the court to direct the attorneys or parties to appear before the court for a **pretrial hearing**, or **settlement conference**. One of the major purposes of these hearings is to facilitate settlement of the case. Pretrial conferences often are held informally in the judge's chambers. If no settlement is reached, the pretrial hearing is used to identify the major trial issues and other relevant factors.

More than 90 percent of all cases are settled before they go to trial. In cases that do proceed to trial, the trial judge may advise the attorneys of the rules or timetable of the individual judge. The judges also will advise the attorneys of any deadlines for discovery and the deadline for submitting any final motions with regard to what may be offered at the trial, called *motions in limine*.

In a number of jurisdictions, cases are referred to arbitration or other forms of alternative dispute resolution. Depending on the amount of money in controversy, some cases are required to be submitted before court-approved panels of attorneys sitting as arbitrators of the dispute. In other courts, the litigants may elect to have the case heard before an arbitration panel. Appeal rights from arbitration panel decisions vary, but cases typically may be appealed *de novo* to the trial court as if no arbitration had occurred, except possibly the payment of an appeal fee to cover part of the cost of the arbitration.

Exhibit 7.9 shows the sequence of key events before trial.

Trial

Pursuant to the Seventh Amendment to the U.S. Constitution, a party to an action at law is guaranteed the right to a **jury trial** in cases in federal court. Most state constitutions contain a similar guarantee for state court actions. If either party requests a jury, the trial will be by jury. If both parties waive their right to a jury, the trial will be without a jury. In non-jury trials, the judge sits as the **trier of fact**. These trials also are called *waiver trials* or **bench trials.** At the time of trial, the parties usually submit to the judge **trial briefs** containing legal support for their side of the case.

Trials usually are divided into the following phases:

- Jury selection
- Opening statements
- Plaintiff's case
- Defendant's case
- Rebuttal and rejoinder

Motion for judgment on the pleadings A motion that alleges that if all the facts presented in the pleadings are taken as true, the party making the motion would win the lawsuit when the proper law is applied to these asserted facts.

Motion for summary judgment A motion that asserts that there are no factual disputes to be decided by the jury and that the judge can apply the proper law to the undisputed facts and decide the case without a jury. These motions are supported by affidavits, documents, and deposition testimony.

 Web Exploration

Go to http://www.legalzoom.com/legal-articles//article11331.html and read the article "Top Ten Frivolous Lawsuits."

Trier of fact The jury in a jury trial; the judge where there is not a jury trial.

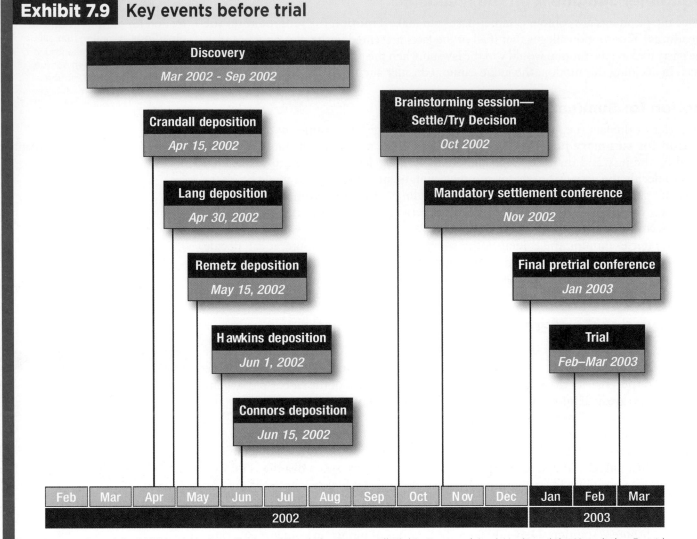

Exhibit 7.9 Key events before trial

Discovery — Mar 2002 - Sep 2002

Crandall deposition — Apr 15, 2002

Lang deposition — Apr 30, 2002

Remetz deposition — May 15, 2002

Hawkins deposition — Jun 1, 2002

Connors deposition — Jun 15, 2002

Brainstorming session— Settle/Try Decision — Oct 2002

Mandatory settlement conference — Nov 2002

Final pretrial conference — Jan 2003

Trial — Feb–Mar 2003

Feb | Mar | Apr | May | Jun | Jul | Aug | Sep | Oct | Nov | Dec | Jan | Feb | Mar

2002 | 2003

- Closing arguments
- Jury instructions
- Jury deliberation
- Entry of judgment

Jury Selection

Voir dire Process whereby prospective jurors are asked questions by the judge and attorneys to determine if they would be biased in their decision.

In **jury selection**, the pool of the potential jurors usually is selected from voter or automobile registration lists. Potential jurors are asked to fill out a questionnaire such as that shown in Exhibit 7.10. Individuals are selected to hear specific cases through the process called *voir dire* ("to speak the truth"). Lawyers for each party and the judge can ask questions of prospective jurors to determine if they would be biased in their decision. Jurors can be "stricken for cause" if the court believes that the potential juror is too biased to render a fair verdict. Lawyers may also use preemptory challenges to exclude a juror from sitting on a particular case without giving any reason for the dismissal. Once the appropriate number of jurors is selected (usually six to twelve jurors), they are impaneled to hear the case and are sworn in. The trial is ready to begin. In cases in which the Court is concerned for the safety of the jury, such as a high-profile murder case, it can **sequester,** or separate it from the outside world. Jurors are paid minimum

Exhibit 7.10   **Sample jury questionnaire**

JURY QUESTIONNAIRE
(Please Print)

NAME _____   JUROR NO. _____

    (Last)   *(First)*   *(Middle initial)*

SECTION OF CITY _____

    (Currently)   *(Other sections of city lived in within past ten years)*

Marital Status   ☐ Married   ☐ Single   ☐ Divorced   ☐ Separated   ☐ Widowed

Occupation _____

    (Currently)   *(Other occupations within past ten years)*

Occupation of ☐ Spouse *(or deceased spouse)*   ☐ Other

_____

    (Currently)   *(Other occupations within past ten years)*

No. of Male Children _____   Ages _____

No. of Female Children _____   Ages _____

Your Level of Schooling Completed _____

Race   ☐ White   ☐ Hispanic   ☐ Black   ☐ Other

STOP HERE
Writing below this line is prohibited until the juror video is shown

---

QUESTIONS TO BE ANSWERED IN THE JURY ASSEMBLY ROOM

1. Do you have any physical or psychological disability or are you presently taking any medication?   ☐ YES   ☐ NO

2. (a) Have you ever been a juror before?   ☐ YES   ☐ NO

   (b) If so, were you ever on a hung jury?   ☐ YES   ☐ NO

Questions 3 through 15 apply to criminal cases only

3. Do you have any religious, moral or ethical beliefs that would prevent you from sitting in judgment in a criminal case and rendering a fair verdict?   ☐ YES   ☐ NO

4. Have you or anyone close to you ever been a victim of a crime?   ☐ YES   ☐ NO

5. Have you or anyone close to you ever been charged with or arrested for a crime, other than a traffic violation?   ☐ YES   ☐ NO

6. Have you or anyone close to you ever been an eyewitness to a crime, whether or not it ever came to Court?   ☐ YES   ☐ NO

(continued)

Exhibit 7.10 **Sample jury questionnaire** *(continued)*

7. Have you, or has anyone close to you, ever worked as a police officer or in other law enforcement jobs? This includes prosecutors, public defenders, private criminal defense lawyers, detectives, and security or prison guards. ❏ YES ❏ NO

8. Would you be more likely to believe the testimony of a police officer or any other law enforcement officer just because of his job? ❏ YES ❏ NO

9. Would you be less likely to believe the testimony of a police officer or any other law enforcement officer just because of his job? ❏ YES ❏ NO

10. Would you have any problem following the Court's instruction that the defendant in a criminal case is presumed to be innocent until proven guilty beyond a reasonable doubt? ❏ YES ❏ NO

11. Would you have any problem following the Court's instruction that the defendant in a criminal case does not have to take the stand or present evidence, and it cannot be held against the defendant if he or she elects to remain silent? ❏ YES ❏ NO

12. Would you have any problem following the Court's instruction in a criminal case that just because someone is arrested, it does not mean that the person is guilty of anything? ❏ YES ❏ NO

13. In general, would you have any problem following and applying the judge's instructions on the law? ❏ YES ❏ NO

14. Would you have any problem during jury deliberations in a criminal case discussing the case fully but still making up your own mind? ❏ YES ❏ NO

15. Is there any other reason you could not be a fair juror in a criminal case? ❏ YES ❏ NO

Questions 16 through 24 apply to civil cases only

16. Have you or anyone close to you ever sued someone, been sued, or been a witness? ❏ YES ❏ NO

17. Have you or anyone close to you been employed as a lawyer or in a law-related job? ❏ YES ❏ NO

18. Have you or anyone close to you been employed as a doctor or nurse or in a medical-related job? ❏ YES ❏ NO

19. In a civil case, would you have any problem following the Court's instruction that the plaintiff has the burden or proof, but unlike in a criminal case, the test is not beyond a reasonable doubt but "more likely than not"? ❏ YES ❏ NO

20. In a civil case, would you have any problem putting aside sympathy for the plaintiff and deciding the case solely on the evidence? ❏ YES ❏ NO

21. In a civil case, would you have any problem following the Court's instruction to award money for damages for things like pain and suffering, loss of life's pleasures, etc., although it is difficult to put a dollar figure on them? ❏ YES ❏ NO

22. Would you have any problem during jury deliberations in a civil case discussing the case fully but still making up your own mind? ❏ YES ❏ NO

23. Is there any reason in a civil case that you cannot follow the Court's instructions on the law? ❏ YES ❏ NO

24. Is there any reason in a civil case that you cannot otherwise be a fair juror? ❏ YES ❏ NO

fees for their service. Courts can hold people in contempt and fine or jail them for willful refusal to serve as a juror.

Opening Statements

Each party's attorney is allowed to make an **opening statement** to the jury. In opening statements, attorneys usually summarize the main factual and legal issues of the case and describe why they believe their client's position is valid. The information given in this statement is not considered as evidence. It is the attorney's opportunity to tell the trier of fact what he or she intends to tell the jury through witnesses and evidence.

Plaintiff's Case

Plaintiffs bear the **burden of proof** to persuade the trier of fact of the merits of their case. This is called the **plaintiff's case**. The plaintiff's attorney calls witnesses to give testimony. After a witness has been sworn in, the plaintiff's attorney examines (questions) the witness. This is called **direct examination**. Documents and other evidence can be introduced through each witness.

After the plaintiff's attorney has completed his or her questions, the defendant's attorney can question the witness in **cross-examination**. The defendant's attorney can ask questions only about the subjects that were brought up during the direct examination. After the defendant's attorney completes his or her questions, the plaintiff's attorney can ask questions of the witness in **redirect examination**. The defendant's attorney then can ask questions of the witness again. This is called **recross examination**. Exhibit 7.11 illustrates this sequence for examining witnesses.

Defendant's Case

After the plaintiff has concluded his or her case, the **defendant's case** proceeds. The defendant's case must

1. rebut the plaintiff's evidence.
2. prove any affirmative defenses asserted by the defendant.
3. prove any allegations contained in the defendant's cross-complaint.

The defendant's witnesses are examined by the defendant's attorney. The plaintiff's attorney can cross-examine each witness. This is followed by redirect examination by the defendant and recross examination of witnesses by the plaintiff.

Rebuttal and Rejoinder

After the defendant's attorney has completed calling witnesses, the plaintiff's attorney can call witnesses and put forth evidence to rebut the defendant's case. This is called a **rebuttal.** The defendant's attorney can call additional witnesses and introduce other evidence to counter the rebuttal. This is called the **rejoinder**.

Closing Arguments

At the conclusion of the evidence, each party's attorney is allowed to make a **closing argument** to the jury. Each attorney tries to convince the jury to render a verdict for his or her clients by pointing out the strengths in the client's case and the weaknesses in the other side's case.

Information given by the attorneys in their closing statements is not evidence. It is a chance for the attorneys to tell the jury what they said they would tell the jury through witnesses and evidence in the opening statements and how they had done that during the trial.

Jury Instructions

Once the closing arguments are completed, the judge reads **jury instructions**, or **charges** to the jury. These instructions inform the jury about what law to apply in deciding the case

Plaintiff's case Process by which the plaintiff calls witnesses and introduces evidence to prove the allegations contained in his or her complaint.

CONDUCTING A COST-BENEFIT ANALYSIS OF A LAWSUIT

A paralegal should have knowledge of how expensive and time-consuming a lawsuit is both for the client and for the lawyer and law office. Therefore, the choice of whether to bring or defend a lawsuit should be analyzed like any other business decision. This includes performing a **cost–benefit analysis** of the lawsuit. For the plaintiff, it may be wise not to sue. For the defendant, or the plaintiff, it may be wise to settle.

The following factors should be considered in deciding whether to bring or settle a lawsuit:

- The probability of winning or losing
- The amount of money to be won or lost
- Lawyers' fees and other costs of litigation
- Loss of time by managers and other personnel
- The long-term effects on the relationship and reputation of the parties
- The amount of prejudgment interest provided by law
- The aggravation and psychological costs associated with a lawsuit
- The unpredictability of the legal system and the possibility of error
- Other factors peculiar to the parties and lawsuit

Exhibit 7.11 Sequence for examining witnesses

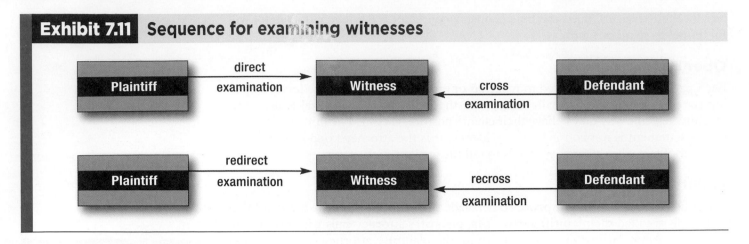

Defendant's case Process by which the defendant calls witnesses and introduces evidence to (1) rebut the plaintiff's evidence, (2) prove affirmative defenses, and (3) prove allegations made in a cross-complaint.

Jury instructions (charges) Instructions given by the judge to the jury that informs them of the law to be applied in the case.

Verdict Decision reached by the jury.

Judgment The official decision of the court.

(see Exhibit 7.12). For example, in a criminal trial the judge will read the jury the statutory definition of the crime charged. In an accident case, the judge will read the jury the legal definition of *negligence*.

Jury Deliberation and Verdict

The jury then goes into the jury room to deliberate its findings. **Jury deliberation** can take from a few minutes to many weeks. After deliberation, the jury announces its **verdict**. In civil cases, the jury also assesses damages. In criminal cases, the judge assesses penalties.

Entry of Judgment

After the jury has returned its verdict, in most cases the judge enters **judgment** to the successful party, based on the verdict. This is the official decision of the court. But the court may overturn the verdict if it finds bias or jury misconduct. This is called a **judgment notwithstanding the verdict**, or **judgment n.o.v.**, or **j.n.o.v.**, for the Latin *judgment non obstante verdicto*.

In a civil case, the judge may reduce the amount of monetary damages awarded by the jury if he or she finds the jury to have been biased, emotional, or inflamed. This is called **remittitur**. The trial court usually issues a **written memorandum** setting forth the reasons for the judgment. This memorandum, together with the trial transcript and evidence introduced at trial, constitutes the permanent *record* of the trial court proceeding.

Appeal The act of asking an appellate court to overturn a decision after the trial court's final judgment has been entered.

Appellant The appealing party in an appeal. Also known as *petitioner*.

Appellee The responding party in an appeal. Also known as *respondent*.

Briefs Documents submitted by the parties' attorneys to the judge that contain legal support for their side of the case.

Appeal

In a civil case, either party can **appeal** the trial court's decision once a final judgment is entered. In a criminal case, only the defendant can appeal. The appeal is made to the appropriate **appellate court** (see Exhibit 7.13). A notice of appeal must be filed within a prescribed time after judgment is entered (usually within 60 or 90 days). The appealing party is called the **appellant**, or **petitioner**. The responding party is called the **appellee**, or **respondent**. The appellant often is required to post an **appeal bond** (e.g., one-and-one-half times the judgment) on appeal.

Briefs and Oral Argument

The parties may designate all or relevant portions of the trial record to be submitted to the appellate court for review. The appellant's attorney may file an **opening brief** with the court, setting forth legal research and other information to support his or her

Exhibit 7.12 **Sample jury instructions**

6.01J (Civ) PROPERTY DAMAGE

The plaintiff is entitled to be compensated for the harm done to his (her) property. If you find that the property was a total loss, damages are to be measured by either its market value or its special value to plaintiff, whichever is greater. If the property was not a total loss, damages are measured by (the difference in value before and after the harm) (the reasonable cost of repairs) and you may consider such evidence produced by defendant by way of defense to plaintiff's claim. In addition, plaintiff is entitled to be reimbursed for incidental costs or losses reasonably incurred because of the damage to the property, such as (rental of a replacement vehicle during repairs), (towing charges), (loss of use of the property), (etc.).

SUBCOMMITTEE NOTE

Damage to property is covered generally by Restatement of Torts, §§ 927 and 928. Section 927 provides for damages to be measured by the "market value" or "damages based upon its special value to [plaintiff] if that is greater than its market value." Restatement of Torts, § 927, Comment c (1934). Section 928 provides, in the case of damages not amounting to total destruction, damages measured by "the difference between the value of the chattel before the harm and the value after the harm or, at plaintiff's election, the reasonable cost of repair or restoration." This accounts for the parenthesized phrases (the difference in value before and after the harm) and (the reasonable cost of repairs).

Incidental costs will depend on the nature of the property damage. Rental of a substitute vehicle has long been recognized as one such compensable item. *Bauer v. Armour & Co.*, 84 Pa.Super. 174 (1924). Compensation for loss of use is specifically authorized by Restatement of Torts, § 928(b), in the case of less than total loss. The Subcommittee can see no logical reason why such damages should not be awarded under Section 927 in the case of total loss. *Nelson v. Johnson*, 55 D. & C. 2d 21 (Somerset C.P. 1970). Any further expense, proximately resulting from the loss or damage is recoverable under general provisions of tort law. *Nelson v. Johnson, supra*, at 33-34.

In the case of damage to automobiles, however, the appellate courts have adhered to the ancient rule requiring testimony of the one who supervised or made the repairs, prior to admission of damage estimates. *Mackiw v. Pennsylvania Threshermen & Farmers Mut. Cas. Ins. Co.*, 201 Pa.Super. 626, 193 A.2d 745 (1963). This rule has been criticized as time-consuming and "technical" by the very courts adhering to it. *Mackiw, supra*, 193 A.2d at 745. It further creates an intolerable burden on the courts, in a period when backlog has led to "compulsory" arbitration in many counties of cases valued below $10,000. E.g., *Loughery v. Barnes*, 181 Pa.Super. 352, 124 A.2d 120 (1956) (appeal after verdict of $341.30 for property damage); *Wilk v. Borough of Mt. Oliver*, 152 Pa.Super. 539, 33 A.2d 73 (1943) (new trial ordered after verdict of $175). The Subcommittee therefore adopts a rule requiring only the submission of a repair bill or estimate in proof of damages to automobiles (such bill being submitted prior to trial to defense counsel); should defendant wish to challenge such an estimate, he may do so through cross-examination and through the introduction of evidence in his own case. See *Watsontown Brick Co. v. Hercules Powder Co.*, 265 F.Supp. 268, 275 (M.D.Pa.), *aff'd*, 387 F.2d 99 (3rd Cir. 1967) (after introduction of damage evidence, burden shifts to defendant to show reduction).

Absent stipulation, the issue of reasonable compensation remains a jury issue.

6.01F (Civ) FUTURE PAIN AND SUFFERING

The plaintiff is entitled to be fairly and adequately compensated for such physical pain, mental anguish, discomfort, inconvenience and distress as you believe he (she) will endure in the future as a result of his (her) injuries. [. . .]

Exhibit 7.13 Form 1 of appellate rules

United States District Court for the _Eastern_

District of _Pennsylvania_

File Number _US3CA 01234_

Ethan Marshall

     v.   )   Notice of Appeal

Sara Elliott

Notice is hereby given that _Ethan Marshall_ (plaintiffs) in the above named case,* hereby appeal to the United States Court of Appeals for the _Third_ Circuit _from the final judgment_ entered in this action on the _06_ day of _February_ , _2011_ .

(s) _[signature]_

Thomas F. Goldman

_____

(Address)

Attorney for _Plaintiff_

Address: _138 North State Street_
Newtown, Pa, 18940

* See Rule 3(c) for permissible ways of identifying appellants.

contentions on appeal. The appellee can file a **responding brief** answering the appellant's contentions.

In some appeals, the attorneys submit their case on "brief" only and ask the court to make a decision based upon the written submission. In other cases, the attorneys on their own or at the request of the court make oral arguments to support their position and clarify what they believe to be the appropriate law. Appellate courts usually permit a brief oral argument at which each party's attorney is heard.

Not every appellate court permits or allows oral argument in every case. Many cases are decided on the brief submitted. In some courts, it is necessary, at the time of filing, to make any desired request for oral argument or indicate a willingness to have the matter decided on the briefs alone. In some cases, the oral argument is allowed automatically, and in other cases a reason for the desired oral argument must be stated.

In the federal court of appeals, oral argument is allowed unless a panel of three judges unanimously agrees, after reviewing the briefs, that the oral argument is unnecessary because the appeal is frivolous, the dispositive issues have been authoritatively decided, or the facts and argument are presented adequately in the briefs and record and the decisional process would not be aided by oral argument [F.R.A.P. 344].

Typically, oral arguments are made before the court without the presence of clients or witnesses. Because no additional fact-finding is permitted, it is merely a matter of making appropriate legal arguments to attempt to persuade the court to rule in favor of the legal position being argued. Many appellate courts establish a time limit for each side. In some courts, the time limit is enforced by a flashing light when the time has expired, and in other courts by a warning light when the time has almost been used. This is done to allow for final statements.

The judges may waive the time limits, particularly when they use up the attorneys' allotted time by asking questions. Local practice, however, is what determines how the court will treat the time limit.

Web Exploration

Check the "Court Rules" of the U.S. Supreme Court, Rule 129, at http://supremecourtus.gov/.

Actions by the Appellate Courts

After review of the briefs, the record in the form of the trial court transcript, and oral arguments by the attorneys, an appellate court may affirm, reverse, or remand the case to the lower court.

If the appellate court believes there had been no errors in application of the procedural law or the substantive law, it will **affirm** the decision of lower court and the lower court decision will stand. If the appellate court rules that the lower court has made a substantial error, either in the procedural law or the substantive law of the case, it may **reverse** the decision of lower court. In other cases when the court finds a reversible error, the court may **reverse and remand** the case. This means that the appellate court feels that based on the correction of the error of law that the case needs to be retried. The retrial will take place in front of a new judge and a new jury.

In the federal court of appeals, oral argument is allowed unless a panel of three judges unanimously agrees, after reviewing the briefs, that the oral argument is unnecessary because the appeal is frivolous, the dispositive issues have been authoritatively decided, or the facts and argument are presented adequately in the briefs and record and the decisional process would not be aided by oral argument [F.R.A.P. 344].

Typically, oral arguments are made before the court without the presence of clients or witnesses. Because no additional fact-finding is permitted, it is merely a matter of making appropriate legal arguments to attempt to persuade the court to rule in favor of the legal position being argued. Many appellate courts establish a time limit for each side. In some courts, the time limit is enforced by a flashing light when the time has expired, and in other courts by a warning light when the time has almost been used. This is done to allow for final statements.

The judges may waive the time limits, particularly when they use up the attorneys' allotted time by asking questions. Local practice, however, is what determines how the court will treat the time limit.

The court also may find that the lower court has made an error that can be corrected, and **remand** the case to the lower court to take additional action or conduct further proceedings. This is called reverse and remand. For example, the lower court may be directed to hold further proceedings in which a jury hears testimony related to the issue of damages and makes an award of monetary damages.

An appellate court will reverse a lower court decision if it finds an **error of law** in the record. An error of law occurs if the jury was improperly instructed by the trial court judge, prejudicial evidence was admitted at trial when it should have been excluded, prejudicial evidence was obtained through an unconstitutional search and seizure, and the like. An appellate court will not reverse a finding of fact unless such finding is unsupported by the evidence or is contradicted by the evidence.

Concept Review *and* Reinforcement

LEGAL TERMINOLOGY

Admitted   251
Affirm   273
Answer   251
Appeal   270
Appeal bond   270
Appellant   270
Appellate court   270
Appellee   270
Bench trial   265
Burden of proof   269
Civil litigation   242
Closing arguments   269
Complaint   245
Consolidation   252
Cost–benefit analysis   269
Cross-complaint   252
Cross-complainant   252
Cross-defendant   252
Cross-examination   269
Default judgment   251
Defendant   245
Defendant's case   269
Denied   251
Demurrer   264
Deponent   260
Deposition   260
Direct examination   269
Discovery   255
E-filing   255

Electronic discovery
  (e-discovery)   263
Error of law   273
Expert witness   260
Extension of time to respond   251
Fact pleading   245
General denial   251
Independent Medical Examination
  (IME)   260
Interrogatories   260
Intervention   252
Judgment   270
Judgment notwithstanding the verdict
  (j.n.o.v.)   270
Jury deliberation   270
Jury instructions (charges)   269
Jury selection   266
Jury trial   265
Litigation   242
Motion for judgment on the
  pleadings   265
Motion for summary judgment   265
Motion to dismiss   264
Notice pleading   245
Opening brief   270
Opening statement   269
Petitioner   270
Physical and mental examination   260
Plaintiff   245
Plaintiff's case   269

Pleadings   242
Pretrial hearing   265
Pretrial motion   264
Pro se   245
Production of documents   260
Rebuttal   269
Recross examination   269
Redirect examination   269
Rejoinder   269
Remand   273
Remittitur   270
Reply   252
Request for admission   263
Respondent   270
Responding brief   272
Reverse   273
Reverse and remand   273
Sequester   266
Settlement conference   265
Statute of limitations   252
Subpoena   260
Summons   245
Trial briefs   265
Trier of fact   265
Verdict   270
Voir dire   266
Witness   260
Written memorandum   270

SUMMARY OF KEY CONCEPTS

Civil Litigation

Description	The legal process for resolving disputes between parties. In civil litigation, the plaintiff sues a defendant to recover monetary damages or other remedy for the alleged harm the defendant caused the plaintiff.

Pleadings

Description	Pleadings consist of paperwork that initiates and responds to a lawsuit.
Complaint	A complaint (petition) is filed by the plaintiff with the court and served, in some states, with a summons on the defendant. It sets forth the basis of the lawsuit.

Fact and Notice Pleading	Depending on the jurisdiction, the complaint must either provide a general allegation of the wrongful conduct alleged, called notice pleading; or plead specific facts alleged, called fact pleading.
Pleading Deadlines	Individual court rules provide a time within which the initial complaint or petition must be served, and responsive pleading must be filed to avoid dismissal of the action or a default judgment.
Responsive Pleadings	The responding party (defendant) must file a responsive pleading within the time limit allowed by rule of court, or request an extension of time to respond from the opposing attorney or from the court.
Answer	An answer is filed by the defendant with the court and served on the plaintiff. It usually denies most allegations of the complaint.
Cross-Complaint	A cross-complaint is filed and served by the defendant if he or she countersues the plaintiff. The defendant is the cross-complainant and the plaintiff is the cross-defendant. The cross-defendant must file and serve a reply (answer).
Intervention	In an intervention, a person who has an interest in a lawsuit becomes a party to the lawsuit.
Consolidation	Consolidation means that the court combines separate cases against the same defendant arising from the same incident into one case if it will not cause prejudice to the parties.
Statute of Limitations	A statute of limitations establishes the period during which a plaintiff must bring a lawsuit against a defendant. If a lawsuit is not filed within this time period, the plaintiff loses his or her right to sue.

Discovery

Description	Discovery is the pretrial litigation process for eliciting facts of the case from the other party and witnesses, for purposes of understanding and evaluating the client's case, focusing the legal team on the strengths and weaknesses of its case; understanding and evaluating the strengths and weaknesses of the opponent's case; preserving testimony; potentially facilitating settlement; and learning information that may be used to impeach a witness.
Depositions	Depositions are oral testimony given by *deponents*, either a party or witness, and transcribed.
Interrogatories	Interrogatories are written questions submitted by one party to the other party. These questions must be answered within a specified period of time.
Production of Documents	A party to a lawsuit may obtain copies of all relevant documents from the other party called a production of documents.
Physical and Mental Examination	Physical and mental examinations of a party are permitted upon order of the court where injuries are alleged that could be verified or disputed by such examination.
Requests for Admission	Written requests issued by one party to the lawsuit to the other asking that certain facts or legal issues be admitted as true.
E-Discovery	In many lawsuits, much of the evidence is in digital form. The winning or losing of lawsuits may lie in the ability of a party to conduct electronic discovery. The lawyer and the paralegal must have a sound understanding of permissible e-discovery.

Pretrial Motions

Motion to Dismiss	A motion to dismiss alleges that even if the facts as presented in the plaintiff's complaint are true, there is no reason to continue the lawsuit. Also called a *demurrer*.

Motion for Judgment on the Pleadings	A motion for judgment on the pleadings alleges that if all facts as pleaded are true, the moving party would win the lawsuit. No facts outside the pleadings may be considered.
Motion for Summary Judgment	A motion for summary judgment alleges that there are no factual disputes, so the judge may apply the law and decide the case without a jury. Evidence outside the pleadings, however, may be considered (e.g., affidavits, documents, depositions).

Settlement Conference

Description	A settlement conference is held prior to trial between the parties in front of the judge to facilitate settlement of the case. Also called *pretrial hearing*. If a settlement is not reached, the case proceeds to trial.

Trial

Jury Selection	Jury selection is done through a process called *voir dire*. Biased jurors are dismissed and replaced.
Opening Statements	The parties' lawyers make opening statements. These do not constitute evidence.
Plaintiff's Case	The plaintiff bears the burden of proof. The plaintiff calls witnesses and introduces evidence to try to prove his or her case.
Defendant's Case	The defendant calls witnesses and introduces evidence to rebut the plaintiff's case and to prove affirmative defenses and cross-complaints.
Rebuttal and Rejoinder	In rebuttal and rejoinder, the plaintiff and defendant may call additional witnesses and introduce additional evidence.
Closing Arguments	Closing arguments are made by the parties' lawyers. Their statements are not evidence.
Jury Instructions	The judge reads instructions to the jury as to what law the jurors are to apply to the case.
Jury Deliberation	The jury retires to the jury room and deliberates until it reaches a *verdict*.
Entry of Judgment	The judge may: a. enter the verdict reached by the jury as the court's *judgment*. b. grant a motion of *judgment* n.o.v. if the judge finds that the jury was biased. This means that the jury's verdict does not stand. c. order *remittitur* (reduction) of any damages awarded if the judge finds the jury to have been biased or emotional.

Appeal

Appellate Court	1. Unlike the trial court, whose main function is to make findings of facts, the appellate court's main function is to make findings of law. 2. In a civil case, unlike a criminal case, either party can appeal the trial court's decision once a final judgment is entered. In a criminal case, only the defendant can appeal. The appeal is made to the appropriate appellate court.
Briefs	In some appeals, the attorneys submit their case on "brief" only, and ask the court to make a decision based upon the written submission.
Oral Arguments	In other cases, the attorneys, on their own or at the request of the court, make an oral argument to support their position and clarify what they believe to be the appropriate law. Not every appellate court permits or allows oral argument in every case.

Actions by the Appellate Courts

Affirm	The appellate court believes there have been no errors in the application of the procedural law or the substantive law and allows the prior decision to stand.
Reverse	The appellate court rules that the lower court has made a substantial error in either the procedural or the substantive law of the case.
Remand	The court finds that the lower court has made an error that can be corrected by sending the case back to the lower court.

WORKING THE WEB

1. Locate the website for your local state trial court that serves your city, if that website is available. If the website is not available, visit the local state trial court. Locate the local rules for filing complaints, answers, and other documents with the court. Are these rules complicated? Explain.
2. Visit the website http://uscourts.gov/. Locate the U.S. District Court that serves the county or parish in which you live. Go to that court's website. Does the court permit electronic filing of documents? If so, review the "user manual" on how to make electronic filings with the court.
3. Visit the website http://supremecourt.us.gov/. Click on "Paid Cases Brief Chart" and review the types of forms that can be filed with the U.S. Supreme Court. How much detail does a paralegal need to know when assisting an attorney to file documents with the U.S. Supreme Court? Explain.
4. Visit the website http://www.lexisone.com/. Click on the feature "Deadlines on Demand." Read about the services available. Are these useful services?
5. Visit the website http://www.lexisone.com/. Click on "Register" and register for the free service to obtain court forms. Find a state form for the state court that serves the county or parish where you live. Find a federal form for the U.S. District Court that serves the county or parish where you live.

CRITICAL THINKING & WRITING QUESTIONS

1. Define "plaintiff." Define "defendant."
2. What is civil litigation? What remedy or remedies are sought by the plaintiff in civil litigation?
3. What are pleadings? Describe the following pleadings: (a) complaint, (b) answer, (c) cross-complaint, and (d) reply.
4. What is a summons? Describe service of process.
5. What is intervention? What is consolidation?
6. Explain statutes of limitations. What purpose do they serve?
7. What is the process of discovery? What purposes does discovery serve? Explain.
8. Describe the following types of discovery: (a) deposition, (b) interrogatories, (c) production of documents, and (d) physical and mental examination.
9. Describe the differences between the following pretrial motions: (a) motion to dismiss, (b) motion for judgment on the pleadings, and (c) motion for summary judgment.
10. What is a settlement conference? What is its purpose?
11. How is a jury selected for a case? What is *voir dire*? What does trier of fact mean?
12. Describe the following phases of a trial: (a) opening statements, (b) plaintiff's case, (c) defendant's case, (d) rebuttal and rejoinder, and (e) closing arguments.
13. What are jury instructions? Explain. What is a verdict? What is a judgment?
14. What is an appeal? Define appellant (petitioner) and appellee (respondent).
15. Describe the following possible decisions by an appellate court: (a) affirm, (b) reverse, and (c) reverse and remand.

Building Paralegal Skills

Videotaped Deposition: Deposing an Expert Witness for Use at Trial

An expert witness whose testimony is critical to the issue of negligence may not be available at time of trial. The parties have agreed to the videotaping of the expert's deposition using a real-time reporting system that provides standard word processing documents simultaneously for the parties.

After viewing the video case study at www.pearsonhighered .com/goldman answer the following:

1. What are the pros and cons to taking a video deposition of an expert witness?
2. Are there any special preparations that need to be made in taking videotaped depositions?
3. How much credibility would you as a juror give to videotaped deposition of an expert witness?

Trial: Direct and Cross-examination of a Witness

The attorneys in a trial ask questions of a fact witness in direct and then in cross-examination to develop the facts of a case.

After viewing the video case study at www.pearsonhighered .com/goldman answer the following:

1. What is the purpose of direct examination?
2. What is the purpose of cross-examination?
3. Why would the attorney ask if it was acceptable to approach the witness?

Preparing for Trial: Preparing a Fact Witness

A paralegal is preparing a witness for deposition and trial and attempts to put the witness at ease by answering the witness's questions and explaining the procedures.

After viewing the video case study at www.pearsonhighered .com/goldman answer the following:

1. Why is it necessary to prepare a person for deposition or for trial?
2. What is the most important advice the paralegal gives the witness?
3. Is preparing a witness the unauthorized practice of law?

1. Is there an ethical obligation not to file certain lawsuits?
2. What is meant by frivolous lawsuit? Are there sanctions for filing frivolous lawsuits? Explain.
3. Should email between lawyers and paralegals be treated as confidential and not subject to use as evidence in a case? Why or why not?
4. A former client of the firm where you work sees you on the street at a local lunch stand and shows you a copy of a judgment rendered against him in a small-claims court. He tells you he is out of work and cannot afford to hire a lawyer. [Pennsylvania comments to Ethics Rule 5.5.] Can you help the client proceed *pro se* (on his own, acting as his own lawyer)? Can you help him prepare the paperwork to appeal the judgment? Does any of this constitute the unauthorized practice of law?
5. You have been advised in your orientation of the ethical rule prohibiting communication with an opponent who is represented by counsel. While surfing the Web, you decide to see if the opposing party has a website. You locate it and check it carefully for any information that might help the investigation of the case assigned to you. You send a request to the site and receive information related to the lawsuit. [Oregon State Bar Op2001–164.] Have you violated the ethical prohibition barring communications with a represented party?

DEVELOPING YOUR COLLABORATION SKILLS

With a group of other students, selected by you or as assigned by your instructor, review the Paralegals at Work at the beginning of the chapter. As a group, discuss the following questions.

1. Identify what document or documents your law firm should prepare on behalf of Rowan, Isis, and their parents to start the lawsuit. Identify what document the trucking company will file with the court to defend the lawsuit.
2. What are the time limits for filing and responding to a complaint? Are there any other local requirements to commence and respond to the lawsuit?
3. Why would the state or federal court be more preferable?

PARALEGAL & PORTFOLIO EXERCISE

Refer to the Paralegals at Work opening scenario. Find online if possible, or if not found online, find in the law library or the federal U.S. District Court, the proper form for filing a complaint for personal injuries in the federal U.S. district court that serves your city. Prepare as best as possible, from the facts of the Paralegals at Work, the complaint and answer in the case presented. If insufficient facts are provided to complete the complaint or answer, make up the missing information and complete these documents.

LEGAL ANALYSIS & WRITING CASES

Swierkiewicz v. Sorema N.A.
534 U.S. 506, 122 S.Ct. 992, 152 L.Ed. 1 2002 U.S. Lexis 1374 (U.S.)

In April 1989, Akos Swierkiewicz, a native of Hungary, began working for Sorema N.A., a reinsurance company headquartered in New York. Swierkiewicz initially was employed as senior vice president and chief underwriting officer. Nearly six years later, the chief executive officer of the company demoted Swierkiewicz to a marketing position, and he was removed from his underwriting responsibilities. Swierkiewicz's underwriting responsibilities were transferred to a 32-year-old employee with less than 1 year of underwriting experience. Swierkiewicz, who was 53 years old at the time and had 26 years of experience in the insurance industry, was dismissed by Sorema.

Swierkiewicz sued Sorema to recover monetary damages for alleged age and national-origin discrimination in violation of federal antidiscrimination laws. Sorema moved to have Swierkiewicz's complaint dismissed. The District Court dismissed Swierkiewicz's complaint for not being specific enough, and the Court of Appeals affirmed. Swierkiewicz appealed to the U.S. Supreme Court.

Question

1. Under the notice pleading system, was plaintiff Swierkiewicz's complaint sufficiently stated to permit the case to go to trial?

Norgart v. The Upjohn Company
21 Cal.4th 383, 87 Cal.Rptr.2nd 453 1999 Cal. Lexis 5308 (Cal.)

Kristi Norgart McBride lived with her husband in Santa Rosa, California. Kristi suffered from manic-depressive mental illness (now called bipolar disorder). In this disease, the person cycles between manic (ultrahappy, expansive, extrovert) episodes to depressive episodes. The disease is often treated with prescription drugs. In April 1984, Kristi attempted suicide. A psychiatrist prescribed an antianxiety drug. In May 1985, Kristi attempted suicide again by overdosing on drugs. The doctor prescribed Halcion, a hypnotic drug, and added Darvocet-N, a mild narcotic analgesic. On October 16, 1985, after descending into a severe depression, Kristi committed suicide by overdosing on Halcion and Darvocet-N.

On October 16, 1991, exactly six years after Kristi's death, Leo and Phyllis Norgart, Kristi's parents, filed a lawsuit against the Upjohn Company, the maker of Halcion, for wrongful death based on Upjohn's alleged failure to warn of the unreasonable dangers of taking Halcion. The trial court granted Upjohn's motion for summary judgment based on the fact that the one-year statute of limitations for wrongful death actions had run. The Court of Appeals reversed, and Upjohn appealed to the Supreme Court of California.

Question

1. Is the plaintiff's action for wrongful death barred by the one-year statute of limitations?

Engler v. Winfrey   201 F.3d 680 2000 U.S. App. Lexis 1723 (5th Cir.)

In early 1996, a disease called Mad Cow Disease was diagnosed in Britain. The disease triggers a deadly brain condition in cattle, which in turn causes degeneration and fatal brain disease in humans who eat beef from infected cattle. Oprah Winfrey hosts a popular television show in the United States, which is produced by Harpo Productions, Inc., a company wholly owned by Winfrey. Producers, editors, and other employees of the Oprah Winfrey Show researched the Mad Cow Disease topic as part of a "Dangerous Foods" episode of the Oprah Winfrey Show. Guests on the show included Dr. Gary Weber, who holds a Ph.D. in animal science and represented the National Cattlemen's Beef Association; Dr. Will Hueston from the U.S. Department of Agriculture and a leading expert on Mad Cow Disease; Dr. James Miller, a physician with experience in treating individuals inflicted with the disease; and Howard Lyman, a former cattle rancher turned vegetarian and an activist for the Humane Society.

On the show, which was aired April 16, 1996, Lyman made several statements regarding the threat that Mad Cow Disease posed to people in the United States. The experts on the show countered that no case of Mad Cow Disease had been reported in the United States and explained the extensive animal testing and oversight employed by the U.S. Department of Agriculture and cattle producers to prevent Mad Cow Disease in the United States.

Following the broadcast of Oprah Winfrey's "Dangerous Foods" show, the cattle market in Texas dropped drastically.

In the week before the show aired, finished cattle sold for approximately $61.90 per hundredweight; after the show, the price dropped to the mid-$50s. The live cattle futures market on the Chicago Mercantile Exchange dropped within an hour of the airing of the Oprah Winfrey Show. The depressed market for finished cattle continued its slump for approximately three months after the show.

Plaintiffs Paul Engler and Cattle Feeders, Inc. filed a lawsuit against defendants Oprah Winfrey and Harpo Productions, Inc., alleging that the defendants had engaged in the intentional tort of business disparagement of the product cattle. After testimony was heard from both sides, the trial court judge submitted the following question to the jury: "Did a named defendant publish a false, disparaging statement that was of and concerning the cattle of a plaintiff?" The trial court jury returned the answer "no" to this question, and the trial court judge entered judgment in favor of the defendants Oprah Winfrey and Harpo Productions, Inc. The plaintiffs appealed this decision to the U.S. Court of Appeals, arguing that the trial court judge's business disparagement instruction was in error.

Question

1. Was the trial court judge's business disparagement instruction to the jury an error that requires the case to be reversed on this issue on appeal?

Ferlito v. Johnson & Johnson Products, Inc.   771 F.Supp. 196 1991 U.S. Dist. Lexis 11747 (E.D.Mich.)

Susan and Frank Ferlito were invited to a Halloween party. They decided to attend as Mary (Mrs. Ferlito) and her little lamb (Mr. Ferlito). Mrs. Ferlito constructed a lamb costume for her husband by gluing cotton batting manufactured by Johnson & Johnson Products, Inc. (JJP), to a suit of long underwear. She used the same cotton batting to fashion a headpiece, complete with ears. The costume covered Mr. Ferlito from his head to his ankles, except for his face and hands, which were blackened with paint. At the party, Mr. Ferlito attempted to light a cigarette with a butane lighter. The flame

passed close to his left arm, and the cotton batting ignited. He suffered burns over one-third of his body. The Ferlitos sued JJP to recover damages, alleging that JJP failed to warn them of the ignitability of cotton batting. The jury returned a verdict for Mr. Ferlito in the amount of $555,000 and for Mrs. Ferlito in the amount of $70,000. JJP filed a motion for judgment notwithstanding the verdict (j.n.o.v.).

Question

1. Should defendant JJP's motion for j.n.o.v. be granted?

Pizza Hut, Inc. v. Papa John's International, Inc.   227 F.3d 489 2000 U.S. App. Lexis 23444 (5th Cir.)

Pizza Hut, Inc., the largest pizza chain in the United States, operates more than 7,000 restaurants. Papa John's International, Inc., is the third-largest pizza chain in the United States, with more than 2,050 locations. In May 1995, Papa John's adopted a new slogan, "Better Ingredients. Better

Pizza," and applied for and received a federal trademark for this slogan. Papa John's spent more than $300 million building customer recognition and goodwill for this slogan. The slogan has appeared on millions of signs, shirts, menus, pizza boxes, napkins, and other items and has regularly appeared as the tag line at the end of Papa John's radio and television advertisements.

On May 1, 1997, Pizza Hut launched a new advertising campaign in which it declared "war" on poor-quality pizza. The advertisements touted the "better taste" of Pizza Hut's pizza and "dared" anyone to find a better pizza. A few weeks later, Papa John's launched a comparative advertising campaign that touted the superiority of Papa John's pizza over Pizza Hut's pizza. Papa John's claimed it had sauce and dough superior to Pizza Hut's. Many of these advertisements were accompanied by Papa John's slogan, "Better Ingredients. Better Pizza."

In 1998, Pizza Hut filed a civil action in federal District Court, charging Papa John's with false advertising in violation of Section 43(a) of the federal Lanham Act. The District Court found that Papa John's slogan "Better Ingredients. Better Pizza," standing alone, was mere puffery and did not constitute false advertising. The District Court found, however, that Papa John's claims of superior sauce and dough were misleading and that Papa John's slogan "Better Ingredients. Better Pizza" became tainted because it was associated with these misleading statements. The District Court enjoined Papa John's from using the slogan "Better Ingredients. Better Pizza." Papa John's appealed.

Question

1. Should the U.S. District Court's opinion in favor of Pizza Hut, Inc. be reversed?

Conrad v. Delta Airlines, Inc.　494 F.2d 914 1974 U.S. App. Lexis 9186 (7th Cir.)

Captain Conrad was a pilot for Delta Airlines. In 1970, the airline forced Conrad to resign. He sued, alleging that he was discharged because of his pro-union activities and not because of poor job performance, as claimed by Delta.

During discovery, a report written by a Delta flight operations manager was produced, stating: "More than a few crew members claimed that Conrad professed to being a leftist-activist. His overactivity with the local pilots' union, coupled with inquiries regarding company files to our secretary, led to the conclusion that potential trouble will be avoided by acceptance of his resignation."

Conrad claims that the report is evidence of the anti-union motivation for his discharge. Delta made a summary judgment motion to the Trial Court.

Question

1. Should its summary judgment motion be granted?

Haviland & Co. v. Montgomery Ward & Co.　31 F.R.D. 578 1962 U.S. Dist. Lexis 5964 (S.D.N.Y.)

Haviland & Company filed suit against Montgomery Ward & Company in U.S. District Court, claiming that Ward used the trademark "Haviland" on millions of dollars worth of merchandise. As the owner of the mark, Haviland & Company sought compensation from Ward. Ward served notice to take the deposition of Haviland & Company's president, William D. Haviland. The attorneys for Haviland told the court that Haviland was 80 years old, lived in Limoges, France, and was too ill to travel to the United States for the deposition. Haviland's physician submitted an affidavit confirming these facts.

Question

1. Must Haviland give his deposition?
2. What other alternative way to take the testimony may be used?

Simblest v. Maynard　427 F.2d1 1970 U.S. App. Lexis 9265 (2nd Cir.)

On November 9, 1965, Mr. Simblest was driving a car that collided with a fire engine at an intersection in Burlington, Vermont. The accident occurred on the night on which a power blackout left most of the state without lights. Mr. Simblest, who was injured in the accident, sued the driver of the fire truck for damages.

During the trial, Simblest testified that when he entered the intersection, the traffic light was green in his favor. All of the other witnesses testified that the traffic light had gone dark at least 10 minutes before the accident. Simblest testified that the accident was caused by the fire truck's failure to use any warning lights or sirens. Simblest's testimony was contradicted by four witnesses who testified that the fire truck had used both its lights and sirens. The jury found that the driver of the fire truck had been negligent and rendered a verdict for Simblest. The defense made a motion for judgment n.o.v.

Question

1. Who wins?

IN RE M.C., 09-08-00465-CV (Tex.App.-Beaumont [9th Dist.] 3-5-2009)

On January 9, 2009, the court notified the parties that the appeal would be dismissed for want of prosecution unless arrangements were made for filing the record or the appellant explained why additional time was needed to file the record. It also notified the parties that the appeal would be dismissed unless the appellant remitted the filing fee for the appeal. The appellant, Blanca Carrillo, did not respond to the Court's notices. The appellant did not file an affidavit of indigence and is not entitled to proceed without payment of costs. There was no satisfactory explanation for the failure to file the record, and no reasonable explanation for the

failure to pay the filing fee for the appeal. The court dismissed the appeal for want of prosecution.

Question

1. Why would a court dismiss a case for failure to meet a time deadline?
2. Why would a court dismiss a case for not paying the filing fees?
3. Is justice served by the court enforcing these time limits and filing requirements?

WORKING WITH THE LANGUAGE OF THE COURT CASE

Gnazzo v. G.D. Searle & Co.

973 F.2d 136 1992
U.S. App. Lexis 19453 United States Court of Appeals, Second Circuit

Read the following case, excerpted from the Court of Appeals opinion. Review and brief the case. In your brief, answer the following questions.

1. What is a statute of limitations? What purposes does such a statute serve?
2. What was the Connecticut statute of limitations for the injury alleged by the plaintiff?
3. What is summary judgment? When will it be granted?
4. What was the decision of the trial court? Of the Court of Appeals?

Pierce, Circuit Judge

On November 11, 1974, Gnazzo had a CU-7 intrauterine device (IUD) inserted in her uterus for contraceptive purposes. The IUD was developed, marketed, and sold by G.D. Searle & Co. (Searle). When Gnazzo's deposition was taken, she stated that her doctor had informed her that "the insertion would hurt, but not for long," and that she "would have uncomfortable and probably painful periods for the first three to four months." On October 11, 1975, Gnazzo found it necessary to return to her physician due to excessive pain and cramping. During this visit she was informed by her doctor that he thought she had pelvic inflammatory disease (PID). She recalled that he stated that the infection was possibly caused by venereal disease or the use of the IUD. The PID was treated with antibiotics and cleared up shortly thereafter. Less than one year later, Gnazzo was again treated for an IUD-associated infection. This infection was also treated with antibiotics. Gnazzo continued using the IUD until it was finally removed in December of 1977.

Following a laparoscopy in March of 1989, Gnazzo was informed by a fertility specialist that she was infertile because of PID-induced adhesions resulting from her prior IUD use. Subsequent to this determination, and at the request of her then-attorneys, Gnazzo completed a questionnaire dated May 11, 1989. In response to the following question, "When and why did you first suspect that your IUD had caused you any harm?" Gnazzo responded "sometime in 1981" and explained: "I was married in April 1981, so I stopped using birth control so I could get pregnant—nothing ever happened (of course), then I started hearing and reading about how damaging IUDs could be. I figured that was the problem; however, my marriage started to crumble, so I never pursued the issue."

On May 4, 1990, Gnazzo initiated the underlying action against Searle. In an amended complaint, she alleged that she had suffered injuries as a result of her use of the IUD developed by Searle. Searle moved for summary judgment on the ground that Gnazzo's claim was time-barred by Connecticut's three-year statute of limitations for product liability actions. Searle argued, inter alia, that Gnazzo knew in 1981 that she had suffered harm caused by her IUD. Gnazzo contended that her cause of action against Searle accrued only when she learned from the fertility specialist that the IUD had caused her PID and subsequent infertility.

In a ruling dated September 18, 1991, the district court granted Searle's motion for summary judgment on the ground that Gnazzo's claim was time-barred by the applicable statute of limitations. In reaching this result, the court determined that Connecticut law provided no support for Gnazzo's contention that she should not have been expected to file her action until she was told of her infertility and the IUD's causal connection. This appeal followed.

On appeal, Gnazzo contends that the district court improperly granted Searle's motion for summary judgment because a genuine issue of material fact exists as to when she discovered, or reasonably should have discovered, her injuries and their causal connection to the defendant's alleged wrongful conduct. Summary judgment is appropriate when there is no genuine issue as to any material fact and the moving party is entitled to judgment as a matter of law. We consider the record in the light most favorable to the non-movant. However, the non-movant "may not rest upon the mere allegations of denials of her pleading, but must set forth specific facts showing that there is a genuine issue for trial."

Under Connecticut law, a product liability claim must be brought within "three years from the date when the injury is first sustained or discovered or in the exercise of reasonable care should have been discovered." In Connecticut, a cause of action accrues when a plaintiff suffers actionable harm. Actionable harm occurs when the plaintiff discovers or should discover, through the exercise of reasonable care, that he or she has been injured and that the defendant's conduct caused such injury.

Gnazzo contends that "the mere occurrence of a pelvic infection or difficulty in becoming pregnant does not necessarily result in notice to the plaintiff of a cause of action." Thus, she maintains that her cause of action did not accrue until 1989 when the fertility specialist informed her both that she was infertile and that this condition resulted from her previous use of the IUD.

Under Connecticut law, however, "the statute of limitations begins to run when the plaintiff discovers some form of actionable harm, not the fullest manifestation thereof." Therefore, as Gnazzo's responses to the questionnaire indicate she suspected "sometime in 1981" that the IUD had caused her harm because she had been experiencing trouble becoming pregnant and had "started hearing and reading about how damaging IUDs could be and had figured that was the problem."

Thus, by her own admission, Gnazzo had recognized, or should have recognized, the critical link between her injury and the defendant's causal connection to it. In other words, she had "discovered, or should have discovered through the exercise of reasonable care, that she had been injured and that Searle's conduct caused such injury." However, as Gnazzo acknowledged in the questionnaire, she did not pursue the "issue" at the time because of her marital problems. Thus, even when viewed in the light most favorable to Gnazzo, the non-moving party, we are constrained to find that she knew by 1981 that she had "some form of actionable harm." Consequently, by the time she commenced her action in 1990, Gnazzo was time-barred by the Connecticut statute of limitations.

Since we have determined that Gnazzo's cause of action commenced in 1981, we need not address Searle's additional contention that Gnazzo's awareness in 1975 of her PID and her purported knowledge of its causal connection to the IUD commenced the running of the Connecticut statute of limitations at that time.

We are sympathetic to Gnazzo's situation and mindful that the unavoidable result we reach in this case is harsh. Nevertheless, we are equally aware that "it is within the Connecticut General Assembly's constitutional authority to decide when claims for injury are to be brought. Where a plaintiff has failed to comply with this requirement, a court may not entertain the suit." The judgment of the district court is affirmed.

Criminal Procedure and Administrative Law

DIGITAL RESOURCES

Chapter 8 Digital Resources at *www.pearsonhighered.com/goldman*

- Video Case Studies:
  - Administrative Agency Hearing: The Role of the Paralegal
- Chapter Summary • Web Links • Court Opinions • Glossary • Comprehension Quizzes
- Technology Resources

> "It is better that ten guilty persons escape, than that one innocent suffer."
>
> *Sir William Blackstone, Commentaries on the Laws of England (1809)*

LEARNING OBJECTIVES

After studying this chapter, you should be able to:

1. Recognize the professional opportunities for paralegals in the criminal law area.
2. Identify and describe the parties and attorneys to a criminal action.
3. Describe criminal procedure, including arrest and arraignment.
4. Describe the functions of a grand jury and what an indictment is.
5. Describe the process of a criminal trial.
6. Explain the Fourth Amendment's protection from unreasonable search and seizure.
7. Describe the Fifth Amendment's privilege against self-incrimination and the *Miranda* rights.
8. Explain the Fifth Amendment's protection against double jeopardy.
9. Recognize the professional opportunities for paralegals in administrative law.
10. List and explain the functions of administrative agencies.
11. Explain the scope of the Administrative Procedure Act.
12. Describe the powers of administrative agencies.
13. Explain a paralegal's duty not to assist in criminal activity.

Paralegals at Work

You are a paralegal at a law firm that does criminal defense work. The law firm specializes in defending executives in white-collar criminal law matters. You work for Ms. Heather Josephson, a renowned attorney in the area of white-collar criminal defense. Ms. Josephson informs you that the law firm has been retained to represent Mr. Keith Day, an executive now facing criminal charges for alleged white-collar crimes. Ms. Josephson informs you that you will assist her in preparing the defense of Mr. Day.

Ms. Josephson explains the following facts and issues to you: Mr. Day was the founder and Chief Executive Officer (CEO) of the E-Run Corporation. The E-Run Corporation was one of the largest companies in the United States and operated an energy business. Mr. Day has been served a complaint, *United States v. Day*, wherein Mr. Day has been charged by the federal government with various crimes, including financial fraud.

Ms. Josephson explains that immediately after being served with the complaint that the federal government agents asked Mr. Day many questions concerning his business affairs as they pertained to his employment at E-Run Corporation and his involvement in the financial affairs of the company. Mr. Day explained to the federal agents how the fraud worked and his involvement in this situation. Ms. Josephson asks Mr. Day if the federal agents read him any rights before they questioned him and Mr. Day answered that they had not. Mr. Day is now concerned that the information he told the federal agents "may come back to haunt him."

The complaint alleges that Mr. Day, as well as Mr. Don Scott, E-Run Corporation's Chief Financial Officer (CFO), and other corporate officers agreed with each other to "cook the books" of the corporation to make the corporation seem like it was making huge profits when it was not. The complaint alleges that the executives failed to report on its financial statements large debts incurred by the corporation causing the corporation to show a large financial profit when in fact the corporation was losing money. When the alleged misdeeds were discovered, the E-Run Corporation failed and had to declare bankruptcy. Shareholders lost their entire investment, and the creditors of the corporation were not paid.

In addition, the complaint alleges that Mr. Day, Mr. Scott, and other corporate officers stole money directly from the corporation and diverted corporate cash and other property to their own personal bank accounts. Mr. Day is alleged to have used the mail, telephones, and computers to implement and operate the entire scheme. The complaint also alleges that Mr. Day had purchased a restaurant and used the restaurant to hide and move the stolen money through it to make it seem that he had another business that generated the stolen property for him.

Ms. Josephson explains to you that the federal government had engaged in a wiretap of Mr. Day's telephones for twelve months but had failed to obtain a warrant to conduct the wiretap on Mr. Day's telephone. Ms. Josephson also explains that Mr. Day had said that his spouse "knows everything" and that she is willing to be a witness against him at trial. Also, the federal government has reached a plea bargain with Mr. Scott that grants Mr. Scott immunity from prosecution in return for his testimony against Mr. Day at trial.

INTRODUCTION FOR THE PARALEGAL

Paralegals often work for criminal lawyers, and therefore require knowledge of the criminal legal process. Some private lawyers specialize in representing clients accused of criminal wrongdoing. Other lawyers work for the government, either for the prosecution team that represents the government in the criminal lawsuit against the defendant, or for a government-appointed defense counsel representing defendants who cannot afford a private attorney to represent them.

For members of society to coexist peacefully and commerce to flourish, people and their property must be protected from injury by other members of society. Federal, state, and local governments' **criminal laws** are intended to accomplish this by providing an incentive for persons to act reasonably in society and imposing penalties on persons who violate them.

A person charged with a crime in the United States is *presumed innocent until proven guilty*. The **burden of proof** is on the government to prove that the accused is guilty of the crime charged. The accused must be found guilty **"beyond a reasonable doubt."** Conviction requires a unanimous jury vote.

Paralegals who work in the criminal law field must have a thorough understanding of the protections in the U.S. Constitution that protect a person charged with a crime in the United States. These include the protections against unreasonable search and seizure, against self-incrimination, against double jeopardy, against cruel and unusual punishment, and the right to a public jury trial.

Many paralegal professionals work in the area of administrative law. This may consist of working for federal administrative agencies such as the Securities and Exchange

Commission (SEC), the Federal Trade Commission (FTC), and other federal agencies. Paralegals also often work for state administrative agencies. These include state environmental protection agencies, corporations departments, and other such agencies.

In the administrative law field paralegals may also work for attorneys who represent clients who are regulated by administrative agencies. For example, if a client has proceedings brought against him or her for violation of federal securities laws by the SEC, an attorney will represent the client at the proceeding. Other attorneys will represent clients who are seeking licenses to conduct business from an administrative agency. For example, clients who wish to form a national bank must obtain permission from the Office of the Comptroller of the Currency. Paralegals often assist attorneys in preparing for administrative agency matters.

This chapter covers criminal litigation and procedure and administrative law.

The following feature discusses the career opportunities for paralegal professionals in criminal law.

CAREER OPPORTUNITIES FOR PARALEGALS IN CRIMINAL LAW AND PROCEDURE

The area of criminal law provides abundant opportunities for jobs for paralegals. The criminal law system in this country is extremely large and requires the services of thousands of lawyers and, thus, thousands of paralegals. The job opportunities for paralegals are quite varied in this area of law.

Most of the crimes prosecuted in the United States involve violations of state laws. These include many physical crimes, such as assault, battery, robbery, rape, and such. In addition, many crimes involve illegal drug sales, fraud, and other violations of criminal law.

In each case when a defendant is charged with a state-law crime, the state brings the lawsuit against the alleged criminal. The lawsuits are brought by prosecutors of the local jurisdiction where the crime has been alleged to have been committed. The prosecutors are lawyers who are state government employees. The prosecutor is responsible for investigating the alleged crime and for assembling the government's case against the defendant. Paralegals have opportunities to work for state government assisting prosecuting attorneys in bringing and pursuing criminal charges.

Paralegals have opportunities to work for the state government or other defense attorneys assisting in the defense of criminally-charged defendants. Many defendants in criminal cases cannot afford their own attorneys, so the government provides defense attorneys to represent the defendant in the criminal case. The defense attorneys frequently are government employees as well. These lawyers often are referred to as public defenders. In this case, paralegals can work as state government employees assisting in the defense in a criminal case. Sometimes the court will appoint an attorney in private practice to represent a defendant. The government, of course, pays the private attorney's fees.

Paralegals who work for the prosecutor's office or for the defense attorneys typically are relied on heavily to conduct investigations, prepare documents that will be filed with the court, conduct legal research, and assist attorneys at criminal trials. Thus, substantial job opportunities are available for paralegals in this criminal law area.

In addition, some defendants—individuals, corporations, and other businesses—are charged with committing white-collar crimes, including criminal fraud, securities fraud, money laundering, racketeering, and such. White-collar criminal defendants can be charged with violating either state or federal criminal laws, depending on the crimes they are alleged to have committed.

In white-collar criminal law cases, whether in state or federal court, the government employs lawyers to represent the government in its case against the accused. In state criminal law cases, the lawyers are state employees. In federal criminal law cases the lawyers are federal employees. There are excellent opportunities for paralegals to become federal government employees and assist attorneys in the prosecution of federal crimes.

On the other side, white-collar defendants often have sufficient funds to employ private attorneys to represent them in white-collar criminal law cases. This could be the case of either wealthy individuals or corporations and businesses. Paralegals can work for the law firms who represent white-collar criminals and businesses or for the legal department of a corporation if it is the defendant in a white-collar criminal case.

White-collar criminal cases are often complex. These cases require substantial investigation, as well as preparation for trial. Paralegals are indispensable in preparing for these complex white-collar criminal cases.

There will always be criminals; therefore, there will always be a need for attorneys to represent the government on one side of the case and the defendant on the other side of the case. In a parallel fashion, there will always be a need for paralegals on the government prosecutor's side of the case, as well as the defendant's side of the case. The area of criminal law will remain an important source of employment for paralegals.

Parties and Attorneys of a Criminal Action

In a criminal lawsuit, the government (not a private party) is the **plaintiff**. The government prosecuting a case can either be the federal government or a state or territory government. The government is represented by a **prosecuting attorney**. The lawyer who prosecutes criminal cases on behalf of a state is called the **district attorney (DA)**. The lawyer who prosecutes federal criminal cases is called the **United States Attorney** (see Exhibit 8.1).

The accused, which is usually an individual or a business, is the **defendant**. The accused is represented by a **defense attorney**. Sometimes the accused will hire a private attorney to represent him or her if he can afford to do so. If the accused cannot afford a private defense lawyer, the government will provide one free of charge. This government defense attorney is often called a **public defender** (see Exhibit 8.1).

Criminal Procedure

The court procedure for initiating and maintaining a criminal action is quite detailed. It encompasses both pretrial procedures and the actual trial. Pretrial criminal procedure consists of several distinct stages: *arrest*, *indictment* or *information*, *arraignment*, and possible *plea bargaining*.

Federal Rules of Criminal Procedure govern all criminal proceedings in the courts of the United States (federal courts) [F.R.C.P. Rule 1]. Each state has its own rules of criminal procedure that govern criminal proceedings in state courts.

Criminal Complaint

In criminal cases the government must file a **criminal complaint** charging the accused with the alleged crimes he or she, or the corporation or other business, is accused of committing. F.R.C.I Rule 3 (Complaint) states "The complaint is a written statement of the essential facts constituting the offense charged. It must be made under oath before a magistrate judge or, if none is reasonably available, before a state or local judicial officer." States have their own requirements for the information to be contained in a criminal complaint

A complaint is usually filed after the government has obtained sufficient evidence to charge the accused with the crime. This government investigation may consist of watching the accused's activities, wiretaps, obtaining information from informants or

---

Exhibit 8.1   **Parties and attorneys involved in a criminal case**

PARTIES TO A CRIMINAL LAWSUIT

Government	Person or Business
(plaintiff)	(defendant)

ATTORNEYS REPRESENTING THE PARTIES

Prosecutor	Defense Attorney
(government attorney)	(private attorney or public defender)

witnesses, and through other means of obtaining sufficient evidence for filing the complaint.

A copy of a criminal complaint filed by the United States government appears as Exhibit 8.2.

Arrest

Before the police can arrest a person for committing a crime, they often must obtain an **arrest warrant** based upon a showing of **probable cause**—the substantial likelihood that the person either committed or is about to commit a crime.

> **Arrest warrant** A document for a person's detainment based upon a showing of probable cause that the person committed the crime.

> **Example** The police are tipped off by a source that a person has been involved in selling illegal drugs. If the judge finds that the information is reliable, and that it constitutes probable cause, the judge will issue an arrest warrant.

If the police do not have time to obtain a warrant the police still may arrest the suspect. **Warrantless arrests**, too, are judged by the probable-cause standard. A warrantless arrest can be made by the police if they arrive during the commission of a crime, when a person is fleeing from the scene of a crime, or when it is likely that evidence will be destroyed.

After a person is arrested, he or she is taken to the police station for *booking*—the administrative proceeding for recording the arrest, fingerprinting, and so on.

Bail

When a person is arrested, a **bail** amount is usually set. If the arrested person "posts" bail, he or she can be released from prison until the date of the trial. The bail can be posted by the arrested person, or a bail bonds person is paid to post the bond. Bail will not be set if the crime is substantial (e.g., murder) or if the arrestee is a flight risk who might not later show up for trial.

Most arrestees (or a relative or friend) pay a professional bail bonds person who operates a bail bonds business to post the **bail bond**. Bail bonds persons usually require payment of 10 percent of the bail in order to post bond. If the bail is set at $100,000, then the amount for payment of the bail bond is $10,000. The bail bonds person keeps this $10,000 payment. The bail bonds person guarantees the court that he or she will pay the court $100,000 if the arrestee does not show up for trial. If this happens, the bail bonds person will attempt the amount of the bond from the arrestee. Bail bonds persons often require collateral (e.g., title to an automobile, second mortgage on a house and such) before they issue a bail bond.

> **Examples** Susan is arrested for possession of an illegal narcotic. The court sets a bail of $100,000. Susan can pay $100,000 to the court and get out of jail until the time of her trial. At the time of her trial she will be paid back the $100,000. If Susan cannot post bail herself, she can pay a bail bonds person $10,000 to post bail.

Indictment or Information

Accused persons must be formally charged with a crime before they can be brought to trial. This usually is done by the issuance of a **grand jury indictment** or a **magistrate's (judge's) information**. Evidence of serious crimes, such as murder, is usually presented to a **grand jury**.

F.R.C.P. Rule 6 (The Grand Jury) states that a federal grand jury shall consist of between 6 and 23 citizens who are charged with evaluating the evidence presented by the government. State grand juries provide for a varying number of grand jurors. Grand jurors sit for a fixed time, such as one year.

Exhibit 8.2 Complaint filed by the United States government in *United States of America v. Bernard L. Madoff*

Approved: *Mar* 08 MAG 2735 COPY
_____
MARC LITT
Assistant United States Attorney

Before: HONORABLE DOUGLAS F. EATON
          United States Magistrate Judge
          Southern District of New York

--x

UNITED STATES OF AMERICA   :   COMPLAINT

          - v. -   :   Violation of
                                                   15 U.S.C. §§ 78·j(b),
BERNARD L. MADOFF,   :   78ff; 17 C.F.R. §
                                                   240.10b-5
          Defendant.   :

                                            :   COUNTY OF OFFENSE:
                                                   NEW YORK
--x

SOUTHERN DISTRICT OF NEW YORK, ss.:

          THEODORE CACIOPPI, being duly sworn, deposes and says
that he is a Special Agent with the Federal Bureau of
Investigation, and charges as follows:

                          COUNT ONE
                       (Securities Fraud)

          1.   From at least in or about December 2008 through the
present, in the Southern District of New York and elsewhere,
BERNARD L. MADOFF, the defendant, unlawfully, wilfully and
knowingly, by the use of the means and instrumentalities of
interstate commerce and of the mails, directly and indirectly, in
connection with the purchase and sale of securities, would and
did use and employ manipulative and deceptive devices and
contrivances in violation of Title 17, Code of Federal
Regulations, Section 240.10b-5, by (a) employing devices,
schemes, and artifices to defraud; (b) making untrue statements
of material facts and omitting to state material facts necessary
in order to make the statements made, in the light of the
circumstances under which they were made, not misleading, and (c)
engaging in acts, practices, and courses of business which
operated and would operate as a fraud and deceit upon persons, to
wit, MADOFF deceived investors by operating a securities business
in which he traded and lost investor money, and then paid certain

Exhibit 8.2 Complaint filed by the United States government in *United States of America v. Bernard L. Madoff* (continued)

investors purported returns on investment with the principal received from other, different investors, which resulted in losses of approximately billions of dollars.

(Title 15, United States Code, Sections 78j(b) & 78ff; Title 17, Code of Federal Regulations, Section 240.10b-5; and Title 18, United States Code, Section 2.)

The bases for my knowledge and the foregoing charges are, in part, as follows:

2.   I have been a Special Agent with the Federal Bureau of Investigation ("FBI") for approximately six and one-half years, and I have been personally involved in the investigation of this matter. The information contained in this Complaint is based upon my personal knowledge, as well as information obtained from other sources, including: a) statements made or reported by various witnesses with knowledge of relevant facts; and b) my review of publicly available information relating to BERNARD L. MADOFF, the defendant. Because this Complaint is being submitted for the limited purpose of establishing probable cause, it does not include every fact that I have learned during the course of the investigation. Where the contents of documents and the actions, statements and conversations of others are reported herein, they are reported in substance and in part, except where otherwise indicated.

3.   I have reviewed the publicly available web site of a securities broker dealer named Bernard L. Madoff Securities LLC, from which I have learned the following: (a) BERNARD L. MADOFF, the defendant, is the founder of Bernard L. Madoff Investment Securities LLC; (b) Bernard L. Madoff Investment Securities LLC is a securities broker dealer with its principal office in New York, New York; (c) Bernard L. Madoff Investment Securities LLC "is a leading international market maker. The firm has been providing quality executions for broker-dealers, banks and financial institutions since its inception in 1960;" (d) "[w]ith more than $700 million in firm capital, Madoff currently ranks among the top 1% of US Securities firms; (e) BERNARD L. MADOFF, the defendant, is a former Chairman of the board of directors of the NASDAQ stock market; and (f) "Clients know that Bernard Madoff has a personal interest in maintaining an unblemished record of value, fair-dealing, and high ethical standards that has always been the firm's hallmark."

4.   I have interviewed two senior employees of Bernard L. Madoff Investment Securities LLC ("Senior Employee No. 1", and "Senior Employee No. 2", collectively the "Senior Employees").

(continued)

The Senior Employees informed me, in substance, of the following:

       a. The Senior Employees are employed by Bernard L. Madoff Investment Securities LLC, in a proprietary trading, and market making capacity. According to the Senior Employees, BERNARD L. MADOFF, the defendant, conducts certain investment advisory business for clients that is separate from the firm's proprietary trading and market making activities. According to the Senior Employees, MADOFF ran his investment adviser business from a separate floor in the New York offices of Bernard L. Madoff Investment Securities LLC. According to Senior Employee No. 1, MADOFF kept the financial statements for the firm under lock and key, and stated that MADOFF was "cryptic" about the firm's investment advisory business.

       b. In or about the first week of December, BERNARD L. MADOFF, the defendant, told Senior Employee No. 2 that there had been requests from clients for approximately $7 billion in redemptions, that he was struggling to obtain the liquidity necessary to meet those obligations, but that he thought that he would be able to do so. According to the Senior Employees, they had previously understood that the investment advisory business had assets under management on the order of between approximately $8-15 billion. According to a Form ADV filed by MADOFF on behalf of Bernard L. Madoff Investment Securities LLC with the SEC on or about January 7, 2008, MADOFF's investment advisory business served between 11 and 25 clients and had a total of approximately $17.1 billion in assets under management.

       c. On or about December 9, 2008, MADOFF informed Senior Employee No. 1 that he wanted to pay bonuses to employees of the firm in December, which was earlier than employee bonuses are usually paid. Accordingly to the Senior Employees, bonuses traditionally have been paid in February of each year. On or about December 10, 2008, the Senior Employees visited MADOFF at the offices of Bernard L. Madoff Investment Securities LLC to discuss the situation further, particularly because it MADOFF had appeared to the Senior Employees to have been under great stress in the prior weeks. At that time, MADOFF informed the Senior Employees that he had recently made profits through business operations, and that now was a good time to distribute it. When the Senior Employees challenged his explanation, MADOFF said that he did not want to talk to them at the office, and arranged a meeting at MADOFF's apartment in Manhattan. According to Senior Employee No. 2, MADOFF stated, in substance, that he "wasn't sure he would be able to hold it together" if they continued to discuss the issue at the office.

Exhibit 8.2 **Complaint filed by the United States government in *United States of America v. Bernard L. Madoff*** *(continued)*

     d. At MADOFF's Manhattan apartment, MADOFF informed the Senior Employees, in substance, that his investment advisory business was a fraud. MADOFF stated that he was "finished," that he had "absolutely nothing," that "it's all just one big lie," and that it was "basically, a giant Ponzi scheme." The Senior Employees understood MADOFF to be saying, in substance, that he had for years been paying returns to certain investors out of the principal received from other, different, investors. MADOFF stated that the business was insolvent, and that it had been for years. MADOFF also stated that he estimated the losses from this fraud to be at least approximately $50 billion. One of the Senior Employees has a personal account at Bernard L. Madoff Investment Securities LLC in which several million had been invested under the management of MADOFF.

     e. At MADOFF's Manhattan apartment, MADOFF further informed the Senior Employees that, in approximately one week, he planned to surrender to authorities, but before he did that, he had approximately $200-300 million left, and he planned to use that money to make payments to certain selected employees, family, and friends.

     f. At MADOFF's Manhattan apartment, MADOFF further informed the Senior Employees that he had also recently informed a third senior employee ("Senior Employee No. 3"), of the facts that MADOFF had just told the Senior Employees.

     5. On December 11, 2008, I spoke to BERNARD L. MADOFF, the defendant. After identifying myself, MADOFF invited me, and the FBI agent who accompanied me, into his apartment. He acknowledged knowing why we were there. After I stated, "we're here to find out if there's an innocent explanation." MADOFF stated, "There is no innocent explanation." MADOFF stated, in substance, that he had personally traded and lost money for institutional clients, and that it was all his fault. MADOFF further stated, in substance, that he "paid investors with money that wasn't there." MADOFF also said that he was "broke" and "insolvent" and that he had decided that "it could not go on," and that he expected to go to jail. MADOFF also stated that he had recently admitted what he had done to Senior Employee Nos. 1, 2, and 3.

(continued)

| **Exhibit 8.2** | **Complaint filed by the United States government in *United States of America v. Bernard L. Madoff*** (continued) |

WHEREFORE, deponent prays that BERNARD L. MADOFF, the defendant, be imprisoned, or bailed, as the case may be.

DEC 11 2008

THEODORE CACIOPPI
Special Agent
Federal Bureau of Investigation

Sworn to before me this
_____ day of December, 2008

HONORABLE DOUGLAS F. EATON
UNITED STATES MAGISTRATE JUDGE
SOUTHERN DISTRICT OF NEW YORK

Indictment The charge of having committed a crime (usually a felony), based on the judgment of a grand jury.

If the grand jury determines that there is sufficient evidence to hold the accused for trial, it issues an **indictment**. Note that the grand jury does not determine guilt. If an indictment is issued, the accused will be held for later trial.

Example Dominick is arrested and accused of the crime of first-degree murder. Usually, in this type of crime, Dominick will not be granted bail and remains in prison. Usually several months later, the government prosecutors will present to the Grand Jury evidence concerning Dominick's alleged crime. Dominick's lawyer will also introduce evidence claiming that Dominick did not commit the crime. After hearing this evidence, the Grand Jury issues an indictment. The indictment means that the Grand Jury found enough evidence to hold Dominick for trial for first-degree murder. The Grand Jury has made no decision whether Dominick is guilty, but has just decided there is enough evidence to hold him for a future trial for the crime of murder. In this case, Dominick will probably be denied bail and will remain in prison until the trial.

Information The charge of having committed a crime (usually a misdemeanor), based on the judgment of a judge (magistrate).

For lesser crimes (burglary, shoplifting and such), the accused will be brought before a **magistrate (judge)**. A magistrate who finds that there is enough evidence to hold the accused for trial will issue **information**. The case against the accused is dismissed if neither an indictment nor information is issued.

Excerpts of a federal grand jury indictment appear as Exhibit 8.3.

Arraignment

Arraignment A hearing during which the accused is brought before a court and is (1) informed of the charges against him or her and (2) asked to enter a plea.

If an indictment or information is issued, the accused is brought before a court for an **arraignment** proceeding during which the accused is (1) informed of the charges against him or her and (2) asked to enter a *plea*. The accused may plead *guilty*, *not guilty*, or *nolo contendere*.

Exhibit 8.3	Grand jury indictment of the Court of Common Pleas, County of Summit, Ohio

COPY

DANIEL M. HORRIGAN

'2008 APR -9 PM 1: 28

IN THE COURT OF COMMON PLEAS
COUNTY OF SUMMIT, OHIO

SUMMIT COUNTY
CLERK OF COURTS

INDICTMENT TYPE: BINDOVER   CASE NO. 2008-03-0968

INDICTMENT FOR: MURDER (1) 2903.02(B) SF; FELONIOUS ASSAULT (1) 2903.11(A)(1) F-2; ENDANGERING CHILDREN (1) 2919.22(B)(1) F-2; ENDANGERING CHILDREN (1) 2919.22(A) F-3

In the Common Pleas Court of Summit County, Ohio, of the term of MARCH in the year of our Lord, Two Thousand and Eight.

The Jurors of the Grand Jury of the State of Ohio, within and for the body of the County aforesaid, being duly impaneled and sworn and charged to inquire of and present all offenses whatever committed within the limits of said County, on their oaths, IN THE NAME AND BY THE AUTHORITY OF THE STATE OF OHIO,

COUNT ONE

DO FIND AND PRESENT That **CRAIG R. WILSON** on or about the 12th day of March, 2008, in the County of Summit and State of Ohio, aforesaid, did commit the crime of **MURDER** in that he did cause the death of C.W. (DOB: 1/1/2008) as a proximate result of **CRAIG R. WILSON** committing or attempting to commit Endangering Children and/or Felonious Assault, an offense of violence that is a felony of the first or second degree, in violation of Section 2903.02(B) of the Ohio Revised Code, A SPECIAL FELONY, contrary to the form of the statute in such case made and provided and against the peace and dignity of the State of Ohio.

COUNT TWO

And the Grand Jurors of the State of Ohio, within and for the body of the County of Summit aforesaid, on their oaths in the name and by the authority of the State of Ohio, DO FURTHER FIND AND PRESENT, that **CRAIG R. WILSON** on or about the 12th day of March, 2008, in the County of Summit aforesaid, did commit the crime of **FELONIOUS ASSAULT** in that he did knowingly cause serious physical harm to C.W. (DOB: 1/1/2008), in violation of Section 2903.11(A)(1) of the Ohio Revised Code, A FELONY OF THE SECOND DEGREE, contrary to the form of the statute in such case made and provided and against the peace and dignity of the State of Ohio.

(continued)

Exhibit 8.3   **Grand jury indictment of the Court of Common Pleas, County of Summit, Ohio** (continued)

COPY

Criminal Indictment
Case No. 2008-03-0968
Page Two of Three

COUNT THREE

And the Grand Jurors of the State of Ohio, within and for the body of the County of Summit aforesaid, on their oaths in the name and by the authority of the State of Ohio, DO FURTHER FIND AND PRESENT, that **CRAIG R. WILSON** on or about the 12th day of March, 2008, in the County of Summit aforesaid, did commit the crime of **ENDANGERING CHILDREN** in that he did recklessly abuse C.W., 2 months, a child under eighteen years of age (DOB: 1/1/2008), resulting in serious physical harm to said child, in violation of Section 2919.22(B)(1) of the Ohio Revised Code, A FELONY OF THE SECOND DEGREE, contrary to the form of the statute in such case made and provided and against the peace and dignity of the State of Ohio.

COUNT FOUR

And the Grand Jurors of the State of Ohio, within and for the body of the County of Summit aforesaid, on their oaths in the name and by the authority of the State of Ohio, DO FURTHER FIND AND PRESENT, that **CRAIG R. WILSON** on or about the 1st day of January, 2008 to the 12th day of March, 2008, in the County of Summit aforesaid, did commit the crime of **ENDANGERING CHILDREN** in that he did being a parent, guardian, custody, person having custody or control, or person in loco parentis of C.W., 2 months, a child under eighteen years of age (DOB: 1/1/2008), did recklessly create a substantial risk to the health or safety of the child by violating a duty of care, protection or support resulting in serious physical harm to said child, in violation of Section 2919.22(A) of the Ohio Revised Code, A FELONY OF THE THIRD DEGREE, contrary to the form of the statute in such case made and provided and against the peace and dignity of the State of Ohio.

SHERRI BEVAN WALSH, Prosecutor/pw

Prosecutor, County of Summit, by

Date: 4-8-08

A TRUE BILL

Grand Jury foreperson/Deputy Foreperson

COPY

Case No. 2008-03-0968
Page Three of Three

ORDER

TO: DREW ALEXANDER, Sheriff
       County of Summit, Ohio

CRAIG R. WILSON

THAT he has been indicted by the Grand Jury of the County of Summit and that the person named in the indictment is hereby ordered to personally appear for the purpose of arraignment at 8 a.m. on the **11th** day of **April, 2008** before the Honorable Magistrate John H. Shoemaker, Judge of the Court of Common Pleas in the County of Summit Courthouse at 209 South High Street, Akron, Ohio, and THAT FAILURE TO APPEAR WILL RESULT IN A WARRANT FOR ARREST, FORFEITURE OF BOND, IF ANY, OR ADDITIONAL CRIMINAL CHARGES FOR FAILURE TO APPEAR UNDER O.R.C. SECTION 2937.99.

I certify that this is a true copy of the original indictment on file in this office.

DANIEL HORRIGAN, Clerk
Court of Common Pleas

By_____
                    Deputy

A plea of *nolo contendere* means that the accused agrees to the imposition of a penalty but does not admit guilt. A *nolo contendere* plea cannot be used as evidence of liability against the accused at a subsequent civil trial. Corporate defendants often enter this plea. The government has the option of accepting a *nolo contendere* plea or requiring the defendant to plead guilty or not guilty. Depending on the nature of the crime, the accused may be released upon posting bail.

> **Example** The U.S. government sues a company for criminally violating federal pollution control laws. The company pleads *nolo contendere* and the government accepts the plea. The government and the company agree that the company must pay $100,000 in criminal fines but the company does not admit guilt.

Plea Bargaining

Plea bargain agreement An agreement in which the accused admits to a lesser crime than charged. In return, the government agrees to impose a lesser sentence than might have been obtained had the case gone to trial.

Sometimes the accused and the government enter into a **plea bargain agreement**. The government engages in plea bargaining to save costs, avoid the risks of a trial, and prevent further overcrowding of the prisons. This arrangement allows the accused to admit to a lesser crime than charged. In return, the government agrees to impose a lesser penalty or sentence than might have been obtained had the case gone to trial. In the federal system, more than 90 percent plead guilty rather than go to trial.

> **Example** Harold is arrested for the crime of felony burglary, which carries a typical penalty of three years in jail if he is found guilty. The government and Harold reach a plea bargain where he will plead guilty to misdemeanor burglary and agrees to a sentence of six months in jail and three years' probation.

Exhibit 8.4 compares the major features of criminal law and civil law.

Criminal Trial

Trier of fact The jury is the trier of fact.

The **criminal trial** and the civil action trial have many similarities. The functions of the judge and jury are the same. The jury acts as the **trier of fact.** In cases in which the defendant exercises the right to proceed without a jury, also known as a **bench trial**, or **waiver trial**, the judge acts as the trier of fact. The judge also acts as the arbiter of procedural rules covering the conduct of the trial, and the judge ultimately is the one who applies the law to findings of fact, and guilt or innocence of the charges and who determines the sentence, fine, or other permitted forfeiture in cases of guilt. In some cases, such as murder trials, the jury also decides the sentence.

Exhibit 8.4	Civil and criminal law compared	
Issue	**Civil Law**	**Criminal Law**
Party who brings the action	The plaintiff	The government
Trial by jury	Yes, except actions for equity	Yes
Burden of proof	Preponderance of the evidence	Beyond a reasonable doubt
Jury vote	Judgment for plaintiff requires specific jury vote (e.g., 9 of 12 jurors)	Conviction requires unanimous jury vote
Sanctions and penalties	Monetary damages and equitable remedies (e.g., injunction, specific performance)	Imprisonment, capital punishment, fine, probation

The order and presentation of evidence also are similar. The prosecution goes first and puts on its case, followed by the defense's presentation of its evidence. Motions for dismissal at the close of the prosecution's case also are similar to those in the civil action.

A significant difference is the concern in many cases to protect the record (the trial transcript). The defense counsel tends to be concerned especially with making appropriate objections on the record that can be used as the basis for an appeal. Prosecutors, too, are concerned that they not say anything on the record that the defendant can use as a basis for appeal in the event of a conviction.

Pretrial Discovery

A limited amount of **pretrial discovery** is permitted, with substantial restrictions to protect the identity of government informants and to prevent intimidation of witnesses. Defense attorneys often file motions to suppress evidence, which ask the court to exclude evidence from trial that the defendant believes the government obtained in violation of the defendant's constitutional rights, statute, or procedural rule. The government is under an obligation to provide **exculpatory evidence** to the defense attorney.

Under the Federal Rules of Criminal Procedure Rule 16, upon the defendant's request, the government must disclose and make available for inspection, copying, or photographing any relevant written or recorded statements made by defendant within the possession, custody, or control of the government, the existence of which is known, or where the exercise of due diligence may become known to the attorney for the government.

Determination of Guilt

At a criminal trial, unlike a civil-action trial, all jurors must agree *unanimously* before the accused is found guilty of the crime charged. If even one juror disagrees (i.e., has reasonable doubt) about the guilt of the accused, the accused is not guilty of the crime charged. If all of the jurors agree that the accused did not commit the crime, the accused is **innocent** of the crime charged.

After trial, the following rules apply:

- If the defendant is found guilty, he or she may appeal.
- If the defendant is found innocent, the government cannot appeal.
- If the jury cannot come to a unanimous decision about the defendant's guilt, the jury is considered a **hung jury**. The government may choose to retry the case before a new judge and jury.

Constitutional Safeguards

When our forefathers drafted the U.S. Constitution, they included provisions that protect persons from unreasonable government intrusion and provide safeguards for those accused of crimes. Although these safeguards originally applied only to federal cases, the Fourteenth Amendment's Due Process Clause made them applicable to state criminal law cases as well. The most important constitutional safeguards and privileges are discussed in the following paragraphs.

Fourth Amendment Protection Against Unreasonable Searches and Seizures

The **Fourth Amendment** to the U.S. Constitution protects persons and corporations from overzealous investigative activities by the government. It protects the rights of the people from **unreasonable search and seizure** by the government and permits people to be secure in their persons, houses, papers, and effects.

Web Exploration

Go to http://www.thelaborers .net/indictments/bellomo/ indictment_criminal_genovese_ family-2006-2-23.htm and read a grand jury indictment of the Genovese Organized Crime Family.

Hung jury A jury that does not come to a unanimous decision about the defendant's guilt. The government may choose to retry the case.

Unreasonable search and seizure Any search and seizure by the government that violates the Fourth Amendment.

Search Warrants

"Reasonable" search and seizure by the government is lawful. **Search warrants** based on probable cause are necessary in most cases. These warrants specifically state the place and scope of the authorized search. General searches beyond the specified area are forbidden.

> **Example** If the police receive a tip from a reasonable source that someone is engaged in criminal activity the police can present this information to a judge who will issue a search warrant if he or she finds probable cause. A copy of a search warrant appears as Exhibit 8.5.

Warrantless Searches

Warrantless searches generally are permitted only (1) incident to arrest, (2) where evidence is in "plain view," or (3) where evidence likely will be destroyed. Warrantless searches also are judged by the probable-cause standard.

> **Example** The police are notified that a person of a certain description has committed a crime in a specific location. The police arrive on the scene and nearby they find a suspect who meets the description. The police may conduct a warrantless search of the individual in order to protect the police from danger.

Search of Business Premises

Generally, the government does not have the right to search business premises without a search warrant on probable cause or pursuant to a warrantless search based on probable cause. However, businesses in certain hazardous and regulated industries are subject to warrantless searches if proper statutory procedures are met.

> **Examples** Sellers of firearms and liquor, coal mines, vehicle dismantling and automobile junkyards, and the like are subject to warrantless searches.

A business also may give consent to search the premises, including employee desks and computers, because of the lack of privacy in those items.

Exclusionary Rule

Exclusionary rule A rule that says evidence obtained from an unreasonable search and seizure can generally be prohibited from introduction at a trial or administrative proceeding against the person searched.

Evidence obtained from an unreasonable search and seizure is considered tainted evidence ("fruit of a poisonous tree"). Under the **exclusionary rule**, such evidence can be prohibited from introduction at a trial or administrative proceeding against the person searched. This evidence, however, is freely admissible against other persons. The U.S. Supreme Court created a *good-faith exception* to the exclusionary rule. This exception allows evidence otherwise obtained illegally to be introduced as evidence against the accused if the police officers who conducted the unreasonable search reasonably believed they were acting pursuant to a lawful search warrant.

Fifth Amendment Privilege Against Self-Incrimination

Self-incrimination The Fifth Amendment states that no person shall be compelled in any criminal case to be a witness against him- or herself.

The **Fifth Amendment** to the U.S. Constitution provides that no person "shall be compelled in any criminal case to be a witness against himself." Thus, a person cannot be compelled to give testimony against himself or herself. A person who asserts this right is described as having "taken the Fifth." This protection applies to federal cases and is extended to state and local criminal cases through the Due Process Clause of the Fourteenth Amendment.

The privilege against **self-incrimination** applies only to natural persons who are accused of crimes. Therefore, artificial persons (such as corporations and partnerships)

Exhibit 8.5   **Search warrant of the federal U.S. district court**

AO 93 (Rev. 01/09) Search and Seizure Warrant

UNITED STATES DISTRICT COURT
for the

In the Matter of the Search of   )
(Briefly describe the property to be searched   )
or identify the person by name and address)   )   Case No.
)
)
)

SEARCH AND SEIZURE WARRANT

To: Any authorized law enforcement officer

An application by a federal law enforcement officer or an attorney for the government requests the search of the following person or property located in the _____ District of _____
(identify the person or describe the property to be searched and give its location):

The person or property to be searched, described above, is believed to conceal *(identify the person or describe the property to be seized)*:

I find that the affidavit(s), or any recorded testimony, establish probable cause to search and seize the person or property.

YOU ARE COMMANDED to execute this warrant on or before _____
                                                                (not to exceed 10 days)

❏ in the daytime 6:00 a.m. to 10 p.m.   ❏ at any time in the day or night as I find reasonable cause has been established.

Unless delayed notice is authorized below, you must give a copy of the warrant and a receipt for the property taken to the person from whom, or from whose premises, the property was taken, or leave the copy and receipt at the place where the property was taken.

The officer executing this warrant, or an officer present during the execution of the warrant, must prepare an inventory as required by law and promptly return this warrant and inventory to United States Magistrate Judge

_____ .
            (name)

❏ I find that immediate notification may have an adverse result listed in 18 U.S.C. § 2705 (except for delay of trial), and authorize the officer executing this warrant to delay notice to the person who, or whose property, will be searched or seized *(check the appropriate box)* ❏ for _____ days *(not to exceed 30).*
                                        ❏ until, the facts justifying, the later specific date of _____ .

Date and time issued: _____   _____
                                                                Judge's signature

City and state: _____   _____
                                                                Printed name and title

(continued)

Exhibit 8.5 **Search warrant of the federal U.S. district court** *(continued)*

AO 93 (Rev. 01/09) Search and Seizure Warrant (Page 2)

Return		
Case No.:	Date and time warrant executed:	Copy of warrant and inventory left with:
Inventory made in the presence of :		
Inventory of the property taken and name of any person(s) seized:		

Certification
I declare under penalty of perjury that this inventory is correct and was returned along with the original warrant to the designated judge.

Date: _____

_____
Executing officer's signature

_____
Printed name and title

cannot raise this protection against incriminating testimony. Thus, business records of corporations and partnerships are not protected from disclosure, even if they incriminate individuals who work for the business. But certain "private papers" of businesspersons (such as personal diaries) are protected from disclosure.

It is improper for a jury to infer guilt from the defendant's exercise of his or her constitutional right to remain silent.

Nontestimonial evidence may be required without violating the Fifth Amendment.

Examples Fingerprints, body fluids, and the like.

Miranda Rights

Most people have not read and memorized the provisions of the U.S. Constitution. The U.S. Supreme Court recognized this fact when it decided the landmark case *Miranda v. Arizona* in 1966 [384 U.S. 436, 86 S.Ct. 1602, 16 L.Ed.2d 694, 1966 U.S. Lexis 2817]. In that case, the Supreme Court held that the Fifth Amendment privilege against self-incrimination is not useful unless a criminal suspect has knowledge of this right. Therefore, the Supreme Court required that the following warning—colloquially called the *Miranda* **rights**—be read to a criminal suspect before he or she is interrogated by the police or other government officials:

- You have the right to remain silent.
- Anything you say can and will be used against you.
- You have the right to consult a lawyer and to have a lawyer present with you during interrogation.
- If you cannot afford a lawyer, a lawyer will be appointed free of charge to represent you.

Many police departments read a more detailed version of the *Miranda* rights, which is designed to cover all issues that a detainee might encounter while in police custody. A detainee may be asked to sign a statement acknowledging that the *Miranda* rights have been read to him or her. A copy of the *Miranda* rights appears as Exhibit 8.6.

Miranda **rights** Rights that a suspect must be informed of before being interrogated, so that the suspect will not unwittingly give up his or her Fifth Amendment right.

Exhibit 8.6 *Miranda* **rights form**

MIRANDA RIGHTS

- You have the right to remain silent and refuse to answer questions. Do you understand?

- Anything you do say may be used against you in a court of law. Do you understand?

- You have the right to consult an attorney before speaking to the police and to have an attorney present during questioning now or in the future. Do you understand?

- If you cannot afford an attorney, one will be appointed for you before any questioning if you wish. Do you understand?

- If you decide to answer questions now without an attorney present you will still have the right to stop answering at any time until you talk to an attorney. Do you understand?

- Knowing and understanding your rights as I have explained them to you, are you willing to answer my questions without an attorney present?

Excluded Admissions

Any statements or confessions obtained from a suspect prior to being read his or her *Miranda* rights can be excluded from evidence at trial. In 2000, the U.S. Supreme Court upheld *Miranda* in *Dickerson v. United States* [530 U.S. 428, 120 S.Ct. 2326, 147 L.Ed.2d 405, 2000 U.S. Lexis 4305]. The Supreme Court stated, "We do not think there is justification for overruling *Miranda*. *Miranda* has become embedded in routine police practice to the point where the warnings have become part of our national culture."

Example Margaret is arrested by the police for suspicion of using and distributing illegal narcotics. The police start asking her questions about these issues before reading Margaret her *Miranda* rights. During this questioning Margaret admits to the offenses. Margaret's statements are inadmissible at court because she had not been read her *Miranda* rights.

The Ethical Perspective discusses a paralegal's ethical duty to conduct careful research in a criminal case.

ETHICAL PERSPECTIVE

Duty to Conduct Careful Research in a Criminal Case

Ms. Smith is a newly hired paralegal who works for attorney Ms. Gutierrez. Ms. Gutierrez represents Mr. Granville, a client who has been charged by the state with dealing in illegal narcotics. Ms. Gutierrez requests that Ms. Smith sit in on her discussions with Mr. Granville when Ms. Gutierrez asks Mr. Granville questions concerning the case.

At the meeting, Mr. Granville discloses that yes he had been dealing and selling illegal narcotics. He explains that the police arrested him as he left his home one evening. The police searched Mr. Granville's person, and found illegal narcotics on his body. The police then questioned Mr. Granville and he admitted that the drugs were his and that he was a distributor of illegal narcotics. Pursuant to this admission, the police also searched Mr. Granville's automobile, where they found illegal narcotics. In addition, the police obtained a search warrant and searched Mr. Granville's home where they also discovered more illegal narcotics.

If all of this evidence is introduced against Mr. Granville at trial, he is most likely to be convicted of the crime of selling narcotics. Ms. Gutierrez gives Ms. Smith the assignment to conduct electronic legal research and find recent case law that affects the possible exclusion of evidence at Mr. Granville's criminal trial. Ms. Gutierrez also informs Ms. Smith that she will be using this research when she conducts settlement talks with the government regarding Mr. Granville's case.

Ms. Smith, who is not that sympathetic to Mr. Granville's situation anyhow, conducts minimal research and reports back to Ms. Gutierrez that she has found no relevant case law that would allow for the suppression of the evidence against Mr. Granville. However, if Ms. Smith had conducted a more thorough research she would have discovered an important case where the court had made a decision that would have been favorable to suppressing much of the evidence against Mr. Granville because of failure of the police to read him the *Miranda* rights before obtaining his confession, and that the further evidence discovered against Mr. Granville would also be inadmissible because of the excludable admission that led to the evidence being discovered.

Here, Ms. Smith has been derelict and negligent in the conduct of her duties as a paralegal. She failed to carry out an important assignment and therefore has jeopardized a case against a client of the lawyer for whom she works. Because of Ms. Smith's negligence, her supervising attorney Ms. Gutierrez may not have all of the relevant information to properly prepare for her settlement conference with the government or to prepare the trial defense for her client.

Immunity from Prosecution

On occasion, the government wants to obtain information from a suspect who has asserted his or her Fifth Amendment privilege against self-incrimination. The government can try to achieve this by offering the suspect **immunity from prosecution**, in which the government agrees not to use any evidence given by a person who has been granted immunity against that person. Once immunity is granted, the suspect loses the right to assert his or her Fifth Amendment privilege.

Grants of immunity often are given when the government wants the suspect to give information that will lead to the prosecution of other, more important criminal suspects. Partial grants of immunity also are available. For example, a suspect may be granted immunity from prosecution for a serious crime but not a lesser crime, in exchange for information. Some persons who are granted immunity are placed in witness protection programs in which they are given a new identity, relocated, and found a job.

Attorney–Client Privilege

To obtain a proper defense, the accused person must be able to tell his or her attorney facts about the case without fear that the attorney will be called as a witness against the accused. The **attorney–client privilege** is protected by the Fifth Amendment. Either the client or the attorney can raise this privilege. For the privilege to apply, the information must be told to the attorney in his or her capacity as an attorney, and not as a friend or neighbor or other such relationship.

> **Example** Cedric is accused of murder. He employs Hillary, a renowned criminal attorney, to represent him. During the course of their discussions Cedric confesses to the murder. Hillary cannot be a witness against Cedric at his criminal trial. Cedric is permitted to tell his lawyer the truth so that the lawyer can prepare the best defense she can for him.

Attorney–client privilege A rule that says a client can tell his or her lawyer anything about the case without fear that the attorney will be called as a witness against the client.

Other Privileges

The following privileges have also been recognized under the Fifth Amendment where the accused may keep the following individuals from being a witness against him or her. The reasons are stated in parentheses.

- **Psychiatrist/psychologist–patient privilege** (so that the accused may tell the truth in order to seek help for his or her condition)
- **Priest/rabbi/minister/imam–penitent privilege** (so that the accused may tell the truth in order to repent, to obtain help, and seek forgiveness for his or her deed)
- **Spouse–spouse privilege** (so that the family will remain together)
- **Parent–child privilege** (so that the family will remain together)

A spouse or child who is injured by a spouse or parent (e.g., domestic abuse) may testify against the accused. In addition, if the accused discloses that he or she is planning to commit a crime in the future (e.g., murder), then the accused's lawyer, psychiatrist, or psychologist, and priest, rabbi, minister, or imam is required to report this to the police or other relevant authorities.

The U.S. Supreme Court has held that there is no accountant–client privilege under federal law. Thus, an accountant could be called as a witness in cases involving federal securities laws, federal mail or wire fraud, or other federal crimes. Nevertheless, approximately 20 states have enacted special statutes that create an **accountant–client privilege**. An accountant cannot be called as a witness against a client in a court action in a state where these statutes are in effect. Federal courts do not recognize these laws, however.

Fifth Amendment Protection Against Double Jeopardy

Double Jeopardy Clause A clause of the Fifth Amendment that protects persons from being tried twice for the same crime.

The **Double Jeopardy Clause** of the Fifth Amendment protects persons from being tried twice for the same crime. For example, if the state tries a suspect for the crime of murder and the suspect is found innocent, the state cannot bring another trial against the accused for the same crime. But if the same criminal act involves several different crimes, the accused may be tried for each of the crimes without violating the Double Jeopardy Clause. Suppose the accused kills two people during a robbery. The accused may be tried for two murders and for the robbery.

If the same act violates the laws of two or more jurisdictions, each jurisdiction may try the accused. For instance, if an accused person kidnaps a person in one state and brings the victim across a state border into another state, the act violates the laws of two states and the federal government. Thus, three jurisdictions can prosecute the accused without violating the Double Jeopardy Clause.

If an accused is tried once and the jury reaches a hung jury—that is, the verdict is not unanimous for either guilty or not guilty—then the government can retry the case against the accused without violating the Double Jeopardy Clause.

Example Suppose the government tries a defendant for the crime of murder and the jury reaches a 10 to 2 verdict, that is, 10 jurors vote for guilty and two jurors vote for not guilty. This is a hung jury. Since no decision has been reached, the government may, if it wants, retry the case against the accused. This does not violate the Double Jeopardy Clause.

Sixth Amendment Right to a Public Trial

The **Sixth Amendment** guarantees that criminal defendants have these rights:

1. The right to be tried by an impartial jury of the state or district in which the alleged crime was committed.
2. The right to confront (cross-examine) the witnesses against the accused.
3. The right to have the assistance of a lawyer.
4. The right to have a speedy trial.

The federal **Speedy Trial Act** requires that a criminal defendant be brought to trial within 70 days after indictment [18 U.S.C. Section 3161(c)(1)]. States have similar acts that require speedy trials for criminal defendants. The court may grant continuances to serve the "ends of justice."

Eighth Amendment Protection Against Cruel and Unusual Punishment

The **Eighth Amendment** protects criminal defendants from **cruel and unusual punishment**.

Example It prohibits the torture of criminals. This clause, however, does not prohibit capital punishment, but does limit the form of capital punishment that is allowed. The U.S. Supreme Court has held that injection by lethal dosage of drugs generally is permitted as a means of capital punishment.

Administrative Law and Agencies

Administrative law Substantive and procedural law that governs the operation of administrative agencies.

Federal and state governments enact laws that regulate business. The legislative and executive branches of government have created numerous administrative agencies to assist in implementing and enforcing these laws. The operation of these administrative agencies is governed by a body of **administrative law**. Because of their importance, administrative agencies are informally referred to as the "fourth branch of government."

The following feature discusses the career opportunities for paralegal professionals in administrative law.

CAREER OPPORTUNITIES FOR PARALEGALS IN ADMINISTRATIVE LAW

Lawyers increasingly employ paralegals in areas of law that involve practice before administrative agencies. Administrative law has become extremely important for businesses and individuals alike. Administrative agencies govern many aspects of general business operations, specific industries, and our personal lives as well.

The number of administrative agencies in this country is staggering. The federal government alone has dozens of administrative agencies. These range from agencies whose powers apply to the country and economy in general, to agencies that regulate specific industries. Some of the major federal administrative agencies are:

- Environmental Protection Agency (EPA): regulates air, water, hazardous waste, and other types of pollution.
- Equal Employment Opportunity Commission (EEOC): enforces many antidiscrimination laws that affect businesses, employees, disabled persons, and others.
- Federal Trade Commission (FTC): enforces many consumer protection laws.
- Food and Drug Administration (FDA): regulates the safety of foods, drugs, cosmetics, and medicinal devices.
- Federal Communications Commission (FCC): regulates radio, television, cable, and other broadcast media.
- National Labor Relations Board (NLRB): regulates labor union formation, elections, bargaining with employers, and other labor issues.
- Securities Exchange Commission (SEC): regulates the issuance, sale, and purchase of securities, including stocks and bonds.
- Department of Homeland Security (DHS): responsible for coordinating certain federal agencies in protecting the country against terrorism and other threats.

In addition to federal administrative agencies, there are thousands of state and local administrative agencies. These include state administrative agencies that regulate corporations, agencies that license and regulate financial institutions, state environmental protection agencies, and other state administrative agencies. At the local level, cities and municipalities have administrative agencies that regulate construction, set building codes, establish zoning regulations, issue water permits, and so forth.

Paralegals often work for lawyers who specialize in making appearances before specific federal, state, and local administrative agencies. For example, lawyers must prepare applications for submission to the Federal Communications Commission (FCC) to obtain a license for a client to operate a radio, television, or cable company. Lawyers must prepare applications for submission to the Federal Food and Drug Administration (FDA) to obtain approval for a client to market a new drug. Lawyers must prepare applications to be submitted to a state banking commission to obtain a license for a client to operate a new commercial bank.

The federal government has enacted the Administrative Procedure Act (APA), which establishes rules for legal practice before federal administrative agencies. The state has similar administrative procedures acts at the state level. In addition, each administrative agency has its own rules and regulations for submitting applications and appearing at hearings before the administrative agency.

Paralegals who work for lawyers specializing in certain administrative law practices must become familiar with that agency's rules and procedures. Paralegals often are called upon to assist in drafting documents that will be submitted to administrative agencies and preparing cases that will be heard and decided by these agencies. Thus, paralegals often become experts in areas of administrative law and, therefore, can be indispensable to lawyers who practice before administrative agencies.

Administrative Agencies

Administrative agencies are created by federal, state, and local governments. They range from large, complex federal agencies, such as the federal Department of Health and Human Services, to city zoning boards. At the federal government level, the legislative branch (Congress) and the executive branch (the president) have created more than 100 administrative agencies. Thousands of other administrative agencies have been created by state and local governments.

When Congress enacts a statute, it often creates an administrative agency to administer and enforce the statute (see Exhibit 8.7). When Congress enacts some statutes, it authorizes an existing administrative agency to administer and enforce the new statute.

Example When Congress enacted the Securities Act of 1933 and the Securities Exchange Act of 1934, it created the Securities and Exchange Commission (SEC), a federal administrative agency, to administer and enforce those statutes.

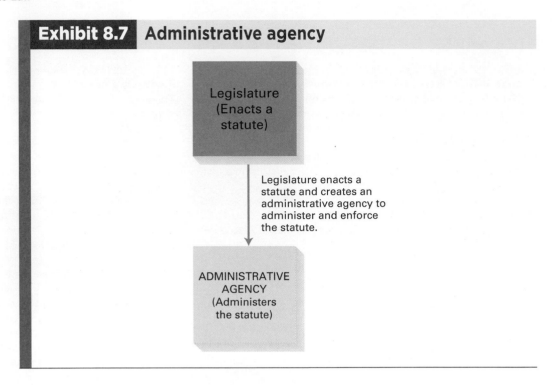

Exhibit 8.7 Administrative agency

Legislature (Enacts a statute)

Legislature enacts a statute and creates an administrative agency to administer and enforce the statute.

ADMINISTRATIVE AGENCY (Administers the statute)

Administrative agencies are established with the overall goal of creating a body of professionals who are experts in a specific field. These experts have delegated authority to regulate an individual industry or a specific area of commerce.

Federal Administrative Agencies

Federal administrative agencies Agencies established by legislative and executive branches of federal and state governments.

Federal administrative agencies can be created by either the *legislative* or the *executive* branch of the federal government.

Congress has established many federal administrative agencies. These agencies have broad regulatory powers over key areas of the national economy.

> **Examples** The Securities and Exchange Commission (SEC), which regulates the issuance of and trading in securities, and the Commodity Futures Trading Commission (CFTC), which regulates trading in commodities futures contracts.

Other federal administrative agencies are created by the president of the United States to operate the federal government.

> **Examples** The U.S. Department of Justice and the Commerce Department.

State Administrative Agencies

State administrative agencies Administrative agencies that states create to enforce and interpret state law.

All states have created administrative agencies to enforce and interpret state law. **State administrative agencies** have a profound effect on business. State administrative agencies are empowered to enforce state statutes. They have the power to adopt rules and regulations to interpret the statutes they are empowered to administer.

> **Example** Most states have a Corporations Department to enforce state corporation law and regulate the issuance of securities, a Banking Department to license and regulate the operation of banks, Fish and Game Departments to regulate fishing and hunting within the state's boundaries, Worker's Compensation Boards to decide workers' compensation claims for injuries that occur on the job, Environment Protection Departments to regulate the land, waterways and other environmental issues, and such.

Local governments and municipalities create administrative agencies to administer local law.

Examples Counties have numerous administrative boards to regulate county activities. Cities and towns have school boards, zoning commissions, and other administrative bodies to regulate city and town matters.

Government Regulation

Many administrative agencies, and the laws they enforce, regulate businesses and industries collectively. This is called **general government regulation**. That is, most of the industries and businesses in the United States are subject to these laws.

> **General government regulation** Government regulation that applies to many industries collectively.

Example The federal National Labor Relations Board (NLRB) is empowered to regulate the formation and operation of labor unions in most industries and businesses in the United States.

Some administrative agencies, and the laws they enforce, are created to regulate specific industries. That is, an industry is subject to administrative laws that are specifically adopted to regulate that industry. This is called **specific government regulation** of business. Administrative agencies, which are industry specific, are created to administer these specific laws.

> **Specific government regulation** Government regulation that applies to individual industries.

Example The Federal Communications Commission (FCC) issues licenses and regulates the operation of television and radio stations.

Administrative Procedure

Administrative law is a combination of *substantive* and *procedural law*. **Substantive law** is the law that has been created that the administrative agency enforces—the federal statute enacted by Congress or the state statute enacted by a state legislature. **Procedural law** establishes the procedures that must be followed by an administrative agency while enforcing substantive administrative laws.

Example The federal Environmental Protection Agency (EPA) has been created by Congress to enforce federal environmental laws that protect the environment. This is an example of substantive law—the laws to protect the environment. In enforcing these laws, the EPA must follow certain established procedural rules (e.g., notice, hearing). These are examples of procedural law.

Administrative Procedure Act (APA)

In 1946, Congress enacted the **Administrative Procedure Act (APA)** [5 U.S.C. Sections 551–706]. This act is very important because it establishes procedures that federal administrative agencies must follow in conducting their affairs. The APA establishes notice requirements of actions the federal agency plans on taking. It requires hearings to be held in most cases and certain procedural safeguards and protocol to be followed at these proceedings.

> **Administrative Procedure Act (APA)** An act that establishes certain administrative procedures that federal administrative agencies must follow in conducting their affairs.

The APA establishes how rules and regulations can be adopted by federal administrative agencies. This includes notice of proposed rule making, granting a time period for receiving comments from the public regarding proposed rule making, and holding hearings to take evidence. The APA provides a procedure for receiving evidence and hearing requests for the granting of federal licenses (e.g., to operate a national bank). The APA also establishes notice and hearing requirements and rules for conducting agency adjudicative actions, such as actions to take away certain parties' licenses (e.g., a securities broker's licenses).

Most states have enacted administrative procedural acts that govern state administrative procedures.

Administrative Law Judge

Administrative law judges (ALJs) preside over administrative proceedings. They decide questions of law and fact concerning a case. There is no jury. An ALJ is an employee of the administrative agency. Both the administrative agency and the respondent may be represented by counsel. Witnesses may be examined and cross-examined, evidence may be introduced, objections may be made, and such.

An ALJ's decision is issued in the form of an **order**. The order must state the reasons for the ALJ's decision. The order becomes final if it is not appealed. An appeal consists of a review by the agency. Further appeal can be made to the appropriate federal court (in federal agency actions) or state court (in state agency actions).

Exhibit 8.8 is an application form for an administrative hearing regarding a Social Security matter.

Powers of Administrative Agencies

When an administrative agency is created, it is delegated certain powers. The agency has only the legislative, judicial, and executive powers that are delegated to it. This is called the **delegation doctrine**. The courts have upheld this combined power of administrative agencies as being constitutional. If an administrative agency acts outside the scope of its delegated powers, it is an unconstitutional act.

The powers of administrative agencies are discussed in the following paragraphs.

Rule Making

Many federal statutes expressly authorize an administrative agency to issue **substantive rules**. A substantive regulation is much like a statute: It has the force of law and must be adhered to by covered persons and businesses. Violators may be held civilly or criminally liable, depending on the rule. The agency must give public notice of a proposed rule and consider public comments before adopting a substantive rule.

> **Example** The Securities and Exchange Commission (SEC) is authorized to prohibit fraud in the purchase and sale of securities. The SEC therefore has the power to adopt rules that define what fraudulent conduct is prohibited by the federal securities laws.

Administrative agencies can issue an **interpretive rule** that interprets existing statutory language. Such rules do not establish new laws. Administrative agencies may also issue a **statement of policy** that announces a proposed course of action that an agency intends to follow in the future. Interpretive rules and statements of policy do not have the force of law and public notice and participation are not required.

Licensing Power

Statutes often require the issuance of a government **license** before a person can enter certain types of industries (e.g., the operation of banks, television and radio stations, and commercial airlines) or professions (e.g., doctors, lawyers, dentists, certified public accountants, and contractors). The administrative agency that regulates the specific area involved is granted the power to determine whether to grant a license to an applicant.

Applicants must usually submit detailed applications to the appropriate administrative agency. In addition, the agency usually accepts written comments from interested parties and holds hearings on the matter. Courts generally defer to the expertise of administrative agencies in licensing matters.

> **Example** A group of persons wants to start a new national bank. To start a new national bank, the applicants must obtain approval from the Office of the

Exhibit 8.8 Application for social security administrative hearing

SOCIAL SECURITY ADMINISTRATION
OFFICE OF HEARINGS AND APPEALS

Form Approved
OMB No. 0960-0269

REQUEST FOR HEARING BY ADMINISTRATIVE LAW JUDGE
[Take or mail original and all copies to your local Social Security Office]

PRIVACY ACT NOTICE
ON REVERSE SIDE OF FORM.

1. CLAIMANT	2. WAGE EARNER, IF DIFFERENT	3. SOC. SEC. CLAIM NUMBER	4. SPOUSE's CLAIM NUMBER

5. I REQUEST A HEARING BEFORE AN ADMINISTRATIVE LAW JUDGE. I disagree with the determination made on my claim because:

An Administrative Law Judge of the Office of Hearings and Appeals will be appointed to conduct the hearing or other proceedings in your case. You will receive notice of the time and place of a hearing at least 20 days before the date set for a hearing.

6. If you have additional evidence to submit check the following block and complete the statement: ☐

I have additional evidence to submit from
(name and address of source): _____

_____

(Please submit it to the Social Security Office within 10 days. Attach an additional sheet if you need more space.)

7. Check one of the blocks:

☐ I wish to appear at a hearing.

☐ I do not wish to appear and I request that a decision be made based on the evidence in my case.
(Complete Waiver Form HA-4608)

You have a right to be represented at the hearing. If you are not represented but would like to be, your Social Security Office will give you a list of legal referral and service organizations. (If you are represented and have not done so previously, complete and submit form SSA-1696 (Appointment of Representative).)

[You should complete No. 8 and your representative (if any) should complete No. 9. If you are represented and your representative is not available to complete this form, you should also print his or her name, address, etc. in No. 9.]

8.	9.
(CLAIMANT'S SIGNATURE)	(REPRESENTATIVE'S SIGNATURE/NAME)
ADDRESS	(ADDRESS) ☐ ATTORNEY; ☐ NON ATTORNEY;
CITY STATE ZIP CODE	CITY STATE ZIP CODE
DATE AREA CODE AND TELEPHONE NUMBER	DATE AREA CODE AND TELEPHONE NUMBER

TO BE COMPLETED BY SOCIAL SECURITY ADMINISTRATION-ACKNOWLEDGMENT OF REQUEST FOR HEARING

10.
Request for Hearing RECEIVED for the Social Security Administration on _____ by: _____

(TITLE) ADDRESS

11. Was the request for hearing received within 65 days of the reconsidered determination?
☐ YES ☐ NO

If no is checked, attach claimant's explanation for delay; and attach copy of appointment notice, letter, or other pertinent material or information in the Social Security Office.

12. Claimant not represented -
☐ list of legal referral and service organizations provided

13. Interpreter needed -
☐ enter language (including sign language): _____

14.
Check one: ☐ Initial Entitlement Case
☐ Disability Cessation Case
☐ Other Postentitlement Case

15.
Check claim type(s):

☐ RSI only --(RSI)
☐ Title II Disability-worker or child----------------------------------(DIWC)
☐ Title II Disability-widow(er) only------------------------------------(DIWW)

16.
HO COPY SENT TO: _____ HO on _____
☐ CF Attached: ☐ Title II; ☐ Title XVI; or
☐ Title II CF held in FO to establish CAPS ORBIT; or
☐ CF requested ☐ Title II; ☐ Title XVI
(Copy of teletype or phone report attached)

☐ SSI Aged only---(SSIA)
☐ SSI Blind only---(SSIB)
☐ SSI Disability only --(SSID)
☐ SSI Aged/Title II ---(SSAC)

17.
CF COPY SENT TO: _____ HO on _____
☐ CF Attached: ☐ Title II; ☐ Title XVI
☐ Other Attached: _____

☐ SSI Blind/Title II --(SSBC)
☐ SSI Disability/Title II --(SSDC)
☐ HI Entitlement --(HIE)
☐ Other-Specify: ( )

FORM HA-501-U5 (5-1996) EF (7-2000)
Issue old stock

CLAIMS FOLDER

Comptroller of Currency (OCC), a federal administrative agency that charters, supervises, and regulates national banks. The group will hire lawyers, economists, accountants, and other professionals needed to prepare the appropriate application. After considering the application, the OCC will either approve or reject the application.

Paralegals *in* Practice

Since 1996, Melvin E. Irvin has worked as a non-attorney Social Security Disability Appeals Representative in the San Jose, California area. He legally represents clients before the Social Security Administration (SSA) in appeals for Social Security disability benefits. In addition to being a Marine Corps veteran, Mel is a graduate from Santa Clara University Law School Institute for Paralegal Studies. He also earned the Certified Paralegal (C.P.) designation from the National Association of Legal Assistants.

As President of my own corporation, Melvin E. Irvin Disability Representative, Inc., I represent about 55–60 clients at any given time. The most important skills needed in my position are above-average communication skills and a good working knowledge of Social Security Law. There are no specific educational requirements to become a non-attorney

Disability Representative except that you cannot be a disbarred attorney, or disallowed by another government administration from practicing. Naturally, a college degree and a paralegal certificate are very helpful.

Over the past 20 years, successful representation has become more difficult as the SSA has significantly reduced its claim allowance rates. SSA representation fees are paid only on a contingency basis, whether you are an attorney or non-attorney. Since the SSA is backlogged on disability cases, currently more than 700,000 nationally, it may take two or more years before a new representative sees the first paycheck. This is due to the length of time it takes for a case to be resolved. Even so, my work is very rewarding because it allows me to help people who really need assistance.

I find that many people in the U.S. today still believe that paralegals can perform work directly for the public. According to Section 6450 of the California Business and Professions Code, those who call themselves paralegals must be attorney supervised, with few exceptions. One exception is legally representing the public in administrative law settings such as the SSA. As the current President of the California Alliance of Paralegal Associations, I help educate others about the paralegal profession. Part of my role is to encourage local paralegal associations to appoint Public Information Officers who can respond to questions from the legal community, the public, and the media.

Judicial Authority

Many administrative agencies have the judicial authority to adjudicate cases through an administrative proceeding. Such a proceeding is initiated when an agency serves a complaint on a party the agency believes has violated a statute or an administrative rule or order.

> **Example** The Occupational Safety and Health Administration (OSHA) is a federal administrative agency empowered to enforce worker safety rules. OSHA can bring an administrative proceeding against an employer for violating a federal worker safety rule. OSHA can make a decision that the employer violated the rule and order the violator to pay a monetary fine.

Procedural due process requires the respondent to be given (1) proper and timely notice of the allegations or charges against him or her and (2) an opportunity to present evidence on the matter.

Executive Power

Administrative agencies are usually granted **executive powers**, such as the power to investigate and prosecute possible violations of statutes, administrative rules, and administrative orders.

> **Example** The Antitrust Division of the United States Department of Justice suspects that three companies in the same line of commerce are engaged in illegal price fixing. The Department of Justice has the authority to investigate whether a criminal violation of the federal Sherman Antitrust Act has occurred. The Department of Justice can prosecute suspected criminal violators of criminal antitrust laws.

Exhibit 8.9 | Appeal of a federal administrative agency rule, order, or decision

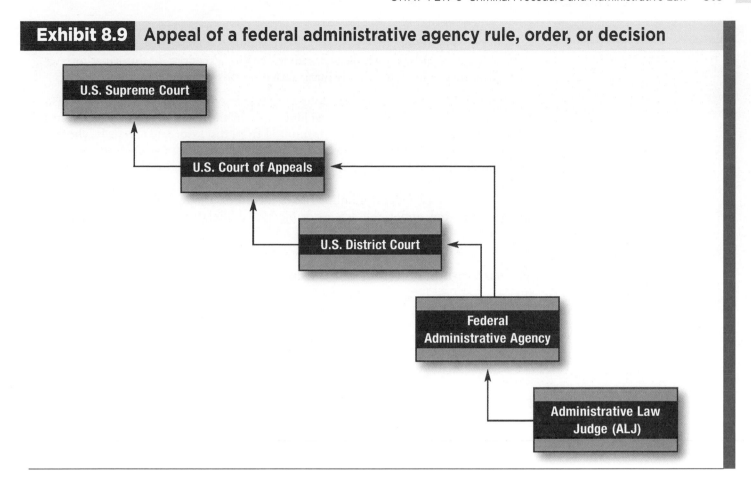

Judicial Review of Administrative Agency Actions

Many federal statutes expressly provide for judicial review of administrative agency actions. Where an enabling statute does not provide for review, the Administrative Procedure Act (APA) authorizes judicial review of federal administrative agency actions. The party appealing the decision of an administrative agency is called the **petitioner**.

Decisions of federal administrative agencies are appealed to the appropriate federal court. Decisions of state administrative agencies may be appealed to the proper state court. The federal appeal process is illustrated in Exhibit 8.9.

Disclosure of Administrative Agency Actions

Public concern over possible secrecy of administrative agency actions led Congress to enact several statutes that promote public disclosure of federal administrative agency actions and protect parties from overly obtrusive agency actions. These statutes are discussed in the paragraphs that follow.

Freedom of Information Act

The **Freedom of Information Act** (FOIA) was enacted to give the public access to most documents in the possession of federal administrative agencies. The act requires federal administrative agencies to publish agency procedures, rules, regulations, interpretations, and other such information in the *Federal Register*. The act also requires agencies to publish quarterly indexes of certain documents. In addition, the act specifies time limits for agencies to respond to requests for information, sets limits on copying charges, and provides for disciplinary action against agency employees who refuse to honor proper requests for information.

Freedom of Information Act
A law that was enacted to give the public access to most documents in the possession of federal administrative agencies.

Web Exploration

Go to http://www.rcfp.org/foiact/ which discusses the Freedom of Information Act. Go to "A brief overview of how the act works." Read it.

Example If a person suspects that he or she, or someone else, was subject to the Federal Bureau of Investigation (FBI) inquiry during the anti-communist McCarthy hearings, that person can submit a Freedom of Information Act request to obtain copies of any information on this subject from the FBI.

For purposes of privacy, the following documents are exempt from disclosure: (1) documents classified by the president to be in the interests of national security; (2) documents that are statutorily prohibited from disclosure; (3) records whose disclosure would interfere with law enforcement proceedings; (4) medical, personnel, and similar files; and (5) documents containing trade secrets or other confidential or privileged information.

Decisions by federal administrative agencies not to publicly disclose documents requested under the act are subject to judicial review in the proper U.S. district court.

Government in the Sunshine Act

Government in the Sunshine Act An act that was enacted to open certain federal administrative agency meetings to the public.

The **Government in the Sunshine Act** was enacted to open most federal administrative agency meetings to the public. There are some exceptions to this rule. These include meetings (1) where a person is accused of a crime, (2) concerning an agency's issuance of a subpoena, (3) where attendance of the public would significantly frustrate the implementation of a proposed agency action, and (4) concerning day-to-day operations. Decisions by federal administrative agencies to close meetings to the public are subject to judicial review in the proper U.S. district courts.

Example The Federal Communications Commission (FCC) is debating whether to grant an applicant permission to purchase a television station license. This meeting is not protected by any of the exceptions to the Government in the Sunshine Act. The FCC must publish a public notice of place, date, and time of the meeting so that persons may appear at the meeting.

Equal Access to Justice Act

Congress enacted the **Equal Access to Justice Act** to protect persons from harassment by federal administrative agencies. Under this act, a private party who is the subject of an unjustified federal administrative agency action can sue to recover attorneys' fees and other costs. The courts have generally held that the agency's conduct must be extremely outrageous before an award will be made under the act. A number of states have similar statutes.

Web Exploration

Find out the threat advisory for the risk of terrorist attacks today at http://dhs.gov/dhspublic/.

Privacy Act

The federal **Privacy Act** concerns individual privacy. It stipulates that federal administrative agencies can maintain only information about an individual that is relevant and necessary to accomplish a legitimate agency purpose. The act affords individuals the right to have access to agency records concerning themselves and to correct these records. Many states have enacted similar privacy acts.

The Ethical Perspective discusses a paralegal's ethical and legal duty not to assist criminal activity.

ETHICAL PERSPECTIVE
Duty Not to Assist Criminal Activity

Mr. Bush is a paralegal who works at a white-collar criminal defense law firm. Mr. Bush works directly for Ms. Swanson, a partner at the law firm.

One day Ms. Swanson requests that Mr. Bush sit in on a meeting with her with a client of the firm. The client, Mr. John White, owns White Enterprises Inc. Mr. White explains that he and White Enterprises Inc. are under investigation by the federal government for engaging in criminal fraud, wire fraud, mail fraud, and racketeering. Mr. White has hired Ms. Swanson to represent him and the company during the federal investigation and criminal lawsuit. At the meeting, Mr. White discloses that he wants "to get the cash out of White Enterprises and put it in a safe place" before the federal government goes any further with its investigation.

Ms. Swanson, who is an expert in white-collar criminal matters, tells Mr. White he can accomplish this if he starts another business that is secretly owned by Mr. White through a front, transfers the cash from White Enterprises to this new business, and then transfers the cash to a bank located in the Cayman Islands in a bank account in Mr. White's name. Ms. Swanson explains that the Cayman Islands has bank secrecy laws that prevent any party, including the United States government, from discovering the owner of and the amount of money in bank accounts that are located in the Cayman Islands.

Mr. White asks Ms. Swanson if she will help him do this, and Ms. Swanson agrees. The actions that Mr. White proposes, and Ms. Swanson has agreed to help accomplish, would constitute criminal conspiracy, criminal fraud, money laundering, racketeering, and other federal and state crimes. Ms. Swanson asks Mr. Bush, the paralegal, to assist her in accomplishing the illegal activities.

What should Mr. Bush do?

A paralegal is under a duty to not knowingly assist in the commission of a criminal act. Model and state paralegal Code of Ethics and Professional Responsibility provide that a paralegal is under an ethical duty to avoid engaging in criminal activity while performing paralegal responsibilities. A paralegal owes an ethical duty not to knowingly engage in criminal conduct. In addition, state and federal laws prohibit a paralegal from engaging in criminal acts.

PARALEGAL'S ETHICAL DECISION

The knowing participation of a paralegal in criminal activity on the job violates the law and the ethical duty of a paralegal. Mr. Bush cannot obey Ms. Swanson's direction to help assist Mr. White in engaging in criminal fraud, money laundering, racketeering, and other federal and state crimes. To do so would violate Mr. Bush's ethical duty as a paralegal. If Mr. Bush participates in the scheme, he would also be guilty of criminal conspiracy and other crimes.

Concept Review *and* Reinforcement

LEGAL TERMINOLOGY

Accountant–client privilege 305
Administrative agency 307
Administrative law 306
Administrative law judge (ALJ) 310
Administrative Procedure Act (APA) 309
Arraignment 294
Arrest warrant 289
Attorney–client privilege 305
Bail 289
Bail bond 289
Bench trial (waiver trial) 298
Beyond a reasonable doubt 286
Burden of proof 286
Criminal complaint 288
Criminal laws 286
Criminal trial 298
Cruel and unusual punishment 306
Defendant 288
Defense attorney 288

SUMMARY OF KEY CONCEPTS

Parties and Attorneys of a Criminal Action

Parties to a Criminal Lawsuit	1. *Plaintiff:* the government. 2. *Defendant:* the person or business accused of the crime.

Attorneys in a Criminal Lawsuit	1. *Prosecuting attorney:* the attorney who represents the government. These can be:
	   a. District attorney (DA), who prosecutes criminal cases on behalf of the state.
	   b. United States Attorney, who prosecutes criminal cases on behalf of the federal government.
	2. *Defense attorney:* the attorney who represents the person or party accused of the crime. These can be:
	   a. Public defender, a government attorney who represents the accused.
	   b. Private attorney, a nongovernment attorney who the accused hires to represent him or her.

Criminal Procedure

Pretrial Criminal Procedure	1. *Arrest:* The person is arrested pursuant to an *arrest warrant* based upon a showing of *probable cause*, or, where permitted, by a *warrentless* arrest. 2. *Indictment or information:* Grand juries issue *indictments*; magistrates (judges) issue *informations*. These formally charge the accused with specific crimes. 3. *Arraignment:* The accused is informed of the charges against him or her and enters a *plea* in court. The plea may be *not guilty*, *guilty*, or *nolo contendere*. 4. *Plea bargaining:* The government and the accused may negotiate a settlement agreement wherein the accused agrees to admit to a lesser crime than charged.

Criminal Trial

Outcomes	1. *Conviction:* requires unanimous vote of jury 2. *Innocent:* requires unanimous vote of jury 3. *Hung jury:* nonunanimous vote of the jury; the government may prosecute the case again
Appeal	1. *Defendant:* may appeal his or her conviction 2. *Plaintiff (government):* may not appeal a verdict of innocent

Constitutional Safeguards

Constitutional Safeguards	The U.S. Constitution includes provisions that protect persons from unreasonable government intrusion and provide safeguards for those accused of crimes.

Fourth Amendment Protection Against Unreasonable Searches and Seizures

Fourth Amendment Protection Against Unreasonable Searches and Seizures	The Fourth Amendment protects persons and corporations from *unreasonable searches and seizures.*
	1. *Reasonable searches and seizures:* based on *probable cause* are lawful:
	  a. Search warrant: stipulates the place and scope of the search
	  b. Warrantless search: permitted only:
	    i. incident to an arrest
	    ii. where evidence is in plain view
	    iii. where it is likely that evidence will be destroyed
	2. *Exclusionary rule:* states that evidence obtained from an unreasonable search and seizure is *tainted evidence* that may not be introduced at a government proceeding against the person searched.
	3. *Business premises:* protected by the Fourth Amendment, except that certain *regulated industries* may be subject to warrantless searches authorized by statute.

Fifth Amendment Privilege Against Self-Incrimination

Fifth Amendment Privilege Against Self-Incrimination	The Fifth Amendment provides that no person "shall be compelled in any criminal case to be a witness against himself." A person asserting this privilege is said to have "taken the Fifth."
	1. *Nontestimonial evidence:* evidence (e.g., fingerprints, body fluids, etc.) that is not protected.
	2. *Businesses:* a privilege that applies only to natural persons; business cannot assert the privilege.
	3. *Miranda rights:* a right of a criminal suspect to be informed of his or her Fifth Amendment rights before the suspect can be interrogated by the police or government officials.
	4. *Immunity from prosecution:* granted by the government to obtain otherwise privileged evidence; the government agrees not to use the evidence given against the person who gave it.
	5. *Attorney–client privilege:* An accused's lawyer cannot be called as a witness against the accused.
	6. *Other privileges:* The following privileges have been recognized, with some limitations:
	  a. psychiatrist/psychologist–patient
	  b. priest/rabbi/minister/imam–penitent
	  c. spouse–spouse
	  d. parent–child
	7. *Accountant–client privilege:* None recognized at the federal level. Some states recognize this privilege in state law actions.

Fifth Amendment Protection Against Double Jeopardy

Fifth Amendment Protection Against Double Jeopardy	The Fifth Amendment protects persons from being tried twice by the same jurisdiction for the same crime. If the act violates the laws of two or more jurisdictions, each jurisdiction may try the accused.

Sixth Amendment Right to a Public Trial

Sixth Amendment Right to a Public Trial	The Sixth Amendment guarantees criminal defendants the following rights: 1. to be tried by an impartial jury 2. to confront the witness 3. to have the assistance of a lawyer 4. to have a speedy trial (Speedy Trial Law)

Eighth Amendment Protection Against Cruel and Unusual Punishment

Eighth Amendment Protection Against Cruel and Unusual Punishment	The Eighth Amendment protects criminal defendants from cruel and unusual punishment. Capital punishment is permitted.

Administrative Law and Agencies

Administrative Agencies	Created by federal and state legislative and executive branches; consist of professionals having expertise in a certain area of commerce, who interpret and apply designated statutes.
General Government Regulation	The government enacts laws that regulate businesses and industries collectively.
Specific Government Regulation	The government also enacts laws that regulate certain industries only.

Administrative Procedure

Administrative Procedure Act (APA)	The APA establishes procedures (e.g., notice, hearing) for federal agencies to follow in conducting their affairs. States have enacted their own procedural acts to govern state agencies.
Administrative Law Judge (ALJ)	The ALJ is an employee of the administrative agency who presides over the administrative proceeding; decides questions of law and fact, issues a decision in the form of an order.
Substantive Rule Making	Administrative agencies have the power to adopt substantive rules that have the force of law and must be adhered to by covered persons and businesses.
Licensing Power	Administrative agencies are authorized to issue licenses before a person or business can enter certain types of industries.

Disclosure of Administrative Agency Actions

Freedom of Information Act	The FOIA is a federal law that gives the public access to most documents in the possession of federal administrative agencies. It also requires federal administrative agencies to publish agency procedures, rules, regulations, interpretations, and other information in the *Federal Register*.
Government in the Sunshine Act	This federal law opens certain federal administrative agency meetings to the public.
Equal Access to Justice Act	This federal law protects persons from harassment by federal administrative agencies and provides certain penalties for its violation.
Privacy Act	The Privacy Act (a) restricts information a federal administrative agency can maintain about an individual, and (b) gives individuals the right to access agency records concerning themselves.

WORKING THE WEB

1. Go to the website of Crime Stoppers USA at http://www.crimestopusa.com/AboutUs.asp#. Read about what the organization does.

2. Go to http://www.thelaborers.net/indictments/bellomo/indictment_criminal_genovese_family-2006-2-23.htm and read a grand jury indictment of the Genovese Organized Crime Family.

3. Go to http://www.fbi.gov/wanted/topten/fugitives/fugitives.htm and find the persons on the most recent FBI's "Ten Most Wanted" criminals list. Pick out two of these individuals and read about the crimes they are wanted for.

4. Go to http:www.dailybreeze.com/ci_9009312 and read the ruling regarding searches of computers at the borders of the United States.

5. Go to http://www.youtube.com/watch?v=Y0oLsEVWwWM to see a video clip of an offer for a reward for reporting a criminal suspect.

6. Go to the website http://www.fda.gov/. This is the website for the Federal Food and Drug Administration (FDA). Click on one of the "Hot Topic" subject matters that interests you and write a one-page report on that information.

7. Using the Food and Drug Administration (FDA) website http://www.fda.gov/, click on the word "Forms." Choose a "Subject" and locate an FDA form. Print the form and write a brief description of what the form is used for.

8. Go to the website http://www.cpsc.gov/. This is the website for the federal Consumer Product Safety Commission (CPSC). Click on "Recent Recalls" for the most current month. Find a recall of a product that interests you and write a half-page report describing the product and its recall.

CRITICAL THINKING & WRITING QUESTIONS

1. Who are the parties to a criminal action?

2. What lawyers are involved in a criminal action?

3. Describe the function of a criminal complaint.

4. Explain the process of arrest. What is a search warrant? When are warrantless arrests permitted?

5. What is bail? What is a bail bond?

6. Describe a grand jury. What is the function of a grand jury? What is an indictment?

7. What is a magistrate judge? What is an information?

8. Describe the process of arraignment.

9. What is a plea? Describe the plea of *nolo contendere*.

10. Describe the process of plea bargaining. Why would an accused agree to a plea bargain agreement? Why would the government agree to a plea bargain agreement?

11. What is a trier of fact? What is its function in a criminal trial?

12. Describe the difference between a finding of *guilty* or *innocent* at a criminal trial.

13. What does the Fourth Amendment's protection against unreasonable search and seizure provide? What is a search warrant?

14. What is required for there to be a reasonable search and seizure? What is *probable cause*?

15. What is unreasonable search and seizure? Explain the exclusionary rule.

16. What does the Fifth Amendment privilege against self-incrimination provide? Describe the *Miranda* rights.

17. Describe the attorney–client privilege. What other privileges are there?

18. Explain the Fifth Amendment's protection against double jeopardy. What is a hung jury? Can the government retry the accused where there has been a hung jury in a criminal trial?

19. Explain the Sixth Amendment's right to a public jury trial.

20. Explain the Eighth Amendment's protection against cruel and unusual punishment.

21. What is an administrative agency? Who creates administrative agencies?

22. What is the purpose of an administrative agency? Explain.

23. Describe the difference between general government regulation and specific government regulation. Give an example of each.

24. What is an administrative law judge (ALJ)? What does an ALJ do?

25. Describe what the following federal statutes provide: (1) Freedom of Information Act, (2) Government in the Sunshine Act, (3) Equal Access to Justice Act, and (4) Privacy Act.

Building Paralegal Skills

Administrative Agency Hearing: The Role of the Paralegal

 A school bus driver has been injured in what he claims to be a work-related injury. His employer—the school district—has raised objections requiring a Workers' Compensation hearing. A paralegal appears before the Workers' Compensation hearing officer representing the school bus driver.

After viewing the video case study at www.pearsonhighered .com/goldman answer the following:

1. Why are matters of this type heard before administrative hearing officers instead of going directly to court?
2. Is the paralegal committing the unauthorized practice of law in representing the school bus driver in this matter?
3. Are paralegals in your jurisdiction permitted to represent clients before administrative agencies?

ETHICS ANALYSIS & DISCUSSION QUESTIONS

1. Is the information given to a paralegal by a criminal client covered under the Fifth Amendment when he or she interviews a criminal?
2. What obligation does a paralegal have to make available exculpatory evidence discovered during the investigation of a case?
3. You are working at a firm with a large client base that does not speak English. You are fluent in three languages, and you are asked to translate for a firm attorney during an interview of a client in a criminal case. You take notes as you translate to be sure you are translating what is said properly [*Von Bulow by Auersperg v. Von Bulow*, 811 F. 2nd 136 1987 U.S. App. Lexis 2048 (2nd Cir. 1987).] Are the notes covered under the

work–product doctrine? Does the attorney–client privilege apply to what you heard?
4. What ethical guidelines apply to the representation of parties before administrative agencies by a paralegal?
5. May paralegals advertise their availability to appear before administrative agencies? Explain.
6. As a recent graduate of a four-year degree program, you wish to get started in your career. You purchase a copy of Quicken Family Lawyer at your local computer store. You invite a group of friends and relatives to your place and offer to use the program to prepare powers of attorney and living wills (advance medical directives) for them. [*Unauthorized Practice of Law v. Parsons Tech.*, 179 F.3d 956 (5th Cir. 1999).] Are there any UPL issues? Explain.

DEVELOPING YOUR COLLABORATION SKILLS

With a group of other students, selected by you or as assigned by your instructor, review the facts of the following case. As a group, discuss the following questions.
1. What does the Fourth Amendment provide regarding searches and seizures of evidence?

2. Was the use of the GPS system in this case a search?
3. If it is not a search can the evidence discovered be used against the defendant at his criminal trial?

PARALEGAL PORTFOLIO EXERCISE

Prepare a memorandum, no longer than three pages, that discusses the general powers of a federal administrative agency and the specific powers of the Federal Food and Drug Administration (FDA).

United States of America v. Garcia

Bernardo Garcia had served time in jail for methamphetamine (meth) offenses. Upon release from prison, a person reported to the police that Garcia had brought meth to her and used it with her. Another person told police that Garcia bragged that he could manufacture meth in front of a police station without being caught. A store's security video system recorded Garcia buying ingredients used in making meth. From someone else the police learned that Garcia was driving a Ford Tempo.

The police found the car parked on the street near where Garcia was staying. The police placed a GPS (global positioning system) tracking device underneath the rear bumper of the car. The device receives and stores satellite signals that indicate the device's location. Using the device, the police learned that Garcia had been visiting a large tract of land. With permission of the owner of the land, the police conducted a search and discovered equipment and materials to manufacture meth. When the police were there, Garcia arrived in his car.

The police had not obtained a search warrant authorizing them to place the GPS tracker on Garcia's car. At Garcia's criminal trial in U.S. district court, the evidence the police obtained using the GPS system was introduced at court. Based upon this evidence, Garcia was found guilty of crimes related to the manufacture of meth. Garcia appealed to the U.S. court of appeals, arguing that the use of the GPS tracking system by the police was an unreasonable search in violation of the Fourth Amendment to the Constitution.

Source: *United States of America v. Garcia*, 474 F.3d 994, **Web** 2007 U.S. App. Lexis 2272 (United States Court of Appeals for the Seventh Circuit, 2007)

LEGAL ANALYSIS & WRITING CASES

Center Art Galleries–Hawaii, Inc. v. United States
875 F.2d 747, Web 1989 U.S. App. Lexis 6983

United States Court of Appeals for the Ninth Circuit
The Center Art Galleries–Hawaii sells artwork. Approximately 20 percent of its business involves art by Salvador Dalí. The federal government, which suspected the center of fraudulently selling forged Dalí artwork, obtained identical search warrants for six locations controlled by the center. The warrants commanded the executing officer to seize items that were "evidence of violations of federal criminal law." The warrants did not describe the specific crimes suspected and did not stipulate that only items pertaining to the sale of Dalí's work could be seized. There was no evidence of any criminal activity unrelated to that artist.

Question
1. Is the search warrant valid?

United States v. John Doe
465 U.S. 605, 104 S.Ct. 1237, 79 L.Ed.2d 552, Web 1984 U.S. Lexis 169

Supreme Court of the United States
John Doe is the owner of several sole-proprietorship businesses. During the course of an investigation of corruption in awarding county and municipal contracts, a federal grand jury served several subpoenas on John Doe, demanding the production of certain business records. The subpoenas demanded the production of the following records: (1) general ledgers and journals, (2) invoices, (3) bank statements and canceled checks, (4) financial statements, (5) telephone-company records, (6) safe-deposit box records, and (7) copies of tax returns. John Doe filed a motion in federal court, seeking to quash the subpoenas, alleging that producing these business records would violate his Fifth Amendment privilege of not testifying against himself.

Question
1. Do the records have to be disclosed?

People v. Paulson
216 Cal.App.3d 1480, 265 Cal. Rptr. 579, Web 1990 Cal.App. Lexis 10

Court of Appeal of California
Lee Stuart Paulson owned the liquor license for My House, a bar in San Francisco. The California Department of Alcoholic Beverage Control is the administrative agency that regulates bars in that state. The California Business and Professions Code, which the department administers, prohibit "any kind of illegal activity on licensed premises." An anonymous informer tipped the department that narcotics sales were occurring on the premises of My House and that the narcotics were kept in a safe behind the bar on the premises. A special department investigator entered the bar during its hours of operation, identified himself, and informed Paulson that he was conducting an inspection. The investigator, who did not have a search warrant, opened the safe without seeking Paulson's consent. Twenty-two bundles of cocaine, totaling 5.5 grams, were found in the safe. Paulson was arrested. At his criminal trial, Paulson challenged the lawfulness of the search.

Question
1. Was the warrantless search of the safe a lawful search?

City of Indianapolis v. Edmond
531 U.S. 32, 121 S.Ct. 447, 148 L.Ed.2d 333, Web 2000 U.S. Lexis 8084 (2000)

Supreme Court of the United States

The police of the city of Indianapolis, Indiana, began to operate vehicle roadblock checkpoints on Indianapolis roads in an effort to interdict unlawful drugs. Once a car had been stopped, police questioned the driver and passengers and conducted an open-view examination of the vehicle from the outside. A narcotics-detection dog walked around outside each vehicle. The police conducted a search and seizure of the occupants and vehicle only if particular suspicion developed from the initial investigation. The overall "hit rate" of the program was approximately 9 percent.

James Edmond and Joel Palmer, each attorneys who had been stopped at one of Indianapolis's checkpoints, filed a lawsuit on behalf of themselves and the class of all motorists who had been stopped or were subject to being stopped at such checkpoints. They claimed that the roadblocks violated the Fourth Amendment to the Constitution. The district court found for Indianapolis, but the court of appeals reversed. The U.S. Supreme Court granted certiorari to hear the appeal.

Question

1. Does Indianapolis's highway checkpoint program violate the Fourth Amendment to the U.S. Constitution?

Donovan, Secretary of Labor v. Dewey
452 U.S. 594, 101 S.Ct. 2534, 69 L.Ed.2d 262, Web 1980 U.S. Lexis 58

Supreme Court of the United States

The Federal Mine Safety and Health Act of 1977 requires the Secretary of Labor to develop detailed mandatory health and safety standards to govern the operation of the nation's mines. The Act provides that federal mine inspectors are to inspect underground mines at least four times a year and surface mines at least twice a year to ensure compliance with these standards and to make the following inspections to determine whether previously discovered violations have been corrected. The Act also grants mine inspectors "a right of entry to, upon or through any coal or other mine" and states that "no advance notice of an inspection shall be provided to any person."

In July 1978, a federal mine inspector attempted to inspect quarries owned by Waukesha Lime and Stone Company (Waukesha) to determine whether all 25 safety and health violations uncovered during a prior inspection had been corrected. Douglas Dewey, Waukesha's president, refused to allow the inspector to inspect the premises without first obtaining a search warrant.

Question

1. Are the warrantless searches of stone quarries authorized by the Mine Safety and Health Act constitutional? Did Dewey act ethically in refusing to allow the inspections?

WORKING WITH THE LANGUAGE OF THE COURT CASE

Department of Justice v. Landano

508 U.S. 165, 113 S.Ct. 2014, 124 L.Ed.2d 84, 1993 U.S. Lexis 3727 (1993)
Supreme Court of the United States

Read the following case, excerpted from the U.S. Supreme Court's opinion. Review and brief the case. In your brief, answer the following questions:

1. Under what circumstances may a defendant obtain information under the Freedom of Information Act (FOIA)?
2. When may the government in a criminal case refuse to divulge information under the FOIA?
3. Is all information provided to the Federal Bureau of Investigation confidential and therefore not available under the FOIA?
4. Who has the burden of proof in FOIA cases?

O'Connor, J., delivered the opinion for a unanimous Court

Exemption 7(D) of the Freedom of Information Act, 5 U.S.C. Section 552 (FOIA), exempts from disclosure agency records "compiled for law enforcement purposes by criminal law enforcement authority in the course of a criminal investigation" if release of those records "could reasonably be expected to disclose" the identity of or information provided by a "confidential source" [Section 552(b)(7)(D)]. This case concerns the evidentiary showing that the Government must make to establish that a source is "confidential" within the meaning of Exemption 7(D). We are asked to decide whether the Government is entitled to a presumption that all sources supplying information to the Federal Bureau of Investigation (FBI or Bureau) in the course of a criminal investigation are confidential sources.

Respondent Vincent Landano was convicted in New Jersey state court for murdering Newark, New Jersey, police officer John Snow in the course of a robbery. The crime received considerable media attention. Evidence at trial showed that the robbery had been orchestrated by Victor Forni and a motorcycle gang known as "the Breed." There was testimony that Landano, though not a Breed member, had been recruited for the job. Landano always has maintained that he did not participate in the robbery, and that Forni, not he, killed Officer Snow. He contends that the prosecution withheld material exculpatory evidence in violation of Brady v. Maryland, 373 U.S. 83 (1963).

Landano apparently is currently pursuing a Brady claim in the state courts. Seeking evidence to support that claim, Landano filed FOIA requests with the FBI for information that the Bureau had compiled in the course of its involvement in the investigation of Officer Snow's murder. Landano sought release of the Bureau's files on both Officer Snow and Forni. The FBI released several hundred pages of documents. The Bureau redacted some of these, however, and withheld several hundred other pages altogether.

The information withheld under Exemption 7(D) included information provided by five types of sources: regular FBI informants; individual witnesses who were not regular informants; state and local law enforcement agencies; other local agencies; and private financial and commercial institutions. In the Government's view, all such sources should be presumed confidential. The deleted portions of the files were coded to indicate which type of source each involved.

Relying on legislative history, the court stated that a source is confidential within the meaning of Exemption 7(D) if the source received an explicit assurance of confidentiality or if there are circumstances "from which such an assurance could reasonably be inferred." An "assurance of confidentiality," the court said, is not a promise of absolute anonymity or secrecy, but "an assurance that the FBI would not directly or indirectly disclose the cooperation of the interviewee with the investigation unless such a disclosure is determined by the FBI to be important to the success of its law enforcement objective."

Exemption 7(D) permits the Government to withhold "records or information compiled for law enforcement purposes, but only to the extent that the production of such law enforcement records or information . . . could reasonably be expected to disclose the identity of a confidential source, including a state, local, or foreign agency or authority or any private institution which furnished information on a confidential basis, and, in the case of a record or information compiled by criminal law enforcement authority in the course of a criminal investigation, information furnished by a confidential source" [§ 552(b)(7)(D)]. The Government bears the burden of establishing that the exemption applies.

When FOIA was enacted in 1966, Exemption 7 broadly protected "'investigatory files compiled for law enforcement purposes except to the extent available by law to a private party.'" Congress adopted the current version of Exemption 7(D) in 1986. The 1986 amendment expanded "records" to "records or information," replaced the word "would" with the phrase "could reasonably be expected to," deleted the word "only" from before "confidential source," and clarified that a confidential source could be a state, local, or foreign agency or a private institution.

Under Exemption 7(D), the question is not whether the requested document is of the type that the agency usually treats as confidential, but whether the particular source spoke with an understanding that the communication would remain confidential. According to the Conference Report on the 1974 amendment, a source is confidential within the meaning of Exemption 7(D) if the source provided information under an express assurance of confidentiality or in circumstances from which such an assurance could be reasonably inferred. In this case, the Government has not attempted to demonstrate that the FBI made explicit promises of confidentiality to particular sources. That sort of proof apparently often is not possible: The FBI does not have a policy of discussing confidentiality with every source, and when such discussions do occur, agents do not always document them.

The precise question before us, then, is how the Government can meet its burden of showing that a source provided information on an implied assurance of confidentiality. The parties dispute two issues: the meaning of the word "confidential," and whether, absent specific evidence to the contrary, an implied assurance of confidentiality always can be inferred from the fact that a source cooperated with the FBI during a criminal investigation.

FOIA does not define the word "confidential." In common usage, confidentiality is not limited to complete anonymity or secrecy. A statement can be made "in confidence" even if the speaker knows the communication will be shared with limited others, as long as the speaker expects that the information will not be

(continued)

published indiscriminately. A promise of complete secrecy would mean that the FBI agent receiving the source's information could not share it even with other FBI personnel. Such information, of course, would be of little use to the Bureau.

We assume that Congress was aware of the Government's disclosure obligations under Brady and applicable procedural rules when it adopted Exemption 7(D). Congress also must have realized that some FBI witnesses would testify at trial. We therefore agree with the Court of Appeals that the word "confidential," as used in Exemption 7(D), refers to a degree of confidentiality less than total secrecy. A source should be deemed confidential if the source furnished information with the understanding that the FBI would not divulge the communication except to the extent the Bureau thought necessary for law enforcement purposes.

Considerations of "fairness" also counsel against the Government's rule. The Government acknowledges that its proposed presumption, though rebuttable in theory, is in practice all but irrebuttable. Once the FBI asserts that information was provided by a confidential source during a criminal investigation, the requester—who has no knowledge about the particular source or the information being withheld—very rarely will be in a position to offer persuasive evidence that the source in fact had no interest in confidentiality.

We agree with the Government that, when certain circumstances characteristically support an inference of confidentiality, the Government similarly should be able to claim exemption under Exemption 7(D) without detailing the circumstances surrounding a particular interview. Neither the language of Exemption 7(D) nor Reporters Committee, Page 178, however, supports the proposition that the category of all FBI criminal investigative sources is exempt.

But Congress did not expressly create a blanket exemption for the FBI; the language that it adopted requires every agency to establish that a confidential source furnished the information sought to be withheld under Exemption 7(D). In short, the Government offers no persuasive evidence that Congress intended for the Bureau to be able to satisfy its burden in every instance simply by asserting that a source communicated with the Bureau during the course of a criminal investigation. Had Congress meant to create such a rule, it could have done so much more clearly.

The Government has argued forcefully that its ability to maintain the confidentiality of all of its sources is vital to effective law enforcement. A prophylactic rule protecting the identities of all FBI criminal investigative sources undoubtedly would serve the Government's objectives, and would be simple for the Bureau and the courts to administer. But we are not free to engraft that policy choice onto the statute that Congress passed. For the reasons we have discussed, and consistent with our obligation to construe FOIA exemptions narrowly in favor of disclosure, we hold that the Government is not entitled to a presumption that a source is confidential within the meaning of Exemption 7(D) whenever the source provides information to the FBI in the course of a criminal investigation.

More narrowly defined circumstances, however, can provide a basis for inferring confidentiality. For example, when circumstances such as the nature of the crime investigated and the witness' relation to it support an inference of confidentiality, the Government is entitled to a presumption. In this case, the Court of Appeals incorrectly concluded that it lacked discretion to rely on such circumstances. Accordingly, we vacate the judgment of the Court of Appeals and remand the case for further proceedings consistent with this opinion. It is so ordered.

Paralegal Skills

The aspiring paralegal professional must develop a set of skills to allow them to understand and work in a supporting role as part of the legal team in the law office, the court, the administrative agency, and in the alternative dispute resolution working environment. Excellent verbal and written skills are crucial for paralegals who will be interviewing clients and witnesses and the general public. Paralegals must develop an ability to think critically and analytically when performing legal research and in writing briefs, memorandums of the law, and general correspondence. Today's paralegal must be familiar with the use of technology to conduct legal and factual research using a digital library and Internet research services, as well as how to use traditional print sources of information. Part III covers the basic skills needed for a paralegal professional to be successful in the job.

Interviewing and Investigation Skills

DIGITAL RESOURCES

Chapter 9 Digital Resources at *www.pearsonhighered.com/goldman*

- Video Case Studies:
  - UPL Issue: Working with a Witness
  - UPL Issue: Interviewing a Client
  - Zealous Representation Issue: When You Are Asked to Lie
- Chapter Summary • Web Links • Court Opinions • Glossary • Comprehension Quizzes
- Technology Resources

It is the spirit and not the form of law that keeps justice alive.

Earl Warren

LEARNING OBJECTIVES

After studying this chapter, you should be able to:

1. Explain the potential issues involved in a screening interview.
2. Describe the issues in preparing for and conducting an interview.
3. Explain the steps and process of conducting an investigation.
4. List and describe sources for obtaining information.
5. Explain the function of the trial notebook and its relationship to case management.

Paralegals at Work

Sara had been working for only a few weeks as a paralegal intern for a small, boutique litigation law firm. Mrs. Weiser, one of the two paralegals supporting the two trial attorneys, told Sara about her long-planned Alaskan cruise that she would be taking with her husband for their 25th anniversary. The reality of the situation started to set in when Sara was advised that the cruise would start from Anchorage the next day and Mrs. Weiser was scheduled to leave within the hour to catch a plane. Sara's concerns heightened when she and Mrs. Weiser reviewed the office calendar and it became obvious that Sara would be alone in the office. The attorneys and the other full-time paralegal were involved in a major medical malpractice case in another state for at least the next two weeks. Clearly, Sara would be in charge of the office, answering the phone and taking care of anyone who came in. Somewhat troubling would be the lack of any contact with Mrs. Weiser for the duration of the cruise, or contact with the other paralegal or attorneys during the trial day.

The instructions left no doubt that Sara would be busy when she was told: "Now remember—we advertise on TV, and Mr. Elliott expects us to screen potential clients without bothering him with loser cases. I've left a couple of files for you to work on while I'm gone. The Morales case just came in. It's an accident case that happened a few years ago, and you need to get her in for an initial interview—get all the necessary facts and see what else we have to do to move it along and either settle it or start suit. Oh, by the way, you do speak Spanish, don't you? Mrs. Morales is from Puerto Rico.

"The LaCorte case is on the trial list for next month. We don't have an expert yet who can substantiate our theory of the case. See what you can find. Oh, and you'd better get that case organized so they can start trial immediately in case the current trial lasts longer than the expected three weeks. All the material is in piles or in boxes in Mr. Martin's office. Prepare a trial notebook, or you can try that new case management software program we just got that is supposed to make life easier. I'm sure, with your computer skills, that you can get it up and running and use it to get the case ready for trial."

Consider the issues involved in this scenario as you read the chapter.

INTRODUCTION FOR THE PARALEGAL

Communication skills are at the heart of paralegals' ability to conduct successful interviews and investigations. The paralegal must be prepared to be the first point of contact with the client. In some practices, clients are interviewed first by the supervising attorney and then referred to the paralegal for a detailed factual interview. In other practices, the paralegal is the first one to meet with the client and conduct the initial interview before referring the client to the supervising attorney.

The paralegal must be able to interview clients, fact witnesses, expert witnesses, investigators, and others, including public records custodians who may have access to information necessary for the preparation of a case. The skill of the interviewer or investigator can determine the accuracy and completeness of the information obtained—and ultimately the outcome of the case. The impressions created and the relationship developed with a new client may be the deciding factor in whether the client stays with the firm or seeks other counsel. Professional relationships developed with public officials, public custodians of records, hospital records librarians, police investigators, and similar independent investigators can make the paralegal's job much easier and ultimately benefit the client.

Interviews

Screening interview Limited first contact with a prospective new client.

Any contact that a paralegal has with a client, or prospective client, constitutes an interview. It may involve limited contact, such as a **screening interview**, or an in-depth initial fact-gathering interview. In each case, the paralegal usually is the first point of contact with the client for the firm. The impression the paralegal makes is the impression the firm makes. As someone once said, we have only one opportunity to make a good first impression.

The initial contact with a client is what is sometimes called a screening interview. This usually begins with an initial telephone call to the firm, although a person may appear at the reception desk, looking for an attorney and wanting to determine if the firm is interested in taking the case, and usually what it will cost.

Also, paralegals frequently make the initial contact with potential witnesses. Again this may be a telephone call to set up a meeting or a telephone interview. The initial meeting with potential witnesses may be in the office or in the field at the witness's home or place of business. The initial contact with a potential witness, just as with a potential client, may set the tone for the interview and the willingness of the person to cooperate.

Screening Interview

Many clients come to a law firm or lawyer from a referral source, such as a current or former client. This source of clients acts as a potential screening. The individual probably has been told by the referral source something about the nature of the practice, the kind of work being done for the referring person, and the perceived reputation or ability of the lawyer or firm. Other potential clients find the firm's name and phone number in the telephone book, on a website listing of attorneys, or from another law firm advertisement or promotional piece.

Finally, some people simply appear at the office door and ask for an appointment or basic information about the firm's ability or interest in taking a case. In smaller offices the paralegal is the one who often takes these calls, doubling as receptionist–phone operator.

The initial contact is filled with potential landmines. If the paralegal solicits too much information or the prospective client volunteers too much information, an **implied attorney–client relationship** may be created. If too little information is obtained, the attorney will not have enough information to decide if he or she wants to talk to the potential client. Therefore, the paralegal or receptionist has to decide how much information to take and how much information to give.

First Meeting

At the very least, it is prudent for the paralegal to advise the potential client that paralegals are not lawyers, and that only a lawyer can give legal advice. Also, anything said to the paralegal may not be subject to the **attorney–client privilege**.

The prospective client may want a quick answer to the question, "Do I have a case?" The answer requires a legal analysis that only the attorney can make. The attorney–employer probably does not want to be bothered with most such early contacts but also does not want to lose a good case. Should the paralegal give advice or have this person speak with a lawyer? Most of these potential problems can be avoided by having a policy or strategy in place. Most offices have a policy on the fee for an initial interview. Many offer a no-cost initial interview to determine the validity of a case and any potential conflict of interests that might require the office to decline a case. In some cases, a nominal fee is charged. This may be a flat rate or an hourly rate. In many jurisdictions, referrals from the local lawyer referral office or legal aid office are charged at a token fee, sometimes as little as $5, or in indigent cases, no fee as part of the local pro bono program. The paralegal must ask the firm's policy before attempting to give and receive information from potential clients.

Implied Attorney–Client Relationship

If too much information is taken, the potential client may think he or she now has a lawyer. The courts have ruled on the side of the prospective client, holding that an implied attorney–client relationship exists. In this "implied" relationship, the client is entitled to expect the same degree of confidentiality under the attorney–client privilege. In this situation, a **conflict of interest** may result if the firm is already representing another party in the same matter, which would result in disqualification of the attorney or the establishment of an **ethical wall** to prevent access to information by members of the legal team with a conflict.

One of the biggest potential areas of potential malpractice is to miss a **statute of limitations** on a client's case. The statute of limitations is a time period within which a case must be filed with the court or the right to use the court for resolution of the case is lost. The statute of limitations is based on statute, and each jurisdiction has the power to set its own statute of limitations for each type of case. For example, in many states the time limit for filing a tort action arising out of an automobile action is two years, and a contract action six years, but in some states the suit must be filed in as little as 30 days. To a client seeking a new lawyer for an appeal, the timeframe may not be important. But to the lawyer, it is potentially critical to prevent malpractice, especially

Implied attorney—client relationship Implied attorney–client relationship may result when a prospective client divulges confidential information during a consultation with an attorney for the purpose of retaining the attorney, even if actual employment does not result.

Attorney–client privilege A client's right to have anything told to a lawyer while seeking legal advice, kept confidential in most instances.

Conflict of interest Representation of another with conflicting rights.

Ethical wall A artificial barrier preventing anyone not authorized who may have a conflict of interest from accessing client information.

Statute of limitations A time limit within which a case must be brought or lose the right to seek redress in court.

Web Exploration

Contrast and compare the Missouri Rule 4-1.18 at http://www.courts.mo.gov/courts/ClerkHandbooks P2RulesOnly.nsf with the ABA Rule 1.18 at www.abanet.org/cpr and the rule in your jurisdiction.

IMPLIED ATTORNEY-CLIENT RELATIONSHIP

SIDEBAR

Implied attorney-client relationship may result when a prospective client divulges confidential information during a consultation with an attorney for the purpose of retaining the attorney, even if actual employment does not result.

Pro-Hand Servs. Trust v. Monthei, 49 P.3d 56, 59 (Mont.2002).

The attorney-client privilege applies to all confidential communications made to an attorney during preliminary discussions of the prospective professional employment, as well as those made during the course of any professional relationship resulting from such discussions.

Hooser v. Superior Court, 101 Cal. Rptr. 2d 341, 346 (Ct. App. 2000).

ETHICAL PERSPECTIVE

Missouri Bar—Rules of Professional Conduct

RULE 4-1.18: DUTIES TO PROSPECTIVE CLIENT

(a) A person who discusses with a lawyer the possibility of forming a client-lawyer relationship with respect to a matter is a prospective client.

(b) Even when no client-lawyer relationship ensues, a lawyer who has had discussions with a prospective client shall not use or reveal information learned in the consultation, except as Rule 4-1.9 would permit with respect to information of a former client.

(c) A lawyer subject to Rule 4-1.18(b) shall not represent a client with interests materially adverse to those of a prospective client in the same or a substantially related matter if the lawyer received information from the prospective client that could be significantly harmful to that person in the matter, except as provided in Rule 4-1.18(d). If a lawyer is disqualified from representation under Rule 4-1.18(c), no lawyer in a firm with which that lawyer is associated may knowingly undertake or continue representation in such a matter, except as provided in Rule 4-1.18(d).

(d) When the lawyer has received disqualifying information as defined in Rule 4-1.18(c), representation is permissible if:

(1) both the affected client and the prospective client have given informed consent, confirmed in writing, or:

(2) the lawyer who received the information took reasonable measures to avoid exposure to more disqualifying information than was reasonably necessary to determine whether to represent the prospective client and the disqualified lawyer is timely screened from any participation in the matter.

when the timeframe is short, such as when the court has allowed a time limit for an appeal of 10 to 45 days, after which time the court order is not appealable barring special relief by the court.

The timing of the statute of limitations deadline always must be considered when taking the initial call or during the first contact with the potential client. If a court holds that an implied attorney–client relationship exists after the statute of limitations has run out (expired), the failure of the attorney to have taken action may be held to be malpractice and subject the lawyer to pay what would have been recovered if the case had gone forward and a recovery obtained. As the first point of potential client contact, the paralegal must be prepared to take appropriate action and refer the matter to the supervising attorney.

Some calls are not from potential clients but, rather, from those attempting to get information about the representation of other clients. This is not unusual. Particularly in family law cases, a party may call as if seeking representation but in reality is trying to find out if the other party has retained the firm.

Preparing for the Interview

The first step in preparing for an interview or conducting an investigation is to understand the outcome desired. One of the desired outcomes in an initial interview with a new client is to instill confidence in the firm and its personnel. The fundamentally desired outcome of any interview is to obtain all of the relevant facts for the case that has been assigned. Understanding the goals of the interview or investigation, the background or cultural issues of the individual, and the nature of the situation will help in structuring a successful interview.

Occasionally an interview has to be conducted without time for preparation, such as when the paralegal is asked to fill in for someone else at the last moment.

IN THE WORDS OF THE COURT

Identity of Clients

HOOSER V. SUPERIOR COURT OF SAN DIEGO COUNTY
84 CAL.APP.4TH 997 (2000) 101 CAL.RPTR.2D 341.

. . . the identity of an attorney's clients is sensitive personal information that implicates the clients' rights of privacy. "[E]very person [has the right] to freely confer with and confide in his attorney in an atmosphere of trust and serenity. . . ." (Willis v. Superior Court (1980) 112 Cal.App.3d 277, 293.)

Clients routinely exercise their right to consult with counsel, seeking to obtain advice on a host of matters that they reasonably expect to remain private. A spouse who consults a divorce attorney may not want his or her spouse or other family members to know that he or she is considering divorce.

Similarly, an employee who is concerned about conduct in his workplace, an entrepreneur planning a new business endeavor, an individual with questions about the criminal or tax consequences of his or her acts, or a family member who desires to rewrite a will may consult an attorney with the expectation that the consultation itself, as well as the matters discussed therein, will remain confidential until such time as the consultation is disclosed to third parties, through the filing of a lawsuit, the open representation of the client in dealing with third parties or in some other manner.

Upon such public disclosure of the attorney-client relationship, the client's privacy concerns regarding the fact of the consultation evaporate and there is no longer a basis for preventing the attorney from identifying the client. (See Satterlee v. Bliss (1869) 36 Cal. 489, 501.) However, until such a public disclosure occurs, the client's identity is itself a matter of privacy, subject to the protection against involuntary disclosure through compelled discovery against the attorney.

Investigation Checklists

The investigation checklist (Exhibit 9.1) should not be viewed as a static document. The checklist should start with a listing of all of the parties involved who should be interviewed, including initial fact witnesses. As additional parties and witnesses are interviewed, more people may have to be added to the list. Exhibit 9.2 is a witness information form. Investigation of locations and physical evidence may result in the need to examine other locations and evidence. Initial interviews also may result in the need to add one or more expert witnesses to the investigation checklist.

A checklist can be a valuable tool to be certain that all the information required for a certain type of case or other legal matter is obtained during the initial interview. The same checklist offers a good foundation for developing a more detailed interview plan when there is time for preparation.

Physical surroundings, clothing, and appearance are important in preparing for interviews and investigations. They merit your attention.

Physical Surroundings

The physical surroundings in the interview location can set the tone for the interview. Depending upon the purpose of the interview and the person being interviewed, the paralegal may wish to create either a formal or an informal environment. You probably can remember a situation in which someone interviewed you from across a desk. Didn't you feel a certain formality and possibly subservience to the interviewer? Contrast that situation with sitting in an informal setting with a low coffee table and living room-style chairs. This setting gives the meeting a more personal tone.

Putting a client at ease may be easier in the informal setting, whereas dealing with opposing counsel might be better handled in the formal, "across the desk" meeting.

Exhibit 9.1   Investigation checklist for auto accident

INVESTIGATION CHECKLIST

Client name _____

Phone (hm) _____ (wk) _____ (cell) _____

Current address _____

Prior address(es) _____

Date of birth _____ Place of birth _____

Social Security No. _____

VEHICLE CLIENT OPERATING/PASSENGER

Owner and type of motor vehicle _____

Insurance Co. _____ Policy number _____

Insurance company contact _____ Phone _____

Date of incident _____ Time of day _____ Weather conditions _____

Location of incident _____

City, State _____ County _____ Municipality _____

Opposing party _____

Address _____

Phone (hm) _____ (wk) _____ (cell) _____

Owner and type of motor vehicle _____

Insurance Co. _____ Policy number _____

FACT WITNESSES

Name _____ Address _____

Name _____ Address _____

Name _____ Address _____

Name of ambulance _____

Name of hospital _____

Police report issued _____ Copy ordered _____

Photographs of scene taken _____

Name of treating physicians _____

EXPERT WITNESSES

Name _____ Address _____

Name _____ Address _____

Summary of cause of action _____

Attach detailed accident/incident description, accident reports and diagrams.

In most cases, the paralegal will want to create the impression of a competent professional, although in some situations, creating a more casual and less professional impression may be beneficial. Some witnesses are more cooperative and helpful when they feel as if they are the ones in charge and are helping the paraprofessional.

Dress and Appearance

Remember the old saying, "First impressions count"? The impression a paralegal makes when walking into the room for the initial interview may set the stage for the entire relationship with the client or witness.

Exhibit 9.2 Witness information form

Witness Information

CLIENT PERSONAL DATA

Client Name	Case No.	File No.

Address	City, State, Zip	Phone

CASE DATA

File Label	Case issue	Date

Responsible Attorney(s)

WITNESS DATA

Witness Name

Aliases, if any	US Citizen ☐ Yes ☐ No

Current Address	City, State, Zip	Phone

Past Address(es)

Date & Place of Birth	Sex	Race	Age	Current Marital Status ☐ Single ☐ Divorced

Name of Spouse	Number/Former Marriages	Number/Children	☐ Married ☐ Widowed ☐ Separated

Name of Children (natural & adopted)	Age	Name	Age

Current Employer

Address	City, State, Zip	Phone

Job Title	Supervisor	From	To

Previous Employer

Address	City, State, Zip	Phone

Job Title	Supervisor	From	To

Education/Name of School	City/State	From	To	Degree
High School				
College				
Technical/Other				

Witness for ☐ Plaintiff ☐ Defendant	Type of Witness ☐ Expert ☐ Character ☐ Eye Witness	Have you ever been a party or witness in a court suit? ☐ No ☐ Yes

If yes, where & when

OTHER PERTINENT DATA

Form 9567 · 9/86 SYCOM Madison, WI Printed in U.S.A.

Clothing, posture, and manner of greeting create the first impression. Clothing sends a nonverbal message about the person and the firm or business. The impression a person makes upon walking into the room can enhance or destroy credibility. In the practice of law, or in a corporate law department, the unexpected can become the norm. Many attorneys, male and female alike, keep a "going-to-court suit" in the office just in case they need to have a more professional appearance at a moment's notice. When the new client comes in, they can change quickly while the receptionist or secretary buys them time to change to the "power" outfit.

A client may be offended by a paralegal's "casual Friday" appearance, believing that the paralegal is not taking the matter seriously. The working paralegal, however, usually doesn't have time to change when the unexpected arises, often being the one to "buy time" for the attorney. Therefore, paralegals always must be prepared to make a good impression and tailor their appearance appropriately as the situation warrants. In the case of field interviews, a casual appearance may be preferred to put the potential witness at ease. In the office, suits with jackets are appropriate for men and women. In the field, removing the jacket may give the impression of less formality.

Communication Skills in a Multicultural Society*

Those with whom paralegals communicate can be addressed in many ways. Clients, witnesses, and others with whom the paralegal comes in contact should never be stereotyped. At the same time, paralegals should be aware of the gender, religious, and ethic sensitivities of people. Paralegals' skills as interviewers depend on their ability to appreciate the differences in how and why individuals act and react differently. They must not assume that everyone in each category believes and acts the same and have to be sensitive to issues that may cause a person not to communicate as might have been anticipated from first impressions of them. We will point out some general differences in the way men and women communicate, followed by some cultural background considerations.

Gender Differences

A man, in comparison to a woman, is more likely to:

- have been socialized to perform more aggressively and boast of his successes;
- have learned from childhood games that winning is desirable;
- be motivated by competition;
- view conflict as impersonal, a necessary part of working relationships;
- be impressed by power, ability, and achievement;
- hear only the literal words and miss the underlying emotion;
- not express his true feelings through facial expressions;
- have a more direct communication style.

A woman is more likely to:

- have been socialized to work cooperatively and to be modest about her success;
- have learned from childhood games to compromise and collaborate, and continue to be motivated by affiliation;
- compete primarily with herself—with her own expectations of what she should be able to accomplish;
- take conflict personally;
- be impressed by personal disclosure and professional courage;
- have the ability to focus on several projects at the same time;
- be proficient at decoding nonverbal meanings and likely to display her feelings through facial expression and body language;
- have an indirect style, except with other women of equal rank.

---

* This section on communication skills is adapted from *Crosstalk: Communicating in a Multicultural Workplace*, by Sherron Kenton and Deborah Valentine, 1997. Reprinted with permission of the Authors.

Considering the receiver's attitudes about the paralegal:

- Man-to-man: He may afford the paralegal instant credibility based on the same gender.
- Woman-to-woman: She may expect the paralegal to be friendly, nurturing, and concerned and may afford the paralegal instant credibility based on same-gender assumptions.
- Paralegal man-to-woman. She may expect that the paralegal will not really listen to her.
- Paralegal woman-to-man: He may expect the paralegal to be friendly and nurturing, even passive-dependent. Any aggressive behavior or deviation from his expectation could cause him discomfort and confusion, or produce negative responses. He may simply disregard the female paralegal.

Cultural Sensitivity

The culturally sensitive person is aware of the reasons for differences in the way people behave, based on religious and ethnic background and belief system. As the cultural makeup of the United States has become more diverse, the need for cultural awareness and sensitivity in the legal and paralegal professions has grown. Just as men and women are said to be different in some ways, so are Europeans, Asians, Latinos, and Africans who have not fully assimilated into the culture of the country.

Interviewing a Latino male, for example, may require a different approach than interviewing an Asian female. Even subtleties of eye contact can affect an interview. Whereas Americans view eye contact as a sign of sincerity, some Asian cultures view this as aggressive. In developing communication skills, paralegals must become sensitive to how they are perceived and learn to fashion their approach to maximize accuracy of communication.

The effectiveness of paralegals also is influenced by how well they "read" the cultural backgrounds of those with whom they interact. This involves manner of speaking, dressing, and acting, and whether one is a man or a woman in that culture. What is heard may not be what was intended. What is perceived may not be what the other person perceives, because of cultural differences that affect the interpretation of words and body language. We will briefly highlight some general characteristics of four cultural groups.

European background. Generally, the countries of Western Europe, including Scandinavia, comprise the group of European background. This group is extraordinarily large and complex, which limits attempts to make cultural generalities. In terms of gender differences, men and women with roots in the European culture may have different initial reactions to the paralegal and attitudes about the topic. Male and female listeners alike tend to perceive men as having more credibility than women of equal rank, experience, and training. Men tend to be more credible to other men, and women may be more credible to other women.

Now consider the cultural implications of graphic pictures of physical injuries from car crashes. These photos are acceptable in the United States, but Germans tend to dislike the sight of blood and the British are likely to be offended by violence.

According to Kenton and Valentine, if the paralegal appears to be European–American, receivers of communication may be concerned that the paralegal will:

- reject their opinions;
- take advantage of them or hold them back;
- consider them different in a negative way;
- deny them equal opportunities.

Latino background. Collectively, Latin America encompasses 51 countries generally considered to be those south of the U.S. border: Mexico and the countries of Central America, South America, and the Caribbean islands. With so vast an area, many differences can be expected from country to country and even from city to city. The languages, too, are not the same. Portuguese is spoken in Brazil, and the Spanish that is spoken in South America differs from the Spanish spoken in Puerto Rico. The Latino–American population has moved closer to becoming the largest minority group in the United States. According to Kenton and Valentine, individuals with roots in the Latino culture tend to:

- value family and loyalty to family;
- honor nationalism;
- exhibit a strong sense of honor;
- have a fatalistic view of the world;
- express passion in speech, manner, and deed.

Asian background.   More than 30 countries can be considered Asian—among them, China, Malaysia, Japan, the Philippines, India, and Korea. They, too, demonstrate vast differences from culture to culture. Some generalizations may be made, however. Asian cultures generally consider that being direct and to the point is rude, and relationships are considered top priority. The Japanese, for example, tend to prefer an indirect style of communication. In communicating with people who have an Asian background, then, it might be best to begin with pleasantries about the weather, sports, or inquire about the well-being of the individual and his or her family.

Roots in the African culture.   African Americans represent the largest ethnic group in the United States. A distinction should be made between African Americans of recent immigration with stronger cultural ties to the African culture and African Americans with long family ties within the United States whose cultural roots are American. According to Kenton and Valentine, some of the African core beliefs and cultural values that may influence attitudes and behavior are:

- a holistic worldview;
- emotion and expressiveness;
- a keen sense of justice or fairness.

Conducting the Interview

In the first meeting, the paralegal must make clear that he or she is a paralegal and not an attorney. During the first few minutes of the interview, paralegals must build a relationship with the interviewees, explain the reason for the interview, and eliminate any barriers that would prevent obtaining the necessary information. Sometimes the interviewees seem to be fully cooperative when in fact they are not cooperating. Or the subject matter may be embarrassing, or they may have a fear of authority figures, or they might be uncomfortable using certain terms necessary to describe the situation.

Effective interviewers learn the verbal and nonverbal cues that help them understand the reasons for interviewees' reluctance to answer questions. In some situations the solution is first to ask easy questions, such as the person's name and address. Once interviewees start speaking, they have less trouble answering well thought-out questions that build logically on the previous information.

This is not always the case, though. In times of great stress, clients have been known to read the name from a nameplate in the office and state it as their own name! The interviewer must be careful to avoid embarrassing the interviewee and have prepared questions that can be answered easily and thereby help the person gain composure, such as, "My records show that you live at 123 South Main Street. Is that correct?" Or "How do you spell your name?"

Listening Skills

A good interviewer must master the skill of listening. Most of us hear the words being said but may not be listening to *what* is being said. Instead of concentrating on what is being said, listeners may be more concerned with the next question they want to

CHECKLIST Listening Skills

☐ Empathize with the person, and try to put yourself in his or her place to help you see the point.

☐ Don't interrupt; allow time for the person to say what he or she is trying to say.

☐ Leave your emotions behind, and control your anger. Emotions will prevent you from listening well.

☐ Get rid of distractions.

☐ Don't argue mentally.

☐ Don't antagonize the speaker. This could cause someone to conceal important ideas, emotions, and attitudes.

☐ Avoid jumping to conclusions. This can get you into trouble. For example, don't assume that the speaker is using the words in the same way that you are interpreting them. If you are unsure, ask for clarification.

© Student Counseling Service, Texas A&M University.

ask, or emotionally influenced by the speaker's message, or distracted by the speaker's physical behavior.

Interviewing clients and witnesses requires listening to what is being said in the context of the speaker's cultural makeup. It also requires an understanding of the type of witness—friendly, hostile, or expert—and the witnesses' bias toward the client or the type of case for which they are being interviewed. Fact witnesses may not want to get involved, or be hostile witnesses, saying what they either think you want to hear or what will move their agenda along. Fact witnesses in criminal matters involving members of different races or religions may not be as concerned for the truth as they are for "someone paying" for committing the crime. Bias and cultural identity may influence what is said.

The professional interviewer must listen to what is really being said in a non-judgmental impartial manner.

When listening, the paralegal must focus on what is said and not how it is said. Some people are not articulate, and the facts may be lost if a person doesn't listen carefully. Others may try to shock or put off the paralegal by buzz words designed to get a reaction. In sports, this is referred to as "trash talk"—saying things to get the listener to react emotionally and lose concentration.

Good listeners avoid distractions. They do not allow themselves to lose focus because of environmental distractions such as noise or activity in the area of the interview, or a speaker's annoying physical habits, such as tapping the fingers or legs, or speech impediments, such as stuttering. Think about how hard it is to concentrate on what is being said in a large classroom. Good listeners focus on the message and block out distractions.

Further, good interviewers do not make assumptions about the facts of the case. They listen with an open mind. Making assumptions about people or facts can lead to attempts to make the facts fit the interviewer's preconceived notions. Sometimes the facts are not what they first seem to be. Look at the number of people released from jail after DNA evidence proves they did not do the crime everyone assumed they committed. Fact witnesses may have been interviewed and been given a version of the incident that the DNA does not prove to be correct, and the person is innocent.

Leading Questions

Leading questions are those that suggest the desired answer. In conducting a cross-examination, lawyers in trial frequently use leading questions to force the witness to answer in a desired manner. An obvious example is, "Have you stopped kicking your dog?"

On direct examination, an attorney might ask a more direct and neutral question: "Have you ever kicked your dog?"

Leading questions do not lead to open-ended answers but are directed toward a desired answer: "You ran the red light, didn't you?"

 Web Exploration

For more information on listening skills see the Texas A&M Website at http://www.scs.tamu.edu/selfhelp/elibrary/listening_skills.asp.

Leading question A question which suggests the answer.

Open-Ended Questions

Open-ended question
A question that usually does not have a yes or no answer.

Narrative opportunity
A question that allows the giving of a full explanation.

Open-ended questions are designed to give interviewees an opportunity to tell their story without the limitation of yes-or-no answers. Open-ended questions create a **narrative opportunity** for the witness. For example: "Tell me about your life"; "Tell me about your life since the accident."

In fact interviews, the witness should receive the opportunity for open-ended narrative answers. Asking a question to solicit an answer that you desire may cut off information that is essential to your case. For example, you may want to know whether your client was at the scene of an accident, and therefore you ask the witness, "Did you see my client at the scene of the accident?" The answer to this question may be "yes" or "no." A better question would be, "Who was present at the scene of the accident?" This kind of question may lead to additional information on additional witnesses you may want to interview.

Similarly, the question, "How fast were the cars going prior to the impact?" is much better than, "Were the cars speeding before the impact?" In this context, the term "speeding" may be interpreted as exceeding the speed limit instead of going too fast for the conditions.

With the witness's statements from the interview in hand at the time of trial, the trial attorney might appropriately ask a leading question such as, "My client wasn't present at the scene of the accident, was she?" Or, "Isn't it true that the defendant was speeding before the impact?" With knowledge of the prior statement, there should be no surprise in the answer at trial. If there is, the prior statement can be used to impeach the credibility of the witness, if desired, as part of the trial strategy.

At times, the interviewer may want to focus clients or witnesses by asking questions that give them a perspective of time or place, such as, "What did you observe at noon on Saturday?" or, "Tell me what happened on September 11, 2001." The tragedy of that day will haunt the memories of Americans and most of the rest of the world, so little stimulus will be needed to elicit where they were and what they observed. This is true of most traumatic events in people's lives—the loss of a loved one, the birth of a child, or a serious accident in which they were injured. Other days and times tend to blur and have to be brought to the consciousness of the witness by questions such as, "Let's think back to August 19, 2001" and, "What happened to you that day?"

Discovery Limitations

Discovery is the more formal term for the pretrial process of learning everything relevant about the case. This includes the investigation phase where basic information is gathered without the formality of statements signed under oath, such as written interrogatories, or before a court reporter authorized to administer oaths such as in a formal deposition.

The scope of the inquiry is only limited generally to that which is relevant. Evidence is relevant if the fact is logically connected and tends to prove or disprove a fact in issue. Under the federal rules of evidence:

Rule 26 (b)

Discovery Scope and Limits.
(1) Scope in General.
Unless otherwise limited by court order, the scope of discovery is as follows: Parties may obtain discovery regarding any nonprivileged matter that is relevant to any party's claim or defense—including the existence, description, nature, custody, condition, and location of any documents or other tangible things and the identity and location of persons who know of any discoverable matter. For good cause, the court may order discovery of any matter relevant to the subject matter involved in the action. Relevant information need not be admissible at the trial if the discovery appears reasonably calculated to lead to the discovery of admissible evidence. All discovery is subject to the limitations imposed by Rule 26(b)(2)(C).

For the investigator or interviewer, the rule then is: Information may be sought, even if it is not admissible, as long as it is relevant and may lead to relevant information that will be admissible at trial. This includes information that may be used in trial to show bias, lack of credibility, and challenges to the qualifications of an expert.

Moral Versus Ethical Considerations

At times in the investigation of a case, it is necessary to consider the difference between a moral consideration and an ethical consideration. A **moral obligation** is one based on one's own conscience or a person's perceived rules of correct conduct, generally in the person's own community. Some communities, for instance, may consider it to be morally improper to ask someone to give information about another person. An **ethical obligation**, for members of the legal team including those acting on behalf of a supervising attorney, are the responsibilities of the legal profession under the ABA Model Rules of Professional Conduct, including thoroughness in representing a client.

Is it ethically improper to ask someone to tell the truth surrounding the facts of a case that may lead to a neighbor, relative, or friend being subjected to liability for his or her actions? For the paralegal and the legal team, the primary ethical obligation is the duty to the client. Some members of the legal team, for example, may be offended to ask a mother to testify against a child. This is a moral issue for the mother, in which the results may cause financial hardship or ruin upon awarding a verdict for causing injury as the result of negligent conduct, but ethics may require this course of conduct for the paralegal.

Privileged Communication

Certain forms of communication are considered privileged and not usable at trial unless the privilege is waived. Forms of **privileged communication** are:

1. Attorney–client communications
2. Doctor–patient communications
3. Priest–penitent communications
4. Spousal communications during marriage

Each of these privileges can be waived but the waiver must come from the client, the patient, the penitent, or the spouse making the statement with the belief that it is privileged. Changes in some of the rules of ethics, and by statute, may permit certain otherwise privileged communications to be revealed to prevent harm or injury to another. The spouse, the priest, or the doctor may have a moral issue in revealing what was communicated.

When the paralegal is acting on behalf of the attorney, communications between a client and the paralegal have the same privilege as those between the client and the attorney. Information gathered from the client as part of representation of

Moral obligation An obligation based on one's own conscience.

Ethical obligation A minimum standard of conduct usually within one's profession.

Privileged communication A communication that the person has a right to be kept confidential based on the relationship with the other part such as attorney and client.

ETHICAL PERSPECTIVE
New Hampshire Rules of Professional Conduct
RULE 1.6. CONFIDENTIALITY OF INFORMATION

(a) A lawyer shall not reveal information relating to the representation of a client unless the client gives informed consent. The disclosure is impliedly authorized in order to carry out the representation or the disclosure is permitted by paragraph (B).

 Web Exploration

Contrast and compare the New Hampshire Rule at http://www .courts.state.NH.US/supreme/ orders/20072507.pdf with the ABA Model Rules at www.abanet.org/cpr and the rule in your jurisdiction.

the client and necessary for rendering competent legal advice is privileged. The paralegal, therefore, is in the same position as the attorney, the doctor, the priest, or the spouse to whom the confidential information has been communicated. Each must carefully guard the confidential information and not inadvertently or intentionally reveal the information. In some cases, such as when another person's life may be in danger, these people may be compelled by a court to testify even when they believe it is a violation of their moral duty to another person from whom they have received information.

Expert Witnesses

Expert witness A person qualified by education or experience to render an opinion based on a set of facts.

Expert witnesses are individuals whose background, education, and experience are such that courts recognize them as qualified to give opinions based on a set of facts. The expert witness may be a doctor certified by a board of medical experts or a scientist or engineer specializing in an area of science such as flammability of fabrics. The report of these experts may be advice based on the facts of a potential case to determine whether there is sufficient evidence to believe that a wrong has occurred or malpractice committed. Without this report, the lawyers may be obligated to advise clients that they have no actionable cause of action.

There is no clear rule on whether what is revealed to an expert in the preparation of a case is protected as part of the attorney–client privilege in the same manner as that revealed to a member of the trial team, including other attorneys, paralegals, and secretarial staff working on the case with the primary trial attorney. Almost certainly, anything revealed to an expert who is listed as an expert witness on the list of witnesses to be called at trial is discoverable.

Some law firms retain an expert to advise them but do not use that expert to testify. The advice and information provided by these experts to help in the preparation

IN THE WORDS OF THE COURT

Federal Rules of Civil Procedure 26 F.R.C.P. 26(b)(4)

(4) Trial Preparation: Experts

(A) A party may depose any person who has been identified as an expert whose opinions may be presented at trial. If a report from the expert is required under subdivision (a)(2)(B), the deposition shall not be conducted until after the report is provided.

(B) A party may, through interrogatories or by deposition, discover facts known or opinions held by an expert who has been retained or specially employed by another party in anticipation of litigation or preparation for trial and who is not expected to be called as a witness at trial, only as provided in Rule 35(b) or upon a showing of exceptional circumstances under which it is impracticable for the party seeking discovery to obtain facts or opinions on the same subject by other means.

(C) Unless manifest injustice would result, (i) the court shall require that the party seeking discovery pay the expert a reasonable fee for time spent in responding to discovery under this subdivision; and (ii) with respect to discovery obtained under subdivision (b)(4)(B) of this rule the court shall require the party seeking discovery to pay the other party a fair portion of the fees and expenses reasonably incurred by the latter party in obtaining facts and opinions from the expert.

for trial may come under the privilege. Although the privilege is the client's, the paralegal and others on the legal team must be careful not to divulge privileged or confidential material without authorization.

The expert retained for background trial advice must have as much confidence in the legal team as the legal team has in the expert's advice and integrity. Some experts fear that the legal team will give them only selected information. With the limited information provided, they might give an expert opinion that is not what they would have given if they had received the complete set of facts.

Exhibit 9.3 indicates factors to be considered in arranging for an expert witness.

Investigating Claims

The legal team must gather all of the relevant information about a cause of action before making a recommendation to a client to file a lawsuit or respond to a claim of wrongdoing. In most cases, before the first interview with the client is conducted, the paralegal has some indication of the area of law or the nature of the claim. It may be from a telephone interview when the client calls for an appointment, or from the referral from the supervising attorney to the paralegal to conduct the interview and investigation. If paralegals specialize in certain areas of law, they are likely to understand the underlying elements of the claims or rights the client wishes to assert. Those in general practice and those entering a new area have to understand the rules of law as they apply to that issue.

For example, in a product liability case, understanding traditional, or common-law, of negligence is not enough. One also must understand the law of **strict liability** for product defect cases as found in the **Restatement of the Law Third, Torts**: Product Liability. Where negligence requires a breach of duty, strict liability is without fault in cases where the doctrine applies. An interview conducted strictly considering negligence as the basis for a legal action could improperly result in the client's being advised that he or she does not have a claim when, under the no-fault strict liability concept for defective products, an action might exist.

The first step is to determine the legal basis of a client's claim. With an understanding of the legal basis of the claim and the applicable law, an investigative plan can be prepared to obtain the necessary witness statements, locate physical evidence, and obtain photographs, reports, and other evidence for use in preparation for and at trial. Where a claim of negligence is to be made, photographic evidence may be essential in demonstrating the nature of the hazard.

For example, when a client has injured himself or herself as the result of a fall in a store, photographs showing the hazardous condition should be obtained as quickly as possible. In the case of strict liability involving a product defect that caused injury or loss, preservation of the defective product or photographic documentation of the defect becomes essential as a matter of proof. Knowing what elements of the action must be proven dictates what evidence must be located in the form of witnesses, photographs, and physical evidence. Knowing the elements of the claim will ensure that the proper questions are asked in the interview, which then will dictate the necessary investigation steps.

One of the most useful tools in the gathering of information about a case is the digital camera. Digital photographs may be shared on computer networks or by Internet transfer to other members of the legal team, clients, and possible witnesses. It also is useful to take pictures of potential witnesses so other members of the legal team may recognize them later at the time of depositions and trial. If the photographs are going to be used at trial, it should be kept in mind that the photographer may be called to authenticate them.

Web Exploration

For more information in the changes in the revised Restatement of the Law Third, visit the American Law Institute http://www.ali.org/ali/promo6081.htm.

Strict liability Liability without fault.

Restatement of the Law Third, Torts A legal treatise with suggested rules of laws relating to torts.

Exhibit 9.3   Expert witness form

EXPERT WITNESS CHECKLIST

BACKGROUND

Full name _____   Date of birth _____

Business address _____

Business telephone number _____   Business fax number _____

Business email address _____   Business website _____

Locations of prior offices _____

Home address _____

Home telephone number _____

EDUCATION

Schools attended _____   Dates of attendance _____

Degrees or honors awarded _____

Continuing education courses _____

WORK HISTORY

Place of employment _____   Dates of employment _____

Job description _____

Reasons for leaving _____

Specific area of expertise _____

Published articles and books _____

Professional affiliations _____

Professional magazines subscribed to _____

Licenses and jurisdictions _____

Litigations or disciplinary action _____

PRIOR LEGAL EXPERIENCE

Ratio of plaintiff/defense cases _____

Prior clients including date (plaintiff or defendant) _____

Types of investigations with dates _____

Deposition testimony given with dates _____

Court testimony with dates _____

Legal references _____

AVAILABILITY

Vacation plans and dates _____   Potential meeting dates _____

In the deposition, verify the accuracy and currency of the expert's professional information, including all resume and curriculum vitae items. Verify the opinions are those of the expert and, if based on the work of others, who these others are and what other experts' writings were consulted. It is important to have on the record the assumptions upon which the expert has formed the opinion and the steps followed in reaching the opinion.

A Defense Perspective

Most people quite naturally think of a lawsuit from the plaintiff's perspective. Most people think in terms of the violation of rights and resulting injury. In a perfect world, only legitimate actions would be filed and the law would provide a perfect remedy for all wrongs. But not every plaintiff is in the right, and some have been known to file frivolous or even fraudulent lawsuits.

The balance in the American legal system is achieved by a vigorous defense on behalf of the defendant. A plaintiff may claim, for example, that she slipped and was injured as a result of the negligence of a storeowner. The defendant storeowner might be innocent of any wrongdoing or breach of any duty. It is well to remember that for every plaintiff there is a defendant, and for each party there is a law firm, an attorney, and a paralegal.

Obtaining Official Reports

Most incidents giving rise to litigation have associated official reports. In the negligence action, it may be a police accident or incident report, emergency medical services report, fire department call report, or incident reports of safety violations by federal, state, or local authorities. These reports are filed in a central depository as public records. A useful starting point is to obtain any official reports associated with the case. These reports frequently indicate time, place, and the names of fact witnesses. In some cases, detailed diagrams or photographs may accompany the reports. Exhibit 9.4 is an example of a police accident report form.

Fact Analysis

Analyzing the facts starts with interviewing the clients and their recitation of the time, place, circumstances, and other people involved as participants or witnesses. Exhibit 9.5 is a sample client interview form. A complete analysis usually requires further field investigation of the location, the object involved, such as an automobile, and interviews of the parties and witnesses. One person's perception may not be reality. A client's recollection and description of the physical surroundings may not be proven by the investigator's visit to the location. What one person describes as a narrow, congested walkway may actually be a standard-width open sidewalk.

The ultimate trier of fact will be the jury, a panel of arbitrators, or a judge acting as the trier of fact. Therefore, analysis of the facts must be sufficient to justify the position taken and the presentation made in pursuing a client's claim or its defense in **arbitration** or in trial.

Arbitration A form of ADR in which the parties choose an impartial third party to hear and decide the dispute.

Locations

Careful analysis of a claim includes verification of the physical aspects of the actual location where the cause of action occurred. Ask any group of people to describe a location, and you're likely to get as many different descriptions as there are people in the group. How the person viewed the location, from the south, from the north, east, or west, may influence their description. Or the driver's view from behind the wheel of a large tractor-trailer might be different from the view from behind the wheel of a small sports car.

Investigation of a case should involve a trip to the location where the incident occurred. The trier of fact will be relying upon the plaintiff's and defendant's counsels to describe in their presentation the characteristics of the physical location. They also will be looking at the location from an impartial, neutral point of view, usually without prior familiarity with the location. The diagrams usually presented at trial are those of an aerial view with its sterile, one-dimensional presentation. Photographs from the points of view of all the participants can make the difference in understanding the duties and responsibilities of the litigants. Unlike diagrams of the location, these photographs more typically will be from the point of view of the plaintiff, defendant, or witness at ground level, or from behind the wheel of a vehicle, or looking out of a building window.

Exhibit 9.4   Sample police accident report form

COMMONWEALTH OF PENNSYLVANIA
POLICE ACCIDENT REPORT

(XX.) REFER TO OVERLAY SHEETS

REPORTABLE ☐   NON - REPORTABLE ☐   PENNDOT USE ONLY

POLICE INFORMATION

1. INCIDENT NUMBER
2. AGENCY NAME
3. STATION/ PRECINCT
4. PATROL ZONE
5. INVESTIGATOR — BADGE NUMBER
6. APPROVED BY — BADGE NUMBER
7. INVESTIGATION DATE
8. ARRIVAL TIME

ACCIDENT INFORMATION

9. ACCIDENT DATE
10. DAY OF WEEK
11. TIME OF DAY
12. NUMBER OF UNITS
13. # KILLED
14. # INJURED
15. PRIV. PROP. ACCIDENT   Y ☐   N ☐
16. DID VEHICLE HAVE TO BE REMOVED FROM THE SCENE?   UNIT 1   Y ☐ N ☐   UNIT 2   Y ☐ N ☐
17. VEHICLE DAMAGE 0 - NONE 1 - LIGHT 2 - MODERATE 3 - SEVERE   UNIT 1 ☐   UNIT 2 ☐
18. HAZARDOUS MATERIALS   Y ☐   N ☐
19. PENNDOT PROPERTY   Y ☐   N ☐

ACCIDENT   LOCATION

20. COUNTY   CODE
21. MUNICIPALITY   CODE

PRINCIPAL   ROADWAY INFORMATION

22. ROUTE NO. OR STREET NAME
23. SPEED LIMIT
24. TYPE HIGHWAY
25. ACCESS CONTROL

INTERSECTING ROAD:

26. ROUTE NO. OR STREET NAME
27. SPEED LIMIT
28. TYPE HIGHWAY
29. ACCESS CONTROL

IF NOT AT INTERSECTION:

30. CROSS STREET OR SEGMENT MARKER
31. DIRECTION FROM SITE   N S E W
32. DISTANCE FROM SITE   FT.   MI.
33. DISTANCE WAS   MEASURED ☐   ESTIMATED ☐
34. CONSTRUCTION ZONE ☐
35. TRAFFIC CONTROL DEVICE   PRINCIPAL ☐   INTERSECTING ☐

UNIT # 1

36. LEGALLY PARKED? Y☐ N☐	37. REG. PLATE	38. STATE
39. PA TITLE OR OUT-OF-STATE VIN		
40. OWNER		
41. OWNER ADDRESS		
42. CITY, STATE & ZIPCODE		
43. YEAR	44. MAKE	
45. MODEL - (NOT BODY TYPE)	46. INS. Y☐ N☐ UNK☐	
47. BODY TYPE	48. SPECIAL USAGE	49. VEHICLE OWNERSHIP
50. INITIAL IMPACT POINT	51. VEHICLE STATUS	52. TRAVEL SPEED
53. VEHICLE GRADIENT	54. DRIVER PRESENCE	55. DRIVER CONDITION
56. DRIVER NUMBER		57. STATE
58. DRIVER NAME		
59. DRIVER ADDRESS		
60. CITY, STATE & ZIPCODE		
61. SEX	62. DATE OF BIRTH	63. PHONE
64. COMM. VEH. Y☐ N☐	65. DRIVER CLASS	66. DRIVER SS#
67. CARRIER		
68. CARRIER ADDRESS		
69. CITY, STATE & ZIPCODE		
70. USDOT #	ICC #	PUC #
72. VEH. CONFIG.	73. CARGO BODY TYPE	74. GVWR
75. NO. OF AXLES	76. HAZARDOUS MATERIALS	77. RELEASE OF HAZ MAT Y☐ N☐ UNK☐

UNIT # 2

36. LEGALLY PARKED? Y☐ N☐	37. REG. PLATE	38. STATE
39. PA TITLE OR OUT-OF-STATE VIN		
40. OWNER		
41. OWNER ADDRESS		
42. CITY, STATE & ZIPCODE		
43. YEAR	44. MAKE	
45. MODEL - (NOT BODY TYPE)	46. INS. Y☐ N☐ UNK☐	
47. BODY TYPE	48. SPECIAL USAGE	49. VEHICLE OWNERSHIP
50. INITIAL IMPACT POINT	51. VEHICLE STATUS	52. TRAVEL SPEED
53. VEHICLE GRADIENT	54. DRIVER PRESENCE	55. DRIVER CONDITION
56. DRIVER NUMBER		57. STATE
58. DRIVER NAME		
59. DRIVER ADDRESS		
60. CITY, STATE & ZIPCODE		
61. SEX	62. DATE OF BIRTH	63. PHONE
64. COMM. VEH. Y☐ N☐	65. DRIVER CLASS	66. DRIVER SS#
67. CARRIER		
68. CARRIER ADDRESS		
69. CITY, STATE & ZIPCODE		
70. USDOT #	ICC #	PUC #
72. VEH. CONFIG.	73. CARGO BODY TYPE	74. GVWR
75. NO. OF AXLES	76. HAZARDOUS MATERIALS	77. RELEASE OF HAZ MAT Y☐ N☐ UNK☐

AA-45 (1/92)   PAGE·   CENTER FOR HIGHWAY SAFETY

Exhibit 9.4 **Sample police accident report form** *(continued)*

78. RESPONDING EMS AGENCY									INCIDENT #:						
79. MEDICAL FACILITY									ACCIDENT DATE:						

80. PEOPLE INFORMATION

A	B	C	D	E	F	G	NAME	ADDRESS	H	I	J	K	L	M

81. ILLUMINATION 82. WEATHER 83. ROAD SURFACE

86. DIAGRAM

84. PENNSYLVANIA SCHOOL DISTRICT (IF APPLICABLE)

85. DESCRIPTION OF DAMAGED PROPERTY

OWNER

ADDRESS

PHONE

87. NARRATIVE - IDENTIFY PRECIPITATING EVENTS, CAUSATION FACTORS, SEQUENCE OF EVENTS, WITNESS STATEMENTS, AND PROVIDE ADDITIONAL DETAILS. LIKE INSURANCE INFORMATION AND LOCATION OF TOWED VEHILCES, IF KNOWN.

INSURANCE INFORMATION UNIT 1 — COMPANY — POLICY NO.
INSURANCE INFORMATION UNIT 2 — COMPANY — POLICY NO.

88. WINTESSES: NAME / ADDRESS / PHONE

	89. VIOLATIONS INDICATED	90. SECTION NUMBERS (ONLY IF CHARGED)	TC NTC
UNIT 1			
UNIT 2			

	91. PROBABLE USE	92. TYPE TEST	93. RESULTS			91. PROBABLE USE	92. TYPE TEST	93. RESULTS		94. INVESTIGATION COMPLETE?
UNIT 1			0.___% NO TEST REFUSE UNK	UNIT 2				0.___% NO TEST REFUSE UNK		YES NO

AA-45 (1/92)   PAGE: CENTER FOR HIGHWAY SAFETY

Source: Pennsylvania Department of Transporatation, Bureau of Highway Safety and Traffic Engineering. Used with permission.

Exhibit 9.5   Initial client interview form

CLIENT INTERVIEW CHECKLIST

CLIENT PERSONAL INFORMATION

Name

Address

City   State   Zip

Phone (hm)   (wk)   (cell)

How long at this address

Date of birth   Place of birth

Social Security No.

Prior address

City   State   Zip

Dates at this address

Employer:

Job description

Marital status   Maiden name

Spouse's name   Date of birth

Child's name   Date of birth

Child's name   Date of birth

Child's name   Date of birth

CASE INFORMATION

Case referred by

Case type: ☐ Appeal   ☐ Business   ☐ Corporate   ☐ Estate   ☐ Litigation
              ☐ Municipal   ☐ Real Estate   ☐ Tax   ☐ Trust   ☐ Other

Opposing party(ies)

Opposing party

Address

Opposing attorney

Address

Date of incident   Statute of limitation date

Summary of facts

_____

_____

_____

_____

Web Exploration

Find your home on Google Earth at http://earth.google.com.

Satellite photos are available of locations around the world. Earth Google™ offers a Web access to images that may be modified to add desired descriptions such as street names, points of interest, including lodgings, restaurants, schools, churches, and many others by the click of the computer mouse. Images from before a loss such as Hurricane Katrina combined with images taken after the devastation may be helpful in submitting claims for damages.

Tangible Evidence

Tangible evidence consists of the physical objects that may have caused the injury. These may include items as small as a giveaway toy from a fast-food restaurant swallowed by a

2-year-old, to a bottle that exploded, to a large automobile whose brakes failed or whose seatbelts snapped. In some cases, the tangible evidence is essential to proving negligence or an element of strict liability in tort.

Much has been written about the effects of the plaintiffs' and defendants' failure to preserve critical evidence of this type. In some cases, failure to preserve the evidence has resulted in loss of the case by the plaintiff, and in other cases by the defendant.

It is important to understand the local rules with regard to **spoliation of evidence** and its effect on a cause of action. In determining the proper penalty for spoliation of evidence, courts are most likely to consider [*Schroeder v. Department of Transportation*, 551 Pa. 243, 710 A.2d 23, 26 (1998)]:

Spoliation of evidence
Destruction of evidence.

1. The degree of fault of the party who altered or destroyed the evidence.
2. The degree of prejudice suffered by the opposing party.
3. The availability of a lesser sanction that will protect the opposing party's rights and deter future similar conduct.

Following a Timeline

Causes of action should be viewed from the events leading up to the incident to the events and occurrences following the incident. (See Exhibit 9.6 for a comparison of conflicting accounts.) Few things in life that give rise to a potential claim occur in a vacuum. Usually some facts lead up to the incident and others follow the incident. The question may be, "Given the time in which the parties allege this happened, could this really have happened?" For example, could the parties have driven the 30 miles in

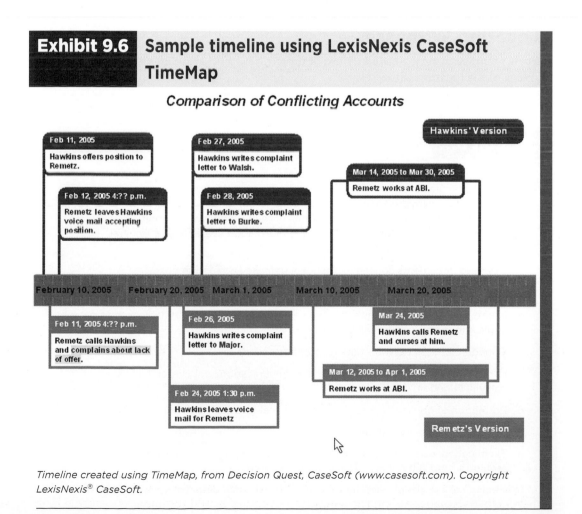

Exhibit 9.6 **Sample timeline using LexisNexis CaseSoft TimeMap**

Comparison of Conflicting Accounts

Hawkins' Version

Feb 11, 2005
Hawkins offers position to Remetz.

Feb 12, 2005 4:?? p.m.
Remetz leaves Hawkins voice mail accepting position.

Feb 27, 2005
Hawkins writes complaint letter to Walsh.

Feb 28, 2005
Hawkins writes complaint letter to Burke.

Mar 14, 2005 to Mar 30, 2005
Remetz works at ABI.

February 10, 2005 — February 20, 2005 — March 1, 2005 — March 10, 2005 — March 20, 2005

Feb 11, 2005 4:?? p.m.
Remetz calls Hawkins and complains about lack of offer.

Feb 26, 2005
Hawkins writes complaint letter to Major.

Feb 24, 2005 1:30 p.m.
Hawkins leaves voice mail for Remetz

Mar 24, 2005
Hawkins calls Remetz and curses at him.

Mar 12, 2005 to Apr 1, 2005
Remetz works at ABI.

Remetz's Version

Timeline created using TimeMap, from Decision Quest, CaseSoft (www.casesoft.com). Copyright LexisNexis® CaseSoft.

Web Exploration

The CPSC FOIA Request form can be completed online at http://xapps.cpsc.gov/FOIA/pages/requestentry.jsp.

Freedom of Information Act
A federal statute permitting access to federal agency records.

Web Exploration

Obtain a copy of the latest CPSC FOIA report at http://www.cpsc.gov/LIBRARY/FOIA/foia.html.

Web Exploration

For information or making an FOIA request to the Department of Justice is available at www.usdoj.gov/04foia/.

20 minutes through crowded rush-hour traffic on city streets? In a food-poisoning case, could ingestion of the food at noon have caused the reaction claimed by 1:00 P.M. The claimant might have been negligent, or the first perceived wrongdoer perhaps was not the correct person, as most food-poisoning cases require 6 to 12 hours from ingestion of the tainted food until onset of symptoms of the illness.

The starting point is the time of the alleged injury. Also important, from a fault standpoint or defense standpoint, is what happened that led up to the incident. From the damages standpoint, what happened after the incident, including treatment and subsequent changes in the person's life or lifestyle, is important.

Freedom of Information Act (FOIA)

The **Freedom of Information Act** is a federal statute designed to open to the public the information possessed by the federal government and its agencies. President Obama issued a memorandum for the heads of executive departments and agencies highlighting the importance of openness of government that resulted in additional information being made available to the public under the FOIA. See Exhibit 9.7.

Many federal agencies do not require a formal FOIA request. Some federal agencies, such as the National Transportation Agency, make information available online (Exhibit 9.8). Other agencies, such as the Consumer Product Safety Commission (CPSC), permit requests to be made on the CPSC website (see Exhibit 9.9). The CPSC site also is helpful in finding information about defective products that may be a cause of a client's injuries. Limitations are placed on the information that an agency may disclose under applicable federal law. See examples in the CPSC limitations shown in the **sidebar** and the NTSB limitations shown in Exhibit 9.10.

Locating Witnesses

Most witnesses can be located by use of directories. The Web has also become a valuable tool for locating witnesses.

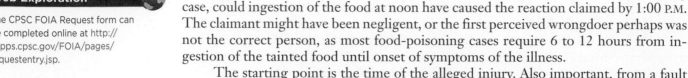

Exhibit 9.7 Freedom of Information Act

The federal government is a good source of information. Many of the documents required to be filed are available through the government, and frequently online, such as corporate filings with the Securities and Exchange Commission. Other information may be available by request, under the provisions of the Freedom of Information Act (FOIA), 5 U.S.C. § 552. Some limitations apply to the information available. The general exceptions, as found in the statute, are:

1. Classified documents concerning national defense and foreign policy.

2. Internal personnel rules and practices.

3. Exemptions under other laws that require information to be withheld, such as patent applications and income-tax returns.

4. Confidential business information and trade secrets.

5. Intra-agency and inter-agency internal communications not available by law to a party in litigation.

6. Protection of privacy of personnel and medical files and private lives of individuals.

7. Law-enforcement investigatory files.

8. Examination, operation, or condition reports of agencies responsible for the regulation and supervision of financial institutions.

9. Geological and geophysical information and data including maps concerning wells.

Exhibit 9.8 Simplified online FOIA form to request information not already available from National Transporation Safety Board (NTSB)

Freedom of Information Act (FOIA) Request

Be sure to read what's available under FOIA before making a request.

Please specify as much detail as possible about the item(s) you are requesting. Depending on the complexity of your request, turnaround could range from 3 weeks to 1 year or more. For assistance, please contact the Records Management Division at (800) 877-6799 or (202) 314-6551.

First Name: _____

Last Name: _____

Street: _____

City: _____

State: [▾]   Zip: _____

Transportation: [- Select Mode - ▾]

Email Addr: _____

Phone No: _____

Business/Affiliation: _____

Country: _____

Please describe your request or comment below - be specific about dates, locations, etc., where applicable:

_____

Directories

Investigators usually keep a collection of telephone books of the areas in which they work. Rarely today does a person not have a telephone of some sort, even if it is an unlisted number. In addition to the standard-issue telephone directories, the cross-reference directory (also known as a "criss-cross directory") is a standard tool; these list phone numbers by address or by phone number instead of by name. Therefore, an address may be checked for a corresponding phone number—for example, determining the phone number located at 123 Main Street, or using the phone numbers listed at an address to determine the physical location or billing address of the phone.

Telephone directories are not limited to just the United States but typically are published in most parts of the world in one form or another. Companies and businesses also can be located by use of commercial or industrial telephone directories, both domestically and internationally.

In addition to telephone directories, directories are published by trade organizations, professional groups, and educational institutions. These directories may be limited to membership but can be useful in cases where the name and the association are known, but not the city, state, or country where the person can be found.

The Web

As paper is replaced by electronic media, directories are being placed online. Search engines can help locate individuals, businesses, and organizations on the Internet. Communications companies and other private firms offer a number of online white pages for individuals and yellow pages for businesses. Many organizations and publishers of professional directories now offer their print directories online. An example is the Web version of Martindale–Hubbell for attorneys. These services may change or cancel their Web address and others may be added, so the list of websites has to be kept up to date.

 Web Exploration

Check frequently requested information at the NTSB website http://www.ntsb.gov/info/foia.htm.

 Web Exploration

Experts can be located using the Lexis Nexis/Martindale–Hubbell free website at http://resources.martindale.com/mhes/index.jsp.

SIDEBAR

CPSC LIMITATIONS OF FOIA DISCLOSURE

15 U.S.C. § 2055. Public disclosure of information release date: 2005-08-01

(a) Disclosure requirements for manufacturers or private labelers; procedures applicable

  (1) Nothing contained in this Act shall be construed to require the release of any information described by subsection (b) of section 552 of title 5 or which is otherwise protected by law from disclosure to the public.

  (2) All information reported to or otherwise obtained by the Commission or its representative under this Act which information contains or relates to a trade secret or other matter referred to in section 1905 of title 18 or subject to section 552 (b)(4) of title 5 shall be considered confidential and shall not be disclosed.

  (3) The Commission shall, prior to the disclosure of any information which will permit the public to ascertain readily the identity of a manufacturer or private labeler of a consumer product, offer such manufacturer or private labeler an opportunity to mark such information as confidential and therefore barred from disclosure under paragraph (2).

  (4) All information that a manufacturer or private labeler has marked to be confidential and barred from disclosure under paragraph (2), either at the time of submission or pursuant to paragraph (3), shall not be disclosed, except in accordance with the procedures established in paragraphs (5) and (6). . . .

Exhibit 9.9 Online Freedom of Information request form for USPSC

US Consumer Product Safety Commission

▸ Consumer Safety   ▸ About CPSC   ▸ Library - FOIA   ▸ Business

New FOIA Request Form
Requestor Information

Name Prefix:
* Last Name:
* First Name:
Phone No:
* Email Address:

If you represent a company or firm, enter it below, otherwise enter personal information.

Company Name:
Website:
* Mailing Address:
* City:
* State:
* ZIP Code:
* Country: United States

Request Detail

* Range of Search Request: 2002   * To   2005
* Subject:
* Request Type:
* Type of Requestor:
Product Description:
Brand/Model:
* Remarks:

* Some requests will include fees. Please check if you accept any fees associated with this request.

Submit   Clear

* Indicates Required Field
Questions on submitting a FOIA request should be directed to aheqgs@cpsc.gov

The Web is also a good source of information about individuals, both expert and lay witnesses. Social networking sites such as Facebook offer information on millions of people who otherwise would not be in a directory. A search of Facebook, the video website YouTube, blogs, and other similar websites may produce information useful for finding people and learning about them, both good and questionable behavior that might demonstrate a credibility issue. For example, the posting of a Web camera image of a high-profile person like Michael Phelps at a party that resulted in a loss of endorsement contract with a cereal company because of questions of improper conduct. Public postings by the potential parties and witnesses may indicate a potential bias, hostility, or in the case of a potential juror, a predisposition or judgment. In some cases, jurors posting to their websites, Facebook, or other social networking sites may show a violation of jury deliberation secrecy that might result in a new trial.

Interviews, Investigations, and Trials

It is never too soon to start preparing for trial. Trial preparation starts with the first client contact and gathering the first document. Good preparation for trial includes an

Exhibit 9.10 Limitations on disclosure by the NTSB

NTSB EXEMPTIONS

The four most common exemptions under which the NTSB withholds information are:

(1) 5 USC 552 (b)(5), draft reports and staff analyses (see 49 CFR 801.54);

(2) 5 USC 552 (b)(6), personal information, where a personal interest in privacy outweighs a public interest in release; this includes graphic photographs of injuries in accidents and autopsy reports (see 49 CFR 801.55);

(3) 5 USC 552 (b)(4), Trade Secrets and/or confidential financial/commercial information submitted by private persons or corporations to the NTSB in the course of an investigation (see 49 CFR 801.59); and

(4) 5 USC 552 (b)(3), information protected from release by another statute (see 49 CFR 801.53). This includes information such as:

- Cockpit Voice Recorder (CVR) tapes. Release of the tapes is prohibited by 49 USC 1114(c). However, the Board will release a CVR transcript [edited or unedited], the timing of such release is also controlled by statute – 49 USC 1114(c)(B);

- Voluntarily provided safety-related information. 49 USC 1114(b)(3) prohibits the release of such information if it is not related to the exercise of the Board's accident or incident investigation authority and if the Board finds that the disclosure would inhibit the voluntary provision of that type of information; and

- Records or information relating to the NTSB's participation in foreign aircraft accident investigations. 49 USC 1114(e) prohibits the release of this information before the country conducting the investigation releases its report or 2 years following the accident, whichever occurs first.

---

assessment of how well clients and witnesses will react in depositions or in court under the pressure of cross-examination and how they will be perceived by opposing counsel, the judge, or the jury. Will they come across sympathetically as being truthful and likeable? Or will they appear sneaky, unpleasant, and trying to hide the truth? These observational notes may be of great interest when the legal team must decide whether to settle or try the case.

A practical consideration in deciding whether to try a case before a jury is how the parties will appear to the jury. If the client appears to be sympathetic and deserving and the opposing party unsympathetic and having adequate financial resources, a jury may try to reward the client with a finding unsupported by the facts or evidence.

Effectively managing a case may involve reviewing, sorting, and marking for identification hundreds or even thousands of documents, photographs, and other graphics. Careful tracking and handling should start at the beginning of the case management process. Good case management requires a thoughtful process for storing, handling, examining, evaluating, and indexing every page. In the computer age, case management includes making decisions on the appropriateness and potential use of electronic display technologies, as well as the fallback on traditional paper exhibit preparation. Demonstrative evidence, physical items, such as defective products in a strict liability action or an automobile in a motor vehicle accident, may have to be obtained and preserved for examination by expert witnesses or for use at trial.

There are almost as many different approaches to setting up case files and managing cases as there are legal teams. One of the traditional approaches includes the case notebook or case **trial notebook**. Summary information about the case is maintained in a notebook with tabs for each major activity, party, expert, or element of proof needed. A sample of the sections is shown in Exhibit 9.11. With the use of a trial notebook comes the responsibility to maintain the case file and file boxes or file cabinets into which the hardcopies of documents, exhibits, and physical evidence are maintained. If only one trial or case notebook is kept for the team, someone working on the case must take responsibility to be certain that there is no duplication of effort and that the most

Trial notebook A summary of the case tabbed for each major activity, witness, or element of proof.

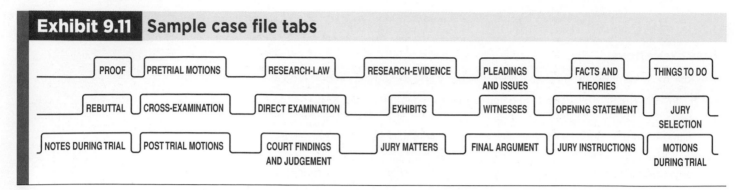

Exhibit 9.11 Sample case file tabs

PROOF	PRETRIAL MOTIONS	RESEARCH-LAW	RESEARCH-EVIDENCE	PLEADINGS AND ISSUES	FACTS AND THEORIES	THINGS TO DO
REBUTTAL	CROSS-EXAMINATION	DIRECT EXAMINATION	EXHIBITS	WITNESSES	OPENING STATEMENT	JURY SELECTION
NOTES DURING TRIAL	POST TRIAL MOTIONS	COURT FINDINGS AND JUDGEMENT	JURY MATTERS	FINAL ARGUMENT	JURY INSTRUCTIONS	MOTIONS DURING TRIAL

current activities are entered. When multiple copies are used, each trial notebook must be updated regularly, again to be sure that there is no duplication of effort and that current activity information is made available for all members of the legal team.

Case and Practice Management Software

The legal team may work on a number of cases at the same time, and each case may be in a different stage of preparation for trial. With the team approach to handling cases, each member of the team must be able to access case information and know what the other members of the team have done and what still needs to be done. In the traditional paper file case management approach, the physical file is the repository of everything from interview notes, to pleadings and exhibits. To work on the case, the physical file has to be located and the needed folder removed. In the **"paperless" office**, everything, in theory, is available on the computer screen. Documents are scanned into an electronic format and saved on the computer, pleadings and notes are saved as word-processor files, and transcripts of depositions and court hearings are stored in electronic

Paperless office An office with electronic documents.

Paralegals *in* Practice

PARALEGAL PROFILE
Kevin D. Gasiewski

Kevin D. Gasiewski is a Certified Legal Assistant Specialist in Intellectual Property. After a career in law enforcement, he obtained his first paralegal job in the City Attorney's Office of Ann Arbor, Michigan. Later, he worked for Ford Global Technologies, LLC, and is now employed by Brooks Kushman P.C. Kevin is an active member of the Legal Assistants Section of the State Bar of Michigan, of which he is a past chairperson and a recipient of its 2003 Mentor Award.

My work focuses mainly on trademark prosecution, maintenance, and protection. During the initial interview with a client interested in registering a trademark, it is important to fully identify all team members, vendors, and third-party manufacturers connected to the proposed mark. I also ask questions regarding the mark itself and who designed it, as well as the goods, services, and countries for which it is intended. This data will be needed if the trademark is challenged, and for future maintenance or protection requirements.

My job also includes protecting trademarks from illegal use. When customs officials notify us that they are detaining suspected counterfeit goods, I initiate an investigation. I examine the subject trademark, determine the origin of the goods, and ascertain the final destination of the goods. The investigation results help me confirm whether or not the suspect goods are genuine.

Interview and investigation data are stored electronically, including contacts' information, specimen images showing use of the trademark, evidence showing the fame of the mark, and documents filed in support of the mark. The databases I use also contain a field for listing key phrases, words, and acronyms to make data searches easier and more efficient.

Although formal education is a definite plus in my field, it is equally important to stress your skills when applying for a paralegal position. Not only were my police investigation and interview skills attractive to employers, these abilities also provided me with the confidence to complete the wide variety of assignments typically encountered as a trademark paralegal.

form. For the case with voluminous paperwork and days or weeks of deposition transcripts, only by use of computer file software can relevant documents or appropriate deposition notes be accessed quickly and efficiently.

A number of software programs can be used to manage the law office and the cases within the office. They generally provide what is sometimes referred to as case management, or practice management. Practice management programs have evolved out of the early programs that tracked time spent on cases, sometimes with a calendar component that could be used to track deadlines such as the statute of limitations for a case. Modern programs may include practice management functions such as time and cost tracking, calendaring, conflict checking, scheduling, and contact management. Others allow for management of the individual cases, tracking of documents, parties, issues, and events.

Software

Case management software is evolving constantly as the various vendors try to meet the demands and needs of their respective customers. Some nonlegal-specific software has case or practice management-type functions. Microsoft Outlook provides a combination contact manager, calendar–scheduler, task "to do" list, and email function. More sophisticated programs such as Practice Manager from Tabs3 provide the same functions, as well as outlining, billing, integrated research management, timelines, and other functions. LexisNexis CaseSoft provides individual programs that can share data, including CaseMap, TimeMap, TextMap, and NoteMap. One of the features of CaseMap is the ability to organize a case by facts, objects or parties, chronology, as shown in Exhibit 9.12, and then seamlessly create timelines from the chronological information by using the TimeMap program (see Exhibit 9.13). Summation's litigation support software allows transcripts, documents, issues, and events to be managed using computer technology.

Web Exploration

The complete set of General Guidelines for Judge Bruce Kauffman may be viewed at www .paed.uscourts .gov/documents/ procedures/kaupol.pdf.

Exhibit 9.12   CaseMap features

Main	Date & Time	Fact Text	Source(s)	Key	Status +	Linked Issues	Eval by CA	Eval
	06/??/1999	William Lang makes decision to reduce size of staff.	Deposition of William Lang, 43:19	☐	Undisputed	Age Discrim Against Hawkins	↘	
Facts	07/??/1999	Susan Sheridan is terminated.	Deposition of Philip Hawkins	☐	Undisputed	Pattern & Practice	↓	
	Sun 07/04/1999	Philip Hawkins allegedly makes derogatory remarks about Linda Collins to Karen Thomas during Anstar Biotech Industries Fourth of	Interview Notes	☑	Disputed by:	Hawkins Deserved Termination	↗	
Obje cts	Mon 07/12/1999	Anstar Biotech Industries second quarter sales announced. Sales have dropped by 8%.		☐	Undisputed	Demotion, Hawkins Deserved Termination	→	
Issue s	Fri 07/30/1999	Philip Hawkins *demoted* to sales manager.	Deposition of Philip Hawkins, p. 24, I15.	☐	Undisputed	Demotion	↘	
	Thu 08/05/1999 #1	Philip Hawkins and William Lang meet.	????	☐	Undisputed	Age Discrim Against Hawkins	→	
	Thu 08/05/1999 #2	Philip Hawkins alleges that William Lang tells him "The old wood must be trimmed back hard."	Complaint, p. 8; Deposition of Philip	☑	Disputed by: Us	Pattern & Practice, Demotion	↓	
	Mon 08/09/1999	Philip Hawkins transferred to Anstar Biotech Industries office in Fresno.	Deposition of Philip Hawkins, p.43, I18.	☐	Undisputed	Transfer, Hawkins Deserved Termination	↘	
	09/23/1999	Philip Hawkins writes letter to William Lang complaining about the way he's being treated and alleging plan to eliminate older staff	Hawkins Letter of 9/23/99	☐	Undisputed	Wrongful Termination, Age Discrim Against Hawkins	↘	
	Fri 11/12/1999	Reduction in force takes place. 55 Anstar Biotech Industries employees are let go including Philip Hawkins.		☑	Undisputed	Wrongful Termination, Age Discrim Against Hawkins	↓	
	Mon 11/22/1999	Philip Hawkins files suit.	Complaint.	☐	Undisputed		→	
	Tue 12/14/1999	Philip Hawkins turns down job offer from Converse Chemical Labs.	Rumor William Lang heard	☐	Prospective	Failure to Mitigate	↗	
	01/??/2000	Philip Hawkins meets with Susan Sheridan	Rumor William Lang heard	☐	Prospective		?	
	01/??/2000	Philip Hawkins is diagnosed as suffering Post Traumatic Stress Disorder.		☐		Mental Anguish	↗	

Source: Copyright LexisNexis® CaseMap.

Exhibit 9.13 | TimeMap features

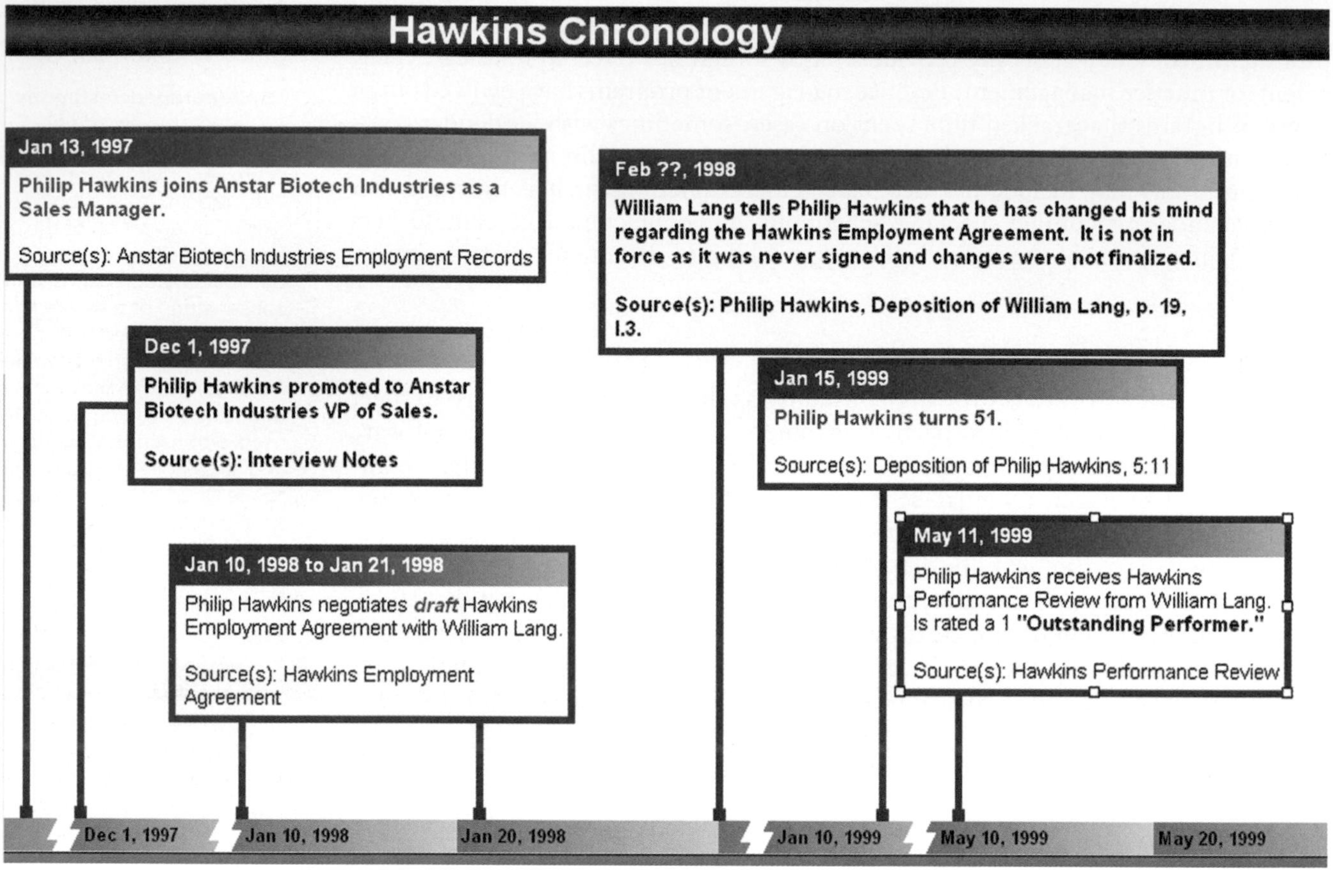

Hawkins Chronology

Jan 13, 1997
Philip Hawkins joins Anstar Biotech Industries as a Sales Manager.

Source(s): Anstar Biotech Industries Employment Records

Dec 1, 1997
Philip Hawkins promoted to Anstar Biotech Industries VP of Sales.

Source(s): Interview Notes

Jan 10, 1998 to Jan 21, 1998
Philip Hawkins negotiates *draft* Hawkins Employment Agreement with William Lang.

Source(s): Hawkins Employment Agreement

Feb ??, 1998
William Lang tells Philip Hawkins that he has changed his mind regarding the Hawkins Employment Agreement. It is not in force as it was never signed and changes were not finalized.

Source(s): Philip Hawkins, Deposition of William Lang, p. 19, l.3.

Jan 15, 1999
Philip Hawkins turns 51.

Source(s): Deposition of Philip Hawkins, 5:11

May 11, 1999
Philip Hawkins receives Hawkins Performance Review from William Lang. Is rated a 1 **"Outstanding Performer."**

Source(s): Hawkins Performance Review

Dec 1, 1997 | Jan 10, 1998 | Jan 20, 1998 | Jan 10, 1999 | May 10, 1999 | May 20, 1999

Source: Copyright LexisNexis® CaseSoft.

Advice *from the* Field

THE 10 AREAS OF INFORMATION YOU SHOULD ALWAYS HAVE AT YOUR FINGERTIPS
Neal R. Bevans

The ultimate paralegal resource guide is the place you save every important piece of information you have gathered in your daily work as a paralegal. This resource should contain telephone numbers, e-mails, important dates, notes about attorneys and judges and much more. The couple of hours you spend creating it will save you hundreds of hours throughout your career, give you a competitive edge and make you an invaluable member of your legal team. In fact, having all of this information at your fingertips will make you seem almost superhuman.

If putting together your own paralegal resource guide sounds unusual, it isn't. Legal professionals have been creating their own handy references for decades. When I first started out as a lawyer, a senior partner at my firm had a ragged manila file folder on his credenza containing copies of complaints he previously used in a wide variety of cases. When he needed a new complaint, he would pull out some of those old pleadings and reuse them. Your system might be a similar large file folder on your desk. Perhaps you keep everything stored in a database on your laptop, or in a network folder. Whatever method you currently use to hang on to your important information, you need to pull it all together and put it in one place. Let these 10 categories be your guide to organizing your resources and making your job easier.

1. COMPLETE CONTACT INFORMATION

Although there are a lot of telephone database programs available, including some basic software programs that came with most computers, many people find simple solutions are better.

A telephone reference is easy to create in any word processing program. The nice thing, about using Corel WordPerfect or Microsoft Word to create these tables is these programs already are running on your computer, you can keep the files open while you work on other materials, you can constantly update your entries and alphabetizing them is a breeze. For instance, Janice Johnson, a paralegal for attorney Russ Becker in Morganton N.C., said she uses a client list she originally created using WordPerfect. Her basic client list includes a chart consisting of the client's name, phone numbers, postal and e-mail addresses and notes.

Johnson said she encourages clients to contact her via e-mail. "I can check on e-mail in an extremely timely manner without having an interruption while a client is in my office," she said. "I also can respond back without getting caught on a call that ends up going entirely too long, Also, I have a word-for-word record of what information was given to the client through the e-mail contacts."

BlackBerry wireless devices are another great way to store contact information and have become very popular among law firms. Dana Martin, a paralegal at Greenbaum, Doll & McDonald, with offices in Ohio, Kentucky, Tennessee and the District of Columbia, likes the fact that with her BlackBerry, she can retrieve her e-mail anywhere, anytime. "We have Microsoft Outlook and [the BlackBerry] gives wireless access to that and my address book." She said she takes the BlackBerry with her wherever she goes.

The notes category is where your telephone reference really shines. You might not think having a notes section is important, but little details about your contacts really can help.

Denise Cunningham, a paralegal for attorney M. Lynne Osterholt in Louisville, Ky., said she lists personal information for many of her contacts. "Along with the addresses, I also put in other information, like birthdays and anniversaries."

Little, personal details, such as remembering a client's birthday or the names of a client or contact's children, can help build personal relationships and provide you with substantial help when you need it most. For instance, one client might be able to help you locate another client who is missing or unavailable. Personal relationships with courthouse personnel will put you on the inside track when it comes to things as simple as when to schedule a hearing or earn you a warning phone call when your firm forgets to file appropriate paperwork in a case.

2. ONE CENTRAL CALENDAR

Everyone knows having a calendar isn't a luxury, it's an absolute necessity. With so much to do and so little time to do it, your calendar must be accurate, easy to access and contain enough information so you can understand what you need to do. "Experts all agree you should have one calendar, not different calendars for work, for play and for the holidays. You should have one calendar for everything," said Cunningham, who has been a paralegal for almost 25 years.

Cunningham said the calendar feature on her Palm is the most used feature and it often comes in handy in court, especially when scheduling court dates. "We write in our appointments or when pleadings are due. We depend on the Palm now, although we also keep a regular calendar. I like the Palm. It's wonderful and I take it everywhere."

Martin has her BlackBerry synced to her office calendar. "If I have an event on my [office] calendar that would notify me that I had an event coming up, I would get the same notification on my BlackBerry."

Whether you use a book-sized calendar, software or the latest handheld device, the important thing is to have one central calendar that is easy to access and update.

3. COURTHOUSE CONTACTS

Whether you decide to go high-tech or stick with low-tech methods to create your paralegal resource, it should contain additional information beyond just telephone contacts and important dates. It should contain plenty of information about the courthouse, including a list of the types of information that can be found in

(continued)

each office, as well as the names of your contact people in those offices. When you find a friendly face at the courthouse, put that person's name in your courthouse reference in as many different places as possible. The next time you call that office, ask for that person.

4. ATTORNEY PECULIARITIES

No ultimate reference would be complete without an "attorney peculiarities" section. This is a section to remind you about the various idiosyncrasies of the people with whom you must interact everyday. If the attorney has a hang up about the way pleadings are prepared (such as never staple, always use paper clips) then make a running list of these preferences. These notes can save you a lot of time, effort and frustration later. If you get new employees in the firm, you also can provide this list to them.

5. JUDGE PECULIARITIES

The basic premise about keeping track of attorney peculiarities applies to judges even more. Every judge with whom I have ever worked has had a different approach to court proceedings, pleadings, drafting orders and even when and where the attorneys should stand in the courtroom. Some judges like to be referred to as "Your Honor" in every context. Some judges have a habit of leaving work everyday at 3 p.m.

Other judges think nothing of making you wait for hours outside their offices before they will sign an order. All of these characteristics should be written down for future reference. Attorneys have been doing this for years. When an attorney has a case pending before an unknown judge, he or she always will call a friend and ask about that judge's characteristics. Then the attorney adapts to that judge's approach. You should do the same thing.

One prosecutor, who preferred to remain anonymous, had a judge who would routinely appear for calendar calls in December wearing a Santa Claus cap. He would then give probation or suspended sentences to nearly every case pending. This is an important piece of information, not only for prosecutors who never wanted to have cases pending before that judge near Christmas, but also for defense attorneys who did.

6. ESSENTIAL FORMS

One of the primary reasons to create an ultimate paralegal resource is for the forms. Forms are the dirty little secret in the legal profession. Every time you come across a good form, put a copy into your paralegal reference guide. Copy the file over to your CD, store it on your flash memory card and put it someplace where you can access it again. There is another reason your forms should be stored in digital format: These days, many federal courts are requiring pleadings to be filed electronically.

"Federal courts are requiring briefs to be filed in Adobe Acrobat," Martin added. With a complete file of forms and pleadings, you will be ready to go in no time.

7. BRIEF AND MEMO BANKS

Your resource also should contain copies of briefs and memoranda used in other cases. We have all had the experience of realizing our current assignment is exactly like a brief we had to prepare last year in another case. Being able to pull up that previous brief can be a huge timesaver and be a real feather in your cap.

Although law firms often have firm-wide brief banks, keeping one of your own always is a good idea. The one time you need access to the law firm's brief bank probably will be the one time the system is down. Having your own brief bank also helps when you have to work at home and have no direct access to the firm's computer system. Your personal brief bank should contain all of the generic appellate briefs and memos you use on a daily basis. For anything more specialized than that, you always can pull it off the main network later.

8. FREQUENTLY ASKED QUESTIONS

If clients ask you the same questions repeatedly, it's time to digitize the answer and keep it available to print at a moment's notice. You might have clients who always ask how to get to the courthouse or what they should wear to court. Give them the answer in written form. It's easier for you and gives them something tangible they can review later.

Lisa Mazzonetto, a paralegal at the McDonald Law Offices in Asheville, N.C., handles domestic cases exclusively. She often gets questions about how long it takes to complete a case, what the basic rules about child visitation are, and what a client should do if he or she wishes to have a Temporary Restraining Order taken out against an unruly spouse. Mazzonetto has this information ready in writing, which frees up her time and gives clients a handy reference if they ever need it.

9. PRIVATE COMPUTER INFORMATION

In these days of Internet legal research and databases, it's important to have a handy reference containing all URLs, passwords and notes about how to access specific sites.

"There is an incredible amount of information out there that is key to day-to-day work in a law office. In my field of work, online tax records and register of deeds, [Department of Motor Vehicles] records, postal addresses, Web sites and people locator sites are very important," Mazzonetto said.

To keep all of your passwords confidential, yet easy to access, you can keep the list in a Word table and update it regularly. You also can password-protect the file to keep the wrong people from accessing it.

10. VENDOR AND SUPPLIER RECORDS

Your ultimate resource should contain information about all your office hardware and software, including vendor names, toll-free support numbers, license numbers and any other information you will need to get help if you have software or hardware problems. Keeping this information in your resource guide can save you a lot of time, especially when a service representative asks you for information contained on the computer or program that isn't currently working.

CREATING A DIGITIZED RESOURCE GUIDE

Now that you know the most important areas to include in your resource guide, you must decide in what format you will keep the information accessible. People have different preferences as to the format that suits them best. Some like to keep a binder with all the information printed out, while others prefer to keep a fully digitized version. Still others prefer a combination of both print and digital records for their resource guides.

There are a lot of different legal software programs available with which you can create a digital paralegal resource guide. They range from simple databases to complete law firm packages containing billing and accounting software, calendar features and complex databases. In high-tech offices, the calendar and case management system is available firm-wide and can be accessed by anyone on the network. However, not all law offices have taken this step into the 21st century. In situations where the office is filled with standalone systems, you will keep this information on your computer and on a backup CD.

David Moyer uses database programs to create lists of clients and documents in his freelance paralegal practice in Cuyahoga, Ohio. "I use database programs, such as Microsoft Access and Excel. I use the databases for client conflict of interest checks, to name just one example."

Use programs that have been tried and tested in the real world or in firms similar in size and structure to your firm. Mazzonetto's firm uses Time & Chaos (www.chaossoftware.com). "It acts as our daily, weekly and monthly calendar; client address book and To-Do lists. It's very inexpensive, but an incredible asset."

Johnson's North Carolina firm uses Abacus Data Systems AbacusLaw (www.abacuslaw.com), which has been around for years and functions as a client database, calendar and docketing system. "We use Abacus as a database and tracking system here at our office," Johnson said. "I don't know how we survived as well as we did before we went to this system. Today, not to have some type of program for client information and management, along with a deadline system is like living in the dark ages and asking for a malpractice suit."

Martin's firm has a separate Information Technology division. "We have a very complex piece of software that keeps track of client information, accounting, billing and case management. Our whole office is really tied together. We are a regional firm and everybody can get to the same documents."

For many firms, tailor-made programs are the best way to go. Norma Schvaneveldt, a paralegal in Chattanooga, Tenn., said her former firm, Eric Buchanan & Associates, relied on software created for the firm's specialty area of law. "We kept track of client information on the computer through a case management software program especially configured to handle Social Security cases. We also used it for our long-term disability cases. If you were out of town and needed to review a file, as long as you had Internet access, you could review any file."

THE POWER OF YOUR RESOURCE GUIDE

The smartest thing you can do with your ultimate paralegal resource is to organize it and keep it all in one place. Let everyone in the firm think you are superhuman, with an incredible memory for names, dates, telephone numbers and the myriad of other information law firms need on a daily basis. Your ultimate paralegal resource can be your secret weapon.

CHECKLIST Investigation Information Sources

Information Source	Web Address	Physical Location	Comments
Police Records–Local	www.		
Police Records–State	www.		
Birth Records	www.		
Death Records	www.		
Drivers License	www.		
Vehicle Registration	www.		
Corporate Records	www.		
Real Estate–Recorder	www.		
Real Estate–Tax	www.		
Real Estate–Land Mapping	www.		
Register of Wills	www.		
Trial Court	www.		
Federal District Court–Clerk's Office	www.	Room Federal Court House	
Federal Bankruptcy Court	www.		
Occupational License	www.		
Weather Reports	www.		

Personalize this list by adding the local or regional office Web addresses, mailing addresses, and room numbers for personal visits, and comments, with any applicable contact people, costs, or hours of operation.

Concept Review *and* Reinforcement

LEGAL TERMINOLOGY

Arbitration   343

Attorney–client privilege   329

Conflict of interest   329

Ethical obligation   339

Ethical wall   329

Expert witnesses   340

Freedom of Information Act (FOIA)   348

Implied attorney–client relationship   329

Leading questions   337

Moral obligation   339

Narrative opportunity   338

Open-ended questions   338

Privileged communication   339

Restatement of the Law Third, Torts   342

Screening interview   328

Spoliation of evidence   347

Strict liability   342

Statute of limitations   329

Trial notebook   352

SUMMARY OF KEY CONCEPTS

Interviews/Interviewing

Interview	Any contact you have with a client, or prospective client is an interview.
Screening Interview	The typical first contact with a client usually is a telephone call, but some people just appear at the office door, asking for an appointment or basic information about the firm's ability or interest in taking a case.

First Meeting	1. The paralegal must be careful to make clear that he or she is a paralegal and not an attorney.
	2. The paralegal must build a relationship with the individual, let him or her understand the purpose of the interview, and eliminate any barriers that would prevent obtaining the necessary information.
Implied Attorney–Client Relationship	If too much information is taken, the potential client will think he or she now has a lawyer. The courts have ruled on the side of the potential client holding that an implied attorney–client relationship exists.
Cultural Sensitivity	The culturally sensitive person is aware of the reasons for differences in the way people behave, based on religious and ethnic background and belief system.

Preparing for the Interview

Outcomes	1. The first step is to understand the outcomes desired, one of which is to instill confidence in the firm and its personnel.
	2. The desired outcome of any interview is to obtain all needed, relevant facts for the case.
Physical Surroundings	Depending upon purpose of interview and the person being interviewed, a formal or an informal environment may be desired.
Dress and Appearance	Clothing worn in an interview sends a nonverbal message about the paralegal and the firm or business, and the initial impression can enhance or destroy credibility.
Communication Skills in a Multicultural Society	Interviewers must appreciate the difference of how and why individuals act and react differently.
Listening Skills	Learning to listen to "What" is being said and not just the words.
Leading Questions	Questions that suggest the desired answer. Lawyers in conducting a cross-examination in trial frequently use leading questions to force the witness to answer in a desired manner.
Open-Ended Questions	Questions designed to create a narrative opportunity for the witness.

Moral Versus Ethical Considerations

| Moral Obligations | Based on one's own conscience or perceived rules of correct conduct, generally in the person's own community. |
| Ethical Obligations | Obligations of legal profession under ABA Model Rules of Professional Conduct, including thoroughness in representing a client. |

Privileged Communications

| Forms of Privileged Communications | Attorney–client communications
Doctor–patient communications
Priest–penitent communications
Spousal communications during marriage |
| Waivers | Privileges can be waived, but the waiver must come from the client, the patient, the penitent, or the spouse making the statement with the belief that it is privileged. |

Investigating Claims

Expert Witnesses

| Definition | Expert witnesses are individuals whose background, education, and experience are such that courts will recognize them as qualified to give opinions based on a set of facts. |

Freedom of Information Act (FOIA)

Definition	FOIA is a federal statute designed to open to the public the information in the possession of the federal government and its agencies.

Locating Witnesses

Directories	1. Phone books 2. Cross-reference directories 3. Membership directories
The Web	Search engines can help locate individuals, businesses, and organizations on the Internet. It is also a source of information about individuals from public sources and social networking sites.

Interviews, Investigations, and Trials

Trial Preparation	Trial preparation starts with the first client contact and the gathering of the first document. Good preparation for trial includes an assessment of how well clients and witnesses will react in depositions or in court under the pressure of cross-examination and how they will be perceived by opposing counsel, the judge, or the jury.
Case Management	Good case management requires a thoughtful process for storing, handling, examining, evaluating, and indexing every page. In the computer age, case management involves decisions on the appropriateness and potential use of electronic display technologies, as well as the fallback on traditional paper exhibit preparation.
Traditional Case Management	Traditional approaches includes the case notebook or case trial notebook.
Case and Practice Management Software	A number of software programs can be used to manage the law office and the cases within the office, in what is sometimes referred to as case management or practice management.

WORKING THE WEB

1. Use MapQuest to print out a map of the local area around your school. www.Mapquest.com
2. Use the MapQuest directions feature to obtain driving directions from your home to your school's main entrance. Don't worry if you live a long distance from your school. Print out the directions and related maps anyway.
3. Repeat items 1 and 2 using Yahoo! Maps. http://maps.yahoo.com and Mapblast from MSN www.mapblast.com. Which gives you the most information?
4. Obtain a satellite image of your school from Google Earth. http://earth.google.com. How might this be more helpful in investigating a case than the other maps available on the Internet?
5. Use Findlaw to locate an accounting expert in your state. www.findlaw.com. Print out a list of experts listed.
6. Use the LexisNexis Martindale–Hubbell website to locate an expert witness for a patent intellectual property case involving electronics. Print out a copy of the contact information you find.
7. Using the search function of your computer browser, find and print out a copy of Rule 26 of the Federal Rules of Civil Procedure.
8. Download a trial copy of TimeMap from LexisNexis on the Technology Resources Website—www.prenhall.com/goldman.
9. Prepare a timeline of the assignments and exams for the courses you currently are taking. Print a copy of the timeline.
10. Assume you have been asked to work on the case of a pedestrian struck by a car going north on the west side of the Flat Iron Building in Manhattan (New York City). Print out a satellite image of the location showing the building and the traffic flow using Earth Google at www.earth.google.com. Note that you will have to download the Earth Google viewer. Check with your instructor before downloading on a school computer. What is the proper direction of the vehicle traffic? Was the crosswalk visible? Were any other potential images available? Prepare a short report memorandum about your findings.

CRITICAL THINKING & WRITING QUESTIONS

1. What are the legal and ethical issues involved for the paralegal when the potential client says he or she just wants a quick answer to the question, "Do I have a case?" Explain fully, including references to your state statute.
2. What is a screening interview? What potential ethical and malpractice issues are involved?
3. How is the implied attorney–client relationship created? What are the critical issues for the law firm when this relationship is established?
4. Does the attorney have a duty to keep the names of clients confidential? Explain the ethical rules that apply.
5. What are the ethical and or legal implications of not advising a party that you are a paralegal and not a lawyer?
6. What is the difference between listening and hearing? Explain.
7. How can stereotypes prevent hearing what is said in interviews?
8. What effect do cultural issues play in the interview process? Explain.
9. What are the strategic reasons for using leading questions and using open-ended questions? Give an example of when each would be better used than the other type.
10. In representing a client, is it acceptable or required to ignore an ethical or moral consideration? Explain, giving an example and reason for breaching each.
11. Explain fully the ultimate reason for conducting a thorough investigation of a case. What ethical issues dictate how an investigation is to be conducted?
12. How can the Internet be used to effectively conduct an investigation of a case? Explain, using examples of traditional methods that also could be used.
13. Using the Facts in the *Palsgraf* case in Appendix A, prepare a list of witnesses who might be called in that case. Prepare an interview checklist for each of the witnesses.
14. Using the Facts in the *Palsgraf* case in Appendix A, prepare an investigative checklist, including a list of the evidence that should be gathered in the case, including a list and description of any photographs needed.
15. In conducting an interview, when would it be appropriate to dress in "Friday casual" attire?
16. Why is it important to visit the site of the accident in a motor-vehicle case being prepared for trial?
17. Under what circumstances might it be advisable for someone other than you in the firm to handle an interview with a client or witness?
18. Why would someone feel a moral obligation not to answer questions in an interview?
19. Why would a law firm hire an expert witness and not call that person as a witness at trial?
20. How useful is the Freedom of Information Act in obtaining state or local government documents? Explain.
21. Can a client restrict the use of information obtained as part of the investigation in preparation for trial even if doing so will have adverse consequences in the opinion of the attorney? Why or why not?
22. What are the issues and potential problems in using a trial notebook?
23. How does the use of case management software improve the effectiveness of the legal team? Who has the ultimate responsibility for managing the case file when using case management software?

Building Paralegal Skills

VIDEO CASE STUDIES

UPL Issue: Interviewing a Client

A lawyer is meeting with a new client when he is called away, leaving his paralegal to complete the interview.

After viewing the video case study at www.pearsonhighered.com/goldman answer the following:

1. Should the paralegal clarify his or her role as a paralegal when meeting a new client?
2. Can a paralegal give a client an opinion of whether a case exists?
3. What kind of questions should be asked in interviewing a new client?

UPL Issue: Working with a Witness

A paralegal investigating an accident case in the field creates the impression that he is acting in an official capacity requesting a fact witness to appear to give a formal statement. When the fact witness appears for the statement, he is offered compensation for his time.

After viewing the video case study at www.pearsonhighered.com/goldman answer the following:

1. Does the paralegal have a duty to divulge his role as a paralegal when interviewing potential witnesses?
2. Is it appropriate to offer compensation to a fact witness?
3. Should the same rules of ethics apply to investigators as well as to paralegals?

Zealous Representation Issue: When You Are Asked to Lie

 A paralegal has been instructed by his supervising attorney to do whatever is necessary to obtain information needed in a particular case.

After viewing the video case study at www.pearsonhighered .com/goldman answer the following:

1. What is pretexting?
2. Is it ethical to lie to obtain needed information?
3. Is a paralegal bound by ethical rules when acting as an investigator?

ETHICS ANALYSIS & DISCUSSION QUESTIONS

1. Review the opening scenario of this chapter. What are the ethical issues involved? Prepare a suggested policy, referencing the specific ethics code sections, to present to the supervising attorney of the firm.

Address the issues of how to answer the phone and what should and should not be said. Your instructor may provide you with specifics, such as the fee for an initial consultation.

DEVELOPING YOUR COLLABORATION SKILLS

Working on your own or with a group of other students assigned by your instructor, review the scenario at the beginning of the chapter and the discussion that takes place between Sara and Mrs. Weiser.

1. a. Prepare a list of questions Sara should prepare before starting work. Discuss who should be asked and what action she should or should not take.
   b. What are the ethical issues facing Sara?
   c. What are the potential malpractice issues facing the firm?
2. Write a summary of the advice the group would give to Sara.

3. Form groups of three. Designate one person who will act as Sara, one as a potential client, and the third as a supervising paralegal.
   a. As the paralegal interviewer for the client who has just walked in the door of the office after being injured in an accident, use the facts of the *Palsgraf* case in the Appendix or one assigned by your instructor.
   b. As the client, you want to be sure that you have a case and that the fee is acceptable.
   c. As the supervising paralegal, comment on the interview, what issues were raised, and what you would have done differently.

PARALEGAL PORTFOLIO EXERCISE

Using the current information for your area or jurisdiction, complete the Investigation Information Source Checklist. Print out a copy for your portfolio.

LEGAL ANALYSIS & WRITING CASES

Limitations on Obtaining Information in Criminal Cases Under the FOIA

The FOIA can be a good source of information in criminal cases as well as civil litigation. As with discovery-limitation exemptions in civil cases, additional exemptions exist under the Act in criminal cases. Landano was convicted in New Jersey state court for murdering a police officer during

what may have been a gang-related robbery. In an effort to support his claim in subsequent state court proceedings that his rights were violated by withholding material exculpatory evidence, he filed Freedom of Information Act requests with the Federal Bureau of Investigation (FBI) for information it had compiled in connection with the murder investigation.

When the FBI redacted some documents and withheld others, Landano filed an action, seeking disclosure of the contents of the requested files. The court held that the government is not entitled to a presumption that all sources supplying information to the FBI in the course of a criminal investigation are confidential sources within the meaning of Exemption 7(D). Further, a source should be deemed "confidential" if the source furnished information with the understanding that the

FBI would not divulge the communication except to the extent it thought necessary for law-enforcement purposes.

Questions

1. Does this unfairly subject an informant to potential harassment?
2. Does limiting information unfairly prevent the defendant from receiving a fair trial?
3. Does the limitation effectively limit any usefulness in making a request under the FOIA?

Department of Justice v. Landano   508 U.S. 165 (1993)

Spoliation of Evidence In Re Daimlerchrysler Ag Securities Litigation (Usdc Del. 2003), Civil Action No. 00-993-JJF

Defendants requested relief in the form of sanctions against the plaintiff for the spoliation of evidence contending that a personal assistant to one of the Plaintiffs, Jaclyn Thode, had destroyed documents that she used to prepare a list of meetings and/or conversations prepared at the request of general counsel, who had failed to instruct her to preserve the documents used in making the list. The court in ruling on the defendant's motion concluded that sanctions were not warranted as a result of the alleged spoliation of evidence. The un-rebutted deposition testimony and affidavit of Ms. Thode establish that she discarded her handwritten notes after converting them into typewritten form, consistent with her practice in the past. Ms. Thode had no information or understanding about the substance of the litigation and no information as to the purpose of counsels' request, and thus she had no reason to alter or omit any information from the documents and that she acted unintentionally when she

discarded the steno pads and pink message notes. The Court also found the Defendants did not suffer any prejudice, because they had a complete and accurate chronology of the contents of the documents that were discarded. The court cited *Son, Inc. v. Louis & Nashville R.R. Co.*, 695 F.2d 253, 259 (7th Cir.1982) (finding that destruction of evidence was not intentional where handwritten notes were discarded after being typed and person handling evidence had no reason to omit or alter necessary information).

Questions

1. Should the investigation of a case where documents include transcription include inquiry to the source of transcripted notes? Why or why not?
2. Why would not knowing the purpose of creating the notes matter in determining the potential spoliation of evidence?
3. What advice would you give to someone who has the responsibility of transcribing or keeping minutes of meetings?

WORKING WITH THE LANGUAGE OF THE COURT CASE

Department of the Interior v. Klamath Water Users Protective Association

532 U.S. 1 (2001)
Supreme Court of the United States

Read, and if assigned, brief this case. In your brief, answer the following questions.

1. What are the two conditions under which a document qualifies for exemption under the Freedom of Information Act, Exemption 5?
2. How is "agency" defined under the FOIA?
3. What is the "deliberative process" privilege? Does non-governmental litigation have an equivalent privilege?

4. What is the purpose of the deliberative process privilege?
5. What is the "general philosophy" behind the FOIA?

(continued)

Justice Souter delivered the opinion of the Court. Documents in issue here, passing between Indian Tribes and the Department of the Interior, addressed tribal interests subject to state and federal proceedings to determine water allocations. The question is whether the documents are exempt from the disclosure requirements of the Freedom of Information Act, as "intra-agency memorandums or letters" that would normally be privileged in civil discovery [5 U.S.C. § 552(b)(5)]. We hold they are not.

I

. . . [T]he Department's Bureau of Indian Affairs (Bureau) filed claims on behalf of the Klamath Tribe alone in an Oregon state-court adjudication intended to allocate water rights. Since the Bureau is responsible for administering land and water held in trust for Indian tribes . . . it consulted with the Klamath Tribe, and the two exchanged written memorandums on the appropriate scope of the claims ultimately submitted. . . . The Bureau does not, however, act as counsel for the Tribe, which has its own lawyers and has independently submitted claims on its own behalf.[1]

. . . [T]he Klamath Water Users Protective Association is a nonprofit association of water users in the Klamath River Basin, most of whom receive water from the Klamath Project, and whose interests are adverse to the tribal interests owing to scarcity of water. The Association filed a series of requests with the Bureau under the Freedom of Information Act (FOIA) [5 U.S.C. § 552] seeking access to communications between the Bureau and the Basin Tribes during the relevant time period. The Bureau turned over several documents but withheld others as exempt under the attorney work-product and deliberative process privileges. These privileges are said to be incorporated in FOIA Exemption 5, which exempts from disclosure "inter-agency or intra-agency memorandums or letters which would not be available by law to a party other than an agency in litigation with the agency" [§ 552(b)(5)]. The Association then sued the Bureau under FOIA to compel release of the documents. . . .

---

[1] The Government is "not technically acting as [the Tribes'] attorney. That is, the Tribes have their own attorneys, but the United States acts as trustee" [Tr. of Oral Arg. 5]. "The United States has also filed claims on behalf of the Project and on behalf of other Federal interests" in the Oregon adjudication [Id. At 6]. The Hoopa Valley, Karuk, and Yurok Tribes are not parties to the adjudication. [Brief for Respondent 7]

Upon request, FOIA mandates disclosure of records held by a federal agency, see 5 U.S.C. § 552, unless the documents fall within enumerated exemptions. . . .

A

Exemption 5 protects from disclosure "inter-agency or intra-agency memorandums or letters which would not be available by law to a party other than an agency in litigation with the agency" [5 U.S.C. § 552(b)(5)]. To qualify, a document must thus satisfy two conditions: Its source must be a Government agency, and it must fall within the ambit of a privilege against discovery under judicial standards that would govern litigation against the agency that holds it.

Our prior cases on Exemption 5 have addressed the second condition, incorporating civil discovery privileges. . . . So far as they might matter here, those privileges include the privilege for attorney work-product and what is sometimes called the "deliberative process" privilege. Work-product protects "mental processes of the attorney" while deliberative process covers "documents reflecting advisory opinions, recommendations and deliberations comprising part of a process by which governmental decisions and policies are formulated." The deliberative process privilege rests on the obvious realization that officials will not communicate candidly among themselves if each remark is a potential item of discovery and front-page news, and its object is to enhance "the quality of agency decisions," . . . by protecting open and frank discussion among those who make them within the Government. . . .

The point is not to protect Government secrecy pure and simple, however, and the first condition of Exemption 5 is no less important than the second; the communication must be "inter-agency or intra-agency" [5 U.S.C. § 552(b)(5)] . . . With exceptions not relevant here, "agency" means "each authority of the Government of the United States," and "includes any executive department, military department, Government corporation, Government- controlled corporation, or other establishment in the executive branch of the Government . . . , or any independent regulatory agency.". . .

Although neither the terms of the exemption nor the statutory definitions say anything about communications with outsiders, some Courts of Appeals have held that in some circumstances a document prepared outside the Government may . . . qualify . . . under Exemption 5. . . .

It is . . . possible . . . to regard as an intra-agency memorandum one that has been received by an agency, to assist it in the performance of its own functions, from a person acting in a governmentally conferred capacity other than on behalf of another agency—e.g., in a capacity as . . . consultant to the agency.

Typically, courts taking the latter view have held that the exemption extends to communications between Government agencies and outside consultants hired by them. . . . In such cases, the records submitted by outside consultants played essentially the same part in an agency's process of deliberation as documents prepared by agency personnel might have done. . . . [T]he fact about the consultant that is constant . . . is that the consultant does not represent an interest of its own, or the interest of any other client, when it advises the agency that hires it. Its only obligations are to truth and its sense of what good judgment calls for, and in those respects the consultant functions just as an employee would be expected to do.

B

. . . The Tribes, on the contrary, necessarily communicate with the Bureau with their own, albeit entirely legitimate, interests in mind. While this fact alone distinguishes tribal communications from the consultants' examples recognized by several Courts of Appeals, the distinction is even sharper, in that the Tribes are self-advocates at the expense of others seeking benefits inadequate to satisfy everyone.

. . . All of this boils down to requesting that we read an "Indian trust" exemption into the statute, a reading that is out of the question for reasons already explored. There is simply no support for the exemption

in the statutory text, which we have elsewhere insisted be read strictly in order to serve FOIA's mandate of broad disclosure, which was obviously expected and intended to affect Government operations. In FOIA, after all, a new conception of Government conduct was enacted into law, "a general philosophy of full agency disclosure." Congress had to realize that not every secret under the old law would be secret under the new.

The judgment of the Court of Appeals is affirmed. *It is so ordered.*

The differences among the various circuits on the use of unpublished opinions was clarified by the Amendment to the Federal Rules of Appellate Procedure approved by the United States Supreme Court on April 12, 2006, when it approved the citation of unpublished opinions.

The proposed new Rule 32.1 as submitted for comment to Congress provided;

> Proposed new Rule 32.1 permits the citation in briefs of opinions, orders, or other judicial dispositions that have been designated as "not for publication," "non-precedential," or the like and supersedes limitations imposed on such citation by circuit rules. New Rule 32.1 takes no position on whether unpublished opinions should have any precedential value, leaving that issue for the circuits to decide. The Judicial Conference amended the proposed rule so as to apply prospectively to unpublished opinions filed on or after January 1, 2007. A court may, by local rule, continue to permit or restrict citation to unpublished opinions filed before that date.

Traditional and Computerized Legal Research

> **" This trial is a travesty; it's a travesty of a mockery of a sham of a mockery of a travesty of two mockeries of a sham. I move for a mistrial. "**
>
> *Woody Allen, Bananas*

LEARNING OBJECTIVES

After studying this chapter, you should be able to:

1. Systematically analyze a research assignment.
2. Create a legal research plan.
3. Explain the differences between conducting legal research using a traditional paper law library and computer-based law resources.
4. Use publisher-specific and generalized legal terminology to create search queries using the computerized resources and traditional book resources.
5. Explain the differences between primary resources, secondary resources, and finding tools.
6. Explain the need for, and the methods of, updating legal research.
7. Read and use legal citations.

Paralegals at Work

As the managing partner of a large multinational law firm, Mr. Mulkeen was preparing for an executive committee meeting with the senior partners from the firm offices around the world. As with all law firms, cost saving was high on the agenda. The diverse group of partners ranged from young partners on the fast track to senior partners concerned more with developing client contacts than working on cases directly. Some firm's newer offices specialize in specific areas of law, such as the five-person health care group in a distant city to the 500-lawyer office in a major metropolitan area.

One of the major cost items on the firm's income statement was designated for the law library. Some partners wanted to expand the library, and others wanted to cut it. Mr. Mulkeen wanted to try to gain a consensus and keep as many members of the firm and support staff happy and have the necessary input from a cross-section of the firm. He invited a cross-section of the firm to a meeting to discuss the issue and get feedback. At the meeting, he indicated that the firm was at something of a crossroads in making a decision about the direction of the firm's law library, what to keep, what to get rid of, and to what to commit resources to. The cost of the space for the library, in the rental cost per square foot, was a major issue for the firm, as well as the increasing cost of law reporters and upkeep services.

Mr. Hains, a senior partner with the firm more than 25 years, reminded everyone that when he started with the firm, it didn't have as many resources as it had currently and that the law book collection was a point of pride he frequently pointed to with new clients. He said the firm could research case law in most jurisdictions where it had offices back to the first volume of the case reporters and the firm had all of the volumes of the state and federal statutes and codes. He indicated that research could be done on weekends if necessary, and pages copied out of the books. He said he didn't feel comfortable eliminating any of the hardbound volumes, and that there is something to be said for thumbing through the pages to find something even if you are not sure what you are looking for.

As one of the senior paralegals, Kathryn indicated that she didn't use the library that much, that it was mostly a place for her to spread things out. She said that she and her supervising attorney did most of their research at their desks, using computers to access the Internet and online research services. She felt limited, she said, in using the hourly-fee research services for research because the cost could not always be billed to the client and the bookkeeping people were critical about not passing on the fees. Kathryn's final point was that the litigation team was always in court or trying cases out of town, so the in-house library didn't really do the litigation team much good anyway.

Kevin, one of the long-term secretaries, expressed concern with eliminating the current library. He explained that in working for one of the general-practice attorneys, many times it was necessary to get up to speed on a new area of law and he had to browse through some of the encyclopedias and treatises just to understand the basic issues and terminology. He said he couldn't do this using the computer—at least until the issues and terminology were understood.

Consider the issues involved in this scenario as you read the chapter.

INTRODUCTION TO RESEARCH FOR THE PARALEGAL

One of the most important skills a paralegal can develop is the ability to find current relevant legal and factual information in a timely manner. Knowing where to look is just as important as knowing what to look for. Clients expect their legal counsel to use the latest law in advising them. The paralegal is expected to be able to understand the relevant facts and find the current statutory law and case law. The frequent changes in court decisions and statutory enactments present a challenge to the legal profession. Traditional law libraries consisting of printed text may not have available the latest case, statute, or regulation for days or weeks because of the time required to assemble, print, and send out updates. Internet and computer technology allows for more rapid access to the latest information. Many courts now issue the electronic version of court opinions at the same time as they distribute printed version. Instant availability is certainly a benefit if the paralegal is working on a similar case and the ethical duty of candor to the court may require the most current decision be used even before the printed version is available.

Although the ability to obtain current case law is important, in many cases an older common law case may still be precedent. The problem is that some electronic or online services, such as VersusLaw, may not have included the older cases in their database of available cases. For example, VersusLaw only includes state appellate court cases from Illinois, Pennsylvania, and Texas from 1950 and the California Court of Appeals from 1944. For that reason, being able to find the case the old-fashioned way by checking through the books is a valuable skill. When using an electronic case service such as VersusLaw, the dates of the available cases should be checked to be certain that they cover the time period needed for the search.

Legal Research

Legal research is a process for finding the answer to a legal question. In practice, the desired answer is usually the answer to a legal question involving a specific set of facts. The answer may include federal, state, and local statutory law, administrative agency regulation, and case law. Before starting, you have to have a clear picture of the legal question and what the person giving you the research assignment needs. With this in mind, proceeding in a systematic way will save time and ensure that all research avenues have been considered. A systematic approach begins with planning the research and knowing what issues must be addressed and covered.

Legal research The process for finding the answer to a legal question.

Creating a Research Plan

The first step in legal research is setting up a research plan. The research plan helps to focus on the issues, sources, and methods for finding the answer and controlling law. A few basic questions should be considered in setting up the research plan.

1. What is the issue or legal question?
   a statute or regulation, or
   a legal question involving a set of facts

Paralegals *in* Practice

PARALEGAL PROFILE
Ann G. Hill

Returning to school after spending over ten years as a legal secretary, Ann G. Hill earned a paralegal certificate at Illinois State University in 2000. She also earned the Insurance Institute of America Certificate in General Insurance in 2003, and obtained her paralegal certification through the National Association of Legal Assistants in 2004. Ann is currently a legal assistant for a major insurance company in Bloomington, Illinois. In her spare time, she serves as a pro bono paralegal providing legal assistance to Social Security clients of the local legal aid society.

I currently specialize in records/information management, legal research, and project management. Legal research is often similar to putting together a massive jigsaw puzzle. When researching a specific issue, I initially review applicable statutes and case law. Then, I look for agency rules, since agencies often have statutory authority to enact rules that carry the force of law. When researching contracts issues, I examine project funding since funds are often tied to federal and state grant programs with many stipulations. I also look at professional organizations' Web sites for legal information relevant to their particular field.

A good research paralegal must be able to "step back," view the issue from different perspectives, and analyze the data. I try to identify factors that could impact the outcome of the legal opinion. I then ask the client more questions. Since clients are not always aware of relevant factors and potential issues, you must be able to "think outside the box" in order to know what questions will prove most helpful to the case.

During the research process, I take advantage of credible research already completed. I use a variety of online search services including Westlaw®, Lexis®, and PACER. Law journal and legal news articles posted on the Internet often contain information about specific laws, regulations, and cases relevant to a particular issue. No matter what research methods are used, I always "shepardize" case law, use annotated statutes when possible, and strive to be thorough.

To be truly successful in the paralegal profession, continue to pursue a variety of learning opportunities. For example, consider helping to fill the need for legal services among low income families and senior citizens who cannot afford private attorneys. By partnering with a legal aid society, you can gain valuable experience while serving your community.

2. What is the appropriate search terminology?
   words
   phrases
   legal terms
   popular names of statutes or cases
3. What type of research material is available?
   traditional
   computer
4. What jurisdiction or jurisdictions are involved?
   federal
   state
   local
5. What is the controlling law?
   statutory
   regulatory
   case law
6. What are the types of resources to be used?
   primary
   secondary
   finding tools
7. Where is the needed research material located?
   in-house traditional materials
   fee-based legal services
   free Web-based remote libraries

Using checklists for each search, such as the Research Plan: Words and Phrases, and Research Sources checklists shown later in the chapter, is a good way to be sure all appropriate terms and sources have been used and a record of the results prepared for follow-up by oneself or a colleague who takes over the research.

What Is the Issue or Legal Question?

Legal research is like a puzzle to be solved. Understanding the question is essential. A lot of time may be wasted if the paralegal takes the wrong research path, because the framer of the question has not been clear or the researcher is not clear on the information needed. At times the question is framed with some specificity:

> **Find the statute . . .**
> **Get me the case of . . .**

More often, however, the question is:

> **Based on these facts, what is the law about . . . ?**

Researchers first must understand the facts that apply to the case they are asked to research. Unlike the cases in textbooks and court opinions, the **relevant facts** and the specific area of substantive or procedural law in real life usually are not so clear. The initial interview information may have focused on what the client or the interviewer thought was the applicable law. Further research may indicate other areas of law that must be considered.

For example, what may seem to be a simple rear-end automobile accident caused by negligent driving may be in actuality a case of product liability caused by a manufacturing defect by the automobile manufacturer or the supplier of a defectively manufactured part, such as the tires. To analyze a case properly, the researcher must know the factual elements of a negligence case and of a product liability case. The researcher must understand the facts of the case at hand. Some facts are crucial to the case; others may or may not be important or have no legal significance.

Relevant facts Facts crucial to the case and having legal significance.

What Is the Appropriate Search Terminology?

Knowing the legal terminology used in the indexes of the research materials is critical. Publishers of legal materials do not always use the same words or legal terms to index the same rules of law. For example, one publisher uses the term "infant" to identify people under the age of majority that another publisher indexes under "minor." Consider the legal question: "What are the contract rights of a person under the age of majority?" Using "minor" will not produce the desired results in some published materials where the information is listed under "infant." Print research materials require finding material based on a printed index of individual words as selected by the editors of the service.

Computer research is not as dependent on an index of terms and may require a completely different set of words or legal terms. Most computer research allows for searches of words found in the documents using a text search of requested words in the **search query**, in which the computer looks through the entire document for every instance of the desired words.

Search query Specific words used in a computerized search.

It is important to keep in mind the differences in terminology used in legal and factual research. Finding cases and statutes requires the use of the legal terminology used by the courts, legal professionals, and authors of legal treatises. These words and phrases may not be the most useful in finding factual information on the Internet. For example, it was noted above that some legal sources use the terms "infant" or "minor" when discussing people under the age of majority. Searches for information on underage drinking by those under the age of majority may require different terms as used in newspaper articles. Or, statutes may use the terms "driving under the influence" while newspaper accounts and laypersons would probably use the terms "drunk driving" or "driving while intoxicated."

What Type of Research Material Is Available?

Traditionally, the law library has consisted of books in paper form, case reporters, legal encyclopedias, legal dictionaries, and a host of finding tools including paper card indexes and digests. Some modern law libraries are completely electronic, using online computer services such as Westlaw, Lexis, and Loislaw. Other libraries combine traditional paper-based materials and electronic materials.

Paralegal students who grew up in the era of the ever-available online research sources provided by some high schools and colleges frequently ask why they need to learn how to use a traditional "paper" law library. In the working world, not every office has access to all the latest computer resources, or the same ones. Ask anyone who has tried a case out of town or in a different courthouse and had to check an unexpected case or resource about the availability of resources or lack of them.

At times, paralegals accompany the lawyer to court. During the trial, they may be asked to slip out of the courtroom and conduct a quick bit of legal research. They may not be able to use a computer for legal research. In some courthouses, computers cannot be connected to outgoing phone lines for security reasons, and even cell phones are retained at the security desk. Other courthouses do not have a public computer terminal available in the law library. In these situations, the paralegal must conduct the research quickly and accurately using traditional book methods. In short, the paralegal must be able to find the information needed when the familiar resources are not available.

Computer research requires the use of appropriate search words to complete a successful search. As with any profession, the legal profession has its own vocabulary. These include words defined by the courts over the years to have specific meaning when used in a legal sense. For example, the legal definition of the term "holder" is "a person to whom a negotiable instrument has been properly negotiated." To the layperson, it may mean people holding something in their hands—not necessarily a negotiable instrument, or with any legal formality. Other words have a different meaning for a number of different groups. For example, to the medical community, the word "head" means the top of a person's body; to the sailor it means a bathroom; and to a bartender it means the top of a beer.

People in all areas of life develop words and phrases that help them understand their fields of interest. In creating laws, legislatures use language in special ways that may not be clear to laypersons or even legal researchers who are not accustomed to the terminology of the lawmakers. The people who create indexes to legal references, such as the professional indexers from the Library of Congress and the indexers of the numerous private legal publications, each have their own vocabulary and method of indexing material. For example, West Publishing Company editors index material using the 450 West Digest Topics (see Exhibit 10.1).

Unless the paralegal understands what items are included under each index classification, it is difficult to find the items even with a fast computer search engine. The word "holder," for example, is listed in the *West Digest* index as being under "Statutes," but the word "holder" as defined above, is actually found under the West Digest Topic "Bills and Notes." *Black's Law Dictionary* defines the same word in the language of the negotiable instrument law. Using the West Topic heading "Bills and Notes" and "holder" in a computer search will not return cases of negotiable instrument holders. But using the terms "negotiable instrument" and "holder" as the search words in a computer search will yield the desired result. Because paralegals cannot be sure whether the research will be done using a traditional paper library or a computer search, they must understand how each resource files the information.

Knowing how to use both traditional and computer methods, and recognizing the strengths and weaknesses of each system, is important in conducting searches. Traditional research may be better when general background research is needed and the paralegal isn't familiar with an area of law. Indexing systems are grouped by concept, and once paralegals get into the right area of law they can browse easily. The ability to flip pages back and forth when they are generally in the right area is particularly helpful in statutory research, as many of the computer-based systems perform that task slowly, if at all—and assuming the paralegal can figure out how the index has been developed to create the computer search term. In contrast, for a narrow, fact-based question, or if the research already has a citation or case name to work from, computer-based research usually is the best approach. Success in research depends on recognizing the best tools for a specific problem and using them efficiently.

What Jurisdiction or Jurisdictions Are Involved?

Research may involve federal, state, or local law. Some questions point to a certain jurisdiction—for example, "What is the age of majority in Florida?" Others are not as clear, "What law controls the situation of an unruly passenger on a flight from Los Angeles to Philadelphia?" Here the paralegal must consider jurisdictional issues related to California, Pennsylvania, and federal statutes. Or consider the case of the driver from Georgia who is driving a truck belonging to a South Carolina company and has an accident in Alabama. The legal team working on that case might want to know the law in each jurisdiction before deciding where to file suit. Focusing on a single jurisdiction or a minimum number of jurisdictions reduces the number of traditional volumes of books necessary and saves online computer search time.

What Is the Controlling Law?

The controlling law is found in primary sources of the law—statutes, regulations, and case law. Knowing which set of materials to use, the statutes of the jurisdiction, the regulation of a certain administrative agency, or the courts of a specific jurisdiction will save time in doing the research. Possibly, the controlling law is a local city, county, or parish ordinance, such as a zoning ordinance or a local plumbing code. Irrelevant sources can be eliminated from consideration and the source of the needed material located if not available onsite or online.

Exhibit 10.1 West Digest Topics and their numerical designations

1	Abandoned and Lost Property	59	Boundaries	103	Counterfeiting	160	Exchanges
2	Abatement and Revival	60	Bounties	104	Counties	161	Execution
4	Abortion and Birth Control	61	Breach of Marriage Promise	105	Court Commissioners	162	Executors and Administrators
5	Absentees	62	Breach of the Peace	106	Courts (see also Topic 170b Federal Courts)	163	Exemptions
6	Abstracts of Title	63	Bribery	107	Covenant, Action of	164	Explosives
7	Accession	64	Bridges	108	Covenants	165	Extortion and Threats
8	Accord and Satisfaction	65	Brokers	108a	Credit Reporting Agencies	166	Extradition and Detainers
9	Account	66	Building and Loan Associations	110	Criminal Law	167	Factors
10	Account, Action on	67	Burglary	111	Crops	168	False Imprisonment
11	Account Stated	68	Canals	113	Customs and Usages	169	False Personation
11a	Accountants	69	Cancellation of Instruments	114	Customs Duties	170	False Pretenses
12	Acknowledgment	70	Carriers	115	Damages	170a	Federal Civil Procedure
13	Action	71	Cemeteries	116	Dead Bodies	170b	Federal Courts
14	Action on the Case	72	Census	117	Death	171	Fences
15	Adjoining Landowners	73	Certiorari	117g	Debt, Action of	172	Ferries
15a	Administrative Law and Procedure	74	Champerty and Maintenance	117t	Debtor and Creditor	174	Fines
16	Admiralty	75	Charities	118a	Declaratory Judgment	175	Fires
17	Adoption	76	Chattel Mortgages	119	Dedication	176	Fish
18	Adulteration	76a	Chemical Dependents	120	Deeds	177	Fixtures
19	Adultery	76h	Children Out-of-Wedlock	122a	Deposits and Escrows	178	Food
20	Adverse Possession	77	Citizens	123	Deposits in Court	179	Forcible Entry and Detainer
21	Affidavits	78	Civil Rights	124	Descent and Distribution	180	Forfeitures
23	Agriculture	79	Clerks of Courts	125	Detectives	181	Forgery
24	Aliens	80	Clubs	126	Detinue	183	Franchises
25	Alteration of Instruments	81	Colleges and Universities	129	Disorderly Conduct	184	Fraud
26	Ambassadors and Consuls	82	Collision	130	Disorderly House	185	Frauds, Statute of
27	Amicus Curiae	83	Commerce	131	District and Prosecuting Attorneys	186	Fraudulent Conveyances
28	Animals	83h	Commodity Futures Trading Regulation	132	District of Columbia	187	Game
29	Annuities	84	Common Lands	133	Disturbance of Public Assemblage	188	Gaming
30	Appeal and Error	85	Common Law	134	Divorce	189	Garnishment
31	Appearance	88	Compounding Offenses	135	Domicile	190	Gas
33	Arbitration	89	Compromise and Settlement	135h	Double Jeopardy	191	Gifts
34	Armed Services	89a	Condominium	136	Dower and Curtesy	192	Good Will
35	Arrest	90	Confusion of Goods	137	Drains	193	Grand Jury
36	Arson	91	Conspiracy	138	Drugs and Narcotics	195	Guaranty
37	Assault and Battery	92	Constitutional Law	141	Easements	196	Guardian and Ward
38	Assignments	92b	Consumer Credit	142	Ejectment	197	Habeas Corpus
40	Assistance, Writ of	92h	Consumer Protection	143	Election of Remedies	198	Hawkers and Peddlers
41	Associations	93	Contempt	144	Elections	199	Health and Environment
42	Assumpsit, Action of	95	Contracts	145	Electricity	200	Highways
43	Asylums	96	Contribution	146	Embezzlement	201	Holidays
44	Attachment	97	Conversion	148	Eminent Domain	202	Homestead
45	Attorney and Client	98	Convicts	148a	Employers' Liability	203	Homicide
46	Attorney General	99	Copyrights and Intellectual Property	149	Entry, Writ of	204	Hospitals
47	Auctions and Auctioneers	100	Coroners	150	Equity	205	Husband and Wife
48	Audita Querela	101	Corporations	151	Escape	205h	Implied and Constructive Contracts
48a	Automobiles	102	Costs	152	Escheat	206	Improvements
48b	Aviation			154	Estates in Property	207	Incest
49	Bail			156	Estoppel	208	Indemnity
50	Bailment			157	Evidence	209	Indians
51	Bankruptcy			158	Exceptions, Bill of		
52	Banks and Banking			159	Exchange of Property		
54	Beneficial Associations						
55	Bigamy						
56	Bills and Notes						
58	Bonds						

(continued)

Exhibit 10.1 West Digest Topics and their numerical designations (continued)

210	Indictment and Information	269	Names	320	Railroads	369	Sunday
211	Infants	270	Navigable Waters	321	Rape	370	Supersedeas
212	Injunction	271	Ne Exeat	322	Real Actions	371	Taxation
213	Innkeepers	272	Negligence	323	Receivers	372	Telecommunications
216	Inspection	273	Neutrality Laws	324	Receiving Stolen Goods	373	Tenancy in Common
217	Insurance	274	Newspapers	325	Recognizances	374	Tender
218	Insurrection and Sedition	275	New Trial	326	Records	375	Territories
219	Interest	276	Notaries	327	Reference	376	Theaters and Shows
220	Internal Revenue	277	Notice	328	Reformation of Instruments	378	Time
221	International Law	278	Novation	330	Registers of Deeds	379	Torts
222	Interpleader	279	Nuisance	331	Release	380	Towage
223	Intoxicating Liquors	280	Oath	332	Religious Societies	381	Towns
224	Joint Adventures	281	Obscenity	333	Remainders	382	Trade Regulation
225	Joint-Stock Companies and Business Trusts	282	Obstructing Justice	334	Removal of Cases	384	Treason
226	Joint Tenancy	283	Officers and Public Employees	335	Replevin	385	Treaties
227	Judges	284	Pardon and Parole	336	Reports	386	Trespass
228	Judgment	285	Parent and Child	337	Rescue	387	Trespass to Try Title
229	Judicial Sales	286	Parliamentary Law	338	Reversions	388	Trial
230	Jury	287	Parties	339	Review	389	Trover and Conversion
231	Justices of the Peace	288	Partition	340	Rewards	390	Trusts
232	Kidnapping	289	Partnership	341	Riot	391	Turnpikes and Toll Roads
232a	Labor Relations	290	Party Walls	342	Robbery	392	Undertakings
233	Landlord and Tenant	291	Patents	343	Sales	393	United States
234	Larceny	292	Paupers	344	Salvage	394	United States Magistrates
235	Levees and Flood Control	294	Payment	345	Schools	395	United States Marshals
236	Lewdness	295	Penalties	346	Scire Facias	396	Unlawful Assembly
237	Libel and Slander	296	Pensions	347	Seals	396a	Urban Railroads
238	Licenses	297	Perjury	348	Seamen	398	Usury
239	Liens	298	Perpetuities	349	Searches and Seizures	399	Vagrancy
240	Life Estates	299	Physicians and Surgeons	349a	Secured Transactions	400	Vendor and Purchaser
241	Limitation of Actions	300	Pilots	349b	Securities Regulation	401	Venue
242	Lis Pendens	302	Pleading	350	Seduction	402	War and National Emergency
245	Logs and Logging	303	Pledges	351	Sequestration	403	Warehousemen
246	Lost Instruments	304	Poisons	352	Set-Off and Counterclaim	404	Waste
247	Lotteries	305	Possessory Warrant	353	Sheriffs and Constables	405	Waters and Water Courses
248	Malicious Mischief	306	Postal Service	354	Shipping	406	Weapons
249	Malicious Prosecution	307	Powers	355	Signatures	407	Weights and Measures
250	Mandamus	307a	Pretrial Procedure	356	Slaves	408	Wharves
251	Manufactures	308	Principal and Agent	356a	Social Security and Public Welfare	409	Wills
252	Maritime Liens	309	Principal and Surety	357	Sodomy	410	Witnesses
253	Marriage	310	Prisons	358	Specific Performance	411	Woods and Forests
255	Master and Servant	311	Private Roads	359	Spendthrifts	413	Workers' Compensation
256	Mayhem	313	Process	360	States	414	Zoning and Planning
257	Mechanics' Liens	313a	Products Liability	361	Statutes	450	Merit Systems Protection (Merit Systems Protection Board Reporter)
257a	Mental Health	314	Prohibition	362	Steam		
258a	Military Justice	315	Property	363	Stipulations		
259	Militia	316	Prostitution	365	Submission of Controversy		
260	Mines and Minerals	316a	Public Contracts	366	Subrogation		
265	Monopolies	317	Public Lands	367	Subscriptions		
266	Mortgages	317a	Public Utilities	368	Suicide		
267	Motions	318	Quieting Title				
268	Municipal Corporations	319	Quo Warranto				
		319h	Racketeer Influenced and Corrupt Organizations				

What Are the Types of Resources to Use?

Law libraries usually have primary and secondary sources of the law. A **primary source** is the actual law itself, which includes the statutes and the case law. The cases you have been briefing in this text are primary sources. **Secondary sources** are not the laws themselves but, instead, are writings about the law, such as legal encyclopedias and digests. This textbook is a secondary source. A third set of resources is referred to as finding tools—publications, such as digests or the *Index to Legal Periodicals*, used to find primary and secondary sources. Frequently, sources contain both secondary sources and **finding tools** in one publication, such as the *American Law Reports*. Some services combine all three into one service or publication. Exhibit 10.2 delineates primary and secondary sources and finding tools.

Ultimately, the primary sources of law are the ones that will be used in preparing the legal memo or brief. Secondary sources are useful, efficient ways to get an overview of an area of law or learn the terminology used in a certain field of law of which you are not familiar. The torts specialist suddenly asked to research an issue related to a different area of law, such as negotiable instruments, may be lost trying to remember the terminology and rules applicable from courses taken long ago.

Secondary sources such as encyclopedias can supply a quick review and point the research to the appropriate primary sources such as the *Uniform Commercial Code* as adopted by the state in question. Legal dictionaries frequently list cases that have defined the words in legal terms that can be a starting point for case research.

Where Is the Needed Research Material Located?

It would be nice to have a complete law school level print and electronic library available onsite to use for legal research. The reality is that law libraries are costly to acquire and maintain. The cost of the materials can run into the hundreds of dollars per volume, and the annual upkeep services not much less for pocket parts, supplemental volumes, and new case reporters. Space in office complexes is another factor. Office space is expensive, and as a library grows, more of the expensive floor space must be used for books instead of people. Finally the cost of filing the updates and keeping the space orderly must be considered. If the collection is large enough, a full-time librarian may be needed. In smaller offices these tasks take the time of paralegals that could be spent performing billable services for clients.

These cost and availability issues have spurred the adoption of electronic libraries such as the fee-based online services provided by Loislaw, Lexis, Westlaw, and VersusLaw, and the free online services provided by some colleges and universities such as the Cornell School of Law. Virtually all primary material is available online. Some certain proprietary secondary materials, such as encyclopedias, are available from some sources and not others. Depending on the resources needed to complete an assignment, the paralegal may have to locate the needed material at a remote library such as a bar association library or a law school library.

Primary source of law The actual law itself.

Secondary source of law Writings about the law.

Finding tools Publications used to find primary and secondary sources.

Exhibit 10.2 | Research materials

Primary Sources	Secondary Sources	Finding Tools
Constitutions	Legal dictionaries	Digests
Statutes	Legal encyclopedias	Citators
Court decisions	Treatises	Indexes
Common-law cases	Law reviews	
Administrative regulations	Textbooks	
Ordinances	Legal periodicals	
Court rules		

Creating a List of Research Terms

The paralegal should create a list of words for online searches and a separate list for traditional print sources. The list should be updated as the paralegal performs research, adding or deleting words and phrases and annotating the list with citations for future research. The word list should be developed from the facts of the question, the parties, locations, case-specific goods and services, and status and relationships between them.

Consider the case of the off-duty police officer who has just come from a doctor's visit and has been given a medication to reduce his blood pressure. He is involved in a rear-end collision with a van of school children returning from a fundraiser selling candy. The driver is one of the mothers, who is also a teacher in the school. A skateboarder darts in front of one of the vehicles. Using a Research Plan: Words and Phrases checklist is a good way to put together a list of the words and phrases to be searched.

What are some of the words and terms with which to start researching the issue of liability? As with most cases, each person has multiple roles or status that must be considered: teacher, parent, driver, police officer, student, child, principal, agent of school, agent of other parents, patient.

Further, the situation may have been caused by any of a number of factors, road conditions, and weather issues, time of day, speed, medical issues, carelessness, and distracted

CHECKLIST Research Plan: Words and Phrases

Concepts and Issues	Generic Words and Phrases	Text-Based Research Terms	Computer-Based Research Terms
Persons			
Status			
Relationship			
Occupation			
Group			
Class			
Item(s) Involved			
Location(s)			
Subject Matter			
Jurisdiction			
Federal			
State			
City			
Locality			
Cause of Action			
Tort			
Contract			
Family Law			
Commercial			
Relief Sought			
Injunction			
Damages			
Compensatory			
Punitive			
Mandamus			
Defenses			

driver. And what about the vehicles' braking ability, recalls of vehicles, and airbag deployment issues? Obviously not every issue relates in every case. Before starting the research, the researcher must identify the relevant terms that apply to the case being researched. The time spent creating the list will save time chasing dead ends or irrelevant issues. In creating the word list, the researcher should think of words, legal terms, and phrases and consider alternatives to those words—synonyms, antonyms, and related terms. Appropriate language may be found using secondary sources and finding tools such as legal dictionaries and legal encyclopedias and treatises.

Executing the Research Plan

Having laid out a plan of action based on answers to the preliminary questions, the research plan now can be executed. As with the execution of any plan, detours can be expected. The law is in a constant evolutionary state as new statutes are enacted and new case interpretations are handed down. During the research process, the researcher must look for changes and potential changes from pending legislation and cases on appeal. Word lists and citation must be updated and new search paths followed.

The time spent creating the list of terms, phrases, and search terms will save time when the research plan is executed. In looking for a statute, knowing the subject matter of the desired law, such as "blood alcohol level for driving," or the popular name of the law, such as "Sarbanes-Oxley," will save time by focusing the search on a specific statutory index or popular name index.

Not every search term will result in a successful search; some may lead to other search terms. The research plan should be executed in a systematic way using a checklist of the terms and research materials. The search is updated with citations, both successful and unsuccessful. When the inevitable circular search brings the researcher back to a previous result, this indicates a dead end, so the researcher can proceed on a more fruitful path.

When the time comes to finalize the research in a written document, the researcher will have the citation references and will not have to go back and find the material again. In the event of additional, similar research assignments, the researcher will have a ready reference to pick up the search and proceed quickly, using relevant terms and citations.

Finding the Law

Finding "the law" should be an easy thing to accomplish. We go to the original source and look at it. But what is the original source, and how is it located in a modern law library? The law is found in the statutes and regulations passed by the **legislative branch** and the case law in court decisions of the **judicial branch**. In the United States, laws are created at the federal, state, and local levels. At the federal legislative level laws are passed by the United States Congress, which is a **bicameral** legislative body—meaning that there are two legislative houses, the House of Representatives and the Senate. At the state government level, all of the state legislatures are bicameral except Nebraska. Local governing bodies include cities, towns, and boroughs. At the judicial level, both federal and state courts create case law through their issuing of court decisions. The law also is found in the regulations enacted by administrative agencies as a result of the authority granted to them by the legislative branch of government, whether federal, state, or local.

Generally, the assignment is to find the current controlling law. Occasionally the research assignment is to find the law that was in control at a point in the past, such as what the blood alcohol limit was last year when the client was cited for driving under the influence. In this case, we might start by asking:

Is there a statute?

Are there administrative regulations?

Is there case law on point?

Legislative branch The part of the government that consists of Congress (the Senate and the House of Representatives).

Judicial branch The court system.

Bicameral In the American system a legislature of a house of representatives and a senate.

CHECKLIST Research

Primary Sources	Secondary Sources
Case ☐ Name ☐ Citation	Encyclopedia—National ☐ Name ☐ Key or descriptive word
Federal statute ☐ Federal citation ☐ Popular name	Encyclopedia—State ☐ Name ☐ Key or descriptive word
State (name) ☐ State citation ☐ Popular name	Treatises ☐ Name ☐ Citation
Local jurisdiction name ☐ Local citation ☐ Popular name	Restatement of law ☐ Name ☐ Citation
Administrative regulations ☐ Federal agency name ☐ Citation	Periodicals ☐ Citation
State agency name ☐ Citation	Practice Books ☐ Name ☐ Citation
Local agency name ☐ Citation	Dictionary ☐ Name
Constitution ☐ Federal citation ☐ State citation	Digest ☐ Name ☐ Citation

If there is a statute in the applicable jurisdiction, it will be controlling. Regulations enacted to enforce the statute also will be controlling subject to compliance with the statutory authority under which they are enacted. Case law may exist to clarify and explain the law under the facts of the cases decided by the courts.

Primary Sources and Authority

Primary sources are the law. Primary sources include constitutions, both federal and state. Primary law includes statutes enacted by the legislative branch of government pursuant to the constitutional limitations and the regulations of the administrative agencies established by the legislature to carry out the statutory enactments. Court rules and court decisions are sources of primary law from the judicial branch of government. Exhibit 10.3 lists the primary sources at the federal level.

Mandatory and Persuasive Authority

Mandatory authority Court decisions that are binding on all lower courts.

Start with primary sources that are **mandatory authority**. Primary authority is the law itself. It is the constitution, the enactments of the legislative branch of government, and the case law decisions of the judicial branch of government. Mandatory authority is legal authority that the courts must follow. In addition to statutes and administrative regulations and ordinances, it includes case law from higher courts. The highest court in the United States is the United States Supreme Court. The decisions of the Supreme Court are mandatory on all lesser federal and state courts. The decisions of the highest appellate court of a state are mandatory authority for all lesser courts of that state.

Persuasive authority Court decisions the court is not required to follow but are well reasoned and from a respected court.

If mandatory authority cannot be found, the researcher should search for **persuasive authority**, authority the courts are not required to follow but is from a respected source and well reasoned. Decisions of some state courts traditionally have

WHEN ARE COURT DECISIONS PRECEDENTS?

Courts may issue published or unpublished opinions. A **published opinion** is a court's written explanation of its decision on a case intended to be relied upon as a statement of the law based on the facts of the case. In some cases, the court will issue an informal statement of its ruling, an **unpublished opinion**, which is intended to apply only to the parties before the court and to the very narrow issue of the particular case based on the specific facts before the court. Unlike published opinions, the courts generally do not intend that unpublished opinions be used as precedent in other cases. It should be made clear that unpublished opinions are not secret opinions, many are available online and others are available from the clerk's office.

There is a controversy with regard to the use of unpublished opinions in other court proceedings. In reviewing the issue, the Court in Anastasoff made the following observations:

Before concluding, we wish to indicate what this case is not about. It is not about whether opinions should be published, whether that means printed in a book or available in some other accessible form to the public in general. Courts may decide, for one reason or another, that some of their cases are not important enough to take up pages in a printed report. Such decisions may be eminently practical and defensible, but in our view they have nothing to do with the authoritative effect of any court decision.

The question presented here is not whether opinions ought to be published, but whether they ought to have precedential effect, whether published or not. We point out, in addition, that "unpublished" in this context has never meant "secret." So far as we are aware, every opinion and every order of any court in this country, at least of any appellate court, is available to the public. You may have to walk into a clerk's office and pay a per-page fee, but you can get the opinion if you want it. Indeed, most appellate courts now make their opinions, whether labeled "published" or not, available to anyone on line. Anastasoff v. U.S. *223 F. 3d 898 (8th cir. 2000)*

Following the publication of the initial opinion, the Anastasoff court declared the issues in the case, about recovery of tax payments, as moot since the taxpayer received her refund, Stating

. . . Here, the case having become moot, the appropriate and customary treatment is to vacate our previous opinion and judgment, remand to the District Court, and direct that Court to vacate its judgment as moot. We now take exactly that action. The constitutionality of that portion of Rule 28A(i) which says that unpublished opinions have no precedential effect remains an open question in this Circuit. . . . Anastasoff v. U.S. No. 99-3917EM, (Dec. 18, 2000)

The controversy has centered on the right of lawyers to use the unpublished opinions in argument to the court. The matter has been resolved with the passage of Rule 32.1 Citing Judicial Dispositions, which permits the inclusion of those published after January 1, 2007.

---

been looked at as being so well reasoned that other courts in other states have been persuaded to follow the legal reasoning in deciding cases for which their own state did not have any previously decided cases or statutes on point.

A good example of a persuasive opinion is that of Justice Cardozo in the New York Court of Appeals case of *Palsgraf* v. *Long Island Railroad Company*, 248 N.Y. 339 (1928) (see Appendix A, How To Brief a Case). Many courts, even today, find the logic and reasoning of Justice Cardozo persuasive and he is frequently quoted by courts in other states.

Constitutions

The United States Constitution is the ultimate primary law that sets the guidelines, limits, and authority of the federal government and the state governments. The individual state constitutions are the ultimate law for the individual state, and set the guidelines, the limits, and the authority of the state government and the local governing bodies of the state. The constitutions are primary sources, the original writing or primary source of law. Finding the United States Constitution is probably the easiest task in legal research. It is reproduced in many publications, including many textbooks, is available in virtually every public library, and is easily available on the Internet from many sources including the National Archives. Finding the Constitution for individual states however, is not as easy. Although some are posted on general-interest websites, most require access to specialty legal research websites, or to the paper version, generally found in the bound volumes of the state statutes.

Published opinion A court's written explanation of its decision on a case intended to be relied upon as a statement of the law based on the facts of the case.

Unpublished opinions Cases which the court does not feel have precedential effect and are limited to a specific set of facts.

 Web Exploration

View a high-resolution version of the original copy of the U.S. Constitution at www.archives.gov.

| Exhibit 10.3 | Federal primary sources | | |

Source	Jurisdiction	Location	URL
Constitution	United States Constitution	U.S. Const. art 1, § 10,cl.3	http://www.gpoaccess.gov/constitution/index.html
Statutes	United States Code	19 U.S.C. § 2411 (2004)	http://www.gpoaccess.gov/uscode/index.html
Administrative Regulations	Code of Federal Regulations	31 C.F.R. § 515.329 (2002)	http://www.gpoaccess.gov/cfr/index.html
Highest Appellate Court	US Supreme Court	*Brown v. Bd. Of Educ.,* 349 U.S. 294 (1955)	http://www.supremecourtus.gov/opinions/opinions.html
Intermediate Appellate Court	US Court of Appeals	*McHenry v. Fla. Bar,* 21 F.3d 1038 (11th Cir. 1994)	http://www.uscourts.gov/courtlinks/
Trial Court	US District Court	*U.S. v. Chairse,* 18 F. Supp. 2d 1021 (D. Minn. 1998)	http://www.uscourts.gov/courtlinks/
Federal Rules of Civil Procedure		Fed. R. Civ. P. 26	http://www.law.cornell.edu/rules/frcp/
Federal Rules of Criminal Procedure		Fed. R. Crim. P. 21(a)	http://www.law.cornell.edu/rules/frcrmp/

Source: *Citations in ALWD Citation format. Copyright © ALWD. Reprinted with permission.*

Web Exploration

Read the latest U.S. Supreme Court opinion at http://www.supremecourtus.gov.
Visit the homepage of the Legal Information Institute at Cornell University Law School to see the information provided. www.cornell.lii.edu.

Bench opinion The initial version of a decision issued from the bench of the court.

Slip opinion A copy of the opinion sent to the printer.

Case syllabus In a court opinion a headnote for the convenience of the reader.

Headnotes The syllabus or summary of the points of law prepared by the editorial staff of a publisher.

Statutes

Statutes enacted by the legislative branch of government are primary sources of the law. The statute of the United States—the United States Code—is available online from a number of free sources including the U.S. Government Printing Office. Many states currently make available their state statutes online through an official state website. Until a few years ago, this free-access source was generally limited to state legislators. Caution should still be the rule in using Web-based resources. Some unofficial sites have posted websites that appear to be an official primary source of the law but in reality are not complete or up-to-date.

Court Decisions

Court decisions also are primary authority. The U.S. Supreme Court and some federal courts provide their current opinions and decisions online. Notably, the Legal Information Institute at Cornell University provides free access to the U.S. Supreme Court opinions, as well as many others. Other court decisions generally are not available from free Web sources and require the use of a paid subscription or fee-based services such as Lexis, Westlaw, Loislaw, and VersusLaw. Exhibit 10.4 shows the homepage of U.S. Courts with judiciary links.

Courts such as the U.S. Supreme Court issue opinions from the "bench" called **bench opinions** and a **slip opinion** that is sent for printing. This second version may contain corrections in the bench opinion. See the U.S. Supreme Court comments on the difference in Exhibit 10.5.

The actual court language is a primary source of the law. The **case syllabus**, summaries, interpretations, or abstracts of the points of law presented by the editorial staff of the publishers of the case law, usually called **headnotes**, are not the primary source of law; rather they are explanations, interpretations, or comments that help the reader understand the legal concepts. As such, they are secondary sources. Note the cautionary

Exhibit 10.4 U.S. Courts website

Source: Administrative Office of the U.S. Courts, Washington, D.C.

comment in the syllabus of the Supreme Court case in Exhibit 10.6. Contrast the syllabus of the case with the opinion of the court in Exhibit 10.7.

Legal dictionaries and encyclopedias use headnotes—short, single-concept definitions and summaries, to provide basic information. When doing research, it should be kept in mind that these short "snippets" are taken out of the context of the case in which they were presented. None of the factual or procedural background is presented that caused the statement to be made.

Taking court statements out of the context in which the case was presented and relying on headnotes or summaries can present many problems for the researcher—the most obvious of which is accuracy. Was the headnote or summary copied correctly from the final version of the opinion? Judges have been known to correct errors in the language of opinions. Did the editor writing the note use the final version of the opinion? More important—does this statement accurately reflect the majority view, or does

 Web Exploration

Search and view full text of Supreme Court decisions issued between 1937 and 1975 at www .fedworld.gov/supcourt.

Exhibit 10.5 Supreme Court explanation on differences between bench and slip opinions

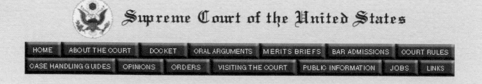

Supreme Court of the United States

| HOME | ABOUT THE COURT | DOCKET | ORAL ARGUMENTS | MERITS BRIEFS | BAR ADMISSIONS | COURT RULES |
| CASE HANDLING GUIDES | OPINIONS | ORDERS | VISITING THE COURT | PUBLIC INFORMATION | JOBS | LINKS |

2005 TERM OPINIONS OF THE COURT

Slip Opinions, *Per Curiams* (PC), and Original Case Decrees (D)

The "slip" opinion is the second version of an opinion. It is sent to the printer later in the day on which the "bench" opinion is released by the Court. Each slip opinion has the same elements as the bench opinion--majority or plurality opinion, concurrences or dissents, and a prefatory syllabus--but may contain corrections not appearing in the bench opinion. The slip opinions collected here are those issued during October Term 2005 (October 3, 2005, through October 1, 2006). These opinions are posted on this Website within hours after the bench opinions are issued and will remain posted until the opinions are published in a bound volume of the United States Reports. For further information, see Column Header Definitions and the file entitled Information About Opinions.

Caution: These electronic opinions may contain computer-generated errors or other deviations from the official printed slip opinion pamphlets. Moreover, a slip opinion is replaced within a few months by a paginated version of the case in the preliminary print, and--one year after the issuance of that print--by the final version of the case in a U. S. Reports bound volume. In case of discrepancies between the print and electronic versions of a slip opinion, the print version controls. In case of discrepancies between the slip opinion and any later official version of the opinion, the later version controls.

Source: *Supreme Court of the United States.*

Exhibit 10.6 Sample of U.S. Supreme Court syllabus

Syllabus

NOTE: Where it is feasible, a syllabus (headnote) will be released, as is being done in connection with this case, at the time the opinion is issued.
The syllabus constitutes no part of the opinion of the Court but has been prepared by the Reporter of Decisions for the convenience of the reader.
See United States v. Detroit Timber & Lumber Co., 200 U.S. 321, 337.

SUPREME COURT OF THE UNITED STATES

ROPER, SUPERINTENDENT, POTOSI CORRECTIONAL CENTER v. SIMMONS

CERTIORARI TO THE SUPREME COURT OF MISSOURI

No. 03—633. Argued October 13, 2004-Decided March 1, 2005

At age 17, respondent Simmons planned and committed a capital murder. After he had turned 18, he was sentenced to death. His direct appeal and subsequent petitions for state and federal postconviction relief were rejected. This Court then held, in *Atkins* v. *Virginia*, 536 U.S. 304, that the Eighth Amendment, applicable to the States through the Fourteenth Amendment, prohibits the execution of a mentally retarded person. Simmons filed a new petition for state postconviction relief, arguing that *Atkins'* reasoning established that the Constitution prohibits the execution of a juvenile who was under 18 when he committed his crime. The Missouri Supreme Court agreed and set aside Simmons' death sentence in favor of life imprisonment without eligibility for release. It held that, although *Stanford* v. *Kentucky*, 492 U.S. 361, rejected the proposition that the Constitution bars capital punishment for juvenile offenders younger than 18, a national consensus has developed against the execution of those offenders since *Stanford*.

Held: The Eighth and Fourteenth Amendments forbid imposition of the death penalty on offenders who were under the age of 18 when their crimes were committed. Pp. 6–25.

(a) The Eighth Amendment's prohibition against "cruel and unusual punishments" must be interpreted according to its text, by considering history,

Source: *Supreme Court of the United States*

Exhibit 10.7 | Sample opinion of the U.S. Supreme Court

Opinion of the Court

NOTICE: *This opinion is subject to formal revision before publication in the preliminary print of the United States Reports. Readers are requested to notify the Reporter of Decisions, Supreme Court of the United States, Washington, D. C. 20543, of any typographical or other formal errors, in order that corrections may be made before the preliminary print goes to press.*

SUPREME COURT OF THE UNITED STATES

No. 03–633

DONALD P. ROPER, SUPERINTENDENT, POTOSI CORRECTIONAL CENTER, PETITIONER v. CHRISTOPHER SIMMONS

ON WRIT OF CERTIORARI TO THE SUPREME COURT OF MISSOURI

[March 1, 2005]

Justice Kennedy delivered the opinion of the Court.

This case requires us to address, for the second time in a decade and a half, whether it is permissible under the Eighth and Fourteenth Amendments to the Constitution of the United States to execute a juvenile offender who was older than 15 but younger than 18 when he committed a capital crime. In *Stanford* v. *Kentucky*, 492 U.S. 361 (1989), a divided Court rejected the proposition that the Constitution bars capital punishment for juvenile offenders in this age group. We reconsider the question.

I

At the age of 17, when he was still a junior in high school, Christopher Simmons, the respondent here, committed murder. About nine months later, after he had turned 18, he was tried and sentenced to death. There is little doubt that Simmons was the instigator of the crime. Before its commission Simmons said he wanted to murder someone. In chilling, callous terms he talked about his plan, discussing it for the most part with two friends, Charles Benjamin and John Tessmer, then aged 15 and 16 respectively. Simmons proposed to commit burglary and murder by breaking and entering, tying up a

Source: Supreme Court of the United States

it reflect a minority or dissenting view? Was it the actual decision on the point of law before the court and, therefore, the "**holding**" of the court having precedential weight, or merely comments having no precedential authority because they are not related directly to the court decision and, therefore, are what are referred to as **dicta**. Contrast the headnote and the full court opinion in the case in Exhibit 10.8.

Doing legal research requires finding the most current and accurate statement of the legislative enactments and of the court. Presenting editorial headnotes, judges' dicta, or a dissenting opinion as accurate current legal authority is a potential career-ending course of action. The members of your legal team may rely on the potentially erroneous information and prepare the case, its prosecution or defense strategy, on the inaccurate information. Notwithstanding the potential effect on the trial of the case, at best it may result in a severe reprimand or dismissal from employment. Presenting the erroneous information to the court is an ethical violation of the duty of candor toward the tribunal under Rule 3.3 of the Model Rules of Professional Conduct.

It does not matter to the court that it was prepared by someone other than the attorney presenting the case, the brief, or the oral argument. It is a breach of the duty of candor to the court by the attorney.

Holding The actual decision on the specific point of law the court was asked to decide.

Dicta Court comments on issues not directly related to the holding and therefore not having precedential effect.

Exhibit 10.8   Regional reporter sample page

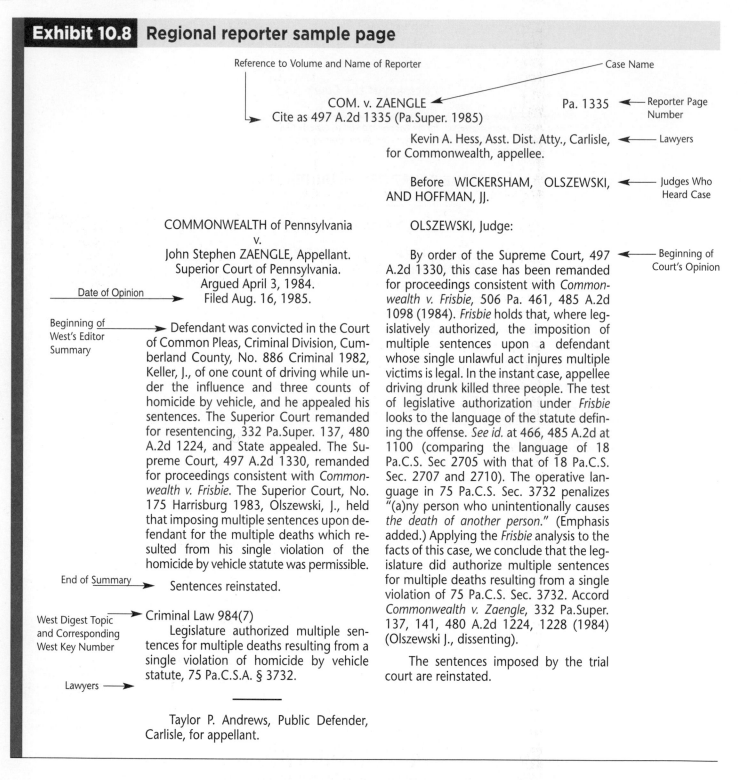

Reference to Volume and Name of Reporter

Case Name

COM. v. ZAENGLE
Cite as 497 A.2d 1335 (Pa.Super. 1985)

Pa. **1335**   ← Reporter Page Number

Kevin A. Hess, Asst. Dist. Atty., Carlisle, ← Lawyers
for Commonwealth, appellee.

Before WICKERSHAM, OLSZEWSKI, ← Judges Who Heard Case
AND HOFFMAN, JJ.

COMMONWEALTH of Pennsylvania
v.
John Stephen ZAENGLE, Appellant.
Superior Court of Pennsylvania.
Argued April 3, 1984.
Filed Aug. 16, 1985.

Date of Opinion →

Beginning of West's Editor Summary →

Defendant was convicted in the Court of Common Pleas, Criminal Division, Cumberland County, No. 886 Criminal 1982, Keller, J., of one count of driving while under the influence and three counts of homicide by vehicle, and he appealed his sentences. The Superior Court remanded for resentencing, 332 Pa.Super. 137, 480 A.2d 1224, and State appealed. The Supreme Court, 497 A.2d 1330, remanded for proceedings consistent with *Commonwealth v. Frisbie*. The Superior Court, No. 175 Harrisburg 1983, Olszewski, J., held that imposing multiple sentences upon defendant for the multiple deaths which resulted from his single violation of the homicide by vehicle statute was permissible.

End of Summary →

Sentences reinstated.

West Digest Topic and Corresponding West Key Number →

Criminal Law 984(7)
Legislature authorized multiple sentences for multiple deaths resulting from a single violation of homicide by vehicle statute, 75 Pa.C.S.A. § 3732.

Lawyers →

Taylor P. Andrews, Public Defender, Carlisle, for appellant.

OLSZEWSKI, Judge:

By order of the Supreme Court, 497 ← Beginning of Court's Opinion
A.2d 1330, this case has been remanded for proceedings consistent with *Commonwealth v. Frisbie*, 506 Pa. 461, 485 A.2d 1098 (1984). *Frisbie* holds that, where legislatively authorized, the imposition of multiple sentences upon a defendant whose single unlawful act injures multiple victims is legal. In the instant case, appellee driving drunk killed three people. The test of legislative authorization under *Frisbie* looks to the language of the statute defining the offense. *See id.* at 466, 485 A.2d at 1100 (comparing the language of 18 Pa.C.S. Sec 2705 with that of 18 Pa.C.S. Sec. 2707 and 2710). The operative language in 75 Pa.C.S. Sec. 3732 penalizes "(a)ny person who unintentionally causes *the death of another person.*" (Emphasis added.) Applying the *Frisbie* analysis to the facts of this case, we conclude that the legislature did authorize multiple sentences for multiple deaths resulting from a single violation of 75 Pa.C.S. Sec. 3732. Accord *Commonwealth v. Zaengle*, 332 Pa.Super. 137, 141, 480 A.2d 1224, 1228 (1984) (Olszewski J., dissenting).

The sentences imposed by the trial court are reinstated.

This is not to say that dissenting opinions and dicta may not be presented or argued to the court. Many of the finest jurists have issued dissenting views that became the law in future cases. And dicta in another case may well be a valid argument in a current case. The researcher's duty is to make clear the source of the information, whether from a primary or a secondary source. Sometimes it is not clear what is an enactment of the court as stated by one court:

What exactly constitutes "dicta" is hotly contested and judges often disagree about what is or is not dicta in a particular case. See *United States v. Johnson*, 256 F.3d 895, 914–16

(9th Cir. 2001) (en banc) (Kozinski, J., concurring). In Johnson, Judge Kozinski explained that, "where a panel confronts an issue germane to the eventual resolution of the case, and resolves it after reasoned consideration in a published opinion, that ruling becomes the law of the circuit, regardless of whether doing so is necessary in some strict logical sense." Id. at 914; accord *Cetacean Cmty. v. Bush*, 386 F.3d 1169,1173 (9th Cir. 2004) (quoting Johnson); *Miranda B. v. Kitzhaber*, 328 F.3d 1181, 1186 (9th Cir. 2003) (per curiam) (same).

Only "[w]here it is clear that a statement is made casually and without analysis, where the statement is uttered in passing without due consideration of the alternatives, or where it is merely a prelude to another legal issue that commands the panel's full attention, it may be appropriate to re-visit the issue in a later case." Johnson, 256 F.3d at 915. Nevertheless, "any such reconsideration should be done cautiously and rarely—only where the later panel is convinced that the earlier panel did not make a deliberate decision to adopt the rule of law it announced." Id. If, however, "it is clear that a majority of the panel has focused on the legal issue presented by the case before it and made a deliberate decision to resolve the issue, that ruling becomes the law of the circuit and can only be overturned by an en banc court or by the Supreme Court." Id. at 916; see also Cetacean Cmty., 386 F.3d at 1173; Miranda B., 328 F.3d at 1186.

This understanding of binding circuit authority was further articulated in *Barapind v. Enomoto*, 400 F.3d 744 (9th Cir. 2005) (en banc) (per curiam), where we said that when a panel has "addressed [an] issue and decided it in an opinion joined in relevant part by a majority of the panel," the panel's decision becomes "law of the circuit." Id. at 750-51 (footnote omitted). PADILLA v. LEVER, 03-56259 (9TH CIR. 2005)

Secondary Sources

Secondary sources explain the law. Trying to understand a new area of law can be difficult. Secondary sources are useful sources of information to learn about the history of an area of law, the issues involved, and in some situations the direction the law may be taking. A secondary source may be the editorial headnotes of a case or an in-depth scholarly interpretation, such as a treatise, a law review, or an article in a scholarly journal or other periodical.

Legal Dictionaries

Legal dictionaries, as opposed to general English or other specialized dictionaries, define words and phrases as used in the law. The "law," as with most professions, trades, and occupations, has developed its own specialized vocabulary. Each specialized area of law further develops a specialized terminology. Lawyers in specialty fields, such as antitrust law, use terms that have developed specialized meaning through case decisions such as the antitrust law term "tying arrangement," used to describe the situation in which one product can be purchased only with another product. This term comes from the 1947 antitrust case of *International Salt v. United States*, which held that a patent is presumed to give the patent holder "market power" (another legal term), making it illegal to "tie the sale of the patented product to the sale of another." Without an understanding of the basic terminology and legal concepts, it is hard to conduct proper legal search using either traditional books or computer-based services. Exhibit 10.9 is a sample page from *Black's Law Dictionary*, illustrating the term "tying."

Secondary Sources-Legal Encyclopedias

Legal encyclopedias, like legal dictionaries, can provide the needed background to understand an area enough to start the research. They can provide an overview of the concepts and history of an area of law, the legal issues involved, and the terminology. The annotations (lists of case citations) can provide a starting point for case law research. National encyclopedias such as *Corpus Juris Secundum* (CJS) and *American*

Exhibit 10.9	*Black's Law Dictionary*, sample page

confesses in open court. U.S. Const. Art. IV, § 2, cl. 2.

tying, *adj. Antitrust.* Of or relating to an arrangement whereby a seller sells a product to a buyer only if the buyer purchases another product from the seller <tying agreement>.

tying arrangement. *Antitrust.* **1.** A seller's agreement to sell one product or service only if the buyer also buys a different product or service. The product or service that the buyer wants to buy is known as the *tying product* or *tying service*; the different product or service that the seller insists on selling is known as the *tied product* or *tied service*. Tying arrangements may be illegal under the Sherman or Clayton Act if their effect is too anticompetitive. **2.** A seller's refusal to sell one product or

service unless the buyer also buys a different product or service. — Also termed *tying agreement; tie-in; tie-in arrangement.* Cf. RECIPROCAL DEALING.

tying product. See TYING ARRANGEMENT (1).

tyranny, *n.* Arbitrary or despotic government; the severe and autocratic exercise of sovereign power, whether vested constitutionally in one ruler or usurped by that ruler by breaking down the division and distribution of governmental powers. — **tyrannical, tyrannous**, *adj.*

tyrant, *n.* A sovereign or ruler, legitimate or not, who wields power unjustly and arbitrarily to oppress the citizenry; a despot.

Source: Black's Law Dictionary, *7e, 1995. Reprinted with permission of Thomson/West Publishing.*

Jurisprudence (AM JUR) provide cases from all jurisdictions for reference and research. Exhibit 10.10 is a sample page from *American Jurisprudence*.

State-specific encyclopedias generally limit case references or citations to that jurisdiction. Where the research is on a new area of law for the jurisdiction, the national coverage may provide information on persuasive authority from other jurisdictions. Exhibit 10.11 is a sample page from a secondary source, *Corpus Juris Secundum*, a national legal encyclopedia.

Treatises, Law Reviews, and Legal Periodicals

Some secondary sources are authoritative or of sufficient scholarly value to be persuasive to the court. For example, the treatise on Torts by Prosser is frequently used in argument as persuasive and accepted as such by most courts. In new areas of the law, such as cyber law, or emerging and changing areas such as privacy rights, courts frequently welcome a well-reasoned scholarly article from a law review or other legal journal that makes a clear and convincing argument with well-researched and reasoned thought. In some instances, these articles are like the *amicus curia* briefs submitted to the court by interested parties that have no actual standing as a party but have a clear interest in the outcome. Examples are Planned Parenthood and a national right-to-life organization in abortion-rights cases.

Amicus curia Briefs submitted by interested parties, as a "friend of the court," who do not have standing in the action.

Finding Tools

Finding tools help to "find" the law. Finding the right case, statute, or regulation can be difficult, particularly if the correct term or phrase is not used to conduct the search. As mentioned previously, West Publishing might use the phrase "Bills and Notes" and another publisher might use the term "holder" to refer to the same cases and material on negotiable instruments.

Indexes and Digests

Indexes and digests offer a way of finding the material.

Citator An index of cases.

1. Indexes and citators. Among the more useful sets of indexes and **citators** are those that cross-reference material. Some indexes use the commonly used or popular name of a case or statute to provide the citation or

Exhibit 10.10 *American Jurisprudence*, sample page

is infected with a contagious disease[90] or has been dangerously exposed to such a disease.[91]

§ 317. —Children infected with the AIDS virus

Acquired Immune Deficiency Syndrome (AIDS) disables victims of the disease by collapsing their immune systems, making them unable to fight infection.[92] State education authorities, rather than local school authorities, are the appropriate parties to promulgate regulations concerning the right of AIDS-infected children to attend public school, since the state's power to regulate on the issue, inferable from its broad grant of authority to supervise the schools, pre-empts any rights of local authorities under their statutory discretion to exclude children from school to prevent the spread of contagious disease.[93]

◆ *Caution:* State statutes and local health regulations concerning contagious diseases in general, which make no specific reference to AIDS, do not apply to the decision whether AIDS-infected students should be allowed to attend public school.[94]

Procedures for determining whether AIDS-infected children should be excluded from a public school have withstood a due process challenge, one court having upheld the constitutionality of a plan which provided for an impartial decision by a medical panel, proper notice, and the opportunity to call and cross-examine witnesses.[95] However, distinguishing between students known to be infected with AIDS and students who were unidentified carriers of AIDS-related complex or asymptomatic carriers is constitutionally unacceptable since the proposed exclusion from public school of only the known AIDS-infected children constitutes an equal protection violation.[96]

◆ *Practice Guide:* Numerous organizations, both medical and educational, have formulated guidelines on when AIDS carriers should be segregated from the rest of the population. In cases concerning the right of a student with AIDS to attend school, courts have received evidence of the guidelines

90. Kenney v. Gurley, 208 Ala. 623, 95 So. 34, 26 A.L.R. 813 (1923); Nutt v. Board of Education of City of Goodland, Sherman County, 128 Kan. 507, 278 P. 1065 (1929).

As to the right to public education, generally, see §§ 242 et seq.
Forms: Answer—Defense—School district providing home teaching to student with contagious or infectious disease pending determination whether student's attendance at school would be danger to others. 22 Am Jur Pl & Pr Forms (Rev), Schools, Form 182.

91. Bright v. Beard, 132 Minn. 375, 157 N.W. 501 (1916).

92. Board of Educ. of City of Plainfield, Union County v. Cooperman, 105 N.J. 587, 523 A.2d 655, 38 Ed. Law Rep. 607, 60 A.L.R.4th 1 (1987).
Law Reviews: AIDS in public schools: Resolved issues and continuing controversy, 24 J Law and Educ 1:69 (1995).

Students with AIDS: Protecting an infected child's right to a classroom education and developing a school's AIDS policy, 40 S Dakota LR 172 (1995).

93. Board of Educ. of City of Plainfield, Union County v. Cooperman, 105 N.J. 587, 523 A.2d 655, 38 Ed. Law Rep. 607, 60 A.L.R.4th 1 (1987).

94. District 27 Community School Bd. by Granirer v. Board of Educ. of City of New York, 130 Misc. 2d 398, 502 N.Y.S.2d 325, 32 Ed. Law Rep. 740 (Sup. Ct. 1986).

95. Board of Educ. of City of Plainfield, Union County v. Cooperman, 105 N.J. 587, 523 A.2d 655, 38 Ed. Law Rep. 607, 60 A.L.R.4th 1 (1987).
Forms: Complaint, petition, or declaration—To enjoin expulsion of student who tested positive for AIDS virus—By guardian. 22 Am Jur Pl & Pr Forms (Rev), Schools, Form 177.

96. District 27 Community School Bd. by Granirer v. Board of Educ. of City of New York, 130 Misc. 2d 398, 502 N.Y.S.2d 325, 32 Ed. Law Rep. 740 (Sup. Ct. 1986).

537

Source: American Jurisprudence, 2e, 2000. Reprinted with permission of Thomson/West Publishing.

Exhibit 10.11   Page from *Corpus Juris Secundum,* a legal encyclopedia

§§ 58–59   SOCIAL SECURITY   81 C.J.S.

individual who died fully insured,[65] and have physical or mental impairments which, under regulations promulgated for the purpose, are deemed to be of such severity as to preclude engaging in any gainful activity.[66]   The requirements for obtaining disability benefits by such persons are more restrictive than requirements for the insured individual himself.[67]   The physical impairment necessary to a finding of disability is placed on a level of severity to be determined administratively,[68] and the regulations adopted to carry out the statutory provisions have been upheld.[69]

A claim for disability is judged solely by medical criteria,[70] without regard to non-medical factors[71] such as age, education, and work experience,[72] in contrast to the considerations given to an insured individual's age, education, and work experience, in determining his ability to engage in substantial gainful activity, as discussed supra § 56.   An individual cannot qualify for disability insurance benefits unless suffering from an impairment listed in the appendix to the regulations applicable to disabilities, or from one or more unlisted impairments that singly or in combination are the medical equivalent of a listed impairment.[73]   The benefits are to be paid only for a disabling medical impairment,[74] and not simply for the inability to obtain employment.[75]

§ 59.   Benefits of Disabled Child

A disabled child of an insured individual who is, or would have been, eligible for social security benefits, may be entitled to disability insurance benefits.

Research Note

Status as child eligible for benefits under statute generally is discussed supra § 41.

Library References

Social Security and Public Welfare ⬅123, 140.5.

Under the provisions of the Social Security Act,[76] disabled children of retired or disabled insured individuals, and of insured individuals who have died, may be paid benefits if they have been disabled since before they reached twenty-two years of age, and if they meet the other conditions of eligibility.[77]   The purpose of the provision is to provide a measure of income and security to those who have lost a wage-earner on whom they depended,[78] or to provide support for the dependents of a disabled wage earner,[79] and not to replace only that support enjoyed by the child prior to the onset of disability.[80]   The liberal perspective of the Act applies to the award of children's disability benefits.[81]

In order to be entitled to recover benefits under this provision, the child must have been disabled,[82] as defined elsewhere in the Act,[83] prior to attaining a specified age,[84] and must be un-

65. U.S.—Sullivan v. Weinberger, C.A. Ga., 493 F.2d 855, certiorari denied 95 S.Ct. 1958, 421 U.S. 967, 44 L.Ed.2d 455.

66. U.S.—Wokojance v. Weinberger, C. A.Ohio, 513 F.2d 210, certiorari denied 96 S.Ct. 106, 423 U.S. 856, 46 L.Ed.2d 82.

Hendrix v. Finch, D.C.S.C., 310 F. Supp. 513.

Baby sitting; domestic work
U.S.—Dixon v. Weinberger, C.A.Ga., 495 F.2d 202.

Time impairment manifest
U.S.—Sullivan v. Weinberger, C.A.Ga., 493 F.2d 855, certiorari denied 95 S.Ct. 1958, 421 U.S. 967, 44 L.Ed.2d 455.

67. U.S.—Wokojance v. Weinberger, C. A.Ohio, 513 F.2d 210, certiorari denied 96 S.Ct. 106, 423 U.S. 856, 46 L.Ed.2d 82.

Solis v. U. S. Secretary of Health, Ed. and Welfare, D.C.Puerto Rico, 372 F.Supp. 1223—Truss v. Richardson, D. C.Mich., 338 F.Supp. 741—Nickles v. Richardson, D.C.S.C., 326 F.Supp. 777.

68. U.S.—Gillock v. Richardson, D.C. Kan., 322 F.Supp. 354.

69. U.S.—Sullivan v. Weinberger, C.A. Ga., 493 F.2d 855, certiorari denied 95 S.Ct. 1958, 421 U.S. 967, 44 L.Ed.2d 455.

Gunter v. Richardson, D.C.Ark., 335 F.Supp. 907—Zanoviak v. Finch, D.C. Pa., 314 F.Supp. 1152—Frasier v. Finch, D.C.Ala., 313 F.Supp. 160, affirmed, C. A., 434 F.2d 597.

70. U.S.—Wokojance v. Weinberger, C. A.Ohio, 513 F.2d 210, certiorari denied 96 S.Ct. 106, 423 U.S. 856, 46 L.Ed.2d 82.

71. U.S.—Sullivan v. Weinberger, C.A. Ga., 493 F.2d 855, certiorari denied 95 S.Ct. 1958, 421 U.S. 967, 44 L.Ed.2d 455.

72. U.S.—Gillock v. Richardson, D.C. Kan., 322 F.Supp. 354.

73. U.S.—Wokojance v. Weinberger, C. A.Ohio, 513 F.2d 210, certiorari denied 96 S.Ct. 106, 423 U.S. 856, 46 L.Ed.2d 82.

Gillock v. Richardson, D.C.Kan., 322 F.Supp. 354—Hendrix v. Finch, D.C.S. C., 310 F.Supp. 513.

74. U.S.—Sullivan v. Weinberger, C.A. Ga., 493 F.2d 855, certiorari denied 95 S.Ct. 1958, 421 U.S. 967, 44 L.Ed.2d 455.

75. U.S.—Sullivan v. Weinberger, C.A. Ga., 493 F.2d 855, certiorari denied 95 S.Ct. 1958, 421 U.S. 967, 44 L.Ed.2d 455.

76. 42 U.S.C.A. § 402(d).

77. U.S.—Lowe v. Finch, D.C.Va., 297 F.Supp. 667—Blevins v. Fleming, D.C. Ark., 180 F.Supp. 287.

78. U.S.—Ziskin v. Weinberger, D.C. Ohio, 379 F.Supp. 124.

79. U.S.—Jimenez v. Weinberger, Ill., 94 S.Ct. 2496, 417 U.S. 628, 41 L.Ed.2d 363, appeal after remand, C.A., 523 F.2d 689, certiorari denied 96 S.Ct. 3200.

80. U.S.—Jimenez v. Weinberger, Ill., 94 S.Ct. 2496, 417 U.S. 628, 41 L.Ed.2d 363, appeal after remand, C.A., 523 F.2d 689, certiorari denied 96 S.Ct. 3200.

81. U.S.—Ziskin v. Weinberger, D.C. Ohio, 379 F.Supp. 124.

82. U.S.—Ziskin v. Weinberger, D.C. Ohio, 379 F.Supp. 124.

83. 42 U.S.C.A. § 423.

84. U.S.—Ziskin v. Weinberger, D.C. Ohio, 379 F.Supp. 124—Moon v. Richardson, D.C.Va., 345 F.Supp. 1182.

Source: From Corpus Juris Secundum, © The West Group, a Thomson Company. Reproduced with permission.

reference to the original source. For example, the commonly used or popular name for the statement of rights read to criminal defendants when arrested is "Miranda Rights." Using a popular name index provides the citation to the case in which the U.S. Supreme Court made mandatory the reading of these rights to defendants—*Miranda v Arizona* 384 US 436 (1966).

2. Legal digests provide lists of cases in subject topic format, with cases generally in chronological order from the earliest to the latest. Digests do not offer the detailed analysis found in encyclopedias. Exhibit 10.12 is a sample page from *West's Digest*.

Personal Research Strategy

Over time, each paralegal develops a personal search strategy based on the nature of the problem or issue to be researched and the resources available. When a legal issue is well defined and a specific case or statute is in question, it may be possible to start with the original primary source. More likely, though, the research assignment will be less defined and may be just a set of facts describing a situation. A possible area of relevant law may be suggested. This could be a specific area of law such as "driving too fast for conditions," or a general area of law such as "personal injury from an automobile accident."

The facts will determine the area of law. If the paralegal is unfamiliar with the area of law, the relevant facts may not be obvious. Secondary sources provide a good reference source to acquire a general understanding about an area of law. As the paralegal learns more about the specifics of the area of law and the essential elements of causes of actions, the relevant facts should become clearer. One of the advantages of using the traditional book form of research is the ability to flip pages back and forth and scan many items that can lead to a specific point of law. This is sometimes referred to as "the serendipity of research."

Computer search engines can lead to specific case law and statutes. The challenge is in how to construct the search query or question. If you do not know the relevant facts to include, the resulting report may not be accurate. Computers, for the most part, are limited to finding only the things the search query specifically asks for. Learning the relevant facts to create the proper question may involve using the print resources first to determine the relevant facts or the proper terminology. For example, in a fair-use doctrine case of alleged copyright violation, is the status of the alleged violator as a nonprofit organization relevant?

Always verify that the law and cases cited in the research and memo of law is current law or current authority. Look for pending cases and legislation that might change the answer to the legal question. Look in legal journals, periodicals, and legal newspapers, as well as newspapers of general circulation, for cases that are on appeal that involve the same legal issues. Check the legislative services for pending legislation that may have an impact on the case. Research that is concerned with giving clients advice on future actions may depend on knowing the changes that may occur that will change the basic parameters of the law. For example, can I have a smoking section in my new restaurant? Are the tax rates for estate planning going to change next year?

A Final Word on Executing the Legal Research Plan

We emphasize this final piece of advice: Know when to ask for help. Everyone on the legal team who has done legal research has at one time or another hit a research dead end. Sometimes taking a few minutes to ask a question will yield the "magic" word, term, or phrase that will result in the answer you seek.

Exhibit 10.12 *West's Federal Digest*, sample page

CRIMINAL LAW

SUBJECTS INCLUDED

Acts and omissions in violation of law punishable as offenses against the public

Nature and elements of crime in general

Capacity to commit crime, nature and extent of responsibility therefore in general, and responsibility of principals, accessories, etc.

Jurisdiction over and place of prosecution of crimes

Limitation of time for prosecution

Preliminary complaints, warrants, examination and commitment

Arraignment and pleas

Evidence in criminal proceedings

Trial, and acquittal or conviction

Motions in arrest of judgment and for new trial

Judgment or sentence and final commitment

Review on appeal, writ of error or certiorari

Prosecution and punishment of successive offenses or of habitual criminals

Modes of punishment and prevention of crime in general

SUBJECTS EXCLUDED AND COVERED BY OTHER TOPICS

Arrest, see ARREST

Bail, see BAIL

Constitutional rights and privileges of accused not peculiar to matters within scope of this topic, see CONSTITUTIONAL LAW, INDICTMENT AND INFORMATION, JURY, SEARCHES AND SEIZURES, WITNESSES and other specific topics

Convicts, disabilities and regulation, see CONVICTS

Costs in criminal prosecutions, see COSTS

Extradition of fugitives, see EXTRADITION AND DETAINERS

Fines in general, see FINES

Grand juries and inquisitions by them, see GRAND JURY

Habeas corpus to obtain discharge from imprisonment, see HABEAS CORPUS

Included offenses, conviction under indictment for broader offense, see INDICTMENT AND INFORMATION

Indictments or other accusations, see INDICTMENT AND INFORMATION and specific topics relating to particular offenses

Injunction against commission of crime, see INJUNCTION

Judgment of acquittal, conviction or sentence, effect as adjudication, see JUDGMENT

Jury trial, right to and waiver, and qualifications and selection of jurors, see JURY

Juvenile offenders, special rules and proceedings, see INFANTS

Source: Federal Digest, West's Federal Digest, 4e. Reprinted with permission of Thomson/West Publishing.

Using Printed Legal Reference Works

Most legal references have a set of common features. They generally have a section, usually in the introduction, that explains the coverage and how to use the specific book or service. This usually includes the abbreviations used throughout the work (see Exhibit 10.13), and the method of pagination—for example, standard page numbering or use of section numbers. A table of contents at the beginning of the work (see Exhibit 10.14) provides a general list of major topics. The index at the end of the work provides the detailed coverage. Multivolume sets might have a separate set of volumes containing the index. Each volume also might contain an index for the specific volume.

Most legal words also contain a table of cases that are mentioned in the text. This is a useful feature when a case seems to be on point or relevant and the paralegal wants to research the area of law and other cases on the same issue. A table of statutes also may be included, to help the researcher find cases or discussions of a statute.

Rule 32.1. Citing Judicial Dispositions

(a) Citation Permitted. A court may not prohibit or restrict the citation of federal judicial opinions, orders, judgments, or other written dispositions that have been:
  (i) designated as "unpublished," "not for publication," "non-precedential," "not precedent," or the like; and
  (ii) issued on or after January 1, 2007.
(b) Copies Required. If a party cites a federal judicial opinion, order, judgment, or other written disposition that is not available in a publicly accessible electronic database, the party must file and serve a copy of that opinion, order, judgment, or disposition with the brief or other paper in which it is cited.

Updates

Print material is updated in a number of ways. One of the most frequent is the use of **pocket parts**, so called because they are slipped into a pocket in the back of the print volume. Usually these are annual updates, but they may be produced more or less frequently depending on the publisher and the need for updates. Also used are supplemental

Pocket parts An update to a book that is a separate document that slips into a pocket in the back of the main volume.

Exhibit 10.13 — Sample list of abbreviations

A.	*Atlantic Reporter*	**Binns' Just.**	*Binns' Justice*
A.2d	*Atlantic Reporter, Second Series*	**Biss.**	*Bissell's Reports, U.S.*
Abb.	*Abbott's Circuit Court Reports, U.S.*	**Black**	*Black's United States Supreme Court Reports*
Abb.Adm.	*Abbott's Admiralty Reports, U.S.*	**Blair**	*Blair County Law Reports*
Adams L.J.	*Adams County Legal Journal*	**Blatchf.C.C.**	*Blatchford's Reports, U.S.*
Add.	*Addison's Reports*	**Bond**	*Bond's Reports, U.S.*
Am.Dec.	*American Decisions*	**B.R.**	*Bankruptcy reports*
Am.L.J., N.S.	*American Law Journal, New Series*	**Bright.E.C.**	*Brightly's Election Cases*
Am.L.J.,O.S.	*American Law Journal, Hall's*	**Bright.N.P.**	*Brightly's Nisi Prius Reports*
Am.L.Reg., N.S.	*American Law Register, New Series*	**Browne**	*P.A. Browne's reports*
Am.L.Reg., O.S.	*American Law Register, Old Series*	**Brock.**	*Brockenbrough's Reports, U.S.*
Am.Rep.	*American Reports*	**Bucks**	*Bucks County Law Reporter*
Am.St.Rep.	*American State Reports*	**C.A.**	*United States Court of Appeals*
Ann.Cas.	*American & English Annotated Cases*	**C.C.A.**	*United States Circuit Court of Appeals*
Ashm.	*Ashmead's Reports*	**Cambria**	*Cambria County Legal Journal*
Baldw.	*Baldwin's Reports, U.S.*	**Cambria C.R.**	*Cambria County Reports*
Beaver	*Beaver County Legal Journal*	**Camp.**	*Campbell's Legal Gazette Reports*
Ben.	*Benedict's Reports, U.S.*	**Cent.**	*Central Reporter*
Berks	*Berks County Legal Journal*	**C.C.**	*(see Pa.C.C.) County Court Reports*
Binn.	*Binney's Reports*	**Chest.**	*Chester County Reports*

Source: From Purdon's Pennsylvania Statutes Annotated, *© 1994 by West Group, a Thomson Company. Reproduced with permission.*

Exhibit 10.14   Sample table of contents

Source: From Pennsylvania Estate Planning and Drafting, *2/E, by Robert J. Weinberg. © George T. Bisel Company, Inc., Reproduced by permission.*

pamphlets, usually paperbacks, to supplement the annual updates. Some are issued monthly, and others quarterly or semi-annually.

It is essential that the pocket part or supplement be consulted. In statutory research, the main volumes may be many years old and sections of the law repealed. The pocket parts or other supplements, not the main volume, contain the latest information. For this reason, some researchers look at the pocket part first, before consulting the main volume. More and more frequently, additional updates are provided online. The paralegal must learn how each resource is updated and the frequency of the updates. Exhibit 10.15 is a sample pocket part supplement.

Constructing a Computer Search Query

Constructing a search query requires one to select a computer search index, then to create the query.

Creating a Computer Search

The three primary full-service online providers of computer research services—Lexis, Loislaw, and Westlaw—provide a broad range of legal materials including cases, statutes, and regulations. In addition, a limited-service search provider, VersusLaw, specializes in providing cases and limited access to additional items, such as the *Code of Federal Regulations*.

In using a limited-service provider, it is important to check the coverage dates and content. In some cases the same information is available at other sources, such as the *United States Code* and the *Code of Federal Regulations*, which are available online through the GPO Access website. In all cases, researchers must be certain that they have checked all the latest update sources.

Search Method and Query

Each of the online providers uses words to find and retrieve documents. As part of the publication process, indexes are prepared of every word in the document, the words are tabulated for frequency, and a word index is prepared. The search you create searches this index. VersusLaw uses a full-text retrieval method that searches every word except "stop words"—words that are used too commonly in documents to be used in a search, such as "the," "not," "of," and "and."

Creating the Query

When you conduct a search, you are asking the search engine to find the indexed words you have chosen. These may be legal specialty words or common English words. Single words may be in any of the Internet or legal search engines. Frequently you will be looking for more detailed information. Using combinations of words in the search can narrow the search results. Usually, the most productive search contains a combination of words, which may consist of terms such as "strict liability," "legal malpractice," "automobile accident," or "reckless indifference," for example.

Using Connectors

Connectors are instructions to the search engine to look for documents containing combinations of words. Connectors may be thought of as instructions to the search engine: Find me documents in which the words "strict" AND "liability" appear. The word AND is a connector that instructs the search not to return the documents in which only one of the words is found. Exhibit 10.16 shows a Loislaw search with the AND connector.

Web Explorations

VersusLaw Research Manual: www.versuslaw.com/Support/R-Manual_Preface.asp
Lexis: www.lexisnexis.com/
Westlaw: www.westlaw.com/about/
VersusLaw: www.versuslaw.com
Loislaw: www.loislaw.com

ELECTRONIC SEARCHING STRATEGY

SIDEBAR

Searching is a process, not an event. . . . Searching a library is not about spending time and mental energy formulating the 'golden query' that retrieves your desired information in a single stroke. In practice, good online searching involves formulating a succession of queries until you are satisfied with the results. As you view results from one search, you'll come across additional leads that you did not identify in your original search. You can incorporate these new terms into your existing query or create a new one. After each query, evaluate its success by asking:

- Did I find what I was looking for?
- What better information could still be out there?
- How can I refine my query to find better information?

Issuing multiple queries can be frustrating or rewarding, depending on how long it takes you to identify the key material you need to answer your research problem

Connectors Instructions in a search query on how to treat the words in the query.

Exhibit 10.15 **Sample pocket part supplement**

13 Pa.C.S.A. § 1105   COMMERCIAL CODE

DIVISION 1
GENERAL PROVISIONS

CHAPTER 11

SHORT TITLE, CONSTRUCTION, APPLICATION
AND SUBJECT MATTER OF TITLE

§ 1105.   Territorial application of title; power of parties to choose applicable law

Notes of Decisions

Bankruptcy 6

———————

1. In general

In re Eagle Enterprises, Inc., Bkrtcy.E.D.Pa. 1998, 223 B.R. 290, [main volume] affirmed 237 B.R. 269.

2. Law governing

When parties agree to apply foreign law, pursuant to which their contract to "lease" goods kept in Pennsylvania will be deemed a true "lease," despite fact that contract does not permit lessor to terminate agreement but affords him an option to purchase goods for nominal consideration, Pennsylvania law will not give effect to that choice. In re Eagle Enterprises, Inc., E.D.Pa.1999, 237 B.R. 269.

4. Third parties

In re Eagle Enterprises, Inc., Bkrtcy.E.D.Pa. 1998, 223 B.R. 290, [main volume] affirmed 237 B.R. 269.

6. Bankruptcy

While Chapter 7 debtor and equipment lessor were generally free, under Pennsylvania statute, to agree what law would govern their rights and duties, debtor and equipment lessor could not impose their choice of law on Chapter 7 trustee, as party who never agreed to choice-of-law provision, in order to prevent trustee from challenging parties' characterization, as equipment "lease," of agreement which required debtor to pay alleged rent throughout full term of lease, and which then allowed debtor to acquire equipment at end of lease for nominal consideration of one dollar, merely because lease would allegedly have been recognized as true lease under law of foreign country that parties chose to govern their agreement. In re Eagle Enterprises, Inc., E.D.Pa.1999, 237 B.R. 269.

CHAPTER 12

GENERAL DEFINITIONS AND PRINCIPLES OF INTERPRETATION

§ 1201.   General definitions

Notes of Decisions

11. Lease or lease intended as security

Under Pennsylvania law, "lease" transaction in which "lessee" cannot terminate "lease" during its term, but may thereafter become owner of "leased" goods for no additional or nominal additional consideration, does not create lease, but rather a security interest. In re Eagle Enterprises, Inc., E.D.Pa.1999, 237 B.R. 269.

When parties agree to apply foreign law, pursuant to which their contract to "lease" goods kept in Pennsylvania will be deemed a true "lease," despite fact that contract does not permit lessor to terminate agreement but affords him an option to purchase goods for nominal consideration, Pennsylvania law will not give effect to that choice. In re Eagle Enterprises, Inc., E.D.Pa.1999, 237 B.R. 269.

13. Security interest

Revised Pennsylvania statute defining term "security interest" seeks to correct shortcomings of its predecessor by focusing inquiry of lease/security interest analysis on economics of the transaction, rather than on intent of the parties. In re Kim, Bkrtcy.E.D.Pa.1999, 232 B.R. 324.

Whether, under Pennsylvania law, lease or security interest is created by a particular transaction is no longer within exclusive control of the parties and subject to possible manipulation through artful document drafting; rather, issue is to be determined by reference to uniform criteria set forth in revised statute defining term "security interest." In re Kim, Bkrtcy.E.D.Pa.1999, 232 B.R. 324.

In determining whether debtor's lease was a disguised security interest or a true lease under Pennsylvania law, bankruptcy court was required to consider entire "transaction" and was not constrained to look solely to documents signed by the parties which were designated "lease" or which made use of terms commonly found in leases, but could examine both parol and extrin-

4

Source: *From Purdon's* Pennsylvania Consolidated Statutes Annotated, 2001 Cumulative Annual Pocket Part. © 2001 by West Group, a Thomson Company. Reproduced with permission.

Exhibit 10.16 Loislaw search with AND connector

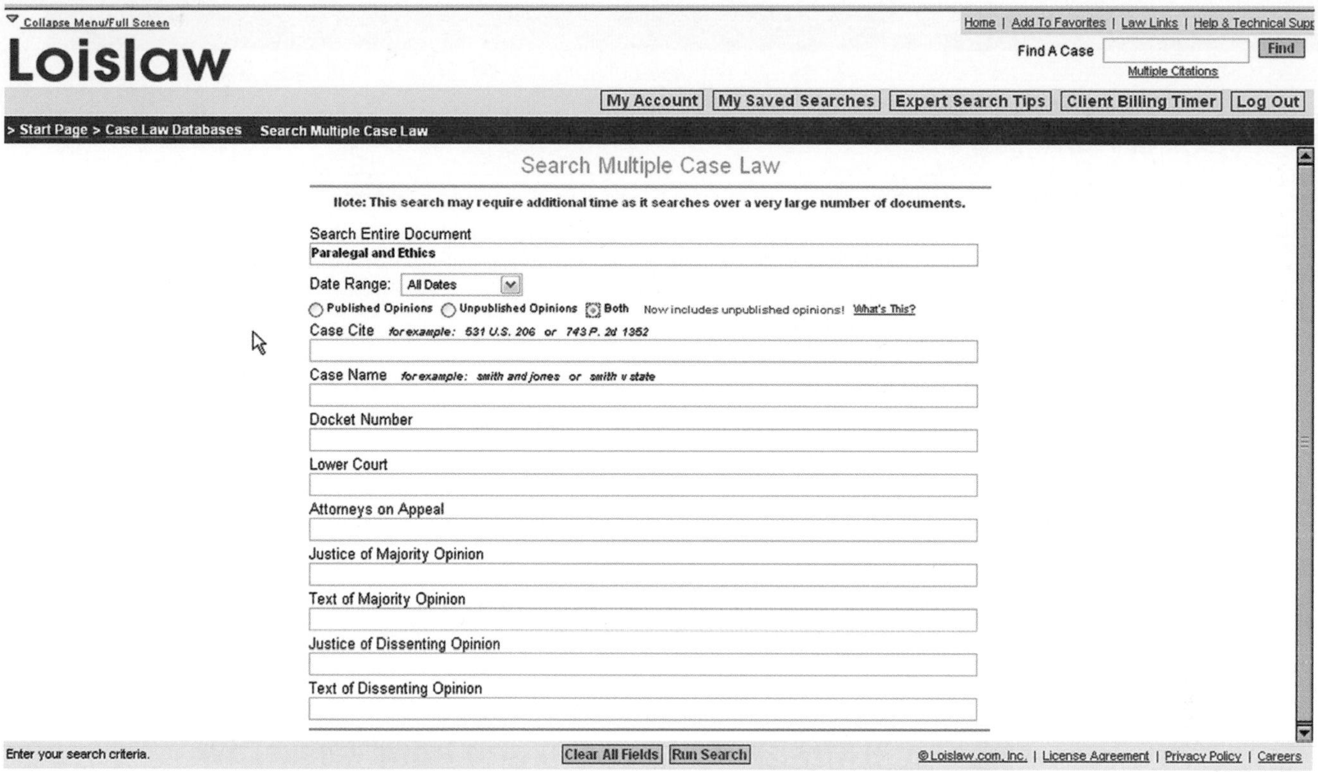

Source: *Reproduced with permission of Aspen Publishers, Loislaw screen shot.*

The connector OR instructs the search engine to find either term—the word "strict" OR the word "liability"—and retrieve the documents. Exhibit 10.17 depicts a Lexis search with the OR connector. The NOT connector instructs the search to eliminate certain words. For example, you may wish to review documents in which the word "malpractice" is found but *not* those with the word "medical."

In some cases it might be assumed that there will be other words between the desired terms, such as in the phrase "Paralegals are bound by the ethics of their profession." The NEAR connector helps to locate documents where the terms are near each other; for example: find "paralegal" NEAR "ethics." The NEAR connector allows the paralegal to search for words near each other by specifying the number of words apart that is acceptable.

Exhibit 10.18 gives a comparison of these concepts, by VersusLaw, and Exhibit 10.19 gives a guide to connectors from Westlaw.

Updating Legal Research

The legal team always must use the most current statutory and case law in advising clients and arguing cases to the court. One of the features of the American legal system is its constant change. Courts attempt to meet the needs of a changing society by reviewing prior case law and, when appropriate, overruling or modifying it as the contemporary American view of justice dictates. The American legal system concept of *stare decisis* provides that we use prior case law as **precedent** but change the law as American society changes. Occasionally, existing case law may be held unconstitutional, such as happened with the landmark case of *Roe v. Wade.*

Stare decisis The legal principle that prior case law should apply unless there is a substantial change in society necessitating a change in the case law.

Precedent Prior case law that is controlling.

Exhibit 10.17 Lexis search with OR connector

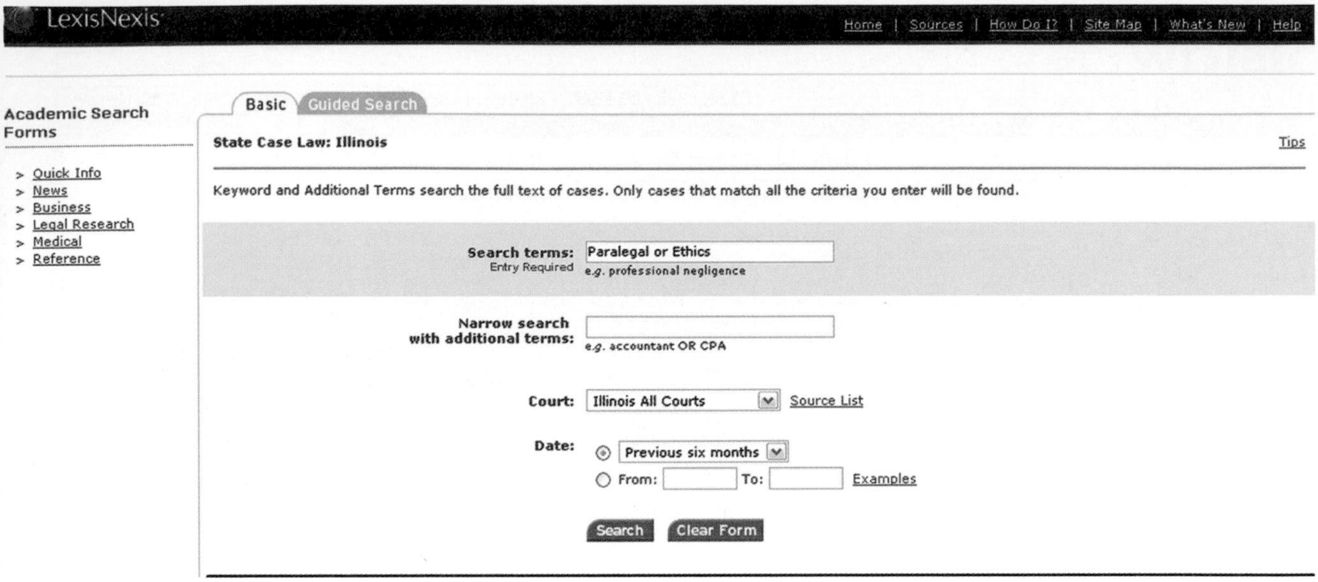

Source: *Copyright 2009 Lexis Nexis, a division of Reed Elsevier Inc. All Rights Reserved. LexisNexis and the Knowledge Burst logo are registered trademarks of Reed Elsevier Properties Inc. and are used with the permission of LexisNexis.*

Exhibit 10.18 Comparison grid from VersusLaw

VersusLaw	LEXIS	Westlaw
Connectors		
and	and	and, &
or	or	or, *space*
not	and not	but not, %
Proximity operators		
w/n	w/n	w/n, /n
w/n	pre/n	pre/n, +n
Exact phrase match		
unlawful entry	unlawful entry	"unlawful entry"
Wild Cards - end of root words		
*	!	!
Wild Cards - single character		
?	*	*
Order of operators		
proximity operators, not, and, or	or, *proximity operators*, and, and not	or, *proximity operators*, and, but not

Source: *© Copyright 2009 VersusLaw, Inc. Redmond, WA, USA. All rights reserved. www.versuslaw.com*

Knowing if the case law being used in a legal argument is the current case law is a vital part of the lawyer's obligation to the client and to the court. Up to the moment before the arguments are made to the court or the brief is submitted, a case that the attorney or the opponent is using as a basis for a legal argument may be overturned. The ethical obligation of candor, shown below in the Ethical Perspective, to the court and of professional competency requires the use of current case law.

Exhibit 10.19 Westlaw guide to connectors

USING CONNECTORS

Connector	You type	Westlaw retrieves documents
AND	&	containing both search terms: **work-place & safety**
OR	a space	containing either search term or both search terms: **landlord lessor**
Grammatical Connectors	/p	containing search terms in the same paragraph: **warrant! /p habitat!**
	/s	containing search terms in the same sentence: **danger! /s defect!**
	+s	in which the first term precedes the second within the same sentence: **capital 1 s gain**
Numerical Connectors	/n (where *n* is a number)	containing search terms with *n* terms of each other: **issues /5 fact**
	+n (where *n* is a number)	in which the first term precedes the second by *n* terms: **20 1 5 1080**
BUT NOT	%	not containing the term or terms following the percent symbol (%): **tax taxation % tax taxation/3 income**

Source: *Reproduced with permission from West Group.*

ETHICAL PERSPECTIVE

Idaho Rules of Professional Conduct

RULE 3.3 CANDOR TOWARD THE TRIBUNAL

(a) A lawyer shall not knowingly:

   (1) make a false statement of fact or law to a tribunal or fail to correct a false statement of material fact or law previously made to the tribunal by the lawyer;

   (2) fail to disclose to the tribunal legal authority in the controlling jurisdiction known to the lawyer to be directly adverse to the position of the client and not disclosed by opposing counsel; or

   (3) offer evidence that the lawyer knows to be false. If a lawyer, the lawyer's client, or a witness called by the lawyer, has offered material evidence and the lawyer comes to know of its falsity, the lawyer shall take reasonable remedial measures, including, if necessary, disclosure to the tribunal. A lawyer may refuse to offer evidence, other than the testimony of a defendant in a criminal matter, that the lawyer reasonably believes is false.

(b) A lawyer who represents a client in an adjudicative proceeding and who knows that a person intends to engage, is engaging or has engaged in criminal or fraudulent conduct related to the proceeding shall take reasonable remedial measures, including, if necessary, disclosure to the tribunal.

(c) The duties stated in paragraphs (a) and (b) continue to the conclusion of the proceeding, and apply even if compliance requires disclosure of information otherwise protected by Rule 1.6.

(d) In an ex parte proceeding, a lawyer shall inform the tribunal of all material facts known to the lawyer that will enable the tribunal to make an informed decision, whether or not the facts are adverse.

 Web Exploration

Contrast and compare the Rhode Island rule at http://www .courts.ri.gov/supreme/pdf-files/ Rules_Of_Professional_Conduct .pdf with the ABA Model Rules of Professional Conduct at www .abanet.org/cpr and the rule in your jurisdiction.

Thus, an essential part of legal research for paralegals is to verify that they have the latest case or statute. The process is complicated by the method by which changes in statutes or case law are released to the public. Ultimately, new statutes and new case law are reported in a published form, both in paper and electronically, but not all publications are able to disseminate the information daily. Paper versions take time to print and distribute. Not all electronic versions are posted immediately. Therefore, it becomes important to know how quickly the reporting or electronic services of the law firm or practice distribute post-statutory changes and new cases. More and more courts have their own websites and release case opinions electronically along with the print versions to the public and publishing companies. For example, you can check decisions of the U.S. Supreme Court daily.

What is difficult is knowing if the new cases or new statutes affect the case being researched. When the court specifically mentions a case being cited in a memo of law or a court brief, the paralegal has to know if the new case follows the older case law, reverses it, or in some way differs from the older case.

As soon as a case is entered into an electronic case law database, such as Westlaw, Lexis, Loislaw, or VersusLaw, a general search can be made for references to the case name or citation. Before it is entered, the same search will not show the newest reference. Even a reference to the case will not tell whether the case law has changed, only that another case has referred to it. Someone must actually read the case to see how the court has used it or referred to it in the opinion.

Shepard's

Long a standard tool of legal research in law libraries, *Shepard's Citations* is a multi-volume set of books listing cases and statutes by their respective citations and giving the citation of every other case in which the listed case was mentioned. The listings originally were compiled by editors who physically read through every case reported to find citations. These then were reported by case citation, with every other mention of the case reported by its citation in chronological fashion, with notations indicating if the opinion was reversed, affirmed, followed, overruled, and so on. The process of using *Shepard's* to check legal citations came to be called "Shepardizing"—a term that many legal assistants still use, even when using other citation-checking services such as Westlaw's KeyCite. An advantage to the *Shepard's Citator* is the editorial symbol system used to indicate how the new case affects the case being checked, as shown in Exhibit 10.20.

The problem with the traditional paper form of *Shepard's* is the lag in time for the print version to be prepared and sent out to subscribers. *Shepard's* now provides the same service online through the Lexis service; subscribers can obtain the latest case information, to the day, by calling a toll-free number. One of the difficulties in using the print version of *Shepard's* is the number of hardbound volumes and paperback updates required to be consulted, and finding the latest update pamphlet if someone has misfiled it in the law library. Exhibit 10.21 is an example of the print version case presentation in *Shepard's*.

Many educational institutions and public libraries subscribe to the Web-based LexisNexis Academic Universe. *Shepard's* citation service (**see** Exhibit 10.22) usually is available for the U.S. Supreme Court as part of the service, but other federal and state *Shepard's* citation services may not be included because of the cost of the additional license fees involved.

GlobalCite™

GlobalCite Loislaw's tool for searching cases containing references to another case.

Loislaw's **GlobalCite** provides a reverse chronological list of the case law, the statutes in the order of the highest number of citation occurrences, the regulations listed in

Exhibit 10.20 *Shepard's* symbols showing effects of new cases

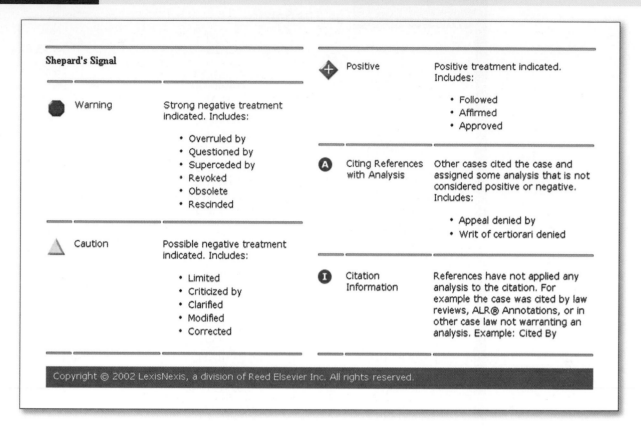

Source: Copyright 2009 LexisNexis, a division of Reed Elsevier Inc. All Rights Reserved. LexisNexis and the Knowledge Burst logo are registered trademarks of Reed Elsevier Properties Inc. and are used with the permission of LexisNexis.

relevancy order, and reference to other databases in the Loislaw library. Exhibit 10.23 shows a GlobalCite screen.

KeyCite™

KeyCite is the Westlaw online citation update service. The Westlaw KeyCite is a combination citator and case finder. Unlike other similar services, KeyCite uses the West Key number system and West Headnotes.

KeyCite Westlaw's tool for searching cases containing references to another case.

V. Cite™

V. Cite, VersusLaw's citation tool, will produce a list of all cases within the selected jurisdictions that have cited the case being searched. The list that a V. Cite search produces will include cases that have cited the initial case, which most likely will discuss similar issues. Using the added V. Cite feature allows the appending of a specific term to the search request. For example, including the word "damages" in the "additional query information" section of the V. Cite form will restrict the search to cases that cite the searched case and also discuss "damages."

V. Cite VersusLaw's tool for searching cases containing references to another case.

Exhibit 10.21	Example of print version case presentation in *Shepard's*

—157—	—558—	—558—
Oregon v Plowman 1992	**Oregon v Plowman 1992**	**Oregon v Plowman 1992**
(838P2d558)	(314Ore157)	(314Ore157)
s 107OrA782	s 813P2d1114	s 813P2d1114
cc 314Ore170	cc 813P2d1115	cc 813P2d1115
e 315Ore375	cc 838P2d566	cc 838P2d566
315Ore380	840P2d1324	840P2d1324
317Ore^{4}258	e 840P2d1325	e 840P2d1325
317Ore451	841P2d650	841P2d650
f 317Ore452	e 845P2d1285	e 845P2d1285
j 317Ore472	845P2d1289	845P2d1289
f 318Ore488	j 851P2d1147	j 851P2d1147
318Ore492	j 852P2d888	j 852P2d888
d 318Ore497	854P2d959	854P2d959
116OrA189	855P2d^{4}625	855P2d^{4}625
e 116OrA192	857P2d107	Calif
h 116OrA265	f 857P2d108	17CaR2d296
j 119OrA303	j 857P2d119	e 19CaR2d448
j 120OrA333	f 871P2d458	e 19CaR2d449
121OrA384	871P2d461	Iowa
j 128OrA14	d 871P2d463	500N W 42
71OLR689	j 874P2d1348	
22A5268n		
Shepard's Oregon Citations, *Oregon Reports division,* shows citations from:	Shepard's Oregon Citations, *Oregon Cases division, shows citations from Oregon as published in the* Pacific Reporter.	Shepard's Pacific Reporter Citations, *P.2d division, shows citations from all cases published in a West regional reporter.*
• state reports • Oregon Law Review • annotations (ALR® 5th)		

Parallel Citations

Parallel citation The citation to the same case in a different publication.

Most cases are reported in more than one service or set of books. A **parallel citation** is a cite to the same material, usually a case, in another source. Frequently a state has an official publication, such as the court's own publication, and a private publication, such as the *West Reporter*. In some cases, *West* was and is the official reporter, and there may not be a parallel print source. One of the many uses of *Shepard's* is to find the parallel citation to other locations for the same case.

Shepard's also provides update information on statutory citations. Amendments and repeals of statutory information are listed in *Shepard's*. Citations to any cases in which the statute has been cited also are listed, with information on how the case law considered the statute.

Exhibit 10.22 LexisNexis Total *Shepard's*® Table of Authorities

Source: Copyright 2009 LexisNexis, a division of Reed Elsevier Inc. All Rights Reserved. LexisNexis and the Knowledge Burst logo are registered trademarks of Reed Elsevier Properties, Inc. and are used with the permission of LexisNexis.

Exhibit 10.23 GlobalCite screen

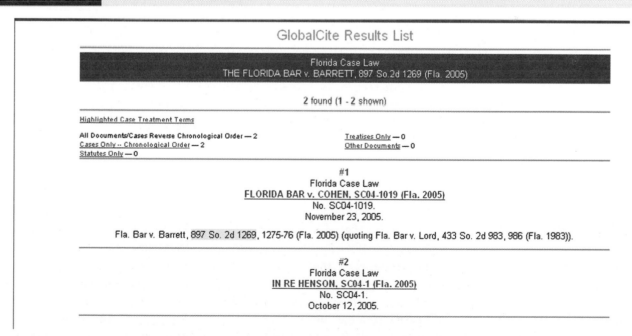

Source: Reprinted with permission of Aspen Publishers, from GlobalCite screen shot.

CHECKLIST Research Search Items

- ☐ Client:
- ☐ Issue:
- ☐ Search terms and phrases:

- ☐ Search combinations used:
- ☐ Date:

CHECKLIST Research Sources Checked

Checked Source	Citation	Pocket Part Checked	∨	Web Location
Primary Sources				
	State statute			www.
	USC			www.
	USCA			www.
	CFR			www.
	Local ordinance			www.
				www.
Secondary Sources				
	State digest			www.
	Federal digest			www.
	ALR			www.
				www.
	Encyclopedia			www.
	State			www.
	C.J.S.			www.
	Periodicals			www.
	Treatises			www.

Concept Review *and* Reinforcement

LEGAL TERMINOLOGY

SUMMARY OF KEY CONCEPTS

Legal Research

Definition	Legal research is a process for finding the answer to a legal question.

Creating a Research Plan

	The research plan helps to focus on the issues, sources, and methods for finding the answer and controlling law.
What Is the Issue or Legal Question?	What are the relevant facts or statutory materials?
What Is the Appropriate Search Terminology?	Print research materials require finding material based on a printed index of individual words as selected by editors of the service. Computer research allows for searches of words found in the documents using a text search of requested words in the search query.
What Type of Research Material Is Available?	The paralegal must be able to find the information needed when the familiar resources are not available. Paralegals cannot be sure whether the research will be done using a traditional paper library or a computer search; they must understand how each resource files the information.
What Jurisdiction or Jurisdictions Are Involved?	Focusing on a single jurisdiction or a minimum number of jurisdictions reduces the numbers of traditional volumes of books necessary and saves online computer search time.
What Is the Controlling Law?	Knowing which set of materials to use, the statutes of the jurisdiction, the regulation of a given administrative agency, or the courts of a given jurisdiction will save time in doing the research.
What Are the Types of Resources to Use?	1. Primary sources of law are used in preparing the legal memo or brief. 2. Secondary sources are useful, efficient ways to get an overview of an area of law or learn the terminology of a particular field of law in which the paralegal is not familiar. 3. Finding tools are publications containing tools for finding both primary and secondary sources.
Where Is the Needed Research Material Located?	The needed material may have to be located at a remote library such as a bar association library or a law school library.
Creating a List of Research Terms	Separate lists should be created for online searches and traditional print sources.
Executing the Research Plan	As with the execution of any plan, detours can be expected, as the law is in a constant evolutionary state. New statutes are enacted, and new case interpretations are handed down. During the research process, the researcher must look for changes and potential changes from pending legislation and cases on appeal.

Finding the Law

The Controlling Law	The controlling law may be found at federal, state, or local legislative or judicial levels.
Primary Sources and Authority	Primary sources include the law, constitutions, statutes, regulations, court rules, and case decisions.
Mandatory and Persuasive Authority	1. Mandatory authority is legal authority that the courts must follow. 2. Persuasive authority is legal authority the courts are not required to follow but is from a respected source and well reasoned.

Constitutions	Constitutions are primary sources that set the guidelines, limits, and authority of the federal government and the state governments.
Statutes	Statutes are enacted by the legislative branch of government.
Court Decisions	The actual court language is a primary source of the law. The syllabus, summaries, interpretations, or abstracts of the points of law presented by the editorial staffs of the publishers of the case law—usually called headnotes—are not the primary source of law.
Secondary Sources	Secondary sources explain the law. 1. Legal dictionaries, as opposed to general English or other specialized dictionaries, define words and phrases as used in the law. 2. Legal encyclopedias provide the background to understand the area enough to start the research. They provide an overview of the concepts and history of an area of law, the legal issues involved, and the terminology. 3. Treatises, Law Reviews, and Legal Periodicals are authoritative or of sufficient scholarly value to be persuasive to the court.
Finding Tools	Finding tools help to "find" the law. 1. Digests provide lists of cases in a subject topic format, with cases generally in chronological order. 2. Indexes and citators cross-reference material, such as by the commonly used or popular name of a case or statute.

Personal Research Strategy

	Over time, each paralegal develops a personal search strategy based on the nature of the problem or issue to be researched and the resources available. Methods of verifying that the law and cases cited in your research and memo of law is current law or current authority, and methods for looking for pending cases and legislation that might change the answer to the legal question.

A Final Word on Executing the Legal Research Plan

	Know when to ask for help.

Using Printed Legal Reference Works

Common Features	Table of abbreviations Table of contents in the front Index of terms in the back Table of cases and citations
Updates	Print material is frequently updated with pocket parts, usually issued annually, slipped into the back of the volume in a pocket. Paperback supplements are issued annually, quarterly, or monthly. Online updates from the publishers are increasingly available for some materials.

Constructing a Computer Search Query

Creating a Computer Search	A combination of words, phrases, and connectors used to search for a desired answer.
Search Method and Query	Each online provider uses words to find and retrieve documents. As part of the publication process, indexes are prepared of every word in the document, the words are tabulated for frequency, and a word index is prepared. The search created searches this index.
Creating the Query	The search engine is used to find the indexed words the paralegal has chosen; they may be legal specialty words or common English words. Using combinations of words in the search can narrow the search results.

Using Connectors	AND instructs the search not to return documents in which only one of the words is found. OR instructs the search engine to find either term. NEAR may be used to find the occurrence of desired words within a set number of words of each other.

Updating Legal Research

1. *Shepard's:* A multivolume set of books listing cases and statutes by their respective citations and giving the citation of every other case in which the listed case was mentioned; checking citations is often called "Shepardizing."
2. GlobalCite (Loislaw): Provides a reverse chronological list of the case law, a list of statutes in the order of the highest number of citation occurrences, regulations in relevancy order, and reference to other databases in Loislaw library.
3. KeyCite (Westlaw): Online citation update service.
4. V. Cite (VersusLaw) Online citation tool.

Parallel Citation

A citation to the same material, usually a case, in another source.

Statutory Law Updates	*Shepard's* provides updated information on amendments and repeals of statutory information. Citations to any cases in which the statute has been cited are also listed, with information on how the case law considered the statute.

WORKING THE WEB

1. Use the Government Printing Office website to find and print out the summary purpose of 21 CFR 404, or any other section assigned by your instructor. www.gpoaccess.gov
2. Make a list of the available federal primary sources available on the Government Printing Office website.
3. From the sitemap of the VersusLaw website, print out for your future computer searches the printable version of the *Versuslaw Research Manual.* http://www.versuslaw.com/features/sitemap.htm
4. Use the Legal Information Institute at the Cornell University website to find title 44 C.F.R. 201 and print out the list of key responsibilities of FEMA and state and local/tribal governments. http://lii.law.cornell.edu/. Does this site provide direct access or a link to another source? Explain. What primary federal sources does this site offer?
5. Conduct a search for information on paralegal ethics using two different search engines, and print out a copy of the first page of each result. Are they the same? What is the difference in results and order of presentation? Possible search engines include: Google, www.google.com; Yahoo, www.yahoo.com; www.ask.com; Findlaw, www.findlaw.com.
6. If you have access to Loislaw, NexisLexis, Westlaw, or VersusLaw, conduct a search for paralegal ethics cases for your jurisdiction. Prepare a list of authorities cited in the search.
7. Print out the current list of opinions of the U.S. Supreme Court at http://www.supremecourt.us.gov.
8. Print out the complete version of Rule 3.3, Candor Toward the Tribunal, of the *ABA Model Rules of Professional Conduct* at http://www.abanet.org/cpr/mrpc/mrpc_toc.html.
9. Under the theory of *stare decisis,* on which courts would the decisions of a court have a binding effect? Would a decision in a case be binding on future cases if the decision were available only in the clerk's office?
10. Would your answer be the same if the decision were available in the clerk's office at first but then available in printed form or online at a later date? When would the decision become effective as precedent?
11. Where is the "law" found?
12. Who makes the "law" under the United States system?
13. What is meant by a "bicameral" legislature?
14. In legal research, what is meant by "primary source?"
15. What is a "treatise?" Is it a primary source? Explain.
16. What is a headnote in legal research? Is it a primary source? Explain.
17. What is dicta? What is its effect on other courts? Explain.
18. Of what weight do courts give secondary sources? Explain fully.
19. Why are finding tools important to the legal researcher? Give an example of how a finding tool might be used.
20. Do unpublished opinions have precedential effect? Explain.

CRITICAL THINKING & WRITING QUESTIONS

1. Using the facts in the *Palsgraf* case in Appendix A, prepare a search query using connectors to locate the law or a similar case in your jurisdiction. Run the search using an online legal research service, if available.
2. Why does a paralegal have to be familiar with both traditional and electronic research tools and methods?
3. Why does the paralegal have to know how quickly changes in statutory and case law are updated by online and traditional primary and secondary sources?
4. Why is knowledge of the underlying law in an area important in constructing a question for online research?
5. How can a researcher be certain that a case that seems to be on point is still the current case law?
6. Why should secondary sources not be relied upon in citing binding authority?
7. Why would a researcher use a traditional paper resource before using an online research tool?
8. How does the use of connectors help in conducting online research? Give an example.
9. Why might an identical search query return different results?
10. Why must researchers clearly understand the question they are being asked to research? How can they be certain they do?

Building Paralegal Skills

VIDEO CASE STUDIES

Legal Research: Are Books Obsolete?

In the middle of a trial, a trial attorney sends his paralegal to the courthouse law library to find a case that has been cited as precedent by opposing counsel in oral argument. Without a valid password, the paralegal is advised to use traditional research methods.

After viewing the video case study at www.pearsonhighered .com/goldman answer the following:

1. What are the differences between using books and electronic legal research?
2. Are traditional paper-based reference materials as current as electronic reference sources?
3. Are there any differences in using the different legal research services such as Lexis, Westlaw, Loislaw, or VersusLaw?

Fees and Billing Issue: Using Time Effectively

A paralegal has responded to the request of her supervising attorney for information on a question of law. After spending considerable time, she is helped by another paralegal who quickly provides surety information she is looking for only to find out that her supervising attorney was merely curious and there was no client against which to bill the research time.

After viewing the video case study at www.pearsonhighered .com/goldman answer the following:

1. What questions should a paralegal ask before commencing to do research?
2. At what point should the paralegal ask for help and from whom should the help be sought?
3. Is there any value in doing legal research when there is no specific client or case to which it will apply?

Fees and Billing Issue: Contemporaneous Timekeeping

A paralegal is trying to reconstruct his time records for the day. Unable to remember everything that he did he arbitrarily assigns time to certain cases.

After viewing the video case study at www.pearsonhighered.com/goldman answer the following:

1. How can well-kept time records document the thoroughness of the research completed on a case?
2. Can time records be used to document the specific citations used in preparing legal research?
3. Is the misapplication of time spent to other clients and cases acceptable behavior for a paralegal?

ETHICS ANALYSIS & DISCUSSION QUESTIONS

1. Is there an ethical obligation under the Model Rules to perform legal research competently? Explain.
2. What is the ethical obligation under the Model Rules to provide the court with legal authority that is not favorable to your client's legal position?

3. What is the ethical obligation to "Shepardize" cases and statutes before submitting a brief or memo of law to the court?

For answers, look at American Bar Association Rule 3.3, Candor Toward the Tribunal, and Rule 1.1, Competence (ABA *Model Rules of Professional Conduct*, 2002).

Confidentiality

There are few certainties in the area of ethics, for paralegals or in any profession. What qualifies as ethical conduct is in most cases based on state law and court interpretation applied to a set of facts. The citation listed below represents one legal opinion and is provided as a research starting point. Do not assume that the same rule applies in your jurisdiction. For the following:

- Prepare a written statement based on your state law.
- Use your state bar association website as a starting point.

You are waiting for a fax needed for a case on which you are working. While you are standing by the fax machine, a fax comes in from an attorney at an opposing firm containing a letter about settlement that was clearly intended for the attorney's client and not for opposing counsel. It was sent by your best friend, the paralegal who is working on that case at the opposing firm. She is stressed out by the case and made the mistake of dialing your fax number rather than the client's. From your reading of the letter it appears the information would greatly help your law office win the case. [*ABA Formal Ethics Opinion, State Compensation Insurance Fund v. The WPS, Inc.*, 70 CA 4644; 82 C.R.2 799 (1999)] Do you quietly return the fax to your friend and say nothing to anyone? Do you read it carefully to be sure of the contents? Do you return it to opposing counsel? Do you tell your supervising attorney about the letter? The contents?

DEVELOPING YOUR COLLABORATION SKILLS

Working on your own or with a group of other students assigned by your instructor, review the scenario at the beginning of the chapter and discuss the different views on law libraries, including traditional versus computer legal research.

1. Write a summary of the potential advantages and disadvantages of each point of view.
2. Prepare a report to the executive committee, considering the different views of members of the firm with a solution that might satisfy most users of the firm's library.
3. The group is divided into two teams. One team will conduct a research assignment using traditional methods and the other will use computer research tools.

   a. Each team is to complete the Research Sources Checked checklist and prepare a copy for the members of the other team and your instructor.
   b. After you have completed the research, prepare a short memorandum of law to submit to your instructor.
4. Complete a second research project with each team now using the other approach to research. The traditional methods team now will use computer tools, and the computer tools team will conduct the research using traditional tools. Prepare a short memorandum and complete the Research Sources Checked checklist.
5. Based on your experience doing traditional and computer research, what recommendations would you make to the managing partner in the opening scenario?

PARALEGAL PORTFOLIO EXERCISE

Complete the "Web Location" section portion of the Research Sources Checked checklist. When preparing the list, include alternative sources where available. Print a copy for your portfolio for future use and a copy for your instructor.

LEGAL ANALYSIS & WRITING CASES

American Geophysical Union v. Texaco Inc.   *37 F.3d 881 (2d Cir. 1994)*

COPYING OF MATERIAL FOR FUTURE RESEARCH AND LAW LIBRARY ARCHIVES FROM COPYRIGHTED MAGAZINES AND JOURNALS

Most researchers understand that misuse of copyright material may subject them to liability under the copyright laws. The case of *American Geophysical Union v. Texaco* illustrates the potential liability in regularly copying copyrighted articles for personal archives. Researchers of Texaco regularly made copies of articles for future reference from the works of the plaintiff and 82 other publishers of scientific and technical journals. Texaco raised the defense of "fair use" as permitted under the copyright law.

Fair use as a defense depends on four tests: (1) the purpose and character of the use—including whether for nonprofit educational purposes or commercial use; (2) the nature of copyright work—the law generally recognizes a greater need to disseminate factual works than works of fiction or fantasy; (3) amount and substantiality of portion used—was the quantity used reasonable in relation to the purpose of the copying? (4) effect on potential market or value—will the copying have an impact on the sale of the works, and is there an efficient mechanism for the licensing of the works?

Questions

1. How does copyright law apply to a student copying copyrighted materials while doing research for a class project?
2. Would the answer be the same if the student were doing the research as part of an assignment while working in a law office?
3. Does it matter if the work copied is a court case or an article by an expert in automobile airbags liability? Why?

WORKING WITH THE LANGUAGE OF THE COURT CASE

Hart v. Massanari

266 F.3d 1155 (2001)
United States Court of Appeals, Ninth Circuit

Read, and if assigned, brief this case. In your brief, answer the following questions.

1. Why are unpublished dispositions (opinion) of courts not valid as precedent in future cases?
2. What is the difference between controlling authority and persuasive authority?
3. How might an unpublished opinion be used in this case?
4. Has the adoption of Rule 32.1 changed the effect of this case?
5. Why does this court believe it is important, in writing an opinion of the court, to recite all the relevant facts?
6. What is the effect of binding precedent on other courts?

Kozinski, Circuit Judge

Appellant's. . . brief cites. . . an unpublished disposition, not reported in the *Federal Reporter*. . . . The full text. . . is marked with the following notice: "This disposition is not appropriate for publication and may not be cited to or by the courts of this circuit. . . ." Unpublished dispositions and orders of this Court are not binding precedent . . .[and generally] may not be cited to or by the courts of this circuit." . . . [9th Cir.R.36-3.]

We ordered counsel to show cause as to why he should not be disciplined for violating Ninth Circuit Rule 36-3. Counsel responds by arguing that Rule 36-3 may be unconstitutional. . . [relying] . . . on the Eighth Circuit's opinion in *Anastasoff v. United States*, [which] while vacated, continues to have persuasive force. . .

A. Anastasoff held that Eighth Circuit Rule 28A(i), . . . that unpublished dispositions are not precedential* . . .

Our rule operates . . . differently from . . . the Eighth Circuit . . . Rule 28A(i) [that] says that "[u]npublished decisions are not precedent." [W]e say that unpublished dispositions are "not binding precedent." . . . Our rule . . . prohibits citation of an unpublished disposition to any of the courts of our circuit. The Eighth Circuit's rule allows citation . . ., but provides that the authority is persuasive rather than binding.

violates Article III of the Constitution. . . . We believe that Anastasoff overstates the case. . . .

Anastasoff focused on one aspect of the way federal courts do business—the way they issue opinions—and held that they are subject to a constitutional limitation derived from the [constitutional] framers' conception of what it means to exercise the judicial power. . . . We question whether the "judicial power" clause contains any limitation at all, separate from the specific limitations of Article III and other parts of the Constitution. . . .The term "judicial power" in Article III is more likely descriptive than prescriptive. . . .

B. Modern federal courts are the successors of the English courts that developed the common law. . . . Common law judges did not make law as we understand that concept; rather, they "found" the law with the help of earlier cases that had considered similar matters. An opinion was evidence of what the law is, but it was not an independent source of law. . . . The idea that judges declared rather than made the law remained firmly entrenched in English jurisprudence until the early nineteenth century. . . . For centuries, the most important sources of law were not judicial opinions themselves, but treatises that restated the law. . . .

The modern concept of binding precedent... came about only gradually over the nineteenth and early twentieth centuries. Lawyers began to believe that judges made, not found, the law. This coincided with monumental improvements in the collection and reporting of case authorities . . . and [as] a more comprehensive reporting system began to take hold, it became possible for judicial decisions to serve as binding authority. . . .

II

Federal courts today do follow some common law traditions. When ruling on a novel issue of law, they will generally consider how other courts have ruled on the same issue. . . . Law on point is the law. If a court must decide an issue governed by a prior opinion that constitutes binding authority, the later court is bound to reach the same result, even if it considers the rule unwise or incorrect. Binding authority must be followed unless and until overruled by a body competent to do so.

In determining whether it is bound by an earlier decision, a court considers not merely the "reason and spirit of cases" but also "the letter of particular precedents.". . . This includes not only the rule announced, but also the facts giving rise to the dispute, other rules considered and rejected, and the views expressed in response to any dissent or concurrence. Thus, when crafting binding authority, the precise language employed is often crucial to the contours and scope of the rule announced.

. . . A decision of the Supreme Court will control that corner of the law unless and until the Supreme Court itself overrules or modifies it. . . . Thus, the first panel to consider an issue sets the law not only for all the inferior courts in the circuit, but also future panels of the court of appeals. Once a panel resolves an issue in a precedential opinion, the matter is deemed resolved, unless overruled by the court itself sitting en banc, or by the Supreme Court. . . .

Controlling authority has much in common with persuasive authority. Using the techniques developed at common law, a court confronted with apparently controlling authority must parse the precedent in light of the facts presented and the rule announced. Insofar as there may be factual differences between the current case and the earlier one, the court must determine whether those differences are material to the application of the rule or allow the precedent to be distinguished on a principled basis. . . . But there are also very important differences between controlling and persuasive authority. . . . [I]f a controlling precedent is determined to be on point, it must be followed. . . . Thus, an opinion of our court is binding within our circuit, not elsewhere. . . .

III

While we agree with Anastasoff that the principle of precedent was well established in the common law courts by the time Article III of the Constitution was written, we do not agree that it was known and applied in the strict sense in which we apply binding authority today. . . .

In writing an opinion, the court must be careful to recite all facts that are relevant to its ruling, while omitting facts that it considers irrelevant. Omitting relevant facts will make the ruling unintelligible to those not already familiar with the case; including inconsequential facts can provide a spurious basis for distinguishing the case in the future. . . .

While federal courts of appeals generally lack discretionary review authority, they use their authority to decide cases by unpublished—and nonprecedential—dispositions to achieve the same end. . . . That a case is decided without a precedential opinion does not mean it is not fully considered. . . . The disposition is not written in a way that makes it suitable for governing future cases. . . . An unpublished disposition is, more or less, a letter from the court to parties familiar with the facts, announcing the result and the essential rationale of the court's decision. . . .

IV

We conclude that Rule 36-3 is constitutional. We also find that counsel violated the rule. Nevertheless, we are aware that Anastasoff may have cast doubt on our rule's constitutional validity. Our rules are obviously not meant to punish attorneys who, in good faith, seek to test a rule's constitutionality. We therefore conclude that the violation was not willful and exercise our discretion not to impose sanctions.

The order to show cause is DISCHARGED.

In a footnote in the case of *Cogan v. Barnhart*, USDC Mass, 03-12421-WGY, the court commented:

"Citation to unpublished opinions has been an issue of considerable debate, which continues until today. The Eighth and Ninth Circuits are on extreme ends of the debate. *Anastasoff v. US*, 223 F. 3d 898. . . (holding that unpublished opinions have precedential effect); *Hart v. Massanari*,. . . (upholding its local rule prohibiting the citation of unpublished decisions as constitutional). . . .

Legal Writing and Critical Legal Thinking

> "Justice is the end of government. It is the end of civil society. It ever has been, and ever will be pursued, until it be obtained, or until liberty be lost in the pursuit."
>
> *James Madison*

LEARNING OBJECTIVES

After studying this chapter, you should be able to:

1. Explain the process of critical legal thinking.
2. Explain the ethical duty of candor toward the tribunal.
3. Describe the similarities and differences between a memorandum of law and a court brief.
4. Explain the reasons for the various citation format rules.
5. Explain and describe the need for, and how to use, proper citation format.

Paralegals at Work

Amanda Chen had worked for the law firm of Douglas and Myers only a few weeks when the senior partner, who specialized in mergers and acquisitions, asked her to sit in on the initial meeting of a long-term client and the client's daughter. One of the more senior paralegals on staff told Amanda that her role was to take notes. The partner never took notes. He conducted the interview, asked the questions, and didn't want anyone else to interfere.

After escorting the client and the client's daughter, Bill and Tonya Johnson, from the reception area to the partner's office, Amanda was asked to take a seat in the corner and record the meeting notes. Bill Johnson made it clear that he was paying the bill and that he expected his attorney to get the charges of driving under the influence against Tonya dropped. Tonya acknowledged that she had been drinking at a country western bar and knew she was well over the legal drinking limit. She had tested her alcohol level on a breath analyzer that the bar made available to its patrons.

Upon leaving the bar, Tonya went out to her car, got in, started it, and then fell asleep at the wheel. A police officer found her in this condition, woke her, and took her to the hospital for a blood alcohol test. The officer cited her for operating a vehicle while under the influence of alcohol, based on her .09% blood alcohol reading.

After the clients left, the partner told Amanda to prepare a memorandum of law that he could use to get the charges against the client's daughter dismissed.

After doing a little research, Amanda realized that the law was against the client's getting the charges dismissed.

411

Furthermore, in the meeting with her father and the partner, Tonya had admitted to being intoxicated. Based on the advice from the other paralegals, Amanda was concerned about putting anything negative into the memo and decided to write a memo presenting a case for dismissal.

Consider the issues involved in this scenario as you read the chapter.

INTRODUCTION FOR THE PARALEGAL

Legal writing and critical legal thinking are intertwined. Legal writing can take a number of forms, memos, letters, opinions, memoranda of law for internal purposes, and briefs for the court. The differences in presentation are determined by the intended audience. The similarities are in the need for clarity and accuracy. Preparation of these documents starts with an understanding of the material facts of a case and identifying the legal issues. Critical legal thinking is used to identify what is material, what law applies, and then to apply the law to the facts and come to a conclusion that answers the issue or issues presented.

Critical Legal Thinking

Critical legal thinking The process of identifying the issue, the material facts, and the applicable law and applying the law to come to a conclusion.

Issue The legal matter in dispute.

Critical legal thinking is the process of identifying the **issue**—the legal matter in dispute—presented by a case, identifying the material (also called key or relevant) facts in the case and the applicable law, and then applying the law to the facts to come to a conclusion that answers the issue or issues presented. Critical legal thinking is the thought process that puts the pieces of the legal puzzle together. The critical thinking process starts with a clear understanding of the facts of the client's case and identifying the legal issues in that case.

Before starting the research, one must have a clear picture of all the material facts. Part of the interview with the client is to determine all the facts. Some of what the client thinks are important facts may in fact not be relevant in deciding the legal issue. And some of the facts that seemed unimportant to the client may in fact be relevant and on which the outcome may depend. For example, it may not seem important that the client was struck by a driver going north. It may be a material fact when it is determined that the street was a one-way street going south.

Consider the timeline on a contract case. Assume that a client signed an employee noncompetition contract three months after starting employment. State law may deny the enforceability of the covenant not to compete unless entered into before commencing employment or unless contemporary, full and adequate consideration is given for signing the agreement after commencing employment.

Understanding the relevant facts enables a review of the court cases and the statutory law to determine applicability to the client case. A difference of one fact may make all the difference in the world in the outcome of the case. Consider the case of the client charged with killing King Kong. The facts indicate that King Kong is not a human being. The murder statute of the jurisdiction defines murder as the taking of the life of a human being by another human being; therefore, the statute has not been violated. Other statutes may have been violated, but not the murder statute. The client may be guilty of hunting out of season, hunting without a license, or killing an endangered species, but not murder.

For these issues, additional facts, immaterial in the murder prosecution, may become material. The material facts also would be different in the civil action by the owner of the animal in a suit for damages for loss of an irreplaceable item. What is relevant as a fact depends on the type of case—civil or criminal—and the wrong committed or the right violated.

IN THE WORDS OF THE COURT

Alaska Case Law

WHITING V. STATE, A-8755 (ALASKA APP. 10-12-2005)

MANNHEIMER, Judge.

Michael T. Whiting appeals his conviction for felony driving under the influence, . . . the facts . . . : Whiting and his girlfriend and his girlfriend's six-year-old son decided to go fishing in Gastineau Channel. Whiting piloted a skiff into the channel and then turned the motor off. The three occupants of the skiff fished while the skiff drifted in the channel; Whiting sat in the rear of the skiff near the motor. While Whiting was fishing, he was also drinking alcoholic beverages.

A Coast Guard vessel approached the skiff . . ., discovered that he was under the influence. Whiting claimed that he had been sober when he piloted the boat into the channel, and that he did not become intoxicated until after he stopped the motor and the fishing began.

. . . Whiting's argument hinges on his assertion that the statutory definition of driving under the influence, AS 28.35.030(a) does not include the situation where an intoxicated person is in control of a watercraft whose engine is not running. Whiting's assertion is incorrect. . . . this Court held that "operating" a watercraft includes being in control of the watercraft, even if its engine is not running.

We addressed essentially the same argument in *Kingsley v. State*, 11 p. 3d 1001 (Alaska App. 2000). The defendant in *Kingsley* drove his car into a snow berm, where it became stuck. Kingsley turned the engine off and decided to remain in the car. According to Kingsley, it was only then that he consumed a bottle of whiskey and became intoxicated.

Kingsley argued that, under these circumstances, he was not intoxicated when he was operating the vehicle, and he was never in "control" of the vehicle after he became intoxicated. We rejected this narrow definition of "control".

As Kingsley acknowledges in his brief to this court, a person who engages the engine of a vehicle and allows it to run is not merely exercising physical control over the vehicle but is also "operating" it. Thus, if the engine of Kingsley's vehicle had been running when the police arrived, the State might have proved that Kingsley was operating the vehicle while intoxicated. But the State had to prove only that Kingsley was in actual physical control of the vehicle while intoxicated.

. . . A person's attempt to operate a vehicle may furnish convincing proof that the person is in actual physical control of the vehicle, but a person may exercise actual physical control over a vehicle without making active attempts to operate it.

Whiting was the one who had piloted the skiff into the channel, and Whiting remained primarily in the rear of the skiff, nearest the motor, while his girlfriend and her son sat in the front of the skiff. Under these facts, as a matter of law, Whiting was in physical control of the skiff, and he was therefore operating the skiff for purposes of the DUI statute.

The American justice system is based on the statutory law and case law. Just as in the criminal law issues discussed above, factual analysis requires determining the elements of the crime, looking at the statute, and applying the facts. It may be necessary to look at case law for precedent on the definition of an operative fact. For example, all states have laws prohibiting driving under the influence of alcohol. Some of these statutes also use the terms "vehicle" and "operating." One of the material facts for the researcher to determine is what is defined as a vehicle and what conduct is defined as "operating."

Defense counsel must look carefully to try to differentiate the client's fact pattern from decided cases. Slight variations in facts can be important in successfully arguing a case, or at least make a compelling argument.

Facts Information or details.

Facts are pieces of information or details that in actuality or reality exist, or have occurred, as opposed to someone's theory, supposition, or conjecture. Facts, in the law, are the circumstances of an event, motion, occurrence, or state of affairs, rather than interpretations of its significance. The car was going south on State Street at 55 miles per hour as shown on the radar unit. This <u>is a</u> fact. Supposition, conjecture, or theory, and not fact is the statement of the witness that everyone speeds down the street in front of their house, that the defendant has done it before, that they heard the car driven by the defendant while they were in the house watching TV facing away from the street, and that they heard the car going south at 55 mph.

Material facts A fact significant or essential to the issue.

Immaterial facts A fact not essential to the matter or issue at hand.

Facts may be divided into **material** (relevant) **facts** and **immaterial** (irrelevant) **facts**. A material fact is a fact that is significant or essential to the issue or matter at hand. An immaterial fact is one that is not essential to the matter at issue. Some facts, while not material, may lead to material facts. Consider the case of the person coming from the doctor's office, driving within the speed limit, who strikes another car in the rear at a red stoplight. Is the fact that he was coming from a doctor's office a material fact in the accident? It may be if he were given medication that caused blurred vision or drowsiness and if the doctor told him not to drive or operate any machinery. Certainly knowing this fact leads to the discovery of other relevant facts.

Legal Writing

There are as many writing styles as there are writers. Writers of novels have a style of writing that may devote pages to setting a stage for the characters and more pages developing the characters. Readers probably come to expect this and look forward to long paragraphs building the scene and setting the stage for the plot.

Writers of short stories are more like skilled legal writers. They must quickly and accurately set the stage in few words and tell the story in a short space. Skilled legal

Paralegals *in* Practice

PARALEGAL PROFILE
Ann L. Atkinson

Ann L. Atkinson is a graduate of the University of Nebraska with a Bachelor of Science Degree in Education. She is also an Advanced Certified Paralegal with over 27 years of legal experience. Her professional memberships include the Nebraska Paralegal Association, the National Association of Legal Assistants, and the National Association of Bond Lawyers. Ann is currently employed by the law firm of Kutak Rock LLP in their Omaha, Nebraska office.

I specialize in public finance law, which generally is transactional in nature—preparing, reviewing, and revising contracts or negotiated "deals" between parties. Specifically, I assist the attorneys as they work with state housing agencies or municipalities when they issue bonds for public purposes. The bonds represent a "loan" of money from bondholders. The attorneys with whom I work often act as bond counsel (where we are counsel for the bond issue itself), or we may also serve as underwriter's counsel (in which we are counsel to the underwriter of the bonds).

Since our department focuses primarily on single-family housing, we prepare all the documents that enable an issuer to issue bonds. These bonds then provide proceeds from which the issuer can offer single-family homes to first-time homebuyers at a "below market" interest rate. Our department also handles transactions for multi-family housing such as apartment buildings being constructed, acquired, and/or rehabilitated.

In my position, I coordinate all the things that need to be done in order for a bond issue to close. In order to do so, I rely heavily on writing and critical thinking skills. Tasks include preparing initial drafts of bond documents, researching statutes, proofing and reviewing offering documents and third-party opinions, and assisting with bond closings including the preparation of closing transcripts. Thus, a knowledge of correct grammar, spelling, and punctuation is essential. Critical thinking skills are very useful when preparing documents because they help you follow document processes—the flow of funds, the timing requirements for notices, and knowing when and how to obtain amendment approvals.

writers are those that can explain, persuade, and state facts for the record accurately, concisely, and clearly. The purpose of writing is to communicate. If the writing does not communicate the subject to the reader, it has not served its purpose. Unlike the novelist or poet, the legal writer must follow a set of guidelines dictated by ethical concerns for honesty and candor, while at the same time clearly present the answer to clients that they may not want to hear, or persuade the court to the advocated point of view.

Writing Styles

Both the brief and the memorandum may be on the exact same set of facts, legal issue, and applicable law, but the writing style is totally different. The **memorandum** is a working document for the legal team to be used in the preparation and presentation of a case. As a result, it has to be an objective analysis of the case, including factual subtleties and analysis of the applicable law with any alternate interpretations. For example, as stated by the Ninth Circuit Court of Appeals in *U.S. v. CASTRILLON*, 716 F.2d 1279 in determining whether consent was voluntary,

> . . . Fed.R.Crim.P. 12(e) states that "[w]here factual issues are involved in determining a [pretrial] motion, the court shall state its essential findings on the record." Such a record is necessary to our review. . . . Compliance with the rule 12(e) requirement is particularly important in a case such as this, where we examine "all the surrounding circumstances" . . . Factual subtleties may well affect a determination of voluntariness under this test. . .

The brief written for the court is designed to provide written advocacy of the client's position and must be written to convince the court to adopt a position favorable to the client. The **opinion letter** to a client requires a different style. The opinion letter must explain to a client, who is generally untrained in the law, what legal options the client has and what can and cannot be done based on a set of facts provided by the client. In some ways it is an educational document, it must be informative and detail the options sufficiently to allow the client to act in an appropriate manner. For example, you have asked us to advise you on whether you may set off a cannon at high noon each day, based on the law in . . .

Memorandum A working legal document for the legal team for use in preparation and presentation of a case.

Opinion letter A formal statement of advice based on the lawyers expert knowledge.

A WORD OF CAUTION

The ready availability and ease of use of email has created a new writing style that uses shorthand terminology such as LOL for "laugh out loud." Those in the legal profession must remember that every email is a potential piece of evidence in an electronic discovery request. Emails are frequently forwarded to others. Shortcuts should not be taken in writing emails. The same formality and care that goes into a hardcopy letter on legal stationery should be used in writing the email. Even greater care should be used when the email may contain privileged or confidential information that may accidentally get into the hands of those not covered by the ethical obligation to keep it confidential and may in some cases, such as accidentally sending it to opposing counsel, result in a breach of the attorney–client or work-product privilege.

CHECKLIST Memorandum of Law Template

- ☐ To:
- ☐ From:
- ☐ Date:
- ☐ Subject:

- ☐ Facts
- ☐ Issue(s)
- ☐ Discussion
- ☐ Conclusion

Duty of candor Honesty to the court.

Duty of Candor

The ethical obligation to be honest with the court is called the **duty of candor**, Rule 3.3 in the Model Rules of Professional Conduct. In some jurisdictions, such as Indiana, the ethical rule is titled. Conduct Toward the Tribunal.

Rule 3.3. Candor Toward the Tribunal

(a) A lawyer shall not knowingly:
  (1) make a false statement of fact or law to a tribunal or fail to correct a false statement of material fact or law previously made to the tribunal by the lawyer;
  (2) fail to disclose to the tribunal legal authority in the controlling jurisdiction known to the lawyer to be directly adverse to the position of the client and not disclosed by opposing counsel; or
  (3) offer evidence that the lawyer knows to be false. If a lawyer, the lawyer's client, or a witness called by the lawyer, has offered material evidence and the lawyer comes to know of its falsity, the lawyer shall take reasonable remedial measures, including, if necessary, disclosure to the tribunal. A lawyer may refuse to offer evidence, other than the testimony of a defendant in a criminal matter, that the lawyer reasonably believes is false.
(b) A lawyer who represents a client in an adjudicative proceeding and who knows that a person intends to engage, is engaging or has engaged in criminal or fraudulent conduct related to the proceeding shall take reasonable remedial measures, including, if necessary, disclosure to the tribunal.
(c) The duties stated in paragraphs (a) and (b) continue to the conclusion of the proceeding, and apply even if compliance requires disclosure of information otherwise protected by Rule 1.6.
(d) In an ex parte proceeding, a lawyer shall inform the tribunal of all material facts known to the lawyer which will enable the tribunal to make an informed decision, whether or not the facts are adverse.

Amended Sep. 30, 2004, effective Jan. 1, 2005.

Source: West Digest Topics. Reprinted with permission of Thomson/West Publishing.

Web Exploration

Contrast and compare the Indiana rule at http://www.state.in.us/judiciary/rules/prof_conduct/index.html#_Rule_3.3._Candor_Toward_the_Tribunal with the ABA Model Rules of Professional Conduct at www.abanet.org/cpr and the rule in your jurisdiction.

The legal team has an ethical obligation not to mislead the court. Just one brief that intentionally distorts or hides the truth or intentionally misleads the court can destroy a legal career. Even if it doesn't result in sanctions, suspension, or disbarment, judges talk with their colleagues, and a bad reputation for integrity to the court is hard to correct. At the least, the court always will remember that the attorney did shoddy work and may give more credibility to the opposing side in the future, even if later cases by the offending attorney are better prepared and more accurately on point.

Preparing Office Memorandums

In doing research and preparing the memorandum of law, the legal assistant must be careful to include all the relevant applicable statutes and case law. Some paralegals are intimidated by the gruff and even downright nasty attitude of certain lawyers, particularly trial counsel in the middle of a stressful case. The paralegals are afraid the lawyer will "shoot the messenger." The reality is that the attorney *must* know the weaknesses in the case along with the strengths. Nothing is more upsetting to the attorney, whether in court or in a meeting with a client or opposing counsel, than to be surprised by a case, facts, or law that has not been covered in the office memorandum of law.

Office memoranda are frequently indexed by subject and filed in the office for future reference. If the same or a similar fact pattern requires research, these provide a good starting point and can be a major time-saver. So that a memorandum may be indexed properly, the facts upon which the conclusion is based must be clearly stated. All statutes, regulations, and cases must be cited properly so anyone reading the memorandum in the future can look them up. Listing relevant websites used in the preparation also is helpful.

Starting Point

The starting point for the legal researcher is to understand the specific assignment. What is it that the researcher has been asked to research? For the memorandum of law, it usually is to answer a question:

What is the current law on . . . ?

What happens if . . . ?

What is the procedure for . . . ?

Before starting an assignment, the paralegal must be certain what is really being asked. Any questions should be resolved by asking the person for whom this is being prepared: "What does the attorney expect?" Where the paralegal's knowledge of the subject area is sufficient, he or she may know that certain facts may change the outcome— such as the requirement in some states that a subscribing witness to a decedent's will cannot be a beneficiary. Before starting, paralegals must be sure to have all the relevant facts, then restate what they believe they are being asked to research in the form of a statement of the question. For example: "You have asked for the law on the rights of individuals to . . . ."

Part of the skill in legal writing is using analytical skills to find the similarities and differences in cases that can be used as persuasive argument for the position being presented for the client. This is the critical legal thinking aspect of the legal writing process. And writing is a process. It requires research, analysis, organization, writing, editing, and proofreading. Sometimes it requires starting over when the final document when viewed from the position of the ultimate reader does not communicate the necessary information or tell the story.

In the legal working environment, time to rethink, re-research, and rewrite is a luxury. The pressure is on developing good skills to minimize the time necessary to produce an acceptable document, whether it is a letter, an office memorandum, or a court brief.

Memorandum of Law Format

A memo is frequently prepared by the supervising attorney with a request for research and an office memorandum of a specific subject or case. A sample of an assignment memo is shown in Exhibit 11.1. Frequently, the assignment is given in a face-to-face meeting. When the assignment is made orally, it is a good idea to confirm the specific assignment if there is any question of the details required.

Exhibit 11.1 **Assignment memo**

MEMORANDUM

To: **Edith Hannah**
From: **Glenn Hains**
Date: **January 23, 2006**
File **Number: GH 06-1002**
Re: **Commonwealth of Pennsylvania vs. Kevin Dones**

Our client was stopped by a police officer at the bottom of the hill on route 332 in Northhampton Township, at 3:30 on Sunday afternoon, January 15, 2006. He was riding a bicycle south on route 332 and was given a citation for speeding. The police used a radar unit and claimed a speed of 35 mph in a 25 mph zone. He administered a field sobriety test, which gave a reading over the legal limit, and client was given a citation for driving under the influence. He tells me he was riding a bike because his license was suspended for a previous DUI.

Please prepare a brief memorandum of law, with citations and cases.

Exhibit 11.2 Word search function

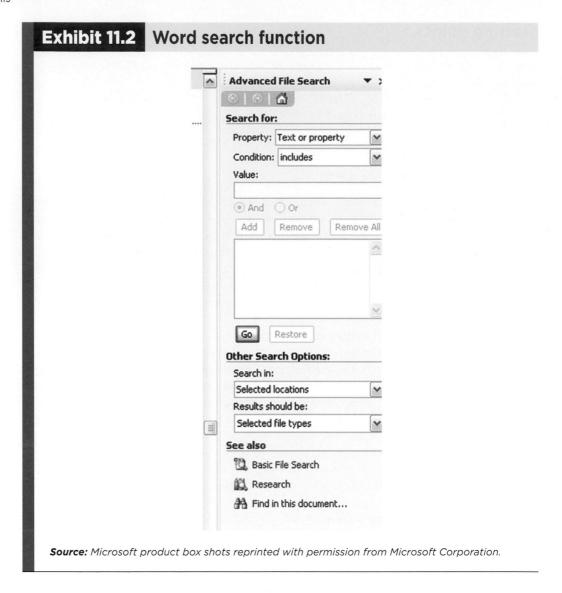

Source: Microsoft product box shots reprinted with permission from Microsoft Corporation.

The format or template for office memoranda is fairly standard, as shown in the Memorandum of Law Template. Some offices may add, for identification purposes, headings such as office file numbers or client identifiers. Some offices that maintain a paper format include subject matter legal terms or areas of law so they can be filed and retrieved if future cases require a memorandum on the same subject. Copies of memorandum are increasingly stored electronically as word processor files. These electronic files can be searched using a search function such as the file search function in Microsoft Word shown in Exhibit 11.2.

When taking an assignment to do research and write a memorandum, a few basics have to be remembered. The attorney, in all probability, will not redo the research or do much more than refer to the material submitted with the memorandum. The memorandum must be an unbiased presentation of the law as it exists, clearly presented. If the content of the memorandum is not accurate and complete, the attorney relying on the analysis and discussion may be, at the least, embarrassed by the opposing counsel or, at the worst, by the court.

Points to remember in preparing a memorandum of law are:

- **Never** rely on case law headnotes. Headnotes are not a primary source of the law.
- **Always** check the language of the court cases. It is the primary authority.

- ■ **Check** the dates of the cases and of the statutes. Be sure they are current law.
- ■ **Shepardize** (GlobalCite, KeyCite, V.Cite) the cases you used and relied on to be certain they have not been overruled by a later case or law.
- ■ **Don't** be afraid to show the cases and law against your client's position.
- ■ **Cite all** sources used. Never plagiarize.
- ■ **Analyze** opposing case law for any differences that may give the attorney a chance to argue that the negative cases are different in some factual or legal way.
- ■ **Ask**, if you don't understand the issues or question involved. It is better to admit that you are having a problem with the research than to give the attorney wrong, incomplete, or unintelligible information.

The format of the memorandum of law is determined by the nature of the assignment, the number of issues, and the ultimate use that will be made of the memorandum, as well as personal preferences of the person making the assignment.

The components of a memorandum of law and the components of a court opinion (case) are similar. Exhibit 11.3 presents a comparison.

Some case opinions have a brief summary or syllabus of the case that is prepared by an editor, such as the West editors or Supreme Court editors, which is not an official part of the case but is provided for reader convenience. Some attorneys prefer to have a Brief Answer under the Statement of the Assignment in a Memorandum of Law. The brief answer is generally a shortened version of the main points of the conclusion.

Samples of a traditional memorandum of law and one prepared for internal government use are shown in Exhibits 11.4 and 11.5.

If you have ever "briefed" a case you will notice the similarity to the list of items shown in the comparison above. A sample of a case and a case brief is provided in Appendix A: How to Brief a Case.

Facts

Paralegals, of course, must have a clear statement of the facts from which to work. The facts relied upon in writing the memo must be part of the ultimate final memorandum. Other people may read the memorandum. They need to understand the specific facts upon which the analysis is based, particularly if they read it at a time when the

Exhibit 11.3 Components of court opinions and memorandums of law

COURT OPINIONS	MEMORANDUMS OF LAW
Caption: Parties, citation, relevant dates	**Heading:** Assigning party, client, file number
Judicial history: Prior proceeding (how the case got to this court)	**Statement of the assignment:** History of what happened and why the client sought representation
Issue: Legal question before the court	**Issue:** Legal issues of clients raised in statement of assignment
Facts: Relevant facts used to decide case	**Statement of facts:** Relevant facts
Analysis and discussion: Discussion of the facts, rules of law, issues, judicial reasons for decision	**Analysis and discussion:** Discussion of each issue, how the applicable law applies, what relevant facts impact the decision
Conclusion: Holding of the Court	**Conclusion:** Restatement of the conclusion to each issue analyzed and discussed above, summarizing the main points

Exhibit 11.4 Sample memorandum of law prepared by leading legal research provider

MEMORANDUM OF LAW

TO: Ellen Holroyd, Esq.

FROM: ███████████████████████

DATE: January 29, 2004

RE: SEC Definitions of Terms Under the Sarbanes-Oxley Act of 2002

QUESTION PRESENTED

With regard to its regulations promulgated pursuant to the Sarbanes-Oxley Act of 2002, how does the Security and Exchange Commission define the concepts "material violation", "credible evidence", and "reasonable behavior" by an attorney?

DISCUSSION

Section 307 of the Sarbanes-Oxley Act of 2002 ("Sarbanes-Oxley") requires the Securities and Exchange Commission ("SEC") to "prescribe minimum standards of professional conduct for attorneys appearing and practicing before the Commission in any way in the representation of issuers." Implementation of Standards of Professional Conduct for Attorneys, Securities Act Release No. 33,8185, 68 Fed. Reg. 6,296 (Feb. 6, 2003.) According to the SEC, these standards "must include a rule requiring an attorney to report evidence of a material violation of securities laws or breach of fiduciary duty or similar violation by the issuer." Id., at 6,296. This memorandum discusses the definitions embraced by the SEC for "material violation," "credible evidence," and "reasonable behavior" by an attorney, three concepts found in the regulations adopted by the SEC pertaining to Sarbanes-Oxley.

Page 4 of 27

| Exhibit 11.4 | Sample memorandum of law prepared by leading legal research provider *(continued)* |

III. Definition of "Reasonable Behavior" By An Attorney

Such a definition necessarily brings up next the question of what the SEC deems to be "reasonable behavior" for attorneys with regard to their duty to report actual or suspected Sarbanes-Oxley violations. In its formulation of what constitutes "reasonable behavior" on the part of an attorney under the Sarbanes-Oxley regulations, the SEC points out that it is not a "bright line" test, and that it is dependent on the circumstances surrounding not just the alleged violation, but also the attorney involved:

> This formulation, while intended to adopt an objective standard, also recognizes that there is a range of conduct in which an attorney may engage without being unreasonable. The "circumstances" are the circumstances at the time the attorney decides whether he or she is obligated to report the information. These circumstances may include, among others, the attorney's professional skills, background and experience, the time constraints under which the attorney is acting, the attorney's previous experience and familiarity with the client, and the availability of other lawyers with whom the lawyer may consult.

Implementation of Standards of Professional Conduct for Attorneys, Securities Act Release No. 33,8185, 68 Fed. Reg. 6,296, 6,302 (Feb. 6, 2003.) Thus, what is deemed reasonable behavior for one attorney could differ significantly from that for another attorney, depending on the various factors laid out by the SEC.

CONCLUSION

While the SEC provided guidance as to the meanings of all three concepts discussed in this memo, it is clear that it intended there to be no "bright line", "one size fits all" definitions for these phrases. That said, a "material violation" for purposes of the SEC's Sarbanes-Oxley rules would appear to be a violation of such consequence that a reasonable and prudent investor would consider it important to know about when determining whether to buy, sell, or hold a particular security. "Credible evidence" would appear to be evidence of a material violation substantial enough that a prudent

Exhibit 11.5 Sample memorandum of law prepared by the U.S. Department of Justice

U.S. Department of Justice
Immigration and Naturalization Service

HQADN 70/23

Office of the Executive Associate Commissioner

425 1 Street NW
Washington, DC 20536

May 24, 2001

MEMORANDUM FOR   Michael A. Pearson
                        Executive Associate Commissioner
                        Office of Field Operations

FROM: Michael D. Cronin /s/
               Acting Executive Associate Commissioner
               Office of Programs

SUBJECT: Public Law 106-378, adjustment of status of certain Syrian nationals.

This memorandum provides eligibility information and adjudication policy guidance for the implementation of Public Law 106-378, which pertains to the adjustment of certain Syrian nationals who were granted asylum after arriving in the United States after December 31, 1991.

ELIGIBILITY

Public Law 106-378 provides for the adjustment of status of a principal alien as well as an alien who is the spouse, child, or unmarried son or daughter of a principal alien.

Principal alien. In order to be eligible for adjustment under this law, the principal alien must:
1. Be a Jewish national of Syria;
2. Have arrived in the United States after December 31, 1991, after being permitted by the Syrian government to depart from Syria;
3. Be physically present in the United States at the time of filing the application to adjust status;
4. Apply for adjustment of status under Public Law 106-378 no later than October 26, 2001, or, have applied for adjustment of status under another provision of law prior to October 27, 2000, and request to have the basis of that application changed to Public Law 106-378;
5. Have been physically present in the United States for at least one year after being granted asylum;
6. Not be firmly resettled in any foreign country; and Memorandum: Public Law 106-378, adjustment of status of certain Syrian nationals.

REQUIRED FIELD OFFICE ACTION

Field offices are to identify all potentially eligible Syrian asylee adjustment applications and forward them and the related A-files to NSC within 30-days of this memorandum. The appropriate code, "SY6, 7 or 8" and reference to Public Law 106-378 must be noted. A-files are to be routed to the NSC in separate batches, with individual cover sheets attached to the outside face of each file reflecting "**SYRIAN ASYLEE P. L. 106-378**". If, for whatever reason, a field office cannot accomplish this goal, they are to provide a report to their respective region identifying each case,
explaining the reason(s), and advising the anticipated date of completion of the A-file transfer. Regions are requested to review the report and take appropriate action.

SERVICE CENTER ACTION ON APPROVED ASYLEE APPLICATIONS

The NSC must review all asylum adjustment cases received via Direct Mail as well as all cases forwarded to them from the field to cull out those Syrian nationals whose applications contain evidence of Syrian nationality, arrival in the United States

Exhibit 11.5	**Sample memorandum of law prepared by the U.S. Department of Justice** *(continued)*

after December 31, 1991, and a grant of asylum or asylee dependent status. The NSC must also retrieve A-files belonging to qualifying Syrian applicants inappropriately coded as "AS" adjustments, and take corrective action. A list containing the names of Syrian asylees has already been provided to the NSC to help in this regard. The NSC will also track the total number of cases approved. After the NSC approves 2,000 principal beneficiaries under this law, the NSC will stop adjudicating applications, and will notify HQ ISD and HQ ADN that the numerical limitation has been reached.

SUPPLEMENTAL FILING INSTRUCTIONS

The Form I-485 supplemental filing instructions are being modified to instruct qualified applicants to identify themselves by writing **"SYRIAN ASYLEE P. L. 106-378"** in Part 2, Block 2. Since many qualified Syrian asylees may be unaware of their special classification or the correct way to claim it, the NSC should review all newly submitted asylee adjustment applications, and, when appropriate, endorse the Form I-485 as described above. When an applicant's eligibility to adjust under Public Law 106-378 has been verified, the adjudicator will check the "other" block in the "Section of Law" portion of the FOR INS USE ONLY Section of Form I-485 and will enter the notation, **"Public Law 106-378."**

CONCLUSION

Segregating the Syrian asylum adjustments for proper adjudication is essential to preserve the use of the 10,000 visa numbers authorized annually for other asylees who are eligible to adjust their status. If you have questions regarding the adjudication of Syrian-processed asylum adjustments, please contact your center or regional representative. If needed, service center. . . .

Source: United States Department of Justice.

---

paralegal is not available to answer questions, such as in the middle of a case, when out ill, on vacation, or if the paralegal has left the firm. It also is frequently necessary to recite other facts not relied upon and the reason for not considering them—that the result would be different. An example is a notation that this fact pattern is based upon the participants' all being over the age of majority for contracting, or over the age to purchase and consume alcoholic beverages.

Analysis

A memorandum must present both sides of the issue and, in that respect, be a neutral, unbiased, objective presentation of applicable laws as they apply to the facts of the case. Issues that the opposing attorney or the judge may raise should be considered and presented. A good analysis will include a discussion of how the fact pattern may differ in cases that are not on point but may be used by opposing counsel.

The memorandum the paralegal prepares may be the basis for the court brief that the attorney or someone else will prepare. To be able to meet the ethical obligation to the court, the person who presents a persuasive argument favoring the client must know all the relevant statutory and case law.

Editing and Rewriting

The written word is a reflection of the writer. Everyone who reads the memorandum will measure the researcher's reputation and skill level. Each person who reads the memorandum will measure the writer's communication skills. The paralegal, however, may be writing for a certain audience, and someone other than that might read the memorandum unaware of the intended reader.

Certain elements of writing style transcend the audience. For example:

- Is it clear?
- Are the words used properly?

- Is the spelling correct?
- Is it written using proper English grammar?
- If it is being written for an audience for whom English is a second language, is that made clear?
- Where there are variations in translation of foreign language terms, have these been clarified? For example, were the facts translated from words spoken by someone from Spain or someone from Puerto Rico, from someone who speaks Northern High German or Bavarian Southern German or Swiss German?

Preparing Court Briefs

Each court has court rules on the requirements for briefs submitted by the parties and by "friends of the court—*amicus curia*." The format and required sections of a brief prepared for the court is determined by these rules, and in some cases the personal preferences of the judge or justices. Before undertaking the task the preparer should always obtain a current copy of the court rules and as a practice pointer, contact the judge's law clerk for any additional limitations or requirements.

At times the court is unable to thoroughly read the brief before oral argument. In these situations the preliminary statement becomes an important part of focusing the court on the issues presented for your side of the case. Being able to state your side of the case briefly is not easy, but it is worth the effort. It requires clear, concise, and careful choice of words that will be remembered as the hearing progresses, and later when the court is making its analysis and decision.

The table of contents, partial table of authorities, summary of the argument, and conclusion of an amicus curia brief submitted in a case to the United States Supreme Court is shown in Exhibit 11.6.

Citations

A legal **citation** is a reference to the source of the information that allows someone else to find the case or other material mentioned in a document. The form of the citation must allow others to find the material. The format must be one that others in the legal community generally accept and use. If a person in California submits a brief to a court, a person in New York or in Florida must be able to use the citation to locate the items referred to in the document in a traditional legal library or electronic law source such as Loislaw, VersusLaw, Lexis, or Westlaw.

All legal authorities can be divided into two groups—primary authority and secondary authority. **Primary authority** includes constitutions, statutes, cases, and administrative regulations. Everything else is a **secondary authority** explaining the primary authority or a finding tool providing a method of locating primary authority. With a consistent citation format, the reader can determine the source of the authority mentioned and find the applicable primary source (constitution, statute, regulation, or case) or secondary source or finding tool (treatise, encyclopedia, digest, or dictionary).

Judges and lawyers in some states are abandoning the longstanding tradition of putting citations in the body of a document and now are putting the citations at the bottom of the document in the footnotes. They claim it makes reading legal opinions easier by eliminating the interference of the citations with the flow of words.

Traditional Sources (Print)

The traditional method for publishing primary and secondary authority is the paper form, including books, collections of books, and series of books. Where a case, statute, or regulation is available in more than one series of books, such as the official reporter of the state and a private publication such as those published by West Publishing, the citation to both locations—known as parallel citations—is required. The citation form is basically the same:

Amicus curia Briefs submitted by interested parties, as a "friend of the court," who do not have standing in the action.

Citation A reference to the source of the information.

Primary authority The actual law itself.

Secondary authority Writings that explain the law.

Volume	Book or Series	Page
232	Atlantic 2d	44

In this example, written as 232 A.2d 44, 232 refers to the volume in the Atlantic 2d series reporter service of West Publishing Company, and 44 refers to the page on which the authority may be found.

Bluebook

The most commonly used guide to citation form is the publication *The Bluebook: A Uniform System of Citation*. This is the generally accepted authority for proper citation form unless the rules of a particular court dictate a different citation format.

Exhibit 11.6 *Amicus curia* brief filed with the U.S. Supreme Court

No. 08-479

In The
Supreme Court of the United States

SAFFORD UNIFIED SCHOOL DISTRICT #1, *et al.*,
Petitioners,

v.

APRIL REDDING,
LEGAL GUARDIAN OF MINOR CHILD,
Respondent.

On Writ of Certiorari to the
United States Court of Appeals
for the Ninth Circuit

BRIEF OF *AMICI CURIAE*
THE RUTHERFORD INSTITUTE,
GOLDWATER INSTITUTE
AND CATO INSTITUTE
IN SUPPORT OF RESPONDENT

John W. Whitehead
Counsel of Record
Douglas R. McKusick
THE RUTHERFORD INSTITUTE
1440 Sachem Place
Charlottesville, VA 22911
(434) 978-3888

Timothy Lynch
Ilya Shapiro
CATO INSTITUTE
1000 Massachusetts Ave., NW
Washington, DC 20001
(202) 218-4600

Clint Bolick
Nicholas C. Dranias
GOLDWATER INSTITUTE
SCHARF-NORTON CENTER
FOR CONSTITUTIONAL
LITIGATION
500 E. Coronado Road
Phoenix, AZ 85004
(602) 462-5000

TABLE OF AUTHORITIES

Cases

Bell v. Wolfish, 441 U.S. 520 (1979)..................7, 9

C.B. by and through Breeding v. Driscoll, 82 F.3d 383 (11th Cir. 1996)..................13

Calabretta v. Floyd, 189 F.3d 808 (9th Cir. 1991).......5

Camara v. Municipal Court, 387 U.S. 523 (1967)..6, 7

Cornfield by Lewis v. Consol. High Sch. Dist. No. 230, 991 F.2d 1316 (7th Cir. 1993) 8, 11, 17

Doe v. Renfrow, 631 F.2d 91 (7th Cir.), *reh'g denied*, 635 F.2d 582 (7th Cir. 1980), *cert. denied*, 451 U.S. 1022 (1981) 5

Edwards v. Aguillard, 482 U.S. 578 (1987)............19

Illinois v. Gates, 462 U.S. 213 (1983)...............16

Leatherman v. Tarrant County Narcotics, Intelligence & Coordination Unit, 507 U.S. 163 (1993) 22

Lilly v. Virginia, 527 U.S. 116 (1999).............12

Mary Beth G. v. City of Chicago, 723 F.2d 1263 (7th Cir. 1983)..................5

Maryland v. Garrison, 480 U.S. 79 (1987) 15

New Jersey v. T.L.O., 469 U.S. 325 (1985) ....passim

O'Connor v. Ortega, 480 U.S. 709 (1987)...............6

Pearson v. Callahan, 129 S.Ct. 808 (2009).........21, 22

Phaneuf v. Fraikin, 448 F.3d 591 (2d Cir. 2006)   5, 8, 11

(continued)

Exhibit 11.6 *Amicus curia* brief filed with the U.S. Supreme Court *(continued)*

SUMMARY OF THE ARGUMENT

In *New Jersey v. T.L.O.*, 469 U.S. 325 (1985), this Court accommodated the interests of public school educators and administrators in maintaining order and discipline in public schools by easing the restrictions on searches normally imposed upon state actors by the Fourth Amendment. In ruling that in-school searches of students in the school setting need not be supported by probable cause, however, the *T.L.O.* decision made clear that the "reasonableness" of a school search largely depends on whether the search is "excessively intrusive in light of the age and sex of the student and nature of the infraction." *Id.* at 342. This Court clearly signaled that the severity of the privacy invasion must be considered when deciding whether school officials have violated a student's Fourth Amendment rights.

In light of *T.L.O.*'s direction to consider the intrusiveness of a search, the *en banc* Ninth Circuit correctly understood here that a strip search of a student will be reasonable only when school officials have clear evidence to justify it. Strip searches are unquestionably privacy invasions of a different order and higher degree than "ordinary" searches and should be undertaken rarely. Only when school officials have highly credible evidence showing (1) the student is in possession of objects posing a significant danger to the school and (2) that the student has secreted the objects in a place only a strip search will uncover is such a search reasonable.

CONCLUSION

Throughout their merits brief, Petitioners decry a regrettable consequence of the decision below: educators must now "school themselves" in Fourth Amendment jurisprudence and allows courts to second-guess their judgment. But, given the seriousness of the intrusion effected by strip searches, this consequence is unavoidable.

School officials must realize that they may conduct strip searches only in extremely limited circumstances, and only on the basis of compelling evidence. The alternative implicit in the Petitioners' suggested resolution of this case is an unblinking deference to school officials that places students' privacy and security in grave jeopardy.

For the above reasons, the Ninth Circuit properly found that the strip search of Savana Redding was not reasonable and therefore violated the Fourth Amendment. That decision should be affirmed as guidance to school officials, and to ensure that the practice of strip-searching students remains appropriately rare.

For example, the executive administrator of the Superior Court of Pennsylvania issued this notice:

> Pennsylvania Superior Court will be issuing opinions containing a Universal Citation. This citation will be as follows:
> Jones v. Smith, 1999 PA Super, 1.
> The second number is a Court-issued number on the opinion. Each opinion will also have numbered paragraphs, to be used for pinpoint citation, e.g., Jones v. Smith, 1999 PA Super, 1, 15. Citation to opinions that have not yet been issued an Atlantic 2d citation are to be in the Universal Citation number. After the official citation has been issued, citation is to be only the official citation, and not the Universal Citation.

Effectively, the old citation format, citing to the book, is still to be used.

ALWD Citation Format

Association of Legal Writing Directors (ALWD) A society for professors who coordinate legal writing instruction.

A citation format, written by the **Association of Legal Writing Directors (ALWD)**, is provided in the *ALWD Citation Manual, A Professional System of Citation*. The ALWD is a society for professors who coordinate legal writing instruction in legal education.

One of the attributes of the manual, as set out in the preface, is that it is "a set of rules that reflects a consensus in the legal profession about how citations should function." The *ALWD Manual* includes, in addition to the general citation rules, an appendix containing court citation rules for the individual states. Exhibit 11.7 shows the comparison between the Bluebook and the ALWD rules for citation format.

Universal Citation Format

The *Universal Citation Guide* represents an attempt by the American Association of Law Libraries (AALL), Committee on Citation Formats, to create a set of universal citation rules for American law that are vendor (publisher) neutral and medium (print and electronic) neutral.

The various formats of electronic distribution require a system of citation that can be applied consistently to allow researchers to find the referenced authority regardless of the research tool used. Whereas the traditional, paper or book-based, citation uses information based on internal page numbers, the **Universal Citation Format** relies upon the courts to use numbered paragraphs in its opinions. Any publisher of the case law then can preserve the information provided by the court including the citation references to the case and paragraph.

Anyone who has read and compared a case in a book with a case online is aware that the page size and the display are different. Unless the online computer display is in a photo-image format, such as Adobe PDF, locating a specific page or reference can be difficult. Librarians and courts are recognizing the need for pinpoint citations for the on-screen user.

The Universal Citation Format represents an attempt to solve this problem. The difficulty with some courts is the requirement that the Universal Citation Format be used only until the hardcopy is published, at which time the traditional citation must be used. As a result, you may see the following citation format within documents:

Jones v. Smith, 1999 Pennsylvania Superior 1, ___Pa Supcr___, ___A2d___(1999)

in which the blank spaces are provided to insert the ultimate volume and page number in the print version when it is available. Appendix D lists court name abbreviations.

Other Citation Formats

Many states, including Pennsylvania, have adopted as their official citation format one that originally was created by publishers such as West Publishing Company. These sometimes are referred to as **vendor-specific citation formats**. The West Publishing Company format is based on the West Regional Reporter system and its publications of federal material.

New methods of electronic information technology, in the form of databases, CD-ROMs, and the Internet, have created a number of problems with the traditional citation format. Some of the vendors have claimed copyright protection for their pagination systems.

In 1985, West Publishing Company, in a case against Mead Data Central, argued successfully that the wholesale use of its *pagination* by a competing online publisher infringed upon West's copyright interest in the arrangement of cases in its court reports. And in a 1998 case involving Matthew Bender & Company and West Publishing Company, the Second Circuit held that West's pagination was not protected by copyright. Obviously, all claims to a pagination system or citation system that is vendor-specific will result in some action to protect the corporate claim for copyright, trademark, or potential patent for some electronic methodology.

Table of Authorities

A **table of authorities** is a listing of the citations or other references in a document and the page numbers where they are located. A Table of Authorities creation tool is included in the two most popular word processor programs used in the law office, WordPerfect and Microsoft Word. Each desired authority is first identified and marked by opening the Table of Authorities menu (pressing ALT+ SHIFT+ I) and organized by category, as shown in Exhibit 11.8. Each authority is marked and an identifier inserted in the document called a TA or Table of Authority Entry in MS Word. These marks are visible when the Hidden Marks button is selected, as shown in Exhibit 11.9.

Web Exploration

Check the ALWD website for the latest updates at www.alwd.org.

Universal Citation Format A system for citation relying on the courts to number the paragraphs in their opinions.

Web Exploration

Download A Draft User Guide to the AALL universal case citation at http://www.allnet.org/committee/citation/case.html.

Vendor-specific citation format Citation format of a legal publisher adopted by a court.

Web Exploration

For a discussion on the use of citations in the traditional format or as footnotes, see the *New York Times* article "Legal Citations on Trial In Innovation v. Tradition" by William Glaberson at http://www.nytimes.com/2001/07/08/us/legal-citations-on-trial-in-innovation-v-traditional.html.

Table of authorities A listing of the citations or other references in a document and the page numbers where they are located.

Exhibit 11.7	Comparison of selected ALWD third edition rules and *The Bluebook* 18th edition rules		
RULE	**ALWD CITATION**	**BLUEBOOK CITATION**	**DIFFERENCES**
Typeface **ALWD:** Rule 1 **BB:** B13 & Rule 2.0	Ordinary type and *italics* (or <u>underlining</u>). No distinctions based on type of document (law review v. court document) or placement of citation within the paper. Rule 1.1 in the third edition indicates that some journals and book publishers that do not follow ALWD require the use of large and small capital letters; Sidebar 23.2 provides examples of how to use large and small capital letters in various circumstances.	Ordinary type, *italics* (or <u>underlining</u>), and SMALL CAPS. Different fonts required depending on type of document and where source is cited within the paper.	ALWD has one set of conventions, not two. ALWD does not use small caps as a typeface.
Abbreviations and Spacing **ALWD:** Rule 2 **BB:** B5.1.1(v), B10.1, & Rule 6.1	F. Supp. F.3d Corp. Govt. Intl. Petr. In citations, ALWD gives the writer the flexibility to abbreviate words found in the appendices.	F. Supp. F.3d Corp. Gov't Int'l Pet'r In citations, the Bluebook requires that words in a case citation (as opposed to a case name used in a textual sentence) be abbreviated if the words appear in the Tables.	No substantial differences on spacing. ALWD abbreviations end with periods; some Bluebook abbreviations include apostrophes. ALWD provides flexibility regarding use of abbreviations.
Capitalization **ALWD:** Rule 3 **BB:** B10.6 & Rule 8	*Federal Civil Procedure before Trial*	*Federal Civil Procedure Before Trial*	ALWD eliminates the "and prepositions of four or fewer letters" part of the Bluebook, which brings legal citation closer to non-legal style.
Numbers **ALWD:** Rule 4 **BB:** Rule 6.2	Indicates that the convention in law is to use words for zero through ninety-nine in all text and notes. However, ALWD provides flexibility on whether to designate numbers with words or numerals. Ordinal contractions are presented as follows: 1st, 2d, 3d, 4th, etc.	Use words for zero through ninety-nine in all text and notes. Ordinal contractions are presented as follows: 1st, 2d, 3d, 4th, etc.	No substantial differences, other than ALWD allows for more flexibility. However, ALWD inserts a comma in some four-digit numerals: 3,000.
Page spans **ALWD:** Rule 5 **BB:** Rule 3.2(a)	125–126 **or** 125–26	125–26	ALWD gives a choice on how to present a page span; you may retain all digits or drop repetitive digits and retain two digits on the right-hand side of the span, as in Bluebook 3.2(a).

Exhibit 11.7	Comparison of selected ALWD third edition rules and *The Bluebook* 18th edition rules *(continued)*		

RULE	ALWD CITATION	BLUEBOOK CITATION	DIFFERENCES
Footnotes and endnotes **ALWD:** Rule 7 **BB:** Rule 3.2(b)–(c)	n. 7 nn. 12–13	n. 7 nn. 12–13	ALWD requires a space after n. or nn. abbreviation.
Supra* and *infra **ALWD:** Rule 10 **BB:** Rule 3.5	*Supra* n. 45.	*Supra* note 45.	Under ALWD, abbreviate note as "n." and place a space after the period.
Id. **ALWD:** Rule 11.3 **BB:** B5.2, Rules 4.1, 10.9 & 12.9	*Id.* at 500.	*Id.* at 500.	Basically similar rules. ALWD eliminates the "5 *id.* in a row" rule found in Bluebook Rule 10.9. In the ALWD Manual, *id.* cannot be used with Practitioner and Court documents. Rule 29.6.
Cases **ALWD:** Rule 12 **BB:** B5 & Rule 10	*Brown v. Bd. of Educ.*, 349 U.S. 294, 297 (1955). *MBNA Am. Bank, N.A. v. Cardoso,* 707 N.E.2d 189 (Ill. App. 1st Dist. 1998). [required inclusion of district court information]	*Brown v. Bd. of Educ.*, 349 U.S. 294, 297 (1955). *MBNA Am. Bank, N.A. v. Cardoso,* 707 N.E.2d 189 (Ill. App. Ct. 1st Dist. 1998). [permissive inclusion of district information]	Under ALWD, case names are always italicized or underlined. Under ALWD, you do not have to abbreviate words in case names. For those who want to abbreviate, Appendix 3 provides a longer list of words that are abbreviated. ALWD requires division and district information for state appellate courts, and eliminates "Ct." from most court abbreviations. For cases cited from Westlaw or LexisNexis, ALWD does not require the docket number of the case. ALWD also requires two asterisks to identify multiple pages of a pinpoint cite.
Constitutions **ALWD:** Rule 13 **BB:** B7 & Rule 11	U.S. Const. amend. V.	U.S. Const. amend. V.	No substantial differences.
Statutes **ALWD:** Rule 14	18 U.S.C. § 1965 (2000).	18 U.S.C § 1965 (2000).	No substantial differences.

(continued)

Exhibit 11.7	Comparison of selected ALWD third edition rules and *The Bluebook* 18th edition rules *(continued)*		
RULE	**ALWD CITATION**	**BLUEBOOK CITATION**	**DIFFERENCES**
BB: B6.1.1, B6.1.2 & Rule 12			
Legislative Materials **ALWD:** Rules 15 & 16 **BB:** B6.1.6 & Rule 13	Sen. Res. 146, 109th Cong. (2005).	S. Res. 146, 109th Cong. (2005).	ALWD abbreviates Senate as "Sen." instead of "S." to avoid confusion with other abbreviations. Most forms are relatively consistent.
Court Rules **ALWD**: Rule 17 **BB:** B6.1.3 & Rule 12.8	Fed. R. Civ. P. 11.	Fed. R. Civ. P. 11.	No substantial differences.
Administrative Materials **ALWD:** Rules 19 and 20 **BB:** B6.1.4 & Rule 14.2	34 C.F.R. § 607.1 (2006). 70 Fed. Reg. 10868 (Mar. 5, 2005).	34 C.F.R. § 607.1 (2006). 70 Fed. Reg. 10868 (Mar. 5, 2005).	C.F.R. citation is the same. Both require an exact date for Fed. Reg. citations. ALWD includes guidance about how to cite C.F.R. references found on unofficial electronic databases, such as Westlaw and LexisNexis. Rule 19.1(d).
Books and Treatises **ALWD**: Rule 22 **BB:** B8 & Rule 15	Charles Alan Wright, Arthur R. Miller & Mary Kay Kane, *Federal Practice and Procedure* vol. 7A, § 1751, 10–17 (3d ed., West 2005). OR Charles Alan Wright et al., *Federal Practice and Procedure* vol. 7A, § 1751, 10–17 (3d ed., West 2005).	7A Charles Alan Wright, Arthur R. Miller & Mary Kay Kane, *Federal Practice and Procedure* § 1751, at 10–17 (3d ed. 2005). OR 7A Charles Alan Wright et al., *Federal Practice and Procedure* § 1751, at 10–17 (3d ed. 2005).	ALWD places volume information after the title, just like any other subdivisions. ALWD separates subdivisions separated with a comma, but no "at." ALWD requires that the publisher be included, no matter what type of document. ALWD uses et al. for three authors or more, compared with the Bluebook which uses et al. for two authors or more.
Legal Periodicals **ALWD**: Rule 23	Geoffrey P. Miller, *Bad Judges*, 83 Tex. L. Rev. 431 (2004). Margaret Graham Tebo, *Duty Calls*, 91 ABA J. 35 (Apr. 2005).	Geoffrey P. Miller, *Bad Judges*, 83 Tex. L. Rev. 431 (2004). Margaret Graham Tebo, *Duty Calls*, A.B.A. J., Apr. 2005, at 35.	ALWD eliminates most distinctions between Consecutively and non-consecutively paginated articles. Include longer date for non-consecutively paginated journals, but do so within the parenthetical.

Exhibit 11.7	Comparison of selected ALWD third edition rules and *The Bluebook* 18th edition rules *(continued)*		

RULE	ALWD CITATION	BLUEBOOK CITATION	DIFFERENCES
BB: B9 & Rule 16	Carrie Ann Wozniak, Student Author, *Difficult Problems Call for New Solutions: Are Guardians Proper for Viable Fetuses of Mentally Incompetent Mothers in State Custody?* 34 Stetson L. Rev. 193 (2004). Jodi Wilgoren, *Prosecution Lays out Case for Harsh Sentencing of B.T.K. Killer in Gory Detail*, 154 N.Y. Times A14 (Aug. 18, 2005).	Carrie Ann Wozniak, Comment, *Difficult Problems Call for New Solutions: Are Guardians Proper for Viable Fetuses of Mentally Incompetent Mothers in State Custody?* 34 Stetson L. Rev. 193 (2004). Jodi Wilgoren, *Prosecution Lays out Case for Harsh Sentencing of B.T.K. Killer in Gory Detail*, N.Y. Times, Aug. 18, 2005, at A14.	ALWD uses the term "Student Author" to replace Note, Comment, Recent Development, etc.
A.L.R. Annotations **ALWD:** Rule 24 **BB:** Rule 16.6.6	Carolyn Kelly MacWilliam, *Individual and Corporate Liability for Libel and Slander in Electronic Communications, Including E-mail, Internet and Websites*, 3 A.L.R.6th 153 (2005).	Carolyn Kelly MacWilliam, Annotation, *Individual and Corporate Liability for Libel and Slander in Electronic Communications, Including E-mail, Internet and Websites*, 3 A.L.R.6th 153 (2005).	ALWD eliminates the "Annotation" reference.
Legal Dictionaries **ALWD**: Rule 25 **BB**: Rule 15.8	*Black's Law Dictionary* 87 (Bryan A. Garner ed., 8th ed., West 2004).	*Black's Law Dictionary* 87 (8th ed. 2004).	ALWD treats dictionaries like books.
Legal Encyclopedias **ALWD:** Rule 26 **BB**: Rule 15.8	98 C.J.S. *Witnesses* § 397 (2002). 68 Am. Jur. 2d *Schools* §§ 20–24 (2000 & Supp. 2005).	98 C.J.S. *Witnesses* § 397 (2002). 68 Am. Jur. 2d *Schools* §§ 20–24 (2000 & Supp. 2005).	No substantial differences; however, ALWD provides expanded coverage and includes a list of many abbreviations for state encyclopedias.
Internet **ALWD:** Rule 40 **BB:** Rule 18.2.3	Fed. Jud. Ctr., *History of the Federal Judiciary*, http://www.fjc.http://www.fjc.gov/history/home.nsf (accessed Aug. 18, 2005).	Federal Judicial Center, *History of the Federal Judiciary* (visited Aug. 18, 2005), at http://www.fjc.gov/history/home.nsf.	ALWD permits the abbreviation of an organizational author's name, to save space. ALWD uses "accessed" instead of "visited" to be consistent with non-legal citation guides. The Bluebook contains different formats for material that appears only on the Web and for material that appears on the Web and in other medium. The position of the date parenthetical moves depending on the type of information cited.

(continued)

Exhibit 11.7	**Comparison of selected ALWD third edition rules and *The Bluebook* 18th edition rules** *(continued)*		
RULE	**ALWD CITATION**	**BLUEBOOK CITATION**	**DIFFERENCES**
Signals **ALWD**: Rule 44 **BB**: B4 & Rule 1.2	Signals are *e.g., accord, see, see also, cf., contra, compare . . . with, but see, but cf.,* and *see generally.*	Signals are *e.g., accord, see, see also, cf., contra, compare . . . with, but see, but cf.,* and *see generally.*	Under ALWD, all signals may be separated with semicolons. Under the Bluebook, a new citation sentence must start when there is a new type of signal. (Signals are categorized by type in the Bluebook—supportive, comparative, contradictory, or background—whereas in ALWD, the signals are ordered individually.) ALWD does not use any punctuation after a signal.
Order of Cited Authority **ALWD**: Rule 45 **BB**: B4.5 & Rule 1.4	ALWD lists federal, state, and foreign court cases first by jurisdiction, then in reverse chronological order.	Federal (appellate and trial) court cases are ordered in reverse chronological order. State court cases are first, alphabetized by state, and then ranked within each state.	Minor differences in the order when looking at the list of specific sources: (1) Under ALWD, statutes (federal and state) come before rules of evidence and procedure, whereas in the Bluebook, federal statutes and rules of evidence and procedure come before state statutes and rules of evidence and procedure. (2) Under the ALWD, the student-authored articles are classified with all other material in law reviews, law journals, and other periodicals, whereas in the Bluebook, the student-authored articles are separate, and cited after the non-student-authored articles.
Quotations **ALWD**: Rule 47 **BB**: B12 & Rule 5	ALWD says to block indent passages if they contain at least fifty words OR if they exceed four lines of typed text.	The *Bluebook* says to block indent passages if they contain at least 50 words.	ALWD does not require you to count the exact number of words in long quotations.

Source: Copyright © 2005, Darby Dickenson. Reprinted with permission.

Exhibit 11.8 Table of Authorities selection menus

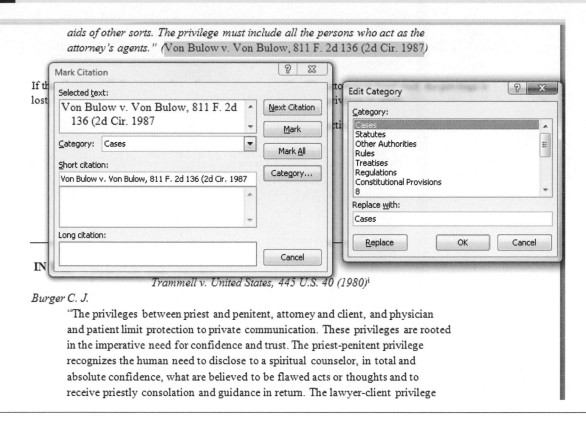

Exhibit 11.9 Table of Authorities hidden characters

The table of authorities may be inserted using the Insert Table of Authorities selection in the Reference tab, as shown in Exhibit 11.10.

Cite Checking

Cite checking is the process of verifying that the proper citation format has been used in a document. The term also means checking the referenced case or statute to determine that it is valid and that it has not been repealed or overturned. The strictness with which the citation rules must be applied, as well as the method—*Bluebook*, *ALWD Citation Manual*, or Universal Citation Format—depends on the wishes and demands of the attorney for whom the document is prepared or the court or judge to

Cite checking The process of verifying proper citation format in a document.

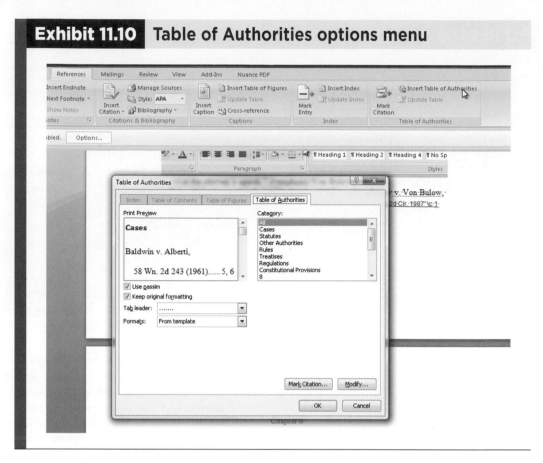

Exhibit 11.10 Table of Authorities options menu

whom it is submitted. Some courts view the presentation of improper citation format with a jaundiced eye, just as they view improper punctuation, improper spelling, and bad grammar. Others are upset if the citation to the paper references or online legal research service available to them is not used.

Bluebook and *ALWD* Compared

Which citation format is used depends on the local custom and courts in which the firm or supervising attorney practices (and the wishes of your instructors!). The two forms used most commonly—the *Bluebook* and the *ALWD Manual*—have a number of similarities. Both of these documents are divided into parts and rules—the *Bluebook* into three parts and the *ALWD Manual* into seven parts.

The parts are further divided into rules. The *Bluebook* has 20 basic rules, and the *ALWD* 50 rules. Most of the rules have a common pattern, and some are the same, such as *Bluebook* Rule 12–Statutes, and *ALWD* Rule 14 on the method of citing the United States Code: 18 U.S.C. § 1965 (1994). Others are minor variations in presentation, such as *Bluebook* Rule 10.2.2, which provides, "Do not abbreviate 'United States,'" and *ALWD* Rule 12.2(g) "United States as party: Cite as U.S. Omit 'America.'"

Sample *Bluebook* citation formats:

Rule 11 Constitutions:	U.S.Const.art.I, § 9, cl.2.
Rule 10 Cases:	United States v Shaffer Equip. Co., 11 F.3d 450 (4th Cir. 1993)
Rule 12 Statutes:	42 U.S.C. § 1983 (1994)

Sample *ALWD* citation formats:

Rule 13 Constitutions:	U.S. Const.art. IV, § 5(b)
Rule 12 Cases:	Brown v. Bd. Of Educ., 349 U.S. 294
	U.S. v. Chairse, 18 F.Supp. 2d 1021
	(D. Minn. 1998)
Rule 14 Statutory Codes:	18 U.S.C. § 1965 (1994)
Session Laws, SlipLaws:	

Advice *from the* Field

PROFESSIONAL COMMUNICATION

by Kathryn L. Myers, Associate Professor and Coordinator of Paralegal Studies at Saint Mary-of-the-Woods College in Saint Mary-of-the-Woods, IN

There are countless misunderstandings, conflicts, and disagreements in every organization in the United States. Effective listening skills are almost extinct in many firms, and gossip among colleagues has become commonplace. The result is lost productivity, hurt feelings, hidden agendas, loss of innovative ideas, and mistrust among coworkers.

The importance of professional communication skills in dealing with these problems cannot be overstressed. *The Wall Street Journal* recently reported a study involving more than one hundred Fortune 500 executives who ranked interpersonal communication first, across the board, as the most valuable skill they considered in hiring or promotion decisions. Lack of interpersonal communication skills impedes professional effectiveness in influencing persuading, and negotiating, all of which are crucial to success.

Professional communication may take the form of written communication, active listening, or nonverbal communication, all of which require interpersonal communication skills. All three skills work together to define professional communication, but this article focuses specifically on written communication.

Writing intimidates many people, but there are times when writing is the best way to communicate and often is the only way to get a message across. Good writers must have access to at least one quality writing guide. Some good choices are: *The Elements of Style*, by William Strunk, Jr., and E.B. White for lawyers, paralegals, and others engaged in formal writing; *The Bedford Handbook*, by Diana T. Hacker; *How 10: A Handbook for Office Professionals*, by James L. and Lyn R. Clark; and *The Associated Press Stylebook* for traditional journalists is the professional bible.

The following tips are offered as examples of what careful writers must consider.

BE CAUTIOUS

Written communication is more concrete than verbal communication and is less forgiving of errors. Once something is written and sent, it cannot be taken back; and it cannot be nuanced or explained away as readily as can be done with the spoken word.

Communicators in writing must meet the challenges of spelling, grammar, punctuation, and style in addition to the actual wording (rhetoric). Modern technology superficially makes writing seem easier by providing grammar and spelling checks, but these tools are not failsafe. They may actually contribute to egregious errors if the writer is not carefully involved with the writing and proofreading the material for sense.

REMEMBER THE ABC'S OF WRITING

Accuracy—Proof and reproof

Brevity—Keep sentences short

Clarity—Use active voice for clear meaning

BEWARE OF COMMON ERRORS

Commas—Use commas after each part of full dates (*e.g.*, "Wednesday, July 13, 2005," or "July 13, 2005," unless the year falls at the end of the sentence. No comma is used with a calendar date expressed alone (*e.g.*, "February 14.") Do not use commas where the year stands by itself (*e.g.*, "the year 2005 was special.")

Restrictive words, phrases, or clauses modify the main idea and are essential to its meaning. These are not set off by commas. Nonrestrictive words, phrases, or clauses, however, do not significantly change the meaning of the sentence and are set off by commas. Place commas inside quotation marks and parentheses.

Semicolons—Use semicolons when there are two or more independent clauses that do not have coordinating conjunctions, or when the clauses are joined by a transitional expression such as "however." Also use them to separate clauses in a series which have internal commas. Place semicolons outside quotation marks and parentheses.

Colons—Use colons after independent clauses that introduce a formal list or enumeration of items, but not if a verb of being precedes the list. Use a colon after a business salutation and to introduce formal quotations (*e.g.*, the court held: "no offense was proven . . .")

Dashes—Use dashes instead of commas to achieve greater pause and emphasis to what follows. Also use them in place of commas with parenthetical expressions or appositives that contain internal commas.

Ellipsis—An ellipsis is a series of three periods to indicate one or more words are missing from the middle of a sentence in the quoted text. If the missing text is at the end of a sentence, this fact is indicated with a fourth period—the sentence period—at the end of the series.

Quotation Marks—Quotation marks are used to show directly quoted speech or text as well as the titles of published articles. Quotations of 50 words or more do not use quotation marks but, rather, are written as separate paragraph(s), single spaced, and indented on the right and left margins greater than the normal text.

Apostrophe—The apostrophe is used to indicate a missing letter in a contraction (*e.g.*, "it's" for "it is" or "don't" for "do not") or to denote singular possession

(continued)

(e.g., "Mary's"), or plural possession (e.g., "the companies' policies.") "Its" is the correct (albeit counterintuitive) possessive form of "it." No apostrophe is used. All possessive case pronouns (my, your, yours, their, its, whose, theirs, ours) are written without apostrophes.

When there is joint ownership, the apostrophe attaches to the last noun (e.g., "it was Dick and Jane's home"). With individual possession where there are two or more nouns, each noun shows ownership (e.g., "it was either Dick's or Jane's").

WATCH YOUR GRAMMAR

Active Voice—Using action verbs and active voice provides clear and readable sentences.

Noun/Pronoun Agreement—A singular noun (legal assistant) must have a singular pronoun (his/her). Plural nouns (legal assistants) must have plural pronouns (their). Avoid confusion by writing in the plural form when possible.

Subjective Case—Use the subjective case of a pronoun (I, he, she, you, we, they, who, it, whoever) for the subject, for the complement of a "being" verb, and after the infinitive "to be" when this verb does not have a subject directly preceding it.

Objective Case—Use the objective case of a pronoun (me, him, her, you, us, them, whom, it, whomever) as the direct or indirect object of a verb, the object of a preposition, the subject of any infinitive, the object of the infinitive "to be" when it has a subject directly preceding it, and the object of any other infinitive.

Noun/Verb Agreement—Singular nouns take singular verbs. Know the difference among present, past, and future tenses. Do not switch verb tenses in documents unless the material requires the switch.

Identifiers (Modifiers)—Place identifiers (modifiers) (e.g., adjectives and adverbs) as close as possible to the words they identify (modify).

Proper Pairs—Certain words (correlative conjunctions) must be used in pairs (e.g., either/or, neither/nor, not only/but also).

Clichés, Slang, and Jargon—Avoid clichés: use them only when there is a sound reason to believe that a particular cliché will strengthen your rhetoric. Use slang and "legalese" only when it would be awkward for the reader not to do so, and only if you are sure the reader will understand the reference. A judge, for example, expects to read some amount of legalese. He or she likely would be disappointed to see none at all in a trial brief.

Spelling—Use your spelling checker, but proofread to make sure you do not have correct spelling of the wrong word (e.g., "she was soaking in the tube.") Great care should be taken to spell the names of people and companies correctly.

Acronyms and Abbreviations—Except for acronyms and abbreviations in common usage and which are self-explanatory in context (e.g., "the Hon. James Parker" or "she is an interpreter with NATO"), give full titles and names when the acronym or abbreviation first is mentioned. Err on the side of spelling it out if there is any doubt.

Numbers—In general, single-digit numbers should be written as words; double digit, as numerals in written materials unless the number is used to begin a sentence (e.g., "I had only 10 reference books when I began five years ago.")

Source Acknowledgement—The source of borrowed material of any kind must be attributed with quotation marks if directly quoted, or by attribution if not directly quoted (e.g., "I shall return," Gen. MacArthur promised, or, "General Douglas MacArthur promised he would be back"). In formal research and in legal writing, complete citations must be provided according to the legal convention or the style prescribed by the particular publication.

LETTERS

Correspondence is a primary form of communication between the law firm and the world. It is vital that correspondence be crafted well to properly reflect both the reputation of the law office and your own professionalism. Correspondence must be free of grammar and spelling errors, and the research and analysis must be absolutely correct.

There are different types of letters for different purposes: informational letters, opinion letters, and demand letters, to name a few. Although paralegals would not sign their names to opinion or demand letters, it is quite common for them to draft substantial portions of this correspondence.

There are certain parts to a letter that are necessary for successful correspondence.

Format—There are three primary formats: 1) full block, 2) modified block with blocked paragraphs, and 3) modified block with indented paragraphs.

Letterhead—Preprinted letterhead needs no additional information; but subsequent pages need to contain an identification of the letter, or a header including the name of the addressee, the date, and the page number.

Date—The full date appears below the letterhead at the left or right margin depending on the format used.

Method of Delivery—This appears at the left margin below the date if delivery other than U.S. Postal Service is used.

Recipient's Address Block—The inside address is placed at the left margin and should include:

The recipient

The recipient's title (if any)

The name of the business (if appropriate)

The address

Reference Line—Usually introduced with "Re:" the reference line identifies the subject of the letter. Depending upon office requirements, it may contain case identification.

Salutation—Legal correspondence generally is formal; and the salutation is followed with a colon, such as "Dear Ms. Myers:" You can use the first name if you know the person well, although it is a safer practice to remain formal. It is best to address the letter to a named individual. This may mean calling the recipient business and identifying a person to whom the letter should be addressed.

Body—The body of the letter should have three components:

1. Introduction: For normal business letters, your letter should start with an overall summary, showing in the first paragraph why the letter is relevant to the reader. Don't make reader go past the first paragraph to find out why the letter was sent.
2. Main section: The body of the letter needs to explain the reason for the correspondence, including any relevant background and current information. Make sure the information flows logically to make your points effectively.
3. Requests/instructions: The closing of the letter is the final impression you leave with the reader. End with an action point such as, "I will call you later this week to discuss the matter."

Closing—Following the body of the letter, the closing consists of a standard statement and/or an action item.

Signature and Title—Clearly identify the writer by name and title.

Initials of Drafter—This is a reference to the author (KLM) and the typist (sbk).

Enclosure Notation—"Enc." or "Encs." notations are used to identify one or more enclosures.

Copies to Others—The traditional "cc" notation, formerly meaning "carbon copy," now means "courtesy copy" and is used universally. Some writers, however, will use only "c" or "copy to," along with the name(s), to identify others receiving copies of the document.

PROOFREADING

Even when you believe your draft is exactly what you want, read it one more time. This rule is for everything you write whether it is a memorandum, letter, proposal, or some other document. It is true no matter how many drafts you have written.

Use both the grammar and spelling checker on your computer, paying very close attention to every word highlighted. Do not place total faith in your computer. Instead, have both a printed dictionary and a thesaurus nearby to double-check everything your computer's editing tools highlight, because the computer tools are not always reliable.

Make sure your document is clear and concise. Is there anything that could be misinterpreted? Does it raise questions or fail to make the point you need to make? Can you reduce the number of words or unnecessarily long words? Do not use a long word when a short one works as well; do not use two words when one will do; and do not waste the reader's time with unnecessary words or phrases.

Is your written communication well organized? Does each idea proceed logically from one paragraph to the next? Make sure written communications are easy to read, contain the necessary information, use facts where needed, and avoid information that is not relevant. Be sure to specify the course of action you expect, such as a return call or an order.

Close appropriately, whether formally or informally, according to the nature of the communication. This may seem obvious, but it is sometimes overlooked and can make written communications look amateurish. This diminishes your chances of meeting your written communication's goals.

Communication is vital to the success of any workplace; and in the legal arena, professionals live or die by the communicated word. Well-crafted documents are a positive step toward being a successful professional.

Reprinted with permission of the National Association of Legal Assistants and Kathryn L. Myers. The article originally appeared in the May 2005 issue of FACTS & FINDINGS, *the quarterly journal for legal assistants. The article is reprinted here in its entirety. For further information, contact NALA at* www.nala.org *or phone 918-587-6828.*

Concept Review *and* Reinforcement

LEGAL TERMINOLOGY

SUMMARY OF KEY CONCEPTS

Critical Legal Thinking: Definitions

Critical Legal Thinking	The process of identifying legal issues, determining the relevant facts, and applying the applicable law to come to a conclusion that answers the legal question the issues present. The paralegal must understand the audience for whom the document is being prepared: the client, the supervising attorney and other members of the legal team, or the court.
Facts	Facts are pieces of information or details that in actuality or reality exist, or have occurred, as opposed to someone's theory, supposition, or conjecture. A fact is, in the law, the circumstances of an event, motion, occurrence, or state of affairs, rather than an interpretation of its significance.
Material (Relevant) Fact	A material fact is a fact that is significant or essential to the issue or matter at hand.
Immaterial (Irrelevant) Fact	An immaterial fact is one that is not essential to the matter at issue.

Legal Writing

Standards	1. The language used must be clear to the intended reader. 2. The writer must make an honest presentation of the facts and argument. 3. Arguments advocating a new interpretation to the existing law, as well as the current law, must be clearly stated. 4. The ethical obligation to the court must be obeyed, including the presentation of adverse authority in the jurisdiction. 5. Factual variation must be presented, and the sources used clearly identified by proper citation in a format acceptable to the reader.
Duty of Candor	There is an obligation to be honest with the court and not to mislead the court.

Preparing Office Memorandums

Purpose	1. The memorandum is a working document for the legal team to be used in preparation and presentation of a case. 2. The paralegal must understand the specific assignment. For the memorandum of law, it usually is the answer to a question. 3. Office memoranda are frequently indexed by subject and filed in the office for future reference; if the same or a similar fact pattern requires research, it is a good starting point and can be a major time-saver. 4. The facts relied upon in writing the memo must be a part of the final memorandum; other people who read the memorandum need to understand the specific facts. 5. A memorandum must present both sides of the issue, and in that respect be a neutral, unbiased, objective presentation of applicable laws as they apply to the facts of the case. Issues that the opposing attorney or the judge may raise should be considered and presented. A good analysis includes a discussion of how the fact pattern may differ in cases that are not on point.

Preparing Court Briefs

	Written for the court, the brief provides written advocacy of the client's position and must be written to convince the court to adopt a position favorable to the client.

Citations

Purpose	A citation should allow someone else to find the case or other material mentioned in a document, and the form of citation must do this. The format must be generally accepted and used by others in the legal community.

Traditional Sources (Print) Citation Format	The basic paper or traditional citation form is: Volume • Book or Series • Page e.g., 232 Atlantic 2d 44 232 refers to the volume in the Atlantic 2d series reporter service of West Publishing Company, and 44 refers to the page on which the authority may be found.
Bluebook Citation Format	*Bluebook* has been the generally accepted authority for proper citation form unless the rules of a particular court dictated a different citation format.
ALWD Citation Format	This citation format authority was written by Association of Legal Writing Directors.
Universal Citation Format	Traditionally, paper or book-based citation used information based on internal page numbers. Universal Citation Format relies upon the courts to provide numbered paragraphs in their opinions.
Table of Authorities	A table of authorities is a listing of the citations or other references in a document and the page numbers where they are located.
Cite Checking	Documents must be checked to verify that they use the proper citation format and that the referenced cases and statutes are valid and the cases have not been repealed or overturned. The strictness with which the citation rules must be applied, as well as the method—*Bluebook*, *ALWD*, or Universal Citation Format—depends on the wishes and demands of the attorney for whom the document is being prepared, or the court or judge to whom it is submitted.

WORKING THE WEB

1. Summarize in a memo the requirements for briefs submitted to the United States Supreme Court, and the citation to the applicable rule. http://www.supremecourt.us.gov/ctrules/rulesofthecourt.pdf or http://www.law.cornell.edu/rules/supct/overview.html

2. Use the Internet to find the information to prepare an internal office memorandum on the requirements for filing briefs in your jurisdiction's highest court. For example, in California at http://www.courtinfo.ca.gov/rules/titleone/title1-1-59.htm, or Kansas at http://www.kscourts.org/ctruls/ctrul610.htm.

3. The Legal Law Institute at Cornell Law School offers a number of sources for the legal writer, including citation information. Use the LII website to download the section from Introduction to Basic Legal Citation by Peter W. Martin—"Who Sets Citation Norms"—at http://www.law.cornell.edu/citation/1-600.htm.

4. Use the homepage link from the Web page in question 3, and download your personal copy of the reference document.

5. If you are using the ALWD manual for citation rules, download a copy of the latest updates at www.alwd.org.

CRITICAL THINKING & WRITING QUESTIONS

1. What is critical legal thinking? Explain and give an example.

2. Why is it important to have all the material facts before beginning the research to prepare a memorandum of law?

3. What is meant by "material facts?" Give an example of a material fact.

4. What is meant by an "immaterial fact?" Give an example.

5. What is the goal of legal writing?

6. Why should headnotes not be used in legal writing?

7. How important is it to Shepardize the cases in a memorandum of law or brief? When should this be done? Why?

8. How are the memorandum of law and the court brief similar, and different? Explain fully.

9. Contrast and compare the fact situation in the opening scenario and the Alaskan case of *Whiting v. State* in the chapter. What are the similarities, and what are the points that could be used to argue that the law does not apply?

10. How does the general duty to inform the court preserve the integrity of the judicial process? (*Hazel-Atlas Glass Co. v. Hartford-Empire Co.*, 322 U.S. 238)

11. Are sanctions against attorneys for failing to observe a duty of candor to the court an appropriate remedy? [*Beam v. IPCO Corp.*, 838 F.2d 242 (7th Cir. 1998)]

12. What are the relevant facts in the *Palsgraf v. LIRR* case found in Appendix A? What facts are interesting but not relevant facts? Create a computer search query using the facts in the *Palsgraf* case, and search the case law of your jurisdiction using these relevant facts. Prepare a short brief of the latest case you find, including proper *Bluebook* and *ALWD* citation format.

13. What questions should a paralegal ask before preparing a memo of law or a brief?
14. Why should both sides of a case be presented in an office memo of law?
15. Why would an attorney request that all parallel citations be listed for each case listed in a memo of law?

16. How would knowing the intended audience influence the writing of a memo of law or a legal brief?
17. What level of confidentiality should be attached to the preparation and handling of a memo of law? Why?

Building Paralegal Skills

VIDEO CASE STUDIES

Zealous Representation Issue: Candor to the Court

 The supervising attorney is due in another courtroom and asks the paralegal to appear for him and submit a brief, which the paralegal has prepared. The lawyer does not read the petition and accepts the paralegal's statement that it is the current law on the subject.

After viewing the video case study at www.pearsonhighered.com/goldman answer the following:
1. What is the duty of the legal team to present up-to-date information to the court when seeking relief?
2. Can legal research from a prior case be used in an argument to the court?
3. Who is responsible for misleading the court on the currency of the information, the paralegal or the attorney?

Zealous Representation Issue: Signing Documents

 Court rules require that pleadings be signed by the attorney. With the court about to close and the statute of limitations running out that day, the paralegal signs the attorney's name and files the paperwork.

After viewing the video case study at www.pearsonhighered.com/goldman answer the following:
1. What is the purpose of having the attorney sign all pleadings?
2. Would electronic filing have avoided this problem?
3. What are the dangers in relying upon electronic filing of documents?

ETHICS ANALYSIS & DISCUSSION QUESTIONS

1. What are the ethical issues in failing to properly cite authorities used in a document?
2. What are the ethical obligations in arguing to the court for a change in the law and not following the current law?
3. What are the ethical obligations to the client when analysis of the law indicates there is no valid claim?
4. Assume you have been working for a legal specialist in estate law for a number of years and have taken a number of advanced courses in the field. You are highly regarded in the paralegal community as the person to call for help in the field. Your supervising attorney decides to take a three-week bicycle trip through the Swiss Alps and leaves you in charge of the office.

    During his absence, you give a talk to a local senior citizens group on the advantages of preparing a will. You meet with most of the people in the audience after the talk and tell them a simple will can be prepared for $25 (your office's standard fee) and proceed to take the information from them for a will. You prepare the individual wills and send copies marked DRAFT to each

person, along with an invoice for the $25 fee with a note to return the fee if they wish to have the will completed. Everyone accepts and sends in the fee.

    Upon his return, the attorney looks over the wills, tells you they are "letter perfect" and says "It's just what I would have done." [*Cincinnati Bar v. Kathman*, 92 Ohio St. 92 (2001) quoting *People v. Cassidy*, 884 P.2d 309 (Colo. 1994).] What are the legal and ethical issues?
5. It is the week between Christmas and New Year's Day. You are the only one covering the office while all of the lawyers and support personnel are on vacation. A client who is traveling in Asia calls and asks you to fax to his hotel a copy of an opinion letter prepared by your supervising attorney. You helped prepare the opinion letter and know that it contains a summary of the facts, including details about the opposing parties, case strategy, and potential violations of law. May you send it? What are the ethical issues, if any?
6. You are working for the local prosecutor as a paralegal. The District Attorney asks you to prepare an office

memorandum of law on the question: Is there any duty to advise the court of any changes in the law or facts after the case has been presented.

7. You prepared a memorandum of law for the firm's trial attorney, and a brief for the court that was used in the case that started today. Closing arguments will be made tomorrow. You now discover that there is case law that is favorable to the other side that effectively overturns the case law you used in the memo of law and brief. What do you do? Are there any ethical issues? Explain fully.

DEVELOPING YOUR COLLABORATION SKILLS

Working on your own or with a group of other students assigned by your instructor, review the scenario at the beginning of the chapter.

1. Divide the group into two teams.
   a. One team is to prepare a memo for the court in the form of a brief.
   b. One team is to prepare a memo of law for the partner.
   c. After the memos are finished, each group should compare and write a report on the differences between the memos.

2. As a group, prepare a memo that Amanda might prepare for the supervising paralegal or other attorney on the handling of the interview and any concerns or recommendations.

3. Discuss any ethical concerns that Amanda might have, based on the interview and the potential handling of the case.

PARALEGAL PORTFOLIO EXERCISE

Prepare a memorandum of law for the supervising attorney using the information in the memorandum assignment below. Use the statutory and case law of your local jurisdiction.

Memorandum Assignment

To: Edith Hannah
From: Glenn Hains
Date: January 23, 2006
File   Number: GH 06-1002
Re: State of (your state) v. Kevin Dones

Our client was stopped by a police officer at the bottom of a 1-mile-long 10% grade hill on state Route 332 in Northhampton Township, at 3:30 p.m. on Sunday afternoon, January 15, 2006. He was riding a bicycle south on State Route 332. He was given a motor vehicle citation for speeding. They used a radar unit and claim a speed of 35 mph in a 25 mph zone. He also was administered a field sobriety test, which gave a reading over the legal limit and was given a citation for driving under the influence. He tells me he was riding a bike because his license was suspended for having two previous DUIs.

Please prepare a brief memorandum of law, with citations and cases.

LEGAL ANALYSIS & WRITING CASES

United States v. Shaffer Equipt. Co.   11 F.3d 450 (4th Cir. 1993)

Issue: Continuing Duty to Inform Court of Changes in the Law

Government counsel learned that its expert witness had lied about his credentials and that the witness had lied in other litigation. The attorney did not immediately notify the court or opposing counsel. In finding against the government, the court extended the duty of candor to include a continuing duty to inform the court of any development that may conceivably affect the outcome of litigation.

Questions

1. Is preserving the integrity of the judicial process more important than the duty to vigorously pursue a client's case?

2. Is there a duty to inform the court when an attorney suspects that a client may have committed perjury?

3. What additional burden is placed on the paralegal in preparing material for a case in light of this decision?

Golden Eagle Distributing Corp. v. Burroughs

801 F.2d. 1531 (9th Cir. 1986)
United States Court of Appeals, Ninth Circuit

Read, and if assigned, brief this case. In your brief, answer the following questions.

1. What is the intent of Federal Rules of Civil Procedure Rule 11?
2. What test does the court use to determine if sanctions should be imposed under FRCP Rule 11?
3. What is meant by the "ethical duty of candor"?
4. Is there a conflict between the attorney's ethical obligations under the ABA Model Rules and the requirements of FRCP 11?
5. Do attorneys have any duty to cite cases adverse to their case? Explain.

Schroeder, Circuit Judge

This is an appeal from the imposition of sanctions under Rule 11 of the Federal Rules of Civil Procedure as amended in 1983. The appellant, a major national law firm, raises significant questions of first impression.

The relevant portions of the amended Rule provide: Every pleading, motion, and other paper of a party represented by an attorney shall be signed by at least one attorney. . . . The signature of an attorney . . . constitutes a certificate by him that he has read the pleading, motion, or other paper; that to the best of his knowledge, information, and belief formed after reasonable inquiry, it is well grounded in fact and is warranted by existing law or a good faith argument for the extension, modification, or reversal of existing law. . . . If a pleading, motion, or other paper is signed in violation of this rule, the court, upon motion or upon its own initiative, shall impose upon the person who signed it, a represented party, or both, an appropriate sanction. . . .

In this appeal, we must decide whether the district court correctly interpreted Rule 11.

. . . Golden Eagle Distributing Corporation filed the underlying action in Minnesota state court for fraud, negligence, and breach of contract against Burroughs, because of an allegedly defective computer system. Burroughs removed the action to the federal district court in Minnesota. Burroughs then moved pursuant to 28 U.S.C. § 1404(a) to transfer the action to the Northern District of California. . . . Burroughs next filed the motion for summary judgment, which gave rise to the sanctions at issue here. It argued that the California, rather than the Minnesota, statute of limitations applied and that all of Golden Eagle's claims were time-barred under California law. It also contended that Golden Eagle's claim for economic loss arising from negligent manufacture lacked merit under California law. Golden Eagle filed a response,

arguing that Minnesota law governed the statute of limitations question and that Burroughs had misinterpreted California law regarding economic loss. . . .

After a hearing, the district judge denied Burroughs' motion and directed the Kirkland & Ellis attorney who had been responsible for the summary judgment motion to submit a memorandum explaining why sanctions should not be imposed under Rule 11. . . . Proper understanding of this appeal requires some comprehension of the nature of Burroughs' arguments and the faults which the district court found with them. . . .

Kirkland & Ellis's opening memorandum argued that Golden Eagle's claims were barred by California's three-year statute of limitations. The question was whether the change of venue from Minnesota to California affected which law applied. . . . In imposing sanctions, the district court held that Kirkland & Ellis's argument was "misleading" because it suggested that there already exists a *forum non conveniens* exception to the general rule that the transferor's law applies. . . . [The case cited] raised the issue but did not decide it. . . . Kirkland & Ellis's corollary argument, that a Minnesota court would have dismissed the case on *forum non conveniens* grounds, was found to be "misleading" because it failed to note that one prerequisite to such a dismissal is that an alternative forum be available. . . .

Kirkland & Ellis also argued that Golden Eagle's claim for negligent manufacture lacked merit because Golden Eagle sought damages for economic loss, and such damages are not recoverable under California law [as demonstrated in the *Seely* case]. . . . The district court sanctioned Kirkland & Ellis for not citing three cases whose holdings it concluded were adverse to *Seely:* . . . The district court held that these omissions violated counsel's duty to disclose adverse authority, embodied in Model Rule 3.3, Model Rules of Professional Conduct Rule 3.3 (1983), which the court viewed as a "necessary corollary to Rule 11."

. . . The district court's application of Rule 11 in this case strikes a chord not otherwise heard in discussion of this Rule. The district court did not focus on whether a sound basis in law and in fact existed for the defendant's motion for summary judgment. Indeed it indicated that the motion itself was nonfrivolous. . . . Rather, the district court looked to the manner in which the motion was presented. The district court in this case held that Rule 11 imposes upon counsel an ethical "duty of candor." . . . It said:

The duty of candor is a necessary corollary of the certification required by Rule 11. A court has a right to expect that counsel will state the controlling law fairly and fully; indeed, unless that is done the court cannot perform its task properly. A lawyer must not misstate the law, fail to disclose adverse authority (not disclosed by his opponent), or omit facts critical to the application of the rule of law relied on. . . .

With the district court's salutary admonitions against misstatements of the law, failure to disclose directly adverse authority, or omission of critical facts, we have no quarrel. It is, however, with Rule 11 that we must deal. The district court's interpretation of Rule 11 requires district courts to judge the ethical propriety of lawyers' conduct with respect to every piece of paper filed in federal court. This gives us considerable pause. . . .

The district court's invocation of Rule 11 has two aspects. The first, which we term "argument identification," is the holding that counsel should differentiate between an argument "warranted by existing law" and an argument for the "extension, modification, or reversal of existing law." The second is the conclusion that Rule 11 is violated when counsel fails to cite what the district court views to be directly contrary authority.

. . . The text of the Rule . . . does not require that counsel differentiate between a position which is supported by existing law and one that would extend it. The Rule on its face requires that the motion be either one or the other. . . . The district court's ruling appears to go even beyond the principle of Rule 3.3 of the ABA Model Rules, which proscribes "knowing" false statements of material fact or law. The district court made no finding of a knowing misstatement, and, given the well-established objective nature of the Rule 11 standard, such a requirement would be inappropriate. Both the earnest advocate exaggerating the state of the current law without knowingly misrepresenting it, and the unscrupulous lawyer knowingly deceiving the court, are within the scope of the district court's interpretation.

This gives rise to serious concerns about the effect of such a rule on advocacy. It is not always easy to decide whether an argument is based on established law or is an argument for the extension of existing law.

Whether the case being litigated is . . . materially the same as earlier precedent is frequently the very issue which prompted the litigation in the first place. Such questions can be close.

Sanctions under Rule 11 are mandatory. . . . In even a close case, we think it extremely unlikely that a judge, who has already decided that the law is not as a lawyer argued it, will also decide that the loser's position was warranted by existing law. Attorneys who adopt an aggressive posture risk more than the loss of the motion if the district court decides that their argument is for an extension of the law which it declines to make. What is at stake is often not merely the monetary sanction but the lawyer's reputation.

The "argument identification" requirement adopted by the district court therefore tends to create a conflict between the lawyer's duty zealously to represent his client, Model Code of Professional Responsibility Canon 7, and the lawyer's own interest in avoiding rebuke. The concern on the part of the bar that this type of requirement will chill advocacy is understandable. . . .

. . . Were the scope of the rule to be expanded as the district court suggests, mandatory sanctions would ride on close decisions concerning whether or not one case is or is not the same as another. We think Rule 11 should not impose the risk of sanctions in the event that the court later decides that the lawyer was wrong. The burdens of research and briefing by a diligent lawyer anxious to avoid any possible rebuke would be great. And the burdens would not be merely on the lawyer. If the mandatory provisions of the Rule are to be interpreted literally, the court would have a duty to research authority beyond that provided by the parties to make sure that they have not omitted something.

The burden is illustrated in this case, where the district court based its imposition of sanctions in part upon Kirkland & Ellis's failure to cite authorities which the court concluded were directly adverse to a case it did cite. The district court charged the appellant with constructive notice of these authorities because they were identified in Shepard's as "distinguishing" the case Kirkland & Ellis relied on.

. . . Amended Rule 11 of the Federal Rules of Civil Procedure does not impose upon the district courts the burden of evaluating under ethical standards the accuracy of all lawyers' arguments. Rather, Rule 11 is intended to reduce the burden on district courts by sanctioning, and hence deterring, attorneys who submit motions or pleadings which cannot reasonably be supported in law or in fact. We therefore reverse the district court's imposition of sanctions for conduct which it felt fell short of the ethical responsibilities of the attorney. Reversed.

How to Brief a Case

CRITICAL LEGAL THINKING

Judges apply legal reasoning in reaching a decision in a case. In doing so, the judge must specify the issue presented by the case, identify the key facts in the case and the applicable law, and then apply the law to the facts to come to a conclusion that answers the issue presented. This process is called **critical legal thinking.** Skills of analysis and interpretation are important in deciding legal cases.

Key Terms

Before embarking upon the study of law, the student should be familiar with the following key legal terms:

Plaintiff The party who originally brought the lawsuit.

Defendant The party against whom the lawsuit has been brought.

Petitioner or Appellant The party who has appealed the decision of the trial court or lower court. The petitioner may be either the plaintiff or the defendant, depending on who lost the case at the trial court or lower court level.

Respondent or Appellee The party who must answer the petitioner's appeal. The respondent may be either the plaintiff or the defendant, depending upon which party is the petitioner. In some cases, both the plaintiff *and* the defendant may disagree with the trial court's or lower court's decision and both parties may appeal the decision.

Briefing a Case

"Briefing" a case is important to clarify the legal issues involved and to gain a better understanding of the case.

The student must summarize (brief) the court's decision in no more than 400 words (some professors may shorten or lengthen this limit). The format is highly structured, consisting of five parts, each of which is numbered and labeled:

Part	Maximum Words
1. Case name and citation	25
2. Summary of key facts in the case	125
3. Issue presented by the case, stated as a one-sentence question answerable only by *yes* or *no*	25
4. Holding—the court's resolution of the issue	25
5. A summary of the court's reasoning justifying the holding	200
Total words	400

446 APPENDIX A How to Brief a Case

1. Case Name and Citation

The name of the case is placed at the beginning of each briefed case. The case name usually contains the names of the parties to the lawsuit. If there are multiple plaintiffs or defendants, however, some of the names of the parties may be omitted from the case name. Abbreviations often are used in case names.

The case citation—which consists of a number plus the year in which the case was decided, such as "126 L.Ed.2d 295 (1993)"—is set forth below the case name. The case citation identifies the book in the law library in which the case may be found. For example, the case in the above citation may be found in volume 126 of the *Supreme Court Reporter Lawyer's Edition (Second)*, page 295. The name of the court that decided the case appears below the case name.

2. Summary of Key Facts in the Case

The important facts of a case are stated briefly. Extraneous facts and facts of minor importance are omitted from the brief. The facts of the case usually can be found at the beginning of the case, but not necessarily. Important facts may be found throughout the case.

3. Issue Presented by the Case

It is crucial in briefing a case to identify the issue presented to the court to decide. The issue on appeal is most often a legal question, although questions of fact sometimes are the subject of an appeal. The issue presented in each case usually is quite specific and should be asked in a one-sentence question that is answerable only by a *yes* or *no*. For example, the issue statement, "Is Mary liable?" is too broad. A more proper statement of the issue would be, "Is Mary liable to Joe for breach of the contract made between them based on her refusal to make the payment due on September 30?"

4. Holding

The holding is the decision reached by the present court. It should be *yes* or *no*. The holding also states which party won.

5. Summary of the Court's Reasoning

When an appellate court or supreme court issues a decision—which often is called an *opinion*—the court normally states the reasoning it used in reaching its decision. The rationale for the decision may be based on the specific facts of the case, public policy, prior law, or other matters. In stating the reasoning of the court, the student should reword the court's language into the student's own language. This summary of the court's reasoning should pick out the meat of the opinions and weed out the nonessentials.

Following are two U.S. Supreme Court opinions for briefing. The case is presented in the language of the U.S. Supreme Court. A "Brief of the Case" follows each of the two cases. A third case, from the New York State Court of Appeals, also is included for briefing.

CASE 1

For Briefing

Harris v. Forklift Systems, Inc.
510 U.S. 17, 114 S.Ct. 367, 126 L.Ed.2d 295

CASE NAME
CITATION   *1993 U.S. LEXIS 7155 (1993)*
COURT   *Supreme Court of the United States*

OPINION OF THE COURT. O'CONNOR, JUSTICE

FACTS. Teresa Harris worked as a manager at Forklift Systems, Inc., an equipment rental company, from April 1985 until October 1987. Charles Hardy was Forklift's president. Throughout Harris's time at Forklift, Hardy often insulted her because of her gender and often made her the target of unwanted sexual innuendos. Hardy told Harris on several occasions, in the presence of other employees, "You're a woman, what do you know" and "We need a man as the rental manager"; at least once, he told her she was "a dumb-ass woman." Again in front of others, he suggested that the two of them "go to the Holiday Inn to negotiate Harris' raise." Hardy occasionally asked Harris and other female employees to get coins from his front pants pocket. He threw objects on the ground in front of Harris and other women, and asked them to pick the objects up. He made sexual innuendos about Harris' and other women's clothing.

In mid-August 1987, Harris complained to Hardy about his conduct. Hardy said he was surprised that Harris was offended, claimed he was only joking, and apologized. He also promised he would stop and based on his assurance Harris stayed on the job. But in early September, Hardy began anew: While Harris was arranging a deal with one of Forklift's customers, he asked her, again in front of other employees, "What did you do, promise the guy some sex Saturday night?" On October 1, Harris collected her paycheck and quit.

LOWER COURTS' OPINIONS. Harris then sued Forklift, claiming that Hardy's conduct had created an abusive work environment for her because of her gender. The United States District Court for the Middle District of Tennessee found this to be "a close case," but held that Hardy's conduct did not create an abusive environment. The court found that some of Hardy's comments offended Harris, and would offend the "reasonable woman," but that they were not "so severe as to be expected to seriously affect Harris' psychological well-being." A reasonable woman manager under like circumstances would have been offended by Hardy, but his conduct would not have risen to the level of interfering with that person's work performance. The United States Court of Appeals for the Sixth Circuit affirmed in a brief unpublished decision.

ISSUE. We granted certiorari to resolve a conflict among the Circuits on whether conduct, to be actionable as "abusive work environment" harassment, must "seriously affect an employee's psychological well-being" or lead the plaintiff to "suffer injury."

STATUTE BEING INTERPRETED. Title VII of the Civil Rights Act of 1964 makes it "an unlawful employment practice for an employer . . . to discriminate against any individual with respect to his compensation, terms, conditions, or privileges of employment, because of such individual's race, color, religion, sex, or national origin." 42 U.S.C. §2000e-2(a)(1).

U.S. SUPREME COURT'S REASONING. When the workplace is permeated with discriminatory intimidation, ridicule, and insult that is sufficiently severe or pervasive to alter the conditions of the victim's employment and create an abusive working environment, Title VII is violated. This standard takes a middle path between making actionable any conduct that is merely offensive and requiring the conduct to cause a tangible psychological injury. Mere utterance of an epithet which engenders offensive feelings in an employee does not sufficiently affect the conditions of employment to implicate Title VII. Conduct that is not severe or pervasive enough to create an objectively hostile or abusive work environment—an environment that a reasonable person would find hostile or abusive—is beyond Title VII's purview. Likewise, if the victim does not subjectively perceive the environment to be abusive, the conduct has not actually altered the conditions of the victim's employment, and there is no Title VII violation.

But Title VII comes into play before the harassing conduct leads to a nervous breakdown. A discriminatorily abusive work environment, even one that does not seriously affect employees' psychological well-being, can and often will detract from employees' job performance, discourage employees from remaining on the job, or keep them from advancing in their careers. Moreover, even without regard to these tangible effects, the very fact that the discriminatory conduct was so severe or pervasive that it created a work environment abusive to employees because of their race, gender, religion, or national origin offends Title VII's broad rule of workplace equality.

HOLDING. We therefore believe the district court erred in relying on whether the conduct "seriously affected plaintiff's psychological well-being" or led her to "suffer injury." Such an inquiry may needlessly focus the factfinder's attention on concrete psychological harm, an element Title VII does not require. So long as the environment would reasonably be perceived, and is perceived, as hostile or abusive, there is no need for it also to be psychologically injurious. This is not, and by its nature cannot be, a mathematically precise test. But we can say that whether an environment is "hostile" or "abusive" can be determined only by looking at all the circumstances.

We therefore reverse the judgment of the Court of Appeals, and remand the case for further proceedings consistent with this opinion.

CONCURRING OPINION. GINSBURG, JUSTICE

The critical issue, Title VII's text indicates, is whether members of one sex are exposed to disadvantageous terms or conditions of employment to which members of the other sex are not exposed. The adjudicator's inquiry should center, dominantly, on whether the discriminatory conduct has reasonably interfered with the plaintiff's work performance. To show such interference, the plaintiff need not prove that his or her tangible productivity has declined as a result of the harassment.

Brief of the Case: *Harris v. Forklift Systems, Inc.*

1. Case Name, Citation, and Court

> Harris v. Forklift Systems, Inc.
>
> 126 L.Ed.2d. 295 (1993)
>
> United States Supreme Court

2. Summary of the Key Facts

A. While Harris worked at Forklift, Hardy continually insulted her because of her gender and made her the target of unwanted sexual innuendos.

B. This conduct created an abusive and hostile work environment, causing Harris to terminate her employment.

C. Harris sued Forklift, alleging sexual harassment in violation of Title VII of the Civil Rights Act of 1964, which makes it an unlawful employment practice for an employer to discriminate in employment because of an individual's sex.

3. The Issue

Must an employee prove that she suffered psychological injury before she can prove a Title VII claim for sexual harassment against her employer?

4. The Holding

No. The Supreme Court remanded the case for further proceedings consistent with its opinion.

5. Summary of the Court's Reasoning

The Supreme Court held that a workplace that is permeated with discriminatory intimidation, ridicule, and insult so severe that it alters the conditions of the victim's employment creates an abusive and hostile work environment that violates Title VII. The Court held that the victim is not required to prove that she suffered tangible psychological injury to prove her Title VII claim. The Court noted that Title VII comes into play before the harassing conduct leads the victim to have a nervous breakdown.

CASE 2

For Briefing

PGA Tour, Inc. v. Martin   **CASE NAME**
121 S.Ct. 1879, 149 L.Ed.2d 904 (2001)   **CITATION**   *2001 U.S. LEXIS 4115*
                                                COURT   *Supreme Court of the United States*

OPINION OF THE COURT. STEVEN, JUSTICE

ISSUE. This case raises two questions concerning the application of the Americans with Disabilities Act of 1990 [42 U.S.C. § 12101 *et seq.*] to a gifted athlete: first, whether the Act protects access to professional golf tournaments by a qualified entrant with a disability; and second, whether a disabled contestant may be denied the use of a golf cart because it would "fundamentally alter the nature" of the tournaments to allow him to ride when all other contestants must walk.

FACTS. Petitioner PGA TOUR, Inc., a nonprofit entity formed in 1968, sponsors and cosponsors professional golf tournaments conducted on three annual tours. About 200 golfers participate in the PGA TOUR; about 170 in the NIKE TOUR; and about 100 in the SENIOR PGA TOUR. PGA TOUR and NIKE TOUR tournaments typically are 4-day events, played on courses leased and operated by petitioner. The revenues generated by television, admissions, concessions, and contributions from cosponsors amount to about $300 million a year, much of which is distributed in prize money. The "Conditions of Competition and Local Rules," often described as the "hard card," apply specifically to petitioner's professional tours. The hard cards for the PGA TOUR and NIKE TOUR require players to walk the golf course during tournaments, but not during open qualifying rounds. On the SENIOR PGA TOUR, which is limited to golfers age 50 and older, the contestants may use golf carts. Most seniors, however, prefer to walk.

RESPONDENT. Casey Martin is a talented golfer. As an amateur, he won 17 Oregon Golf Association junior events before he was 15, and won the state championship as a high school senior. He played on the Stanford University golf team that won the 1994 National Collegiate Athletic Association (NCAA) championship. As a professional, Martin qualified for the NIKE TOUR in 1998 and 1999, and based on his 1999 performance, qualified for the PGA TOUR in 2000. In the 1999 season, he entered 24 events, made the cut 13 times, and had 6 top-10 finishes, coming in second twice and third once.

Martin is also an individual with a disability as defined in the Americans with Disabilities Act of 1990 (ADA or Act). Since birth he has been afflicted with Klippel-Trenaunay-Weber Syndrome, a degenerative circulatory disorder that obstructs the flow of blood from his right leg back to his heart. The disease is progressive; it causes severe pain and has atrophied his right leg. During the latter part of his college career, because of the progress of the disease, Martin could no longer walk an 18-hole golf course. Walking not only caused him pain, fatigue, and anxiety, but also created a significant risk of hemorrhaging,

developing blood clots, and fracturing his tibia so badly that an amputation might be required.

When Martin turned pro and entered the petitioner's Qualifying-School, the hard card permitted him to use a cart during his successful progress through the first two stages. He made a request, supported by detailed medical records, for permission to use a golf cart during the third stage. Petitioner refused to review those records, or to waive its walking rule for the third stage. Martin therefore filed this action.

DISTRICT COURT'S DECISION 994 F.SUPP. 1242 [DISTRICT: OREGON (1998)]. At trial, petitioner PGA TOUR did not contest the conclusion that Martin has a disability covered by the ADA, or the fact that his disability prevents him from walking the course during a round of golf. Rather, petitioner asserted that the condition of walking is a substantive rule of competition, and that waiving it as to any individual for any reason would fundamentally alter the nature of the competition. Petitioner's evidence included the testimony of a number of experts, among them some of the greatest golfers in history. Arnold Palmer, Jack Nicklaus, and Ken Venturi explained that fatigue can be a critical factor in a tournament, particularly on the last day when psychological pressure is at a maximum. Their testimony makes it clear that, in their view, permission to use a cart might well give some players a competitive advantage over other players who must walk.

The judge found that the purpose of the rule was to inject fatigue into the skill of shot-making, but that the fatigue injected "by walking the course cannot be deemed significant under normal circumstances." Furthermore, Martin presented evidence, and the judge found, that even with the use of a cart, Martin must walk over a mile during an 18-hole round, and that the fatigue he suffers from coping with his disability is "undeniably greater" than the fatigue his able-bodied competitors endure from walking the course. As a result, the judge concluded that it would "not fundamentally alter the nature of the PGA Tour's game to accommodate him with a cart." The judge accordingly entered a permanent injunction requiring petitioner to permit Martin to use a cart in tour and qualifying events.

COURT OF APPEALS DECISION 204 F.3D 994 [9TH CIRCUIT (2000)]. The Court of Appeals concluded that golf courses remain places of public accommodation during PGA tournaments. On the merits, because there was no serious dispute about the fact that permitting Martin to use a golf cart was both a reasonable and a necessary solution to the problem of providing him access to the tournaments, the Court of Appeals regarded the central dispute as whether such permission would "fundamentally alter" the nature of the PGA TOUR or NIKE

TOUR. Like the District Court, the Court of Appeals viewed the issue not as "whether use of carts generally would fundamentally alter the competition, but whether the use of a cart by Martin would do so." That issue turned on "an intensively fact-based inquiry," and, the court concluded, had been correctly resolved by the trial judge. In its words, "all that the cart does is permit Martin access to a type of competition in which he otherwise could not engage because of his disability."

FEDERAL STATUTE BEING INTERPRETED. Congress enacted the ADA in 1990 to remedy widespread discrimination against disabled individuals. To effectuate its sweeping purpose, the ADA forbids discrimination against disabled individuals in major areas of public life, among them employment (Title I of the Act), public services (Title II), and public accommodations (Title III). At issue now is the applicability of Title III to petitioner's golf tours and qualifying rounds, in particular to petitioner's treatment of a qualified disabled golfer wishing to compete in those events.

U.S. SUPREME COURT'S REASONING. It seems apparent, from both the general rule and the comprehensive definition of "public accommodation," that petitioner's golf tours and their qualifying rounds fit comfortably within the coverage of Title III, and Martin within its protection. The events occur on "golf courses," a type of place specifically identified by the Act as a public accommodation. Section 12181(7)(L). In this case, the narrow dispute is whether allowing Martin to use a golf cart, despite the walking requirement that applies to the PGA TOUR, the NIKE TOUR, and the third stage of the Qualifying-School, is a modification that would "fundamentally alter the nature" of those events.

As an initial matter, we observe that the use of carts is not itself inconsistent with the fundamental character of the game of golf. From early on, the essence of the game has been shot-making—using clubs to cause a ball to progress from the teeing ground to a hole some distance away with as few strokes as possible. Golf carts started appearing with increasing regularity on American golf courses in the 1950's. Today they are everywhere. And they are encouraged. For one thing, they often speed up play, and for another, they are great revenue producers. There is nothing in the Rules of Golf that either forbids the use of carts, or penalizes a player for using a cart.

Petitioner, however, distinguishes the game of golf as it is generally played from the game that it sponsors in the PGA TOUR, NIKE TOUR, and the last stage of the Qualifying-School—golf at the "highest level." According to petitioner, "the goal of the highest-level competitive athletics is to assess and compare the performance of different competitors, a task that is meaningful only if the competitors are subject to identical substantive rules." The waiver of any possibly "outcome-affecting" rule for a contestant would violate this principle and therefore, in petitioner's view, fundamentally alter the nature of the highest level athletic event. The walking rule is one such rule, petitioner submits, because its purpose is "to inject the element of fatigue into the skill of shot-making," and thus its effect may be the critical loss of a stroke. As a consequence, the reasonable modification Martin seeks would fundamentally alter the nature of petitioner's highest level tournaments.

The force of petitioner's argument is, first of all, mitigated by the fact that golf is a game in which it is impossible to guarantee that all competitors will play under exactly the same conditions or that an individual's ability will be the sole determinant of the outcome. For example, changes in the weather may produce harder greens and more head winds for the tournament leader than for his closest pursuers. A lucky bounce may save a shot or two. Whether such happenstance events are more or less probable than the likelihood that a golfer afflicted with Klippel-Trenaunay-Weber Syndrome would one day qualify for the NIKE TOUR and PGA TOUR, they at least demonstrate that pure chance may have a greater impact on the outcome of elite golf tournaments than the fatigue resulting from the enforcement of the walking rule.

Further, the factual basis of petitioner's argument is undermined by the District Court's finding that the fatigue from walking during one of petitioner's 4-day tournaments cannot be deemed significant. The District Court credited the testimony of a professor in physiology and expert on fatigue, who calculated the calories expended in walking a golf course (about five miles) to be approximately 500 calories—"nutritionally less than a Big Mac." What is more, that energy is expended over a 5-hour period, during which golfers have numerous intervals for rest and refreshment. In fact, the expert concluded, because golf is a low intensity activity, fatigue from the game is primarily a psychological phenomenon in which stress and motivation are the key ingredients. And even under conditions of severe heat and humidity, the critical factor in fatigue is fluid loss rather than exercise from walking. Moreover, when given the option of using a cart, the majority of golfers in petitioner's tournaments have chosen to walk, often to relieve stress or for other strategic reasons. As NIKE TOUR member Eric Johnson testified, walking allows him to keep in rhythm, stay warmer when it is chilly, and develop a better sense of the elements and the course than riding in a cart. As we have demonstrated, the walking rule is at best peripheral to the nature of petitioner's athletic events, and thus it might be waived in individual cases without working a fundamental alteration.

HOLDING AND REMEDY. Under the ADA's basic requirement that the need of a disabled person be evaluated on an individual basis, we have no doubt that allowing Martin to use a golf cart would not fundamentally alter the nature of petitioner's tournaments. As we have discussed, the purpose of the walking rule is to subject players to fatigue, which in turn may influence the outcome of tournaments. Even if the rule does serve that purpose, it is an uncontested finding of the District Court that Martin "easily endures greater fatigue even with a cart than his able-bodied competitors do by walking." The purpose of the walking rule is therefore not compromised in the slightest by allowing Martin to use a cart. A modification that provides an exception to a peripheral tournament rule without impairing its purpose cannot be said to "fundamentally alter" the tournament. What it can be said to do, on the other hand, is to allow Martin the chance to qualify for and compete in the athletic events petitioner offers to those members of the public who have the skill and desire to enter. That is exactly what the ADA requires. As a result, Martin's request for a waiver of the walking rule should have been granted.

The judgment of the Court of Appeals is affirmed. It is so ordered.

DISSENTING OPINION. SCALIA, JUSTICE

In my view, today's opinion exercises a benevolent compassion that the law does not place it within our power to impose. The judgment distorts the text of Title III, the structure of the ADA, and common sense. I respectfully dissent.

The Court, for its part, assumes that conclusion for the sake of argument, but pronounces respondent to be a "customer" of the PGA TOUR or of the golf courses on which it is played. That seems to me quite incredible. The PGA TOUR is a professional sporting event, staged for the entertainment of a live and TV audience. The professional golfers on the tour are no more "enjoying" (the statutory term) the entertainment that the tour provides, or the facilities of the golf courses on which it is held, than professional baseball players "enjoy" the baseball games in which they play or the facilities of Yankee Stadium. To be sure, professional baseball players *participate* in the games, and *use* the ballfields, but no one in his right mind would think that they are *customers* of the American League or of Yankee Stadium. They are themselves the entertainment that the customers pay to watch. And professional golfers are no different. A professional golfer's practicing his profession is not comparable to John Q. Public's frequenting "a 232-acre amusement area with swimming, boating, sun bathing, picnicking, miniature golf, dancing facilities, and a snack bar."

Having erroneously held that Title III applies to the "customers" of professional golf who consist of its practitioners, the Court then erroneously answers—or to be accurate simply ignores—a second question. The ADA requires covered businesses to make such reasonable modifications of "policies, practices, or procedures" as are necessary to "afford" goods, services, and privileges to individuals with disabilities; but it explicitly does not require "modifications that would fundamentally alter the nature" of the goods, services, and privileges. Section 12182(b)(2)(A)(ii). In other words, disabled individuals must be given *access* to the same goods, services, and privileges that others enjoy.

A camera store may not refuse to sell cameras to a disabled person, but it is not required to stock cameras specially designed for such persons. It is hardly a feasible judicial function to decide whether shoe stores should sell single shoes to one-legged persons and if so at what price, or how many Braille books the Borders or Barnes and Noble bookstore chains should stock in each of their stores. Eighteen-hole golf courses, 10-foot-high basketball hoops, 90-foot baselines, 100-yard football fields—all are arbitrary and none is essential. The only support for any of them is tradition and (in more modern times) insistence by what has come to be regarded as the ruling body of the sport—both of which factors support the PGA TOUR's position in the present case. One can envision the parents of a Little League player with attention deficit disorder trying to convince a judge that their son's disability makes it at least 25% more difficult to hit a pitched ball. (If they are successful, the only thing that could prevent a court order giving a kid four strikes would be a judicial determination that, in baseball, three strikes are metaphysically necessary, which is quite absurd.)

Agility, strength, speed, balance, quickness of mind, steadiness of nerves, intensity of concentration—these talents are not evenly distributed. No wild-eyed dreamer has ever suggested that the managing bodies of the competitive sports that test precisely these qualities should try to take account of the uneven distribution of God-given gifts when writing and enforcing the rules of competition. And I have no doubt Congress did not authorize misty-eyed judicial supervision of such revolution. The year was 2001, and "everybody was finally equal." K. Vonnegut, Harrison Bergeron, in *Animal Farm and Related Readings* 129 (1997).

Brief of the Case: *PGA TOUR, Inc. v. Martin*

1. Case Name, Citation, and Court

PGA TOUR, Inc. v. Martin

121 S.Ct. 1879, 2001 LEXIS 415 (2001)

Supreme Court of the United States

2. Summary of the Key Facts

A. PGA TOUR, Inc. is a nonprofit organization that sponsors professional golf tournaments.
B. The PGA establishes rules for its golf tournaments. A PGA rule requires golfers to walk the golf course, and not use golf carts.
C. Casey Martin is a professional golfer who suffers from Klippel-Trenaunay-Weber Syndrome, a degenerative circulatory disorder that atrophied Martin's right leg and causes him pain, fatigue, and anxiety when walking.
D. When Martin petitioned the PGA to use a golf cart during golf tournaments, the PGA refused.
E. Martin sued the PGA, alleging discrimination against a disabled individual in violation of the American with Disabilities Act of 1990, a federal statute.

3. Issue

Does the Americans with Disabilities Act require the PGA to accommodate Martin by permitting him to use a golf cart while playing in PGA golf tournaments?

4. Holding

Yes. The Supreme Court held that the PGA must allow Martin to use a golf cart when competing in PGA golf tournaments. Affirmed.

5. Court's Reasoning

The Supreme Court held that:

A. Martin was disabled and covered by the Act.
B. Golf courses are "public accommodations" covered by the Act.
C. The use of golf carts is not a fundamental characteristic of the game of golf.
D. Other than the PGA rule, no Rule of Golf forbids the use of golf carts.
E. It is impossible to guarantee all players in golf will play under the exact same conditions, so allowing Martin to use a golf cart gives him no advantage over other golfers.
F. Martin, because of his disease, will probably suffer more fatigue playing golf using a golf cart than other golfers will suffer without using a cart.
G. The PGA's "walking rule" is only peripheral to the game of golf and not a fundamental part of golf.
H. Allowing Martin to use a golf cart will not fundamentally alter the PGA's highest-level professional golf tournaments.

CASE 3

For Briefing

Palsgraf v. Long Island R.R. Co.	**CASE NAME**	
248 N.Y. 339 (1928)	**CITATION**	*162 N.E. 99*
	COURT	*Court of Appeals of the State of New York*

OPINION OF THE COURT. CARDOZO, Ch. J.

FACTS. Plaintiff was standing on a platform of defendant's railroad after buying a ticket to go to Rockaway Beach. A train stopped at the station, bound for another place. Two men ran forward to catch it. One of the men reached the platform of the car without mishap, though the train was already moving. The other man, carrying a package, jumped aboard the car, but seemed unsteady as if about to fall. A guard on the car, who had held the door open, reached forward to help him in, and another guard on the platform pushed him from behind. In this act, the package was dislodged, and fell upon the rails. It was a package of small size, about fifteen inches long, and was covered by a newspaper. In fact it contained fireworks, but there was nothing in its appearance to give notice of its contents. The fireworks when they fell exploded. The shock of the explosion threw down some scales at the other end of the platform, many feet away. The scales struck the plaintiff, causing injuries for which she sues.

The conduct of the defendant's guard, if a wrong in its relation to the holder of the package, was not a wrong in its relation to the plaintiff, standing far away. Relatively to her it was not negligence at all. Nothing in the situation gave notice that the falling package had in it the potency of peril to persons thus removed. Negligence is not actionable unless it involves the invasion of a legally protected interest, the violation of a right. "Proof of negligence in the air, so to speak, will not do" (Pollock, *Torts* [11th ed.], p. 455; *Martin v. Herzog*, 228 N.Y. 164, 170; cf. Salmond, Torts [6th ed.], p.24). "Negligence is the absence of care, according to the circumstances" (WILLES, J., in *Vaughan v. Taff Vale Ry. Co.*, 5 H. & N. 679, 688; 1 Beven, Negligence

[4th ed.], 7; *Paul v. Consol. Fireworks Co.*, 212 N.Y. 117; *Adams v. Bullock*, 227 N.Y. 208, 211; *Parrott v. Wells-Fargo Co.*, 15 Wall. [U.S.] 524). The plaintiff as she stood upon the platform of the station might claim to be protected against intentional invasion of her bodily security. Such invasion is not charged. She might claim to be protected against unintentional invasion by conduct involving in the thought of reasonable men an unreasonable hazard that such invasion would ensue. These, from the point of view of the law, were the bounds of her immunity, with perhaps some rare exceptions, survivals for the most part of ancient forms of liability, where conduct is held to be at the peril of the actor (*Sullivan v. Dunham*, 161 N.Y. 290 Page 342). If no hazard was apparent to the eye of ordinary vigilance, an act innocent and harmless, at least to outward seeming, with reference to her, did not take to itself the quality of a tort because it happened to be a wrong, though apparently not one involving the risk of bodily insecurity, with reference to some one else. "In every instance, before negligence can be predicated of a given act, back of the act must be sought and found a duty to the individual complaining, the observance of which would have averted or avoided the injury" (McSHERRY, C.J., in *W. Va. Central R. Co. v. State*, 96 Md. 652, 666; cf. *Norfolk & Western Ry. Co. v. Wood*, 99 Va. 156, 158, 159; *Hughes v. Boston & Maine R.R. Co.*, 71 N.H. 279, 284; *U.S. Express Co. v. Everest*, 72 Kan. 517; *Emry v. Roanoke Nav. Co.*, 111 N.C. 94, 95; *Vaughan v. Transit Dev. Co.*, 222 N.Y. 79; *Losee v. Clute*, 51 N.Y. 494; *DiCaprio v. N.Y.C.R.R. Co.*, 231 N.Y. 94; 1 Shearman & Redfield on Negligence, § 8, and cases cited; Cooley on Torts [3d ed.], p. 1411; Jaggard on Torts, vol. 2, p. 826; Wharton, *Negligence*, § 24; Bohlen, *Studies in the Law of Torts*, p. 601). "The ideas of negligence and duty are strictly correlative" (BOWEN, L.J., in *Thomas v. Quartermaine*, 18 Q.B.D. 685, 694). The plaintiff sues in her own right for a wrong personal to her, and not as the vicarious beneficiary of a breach of duty to another.

A different conclusion will involve us, and swiftly too, in a maze of contradictions. A guard stumbles over a package which has been left upon a platform. It seems to be a bundle of newspapers. It turns out to be a can of dynamite. To the eye of ordinary vigilance, the bundle is abandoned waste, which may be kicked or trod on with impunity. Is a passenger at the other end of the platform protected by the law against the unsuspected hazard concealed beneath the waste? If not, is the result to be any different, so far as the distant passenger is concerned, when the guard stumbles over a valise which a truckman or a porter has left upon the walk? The passenger far away, if the victim of a wrong at all, has a cause of action, not derivative, but original and primary. His claim to be protected against invasion of his bodily security is neither greater nor less because the act resulting in the invasion is a wrong to another far removed. In this case, the rights that are said to have been violated, the interests said to have been invaded, are not even of the same order. The man was not injured in his person nor even put in danger. The purpose of the act, as well as its effect, was to make his person safe. If there was a wrong to him at all, which may very well be doubted, it was a wrong to a property interest only, the safety of his package. Out of this wrong to property, which threatened injury to nothing else, there has passed, we are told, to the plaintiff by derivation or succession a right of action for the invasion of an interest of another order, the right to bodily security. The diversity of interests emphasizes the futility of the effort to build the plaintiff's right upon the basis of a wrong to some one else. The gain is one of emphasis, for a like result would follow if the interests were the same. Even then, the orbit of the danger as disclosed to the eye of reasonable vigilance would be the orbit of the duty. One who jostles one's neighbor in a crowd does not invade the rights of others standing at the outer fringe when the unintended contact casts a bomb upon the ground. The wrongdoer as to them is the man who carries the bomb, not the one who explodes it without suspicion of the danger. Life will have to be made over, and human nature transformed, before prevision so extravagant can be accepted as the norm of conduct, the customary standard to which behavior must conform. The argument for the plaintiff is built upon the shifting meanings of such words as "wrong" and "wrongful," and shares their instability. What the plaintiff must show is "a wrong" to herself, i.e., a violation of her own right, and not merely a wrong to some one else, nor conduct "wrongful" because unsocial, but not "a wrong" to any one. We are told that one who drives at reckless speed through a crowded city street is guilty of a negligent act and, therefore, of a wrongful one irrespective of the consequences. Negligent the act is, and wrongful in the sense that it is unsocial, but wrongful and unsocial in relation to other travelers, only because the eye of vigilance perceives the risk of damage. If the same act were to be committed on a speedway or a race course, it would lose its wrongful quality. The risk reasonably to be perceived defines the duty to be obeyed, and risk imports relation; it is risk to another or to others within the range of apprehension (Seavey, Negligence, Subjective or Objective, 41 H.L. Rv. 6; *Boronkay v. Robinson & Carpenter*, 247 N.Y. 365). This does not mean, of course, that one who launches a destructive force is always relieved of liability if the force, though known to be destructive, pursues an unexpected path. "It was not necessary that the defendant should have had notice of the particular method in which an accident would occur, if the possibility of an accident was clear to the ordinarily prudent eye" (*Munsey v. Webb*, 231 U.S. 150, 156; *Condran v. Park & Tilford*, 213 N.Y. 341, 345; *Robert v. U.S.E.F. Corp.*, 240 N.Y. 474, 477). Some acts, such as shooting, are so imminently dangerous to any one who may come within reach of the missile, however unexpectedly, as to impose a duty of prevision not far from that of an insurer. Even today, and much oftener in earlier stages of the law, one acts sometimes at one's peril (Jeremiah Smith, Tort and Absolute Liability, 30 H.L. Rv. 328; Street, *Foundations of Legal Liability*, vol. 1, pp. 77, 78). Under this head, it may be, fall certain cases of what is known as transferred intent, an act willfully dangerous to A resulting by misadventure in injury to B (*Talmage v. Smith*, 101 Mich. 370, 374) These cases aside, wrong is defined in terms of the natural or probable, at least when unintentional (*Parrot v. Wells-Fargo Co.* [The Nitro-Glycerine Case], 15 Wall. [U.S.] 524). The range of reasonable apprehension is at times a question for the court, and at times, if varying inferences are possible, a question for the jury. Here, by concession, there was nothing in the situation to suggest to the most cautious mind that the parcel wrapped in newspaper would spread wreckage through the station. If the guard had thrown it down knowingly and willfully, he would not have threatened the plaintiff's safety, so far as appearances could warn him. His conduct would not have involved, even then, an unreasonable probability of invasion of her bodily security. Liability can be no greater where the act is inadvertent.

Negligence, like risk, is thus a term of relation. Negligence in the abstract, apart from things related, is surely not a tort, if indeed it is understandable at all (BOWEN, L.J., in *Thomas v. Quartermaine*, 18 Q.B.D. 685, 694). Negligence is not a tort unless it results in the commission of a wrong, and the commission of a wrong imports the violation of a right, in this case, we are told, the right to be protected against interference with one's bodily security. But bodily security is protected, not against all forms of interference or aggression, but only against some. One who seeks redress at law does not make out a cause of action by showing without more that there has been damage to his person. If the harm was not willful, he must show that the act as to him had possibilities of danger so many and apparent as to entitle him to be protected against the doing of it though the harm was unintended. Affront to personality is still the keynote of the wrong. Confirmation of this view will be found in the history and development of the action on the case. Negligence as a basis of civil liability was unknown to mediaeval law (8 Holdsworth, *History of English Law*, p. 449; Street, *Foundations of Legal Liability*, vol. 1, pp. 189, 190). For damage to the person, the sole remedy was trespass, and trespass did not lie in the absence of aggression, and that direct and personal (Holdsworth, op. cit. p. 453; Street, op. cit. vol. 3, pp. 258, 260, vol. 1, pp. 71, 74.) Liability for other damage, as where a servant without orders from the master does or omits something to the damage of another, is a plant of later growth (Holdsworth, op. cit. 450, 457; Wigmore, *Responsibility or Tortious Acts*, vol. 3, *Essays in Anglo- American Legal History*, 520, 523, 526, 533). When it emerged out of the legal soil, it was thought of as a variant of trespass, an offshoot of the parent stock. This appears in the form of action, which was known as trespass on the case (Holdsworth, op. cit. p. 449; cf. *Scott v. Shepard*, 2 Wm. Black. 892; Green, *Rationale of Proximate Cause*, p. 19). The victim does not sue derivatively, or by right of subrogation, to vindicate an interest invaded in the person of another. Thus to view his cause of action is to ignore the fundamental difference between tort and crime (Holland, *Jurisprudence* [12th ed.], p. 328). He sues for breach of a duty owing to himself.

The law of causation, remote or proximate, is thus foreign to the case before us. The question of liability is always anterior to the question of the measure of the consequences that go with liability. If there is no tort to be redressed, there is no occasion to consider what damage might be recovered if there were a finding of a tort. We may assume, without deciding, that negligence, not at large or in the abstract, but in relation to the plaintiff, would entail liability for any and all consequences, however novel or extraordinary (*Bird v. St. Paul F. & M. Ins. Co.*, 224 N.Y. 47, 54; *Ehrgott v. Mayor, etc., of N Y*, 96 N.Y. 264; *Smith v. London & S.W. Ry. Co.*, L.R. 6 C.P. 14; 1 Beven, Negligence, 106; Street, op. cit. vol. 1, p. 90; Green, *Rationale of Proximate Cause*, pp. 88, 118; cf. *Matter of Polemis*, L.R. 1921, 3 K.B. 560; 44 *Law Quarterly Review*, 142). There is room for argument that a distinction is to be drawn according to the diversity of interests invaded by the act, as where conduct negligent in that it threatens an insignificant invasion of an interest in property results in an unforeseeable invasion of an interest of another order, as, e.g., one of bodily security. Perhaps other distinctions may be necessary. We do not go into the question now. The consequences to be followed must first be rooted in a wrong.

HOLDING. The judgment of the Appellate Division and that of the Trial Term should be reversed, and the complaint dismissed, with costs in all courts.

DISSENTING OPINION. ANDREWS, J.
Assisting a passenger to board a train, the defendant's servant negligently knocked a package from his arms. It fell between the platform and the cars. Of its contents the servant knew and could know nothing. A violent explosion followed. The concussion broke some scales standing a considerable distance away. In falling they injured the plaintiff, an intending passenger.

Upon these facts may she recover the damages she has suffered in an action brought against the master? The result we shall reach depends upon our theory as to the nature of negligence. Is it a relative concept—the breach of some duty owing to a particular person or to particular persons? Or where there is an act which unreasonably threatens the safety of others, is the doer liable for all its proximate consequences, even where they result in injury to one who would generally be thought to be outside the radius of danger? This is not a mere dispute as to words. We might not believe that to the average mind the dropping of the bundle would seem to involve the probability of harm to the plaintiff standing many feet away whatever might be the case as to the owner or to one so near as to be likely to be struck by its fall. If, however, we adopt the second hypothesis we have to inquire only as to the relation between cause and effect. We deal in terms of proximate cause, not of negligence.

Negligence may be defined roughly as an act or omission which unreasonably does or may affect the rights of others, or which unreasonably fails to protect oneself from the dangers resulting from such acts. Here I confine myself to the first branch of the definition. Nor do I comment on the word "unreasonable." For present purposes it sufficiently describes that average of conduct that society requires of its members.

There must be both the act or the omission, and the right. It is the act itself, not the intent of the actor, that is important. (*Hover v. Barkhoof*, 44 N.Y. 113; *Mertz v. Connecticut Co.*, 217 N.Y. 475.) In criminal law both the intent and the result are to be considered. Intent again is material in tort actions, where punitive damages are sought, dependent on actual malice—not on merely reckless conduct. But here neither insanity nor infancy lessens responsibility. (*Williams v. Hays*, 143 N.Y. 442.)

As has been said, except in cases of contributory negligence, there must be rights which are or may be affected. Often though injury has occurred, no rights of him who suffers have been touched. A licensee or trespasser upon my land has no claim to affirmative care on my part that the land be made safe. (*Meiers v. Koch Brewery*, 229 N.Y. 10.) Where a railroad is required to fence its tracks against cattle, no man's rights are injured should he wander upon the road because such fence is absent. (*DiCaprio v. N.Y.C.R.R.*, 231 N.Y. 94.) An unborn child may not demand immunity from personal harm. (Drobner v. Peters, 232 N.Y. 220.)

But we are told that "there is no negligence unless there is in the particular case a legal duty to take care, and this duty must be one which is owed to the plaintiff himself and not merely to others." (Salmond Torts [6th ed.], 24.) This, I think too narrow a conception. Where there is the unreasonable act, and some right that may be affected there is negligence whether damage does or does not result. That is immaterial. Should we drive down Broadway at a reckless speed, we are negligent whether we strike an approaching car or miss it by an inch. The act itself is wrongful. It is a wrong not only to those who happen to be within the radius of danger but to all who might have been there—a wrong to the public at large. Such is the language of the street. Such the language of the courts when speaking of contributory negligence. Such again and again their language in speaking of the duty of some defendant and discussing proximate cause in cases where such a discussion is wholly irrelevant on any other theory. (*Perry v. Rochester Line Co.*, 219 N.Y. 60.) As was said by Mr. Justice HOLMES many years ago, "the measure of the defendant's duty in determining whether a wrong has been committed is one thing, the measure of liability when a wrong has been committed is another." (*Spade v. Lynn & Boston R.R. Co.*, 172 Mass. 488.) Due care is a duty imposed on each one of us to protect society from unnecessary danger, not to protect A, B or C alone.

It may well be that there is no such thing as negligence in the abstract. "Proof of negligence in the air, so to speak, will not do." In an empty world negligence would not exist. It does involve a relationship between man and his fellows. But not merely a relationship between man and those whom he might reasonably expect his act would injure. Rather, a relationship between him and those whom he does in fact injure. If his act has a tendency to harm some one, it harms him a mile away as surely as it does those on the scene. We now permit children to recover for the negligent killing of the father. It was never prevented on the theory that no duty was owing to them. A husband may be compensated for the loss of his wife's services. To say that the wrongdoer was negligent as to the husband as well as to the wife is merely an attempt to fit facts to theory. An insurance company paying a fire loss recovers its payment of the negligent incendiary. We speak of subrogation—of suing in the right of the insured. Behind the cloud of words is the fact they hide, that the act, wrongful as to the insured, has also injured the company. Even if it be true that the fault of father, wife or insured will prevent recovery, it is because we consider the original negligence not the proximate cause of the injury. (Pollock, *Torts* [12th ed.], 463.)

In the well-known *Polemis* case (1921, 3 K.B. 560), SCRUTTON, L.J., said that the dropping of a plank was negligent for it might injure "workman or cargo or ship." Because of either possibility the owner of the vessel was to be made good for his loss. The act being wrongful the doer was liable for its proximate results. Criticized and explained as this statement may have been, I think it states the law as it should be and as it is. (*Smith v. London & Southwestern Ry. Co.*, [1870-71] 6 C.P. 14; *Anthony v. Slaid*, 52 Mass. 290; *Wood v. Penn. R.R.Co.*, 177 Penn. St. 306; *Trashansky v. Hershkovitz*, 239 N.Y. 452.)

The proposition is this. Every one owes to the world at large the duty of refraining from those acts that may unreasonably threaten the safety of others. Such an act occurs. Not only is he wronged to whom harm might reasonably be expected to result, but he also who is in fact injured, even if he be outside what would generally be thought the danger zone. There needs be duty due the one complaining but this is not a duty to a particular individual because as to him harm might be expected. Harm to some one being the natural result of the act, not only that one alone, but all those in fact injured may complain. We have never, I think, held otherwise. Indeed in the Di Caprio case we said that a breach of a general ordinance defining the degree of care to be exercised in one's calling is evidence of negligence as to every one. We did not limit this statement to those who might be expected to be exposed to danger. Unreasonable risk being taken, its consequences are not confined to those who might probably be hurt.

If this be so, we do not have a plaintiff suing by "derivation or succession." Her action is original and primary. Her claim is for a breach of duty to herself—not that she is subrogated to any right of action of the owner of the parcel or of a passenger standing at the scene of the explosion.

The right to recover damages rests on additional considerations. The plaintiff's rights must be injured, and this injury must be caused by the negligence. We build a dam, but are negligent as to its foundations. Breaking, it injures property down stream. We are not liable if all this happened because of some reason other than the insecure foundation. But when injuries do result from our unlawful act we are liable for the consequences. It does not matter that they are unusual, unexpected, unforeseen and unforeseeable. But there is one limitation. The damages must be so connected with the negligence that the latter may be said to be the proximate cause of the former.

These two words have never been given an inclusive definition. What is a cause in a legal sense, still more what is a proximate cause, depend in each case upon many considerations, as does the existence of negligence itself. Any philosophical doctrine of causation does not help us. A boy throws a stone into a pond. The ripples spread. The water level rises. The history of that pond is altered to all eternity. It will be altered by other causes also. Yet it will be forever the resultant of all causes combined. Each one will have an influence. How great only omniscience can say. You may speak of a chain, or if you please, a net. An analogy is of little aid. Each cause brings about future events. Without each the future would not be the same. Each is proximate in the sense it is essential. But that is not what we mean by the word. Nor on the other hand do we mean sole cause. There is no such thing.

Should analogy be thought helpful, however, I prefer that of a stream. The spring, starting on its journey, is joined by tributary after tributary. The river, reaching the ocean, comes from a hundred sources. No man may say whence any drop of water is derived. Yet for a time distinction may be possible. Into the clear creek, brown swamp water flows from the left. Later, from the right comes water stained by its clay bed. The three may remain for a space, sharply divided. But at last, inevitably no trace of separation remains. They are so commingled that all distinction is lost.

As we have said, we cannot trace the effect of an act to the end, if end there is. Again, however, we may trace it part of the way. A murder at Sarajevo may be the necessary antecedent to an assassination in London twenty years hence. An overturned lantern may burn all Chicago. We may follow the fire from the shed to the last building. We rightly say the fire started by the lantern caused its destruction.

A cause, but not the proximate cause. What we do mean by the word "proximate" is, that because of convenience, of public policy, of a rough sense of justice, the law arbitrarily declines to trace a series of events beyond a certain point. This is not logic. It is practical politics. Take our rule as to fires. Sparks from my burning haystack set on fire my house and my neighbor's. I may recover from a negligent railroad. He may not. Yet the wrongful act as directly harmed the one as the other. We may regret that the line was drawn just where it was, but drawn somewhere it had to be. We said the act of the railroad was not the proximate cause of our neighbor's fire. Cause it surely was. The words we used were simply indicative of our notions of public policy. Other courts think differently. But somewhere they reach the point where they cannot say the stream comes from any one source.

Take the illustration given in an unpublished manuscript by a distinguished and helpful writer on the law of torts. A chauffeur negligently collides with another car which is filled with dynamite, although he could not know it. An explosion follows. A, walking on the sidewalk nearby, is killed. B, sitting in a window of a building opposite, is cut by flying glass. C, likewise sitting in a window a block away, is similarly injured. And a further illustration. A nursemaid, ten blocks away, startled by the noise, involuntarily drops a baby from her arms to the walk. We are told that C may not recover while A may. As to B it is a question for court or jury. We will all agree that the baby might not. Because, we are again told, the chauffeur had no reason to believe his conduct involved any risk of injuring either C or the baby. As to them he was not negligent.

But the chauffeur, being negligent in risking the collision, his belief that the scope of the harm he might do would be limited is immaterial. His act unreasonably jeopardized the safety of any one who might be affected by it. C's injury and that of the baby were directly traceable to the collision. Without that, the injury would not have happened. C had the right to sit in his office, secure from such dangers. The baby was entitled to use the sidewalk with reasonable safety.

The true theory is, it seems to me, that the injury to C, if in truth he is to be denied recovery, and the injury to the baby is that their several injuries were not the proximate result of the negligence. And here not what the chauffeur had reason to believe would be the result of his conduct, but what the prudent would foresee, may have a bearing. May have some bearing, for the problem of proximate cause is not to be solved by any one consideration.

It is all a question of expediency. There are no fixed rules to govern our judgment. There are simply matters of which we may take account. We have in a somewhat different connection spoken of "the stream of events." We have asked whether that stream was deflected—whether it was forced into new and unexpected channels. (*Donnelly v. Piercy Contracting Co.*, 222 N.Y. 210.) This is rather rhetoric than law. There is in truth little to guide us other than common sense.

There are some hints that may help us. The proximate cause, involved as it may be with many other causes, must be, at the least, something without which the event would not happen. The court must ask itself whether there was a natural and continuous sequence between cause and effect. Was the one a substantial factor in producing the other? Was there a direct connection between them, without too many intervening causes? Is the effect of cause on result not too attenuated? Is the cause likely, in the usual judgment of mankind, to produce the result? Or by the exercise of prudent foresight could the result be foreseen? Is the result too remote from the cause, and here we consider remoteness in time and space. (*Bird v. St. Paul F. & M. Ins. Co.*, 224 N.Y. 47, where we passed upon the construction of a contract—but something was also said on this subject.) Clearly we must so consider, for the greater the distance either in time or space, the more surely do other causes intervene to affect the result. When a lantern is overturned the firing of a shed is a fairly direct consequence. Many things contribute to the spread of the conflagration—the force of the wind, the direction and width of streets, the character of intervening structures, other factors. We draw an uncertain and wavering line, but draw it we must as best we can.

Once again, it is all a question of fair judgment, always keeping in mind the fact that we endeavor to make a rule in each case that will be practical and in keeping with the general understanding of mankind.

Here another question must be answered. In the case supposed it is said, and said correctly, that the chauffeur is liable for the direct effect of the explosion although he had no reason to suppose it would follow a collision. "The fact that the injury occurred in a different manner than that which might have been expected does not prevent the chauffeur's negligence from being in law the cause of the injury." But the natural results of a negligent act—the results which a prudent man would or should foresee—do have a bearing upon the decision as to proximate cause. We have said so repeatedly. What should be foreseen? No human foresight would suggest that a collision itself might injure one a block away. On the contrary, given an explosion, such a possibility might be reasonably expected. I think the direct connection, the foresight of which the courts peak, assumes prevision of the explosion, for the immediate results of which, at least, the chauffeur is responsible.

It may be said this is unjust. Why? In fairness he should make good every injury flowing from his negligence. Not because of tenderness toward him we say he need not answer for all that follows his wrong. We look back to the catastrophe, the fire kindled by the spark, or the explosion. We trace the consequences—not indefinitely, but to a certain point. And to aid us in fixing that point we ask what might ordinarily be expected to follow the fire or the explosion.

This last suggestion is the factor which must determine the case before us. The act upon which defendant's liability rests is knocking an apparently harmless package onto the platform. The act was negligent. For its proximate consequences the defendant is liable. If its contents were broken, to the owner; if it fell upon and crushed a passenger's foot, then to him. If it exploded and injured one in the immediate vicinity, to him also as to A in the illustration. Mrs. Palsgraf was standing some distance away. How far cannot be told from the record—apparently twenty-five or thirty feet. Perhaps less. Except for the explosion, she would not have been injured. We are told by the appellant in his brief "it cannot be denied that the explosion was the direct cause of the plaintiff's injuries." So it was a substantial factor in producing the result—there was here a natural and continuous sequence—direct connection. The only intervening cause was that instead of blowing her to the ground the concussion smashed the weighing machine which in turn fell upon her. There was no remoteness in time, little in space. And surely, given such an explosion as here it needed no great foresight to predict that the natural result would be to injure one on the platform at no greater distance from its scene than was the plaintiff. Just how no one might be able to predict. Whether by flying fragments, by broken glass, by wreckage of machines or structures no one could say. But injury in some form was most probable.

Under these circumstances I cannot say as a matter of law that the plaintiff's injuries were not the proximate result of the negligence. That is all we have before us. The court refused to so charge. No request was made to submit the matter to the jury as a question of fact, even would that have been proper upon the record before us.

The judgment appealed from should be affirmed, with costs.

National Federation of Paralegal Associations, Inc.

Model Code of Ethics and Professional Responsibility and Guidelines for Enforcement

PREAMBLE

The National Federation of Paralegal Associations, Inc.("NFPA") is a professional organization comprised of paralegal associations and individual paralegals throughout the United States and Canada. Members of NFPA have varying backgrounds, experiences, education, and job responsibilities that reflect the diversity of the paralegal profession. NFPA promotes the growth, development, and recognition of the paralegal profession as an integral partner in the delivery of legal services.

In May 1993 NFPA adopted its Model Code of Ethics and Professional Responsibility ("Model Code") to delineate the principles for ethics and conduct to which every paralegal should aspire.

Many paralegal associations throughout the United States have endorsed the concept and content of NFPA's Model Code through the adoption of their own ethical codes. In doing so, paralegals have confirmed the profession's commitment to increase the quality and efficiency of legal services, as well as recognized its responsibilities to the public, the legal community, and colleagues.

Paralegals have recognized, and will continue to recognize, that the profession must continue to evolve to enhance their roles in the delivery of legal services. With increased levels of responsibility comes the need to define and enforce mandatory rules of professional conduct. Enforcement of codes of paralegal conduct is a logical and necessary step to enhance and ensure the confidence of the legal community and the public in the integrity and professional responsibility of paralegals.

In April 1997 NFPA adopted the Model Disciplinary Rules ("Model Rules") to make possible the enforcement of the Canons and Ethical Considerations contained in the NFPA Model Code. A concurrent determination was made that the Model Code of Ethics and Professional Responsibility, formerly aspirational in nature, should be recognized as setting forth the enforceable obligations of all paralegals.

Reprinted by permission from The National Federation of Paralegal Associations, Inc., www.paralegals.org

The Model Code and Model Rules offer a framework for professional discipline, either voluntarily or through formal regulatory programs.

§1 NFPA Model Disciplinary Rules and Ethical Considerations

1.1 A Paralegal Shall Achieve and Maintain a High Level of Competence.

Ethical Considerations

EC-1.1 (a) A paralegal shall achieve competency through education, training, and work experience.

EC-1.1 (b) A paralegal shall aspire to participate in a minimum of twelve (12) hours of continuing legal education, to include at least one (1) hour of ethics education, every two (2) years in order to remain current on developments in the law.

EC-1.1 (c) A paralegal shall perform all assignments promptly and efficiently.

1.2 A Paralegal Shall Maintain a High Level of Personal and Professional Integrity.

Ethical Considerations

EC-1.2 (a) A paralegal shall not engage in any ex parte communications involving the courts or any other adjudicatory body in an attempt to exert undue influence or to obtain advantage or the benefit of only one party.

EC-1.2 (b) A paralegal shall not communicate, or cause another to communicate, with a party the paralegal knows to be represented by a lawyer in a pending matter without the prior consent of the lawyer representing such other party.

EC-1.2 (c) A paralegal shall ensure that all timekeeping and billing records prepared by the paralegal are thorough, accurate, honest, and complete.

EC-1.2 (d) A paralegal shall not knowingly engage in fraudulent billing practices. Such practices may include, but are not limited to: inflation of hours billed to a client or employer; misrepresentation of the nature of tasks performed; and/or submission of fraudulent expense and disbursement documentation.

EC-1.2 (e) A paralegal shall be scrupulous, thorough, and honest in the identification and maintenance of all funds, securities, and other assets of a client and shall provide accurate accounting as appropriate.

EC-1.2 (f) A paralegal shall advise the proper authority of non-confidential knowledge of any dishonest or fraudulent acts by any person pertaining to the handling of the funds, securities or other assets of a client. The authority to whom the report is made shall depend on the nature and circumstances of the possible misconduct, (e.g., ethics committees of law firms, corporations and/or paralegal associations, local or state bar associations, local prosecutors, administrative agencies, etc.). Failure to report such knowledge is in itself misconduct and shall be treated as such under these rules.

1.3 A Paralegal Shall Maintain a High Standard of Professional Conduct.

Ethical Considerations

EC-1.3 (a) A paralegal shall refrain from engaging in any conduct that offends the dignity and decorum of proceedings before a court or other adjudicatory body and shall be respectful of all rules and procedures.

EC-1.3 (b) A paralegal shall avoid impropriety and the appearance of impropriety and shall not engage in any conduct that would adversely affect his/her fitness to practice. Such conduct may include, but is not limited to: violence, dishonesty, interference with the administration of justice, and/or abuse of a professional position or public office.

EC-1.3 (c) Should a paralegal's fitness to practice be compromised by physical or mental illness, causing that paralegal to commit an act that is in direct violation of the Model Code/Model Rules and/or the rules and/or laws governing the jurisdiction in which the paralegal practices, that paralegal may be protected from sanction upon review of the nature and circumstances of that illness.

EC-1.3 (d) A paralegal shall advise the proper authority of non-confidential knowledge of any action of another legal professional that clearly demonstrates fraud, deceit, dishonesty, or misrepresentation. The authority to whom the report is made shall depend on the nature and circumstances of the possible misconduct (e.g., ethics committees of law firms, corporations and/or paralegal associations, local or state bar associations, local prosecutors, administrative agencies, etc.). Failure to report such knowledge is in itself misconduct and shall be treated as such under these rules.

EC-1.3 (e) A paralegal shall not knowingly assist any individual with the commission of an act that is in direct violation of the Model Code/Model Rules and/or the rules and/or laws governing the jurisdiction in which the paralegal practices.

EC-1.3 (f) If a paralegal possesses knowledge of future criminal activity, that knowledge must be reported to the appropriate authority immediately.

1.4 A Paralegal Shall Serve the Public Interest by Contributing to the Improvement of the Legal System and Delivery of Quality Legal Services, Including Pro Bono Publico Services.

Ethical Considerations

EC-1.4 (a) A paralegal shall be sensitive to the legal needs of the public and shall promote the development and implementation of programs that address those needs.

EC-1.4 (b) A paralegal shall support efforts to improve the legal system and access thereto and shall assist in making changes.

EC-1.4 (c) A paralegal shall support and participate in the delivery of Pro Bono Publico services directed toward implementing and improving access to justice, the law, the legal system or the paralegal and legal professions.

EC-1.4 (d) A paralegal should aspire annually to contribute twenty-four (24) hours of Pro Bono Publico services under the supervision of an attorney or as authorized by administrative, statutory or court authority to:

1. persons of limited means; or
2. charitable, religious, civic, community, governmental and educational organizations in matters that are designed primarily to address the legal needs of persons with limited means; or
3. individuals, groups or organizations seeking to secure or protect civil rights, civil liberties or public rights.

The twenty-four (24) hours of Pro Bono Publico services contributed annually by a paralegal may consist of such services as detailed in this EC-1.4(d), and/or administrative matters designed to develop and implement the attainment of this aspiration as detailed above in EC-1.4(a) or (c), or any combination of the two.

1.5 A Paralegal Shall Preserve all Confidential Information Provided by the Client or Acquired from Other Sources Before, During, and After the Course of the Professional Relationship.

Ethical Considerations

EC-1.5 (a)   A paralegal shall be aware of and abide by all legal authority governing confidential information in the jurisdiction in which the paralegal practices.

EC-1.5 (b)   A paralegal shall not use confidential information to the disadvantage of the client.

EC-1.5 (c)   A paralegal shall not use confidential information to the advantage of the paralegal or of a third person.

EC-1.5 (d)   A paralegal may reveal confidential information only after full disclosure and with the client's written consent; or, when required by law or court order; or, when necessary to prevent the client from committing an act that could result in death or serious bodily harm.

EC-1.5 (e)   A paralegal shall keep those individuals responsible for the legal representation of a client fully informed of any confidential information the paralegal may have pertaining to that client.

EC-1.5 (f)   A paralegal shall not engage in any indiscreet communications concerning clients.

1.6 A Paralegal Shall Avoid Conflicts of Interest and Shall Disclose any Possible Conflict to the Employer or Client, as Well as to the Prospective Employers or Clients.

Ethical Considerations

EC-1.6 (a)   A paralegal shall act within the bounds of the law, solely for the benefit of the client, and shall be free of compromising influences and loyalties. Neither the paralegal's personal or business interest, nor those of other clients or third persons, should compromise the paralegal's professional judgment and loyalty to the client.

EC-1.6 (b)   A paralegal shall avoid conflicts of interest that may arise from previous assignments, whether for a present or past employer or client.

EC-1.6 (c)   A paralegal shall avoid conflicts of interest that may arise from family relationships and from personal and business interests.

EC-1.6 (d)   In order to be able to determine whether an actual or potential conflict of interest exists, a paralegal shall create and maintain an effective record-keeping system that identifies clients, matters, and parties with which the paralegal has worked.

EC-1.6 (e)   A paralegal shall reveal sufficient non-confidential information about a client or former client to reasonably ascertain if an actual or potential conflict of interest exists.

EC-1.6 (f)   A paralegal shall not participate in or conduct work on any matter where a conflict of interest has been identified.

EC-1.6 (g)   In matters where a conflict of interest has been identified and the client consents to continued representation, a paralegal shall comply fully with the implementation and maintenance of an Ethical Wall.

1.7 A Paralegal's Title Shall be Fully Disclosed.

Ethical Considerations

EC-1.7 (a) A paralegal's title shall clearly indicate the individual's status and shall be disclosed in all business and professional communications to avoid misunderstandings and misconceptions about the paralegal's role and responsibilities.

EC-1.7 (b) A paralegal's title shall be included if the paralegal's name appears on business cards, letterhead, brochures, directories, and advertisements.

EC-1.7 (c) A paralegal shall not use letterhead, business cards or other promotional materials to create a fraudulent impression of his/her status or ability to practice in the jurisdiction in which the paralegal practices.

EC-1.7 (d) A paralegal shall not practice under color of any record, diploma, or certificate that has been illegally or fraudulently obtained or issued or which is misrepresentative in any way.

EC1.7 (e) A paralegal shall not participate in the creation, issuance, or dissemination of fraudulent records, diplomas, or certificates.

1.8 A Paralegal Shall Not Engage in the Unauthorized Practice of Law.

Ethical Considerations

EC-1.8 (a) A paralegal shall comply with the applicable legal authority governing the unauthorized practice of law in the jurisdiction in which the paralegal practices.

§2 NFPA Guidelines for the Enforcement of the Model Code of Ethics and Professional Responsibility

2.1 Basis for Discipline

2.1(a) Disciplinary investigations and proceedings brought under authority of the Rules shall be conducted in accord with obligations imposed on the paralegal professional by the Model Code of Ethics and Professional Responsibility.

2.2 Structure of Disciplinary Committee

2.2(a) The Disciplinary Committee ("Committee") shall be made up of nine (9) members including the Chair.

2.2(b) Each member of the Committee, including any temporary replacement members, shall have demonstrated working knowledge of ethics/professional responsibility-related issues and activities.

2.2(c) The Committee shall represent a cross-section of practice areas and work experience. The following recommendations are made regarding the members of the Committee.

1. At least one paralegal with one to three years of law-related work experience.
2. At least one paralegal with five to seven years of law related work experience.
3. At least one paralegal with over ten years of law related work experience.
4. One paralegal educator with five to seven years of work experience; preferably in the area of ethics/professional responsibility.

5. One paralegal manager.
6. One lawyer with five to seven years of law-related work experience.
7. One lay member.

2.2(d)   The Chair of the Committee shall be appointed within thirty (30) days of its members' induction. The Chair shall have no fewer than ten (10) years of law-related work experience.

2.2(e)   The terms of all members of the Committee shall be staggered. Of those members initially appointed, a simple majority plus one shall be appointed to a term of one year, and the remaining members shall be appointed to a term of two years. Thereafter, all members of the Committee shall be appointed to terms of two years.

2.2(f)   If for any reason the terms of a majority of the Committee will expire at the same time, members may be appointed to terms of one year to maintain continuity of the Committee.

2.2(g)   The Committee shall organize from its members a three-tiered structure to investigate, prosecute, and/or adjudicate charges of misconduct. The members shall be rotated among the tiers.

2.3 Operation of Committee

2.3(a)   The Committee shall meet on an as-needed basis to discuss, investigate, and/or adjudicate alleged violations of the Model Code/Model Rules.

2.3(b)   A majority of the members of the Committee present at a meeting shall constitute a quorum.

2.3(c)   A Recording Secretary shall be designated to maintain complete and accurate minutes of all Committee meetings. All such minutes shall be kept confidential until a decision has been made that the matter will be set for hearing as set forth in Section 6.1 below.

2.3(d)   If any member of the Committee has a conflict of interest with the Charging Party, the Responding Party, or the allegations of misconduct, that member shall not take part in any hearing or deliberations concerning those allegations. If the absence of that member creates a lack of a quorum for the Committee, then a temporary replacement for the member shall be appointed.

2.3(e)   Either the Charging Party or the Responding Party may request that, for good cause shown, any member of the Committee not participate in a hearing or deliberation. All such requests shall be honored. If the absence of a Committee member under those circumstances creates a lack of a quorum for the Committee, then a temporary replacement for that member shall be appointed.

2.3(f)   All discussions and correspondence of the Committee shall be kept confidential until a decision has been made that the matter will be set for hearing as set forth in Section 6.1 below.

2.3(g)   All correspondence from the Committee to the Responding Party regarding any charge of misconduct and any decisions made regarding the charge shall be mailed certified mail, return receipt requested, to the Responding Party's last known address and shall be clearly marked with a "Confidential" designation.

2.4 Procedure for the Reporting of Alleged Violations of the Model Code/Disciplinary Rules

2.4(a)   An individual or entity in possession of non-confidential knowledge or information concerning possible instances of misconduct shall make a confidential written report to the Committee within thirty (30) days of obtaining same. This report shall include all details of the alleged misconduct.

2.4(b)   The Committee so notified shall inform the Responding Party of the allegation(s) of misconduct no later than ten (10) business days after receiving the confidential written report from the Charging Party.

2.4(c)   Notification to the Responding Party shall include the identity of the Charging Party, unless, for good cause shown, the Charging Party requests anonymity.

2.4(d)   The Responding Party shall reply to the allegations within ten (10) business days of notification.

2.5 Procedure for the Investigation of a Charge of Misconduct

2.5(a)   Upon receipt of a Charge of Misconduct ("Charge"), or on its own initiative, the Committee shall initiate an investigation.

2.5(b)   If, upon initial or preliminary review, the Committee makes a determination that the charges are either without basis in fact or, if proven, would not constitute professional misconduct, the Committee shall dismiss the allegations of misconduct. If such determination of dismissal cannot be made, a formal investigation shall be initiated.

2.5(c)   Upon the decision to conduct a formal investigation, the Committee shall:
1. mail to the Charging and Responding Parties within three (3) business days of that decision notice of the commencement of a formal investigation. That notification shall be in writing and shall contain a complete explanation of all Charge(s), as well as the reasons for a formal investigation and shall cite the applicable codes and rules;
2. allow the Responding Party thirty (30) days to prepare and submit a confidential response to the Committee, which response shall address each charge specifically and shall be in writing; and
3. upon receipt of the response to the notification, have thirty (30) days to investigate the Charge(s). If an extension of time is deemed necessary, that extension shall not exceed ninety (90) days.

2.5(d)   Upon conclusion of the investigation, the Committee may:
1. dismiss the Charge upon the finding that it has no basis in fact;
2. dismiss the Charge upon the finding that, if proven, the Charge would not constitute Misconduct;
3. refer the matter for hearing by the Tribunal; or
4. in the case of criminal activity, refer the Charge(s) and all investigation results to the appropriate authority.

2.6 Procedure for a Misconduct Hearing Before a Tribunal

2.6(a)   Upon the decision by the Committee that a matter should be heard, all parties shall be notified and a hearing date shall be set. The hearing shall take place no more than thirty (30) days from the conclusion of the formal investigation.

2.6(b)   The Responding Party shall have the right to counsel. The parties and the Tribunal shall have the right to call any witnesses and introduce any documentation that they believe will lead to the fair and reasonable resolution of the matter.

2.6(c)   Upon completion of the hearing, the Tribunal shall deliberate and present a written decision to the parties in accordance with procedures as set forth by the Tribunal.

2.6(d)   Notice of the decision of the Tribunal shall be appropriately published.

2.7 Sanctions

2.7(a)   Upon a finding of the Tribunal that misconduct has occurred, any of the following sanctions, or others as may be deemed appropriate, may be imposed upon the Responding Party, either singularly or in combination:
1. letter of reprimand to the Responding Party; counseling;
2. attendance at an ethics course approved by the Tribunal; probation;
3. suspension of license/authority to practice; revocation of license/authority to practice;
4. imposition of a fine; assessment of costs; or
5. in the instance of criminal activity, referral to the appropriate authority.

2.7(b)   Upon the expiration of any period of probation, suspension, or revocation, the Responding Party may make application for reinstatement. With the application for reinstatement, the Responding Party must show proof of having complied with all aspects of the sanctions imposed by the Tribunal.

2.8 Appellate Procedures

2.8(a)   The parties shall have the right to appeal the decision of the Tribunal in accordance with the procedure as set forth by the Tribunal.

DEFINITIONS

"Appellate Body" means a body established to adjudicate an appeal to any decision made by a Tribunal or other decision-making body with respect to formally-heard Charges of Misconduct.

"Charge of Misconduct" means a written submission by any individual or entity to an ethics committee, paralegal association, bar association, law enforcement agency, judicial body, government agency, or other appropriate body or entity, that sets forth non-confidential information regarding any instance of alleged misconduct by an individual paralegal or paralegal entity.

"Charging Party" means any individual or entity who submits a Charge of Misconduct against an individual paralegal or paralegal entity.

"Competency" means the demonstration of: diligence, education, skill, and mental, emotional, and physical fitness reasonably necessary for the performance of paralegal services.

"Confidential Information" means information relating to a client, whatever its source, that is not public knowledge nor available to the public.("Non-Confidential Information" would generally include the name of the client and the identity of the matter for which the paralegal provided services.)

"Disciplinary Hearing" means the confidential proceeding conducted by a committee or other designated body or entity concerning any instance of alleged misconduct by an individual paralegal or paralegal entity.

"Disciplinary Committee" means any committee that has been established by an entity such as a paralegal association, bar association, judicial body, or government agency to: (a) identify, define, and investigate general ethical considerations and concerns with respect to paralegal practice; (b) administer and enforce the Model Code and Model Rules and; (c) discipline any individual paralegal or paralegal entity found to be in violation of same.

"Disclose" means communication of information reasonably sufficient to permit identification of the significance of the matter in question.

"Ethical Wall" means the screening method implemented in order to protect a client from a conflict of interest. An Ethical Wall generally includes, but is not limited to, the following elements: (1) prohibit the paralegal from having any connection with the matter; (2) ban discussions with or the transfer of documents to or from the paralegal; (3) restrict access to files; and (4) educate all members of the firm, corporation, or entity as to the separation of the paralegal (both organizationally and physically) from the pending matter. For more information regarding the Ethical Wall, see the NFPA publication entitled "The Ethical Wall—Its Application to Paralegals."

"Ex parte" means actions or communications conducted at the instance and for the benefit of one party only, and without notice to, or contestation by, any person adversely interested.

"Investigation" means the investigation of any charge(s) of misconduct filed against an individual paralegal or paralegal entity by a Committee.

"Letter of Reprimand" means a written notice of formal censure or severe reproof administered to an individual paralegal or paralegal entity for unethical or improper conduct.

"Misconduct" means the knowing or unknowing commission of an act that is in direct violation of those Canons and Ethical Considerations of any and all applicable codes and/or rules of conduct.

"Paralegal" is synonymous with "Legal Assistant" and is defined as a person qualified through education, training, or work experience to perform substantive legal work that requires knowledge of legal concepts and is customarily, but not exclusively, performed by a lawyer. This person may be retained or employed by a lawyer, law office, governmental agency, or other entity or may be authorized by administrative, statutory, or court authority to perform this work.

"Pro Bono Publico" means providing or assisting to provide quality legal services in order to enhance access to justice for persons of limited means; charitable, religious, civic, community, governmental, and educational organizations in matters that are designed primarily to address the legal needs of persons with limited means; or individuals, groups or organizations seeking to secure or protect civil rights, civil liberties or public rights.

"Proper Authority" means the local paralegal association, the local or state bar association, Committee(s) of the local paralegal or bar association(s), local prosecutor, administrative agency, or other tribunal empowered to investigate or act upon an instance of alleged misconduct.

"Responding Party" means an individual paralegal or paralegal entity against whom a Charge of Misconduct has been submitted.

"Revocation" means the recision of the license, certificate or other authority to practice of an individual paralegal or paralegal entity found in violation of those Canons and Ethical Considerations of any and all applicable codes and/or rules of conduct.

"Suspension" means the suspension of the license, certificate or other authority to practice of an individual paralegal or paralegal entity found in violation of those Canons and Ethical Considerations of any and all applicable codes and/or rules of conduct.

"Tribunal" means the body designated to adjudicate allegations of misconduct.

Model Standards and Guidelines for Utilization of Legal Assistants— Paralegals

Table of Contents:

INTRODUCTION

The purpose of this annotated version of the National Association of Legal Assistants, Inc. Model Standards and Guidelines for the Utilization of Legal Assistants (the "Model," "Standards" and/or the "Guidelines") is to provide references to the existing case law and other authorities where the underlying issues have been considered. The authorities cited will serve as a basis upon which conduct of a legal assistant may be analyzed as proper or improper.

The Guidelines represent a statement of how the legal assistant may function. The Guidelines are not intended to be a comprehensive or exhaustive list of the proper duties of a legal assistant. Rather, they are designed as guides to what may or may not be proper conduct for the legal assistant. In formulating the Guidelines, the reasoning and rules of law in many reported decisions of disciplinary cases and unauthorized practice of law cases have been analyzed and considered. In addition, the provisions of the American Bar Association's Model Rules of Professional Conduct, as well as the ethical promulgations of various state courts and bar associations, have been considered in the development of the Guidelines.

These Guidelines form a sound basis for the legal assistant and the supervising attorney to follow. This Model will serve as a comprehensive resource document and as a definitive, well-reasoned guide to those considering voluntary standards and guidelines for legal assistants.

I
PREAMBLE

Proper utilization of the services of legal assistants contributes to the delivery of cost-effective, high-quality legal services. Legal assistants and the legal profession should be assured that measures exist for identifying legal assistants and their role in assisting attorneys in the delivery of legal services. Therefore, the National Association of Legal Assistants, Inc., hereby adopts these Standards and Guidelines as an educational document for the benefit of legal assistants and the legal profession.

Comment

The three most frequently raised questions concerning legal assistants are (1) How do you define a legal assistant; (2) Who is qualified to be identified as a legal assistant; and (3) What duties may a legal assistant perform? The definition adopted in 1984 by the National Association of Legal Assistants answers the first question. The Model sets forth minimum education, training, and experience through standards which will assure that an individual utilizing the title "legal assistant" or "paralegal" has the qualifications to be held out to the legal community and the public in that capacity. The Guidelines identify those acts which the reported cases hold to be proscribed and give examples of services which the legal assistant may perform under the supervision of a licensed attorney.

These Guidelines constitute a statement relating to services performed by legal assistants, as defined herein, as approved by court decisions and other sources of authority. The purpose of the Guidelines is not to place limitations or restrictions on the legal assistant profession. Rather, the Guidelines are intended to outline for the legal profession an acceptable course of conduct. Voluntary recognition and utilization of the Standards and Guidelines will benefit the entire legal profession and the public it serves.

II
DEFINITION

The National Association of Legal Assistants adopted the following definition in 1984:

> Legal assistants, also known as paralegals, are a distinguishable group of persons who assist attorneys in the delivery of legal services. Through formal education, training, and experience, legal assistants have knowledge and expertise regarding the legal system and substantive and procedural law which qualify them to do work of a legal nature under the supervision of an attorney.

In recognition of the similarity of the definitions and the need for one clear definition, in July 2001, the NALA membership approved a resolution to adopt the definition of the American Bar Association as well. The ABA definition reads as follows:

> A legal assistant or paralegal is a person qualified by education, training or work experience who is employed or retained by a lawyer, law office, corporation, governmental agency or other entity who performs specifically delegated substantive legal work for which a lawyer is responsible. (Adopted by the ABA in 1997)

Comment

These definitions emphasize the knowledge and expertise of legal assistants in substantive and procedural law obtained through education and work experience. They further define the legal assistant or paralegal as a professional working under the supervision of an attorney as distinguished from a non-lawyer who delivers services directly to the public without any intervention or review of work product by an attorney. Such unsupervised services, unless authorized by court or agency rules, constitute the unauthorized practice of law.

Statutes, court rules, case law, and bar association documents are additional sources for legal assistant or paralegal definitions. In applying the Standards and Guidelines, it is important to remember that they were developed to apply to the legal assistant as defined herein. Lawyers should refrain from labeling those as paralegals or legal assistants who do not meet the criteria set forth in these definitions and/or the definitions set forth by state rules, guidelines or bar associations. Labeling secretaries and other administrative staff as legal assistants/paralegals is inaccurate.

For billing purposes, the services of a legal secretary are considered part of overhead costs and are not recoverable in fee awards. However, the courts have held that fees for paralegal services are recoverable as long as they are not clerical functions, such as organizing files, copying documents, checking docket, updating files, checking court dates, and delivering papers. As established in *Missouri v. Jenkins*, 491 U.S.274, 109 S.Ct. 2463, 2471, n.10 (1989) tasks performed by legal assistants must be substantive in nature which, absent the legal assistant, the attorney would perform.

There are also case law and Supreme Court Rules addressing the issue of a disbarred attorney serving in the capacity of a legal assistant.

III
STANDARDS

A legal assistant should meet certain minimum qualifications. The following standards may be used to determine an individual's qualifications as a legal assistant:

1. Successful completion of the Certified Legal Assistant (CLA)/Certified Paralegal (CP) certifying examination of the National Association of Legal Assistants, Inc.;
2. Graduation from an ABA approved program of study for legal assistants;
3. Graduation from a course of study for legal assistants which is institutionally accredited but not ABA approved, and which requires not less than the equivalent of 60 semester hours of classroom study;
4. Graduation from a course of study for legal assistants, other than those set forth in (2) and (3) above, plus not less than six months of in-house training as a legal assistant;
5. A baccalaureate degree in any field, plus not less than six months in-house training as a legal assistant;
6. A minimum of three years of law-related experience under the supervision of an attorney, including at least six months of in-house training as a legal assistant; or
7. Two years of in-house training as a legal assistant.

For purposes of these Standards, "in-house training as a legal assistant" means attorney education of the employee concerning legal assistant duties and these Guidelines. In addition to review and analysis of assignments, the legal assistant should receive a reasonable amount of instruction directly related to the duties and obligations of the legal assistant.

Comment

The Standards set forth suggest minimum qualifications for a legal assistant. These minimum qualifications, as adopted, recognize legal related work backgrounds and formal education backgrounds, both of which provide the legal assistant with a broad base in exposure to and knowledge of the legal profession. This background is necessary to assure the public and the legal profession that the employee identified as a legal assistant is qualified.

The Certified Legal Assistant (CLA) /Certified Paralegal (CP) examination established by NALA in 1976 is a voluntary nationwide certification program for legal assistants. (*CLA and CP are federally registered certification marks owned by NALA.*) The CLA/CP designation is a statement to the legal profession and the public that the legal assistant has met the high levels of knowledge and professionalism required by NALA's certification program. Continuing education requirements, which all certified legal assistants must meet, assure that high standards are maintained. The CLA/CP designation has been recognized as a means of establishing the qualifications of a legal assistant in supreme court rules, state court and bar association standards, and utilization guidelines.

Certification through NALA is available to all legal assistants meeting the educational and experience requirements. Certified Legal Assistants may also pursue advanced certification in specialty practice areas through the APC, Advanced Paralegal Certification, credentialing program. Legal assistants/paralegals may also pursue certification based on state laws and procedures in California, Florida, Louisiana, and Texas.

IV
GUIDELINES

These Guidelines relating to standards of performance and professional responsibility are intended to aid legal assistants and attorneys. The ultimate responsibility rests with an attorney who employs legal assistants to educate them with respect to the duties they are assigned and to supervise the manner in which such duties are accomplished.

Comment

In general, a legal assistant is allowed to perform any task which is properly delegated and supervised by an attorney, as long as the attorney is ultimately responsible to the client and assumes complete professional responsibility for the work product.

ABA Model Rules of Professional Conduct, Rule 5.3 provides:

With respect to a non-lawyer employed or retained by or associated with a lawyer:

a. a partner in a law firm shall make reasonable efforts to ensure that the firm has in effect measures giving reasonable assurance that the person's conduct is compatible with the professional obligations of the lawyer;
b. a lawyer having direct supervisory authority over the non-lawyer shall make reasonable efforts to ensure that the person's conduct is compatible with the professional obligations of the lawyer; and
c. a lawyer shall be responsible for conduct of such a person that would be a violation of the rules of professional conduct if engaged in by a lawyer if:
   1. the lawyer orders or, with the knowledge of the specific conduct ratifies the conduct involved; or
   2. the lawyer is a partner in the law firm in which the person is employed, or has direct supervisory authority over the person, and knows of the conduct at a time when its consequences can be avoided or mitigated but fails to take remedial action.

There are many interesting and complex issues involving the use of legal assistants. In any discussion of the proper role of a legal assistant, attention must be directed to what constitutes the practice of law. Proper delegation to legal assistants is further complicated and confused by the lack of an adequate definition of the practice of law.

Kentucky became the first state to adopt a Paralegal Code by Supreme Court Rule. This Code sets forth certain exclusions to the unauthorized practice of law:

> For purposes of this rule, the unauthorized practice of law shall not include any service rendered involving legal knowledge or advice, whether representation, counsel or advocacy, in or out of court, rendered in respect to the acts, duties, obligations, liabilities or business relations of the one requiring services where:
> a. The client understands that the paralegal is not a lawyer;
> b. The lawyer supervises the paralegal in the performance of his or her duties; and
> c. The lawyer remains fully responsible for such representation including all actions taken or not taken in connection therewith by the paralegal to the same extent as if such representation had been furnished entirely by the lawyer and all such actions had been taken or not taken directly by the attorney. Paralegal Code, Ky.S.Ct.R3.700, Sub-Rule 2.

South Dakota Supreme Court Rule 97-25 Utilization Rule a(4) states:

> The attorney remains responsible for the services performed by the legal assistant to the same extent as though such services had been furnished entirely by the attorney and such actions were those of the attorney.

GUIDELINE 1

Legal assistants should:

1. Disclose their status as legal assistants at the outset of any professional relationship with a client, other attorneys, a court or administrative agency or personnel thereof, or members of the general public;
2. Preserve the confidences and secrets of all clients; and
3. Understand the attorney's Rules of Professional Responsibility and these Guidelines in order to avoid any action which would involve the attorney in a violation of the Rules, or give the appearance of professional impropriety.

Comment

Routine early disclosure of the paralegal's status when dealing with persons outside the attorney's office is necessary to assure that there will be no misunderstanding as to the responsibilities and role of the legal assistant. Disclosure may be made in any way that avoids confusion. If the person dealing with the legal assistant already knows of his/her status, further disclosure is unnecessary. If at any time in written or oral communication the legal assistant becomes aware that the other person may believe the legal assistant is an attorney, immediate disclosure should be made as to the legal assistant's status.

The attorney should exercise care that the legal assistant preserves and refrains from using any confidence or secrets of a client, and should instruct the legal assistant not to disclose or use any such confidences or secrets.

The legal assistant must take any and all steps necessary to prevent conflicts of interest and fully disclose such conflicts to the supervising attorney. Failure to do so may jeopardize both the attorney's representation of the client and the case itself.

Guidelines for the Utilization of Legal Assistant Services adopted December 3, 1994 by the Washington State Bar Association Board of Governors states:

> Guideline 7: A lawyer shall take reasonable measures to prevent conflicts of interest resulting from a legal assistant's other employment or interest insofar as such other employment or interests would present a conflict of interest if it were that of the lawyer.

In Re Complex Asbestos Litigation, 232 Cal. App. 3d 572 (Cal. 1991), addresses the issue wherein a law firm was disqualified due to possession of attorney-client confidences by a legal assistant employee resulting from previous employment by opposing counsel.

In Oklahoma, in an order issued July 12, 2001, in the matter of *Mark A. Hayes, M.D. v. Central States Orthopedic Specialists, Inc.*, a Tulsa County District Court Judge disqualified a law firm from representation of a client on the basis that an ethical screen was an impermissible device to protect from disclosure confidences gained by a non-lawyer employee while employed by another law firm. In applying the same rules that govern attorneys, the court found that the Rules of Professional Conduct pertaining to confidentiality apply to nonlawyers who leave firms with actual knowledge of material, confidential information, and a screening device is not an appropriate alternative to the imputed disqualification of an incoming legal assistant who has moved from one firm to another during ongoing litigation and has actual knowledge of material, confidential information. The decision was appealed and the Oklahoma Supreme Court determined that, under certain circumstances, screening is an appropriate management tool for non-lawyer staff.

In 2004 the Nevada Supreme Court also addressed this issue at the urging of the state's paralegals. The Nevada Supreme Court granted a petition to rescind the Court's 1997 ruling in *Ciaffone v. District Court.* In this case, the court clarified the original ruling, stating "mere opportunity to access confidential information does not merit disqualification." The opinion stated instances in which screening may be appropriate, and listed minimum screening requirements. The opinion also set forth guidelines that a district court may use to determine if screening has been or may be effective. These considerations are:

1. substantiality of the relationship between the former and current matters
2. the time elapsed between the matters
3. size of the firm
4. number of individuals presumed to have confidential information
5. nature of their involvement in the former matter
6. timing and features of any measures taken to reduce the danger of disclosure
7. whether the old firm and the new firm represent adverse parties in the same proceeding rather than in different proceedings.

The ultimate responsibility for compliance with approved standards of professional conduct rests with the supervising attorney. The burden rests upon the attorney who employs a legal assistant to educate the latter with respect to the duties which may be assigned and then to supervise the manner in which the legal assistant carries out such duties. However, this does not relieve the legal assistant from an independent obligation to refrain from illegal conduct. Additionally, and notwithstanding that the Rules are not binding upon non-lawyers, the very nature of a legal assistant's employment imposes an obligation not to engage in conduct which would involve the supervising attorney in a violation of the Rules.

The attorney must make sufficient background investigation of the prior activities and character and integrity of his or her legal assistants.

Further, the attorney must take all measures necessary to avoid and fully disclose conflicts of interest due to other employment or interests. Failure to do so may jeopardize both the attorney's representation of the client and the case itself.

Legal assistant associations strive to maintain the high level of integrity and competence expected of the legal profession and, further, strive to uphold the high standards of ethics.

NALA's Code of Ethics and Professional Responsibility states "A legal assistant's conduct is guided by bar associations' codes of professional responsibility and rules of professional conduct."

GUIDELINE 2

Legal assistants should not:

1. Establish attorney-client relationships; set legal fees; give legal opinions or advice; or represent a client before a court, unless authorized to do so by said court; nor
2. Engage in, encourage, or contribute to any act which could constitute the unauthorized practice of law.

Comment

Case law, court rules, codes of ethics and professional responsibilities, as well as bar ethics opinions now hold which acts can and cannot be performed by a legal assistant. Generally, the determination of what acts constitute the unauthorized practice of law is made by state supreme courts.

Numerous cases exist relating to the unauthorized practice of law. Courts have gone so far as to prohibit the legal assistant from preparation of divorce kits and assisting in preparation of bankruptcy forms and, more specifically, from providing basic information about procedures and requirements, deciding where information should be placed on forms, and responding to questions from debtors regarding the interpretation or definition of terms.

Cases have identified certain areas in which an attorney has a duty to act, but it is interesting to note that none of these cases state that it is improper for an attorney to have the initial work performed by the legal assistant. This again points out the importance of adequate supervision by the employing attorney.

An attorney can be found to have aided in the unauthorized practice of law when delegating acts which cannot be performed by a legal assistant.

GUIDELINE 3

Legal assistants may perform services for an attorney in the representation of a client, provided:

1. The services performed by the legal assistant do not require the exercise of independent professional legal judgment;
2. The attorney maintains a direct relationship with the client and maintains control of all client matters;
3. The attorney supervises the legal assistant;
4. The attorney remains professionally responsible for all work on behalf of the client, including any actions taken or not taken by the legal assistant in connection therewith; and
5. The services performed supplement, merge with, and become the attorney's work product.

Comment

Paralegals, whether employees or independent contractors, perform services for the attorney in the representation of a client. Attorneys should delegate work to legal assistants commensurate with their knowledge and experience and provide appropriate instruction and supervision concerning the delegated work, as well as ethical acts of their employment. Ultimate responsibility for the work product of a legal assistant rests with the attorney. However, a legal assistant must use discretion and professional judgment and must not render independent legal judgment in place of an attorney.

The work product of a legal assistant is subject to civil rules governing discovery of materials prepared in anticipation of litigation, whether the legal assistant is viewed as an extension of the attorney or as another representative of the party itself. Fed.R.Civ.P. 26 (b) (3) and (5).

GUIDELINE 4

In the supervision of a legal assistant, consideration should be given to

1. Designating work assignments that correspond to the legal assistant's abilities, knowledge, training, and experience;
2. Educating and training the legal assistant with respect to professional responsibility, local rules and practices, and firm policies;
3. Monitoring the work and professional conduct of the legal assistant to ensure that the work is substantively correct and timely performed;
4. Providing continuing education for the legal assistant in substantive matters through courses, institutes, workshops, seminars and in-house training; and
5. Encouraging and supporting membership and active participation in professional organizations.

Comment

Attorneys are responsible for the actions of their employees in both malpractice and disciplinary proceedings. In the vast majority of cases, the courts have not censured attorneys for a particular act delegated to the legal assistant, but rather, have been critical of and imposed sanctions against attorneys for failure to adequately supervise the legal assistant. The attorney's responsibility for supervision of his or her legal assistant must be more than a willingness to accept responsibility and liability for the legal assistant's work. Supervision of a legal assistant must be offered in both the procedural and substantive legal areas. The attorney must delegate work based upon the education, knowledge, and abilities of the legal assistant and must monitor the work product and conduct of the legal assistant to insure that the work performed is substantively correct and competently performed in a professional manner.

Michigan State Board of Commissioners has adopted Guidelines for the Utilization of Legal Assistants (April 23, 1993). These guidelines, in part, encourage employers to support legal assistant participation in continuing education programs to ensure that the legal assistant remains competent in the fields of practice in which the legal assistant is assigned.

The working relationship between the lawyer and the legal assistant should extend to cooperative efforts on public service activities wherever possible. Participation in pro bono activities is encouraged in ABA Guideline 10.

GUIDELINE 5

Except as otherwise provided by statute, court rule or decision, administrative rule or regulation, or the attorney's rules of professional responsibility, and within the preceding parameters and proscriptions, a legal assistant may perform any function delegated by an attorney, including, but not limited to the following:

1. Conduct client interviews and maintain general contact with the client after the establishment of the attorney-client relationship, so long as the client is aware of the

status and function of the legal assistant, and the client contact is under the supervision of the attorney.
2. Locate and interview witnesses, so long as the witnesses are aware of the status and function of the legal assistant.
3. Conduct investigations and statistical and documentary research for review by the attorney.
4. Conduct legal research for review by the attorney.
5. Draft legal documents for review by the attorney.
6. Draft correspondence and pleadings for review by and signature of the attorney.
7. Summarize depositions, interrogatories and testimony for review by the attorney.
8. Attend executions of wills, real estate closings, depositions, court or administrative hearings and trials with the attorney.
9. Author and sign letters providing the legal assistant's status is clearly indicated and the correspondence does not contain independent legal opinions or legal advice.

Comment

The United States Supreme Court has recognized the variety of tasks being performed by legal assistants and has noted that use of legal assistants encourages cost-effective delivery of legal services, *Missouri v. Jenkins*, 491 U.S.274, 109 S.Ct. 2463, 2471, n.10 (1989). In *Jenkins*, the court further held that legal assistant time should be included in compensation for attorney fee awards at the market rate of the relevant community to bill legal assistant time.

Courts have held that legal assistant fees are not a part of the overall overhead of a law firm. Legal assistant services are billed separately by attorneys, and decrease litigation expenses. Tasks performed by legal assistants must contain substantive legal work under the direction or supervision of an attorney, such that if the legal assistant were not present, the work would be performed by the attorney.

In *Taylor v. Chubb*, 874 P.2d 806 (Okla. 1994), the Court ruled that attorney fees awarded should include fees for services performed by legal assistants and, further, defined tasks which may be performed by the legal assistant under the supervision of an attorney including, among others: interview clients, draft pleadings and other documents; carry on legal research, both conventional and computer aided; research public records; prepare discovery requests and responses; schedule depositions and prepare notices and subpoenas; summarize depositions and other discovery responses; coordinate and manage document production; locate and interview witnesses; organize pleadings, trial exhibits and other documents; prepare witness and exhibit lists; prepare trial notebooks; prepare for the attendance of witnesses at trial; and assist lawyers at trials.

Except for the specific proscription contained in Guideline 1, the reported cases do not limit the duties which may be performed by a legal assistant under the supervision of the attorney.

An attorney may not split legal fees with a legal assistant, nor pay a legal assistant for the referral of legal business. An attorney may compensate a legal assistant based on the quantity and quality of the legal assistant's work and value of that work to a law practice.

CONCLUSION

These Standards and Guidelines were developed from generally accepted practices. Each supervising attorney must be aware of the specific rules, decisions, and statutes applicable to legal assistants within his/her jurisdiction.

ADDENDUM

For further information, the following cases may be helpful to you:

Duties

Taylor v. Chubb, 874 P.2d 806 (Okla. 1994)

McMackin v. McMackin, 651 A.2d 778 (Del.Fam Ct 1993)

Work Product

Fine v. Facet Aerospace Products Co., 133 F.R.D. 439 (S.D.N.Y. 1990)

Unauthorized Practice of Law

Akron Bar Assn. v. Green, 673 N.E.2d 1307 (Ohio 1997)

In Re Hessinger & Associates, 192 B.R. 211 (N.D. Calif. 1996)

In the Matter of Bright, 171 B.R. 799 (Bkrtcy. E.D. Mich)

Louisiana State Bar Assn v. Edwins, 540 So.2d 294 (La. 1989)

Attorney/Client Privilege

In Re Complex Asbestos Litigation, 232 Cal. App. 3d 572 (Calif. 1991)

Makita Corp. v. U.S., 819 F.Supp. 1099 (CIT 1993)

Conflicts

In Re Complex Asbestos Litigation, 232 Cal. App. 3d 572 (Calif. 1991)

Makita Corp. v. U.S., 819 F.Supp. 1099 (CIT 1993)

Phoenix Founders, Inc., v. Marshall, 887 S.W.2d 831 (Tex. 1994)

Smart Industries v. Superior Court, 876 P.2d 1176 (Ariz. App. Div.1 1994)

Supervision

Matter of Martinez, 754 P.2d 842 (N.M. 1988)

State v. Barrett, 483 P.2d 1106 (Kan. 1971)

Hayes v. Central States Orthopedic Specialists, Inc., 2002 OK 30, 51 P.3d 562

Liebowitz v. Eighth Judicial District Court of Nevada Nev Sup Ct., No 39683, November 3, 2003 clarified in part and overrules in part *Ciaffone v. District Court*, 113 Nev 1165, 945. P2d 950 (1997)

Fee Awards

In Re Bicoastal Corp., 121 B.R. 653 (Bktrcy.M.D.Fla. 1990)

In Re Carter, 101 B.R. 170 (Bkrtcy.D.S.D. 1989)

Taylor v. Chubb, 874 P.2d 806 (Okla.1994)

Missouri v. Jenkins, 491 U.S. 274, 109 S.Ct. 2463, 105 L.Ed.2d 229 (1989) 11 U.S.C.A.§ 330

McMackin v. McMackin, Del.Fam.Ct. 651 A.2d 778 (1993)

Miller v. Alamo, 983 F.2d 856 (8th Cir. 1993)

Stewart v. Sullivan, 810 F.Supp. 1102 (D.Hawaii 1993)

In Re Yankton College, 101 B.R. 151 (Bkrtcy. D.S.D. 1989)

Stacey v. Stroud, 845 F.Supp. 1135 (S.D.W.Va. 1993)

Court Appearances

Louisiana State Bar Assn v. Edwins, 540 So.2d 294 (La. 1989)

In addition to the above referenced cases, you may contact your state bar association for information regarding guidelines for the utilization of legal assistants that may have been adopted by the bar, or ethical opinions concerning the utilization of legal assistants. The following states have adopted a definition of "legal assistant" or "paralegal" either through bar association guidelines, ethical opinions, legislation or case law:

Legislation

California
Florida
Illinois
Indiana
Maine
Pennsylvania

Supreme Court Cases or Rules

Kentucky
New Hampshire
New Mexico
North Dakota
Rhode Island
South Dakota
Virginia

Cases

Arizona
New Jersey
Oklahoma

Cases (Cont.)

South Carolina
Washington

Guidelines

Colorado
Connecticut
Georgia
Idaho
New York
Oregon
Utah
Wisconsin

Bar Association Activity

Alaska
Arizona
Colorado
Connecticut
Florida
Illinois

Bar Association Activity (Cont.)

Iowa
Kansas
Kentucky
Massachusetts
Michigan
Minnesota
Missouri
Nevada
New Mexico
New Hampshire
North Carolina
North Dakota
Ohio
Oregon
Rhode Island
South Carolina
South Dakota
Tennessee
Texas
Virginia
Wisconsin

Federal Court Name Abbreviations

Court	Abbrev.
United States Supreme Court	U.S.

UNITED STATES COURTS OF APPEALS

First Circuit	1st Cir.
Second Circuit	2d Cir.
Third Circuit	3d Cir.
Fourth Circuit	4th Cir.
Fifth Circuit	5th Cir.
Sixth Circuit	6th Cir.
Seventh Circuit	7th Cir.
Eighth Circuit	8th Cir.
Ninth Circuit	9th Cir.
Tenth Circuit	10th Cir.
Eleventh Circuit	11th Cir.
D.C. Circuit	D.C. Cir.
Federal Circuit	Fed. Cir.

UNITED STATES DISTRICT COURTS

Middle District of Alabama	**M.D. Ala.**
Northern District of Alabama	**N.D. Ala.**
Southern District of Alabama	**S.D. Ala.**
District of Alaska	**D. Alaska**
District of Arizona	**D. Ariz.**
Eastern District of Arkansas	**E.D. Ark.**
Western District of Arkansas	**W.D. Ark.**
Central District of California	**C.D. Cal.**
Eastern District of California	**E.D. Cal.**

(Note: The D.C.Z. ceased to exist on March 31, 1982.)

Reprinted with permission of Aspen Publishers, from ALWD Citation Manual: A Professional System of Citation.

Court	Abbrev.
Northern District of California	**N.D. Cal.**
Southern District of California	**S.D. Cal.**
District of the Canal Zone	**D.C.Z.**
District of Colorado	**D. Colo.**
District of Connecticut	**D. Conn.**
District of Delaware	**D. Del.**
District of D.C.	**D.D.C.**
Middle District of Florida	**M.D. Fla.**
Northern District of Florida	**N.D. Fla.**
Southern District of Florida	**S.D. Fla.**
Middle District of Georgia	**M.D. Ga.**
Northern District of Georgia	**N.D. Ga.**
Southern District of Georgia	**S.D. Ga.**
District of Guam	**D. Guam**
District of Hawaii	**D. Haw.**
District of Idaho	**D. Idaho**
Central District of Illinois	**C.D. Ill.**
Northern District of Illinois	**N.D. Ill.**
Southern District of Illinois	**S.D. Ill.**
Northern District of Indiana	**N.D. Ind.**
Southern District of Indiana	**S.D. Ind.**
Northern District of Iowa	**N.D. Iowa**
Southern District of Iowa	**S.D. Iowa**
District of Kansas	**D. Kan.**
Eastern District of Kentucky	**E.D. Ky.**
Western District of Kentucky	**W.D. Ky.**
Eastern District of Louisiana	**E.D. La.**
Middle District of Louisiana	**M.D. La.**
Western District of Louisiana	**W.D. La.**
District of Maine	**D. Me.**
District of Maryland	**D. Md.**
District of Massachusetts	**D. Mass.**
Eastern District of Michigan	**E.D. Mich.**
Western District of Michigan	**W.D. Mich.**
District of Minnesota	**D. Minn.**
Northern District of Mississippi	**N.D. Miss.**
Southern District of Mississippi	**S.D. Miss.**
Eastern District of Missouri	**E.D. Mo.**
Western District of Missouri	**W.D. Mo.**
District of Montana	**D. Mont.**
District of Nebraska	**D. Neb.**

Court	Abbrev.
District of Nevada	**D. Nev.**
District of New Hampshire	**D.N.H.**
District of New Jersey	**D.N.J.**
District of New Mexico	**D.N.M.**
Eastern District of New York	**E.D.N.Y.**
Northern District of New York	**N.D.N.Y.**
Southern District of New York	**S.D.N.Y.**
Western District of New York	**W.D.N.Y.**
Eastern District of North Carolina	**E.D.N.C.**
Middle District of North Carolina	**M.D.N.C.**
Western District of North Carolina	**W.D.N.C.**
District of North Dakota	**D.N.D.**
District of the Northern Mariana Islands	**D.N. Mar. I.**
Northern District of Ohio	**N.D. Ohio**
Southern District of Ohio	**S.D. Ohio**
Eastern District of Oklahoma	**E.D. Okla.**
Northern District of Oklahoma	**N.D. Okla.**
Western District of Oklahoma	**W.D. Okla.**
District of Oregon	**D. Or.**
Eastern District of Pennsylvania	**E.D. Pa.**
Middle District of Pennsylvania	**M.D. Pa.**
Western District of Pennsylvania	**W.D. Pa.**
District of Puerto Rico	**D.P.R.**
District of Rhode Island	**D.R.I.**
District of South Carolina	**D.S.C.**
District of South Dakota	**D.S.D.**
Eastern District of Tennessee	**E.D. Tenn.**
Middle District of Tennessee	**M.D. Tenn.**
Western District of Tennessee	**W.D. Tenn.**
Eastern District of Texas	**E.D. Tex.**
Northern District of Texas	**N.D. Tex.**
Southern District of Texas	**S.D. Tex.**
Western District of Texas	**W.D. Tex.**
District of Utah	**D. Utah**
District of Vermont	**D. Vt.**
Eastern District of Virginia	**E.D. Va.**
Western District of Virginia	**W.D. Va.**
District of the Virgin Islands	**D.V.I.**
Eastern District of Washington	**E.D. Wash.**
Western District of Washington	**W.D. Wash.**
Northern District of West Virginia	**N.D.W. Va.**

Court	Abbrev.
Southern District of West Virginia	**S.D.W. Va.**
Eastern District of Wisconsin	**E.D. Wis.**
Western District of Wisconsin	**W.D. Wis.**
District of Wyoming	**D. Wyo.**

MILITARY COURTS

United States Court of Appeals for the Armed Forces	**Armed Forces App.**
United States Court of Veterans Appeals	**Vet. App.**
United States Air Force Court of Criminal Appeals	**A.F. Crim. App.**
United States Army Court of Criminal Appeals	**Army Crim. App.**
United States Coast Guard Court of Criminal Appeals	**Coast Guard Crim. App.**
United States Navy-Marine Corps Court of Criminal Appeals	**Navy-Marine Crim. App.**

BANKRUPTCY COURTS

Each United States District Court has a corresponding bankruptcy court. To cite a bankruptcy court, add Bankr. to the district court abbreviation.

Examples:

Bankr. N.D. Ala.

Bankr. D. Mass.

OTHER FEDERAL COURTS

Court of Federal Claims	**Fed. Cl.**
Court of Customs and Patent Appeals	**Cust. & Pat. App.**
Court of Claims	**Ct. Cl.**
Claims Court	**Cl. Ct.**
Court of International Trade	**Ct. Intl. Trade**
Tax Court	**Tax**

Effective Learning
How to Study

Everyone learns differently. Some people seem to absorb information like a sponge while others must work hard to soak up any information. Although some people truly do have photographic memories, they are few and far between. Most likely, the people who seem to absorb information "like a sponge" have learned how to maximize their learning experiences. Most of us do not take the time to figure out how we learn best and, as a result, probably spend more time than necessary to achieve the same results as more proficient learners.

Have you ever wondered how some people who are just average students seem to always get A's? If you were to ask them, they probably would tell you that they spend more time than most people studying and preparing, or that they have learned how to study more effectively and efficiently in the time they have available. A good starting point is to determine how you learn best and work out methods to maximize the time and effort you have available.

LEARNING STYLES

A learning style is the way you learn most effectively. Everyone has his or her own learning style, and there are no "better" or "correct" ways to learn. Somewhere in your school career you may have been given tests—such as the Hogan/Champagne Personal Style Indicator or the Kolb Learning Style Inventory—to determine your personal learning styles. These and similar assessments are available through most school advisors and guidance counselors. If you want help in determining your learning styles, take the initiative for your own success and make an appointment with someone who can administer an assessment.

Learning styles fall into these categories:

- independent (competitive) versus collaborative
- structured versus unstructured
- auditory versus visual
- spatial versus verbal
- practical versus creative
- applied versus conceptual
- factual versus analytical
- emotional versus logical

This sounds like a lot to consider, but taking a few minutes to determine which learning style best suits you can save you countless hours of frustration—hours that could be better devoted to studying or other activities.

Independent Versus Collaborative

Do you prefer to work with a group or independently? Some people like to avoid all distractions by working alone. Others prefer to work in a study group and share information.

If you prefer to work independently, you may want to obtain additional course information from study guides and computer-assisted instruction. You may prefer lecture-format classes to small discussion courses. If you prefer to work collaboratively, you may wish to form study groups early in the semester or find a tutor to work with, and you should choose courses that include small discussion groups or group projects.

Structured Versus Unstructured

Structured learners feel more comfortable when they formalize their study habits—for example, by selecting a definite time and place in which to study every day. If you are a structured learner, you may find it useful to create "to-do" lists and keep a written schedule of classes, study times, and activities.

Unstructured learners tend to resist formalizing their study plan and try to avoid feeling "locked-in." They tend to procrastinate. Procrastinators need to find ways to give more structure to their learning activities. One method is to join a study group of students who are more organized.

Auditory Versus Visual

Auditory learners learn best by listening. Visual learners learn best from what they see. Visual learners cannot always learn everything by listening to lectures or by reading and watching video presentations. Auditory learners may find it more efficient to listen to lectures and then read related material. Visual learners may do better reading the book first, and then attending lectures. Auditory learners may also find group discussion and study group activities beneficial.

Spatial Versus Verbal

Spatial learners are better then verbal learners at reading and interpreting maps, charts, and other graphics. Verbal learners prefer to read words than to interpret graphics. Spatial learners need to create and incorporate their own diagrams, maps, timelines, and other graphics into their notes.

Verbal learners need to translate or obtain translations of graphics into words. A useful technique for verbal learners is to take notes that describe the material, including the graphics, in such a way that a visually impaired student could understand the graphic representation from the verbal description. Teaming up with a visually impaired student may be mutually beneficial.

Practical Versus Creative

Practical learners tend to be methodical and systematic. They prefer specific instruction that is directed and focused. Creative learners prefer experimentation and creative activities. Practical learners may benefit from creating an organized study plan for each course, including detailed "to-do" lists and a calendar. For creative learners, courses that allow writing and other creative approaches may be more satisfying.

Applied Versus Conceptual

Applied learners want to know how information can be transferred to given situations. Conceptual learners are not so much concerned with the application as with the underlying concepts. Applied learners need to focus on ways in which the ideas presented in courses and lectures can be applied. Taking notes that include examples for applying the concepts helps them recall the concepts later. Conceptual learners may find it useful to consider the concepts in a broader context than that of the narrow lecture presentation.

Factual Versus Analytical

Factual learners are good with details and enjoy learning interesting and unusual facts. They prefer objective tests. Analytical learners like to break down a topic into its component parts to understand how the parts relate to each other. Analytical learners prefer essay exams that allow them to demonstrate how their knowledge relates to the question. Factual learners may want to make lists of facts, which they can associate with prior knowledge. Analytical learners may want to analyze the organization as they read a textbook, looking for trends and patterns.

Emotional Versus Logical

Emotional learners tend to prefer human-interest stories to material that presents just facts and logic. Logical learners want to understand the factual basis, including statistics, of an argument. Emotional learners may find that reading biographical sketches helps them understand factual subjects.

PUTTING IT ALL TOGETHER

1. *Understand yourself.* From the previous list of types of learners, select the descriptions in each category that best fit your style of learning. Look back at courses and classes you have taken in which you have done well or that you enjoyed the most. You may see a pattern that will help you understand your learning style.

2. *Set goals.* Determine your personal and occupational goals. Do you want a career working with people or with things? Do you want a professional career working directly with people or behind the scenes supporting others? What courses will help you acquire the skills and knowledge you need to achieve these goals?

3. *Make a plan.* Your educational path should lead to a goal. It may be a personal goal to be an outstanding parent or partner, or it may be a goal to be a generalist or a specialist in an occupation or profession. To achieve these goals, you will have to focus on courses that give you the necessary skills and knowledge. Within the courses may be options that accommodate your learning style, such as large lecture classes versus small-group discussion classes, face-to-face courses versus distance-learning courses, and so on.

Create a personal plan that allows for flexibility as your goals or interests change. A good foundation will allow you more flexibility in courses and curriculum. Don't be afraid to admit that you did not enjoy some courses you expected to enjoy or that you enjoyed some classes you didn't think would give you pleasure. These insights may help you fine-tune your personal and professional goals.

4. *Check your progress.* Periodically assess how well you are doing in individual classes, as well as in your overall program of study. Use the opportunity to assess why you are doing better than you expected in some classes and not as well in others. You may have to adjust your overall plan or merely your learning methods. Or outside influences such as work, family, or personal issues may be interfering with your learning. Periodic self-assessment is the first step in modifying your goals.

5. *Make adjustments.* As your goals change, so will your plan. Don't be afraid to make the adjustments necessary to achieve your goals or to change your goals as your interests change. Life rarely follows a straight path. Be adaptable and make adjustments when necessary.

SCHEDULING TIME

Most people use a calendar to keep track of information such as birthdays, appointments, or upcoming events. Calendars may include vacations, concerts, and other special events or activities. Depending on your personal style, you might include "to-do" lists or an hour-by-hour schedule of classes and other activities. Scheduling school and study time is helpful to most students.

Whichever method works best for you, use it to track the amount of time you spend in all of your activities so you can budget your time more accurately. When scheduling, keep in mind that the power of concentration has a limitation for everyone. Don't schedule so many activities that they exceed your mental or physical abilities.

SUPPLEMENTAL LEARNING AIDS

1. *Study guides.* Many textbooks have a study guide that will give you additional information, including sample tests and quizzes. Your instructor may or may not require the use of a study guide. If you need additional reinforcement, you may want to purchase a study guide even if it is not a required part of the course.

2. *Flash cards.* Flash cards are available in college bookstores for many courses. But you will learn more by preparing your own and customizing them to the course you are taking. On the front side of an index card, write a word, phrase, or concept, and write the definition or explanation on the reverse side. With a properly prepared set of flash cards, you may not have to refer to the text or your notes when studying for a test.

3. *Companion websites.* Many publishers offer companion websites for their textbooks. These websites frequently are available on the publisher's website without cost or for a nominal fee. Often these websites are the equivalent of an online study guide. Others offer self-tests. The publisher may post information that has become available since the publication of the textbook.

4. *Outlining.* Few people have a photographic memory or the ability to absorb material on one reading. The following approach can help you use your textbook effectively.

  a. *How long is the chapter?* Before you start, check the length of the chapter and your reading assignment. Most textbooks are filled with graphics and illustrations that reduce the amount of actual reading time to a manageable level.
  b. *Scan the chapter.* Look over the material quickly to get a sense of what will be covered.
  c. *Chapter objectives.* At the beginnings of each chapter, most textbooks list what you should learn from reading the chapter. These chapter objectives help you focus on important topics, information, and themes.
  d. *Read the chapter.* Quickly read through the chapter to get an overall sense of the material and how the sections relate to each other.
  e. *Underline the important items.* After you have done this go back over the material and underline in pencil the items you believe are important.
  f. *Go to class.* From the instructor's lecture and class discussion, you may find that what you think is important changes.
  g. *Highlight the important material.* After class, use a highlighter to highlight what you now believe to be the important information in the text. You probably will find that it is substantially less than what you underlined in pencil.
  h. *Make your flash cards.* From the highlighted information, create a set of flash cards for each chapter.

5. *Tutors.* Not everyone can afford the luxury of a personal tutor, but most colleges and universities have a tutoring center or offer some form of tutoring assistance. If you are having difficulty, don't be afraid to ask for help before it is too late. At the beginning of the semester determine what personalized help is available for each course. You may not need to use this information, but having it available will reduce your anxiety and panic if you realize that you need some help.

Don't be afraid to ask your instructor for help. Your instructor wants you to succeed. If you are doing everything you can to be successful in a class, the instructor should be more than happy to help you or direct you for help.

6. *Study groups.* If you are the type of learner who benefits from working with others, form a study group at the beginning of each semester in each course. After the first class, ask if others wish to form a study group, or post a notice on the course bulletin board website.

One advantage of study groups is the opportunity to share class notes as well as ideas. Verbal learners can benefit from having visual learners in the study group to interpret and explain charts, graphs, and maps. Study groups can motivate procrastinators to complete tasks on time.

7. *Tests.* Most students suffer from some form of test anxiety. At the beginning of each course, ask the instructor for the exam schedule and the type of tests he or she will be giving. Some schools maintain copies of all tests that students can use for practice. If your school does not maintain these, ask your instructors if they will make available sample tests and quizzes. Practice tests may be available in the study guide for the text or on a companion website. If you are in a study group, members can prepare practice tests as part of test preparation.

For more detailed information about study skills, see *Effective Study Skills: Maximizing Your Academic Potential,* by Judy M. Roberts (Prentice Hall, 1998).

The Constitution of the United States of America

PREAMBLE

We the People of the United States, in Order to form a more perfect Union, establish Justice, insure domestic Tranquility, provide for the common defense, promote the general Welfare, and secure the Blessings of Liberty to ourselves and our Posterity, do ordain and establish this Constitution for the United States of America.

ARTICLE I

Section 1. All legislative Powers herein granted shall be vested in a Congress of the United States, which shall consist of a Senate and House of Representatives.

Section 2. The House of Representatives shall be composed of Members chosen every second Year by the People of the several States, and the Electors in each State shall have the Qualifications requisite for Electors of the most numerous Branch of the State Legislature.

No Person shall be a Representative who shall not have attained to the Age of twenty five Years, and been seven Years a Citizen of the United States, and who shall not, when elected, be an Inhabitant of that State in which he shall be chosen.

Representatives and direct Taxes shall be apportioned among the several States which may be included within this Union, according to their respective Numbers, which shall be determined by adding to the whole Number of free Persons, including those bound to Service for a Term of Years, and excluding Indians not taxed, three fifths of all other Persons. The actual Enumeration shall be made within three Years after the first Meeting of the Congress of the United States, and within every subsequent Term of ten Years, in such Manner as they shall by Law direct. The Number of Representatives shall not exceed one for every thirty Thousand, but each State shall have at Least one Representative; and until such enumeration shall be made, the State of New Hampshire shall be entitled to chuse three, Massachusetts eight, Rhode Island and Providence Plantations one, Connecticut five, New York six, New Jersey four, Pennsylvania eight, Delaware one, Maryland six, Virginia ten, North Carolina five, South Carolina five, and Georgia three.

When vacancies happen in the Representation from any State, the Executive Authority thereof shall issue Writs of Election to fill such Vacancies.

The House of Representatives shall chuse their Speaker and other Officers; and shall have the sole Power of Impeachment.

Section 3. The Senate of the United States shall be composed of two Senators from each State, chosen by the Legislature thereof for six Years; and each Senator shall have one Vote.

Immediately after they shall be assembled in Consequence of the first Election, they shall be divided as equally as may be into three Classes. The Seats of the Senators of the first Class shall be vacated at the Expiration of the second Year, of the second Class at the Expiration of the fourth Year, and of the third Class at the Expiration of the sixth Year, so that one third may be chosen every second Year; and if Vacancies happen by Resignation, or otherwise, during the Recess of the Legislature of any State, the Executive thereof may make temporary Appointments until the next Meeting of the Legislature, which shall then fill such Vacancies.

No Person shall be a Senator who shall not have attained to the Age of thirty Years, and been nine Years a Citizen of the United States, and who shall not, when elected, be an Inhabitant of that State for which he shall be chosen.

The Vice President of the United States shall be President of the Senate, but shall have no Vote, unless they be equally divided.

The Senate shall chuse their other Officers, and also a President pro tempore, in the Absence of the Vice President, or when he shall exercise the Office of President of the United States.

The Senate shall have the sole Power to try all Impeachments. When sitting for that Purpose, they shall be on Oath or Affirmation. When the President of the United States is tried, the Chief Justice shall preside: And no Person shall be convicted without the Concurrence of two thirds of the Members present.

Judgment in Cases of Impeachment shall not extend further than to removal from Office, and disqualification to hold and enjoy any Office of honor, Trust or Profit under the United States: but the Party convicted shall nevertheless be liable and subject to Indictment, Trial, Judgment and Punishment, according to Law.

Section 4. The Times, Places and Manner of holding Elections for Senators and Representatives, shall be prescribed in each State by the Legislature thereof; but the Congress may at any time by Law make or alter such Regulations, except as to the Places of chusing Senators.

The Congress shall assemble at least once in every Year, and such Meeting shall be on the first Monday in December, unless they shall by Law appoint a different Day.

Section 5. Each House shall be the Judge of the Elections, Returns and Qualifications of its own Members, and a Majority of each shall constitute a Quorum to do Business; but a smaller Number may adjourn from day to day, and may be authorized to compel the Attendance of absent Members, in such Manner, and under such Penalties as each House may provide.

Each House may determine the Rules of its Proceedings, punish its Members for disorderly Behaviour, and, with the Concurrence of two thirds, expel a Member.

Each House shall keep a Journal of its Proceedings, and from time to time publish the same, excepting such Parts as may in their Judgment require Secrecy; and the Yeas and Nays of the Members of either House on any question shall, at the Desire of one fifth of those Present, be entered on the Journal.

Neither House, during the Session of Congress, shall, without the Consent of the other, adjourn for more than three days, nor to any other Place than that in which the two Houses shall be sitting.

Section 6. The Senators and Representatives shall receive a Compensation for their Services, to be ascertained by Law, and paid out of the Treasury of the United States. They shall in all Cases, except Treason, Felony and Breach of the Peace, be privileged from Arrest during their Attendance at the Session of their respective Houses, and in going to and returning from the same; and for any Speech or Debate in either House, they shall not be questioned in any other Place.

No Senator or Representative shall, during the Time for which he was elected, be appointed to any civil Office under the Authority of the United States, which shall have been created, or the Emoluments whereof shall have been encreased during such time; and no Person holding any Office under the United States, shall be a Member of either House during his Continuance in Office.

Section 7. All Bills for raising Revenue shall originate in the House of Representatives; but the Senate may propose or concur with Amendments as on other Bills.

Every Bill which shall have passed the House of Representatives and the Senate, shall, before it become a Law, be presented to the President of the United States: If he approve he shall sign it, but if not he shall return it, with his Objections to that House in which it shall have originated, who shall enter the Objections at large on their Journal, and proceed to reconsider it. If after such Reconsideration two thirds of that House shall agree to pass the Bill, it shall be sent, together with the Objections, to the other House, by which it shall likewise be reconsidered, and if approved by two thirds of that House, it shall become a Law. But in all such Cases the Votes of both Houses shall be determined by yeas and Nays, and the Names of the Persons voting for and against the Bill shall be entered on the Journal of each House respectively. If any Bill shall not be returned by the President within ten Days (Sundays excepted) after it shall have been presented to him, the Same shall be a Law, in like Manner as if he had signed it, unless the Congress by their Adjournment prevent its Return, in which Case it shall not be a Law.

Every Order, Resolution, or Vote to which the Concurrence of the Senate and House of Representatives may be necessary (except on a question of Adjournment) shall be presented to the President of the United States; and before the Same shall take Effect, shall be approved by him, or being disapproved by him, shall be repassed by two thirds of the Senate and House of Representatives, according to the Rules and Limitations prescribed in the Case of a Bill.

Section 8. The Congress shall have Power To lay and collect Taxes, Duties, Imposts and Excises, to pay the Debts and provide for the common Defence and general Welfare of the United States; but all Duties, Imposts and Excises shall be uniform throughout the United States;

To borrow Money on the credit of the United States;

To regulate Commerce with foreign Nations, and among the several States, and with the Indian Tribes;

To establish an uniform Rule of Naturalization, and uniform Laws on the subject of Bankruptcies throughout the United States;

To coin Money, regulate the Value thereof, and of foreign Coin, and fix the Standard of Weights and Measures;

To provide for the Punishment of counterfeiting the Securities and current Coin of the United States;

To establish Post Offices and post Roads;

To promote the Progress of Science and useful Arts, by securing for limited Times to Authors and Inventors the exclusive Right to their respective Writings and Discoveries;

To constitute Tribunals inferior to the supreme Court;

To define and punish Piracies and Felonies committed on the high Seas, and Offences against the Law of Nations;

To declare War, grant Letters of Marque and Reprisal, and make Rules concerning Captures on Land and Water;

To raise and support Armies, but no Appropriation of Money to that Use shall be for a longer Term than two Years; To provide and maintain a Navy;

To make Rules for the Government and Regulation of the land and naval Forces;

To provide for calling forth the Militia to execute the Laws of the Union, suppress Insurrections and repel Invasions;

To provide for organizing, arming, and disciplining, the Militia, and for governing such Part of them as may be employed in the Service of the United States, reserving to the States respectively, the Appointment of the Officers, and the Authority of training the Militia according to the discipline prescribed by Congress;

To exercise exclusive Legislation in all Cases whatsoever, over such District (not exceeding ten Miles square) as may, by Cession of particular States, and the Acceptance of Congress, become the Seat of the Government of the United States, and to exercise like Authority over all Places purchased by the Consent of the Legislature of the State in which the Same shall be, for the Erection of Forts, Magazines, Arsenals, dockYards, and other needful Buildings;—And

To make all Laws which shall be necessary and proper for carrying into Execution the foregoing Powers, and all other Powers vested by this Constitution in the Government of the United States, or in any Department or Officer thereof.

Section 9. The Migration or Importation of such Persons as any of the States now existing shall think proper to admit, shall not be prohibited by the Congress prior to the Year one thousand eight hundred and eight, but a Tax or duty may be imposed on such Importation, not exceeding ten dollars for each Person.

The Privilege of the Writ of Habeas Corpus shall not be suspended, unless when in Cases of Rebellion or Invasion the public Safety may require it.

No Bill of Attainder or ex post facto Law shall be passed.

No Capitation, or other direct, Tax shall be laid, unless in Proportion to the Census or enumeration herein before directed to be taken.

No Tax or Duty shall be laid on Articles exported from any State.

No Preference shall be given by any Regulation of Commerce or Revenue to the Ports of one State over those of another; nor shall Vessels bound to, or from, one State, be obliged to enter, clear, or pay Duties in another.

No Money shall be drawn from the Treasury, but in Consequence of Appropriations made by Law; and a regular Statement and Account of the Receipts and Expenditures of all public Money shall be published from time to time.

No Title of Nobility shall be granted by the United States: And no Person holding any Office of Profit or Trust under them, shall, without the Consent of the Congress, accept of any present, Emolument, Office, or Title, of any kind whatever, from any King, Prince, or foreign State.

Section 10. No State shall enter into any Treaty, Alliance, or Confederation; grant Letters of Marque and Reprisal; coin Money; emit Bills of Credit; make any Thing but gold and silver Coin a Tender in Payment of Debts; pass any Bill of Attainder, ex post facto Law, or Law impairing the Obligation of Contracts, or grant any Title of Nobility.

No State shall, without the Consent of the Congress, lay any Imposts or Duties on Imports or Exports, except what may be absolutely necessary for executing it's inspection Laws: and the net Produce of all Duties and Imposts, laid by any State on Imports or Exports, shall be for the Use of the Treasury of the United States; and all such Laws shall be subject to the Revision and Controul of the Congress.

No State shall, without the Consent of Congress, lay any Duty of Tonnage, keep Troops, or Ships of War in time of Peace, enter into any Agreement or Compact with another State, or with a foreign Power, or engage in War, unless actually invaded, or in such imminent Danger as will not admit of delay.

ARTICLE II

Section 1. The executive Power shall be vested in a President of the United States of America. He shall hold his Office during the Term of four Years, and, together with the Vice President, chosen for the same Term, be elected, as follows:

Each State shall appoint, in such Manner as the Legislature thereof may direct, a Number of Electors, equal to the whole Number of Senators and Representatives to which the State may be entitled in the Congress: but no Senator or Representative, or Person holding an Office of Trust or Profit under the United States, shall be appointed an Elector.

The Electors shall meet in their respective States, and vote by Ballot for two Persons, of whom one at least shall not be an Inhabitant of the same State with themselves. And they shall make a List of all the Persons voted for, and of the Number of Votes for each; which List they shall sign and certify, and transmit sealed to the Seat of the Government of the United States, directed to the President of the Senate. The President of the Senate shall, in the Presence of the Senate and House of Representatives, open all the Certificates, and the Votes shall then be counted. The Person having the greatest Number of Votes shall be the President, if such Number be a Majority of the whole Number of Electors appointed; and if there be more than one who have such Majority, and have an equal Number of Votes, then the House of Representatives shall immediately chuse by Ballot one of them for President; and if no Person have a Majority, then from the five highest on the List the said House shall in like Manner chuse the President. But in chusing the President, the Votes shall be taken by States, the Representation from each State having one Vote; A quorum for this purpose shall consist of a Member or Members from two thirds of the States, and a Majority of all the States shall be necessary to a Choice. In every Case, after the Choice of the President, the Person having the greatest Number of Votes of the Electors shall be the Vice President. But if there should remain two or more who have equal Votes, the Senate shall chuse from them by Ballot the Vice President.

The Congress may determine the Time of chusing the Electors, and the Day on which they shall give their Votes; which Day shall be the same throughout the United States.

No Person except a natural born Citizen, or a Citizen of the United States, at the time of the Adoption of this Constitution, shall be eligible to the Office of President; neither shall any Person be eligible to that Office who shall not have attained to the Age of thirty five Years, and been fourteen Years a Resident within the United States.

In Case of the Removal of the President from Office, or of his Death, Resignation, or Inability to discharge the Powers and Duties of the said Office, the Same shall devolve on the Vice President, and the Congress may by Law provide for the Case of Removal, Death, Resignation or Inability, both of the President and Vice President, declaring what Officer shall then act as President, and such Officer shall act accordingly, until the Disability be removed, or a President shall be elected.

The President shall, at stated Times, receive for his Services, a Compensation, which shall neither be increased nor diminished during the Period for which he shall have been elected, and he shall not receive within that Period any other Emolument from the United States, or any of them.

Before he enter on the Execution of his Office, he shall take the following Oath or Affirmation:—"I do solemnly swear (or affirm) that I will faithfully execute the Office of President of the United States, and will to the best of my Ability, preserve, protect and defend the Constitution of the United States."

Section 2. The President shall be Commander in Chief of the Army and Navy of the United States, and of the Militia of the several States, when called into the actual Service of the United States; he may require the Opinion, in writing, of the principal

Officer in each of the executive Departments, upon any Subject relating to the Duties of their respective Offices, and he shall have Power to grant Reprieves and Pardons for Offences against the United States, except in Cases of Impeachment.

He shall have Power, by and with the Advice and Consent of the Senate, to make Treaties, provided two thirds of the Senators present concur; and he shall nominate, and by and with the Advice and Consent of the Senate, shall appoint Ambassadors, other public Ministers and Consuls, Judges of the supreme Court, and all other Officers of the United States, whose Appointments are not herein otherwise provided for, and which shall be established by Law: but the Congress may by Law vest the Appointment of such inferior Officers, as they think proper, in the President alone, in the Courts of Law, or in the Heads of Departments.

The President shall have Power to fill up all Vacancies that may happen during the Recess of the Senate, by granting Commissions which shall expire at the End of their next Session.

Section 3. He shall from time to time give to the Congress Information of the State of the Union, and recommend to their Consideration such Measures as he shall judge necessary and expedient; he may, on extraordinary Occasions, convene both Houses, or either of them, and in Case of Disagreement between them, with Respect to the Time of Adjournment, he may adjourn them to such Time as he shall think proper; he shall receive Ambassadors and other public Ministers; he shall take Care that the Laws be faithfully executed, and shall Commission all the Officers of the United States.

Section 4. The President, Vice President and all civil Officers of the United States, shall be removed from Office on Impeachment for, and Conviction of, Treason, Bribery, or other high Crimes and Misdemeanors.

ARTICLE III

Section 1. The judicial Power of the United States shall be vested in one supreme Court, and in such inferior Courts as the Congress may from time to time ordain and establish. The Judges, both of the supreme and inferior Courts, shall hold their Offices during good Behaviour, and shall, at stated Times, receive for their Services a Compensation, which shall not be diminished during their Continuance in Office.

Section 2. The judicial Power shall extend to all Cases, in Law and Equity, arising under this Constitution, the Laws of the United States, and Treaties made, or which shall be made, under their Authority;—to all Cases affecting Ambassadors, other public Ministers and Consuls;—to all Cases of admiralty and maritime Jurisdiction;—to Controversies to which the United States shall be a Party;—to Controversies between two or more States;—between a State and Citizens of another State;—between Citizens of different States;—between Citizens of the same State claiming Lands under Grants of different States, and between a State, or the Citizens thereof, and foreign States, Citizens or Subjects.

In all Cases affecting Ambassadors, other public Ministers and Consuls, and those in which a State shall be Party, the supreme Court shall have original Jurisdiction. In all the other Cases before mentioned, the supreme Court shall have appellate Jurisdiction, both as to Law and Fact, with such Exceptions, and under such Regulations as the Congress shall make.

The Trial of all Crimes, except in Cases of Impeachment, shall be by Jury; and such Trial shall be held in the State where the said Crimes shall have been committed; but when not committed within any State, the Trial shall be at such Place or Places as the Congress may by Law have directed.

Section 3. Treason against the United States, shall consist only in levying War against them, or in adhering to their Enemies, giving them Aid and Comfort. No Person shall be convicted of Treason unless on the Testimony of two Witnesses to the same overt Act, or on Confession in open Court.

The Congress shall have Power to declare the Punishment of Treason, but no Attainder of Treason shall work Corruption of Blood, or Forfeiture except during the Life of the Person attainted.

ARTICLE IV

Section 1. Full Faith and Credit shall be given in each State to the public Acts, Records, and judicial Proceedings of every other State. And the Congress may by general Laws prescribe the Manner in which such Acts, Records and Proceedings shall be proved, and the Effect thereof.

Section 2. The Citizens of each State shall be entitled to all Privileges and Immunities of Citizens in the several States.

A Person charged in any State with Treason, Felony, or other Crime, who shall flee from Justice, and be found in another State, shall on Demand of the executive Authority of the State from which he fled, be delivered up, to be removed to the State having Jurisdiction of the Crime.

No Person held to Service or Labour in one State, under the Laws thereof, escaping into another, shall, in Consequence of any Law or Regulation therein, be discharged from such Service or Labour, but shall be delivered up on Claim of the Party to whom such Service or Labour may be due.

Section 3. New States may be admitted by the Congress into this Union; but no new State shall be formed or erected within the Jurisdiction of any other State; nor any State be formed by the Junction of two or more States, or Parts of States, without the Consent of the Legislatures of the States concerned as well as of the Congress.

The Congress shall have Power to dispose of and make all needful Rules and Regulations respecting the Territory or other Property belonging to the United States; and nothing in this Constitution shall be so construed as to Prejudice any Claims of the United States, or of any particular State.

Section 4. The United States shall guarantee to every State in this Union a Republican Form of Government, and shall protect each of them against Invasion; and on Application of the Legislature, or of the Executive (when the Legislature cannot be convened), against domestic Violence.

ARTICLE V

The Congress, whenever two thirds of both Houses shall deem it necessary, shall propose Amendments to this Constitution, or, on the Application of the Legislatures of two thirds of the several States, shall call a Convention for proposing Amendments, which, in either Case, shall be valid to all Intents and Purposes, as Part of this Constitution, when ratified by the Legislatures of three fourths of the several States, or by Conventions in three fourths thereof, as the one or the other Mode of Ratification may be proposed by the Congress; Provided that no Amendment which may be made prior to the Year One thousand eight hundred and eight shall in any Manner affect the first and fourth Clauses in the Ninth Section of the first Article; and that no State, without its Consent, shall be deprived of its equal Suffrage in the Senate.

ARTICLE VI

All Debts contracted and Engagements entered into, before the Adoption of this Constitution, shall be as valid against the United States under this Constitution, as under the Confederation.

This Constitution, and the Laws of the United States which shall be made in Pursuance thereof; and all Treaties made, or which shall be made, under the Authority of the United States, shall be the supreme Law of the Land; and the Judges in every State shall be bound thereby, any Thing in the Constitution or Laws of any State to the Contrary notwithstanding.

The Senators and Representatives before mentioned, and the Members of the several State Legislatures, and all executive and judicial Officers, both of the United States and of the several States, shall be bound by Oath or Affirmation, to support this Constitution; but no religious Test shall ever be required as a Qualification to any Office or public Trust under the United States.

ARTICLE VII

The Ratification of the Conventions of nine States, shall be sufficient for the Establishment of this Constitution between the States so ratifying the Same.

AMENDMENTS TO THE CONSTITUTION OF THE UNITED STATES

[Amendments I–X make up the Bill of Rights]

AMENDMENT I

Congress shall make no law respecting an establishment of religion, or prohibiting the free exercise thereof; or abridging the freedom of speech, or of the press; or the right of the people peaceably to assemble, and to petition the Government for a redress of grievances.

AMENDMENT II

A well regulated Militia, being necessary to the security of a free State, the right of the people to keep and bear Arms, shall not be infringed.

AMENDMENT III

No Soldier shall, in time of peace be quartered in any house, without the consent of the Owner, nor in time of war, but in a manner to be prescribed by law.

AMENDMENT IV

The right of the people to be secure in their persons, houses, papers, and effects, against unreasonable searches and seizures, shall not be violated, and no Warrants shall issue, but upon probable cause, supported by Oath or affirmation, and particularly describing the place to be searched, and the persons or things to be seized.

AMENDMENT V

No person shall be held to answer for a capital, or otherwise infamous crime, unless on a presentment or indictment of a Grand Jury, except in cases arising in the land or naval forces, or in the Militia, when in actual service in time of War or public danger; nor shall any person be subject for the same offence to be twice put in jeopardy of life or limb; nor shall be compelled in any criminal case to be a witness against himself, nor be deprived of life, liberty, or property, without due process of law; nor shall private property be taken for public use, without just compensation.

AMENDMENT VI

In all criminal prosecutions, the accused shall enjoy the right to a speedy and public trial, by an impartial jury of the State and district wherein the crime shall have been committed, which district shall have been previously ascertained by law, and to be informed of the nature and cause of the accusation; to be confronted with the witnesses against him; to have compulsory process for obtaining witnesses in his favor, and to have the Assistance of Counsel for his defence.

AMENDMENT VII

In suits at common law, where the value in controversy shall exceed twenty dollars, the right of trial by jury shall be preserved, and no fact tried by a jury, shall be otherwise reexamined in any Court of the United States, than according to the rules of the common law.

AMENDMENT VIII

Excessive bail shall not be required, nor excessive fines imposed, nor cruel and unusual punishments inflicted.

AMENDMENT IX

The enumeration in the Constitution, of certain rights, shall not be construed to deny or disparage others retained by the people.

AMENDMENT X

The powers not delegated to the United States by the Constitution, nor prohibited by it to the States, are reserved to the States respectively, or to the people.

AMENDMENT XI

The Judicial power of the United States shall not be construed to extend to any suit in law or equity, commenced or prosecuted against one of the United States by Citizens of another State, or by Citizens or Subjects of any Foreign State.

AMENDMENT XII

The Electors shall meet in their respective states and vote by ballot for President and Vice-President, one of whom, at least, shall not be an inhabitant of the same state with themselves; they shall name in their ballots the person voted for as President, and in distinct ballots the person voted for as Vice-President, and they shall make distinct lists of all persons voted for as President, and of all persons voted for as Vice-President, and of the number of votes for each, which lists they shall sign and certify, and transmit sealed to the seat of the government of the United States, directed to the President of the Senate;—the President of the Senate shall, in the presence of the Senate and House of Representatives, open all the certificates and the votes shall then be counted;—The person having the greatest number of votes for President, shall be the President, if such number be a majority of the whole number of Electors appointed; and if no person have such majority, then from the persons having the highest numbers not exceeding three on the list of those voted for as President, the House of Representatives shall choose immediately, by ballot, the President. But in choosing the President, the votes shall be taken by states, the representation from each state having one vote; a quorum for this purpose shall consist of a member or members from two-thirds of the states, and a majority of all the states shall be necessary to a choice. [And if the House of Representatives shall not choose a President whenever the right of choice shall devolve upon them, before the fourth day of March next following, then the Vice-President shall act as President, as in case of the death or other constitutional disability of the President.—]* The person having the greatest number of votes as Vice-President, shall be the Vice-President, if such number be a majority of the whole number of Electors appointed, and if no person have a majority, then from the two highest numbers on the list, the Senate shall choose the Vice-President; a quorum for the purpose shall consist of two-thirds of the whole number of Senators, and a majority of the whole number shall be necessary to a choice. But no person constitutionally ineligible to the office of President shall be eligible to that of Vice-President of the United States.

AMENDMENT XIII

Section 1. Neither slavery nor involuntary servitude, except as a punishment for crime whereof the party shall have been duly convicted, shall exist within the United States, or any place subject to their jurisdiction.

Section 2. Congress shall have power to enforce this article by appropriate legislation.

AMENDMENT XIV

Section 1. All persons born or naturalized in the United States, and subject to the jurisdiction thereof, are citizens of the United States and of the State wherein they reside. No State shall make or enforce any law which shall abridge the privileges or immunities of citizens of the United States; nor shall any State deprive any person of life, liberty, or property, without due process of law; nor deny to any person within its jurisdiction the equal protection of the laws.

Section 2. Representatives shall be apportioned among the several States according to their respective numbers, counting the whole number of persons in each State, excluding Indians not taxed. But when the right to vote at any election for the choice of electors for President and Vice-President of the United States, Representatives in Congress, the

Executive and Judicial officers of a State, or the members of the Legislature thereof, is denied to any of the male inhabitants of such State, being twenty-one years of age,* and citizens of the United States, or in any way abridged, except for participation in rebellion, or other crime, the basis of representation therein shall be reduced in the proportion which the number of such male citizens shall bear to the whole number of male citizens twenty-one years of age in such State.

Section 3. No person shall be a Senator or Representative in Congress, or elector of President and Vice-President, or hold any office, civil or military, under the United States, or under any State, who, having previously taken an oath, as a member of Congress, or as an officer of the United States, or as a member of any State legislature, or as an executive or judicial officer of any State, to support the Constitution of the United States, shall have engaged in insurrection or rebellion against the same, or given aid or comfort to the enemies thereof. But Congress may by a vote of two-thirds of each House, remove such disability.

Section 4. The validity of the public debt of the United States, authorized by law, including debts incurred for payment of pensions and bounties for services in suppressing insurrection or rebellion, shall not be questioned. But neither the United States nor any State shall assume or pay any debt or obligation incurred in aid of insurrection or rebellion against the United States, or any claim for the loss or emancipation of any slave; but all such debts, obligations and claims shall be held illegal and void.

Section 5. The Congress shall have the power to enforce, by appropriate legislation, the provisions of this article.

AMENDMENT XV

Section 1. The right of citizens of the United States to vote shall not be denied or abridged by the United States or by any State on account of race, color, or previous condition of servitude—

Section 2. The Congress shall have the power to enforce this article by appropriate legislation.

AMENDMENT XVI

The Congress shall have power to lay and collect taxes on incomes, from whatever source derived, without apportionment among the several States, and without regard to any census or enumeration.

AMENDMENT XVII

The Senate of the United States shall be composed of two Senators from each State, elected by the people thereof, for six years; and each Senator shall have one vote. The electors in each State shall have the qualifications requisite for electors of the most numerous branch of the State legislatures.

When vacancies happen in the representation of any State in the Senate, the executive authority of such State shall issue writs of election to fill such vacancies:

Provided, That the legislature of any State may empower the executive thereof to make temporary appointments until the people fill the vacancies by election as the legislature may direct.

This amendment shall not be so construed as to affect the election or term of any Senator chosen before it becomes valid as part of the Constitution.

AMENDMENT XVIII

Section 1. After one year from the ratification of this article the manufacture, sale, or transportation of intoxicating liquors within, the importation thereof into, or the exportation thereof from the United States and all territory subject to the jurisdiction thereof for beverage purposes is hereby prohibited.

Section 2. The Congress and the several States shall have concurrent power to enforce this article by appropriate legislation.

Section 3. This article shall be inoperative unless it shall have been ratified as an amendment to the Constitution by the legislatures of the several States, as provided in the Constitution, within seven years from the date of the submission hereof to the States by the Congress.

AMENDMENT XIX

The right of citizens of the United States to vote shall not be denied or abridged by the United States or by any State on account of sex.

Congress shall have power to enforce this article by appropriate legislation.

AMENDMENT XX

Section 1. The terms of the President and the Vice President shall end at noon on the 20th day of January, and the terms of Senators and Representatives at noon on the 3d day of January, of the years in which such terms would have ended if this article had not been ratified; and the terms of their successors shall then begin.

Section 2. The Congress shall assemble at least once in every year, and such meeting shall begin at noon on the 3d day of January, unless they shall by law appoint a different day.

Section 3. If, at the time fixed for the beginning of the term of the President, the President elect shall have died, the Vice President elect shall become President. If a President shall not have been chosen before the time fixed for the beginning of his term, or if the President elect shall have failed to qualify, then the Vice President elect shall act as President until a President shall have qualified; and the Congress may by law provide for the case wherein neither a President elect nor a Vice President shall have qualified, declaring who shall then act as President, or the manner in which one who is to act shall be selected, and such person shall act accordingly until a President or Vice President shall have qualified.

Section 4. The Congress may by law provide for the case of the death of any of the persons from whom the House of Representatives may choose a President whenever the right of choice shall have devolved upon them, and for the case of the death of any of the persons from whom the Senate may choose a Vice President whenever the right of choice shall have devolved upon them.

Section 5. Sections 1 and 2 shall take effect on the 15th day of October following the ratification of this article.

Section 6. This article shall be inoperative unless it shall have been ratified as an amendment to the Constitution by the legislatures of three-fourths of the several States within seven years from the date of its submission.

AMENDMENT XXI

Section 1. The eighteenth article of amendment to the Constitution of the United States is hereby repealed.

Section 2. The transportation or importation into any State, Territory, or Possession of the United States for delivery or use therein of intoxicating liquors, in violation of the laws thereof, is hereby prohibited.

Section 3. This article shall be inoperative unless it shall have been ratified as an amendment to the Constitution by conventions in the several States, as provided in the Constitution, within seven years from the date of the submission hereof to the States by the Congress.

AMENDMENT XXII

Section 1. No person shall be elected to the office of the President more than twice, and no person who has held the office of President, or acted as President, for more than two years of a term to which some other person was elected President shall be elected to the office of President more than once. But this Article shall not apply to any person holding the office of President when this Article was proposed by Congress, and shall not prevent any person who may be holding the office of President, or acting as President, during the term within which this Article becomes operative from holding the office of President or acting as President during the remainder of such term.

Section 2. This article shall be inoperative unless it shall have been ratified as an amendment to the Constitution by the legislatures of three-fourths of the several States within seven years from the date of its submission to the States by the Congress.

AMENDMENT XXIII

Section 1. The District constituting the seat of Government of the United States shall appoint in such manner as Congress may direct:

A number of electors of President and Vice President equal to the whole number of Senators and Representatives in Congress to which the District would be entitled if it were a State, but in no event more than the least populous State; they shall be in addition to those appointed by the States, but they shall be considered, for the purposes of the election of President and Vice President, to be electors appointed by a State; and they shall meet in the District and perform such duties as provided by the twelfth article of amendment.

Section 2. The Congress shall have power to enforce this article by appropriate legislation.

AMENDMENT XXIV

Section 1. The right of citizens of the United States to vote in any primary or other election for President or Vice President, for electors for President or Vice President, or for Senator or Representative in Congress, shall not be denied or abridged by the United States or any State by reason of failure to pay poll tax or other tax.

Section 2. The Congress shall have power to enforce this article by appropriate legislation.

AMENDMENT XXV

Section 1. In case of the removal of the President from office or of his death or resignation, the Vice President shall become President.

Section 2. Whenever there is a vacancy in the office of the Vice President, the President shall nominate a Vice President who shall take office upon confirmation by a majority vote of both Houses of Congress.

Section 3. Whenever the President transmits to the President pro tempore of the Senate and the Speaker of the House of Representatives his written declaration that he is unable to discharge the powers and duties of his office, and until he transmits to them a written declaration to the contrary, such powers and duties shall be discharged by the Vice President as Acting President.

Section 4. Whenever the Vice President and a majority of either the principal officers of the executive departments or of such other body as Congress may by law provide, transmit to the President pro tempore of the Senate and the Speaker of the House of Representatives their written declaration that the President is unable to discharge the powers and duties of his office, the Vice President shall immediately assume the powers and duties of the office as Acting President.

Thereafter, when the President transmits to the President pro tempore of the Senate and the Speaker of the House of Representatives his written declaration that no inability exists, he shall resume the powers and duties of his office unless the Vice President and a majority of either the principal officers of the executive department or of such other body as Congress may by law provide, transmit within four days to the President pro tempore of the Senate and the Speaker of the House of Representatives their written declaration that the President is unable to discharge the powers and duties of his office. Thereupon Congress shall decide the issue, assembling within forty-eight hours for that purpose if not in session. If the Congress, within twenty-one days after receipt of the latter written declaration, or, if Congress is not in session, within twenty-one days after Congress is required to assemble, determines by two-thirds vote of both Houses that the President is unable to discharge the powers and duties of his office, the Vice President shall continue to discharge the same as Acting President; otherwise, the President shall resume the powers and duties of his office.

AMENDMENT XXVI

Section 1. The right of citizens of the United States, who are eighteen years of age or older, to vote shall not be denied or abridged by the United States or by any State on account of age.

Section 2. The Congress shall have power to enforce this article by appropriate legislation.

AMENDMENT XXVII

No law, varying the compensation for the services of the Senators and Representatives, shall take effect, until an election of representatives shall have intervened.

Internet Resources

Courts—Alternative Dispute Resolution—Government

U.S. Courts	www.uscourts.gov
U.S. Tax Court	www.ustaxcourt.gov/ustcweb.htm
U.S. Court of Federal Claims	www.uscfc.uscourts.gov/
U.S. Court of International Trade	www.uscit.gov/
U.S Court for the Federal Circuit	www.fedcir.gov/
U.S. Supreme Court	www.supremecourtus.gov
National Mediation Board	www.nmb.gov
American Arbitration Association	www.adr.org
Pacer System	http://pacer.psc.uscourts.gov/
U.S. Court of Appeals	www.uscourts.gov/courtsofappeals.html
Internal Revenue Service	www.irs.gov
Government Printing Office	www.gpo.gov/
Code of Federal Regulations	www.access.gpo.gov/nara/cfr/index.html

Legal Research

VersusLaw	www.versuslaw.com/
Lexis	www.lexisnexis.com/
Westlaw	www.westlaw.com/
Library of Congress	www.loc.gov
Loislaw	www.loislaw.com
Cornell University LII	www.law.cornell.edu/citation
ALWD Manual	www.alwd.org

Legal Organizations

American Bar Association	www.abanet.org
National Federation of Paralegal Associations, Inc.	www.paralegals.org
National Association of Legal Assistants	www.nala.org
American Association of Legal Administrators	www.alanet.org/home.html
American Association for Paralegal Education	www.aafpe.org
ABA Standing Committee on Legal Assistants	www.abanet.org/legalassts
Legal Nurse Consultants	www.aalnc.org

State Bar Associations

Alabama	www.alabar.org
Alaska	www.alaskabar.org
Arizona	www.azbar.org.org
Arkansas	www.arkbar.org
California	www.calbar.org
Colorado	www.cobar.org
Connecticut	www.ctbar.org
Delaware	www.dsba.org
District of Columbia	www.dcbar.org
Florida	www.flabar.org
Georgia	www.gabar.org
Hawaii	www.hsba.org
Idaho	www2.state.id.us/isb/
Illinois	www.isba.org
Indiana	www.inbar.org
Iowa	www.iowabar.org
Kansas	www.ksbar.org
Kentucky	www.kybar.org
Louisiana	www.lsba.org
Maine	www.maine.org
Maryland	www.msba.org
Massachusetts	www.massbar.org
Michigan	www.michbar.org
Minnesota	www.mnbar.org
Mississippi	www.msbar.org
Missouri	www.mobar.org
Montana	www.montanabar.org
Nebraska	www.nebar.org
Nevada	www.nvbar.org
New Hampshire	www.nhbar.org
New Jersey	www.njsba.com
New Mexico	www.nmbar.org
New York	www.nysba.org
North Carolina	www.ncbar.com
North Dakota	www.sband.org
Ohio	www.ohiobar.org
Oklahoma	www.okbar.org
Oregon	www.osbar.org
Pennsylvania	www.pa-bar.org
Rhode Island	www.ribar.com
South Carolina	www.scbar.org

South Dakota	www.sdbar.org
Tennessee	www.tba.org
Texas	www.texasbar.com
Utah	www.utahbar.org
Vermont	www.vtbar.org
Virginia	www.vsb.org
Washington	www.wsba.org
West Virginia	www.wvbar.org
Wisconsin	www.wisbar.org
Wyoming	www.wyomingbar.org

Other

Religious calendar	www.interfaithcalendar.org/
AOL	www.aol.com
Compuserve	www.compuserve.com
The Affiliate	www.futurelawoffice.com/practice.html
Adobe Systems	www.adobe.com
Mapquest	www.mapquest.com

Internet Search Engines

AltaVista	www.altavista.com
Ask Jeeves	www.askjeeves.com
Dogpile	www.dogpile.com
Excite	www.excite.com
Google	www.google.com
Metacrawler	www.metacrawler.com
Netscape	www.netscape.com
Yahoo!	www.yahoo.com
Findlaw	www.findlaw.com

Glossary of Spanish Equivalents for Important Legal Terms

A

a priori   Desde antes, del pasado.

AAA   Siglas para **American Arbitration Association** Asociación de Arbitraje.

ABA   Siglas para **American Bar Association** Colegio de Abogados Estadounidenses.

accept   Aceptar, admitir, aprobar, recibir reconocer.

accession   Accesión, admisión, aumento, incremento.

accord   Acuerdo, convenio, arreglo, acordar, conceder.

acquittal   Absolución, descargo, veredicto de no culpable.

act   Acto, estatuto, decreto, actuar, funcionar.

actionable   Justiciable, punible, procesable.

adjourn   Levantar, posponer, suspender la sesión.

adjudicate   Adjudicar, decidir, dar fallo a favor de, sentenciar, declarar.

administrative   Administrativo, ejecutivo.

administrative agency   Agencia administrativa.

administrative hearing   Juicio administrativo.

administrative law   Derecho administrativo.

administrative law judge   Juez de derecho, Administrativo.

administrator   Administrador.

admit   Admitir, conceder, reconocer, permitir entrada, confesar, asentir.

adverse   Adverso, contrario, opuesto.

adverse possession   Posesión adversa.

advice   Consejo, asesoramiento, notificación.

affected class   Clase afectada, grupo iscriminado.

affidavit   Declaración voluntaria, escrita y bajo uramento, afidávit, atestiguación, testificata.

affirmative action   Acción positiva.

affirmative defense   Defensa justificativa.

after acquired property   Propiedad adquirida con garantía adicional.

against   En contra.

agency   Agencia, oficina, intervención.

agent   Agente, representante autorizado.

aggrieved party   Parte dañada, agraviada, perjudicada.

agreement   Acuerdo, arreglo, contrato, convenio, pacto.

alibi   Coartada.

alien   Extranjero, extraño, foráneo.

annul   Anular, cancelar, invalidar, revocar, dejar sin efecto.

answer   Contestación, réplica, respuesta, alegato.

antecedent   Antecedente, previo, preexistente.

appeal   Apelar, apelación.

appear   Aparecer, comparecer.

appellate court   Tribunal de apelaciones.

appellate jurisdiction   Competencia de apelación.

applicable   Aplicable, apropiado, pertinente a, lo que puede ser aplicado.

arraign   Denunciar, acusar, procesar, instruir de cargos hechos.

arrears   Retrasos, pagos atrasados, decursas.

arrest   Arresto, arrestar, aprehensión, aprehender, detener.

arson   Incendio intencional.

articles of incorporation   Carta de organización corporativa.

assault   Agresión, asalto, ataque, violencia carnal, agredir, atacar, acometer.

assault and battery   Amenazas y agresión, asalto.

assign   Asignar, ceder, designar, hacer cesión, traspasar, persona asignada un derecho.

attachment   Secuestro judicial.

attorney   Abogado, consejero, apoderado.

award   Fallo, juicio, laudo, premio.

B

bail Caución, fianza.

bail bondsman Fiador, fiador judicial.

bailee Depositario de bienes.

bailment Depósito, encargo, depósito mercantil, depósito comercial.

bailment For hire, depósito oneroso.

bailor Fiador.

bankruptcy Bancarrota, quiebra, insolvencia.

battery Agravio, agresión.

bearer bond Título mobiliario.

bearer instrument Título al portador.

bench Tribunal, los jueces, la magistratura.

beneficiary Beneficiario, legatario.

bequeath Legar.

bilateral contract Contrato bilateral.

bill of lading Póliza de embarque, boleto de carga, documento de tránsito.

bill of rights Las primeras diez enmiendas a la Constitución de los Estados Unidos de América.

binder Resguardo provisional, recibo para garantizar el precio de un bien inmueble.

birth certificate Acta de nacimiento, partida de nacimiento, certificado de nacimiento.

blue sky laws Estatutos para prevenir el fraude en la compraventa de valores.

bond Bono, título, obligación, deuda inversionista, fianza.

booking Término dado en el cuartel de policía al registro de arresto y los cargos hechos al arrestado.

breach of contract Violación, rotura, incumplimiento de contrato.

brief Alegato, escrito memorial.

burglary Escalamiento, allanamiento de morada.

buyer Comprador.

bylaws Estatutos sociales, reglamentos internos.

C

capacity to contract Capacidad contractual.

case Causa, caso, acción legal, proceso, proceso civil, asunto, expediente.

case law Jurisprudencia.

cashier's check Cheque bancario.

cease and desist order Orden judicial de cese.

censure Censura.

certificate of deposit Certificado de depósito.

certified check Cheque certificado.

certify Certificar, atestiguar.

charge Cobrar, acusar, imputar.

charitable trust Fideicomiso caritativo.

chattel Bienes muebles, bártulos.

cheat Fraude, engaño, defraudador, trampa, tramposo, estafar.

check Cheque, talón, comprobación.

cite Citación, citar, referir, emplazar.

citizenship Ciudadanía.

civil action Acción, enjuiciamiento civil, demanda.

civil law Derecho civil.

Claims Court Tribunal federal de reclamaciones.

client Cliente.

closing arguments Alegatos de clausura.

closing costs Gastos ocasionados en la venta de bienes raíces.

clue Pista, indicio.

codicil Codicilo.

coercion Coerción, coacción.

collateral Colateral, auxiliar, subsidiario, seguridad colateral, garantía prendaria.

collect Cobrar, recobrar, recaudar.

collision Choque, colisión.

common law Derecho consuetudinario.

comparative negligence Negligencia comparativa.

compensatory damages Indemnización compensatoria por daños y perjuicios, daños compensatorios.

competency Competencia, capacidad legal.

concurrent conditions Condiciones concurrentes.

concurrent jurisdiction Jurisdicción simultanea, conocimiento acumulativo.

concurrent sentences Sentencias que se cumplen simultáneamente.

concurring opinion Opinión coincidente.

condemn Condenar, confiscar, expropiar.

condition precedent Condición precedente.

condition subsequent Condición subsecuente.

confession Confesión, admisión.

confidential Confidencial, íntimo, secreto.

confiscation Confiscación, comiso, decomiso.

consent decree Decreto por acuerdo mutuo.

consequential damages Daños especiales.

consideration Contraprestación.

consolidation Consolidación, unión, concentración.

constructive delivery Presunta entrega.

contempt of court Desacato, contumacia o menosprecio a la corte.

contract Contrato, convenio, acuerdo, pacto.

contributory negligence Negligencia contribuyente.

conversion Conversión, canje.

conviction Convicción, fallo de culpabilidad, convencimiento, sentencia condenatoria, condena.

copyright Derecho de autor, propiedad literaria, propiedad intelectual, derecho de impresión.

corroborate Corroborar, confirmar.

counterclaim   Contrademanda, excepción de compensación.

counteroffer   Contra oferta.

courts   Cortes o tribunales establecidas por la constitución.

covenant for quiet enjoyment   Convenio de disfrute y posesión pacífica.

creditor   Acreedor.

crime   Crimen, delito.

criminal act   Acto criminal.

criminal law   Derecho penal.

cross examination   Contrainterrogatorio, repregunta.

cure   Curar, corregir.

D

damages   Daños y perjuicios, indemnización pecuniaria.

DBA   Sigla para **doing business as** En negociación comercial.

deadly force   Fuerza mortífera.

debt   Deuda, débito.

debtor   Deudor.

decision   Decisión judicial, fallo, determinación auto, sentencia.

deed   Escritura, título de propiedad, escritura de traspaso.

defamation   Difamación, infamación.

default   Incumplir, faltar, no comparecer, incumplimiento.

defendant   Demandado, reo, procesado, acusado.

delinquent   Delincuente, atrasado en pagos, delictuoso.

denial   Denegación, negación, denegatoria.

deponent   Deponente, declarante.

deportation   Deportación, destierro.

deposition   Deposición, declaración bajo juramento.

detain   Detener, retardar, retrasar.

devise   Legado de bienes raíces.

direct examination   Interrogatorio directo, interrogatorio a testigo propio.

directed verdict   Veredicto expedido por el juez, veredicto por falta de pruebas.

disaffirm   Negar, rechazar, repudiar, anular.

discharge   Descargo, cumplimiento, liberación.

disclose   Revelar.

discovery   Revelación de prueba, exposición reveladora.

discriminate   Discriminar.

dismiss   Despedir, desechar, desestimar.

dissenting opinion   Opinión en desacuerdo.

dissolution   Disolución, liquidación.

diversity of citizenship   Diversidad de ciudadanías, ciudadanías diferentes.

dividend   Acción librada, dividendo.

divorce   Divorcio, divorciar.

docket   Orden del día, lista de casos en la corte.

double jeopardy   Non bis in idem.

driving under the influence   Manejar bajo los efectos de bebidas alcohólicas o drogas.

duress   Coacción.

E

earnest money   Arras, señal.

easement   Servidumbre.

edict   Edicto, decreto, auto.

embezzlement   Malversación de fondos.

eminent domain   Dominio eminente.

encroachment   Intrusión, usurpación, invasión, uso indebido.

encumbrance   Gravamen, afectación, cargo.

enforce   Hacer cumplir, dar valor, poner en efecto.

entitlement   Derecho, título.

equal protection clause   Cláusula de protección de igualdad ante la ley.

equal protection of the law   Igualdad ante la ley.

equity   Equidad. Derecho equitativo.

escheat   Reversión al estado al no haber herederos.

estate   Bienes, propiedad, caudal hereditario, cuerpo de la herencia, caudal, derecho, título, interés sobre propiedad.

estop   Impedir, detener, prevenir.

ethics   Sistema ético.

eviction   Evicción, desalojo, desalojamiento, desahucio, lanzamiento.

evidence   Testimonio, prueba, pruebas documentales, pieza de prueba.

examination   Examen, reconocimiento, interrogatorio.

executed contract   Contrato firmado, contrato ejecutado.

execution   Ejecución, desempeño, cumplimiento.

executory contract   Contrato por cumplirse.

executory interests   Intereses futuros.

exempt   Franquear, exentar, exencionar, eximir, libre, franco, exento, inmune.

exoneration   Exoneración, descargo, liberación.

expert witness   Testigo perito.

express contract   Contrato explícito.

expropriation   Expropiación, confiscación.

eyewitness   Testigo ocular o presencial.

F

fact   Hecho falsificado.

failure to appear   Incomparecencia.

fault   Falta, defecto, culpa, negligencia.

fee   Honorarios, retribución, cuota, cargo, derecho, dominio, asesoría, propiedad, bienes raíces.

fee simple estate   Propiedad en dominio pleno.

felon   Felón, autor de un delito.

felony   Delito mayor o grave.

fiduciary Fiduciario.

find against Fallar o decidir en contra.

find for Fallar o decidir a favor.

finding Determinación de los hechos.

fine Multa, castigo.

fixture Accesorio fijo.

foreclose Entablar juicio hipotecario, embargar bienes hipotecados.

forgery Falsificación.

franchise Franquicia, privilegio, patente, concesión social, derecho de votar.

fraud Fraude, engaño, estafa, trampa, embuste, defraudación.

full disclosure Revelación completa.

G

garnishment Embargo de bienes.

gift Regalo, dádiva, donación.

gift causa mortis Donación de propiedad en expectativa de muerte.

gift inter vivos Donación entre vivos.

gift tax Impuesto sobre donaciones.

good and valid consideration Causa contractual válida.

good faith Buena fe.

goods Mercaderías, bienes, productos.

grace period Período de espera.

grantee Concesionario, cesionario.

grantor Otorgante, cesionista.

grievance Agravio, injuria, ofensa, queja formal.

gross negligence Negligencia temeraria, negligencia grave.

H

habitation Habitación, lugar donde se vive.

harassment Hostigamiento.

hearing Audiencia, vista, juicio.

hearsay Testimonio de oídas.

holder Tenedor, poseedor.

holding Decisión, opinión, tenencia posesión, asociación, grupo industrial.

holographic will Testamento hológrafo.

homeowner Propietario, dueño de casa.

homestead Casa, solariega, hogar, heredad, excepción de embargo, bien de familia.

hung jury Jurado sin veredicto.

I

identify Identificar, verificar, autenticar.

illegal Ilegal, ilícito, ilegítimo.

illegal entry Entrada ilegal.

illegal search Registro domiciliario, allanamiento ilegal, cacheo ilegal.

immunity Inmunidad, exención.

implied warranty Garantía implícita.

impossibility of performance Imposibilidad de cumplimiento.

impound Embargar, incautar, confiscar, secuestrar.

inadmissible Inadmisible, inaceptable.

income Ingreso, ganancia, entrada, renta, rédito.

incriminate Incriminar, acriminar.

indictment Procesamiento, acusación por jurado acusatorio, inculpatoria.

indorsement Endose, endoso, respaldo, garantía.

informant Informador, denunciante, delator.

information Información, informe, acusación por el fiscal, denuncia.

informed consent Conformidad por información.

inherit Heredar, recibir por herencia.

injunction Mandato judicial, amparo, prohibición judicial, interdicto.

innocent Inocente, no culpable.

inquiry Indagatoria judicial, pesquisa.

insufficient evidence Prueba insuficiente.

interrogation Interrogación.

interstate commerce Comercio interestatal.

intestate Intestado, intestar, sin testamento.

intestate succession Sucesión hereditaria.

investigation Investigación, indagación, encuesta.

issue Emisión, cuestión, punto, edición, número, tirada, sucesión, descendencia, resultado, decisión.

J

jail Cárcel, calabozo, encarcelar.

joint tenancy Condominio.

judge Magistrado, juez, juzgar, adjudicar, enjuiciar, fallar.

judgment Sentencia, fallo, juicio, decisión, dictamen, criterio.

judicial proceeding Proceso o diligencia judicial.

judicial review Revisión judicial.

jump bail Fugarse bajo fianza.

jurisdiction Jurisdicción, fuero competencia.

jury Jurado

L

landlord Arrendatario, propietario.

larceny Hurto, latrocinio, ladronicio.

law Ley, derecho.

lease Contrato de arrendamiento, arrendamiento, arriendo, contrato de locación, arrendar, alquilar.

leasehold estate Bienes forales.

legatee Legatario, asignatario.

lender Prestamista.

lessee Arrendatario, locatario, inquilino.

lessor Arrendatario, arrendador, arrendante, locador.

letter of credit Letra de crédito.

liability Responsiva, responsabilidad.

libel Libelo por difamación por escrito.

license Licencia, permiso, privilegio, matrícula, patente, título, licenciar, permitir.

lien Gravamen, derecho prendario o de retención, embargo preventivo.

life estate Hipoteca legal, dominio vitalicio.

limited liability company Sociedad de responsabilidad limitada.

limited partnership Sociedad en comandita, sociedad comanditaria.

litigated Pleiteado, litigado, sujeto a litigación.

M

majority opinion Opinión que refleja la mayoría de los miembros de la corte de apelaciones.

maker Otorgante, girador.

malice Malicia, malignidad, maldad.

malpractice Incompetencia profesional.

manslaughter Homicidio sin premeditación.

material witness Testigo esencial.

mechanics lien Gravamen de construcción.

mediation Mediación, tercería, intervención, interposición.

medical examiner Médico examinador.

merger Fusión, incorporación, unión, consolidación.

minor Menor, insignificante, pequeño, trivial.

misdemeanor Delito menor, fechoría.

mitigation of damages Mitigación de daños, minoración, atenuación.

monetary damages Daños pecuniarios.

mortgage Hipoteca, gravamen, hipotecar, gravar.

motion to dismiss Petición para declaración sin lugar.

motion to suppress Moción para suprimir, reprimir o suspender.

motive Motivo.

murder Asesinato, asesinar, homicidio culposo.

N

naturalization Naturalización.

negligence Negligencia, descuido, imprudencia.

negotiable Negociable.

negotiate Negociar, agenciar, hacer efectivo, traspasar, tratar.

net assets Haberes netos.

notice Aviso, notificación, advertencia, conocimiento.

novation Novación, delegación de crédito.

nuisance Daño, molestia, perjuicio.

nuncupative will Testamento abierto.

O

oath Juramento.

objection Objeción, oposición, disconformidad, recusación, impugnación, excepción, réplica, reclamación.

obstruction of justice Encubrimiento activo.

offer Oferta, ofrecimiento, propuesta, ofrecer, proponer.

omission Omisión, falla, falta.

opinion Opinión, dictamen, decisión de la corte.

oral argument Alegato oral.

order instrument Instrumento de pago a la orden.

owe Deber, estar en deuda, adeudo.

owner Dueño, propietario, poseedor.

P

pain and suffering Angustia mental y dolor físico.

pardon Perdón, indulto, absolución, indultar, perdonar.

parol evidence rule Principio que prohíbe la modificación de un contrato por prueba verbal.

parole Libertad vigilada.

partnership Sociedad, compañía colectiva, aparcería, consorcio, sociedad personal.

patent Patente, obvio, evidente, aparente, privilegio de invención, patentar.

penalty Pena, multa, castigo, penalidad, condena.

pending Pendiente, en trámite, pendiente de, hasta que.

per capita Por cabeza.

performance Cumplimiento, desempeño, ejecución, rendimiento.

perjury Perjurio, testimonio falso, juramento falso.

personal property Bienes personales, bienes mobiliarios.

plea bargain Declaración de culpabilidad concertada.

plea of guilty Alegación de culpabilidad.

pleadings Alegatos, alegaciones, escritos.

pledge Prenda, caución, empeño, empeñar, dar en prenda, pignorar.

police power Poder policial.

policy Póliza, escritura, práctica política.

possession Posesión, tenencia, goce, disfrute.

possibility of reverter Posibilidad de reversión.

power of attorney Poder de representación, poder notarial, procura.

precedent Precedente, decisión previa por el mismo tribunal.

preemptive right Derecho de prioridad.

prejudicial Dañoso, perjudicial.

preliminary hearing Audiencia preliminar.

premeditation Premeditación.

presume Presumir, asumir como hecho basado en la experiencia, suponer.

prevail Prevalecer, persuadir, predominar, ganar, triunfar.

price discrimination   Discriminación en el precio.

principal   Principal, jefe, de mayor importancia, valor actual.

privileged communication   Comunicación privilegiada.

privity   Coparticipación, intereses comunes.

procedural   Procesal.

proceeds   Ganancias.

profit   Ganancia, utilidad, lucro, beneficio.

prohibited   Prohibido.

promise   Promesa.

promissory estoppel   Impedimento promisorio.

promissory note   Pagaré, vale, nota de pago.

proof   Prueba, comprobación, demostración.

prosecutor   Fiscal, abogado público acusador.

proximate cause   Causa relacionada.

proxy   Poder, delegación, apoderado, mandatario.

punishment   Pena, castigo.

punitive damages   Indemnización punitiva por daños y perjuicios, daños ejemplares.

Q

qualification   Capacidad, calidad, preparación.

qualified indorsement   Endoso limitado endoso con reservas.

quasi contract   Cuasicontrato.

query   Pregunta, interrogación.

question of fact   Cuestión de hecho.

question of law   Cuestión de derecho.

quiet enjoyment   Uso y disfrute.

quitclaim deed   Escritura de traspaso de finiquito.

R

race discrimination   Discriminación racial.

rape   Estupro, violación, ultraje, rapto, violar.

ratification   Ratificación, aprobación, confirmación.

ratify   Aprobar, confirmar, ratificar, convalidar, adoptar.

real property   Bienes raíces, bienes inmuebles, arraigo.

reasonable doubt   Duda razonable.

rebut   Rebatir, refutar, negar, contradecir.

recognizance   Obligación impuesta judicialmente.

recordation   Inscripción oficial, grabación.

recover   Recobrar, recuperar, obtener como resultado de decreto.

redress   Reparación, compensación, desagravio, compensar, reparar, satisfacer, remediar.

regulatory agency   Agencia reguladora.

reimburse   Reembolsar, repagar, compensar, reintegrar.

rejoinder   Respuesta, réplica, contrarréplica.

release   Descargo, liberación, librar, relevar, descargar, libertar.

relevance   Relevancia.

remainder   Resto, restante, residuo, derecho expectativo a un bien raíz.

remedy   Remedio, recurso.

remuneration   Remuneración, compensación.

reply   Réplica, contestación, contestar, responder.

reprieve   Suspensión de la sentencia, suspensión, indulto, indultar, suspender.

reprimand   Reprender, regañar, reprimenda, represión.

repudiate   Repudiar, renunciar, rechazar.

rescission   Rescisión, abrogación, cancelación de un contrato.

respondeat superior   Responsabilidad civil al supervisor.

respondent   Apelado, demandado.

restitution   Restitución, devolución.

restraining order   Inhibitoria, interdicto, orden de amparo.

retain   Retener, emplear, guardar.

reversion   Reversión, derecho de sucesión.

revocation   Revocación, derogación, anulación.

reward   Premio.

right of first refusal   Retracto arrendaticio.

right of subrogation   Derecho de sustituir.

right of survivorship   Derecho de supervivencia entre dueños de propiedad mancomunada.

right to work laws   Leyes que prohíben la filiación sindical como requisito para poder desempeñar un puesto, derecho de trabajo.

rights   Derechos.

robbery   Robo, atraco.

ruling   Determinación oficial, auto judicial.

S

sale   Venta.

sale on approval   Venta por aprobación.

satisfaction   Satisfacción, liquidación, cumplimiento, pago, finiquito.

scope of authority   Autoridad explícitamente otorgada o implícitamente concedida.

search and seizure   Allanamiento, registro e incautación.

search warrant   Orden de registro o de allanamiento.

secured party   Persona con interés asegurado.

secured transaction   Transacción con un interés asegurado.

securities   Valores, títulos, obligaciones.

security agreement   Acuerdo que crea la garantía de un interés.

security deposit   Deposito de seguridad.

seize   Arrestar, confiscar, secuestrar, incautar.

settlement   Arreglo, composición, ajuste, liquidación, componenda, acomodo.

sex discrimination   Discriminación sexual.

sexual harassment   Acoso sexual.

shoplifting   Ratería en tiendas.

signature   Firma.

slander   Calumnia, difamación oral, calumniar.

source of income   Fuente de ingresos.

specific performance   Prestación específica contractual.

split decision   Decisión con opiniones mixtas.

spousal abuse   Abuso conyugal.

stare decisis   Vinculación con decisiones judiciales anteriores.

state of mind   Estado de ánimo, estado mental.

statement   Alegación, declaración, relato, estado de cuentas.

statutory foreclosure   Ejecución hipotecaria estatutaria.

statutory law   Derecho estatutario.

statutory rape   Estupro, violación de un menor de edad.

steal   Robar, hurtar, robo, hurto.

stock   Acciones, capital, existencias, semental.

stock option   Opción de comprar o vender acciones.

stop payment order   Suspensión de pago.

strict liability   Responsabilidad rigurosa.

sublease   Subarriendo, sublocación, subarrendar.

subpoena   Citación, citatorio, comparendo, cédula de citación, citación judicial, subpoena.

sue   Demandar, procesar.

summary judgment   Sentencia sumaria.

summon   Convocar, llamar, citar.

suppress   Suprimir, excluir pruebas ilegalmente obtenidas, reprimir, suspender.

surrender   Rendir, entregar, entrega, rendirse, entregarse.

surviving spouse   Cónyuge sobreviviente.

suspect   Sospecha, sospechar, sospechoso.

T

tangible evidence   Prueba real.

tangible property   Propiedad tangible, bienes tangibles.

tenancy at sufferance   Tenencia o posesión por tolerancia.

tenancy at will   Tenencia o inquilinato sin plazo fijo.

tenancy by the entirety   Tenencia conyugal.

tenancy for life   Tenencia vitalicia.

tenancy for years   Inquilinato por tiempo fijo.

tender   Propuesta, oferta, presentar.

testator   Testador.

testify   Atestar, atestiguar, dar testimonio.

theft   Hurto.

title   Título, derecho de posesión, rango, denominación.

tort   Agravio, torticero, entuerto, daño legal, perjuicio, acto ilícito civil.

Totten trust   Fideicomiso bancario Totten.

trade name   Nombre comercial, marca de fábrica, marca comercial.

trademark   Marca registrada, marca industrial.

transgression   Ofensa, delito, transgresión.

trespass   Transgresión, violación de propiedad ajena, translimitación, traspasar, violar, infringir, transgredir.

trial court   Tribunal de primera instancia.

trust   Fideicomiso, confianza, confidencia, confianza, crédito, combinación, consorcio, grupo industrial.

truth   Verdad, verdadero, veracidad.

try   Probar, juzgar.

U

ultra vires   Mas allá de la facultad de actuar.

unanimous verdict   Veredicto unánime.

unbiased   Imparcial, neutral.

unconditional pardon   Perdón, amnistía, indulto incondicional.

unconscionable   Reprochable, repugnante, desmedido.

under arrest   Arrestado, bajo arresto.

underwrite   Subscribir, asegurar, firmar.

undisclosed   Escondido, no revelado.

undue influence   Influencia indebida, coacción, abuso de poder.

unenforceable   Inejecutable.

unilateral contract   Contrato unilateral.

unlawful   Ilegal, ilícito, ilegítimo.

unsound mind   Privado de razón, de mente inestable.

usury   Usura, agiotaje, logrería.

V

vagrancy   Vagancia, vagabundeo.

validity   Validez, vigencia.

valuable consideration   Causa contractual con cierto valor, causa contractual onerosa.

venue   Partido judicial.

verbal contract   Contrato verbal.

verbatim   Al pié de la letra.

verdict   Veredicto, fallo, sentencia, decisión.

victim   Víctima.

voidable   Anulable, cancelable.

W

wage   Salario, jornal, sueldo.

waive   Renunciar, ceder, suspender, abdicar.

waiver   Renunciar, desistir, ceder, suspender, abdicar, renuncia.

warrant   Autorización, resguardo, comprobante, certificado, justificación, decisión judicial.

warranty   Garantía, seguridad.

warranty of habitability   Garantía de habitabilidad.

welfare   Asistencia pública.

will   Testamento, voluntad.

willful misconduct   Mala conducta intencional.

withhold   Retener, detener.

witness   Testigo, declarante, atestar, testificar, atestiguar.

writ of attachment   Mandamiento de embargo.

writ of certiorari   Pedimento de avocación.

writ of execution   Auto de ejecución, ejecutoria.

Glossary

ABA Model Rules of Professional Conduct   A recommended set of ethics and professional conduct guidelines for lawyers, prepared by American Bar Association, originally released in 1983; prior release was Model Code of Professional Conduct.

Administrative agencies   Agencies that the legislative and executive branches of federal and state governments establish.

Administrative law   Substantive and procedural law that governs the operation of administrative agencies.

Administrative law judge (ALJ)   A judge who presides over an administrative proceeding and who decides the questions of law and fact that arise in the proceeding.

Administrative Procedure Act (APA)   An act that establishes certain administrative procedures that federal administrative agencies must follow in conducting their affairs.

Admitted   A possible response of the defendant to the complaint which accepts the facts of the averment are true.

Affirm   The appellate court agrees with the outcome of trial and can find no reversible error and the decision of the trial court stands.

Agent   A party who agrees to act on behalf of another.

ALS (Acredited Legal Secretary)   The basic certification for legal professionals from NALS.

Alternative dispute resolution (ADR)   Methods of resolving disputes other than litigation.

American Arbitration Association (AAA)   A private nonprofit organization providing lists of potential arbitrators for the parties to select from and a set of rules for conducting the private arbitration.

American Association for Paralegal Education (AAfPE)   National organization of paralegal educators and institutions offering paralegal education programs.

American Bar Association (ABA)   Largest professional legal organization in the United States.

Amicus curia   Briefs submitted by interested parties who do not have standing in the action as a "friend of the court."

Answer   Document by which the defendant responds to the allegations contained in the plaintiff's complaint.

Appeal   The act of asking an appellate court to overturn a decision after the trial court's final judgment has been entered.

Appellant   The appealing party in an appeal. Also known as *petitioner*.

Appellate courts   Courts which review the record from the trial court to determine if the trial judge made an error in applying the procedural or substantive law.

Appellee   The responding party in an appeal. Also known as *respondent*.

Applications software   Applications programs are software that perform generic tasks such as word processing.

Arbitration   A form of ADR in which the parties choose an impartial third party to hear and decide the dispute.

Arbitration clause   A clause in contracts that requires disputes arising out of the contract to be submitted to arbitration. A clause contained in many international contracts that stipulates that any dispute between the parties concerning the performance of the contract will be submitted to an arbitrator or arbitration panel for resolution.

Arraignment   A hearing during which the accused is brought before a court and is (1) informed of the charges against him or her and (2) asked to enter a plea.

Arrest warrant   A document for a person's detainment based upon a showing of probable cause that the person committed the crime.

Associate's degree   A college degree in science (AS) arts (AA), or applied arts (AAS), generally requiring two years of full-time study.

Association of Legal Writing Directors (ALWD)   A society for professors who coordinate legal writing instruction.

Attachment   A popular method of transmitting text files and graphic images by attaching the file to an email.

Attorney–client privilege   A client's right to have anything told to a lawyer while seeking legal advice, kept confidential in most instances.

Bachelor's degree   A college degree generally requiring four years of full-time study.

Backup of data   Making a copy of critical files and programs in case of a loss of the original computer files.

Bench opinions   The initial version of a decision issued from the bench of the court.

Bicameral   In the American system a legislature of a house of representatives and a senate.

Bill of Rights   The first 10 amendments to the Constitution. They were added to the U.S. Constitution in 1791.

Briefs   Documents submitted by the parties' attorneys to the judge that contain legal support for their side of the case.

Burden of proof   The level of proof required to establish an entitlement to recovery.

Candor   A duty of honesty to the court.

Case and litigation management software   Case and litigation management programs are used to manage documents and the facts and issues of cases.

Case syllabus   In a court opinion a headnote for the convenience of the reader.

Central processing unit (CPU)   The computer chip and memory module that perform the basic computer functions.

Certificate   A recognition of the completion of a program of study that requires less than that needed for a degree.

Certified Legal Assistant (CLA) Designation by National Association of Legal Assistants for those who take and pass NALA certification program two-day comprehensive examination.

Choice-of-law clause Clause in an international contract that designates which nation's laws will be applied in deciding a dispute.

Chronological resume format Presents education and job history in chronological order with the most recent experience listed first.

Citation A reference to the source of the information.

Citator An index of cases.

Cite checking The process of verifying proper citation format in a document.

Civil litigation Resolution of legal disputes between parties seeking a remedy for a civil wrong or to enforce a contract.

Closing arguments The last opportunity for the attorneys to address the jury, summing up the client's case and persuading the jury to decide in his client's favor.

Commerce Clause A clause of the U.S. Constitution that grants Congress the power "to regulate commerce with foreign nations, and among the several states, and with Indian tribes."

Commercial speech Speech used by businesses, such as advertising. It is subject to time, place, and manner restrictions.

Common interest privilege To permit a client to share confidential information with the attorney for another who shares a common legal interest.

Common law Developed by judges who issue their opinions when deciding cases. The principles announced in these cases became precedent for later judges deciding similar cases.

Competence/competent The minimum level of knowledge and skill required of a professional.

Complaint The document the plaintiff files with the court and serves on the defendant to initiate a lawsuit.

Complex litigation Cases involving many parties as in a class action or multiple or complex legal issues.

Computer addresses and locations The modern equivalent of a person's telephone number is the email address. Pages on the Internet also have addresses known as the Uniform Resource Locator (URL), made up of three parts: protocol, computer, and path.

Computer hardware Hardware is the term that encompasses all of the tangible or physical items including computers, monitors, printers, fax machines, duplicators, and similar items that usually have either an electrical connection or use batteries as a power source.

Computer network A set of workstations connected together.

Computer system A combination of an input device, a processor, and an output device.

Computer viruses Viruses are programs that attack and destroy computer programs, internal computer operating systems, and occasionally the hard disk drives of computers.

Conciliation A form of dispute resolution in which a conciliator transmits offers and counteroffers between the disputing parties in helping to reach a settlement of their dispute.

Conciliator A third party in a conciliation proceeding who assists the disputing parties in reaching a settlement of their dispute. The conciliator cannot make a decision or an award.

Concurrent jurisdiction Jurisdiction shared by two or more courts.

Confidentiality A duty imposed on the attorney to enable clients to obtain legal advice by allowing the client to freely and openly give the attorney all the relevant facts.

Conflict checking Verifying that the attorneys in the firm do not have a personal conflict and have not previously represented and are not currently representing any party with an adverse interest or conflict with the potential client.

Conflict of interest The representation of one client being directly adverse to the interest of another client.

Connectors Instructions in a search query on how to treat the words in the query.

Consolidation The act of a court to combine two or more separate lawsuits into one lawsuit. Occurs when two or more corporations combine to form an entirely new corporation.

Constitution of the United States of America The supreme law of the United States. The Constitution of the United States of America establishes the structure of the federal government, delegates powers to the federal government, and guarantees certain fundamental rights.

Cost-benefit analysis Process by which a litigant determines the costs of pursuing litigation and compares that to what is likely to be gained.

Counteroffer A response by an offeree that contains terms and conditions different from or in addition to those of the offer. A counteroffer terminates an offer.

Court accounting An accounting with the local court that administers or supervises trust and estate matters. These reports are designed to show that the fiduciary has properly administered the estate or trust.

Court of Appeals for the Federal Circuit A court of appeals in Washington, DC, that has special appellate jurisdiction to review the decisions of the Claims Court, the Patent and Trademark Office, and the Court of International Trade.

Court of Chancery Court that granted relief based on fairness. Also called *equity court*.

Courts of record Those courts in which the testimony and evidence presented are recorded and preserved.

Cover letter A brief letter sent with a document identifying the intended recipient and the purpose of the attachment.

Criminal laws A violation of a statute for which the government imposes a punishment.

Criminal trial A trial to determine if a person has violated a statue for which the government imposes a penalty.

Critical legal thinking The process of identifying the issue, the material facts, and the applicable law and applying the law to come to a conclusion.

Cross-complaint Filed by the defendant against the plaintiff to seek damages or some other remedy.

Cross-examination Opportunity of defense (opposing) counsel to question a witness after the direct examination of the witness.

Cruel and unusual punishment A clause of the Eighth Amendment that protects criminal defendants from torture or other abusive punishment.

Database program A database program is an electronic repository of information of all types that can be sorted and presented in a meaningful manner.

Default judgment Judgment obtained by the plaintiff against the defendant where the defendant has failed to respond in a timely fashion to the complaint.

Defendant   The party who files the answer.

Defendant's case   Process by which the defendant calls witnesses and introduces evidence to (1) rebut the plaintiff's evidence, (2) prove affirmative defenses, and (3) prove allegations made in a cross-complaint.

Delegation doctrine   A doctrine that says when an administrative agency is created, it is delegated certain powers; the agency can only use those legislative, judicial, and executive powers that are delegated to it.

Denied   A possible response of the defendant to the complaint which asserts the facts of the averment are not true.

Deponent   Party who gives his or her deposition.

Deposition   Oral testimony given by a party or witness prior to trial. The testimony is given under oath and is transcribed.

Dicta   Court comments on issues not directly related to the holding and therefore not having precedential effect.

Digital format   A computerized format utilizing a series of 0's and 1's.

Direct examination   Questions addressed to a witness by the attorney who has called that witness to testify on behalf of his client.

Discovery   A legal process during which both parties engage in various activities to elicit facts of the case from the other party and witnesses prior to trial.

Diversity of citizenship   A case between (1) citizens of different states, (2) a citizen of a state and a citizen or subject of a foreign country, and (3) a citizen of a state and a foreign country where a foreign country is the plaintiff.

Double Jeopardy Clause   A clause of the Fifth Amendment that protects persons from being tried twice for the same crime.

Due Process Clause   A clause that provides that no person shall be deprived of "life, liberty, or property" without due process of the law.

Duty of candor   Honesty to the court.

E-discovery   The discovery of emails, electronically stored data, e-contracts, and other electronically stored records.

E-filing   The electronic filing of pleadings, briefs, and other documents related to a lawsuit with the court.

Elder law   Advocacy for the elderly.

Electronic repository   A secure protected file server to which everyone authorized has access over the internet.

Encryption   Encryption is technology that allows computer users to put a "lock" around information to prevent discovery by others.

Enumerated powers   Certain powers delegated to the federal government by the states.

Environmental law   An area of the law dealing with the protection of the environment.

Equal Access to Justice Act   An act that was enacted to protect persons from harassment by federal administrative agencies.

Equal Protection Clause   A clause that provides that state, local, and federal governments cannot deny to any person the "equal protection of the laws."

Establishment Clause   A clause to the First Amendment that prohibits the government from either establishing a state religion or promoting one religion over another.

Ethical wall   An environment in which an attorney or a paralegal is isolated from a particular case or client to avoid a conflict of interest or to protect a client's confidences and secrets.

Exclusionary rule   A rule that says evidence obtained from an unreasonable search and seizure can generally be prohibited from introduction at a trial or administrative proceeding against the person searched.

Exculpatory evidence   Evidence which tends to prove the innocence of the accused or prove the facts of the defendant's case.

Executive branch   One of the three co-equal branches of government represented by the president and administrative agencies.

Expert witness   A person qualified by education or experience to render an opinion based on a set of facts.

Extension of time to respond   Request by the defendant to enlarge the time to respond to the complaint beyond that which is permitted under the rules.

Fact pleading   Pleadings required to include all relevant facts in support of all claims asserted.

Facts   Information or details.

Federal administrative agencies   Agencies established by legislative and executive branches of federal and state governments.

Federal Arbitration Act (FAA)   A federal statute that provides that arbitration agreements in commercial contracts are valid, irrevocable, and enforceable unless some legal or equitable (fraud, duress) grounds exist to invalidate them.

Federal question   A case arising under the U.S. Constitution, treaties, or federal statutes and regulations.

Federalism   The U.S. form of government; the federal government and the 50 state governments share powers.

Fiduciary relationship   A relationship under which one party has a duty to act for the interest and benefit of another while acting within the scope of the relationship.

File attachment   The attachment is a popular method for transmitting text files, and occasionally graphic images, by attaching the file to an email.

File extension   When a file is saved, a file extension (a period followed by three characters) is added to the end of the filename to identify the program or format in which the file has been saved.

Finding tools   Publications used to find primary and secondary sources.

Firewalls   Programs designed to limit access to authorized users and applications.

Forum-selection clause   Contract provision that designates a certain court to hear any dispute concerning nonperformance of the contract.

Free Exercise Clause   A clause to the First Amendment that prohibits the government from interfering with the free exercise of religion in the United States.

Freedom of Information Act   A law that was enacted to give the public access to most documents in the possession of federal administrative agencies.

Freedom of speech   The right to engage in oral, written, and symbolic speech protected by the First Amendment.

Functional resume format Lists a summary of the individual's qualifications with current experience and education without any emphasis on dates of employment.

General denial In some jurisdictions, the word "Denied" alone is insufficient and the averment of the complaint is treated as if it were "Admitted."

General government regulation Government regulation that applies to many industries collectively.

General law practice A general law practice is one that handles all types of cases.

General-jurisdiction trial court (courts of record) A court that hears cases of a general nature that are not within the jurisdiction of limited-jurisdiction trial courts.

GlobalCite Loislaw's tool for searching cases containing references to another case.

Government employment Working for federal, state, and local government agencies and authorities.

Government in the Sunshine Act An act that was enacted to open certain federal administrative agency meetings to the public.

Graphic user interface (GUI) A set of screen presentations and metaphors that utilize graphic elements such as icons in an attempt to make an operating system easier to operate.

Hacking Unauthorized access to a computer or computer network.

Hardcopy Paper copies of documents.

Headnotes The syllabus or summary of the points of law prepared by the editorial staff of a publisher.

Highest state court The top court in a state court system; it hears appeals from intermediate state courts and certain trial courts.

Holding The actual decision on the specific point of law the court was asked to decide.

Hot spot A wireless access point, generally in a public area.

Hung jury A jury that does not come to a unanimous decision about the defendant's guilt. The government may choose to retry the case.

Immaterial facts A fact not essential to the matter or issue at hand.

Immunity from prosecution The government agrees not to use any evidence given by a person granted immunity against that person.

Implied attorney–client relationship Implied attorney–client relationship may result when a prospective client divulges confdential information during a consultation with an attorney for the purpose of retaining the attorney, even if actual employment does not result.

***In personam* (personal) jurisdiction** Jurisdiction over the parties to a lawsuit.

***In rem* jurisdiction** Jurisdiction to hear a case because of jurisdiction over the property of the lawsuit.

Independent Medical Examination (IME) Term formerly used to describe a defense medical evaluation.

Indictment The charge of having committed a crime (usually a felony), based on the judgment of a grand jury.

Information The charge of having committed a crime (usually a misdemeanor), based on the judgment of a judge (magistrate).

Intellectual property and information rights Patents, copyrights, trademarks, trade secrets, trade names, domain names, and other valuable business assets. Federal and state laws protect intellectual property rights from misappropriation and infringement.

Intermediate appellate court An intermediate court that hears appeals from trial courts.

Intermediate scrutiny test Test that is applied to classifications based on protected classes other than race (e.g., sex or age).

International Paralegal Management Association (IPMA) A North American association for legal assistant managers.

Internet A collection of millions of computers that provide a network of electronic connections between the computers.

Internet (Web) browsers An Internet or Web browser is a software program that allows a person to use a computer to access the Internet. The two most popular Web browsers are Microsoft Internet Explorer and AOL.

Internet search engine An Internet search engine is a program designed to take a word or set of words and locate websites on the Internet.

Internet service provider (ISP) The company providing the connection between the user and the Internet.

Interpretive rules Rules issued by administrative agencies that interpret existing statutory language.

Interrogatories Written questions submitted by one party to another party. The questions must be answered in writing within a stipulated time.

Interstate commerce Commerce that moves between states or that affects commerce between states.

Intervention The act of others to join as parties to an existing lawsuit.

IOLTA account Where the amount is too small to earn interest, court rules require the funds be deposited into a special interest-bearing account, and the interest generally paid to support legal aid projects (Interest on Lawyers Trust Accounts).

Judgment The official decision of the court.

Judicial branch The court system.

Judicial decision A ruling about an individual lawsuit issued by federal and state courts.

Jurisdiction The authority of the court to hear disputes and impose resolution of the dispute upon the litigants.

Jurisprudence The philosophy or science of law.

Jury deliberation The process where the jury meets to discuss and resolve the dispute.

Jury instructions (charges) Instructions given by the judge to the jury that informs them of the law to be applied in the case.

Jury selection Process by which a group of six or more people is chosen to serve on the jury.

Just Compensation Clause A clause of the U.S. Constitution that requires the government to compensate the property owner, and possibly others, when the government takes property under its power of eminent domain.

KeyCite Westlaw's tool for searching cases containing references to another case.

Large law offices Large law offices are an outgrowth of traditional law offices that have expanded over the years, adding partners and associates along the way.

Law That which must be obeyed and followed by citizens subject to sanctions or legal consequences; a body of rules of action or conduct prescribed by controlling authority, and having binding legal force.

Law court A court that developed and administered a uniform set of laws decreed by the kings and queens after William the Conqueror; legal procedure was emphasized over merits at this time.

Leading question A question which suggests the answer.

Legal assistant See *Paralegal*.

Legal research The process for finding the answer to a legal question.

Legislative branch The part of the government that consists of Congress (the Senate and the House of Representatives).

Limited-jurisdiction trial courts Courtsauthorized to hear certain types of disputes such as divorce or bankruptcy.

Litigation The process of bringing, maintaining, and defending a lawsuit.

Local area network (LAN) A network of computers at one location.

Long-arm statute A statute that extends a state's jurisdiction to nonresidents who were not served a summons within the state.

Mainframe A large computer system used primarily for bulk processing of data and financial information.

Mandatory authority Court decisions that are binding on all lower courts.

Material facts A fact significant or essential to the issue.

Mediation A form of negotiation in which a neutral third party assists the disputing parties in reaching a settlement of their dispute.

Mediator A neutral third party who assists the disputing parties in reaching a settlement of their dispute. The mediator cannot make a decision or an award.

Memorandum A working legal document for the legal team for use in preparation and presentation of a case.

Minitrial A voluntary private proceeding in which the lawyers for each side present a shortened version of their case to representatives of the other side, and usually to a neutral third party, in an attempt to reach a settlement of the dispute.

Miranda rights Rights that a suspect must be informed of before being interrogated, so that the suspect will not unwittingly give up his or her Fifth Amendment right.

Model Guidelines for the Utilization of Legal Assistant Services A set of guidelines by ABA policymaking body, the House of Delegates, intended to govern conduct of lawyers when utilizing paralegals or legal assistants.

Modem A device to translate electrical signals to allow computers to communicate with each other.

Moral obligation An obligation based on one's own conscience.

Motion for judgment on the pleadings A motion that alleges that if all the facts presented in the pleadings are taken as true, the party making the motion would win the lawsuit when the proper law is applied to these asserted facts.

Motion for summary judgment A motion that asserts that there are no factual disputes to be decided by the jury and that the judge can apply the proper law to the undisputed facts and decide the case without a jury. These motions are supported by affidavits, documents, and deposition testimony.

Motion to dismiss A motion that alleges that the plaintiff's complaint fails to state a claim for which relief can be granted. Also called a *demurrer*.

Narrative opportunity A question that allows the giving of a full explanation.

National Association of Legal Assistants (NALA) Professional organization for legal assistants that provides continuing education and professional certification for paralegals, incorporated in 1975.

National Association of Legal Secretaries (NALS) Since 1999, an association for legal professionals, originally formed in 1949 as an association for legal secretaries.

National Federation of Paralegal Associations (NFPA) Professional organization of state and local paralegal associations founded in 1974.

Negotiation A procedure in which the parties to a dispute engage in negotiations to try to reach a voluntary settlement of their dispute.

Network administrator The network administrator usually is the person with the highest-level access to the network file server.

Network file server A separate computer in a network that acts as the traffic cop of the system controlling the flow of data.

Network rights and privileges Rights or privileges determine who has access to the server, the data stored on the server, and the flow of information between connections.

Networking The establishment of contact with others with whom questions and information are shared.

Notice pleading Pleadings required to include sufficient facts to put the parties on notice of the claims asserted against them.

Nurse paralegals Nurses who have gained medical work experience and combine it with paralegal skills. Also referred to as *legal nurse consultants*.

Obscene speech Speech that (1) appeals to the prurient interest, (2) depicts sexual conduct in a patently offensive way, and (3) lacks serious literary, artistic, political, or scientific value.

Offensive speech Speech that is offensive to many members of society. It is subject to time, place, and manner restrictions.

Office software suites This software consists of commonly used office software programs that manage data and database programs; manipulate financial or numeric information, spreadsheet programs; or display images and presentation graphics programs.

Online collaboration Using the internet to conduct meetings and share documents.

Open-ended question A question that usually does not have a yes or no answer.

Opening brief The first opportunity for the attorneys to address the jury and describe the nature of the lawsuit.

Operating system The operating system is a basic set of instructions to the computer on how to handle basic functions—how to process input from "input devices" such as the keyboard and mouse, the order in which to process information, and what to show on the computer monitor.

Opinion letter A formal statement of advice based on the lawyers expert knowledge.

Order Decision issued by an administrative law judge.

Ordinances Laws enacted by local government bodies such as cities and municipalities, countries, school districts, and water districts.

Outsourcing Use of persons or services outside of the immediate office staff.

Paperless office The paperless office is one in which documents are created and stored electronically.

Paralegal A person qualified by education, training, or work experience who is employed or retained by a lawyer, law office, corporation, governmental agency, or other entity who performs specifically delegated substantive legal work for which a lawyer is responsible. Also referred to as *legal assistant*.

Paralegal Advanced Competency Exam (PACE) National Association of Paralegal Association's certification program that requires the paralegal to have two years of experience and a bachelor's degree and have completed a paralegal course at an accredited school.

Paralegal manager Someone who hires, supervises, trains, and evaluates paralegals.

Parallel citation The citation to the same case in a different publication.

Partnership Two or more natural (human) or artificial (corporation) persons who have joined together to share ownership and profit or loss.

Personal jurisdiction Requires the court to have authority over the persons as well as the subject matter of the lawsuit.

Persuasive authority Court decisions the court is not required to follow but are well reasoned and from a respected court.

Petition for *certiorari* A petition asking the Supreme Court to hear one's case.

Petitioner The party appealing the decision of an administrative agency.

Physical and mental examination A form of discovery that permits the physical or mental examination of a party by a qualified expert of the opposing party's choosing where the physical or mental condition of the party is at issue in the lawsuit.

Plaintiff The party who files the complaint.

Plaintiff's case Process by which the plaintiff calls witnesses and introduces evidence to prove the allegations contained in his or her complaint.

Plea bargain agreement An agreement in which the accused admits to a lesser crime than charged. In return, the government agrees to impose a lesser sentence than might have been obtained had the case gone to trial.

Pleadings The paperwork that is filed with the court to initiate and respond to a lawsuit.

Pocket parts An update to a book that is a separate document that slips into a pocket in the back of the main volume.

Police power The power of states to regulate private and business activity within their borders.

Precedent Prior case law that is controlling.

Preemption doctrine The concept that federal law takes precedence over state or local law.

Pretrial hearing A hearing before the trial in order to facilitate the settlement of a case. Also called a settlement conference.

Pretrial motion A motion a party can make to try to dispose of all or part of a lawsuit prior to trial.

Primary authority The actual law itself.

Primary source of law The actual law itself.

Principal A party who employs another person to act on his or her behalf.

Privacy Act An act stipulating that federal administrative agencies can maintain only information about an individual that is relevant and necessary to accomplish a legitimate agency purpose.

Privilege A special legal right.

Privileged communication A communication that the person has a right to be kept confidential based on the relationship with the other part such as attorney and client.

Pro bono Working without compensation on behalf of individuals and organizations that otherwise could not afford legal assistance.

Pro se Parties represent themselves.

Procedural due process Due process that requires the respondent to be given (1) proper and timely notice of the allegations or charges against him or her and (2) an opportunity to present evidence on the matter.

Procedural law Law which realtes to how the trial is conducted and is usually based upon Rules of Court and Rules of Evidence.

Production of documents Request by one party to another party to produce all documents relevant to the case prior to the trial.

Professional Legal Secretary (PLS) The advanced certification for legal professionals from NALS.

Professional Paralegal (PP) Certification from NALS for those performing paralegal duties.

Proprietary school Private, as opposed to public, institution, generally for profit, offering training and education.

Protocol In a URL the required format of the Web address.

Published opinion A court's written explanation of its decision on a case intended to be relied upon as a statement of the law based on the facts of the case.

Quasi in rem (attachment) jurisdiction Jurisdiction allowed a plaintiff who obtains a judgment in one state to try to collect the judgment by attaching property of the defendant located in another state.

Random access memory (RAM) Temporary computer memory that stores work in processs.

Rational basis test Test that is applied to classifications not involving a suspect or protected class.

Rebuttal Phase of the trial that gives the plaintiff the chance to address or respond to information contained in the defendant's case-in-chief.

Recross examination Permits opposing counsel to again challenge the credibility of the witness but only as to matters questioned on redirect examination.

Redirect examination After cross-examination, counsel who originally called the witness on direct examination may ask the witness additional questions.

Relevant facts Facts crucial to the case and having legal significance.

Remand When the basis of federal jurisdiction is resolved and only state claims remain to be litigated, the federal court must send the matter back to the state trial court. Also, when the appellate court disagrees with the outcome of the trial court but sends the matter back to the trial court for further proceeding in accordance with its opinion, which may include additional proceedings or a new trial to correct the error, in accordance with the appellate court's decision.

Remote collaboration   Working on a common document utilizing remote access by two or more parties.

Reply   Filed by the original plaintiff to answer the defendant's cross-complaint.

Request for admission   A form of discovery in which written requests are made to the opposing party asking him to admit the truth of certain facts or liability.

Respondent   The party who must respond to the appeal, usually the verdict winner at trial.

Restatement of the Law Third, Torts   A legal treatise with suggested rules of laws relating to torts.

Resume   A short description of a person's education, a summary of work experience, and other related and supporting information that potential employers use in evaluating a person's qualifications for a position in a firm or an organization.

Retainer   A payment at the beginning of the handling of a new matter for a client. This amount may be used to offset the fees for services rendered or costs advanced on behalf of the client.

Reverse   The appellate court disagrees with the outcome of the trial and finds reversible error was made and judgment should be overturned and entered in favor of the appellant.

Rules of court   A court's rules for the processing and presentation of cases.

Screening interview   Limited first contact with a prospective new client.

Search query   Specific words used in a computerized search.

Search warrant   A warrant issued by a court that authorizes the police to search a designated place for specified contraband, articles, items, or documents. The search warrant must be based on probable cause.

Secondary authority   Writings that explain the law.

Secondary source of law   Writings about the law.

Self-employment   Working independently either as a freelance paralegal for different lawyers or, when authorized by state or federal law, performing services for the public.

Self-incrimination   The Fifth Amendment states that no person shall be compelled in any criminal case to be a witness against him or herself.

Service of process   A summons is served on the defendant to obtain personal jurisdiction over him or her.

Slip opinion   A copy of the opinion sent to the printer.

Small offices   Small-office arrangements range from individual practitioners sharing space to partnerships.

Small-claims court   A court that hears civil cases involving small dollar amounts.

Software   Refers to programs containing sets of instructions that tell the computer and the other computer-based electronic devices what to do and how to do it.

Solo practice   One lawyer practicing alone without the assistance of other attorneys.

Special federal courts   Federal courts that hear matters of specialized or limited jurisdiction.

Specialty application programs   Specialty programs combine many of the basic functions found in software suites, word processing, database management, spreadsheets, and graphic presentations to perform law office, case, and litigation management.

Specialty practice   A specialty practice is involved in practice in one area of law.

Specific government regulation   Government regulation that applies to individual industries.

Spreadsheet programs   Programs that permit the calculation and presentation of financial information in a grid format of rows and columns.

Standing to sue   The plaintiff must have some stake in the outcome of the lawsuit.

Stare decisis   Latin: "to stand by the decision." Adherence to precedent. The legal principle that prior case law should apply unless there is a substantial change in society necessitating a change in the case law.

State administrative agencies   Administrative agencies that states create to enforce and interpret state law.

Statement of policy   A statement issued by administrative agencies announcing a proposed course of action that an agency intends to follow in the future.

Statute   Written law enacted by the legislative branch of the federal and state governments that establishes certain courses of conduct that the covered parties must adhere to.

Statute of limitations   A time limit within which a case must be brought or lose the right to seek redress in court.

Strict liability   A tort doctrine that makes manufacturers, distributors, wholesalers, retailers, and others in the chain of distribution of a defective product liable for the damages caused by the defect *irrespective of fault*. Also, liability without fault.

Strict scrutiny test   Test that is applied to classifications based on race.

Subject-matter jurisdiction   Jurisdiction over the subject matter of a lawsuit.

Subpoena   A court order compelling a witness to attend and testify, must accompany a Notice of deposition served on a non-party witness.

Substantive due process   Due process that requires that the statute or rule that the respondent is charged with violating be clearly stated.

Substantive law   Law which relates to the law of the case, such as the law of negligence or contract.

Substantive rule   A rule issued by an administrative agency that has much the same power as a statute: It has the force of law and must be adhered to by covered persons and businesses.

Summons   A court order directing the defendant to appear in court and answer the complaint.

Supervising attorney   The member of the legal team to whom all others on the team report and who has the ultimate responsibility for the actions of the legal team.

Supremacy Clause   A clause of the U.S. Constitution that establishes that the federal Constitution, treaties, federal laws, and federal regulations are the supreme law of the land.

Teleworker People who work from remote locations, typically home.

Thin client A computer system where programs and files are maintained on a centralized server.

Third-party documents Documents prepared by a third party in the ordinary course of business that would have been prepared in similar form if there was no litigation.

Track Changes Track Changes, as found in MS Word, shows the original text, the deleted text, and the new text as well as a strike through for deleted text, underlining or highlighting of new text, as well as margin notes on the document.

Treaty A compact made between two or more nations.

Trial brief Document presented to the court setting forth a legal argument to persuade the court to rule in a particular way on a procedural or substantive legal issue.

Trial notebook A summary of the case tabbed for each major activity, witness, or element of proof.

Trier of facts The trier of facts decides what facts are to be accepted and used in making the decision. It is usually a jury, but may be a judge who hears a case without a jury and decides the facts and applies the law.

Trust account The funds of the client.

U.S. Courts of Appeals The federal court system's intermediate appellate courts.

U.S. District Courts The federal court system's trial courts of general jurisdiction.

U.S. Supreme Court The Supreme Court was created by Article III of the U.S. Constitution. The Supreme Court is the highest court in the land. It is located in Washington, DC.

Unauthorized Practice of Law (UPL) Giving legal advice, if legal rights may be affected, by anyone not licensed to practice law.

Uniform Arbitration Act A uniform act adopted by more than half of the states, similar to the Federal Arbitration Act it describes procedures that must be followed for arbitration to be initiated, how the panel of arbitrators is to be selected, and the procedures for conducting arbitration hearings.

Uniform resource locator (URL) The address of a site on the Internet.

Uninterruptable power supply (UPS) A battery system that can supply power to a computer or computer peripheral for a short period of time.

Universal Citation Format A system for citation relying on the courts to number the paragraphs in their opinions.

Unprotected speech Speech that is not protected by the First Amendment and may be forbidden by the government.

Unpublished opinions Cases which the court does not feel have precedential effect and are limited to a specific set of facts.

Unreasonable search and seizure Any search and seizure by the government that violates the Fourth Amendment.

V. Cite VersusLaw's tool for searching cases containing references to another case.

Vendor-specific citation format Citation format of a legal publisher adopted by a court.

Venue A concept that requires lawsuits to be heard by the court with jurisdiction that is nearest the location in which the incident occurred or where the parties reside.

Verdict Decision reached by the jury.

Videoconferencing Conferencing from multiple locations using high speed Internet connections to transmit sound and images.

Voice recognition Computer programs for converting speech into text or commands without the use of other inout devices such as keyboards.

VoIP Voice over internet protocol is a computer internet replacement for traditional telephone connections.

Voir dire Process whereby prospective jurors are asked questions by the judge and attorneys to determine if they would be biased in their decision.

Wide area network A wide area network is a network of networks. Each network is treated as if it were a connection on the network.

Wireless computer networks A wireless network uses wireless technology in place of wires for connecting to the network.

Wireless network A wireless network uses wireless technology instead of wires for connecting to the network.

Work-product doctrine A qualified immunity from discovery for "work product of the lawyer" except on a substantial showing of "necessity or justification" of certain written statements and memoranda prepared by counsel in representation of a client, generally in preparation for trial.

Workstation A computer connected to a network that is used for access consisting of a monitor, input device, and computer.

Writ of certiorari An official notice that the Supreme Court will review one's case.

Case Index

Subject Index